Historical Dictionaries of Asia, Oceania, and the Middle East

Edited by Jon Woronoff

Asia

1. *Vietnam*, by William J. Duiker. 1989. *Out of print. See No. 27.*
2. *Bangladesh*, 2nd ed., by Craig Baxter and Syedur Rahman. 1996. *Out of print. See No. 48.*
3. *Pakistan*, by Shahid Javed Burki. 1991. *Out of print. See No. 33.*
4. *Jordan*, by Peter Gubser. 1991
5. *Afghanistan*, by Ludwig W. Adamec. 1991. *Out of print. See No. 47.*
6. *Laos*, by Martin Stuart-Fox and Mary Kooyman. 1992. *Out of print. See No. 35.*
7. *Singapore*, by K. Mulliner and Lian The-Mulliner. 1991
8. *Israel*, by Bernard Reich. 1992
9. *Indonesia*, by Robert Cribb. 1992. *Out of print. See No. 51.*
10. *Hong Kong and Macau*, by Elfed Vaughan Roberts, Sum Ngai Ling, and Peter Bradshaw. 1992
11. *Korea*, by Andrew C. Nahm. 1993. *Out of print. See No. 52.*
12. *Taiwan*, by John F. Copper. 1993. *Out of print. See No. 34.*
13. *Malaysia*, by Amarjit Kaur. 1993. *Out of print. See No. 36.*
14. *Saudi Arabia*, by J. E. Peterson. 1993. *Out of print. See No. 45.*
15. *Myanmar*, by Jan Becka. 1995
16. *Iran*, by John H. Lorentz. 1995
17. *Yemen*, by Robert D. Burrowes. 1995
18. *Thailand*, by May Kyi Win and Harold Smith. 1995
19. *Mongolia*, by Alan J. K. Sanders. 1996. *Out of print. See No. 42.*
20. *India*, by Surjit Mansingh. 1996
21. *Gulf Arab States*, by Malcolm C. Peck. 1996
22. *Syria*, by David Commins. 1996. *Out of print. See No. 50.*
23. *Palestine*, by Nafez Y. Nazzal and Laila A. Nazzal. 1997
24. *Philippines*, by Artemio R. Guillermo and May Kyi Win. 1997. *Out of print. See No. 54.*

Oceania

1. *Australia*, by James C. Docherty. 1992. *Out of print. See No. 32.*
2. *Polynesia*, by Robert D. Craig. 1993. *Out of print. See No. 39.*
3. *Guam and Micronesia*, by William Wuerch and Dirk Ballendorf. 1994

4. *Papua New Guinea*, by Ann Turner. 1994. *Out of print. See No. 37.*
5. *New Zealand*, by Keith Jackson and Alan McRobie. 1996

New Combined Series
25. *Brunei Darussalam*, by D. S. Ranjit Singh and Jatswan S. Sidhu. 1997
26. *Sri Lanka*, by S. W. R. de A. Samarasinghe and Vidyamali Samarasinghe. 1998
27. *Vietnam*, 2nd ed., by William J. Duiker. 1998
28. *People's Republic of China: 1949–1997*, by Lawrence R. Sullivan, with the assistance of Nancy Hearst. 1998
29. *Afghanistan*, 2nd ed., by Ludwig W. Adamec. 1997. *Out of print. See No. 47.*
30. *Lebanon*, by As'ad AbuKhalil. 1998
31. *Azerbaijan*, by Tadeusz Swietochowski and Brian C. Collins. 1999
32. *Australia*, 2nd ed., by James C. Docherty. 1999
33. *Pakistan*, 2nd ed., by Shahid Javed Burki. 1999
34. *Taiwan (Republic of China)*, 2nd ed., by John F. Copper. 2000
35. *Laos*, 2nd ed., by Martin Stuart-Fox. 2001
36. *Malaysia*, 2nd ed., by Amarjit Kaur. 2001
37. *Papua New Guinea*, 2nd ed., by Ann Turner. 2001
38. *Tajikistan*, by Kamoludin Abdullaev and Shahram Akbarzedeh. 2002
39. *Polynesia*, 2nd ed., by Robert D. Craig. 2002
40. *North Korea*, by Ilpyong J. Kim. 2003
41. *Armenia*, by Rouben Paul Adalian. 2002
42. *Mongolia*, 2nd ed., by Alan J. K. Sanders. 2003
43. *Cambodia*, by Justin Corfield and Laura Summers. 2003
44. *Iraq*, by Edmund A. Ghareeb with the assistance of Beth K. Dougherty. 2004
45. *Saudi Arabia*, 2nd ed., by J. E. Peterson. 2003
46. *Nepal,* by Nanda R. Shrestha and Keshav Bhattarai. 2003
47. *Afghanistan*, 3rd ed., by Ludwig W. Adamec. 2003
48. *Bangladesh*, 3rd ed., by Craig Baxter and Syedur Rahman. 2003
49. *Kyrgyzstan*, by Rafis Abazov. 2004
50. *Syria*, 2nd ed., by David Commins. 2004
51. *Indonesia*, 2nd ed., by Robert Cribb and Audrey Kahin. 2004
52. *Republic of Korea*, 2nd ed., by Andrew C. Nahm and James E. Hoare. 2004
53. *Turkmenistan*, by Rafis Abazov. 2005
54. *Philippines*, 2nd ed., by Artemio Guillermo. 2005

Historical Dictionary of the Philippines

Second Edition

Artemio R. Guillermo
and
May Kyi Win

*Historical Dictionaries of Asia,
Oceania, and the Middle East, No. 54*

The Scarecrow Press, Inc.
Lanham, Maryland • Toronto • Oxford
2005

SCARECROW PRESS, INC.

Published in the United States of America
by Scarecrow Press, Inc.
A wholly owned subsidary of
The Rowman & Littlefield Publishing Group, Inc.
4501 Forbes Boulevard, Suite 200, Lanham, Maryland 20706
www.scarecrowpress.com

PO Box 317
Oxford
OX2 9RU, UK

Copyright © 2005 by Artemio R. Guillermo

British Library Cataloguing in Publication Information Available

Library of Congress Cataloging-in-Publication Data
Guillermo, Artemio R.
  Historical dictionary of the Philippines / Artemio R. Guillermo.—2nd ed.
    p. cm.—(Historical dictionaries of Asia, Oceania, and the Middle East ; no. 54)
  Includes bibliographical references and indexes.
  ISBN 0-8108-5490-2 (hardcover : alk. paper)
    1. Philippines—History—Dictionaries. I. Title. II. Series: Historical
dictionaries of Asia, Oceania, and the Middle East ; 54.
DS667.G85 2005
959.9—dc22
                                                                2004030020

Contents

List of Tables

Editor's Foreword

The Philippines is Asia with a difference. Or rather, many differences. It was colonized earlier and remained under foreign domination longer than its neighbors. The policies imposed by the Spanish and Americans were different, and as Filipinos adapted them, these differences were further accentuated. Alone among Asian countries, the Philippines embraced Catholicism, and the church plays a notable role. Almost inexplicably, despite its fertile soil and plentiful natural resources, it did not partake in the Asian "economic miracle" and economic growth barely keeps up with population growth. Still, although some differences are negative, others are positive. The present political system is exceptionally open and democratic, the media are the freest in the region, and its culture is certainly one of the richest anywhere.

This book presents the Philippines in many aspects, showing what it has in common with other Asian countries and what makes it special. Some entries cover the time of Spanish and American domination, but also on earlier practices, some of which have survived. There are entries on the long struggle for independence and the very distinctive periods since then. Other entries focus on many decisive events and essential institutions. Numerous entries cover its cities, provinces, and geography. Above all, there are entries on the people, patriots and politicians, soldiers and businessmen, and writers and artists. The chronology helps us look back over time while the bibliography enables us find out more about this country, which is all the more fascinating for its differences.

The second edition of the *Historical Dictionary of the Philippines* was updated and expanded by Artemio R. Guillermo, one of the authors of the first edition. Dr. Guillermo, who was born in the Philippines, studied in the United States, specializing in journalism and communication. From 1955 to 1968, he worked as a journalist, businessman, and educator in the Philippines, before returning to the United States to teach journalism and communication. He has since retired but very obviously, to judge by the many additions, keeps thoroughly abreast of events. Alas, May Kyi Win, the other author, passed away in 2002 after many years as curator of the Donn V. Hart Southeast Asia Collection at Northern Illinois University. This book is, in some ways, a tribute to her, but especially to one of Asia's most fascinating and unique countries.

Jon Woronoff
Series Editor

Preface

This revised and updated edition offers a wider range of subjects in order to present a concise and fair account of the historical context of the Philippines. Filipinos have been led to believe that their history started only when Western colonizers "discovered" them. These invaders tried their best to wipe out evidences of a literate and highly developed society. Only later researches by Filipinos, foreign scholars, and archaeologists have turned up trenchant evidences of a civilized society. They had laws, a government in the form of the barangay, and a system of writing. The Laguna Copper Plate Inscription, ancient syllabary, and Tabon Caves artifacts are proofs that pre-Hispanic Filipinos had a distinctive ethos, folk epics, language, and most of the criteria of a functioning society. Epic poetry was the highest form of ancient Filipino literary heritage. The past and present periods yielded a plethora of historical events, dynamic personalities, and institutions that provided the high points of the country's arduous journey in democracy and the road to civilization. Particular attention was devoted to persons who made up the society, their contribution, dominant beliefs and values, the issues on which they were divided or united, the nature and extent of their involvement with national institutions, and their attitudes toward the social system and political order.

Because of new and interesting information that was found, many entries were updated and also new entries were added and extensively written to give more depth and provide the reader/researcher a better knowledge of the subject. Words in bold type indicate the titles of related topics for further elucidation. Filipino terms in many entries are properly given their English meanings. And because the Philippines is an archipelago of 7,100 islands, naturally, there are entries about intriguing places, geographical sites, and geological phenomenon that all add up to the country's prehistoric past. Researches by the author have revealed many more historical facts and data. Some historians tend to omit information that does not suit their point of view, such as the Balangiga massacre and other items that were deserted in describing the epic odyssey of the Filipino people. Since this is a historical dictionary of the Philippines, this author endeavored to err on the side of inclusion, rather than exclusion.

In the first edition, the bibliography was masterfully constructed by my late coauthor May Kyi Win, who did a magnificent job, and my task in this revised edition was simply to build on the foundation by extensively updating it with many new publications. Sources of information include scholarly works, domestic newspapers, and foreign periodicals. Full references of these and other sources used by the author to develop the entries are listed in the bibliography. The bibliography was culled from a wide range of materials with priority given to English, Filipino, and Spanish. Most of these materials are found in the library of the University of the Philippines, National Library of the Philippines, and U.S. Library of Congress. However, many of the items may also be found in several university libraries in the United States that have sections on Southeast Asia, such as the University of Northern Illinois, University of Hawaii-East West Center, University of Michigan, and the University of Wisconsin.

Acknowledgments

The author wishes to gratefully acknowledge the following persons who made this revised edition possible:

- Gregory Green, curator, Donn V. Hart Southeast Asia Collection, Northern Illinois University, for his major contribution in the expansion of the bibliography.
- Alex Lawrence-Richards and Mike Rothamel, for their superb formatting work.
- Sue Davis and Donna Turnball, for their technical and mechanical assistance.
- Corazon B. Guillermo, for her faithful encouragement and wholehearted support in this worthwhile endeavor.
- My late coauthor May Kyi Win, former curator of the Donn V. Hart Southeast Asia Collection, Northern Illinois University, whose excellent bibliographical work in the first edition will remain her enduring contribution to the family of historical dictionaries.
- Jon Woronoff, for his invaluable editing, wise counsel, and insights to make this book fit to join the cavalcade of historical dictionaries.
- And finally my special thanks to the Filipino reporters, writers, historians, professors, scholars, and librarians whose names are too numerous to mention and whose works have immensely helped me in the development of many significant entries.

Acronyms and Abbreviations

AFP	Armed Forces of the Philippines
AFTA	Asian Free Trade Area
AGILE	Accelerated Growth Investment and Liberalization with Equity
AI	Amnesty International
AMLA	Anti-money Laundering Law
ARMM	Autonomous Region of Muslim Mindanao
ASEAN	Association of Southeast Asian Nations
AusAid	Australian Agency for International Development
BCC	Biodiversity Conservation Center
BMP	Bukluran Ng Mangagawang Pilipino
CAR	Cordillera Autonomous Region
CPP	Communist Party of the Philippines
CHAMPS	Competence, Health, Agricultural Productivity, Maintenance of Peace and Order, Preservation of the Environment
COMELEC	Commission on Election
DECS	Department of Education, Culture, and Sports
DWB	Doctors Without Borders
ECOP	Employers Confederation of the Philippines
EDCOR	Economic Development Corps
EDSA	Epifanio de los Santos Avenue
FATF	Financial Action Task Force
FDI	Foreign Direct Investment
GABRIELA	General Assembly Binding Women for Reforms, Integrity, Equality, Leadership, and Action
GDP	Gross Domestic Product
GIFT	Genetically improved form of tilapia
GOMBURZA	Gomez, Burgos, and Zamora

HUKBALAHAP	Hukbo ng Bayan Laban Sa Hapon
INC	Iglesia Ni Cristo
IPD	Institute of Popular Democracy
IPRA	Indigenous People's Right Act
IRRI	International Rice Research Institute
IUCN	International Union of Conservation of Nature
JI	Jemaah Islamiyah
JUSMAG	Joint U.S.Military Assistance Group
KAAKBAY	Kilusan Sa Kapangyarihan at Karapatan ng Bayan (Movement for the Power and Rights of the Nation)
KAKAMPI	Kapisanan ng mga Kamag-anak ng Migrating Mangagawang Pilipino (Organization of Relatives of Migrant Workers)
KAISA	Kaisa Para sa Kaunlaran (United in Progress)
KAMPI	Kabalikat ng Mamamayang Pilipino
KAPATID	Association of Relatives and Friends of Political Detainees
KARAPATAN	Alliance for the Advancement of Human Rights
KBL	Kilusang Bagong Lipunan (New Society Movement)
KMP	Kilusang Magbubukid ng Pilipinas (Peasant Movement of the Philippines)
KMU	Kilusang Mayo Uno (May 1st Movement)
KOMPIL	Kongreso ng Mamamayang Pilipino (Council of Philippine Affairs)
LABAN	Laban ng Demokratikong Pilipino (Fight for Democratic Philippines)
LAKAS	Lakas ng Bayan (Strength of the Nation)
LAKAS-CMD	Lakas ng EDSA-National Union of Christian and Muslim Democrats
LAMP	Laban ng Mamayang Pilipino (Fight for the Pilipino People)
MAKIBAKA	Malayang Kilusan ng Bagong Kababa-ihan (Free Movement of New Women)
MAN	Movement for the Advancement of Nationalism
MILF	Moro Islamic Liberation Front
MNLF	Muslim National Liberation Front

MMDA	Metro Manila Development Authority
MSF	Médecins Sans Frontiéres
NAIA	Ninoy Aquino International Airport
NAMFREL	National Citizen's Movement for Free Elections
NAN	Non-aligned Nations
NBI	National Bureau of Investigation
NCCA	National Commission of Culture and Arts
NDP	National Democratic Party
NFSW	National Federation of Sugar Workers
NGO	Nongovernmental Organization
NPA	New Peoples' Army
OFW	Overseas Foreign Workers
OIC	Organization of Islamic Conference
PACAP	Philippine-Australian Community Assistance Program
PAEC	Philippine Atomic Energy Commission
PAOCTF	Presidential Anti-Organized Crime Task Force
PCGG	Presidential Commission on Good Government
PDP	Pilipino Democratic Party
PEPE	Popular Education for People Empowerment
PESC	Philippine–European Solidarity Center
PLCPM	Philippine Legislators Committee on Population and Management
PNP	Philippine National Police
PRRM	Philippine Rural Reconstruction Movement
PSAP	Philippine-Singapore Plan
RAM	Rebolusyong Alyasang Makabayan (Reform the Armed Forces Movement)
REZA	Regional Economic Zone Authority
SEATO	Southeast Asia Treaty Organization
SIL	Summer Institute of Linguistics
SOCSKSARGEN	Southern Cotabato, Sultan Kudarat, Sarangani, Gen. Santos
SPCPD	Southern Philippine Council for Peace and Development
TESDA	Technical Education and Development Authority
TNC	Transnational Corporations
TUCP	Trade Union Congress of the Philippines

UNA	United National Alliance
UNIDO	United Nationalist Democratic Organization
USAID	U.S. Agency for International Development
WTO	World Trade Organization

Chronology

30,500 B.C. Ancestors of the Aetas (Negritoes) migrate by land bridges to the islands.

22,000 B.C. Early Homo sapiens inhabit Tabon caves, Palawan.

3,000 B.C. Austronesians reach the islands on outrigger canoes.

1 B.C. Ancient Filipinos build rice terraces in Luzon.

585 A.D. Ancient Manobo pottery found in Kulaman, Cotabato.

900 A.D. Laguna copper plates inscription (Old Tagalog and Sanskrit).

8–1377 A.D. Sri Vijaya Hinduized Malay empire based in Palembang, Sumatra, included Sulu and Visayan islands under its rule.

140 A.D. Ancient wooden coffins and trade ceramics found in Panhu-tongan, Surigao del Sur, are carbon-dated to this period.

1292–1478 Majapahit empire included Sabah and the Visayas.

ca. 1200 Ancient burial jars found in Huluga caves, Cagayan de Oro.

ca. 1212 Arrival of legendary 10 Bornean datus fleeing from Sabah and settling in Panay Island.

1402 Chinese merchants establish trading posts on Luzon.

ca. 1515 Sharif Kabungsuan brings Islamic faith to Cotabato.

1519 Ferdinand Magellan leaves Spain to search for new trade routes.

1521 **16 March:** Magellan lands in Cebu and claims the land for Spain. He is killed on Mactan Island by Chief Lapu-lapu.

1543 Ruy Lopez de Villalobos names Leyte-Samar Islands Filipinas.

1565   Miguel Lopez de Legaspi claims the archipelago for Spain.

1571   Rajah Sulayman killed defending Manila against the Spanish.

1574   Uprising of Rajah Lakandula of Tondo against the Spanish.

1585   First rebellion by Filipinos, called Indios, against the Spanish.

1589   Revolt in Cagayan valley and Ilocos provinces.

1593   First book *Doctrina Cristiana* published in Manila.

1595   Naval battle between Dutch and Spanish in Manila Bay.

1603   First Chinese revolt in Manila.

1611   Dominicans establish University of Santo Tomas, Manila.

1615   Start of galleon trade between Manila and Acapulco.

1621   Tamblot revolt in Bohol.

1622   Chinese pirate Limahong occupies Corregidor Island.

1625   Miguel Lanab lead revolt in Cagayan.

1636   Dutch invaders burn Cagsawa church, Albay.

1637   Tomas Pinpin publishes first newsletter *Succesos Felices*.

1638   Jolo falls to Spanish forces.

1647   Dutch fleet besieges Manila.

1649   Sumuroy revolt in Samar to protest forced labor.

1660   Andres Malong revolt in Pangasinan.

1716   Eruption of Taal volcano.

1723   Diego Silang revolt in Ilocos.

1744–1829   Francisco Dagohoy revolt in Bohol.

1755   Expulsion of the Chinese from the Philippines.

1762   Juan de la Cruz Palaris revolt in Pangasinan.

1762–64   British occupation of Manila.

1768   Expulsion of the Jesuits from the Philippines.

1788 Manila becomes an open port.

1796 First American trading vessel visits Manila.

1800 Governor Jose Blanco introduces sugar cane and tobacco as cash crops.

1811 First newspaper *Del Superior Govierno* published in Manila.

1814 Eruption of Mayon volcano burying town of Cagsawa, Albay.

1815 End of galleon trade between Mexico and the Philippines.

1821 Start of direct mail between Spain and the Philippines.

1837 Philippine representation to the Spanish Cortes.

1839 Jesuits return to the Philippines.

1850 **30 August:** Birth of Marcelo H. Del Pilar in Bulacan.

1861 **19 June:** Birth of Jose Rizal in Calamba, Laguna.

1862 **30 November:** Birth of Andres Bonfacio in Tondo, Manila.

1864 **23 July:** Birth of Apolinario Mabini, the "Brains of the Revolution," in Tanauan, Batangas.

1869 **30 March:** Birth of Emilio Aguinaldo in Kawit, Cavite.

1872 **17 February:** Execution of Filipino priests: Jose Burgos, Mariano Gomez, and Jacinto Zamora, known champions of the secularization movement.

1872–1894 Filipino Propaganda movement in Spain.

1875 **15 December:** Birth of Emilio Jacinto.

1887 Establishment of Museo-Biblioteca de Filipinas in Manila. Jose Rizal's first novel *Noli Me Tangere* published in Berlin.

1888 Filipinos petition expulsion of Spanish friars and secularization of parishes.

1889 Spanish civil code introduced in the Philippines. *La Soladaridad* published in Spain.

1891 Jose Rizal published second novel *El Filibusterismo* in Ghent, Belgium.

1892   Jose Rizal founds *La Liga Filipina* in Manila. Opening of first railroad between Manila and Dagupan. Jose Rizal deported to Dapitan, Zamboanga. First Tagalog newspaper *Diariong Tagalog* appears in Manila. **7 July:** Founding of the Katipunan by Andres Bonifacio in Tondo, Manila.

1896   **23 August:** Cry of Balintawak Pugad Lawin. Outbreak of Philippine–Spanish Revolution. Filipino forces under Emilio Aguinaldo capture Cavite.

1897   **15 December:** Pact of Biak Na Bato temporarily suspends fighting between Filipinos and Spanish. Aguinaldo and his military staff go into exile to Hong Kong.

1896   **30 December:** Execution of Jose Rizal at Bagumbayan (Luneta) Manila.

1897   **10 May:** Emilio Aguinaldo orders execution of Andres and Procopio Bonifacio.

1898   **1 May:** Admiral George Dewey defeats Spanish naval fleet in Manila Bay. **12 June:** Aguinaldo declares Philippine independence in Kawit, Cavite. **13 August:** American Expeditionary forces occupy Manila. **15 September:** Malolos Congress convenes at Malolos and ratifies constitution. **10 December:** Treaty of Paris. Spain cedes the Philippines to the United States for the sum of $20 million following its defeat by combined Filipino and American forces.

1899   **23 January:** Aguinaldo inaugurated as president of the first republic in Kawit, Cavite. **4 February:** American soldier kills Filipino soldier and triggers Philippine–American Revolution. **6 February:** U.S. Senate votes to annex the Philippines. **4 March:** First Philippine Commission arrives in Manila to set up American colonization. **15 April:** Apolinario Mabini issues manifesto debunking Philippine Commission report. **15 June:** General Antonio Luna assassinated in Cabanatuan, Nueva Ecija. **21 November:** General Emilio Aguinaldo retreats to the mountains of Northern Luzon. **2 December:** General Gregorio del Pilar and his 60 men are killed in the battle of Tirad Pass while defending Aguinaldo against pursuing American forces.

1900   *Manila Bulletin*, first English newspaper, appears in Manila. **16 March:** Appointment of Second Philippine Commission headed by

William Howard Taft, who was also appointed first civilian governor. **1 September:** Taft Commission becomes the colonial legislative body.

1901 Silliman University founded in Dumaguete, Negros Oriental. First Protestant institution of higher learning in the Philippines. **7 January:** Apolinario Mabini and General Artemio Ricarte exiled in Guam for refusing to take oath of allegiance to the United States. **23 March 23:** Aguinaldo captured in Palanan, Isabela. **23 August:** Arrival of American teachers aboard U.S. transport USS *Thomas*. **1 September:** *El Renacimiento* published in Manila.

1902 End of Philippine–American revolution, after Aguinaldo takes oath of allegiance. U.S. Congress passed Organic Act governing Philippine islands. **3 August:** Gregorio Aglipay founds Iglesia Filipina Independiente.

1903 First census taken under American administration shows 7.6 million population. First Philippine election law enacted (Act 1582) by the Philippine Commission.

1905 Philippine feminist movement wins right to vote.

1907 Nacionalista Party formed.

1908 University of the Philippines granted charter. First public institution of higher learning.

1913 Francis Burton Harrison starts Filipinization program.

1916 Jones Act grants election of Philippine Senate and House of Representatives.

1920 **17 July:** Resignation of Filipino cabinet members to protest Governor-General Leonard Wood's administration.

1927 Philippine Independence bill passed by U.S. Congress.

1930 Sakdalista Farmers movement to protest harsh tenant–landlord relations.

1931 Tayug uprising of tenant farmers to protest *kasama* system.

1933 Suffrage bill passed by Philippine Congress.

1934 Tydings-McDuffie Act passed by U.S. Congress setting Commonwealth government in 1935.

1935 Manuel L. Quezon elected president of Philippine Commonwealth.

1937 Filipino women attain right to vote. The first women in Southeast Asia to obtain the right of suffrage.

1940 President Quezon proclaims Tagalog as one of the official languages beginning July 4, 1946.

1941 **7 December:** Japanese attack Pearl Harbor and Clark Field in the Philippines. **8 December:** Japanese invasion forces land in various parts of the Philippines. Filipino–American forces withdraw to Bataan-Corregidor.

1942 Japanese forces occupy Manila. **20 February:** President Quezon and family leave Corregidor by submarine for Australia. **12 March:** General Douglas MacArthur and family escape to Australia. **9 April:** General Jonathan Wainwright surrenders Filipino–American forces to General Masaharu Homma. Captured soldiers forced to march to concentration camp in Tarlac.

1943 **14 October:** Japanese puppet Philippine Republic established. Jose P. Laurel appointed president by Japanese.

1944 **1 August:** Death of President Manuel L. Quezon at Saranac Lake, N.Y. **20 October:** U.S. Sixth Army lands in Leyte followed by other liberation forces landings in Mindoro and Lingayen Gulf. **23 October:** Philippine Commonwealth re-established with Sergio Osmeña as president.

1945 **7 February:** Liberation of Manila from Japanese forces. **2 March:** American paratroopers retake Corregidor. **4 July:** General Macarthur declares liberation of the Philippines.

1946 Liberal Party formed by Manuel Roxas. **4 April:** Japanese General Masaharu Homma executed in Manila for war crimes. **28 May:** Manuel Roxas inaugurated as president. **4 July:** Philippine independence proclaimed by virtue of an act passed by the U.S. Congress in 1934.

1947 Collaborators with Japanese pardoned by President Manuel Roxas. **11 March:** Parity rights amendment ratified. **14 March:** Military bases agreement signed with United States for 99-year term.

1948   15 April: President Manuel Roxas dies in office, succeeded by Vice President Elpidio Quirino. **17 April:** Elpidio Quirino sworn in as president.

1949   8 November: Elpidio Quirino elected president.

1951   16 June: National Movement for Free Elections organized.

30 August: U.S. Philippine Mutual Defense Treaty signed.

1953   10 November: Ramon Magsaysay defeats Quirino for the presidency.

1954   15 May: Hukbalahap Supremo Luis Taruc surrenders to the government.

1955 Bell Trade Act replaced with Laurel-Langley Agreement. **17 August:** Japan signs $800 million reparation bill.

1956 Congress approves Rizal law requiring study of Jose Rizal in college. **26 May:** Congress approves New National Anthem in Pilipino.

1957   17 March: President Ramon Magsaysay dies in plane crash in Cebu. **18 March:** Vice President Carlos P. Garcia sworn in as president. **12 November:** Carlos P. Garcia elected president.

1959   12 October: Bohlen-Serrano agreement on military bases.

1961   14 November: Garcia defeated for presidency by Diosdado Macapagal.

1962   12 June: New Philippine independence day declared by President Diosdado Macapagal.

1963   8 August: President Macapagal removes import controls and signs land code into law.

1964   6 February: Death of General Emilio Aguinaldo.

1965   9 November: Ferdinand Marcos defeats Macapagal for the presidency.

1966   16 September: United States agrees on the reduction of the 99-year term of the bases to 25 years plus $45 million in economic aid.

1967 Constitution Convention bill passed by Congress.

1968 New Peoples' Army formed by Jose Maria Sison.

1969 **11 November:** Marcos reelected president.

1970 **30 January:** Massive student demonstrations in Manila against Marcos and U.S government. **7 April:** Trade unions lead general strike to protest increased oil prices.

1971 **21 August.** Plaza Miranda massacre. President Marcos suspends writ of habeas corpus.

1972 **22 September:** Marcos declares martial law and assumes all powers of government. **20 October:** New Constitution approved opening way for Marcos to stay in power indefinitely. **16 November:** Six thousand people arrested under martial law.

1973 **17 January:** Marcos signs two decrees extending martial law. **13 July:** Marcos lifts curfew and eases restrictions on free speech. **31 December:** National referendum approves Batasang Pambansa (National Constitution) that included a parliamentary form of government.

1974 **1 September:** Roman Catholic bishops petition Marcos to end martial law.

1975 **12 January:** Benigno Aquino Jr. and Roman Catholic bishops file petition to block implementation of Batasang Pambansa.

1976 **21 January:** Marcos postpones national elections.

1977 **12 August:** Marcos announces measures to ease martial law. **25 November:** Military tribunal sentences Benigno Aquino Jr. to death by musketry. Sentence was not carried out due to worldwide protests.

1978 **7 April:** Marcos' Kilusang Bagong Lipunan wins control of Congress. **12 June:** Marcos sworn in as prime minister in addition to post as president. Imelda Marcos appointed to cabinet position.

1979 Jaime Cardinal Sin delivers protest against martial law and asks release of Benigno Aquino Jr.

1980 **20 January:** Kilusang Bagong Lipunan win majority in local election.

1981 **17 January:** Marcos declares end of nine years of martial law. **16 June:** Marcos becomes president in elections boycotted by most of his opponents.

1982   Marcos appoints wife Imelda to executive council.

1983   **21 August:** Benigno Aquino Jr. assassinated at Manila International Airport. **15 September:** Corazon Aquino leads national rally to protest Marcos dictatorship.

1984   **14 May:** National elections. Marcos' party wins majority seats in congress.

1985   **23 January:** Government investigatory commission charges Armed Forces Chief of Staff General Fabian Ver and 20 soldiers for slaying of Benigno Aquino Jr. **3 November:** Marcos announces plan to hold "snap election." **3 December:** Corazon Aquino declares intention to run for president.

1986   **7 February:** Snap election. Marcos claims early win while widespread fraud reported. **8 February:** NAMFREL reports Corazon Aquino ahead in election count. **22 February:** Juan Ponce Enrile and Fidel Ramos defect to Aquino Camp. **25 February:** Corazon Aquino sworn in as president. Marcos also takes oath of office in Malacañang. Then, Marcos, his family, and some staff were flown out of the country to exile in Hawaii. **25 March:** President Aquino issues Proclamation No. 3 Freedom Constitution. **6 July:** Arturo Tolentino leads coup d'etat and declares himself acting president. **15 October:** Congress adopts draft of new constitution.

2 February: Voters approve new constitution. **11 May:** National election. President Aquino's party gains majorities in congress. **28 August:** Military coup against President Aquino. **9 September:** President Aquino dismisses entire cabinet.

1988   **1 January:** Fidel Ramos appointed secretary of national defense. **4 February:** Top Communist leaders arrested. **10 June:** President Corazon Aquino signs comprehensive agrarian reform law. **17 October:** Interim base agreement between Philippines and United States

1989   First elections in the Autonomous Region in Muslim Mindanao. **1 December:** Coup attempt against President Aquino.

1990   **6 October:** Seventh coup d'etat against President Aquino fails. **6 November:** Inauguration of Autonomous Region of Muslim Mindanao. **29 November:** U.S. citizenship granted to Filipino veterans.

1991   Philippine Senate votes to terminate the U.S.–RP Military Bases Agreement, initiating the pullout of all U.S. military troops in the country.

12 June: Mt. Pinatubo eruption after 600 years of dormancy. **17 July:** Multilateral Assistance Program signed between Philippines and United States.

30 June: Fidel Ramos succeeds Corazon Aquino as president. **16 September:** Philippine Senate rejects extension of Subic Bay Naval Base and Cubi Point Naval Air Station. **24 November:** United States turns over Subic Bay Naval Base to Philippine government.

1993   25 April: Trade agreement between Philippines and China signed. **1 June.** United States approves Mutual Aid Initiative (Philippine Assistance Plan). **21 September:** Southeast Asian Free Trade Agreement signed between President Fidel Ramos and President Soeharto.

1994   2 February: Extradition treaty between United States and Philippines signed. **15 April:** Philippines and Vietnam sign trade pact. **28 May:** Value-added tax law takes effect. **31 May:** Amnesty for communist insurgents and military rebels. **29 September:** Second eruption of Mt. Pinatubo. **25 October:** Philippines and Malaysia Defense Agreement signed.

1995   12 January: Pope John Paul visits the Philippines. **22 July:** First International Conference of Philippines–Japan Relations. **1 September.** Swiss Bank returns $500 million left by late President Marcos to the Philippines.

1996   Oil Deregulation Act signed by President Ramos. **18 July:** Mactan International Airport opens. **25 August:** Philippine Consulate opens in Ho Chi Minh City, Vietnam.

1997   January–June Balikatan (Joint Military Exercises) held in Basilan. **29 October:** Indigenous Peoples' Right Act signed into law.

1998   Philippine Centennial Celebration. First party-list elections. **14 May:** Joseph Ejercito Estrada elected president.

2000   Balikatan Exercises in Mindano and Luzon. **13 November.** House impeaches President Joseph Ejercito Estrada.

2001   Visiting Forces Agreement signed. **16 January:** EDSA II People Power protest against President Estrada. **19 January:** President Estrada ousted by People Power. **20 January:** Gloria Macapagal Arroyo sworn in as president. **1 November:** 50th Anniversary of United States–Philippine Mutual Defense Treaty.

2002   Sectoral parties field candidates in national election. **1 January:** Balikatan Military Exercises held in Basilan Island. **19 June:** Philippine Armed Forces captures MILF camps in Mindanao.

2003   July–October: Balikatan Military exercises, which included civil military operation. **18 October:** President George W. Bush addresses Philippine Congress. **24 October:** House impeaches Supreme Court Justice Hilario Davide Jr. Supreme Court declares impeachment violated constitution.

2004   10 May: National elections. President Gloria Macapagal Arroyo competes against three opponents in the presidential race. **30 May:** Gloria Macapagal Arroyo and Noli De Castro declared winners in the presidential and vice presidential elections. **June 30:** President Gloria Macapagal Arroyo inaugurated 14th president at Cebu City. **July:** President Arroyo orders withdrawal of Philippine troops from Iraq, bowing to terrorist threats to behead Filipino hostage.

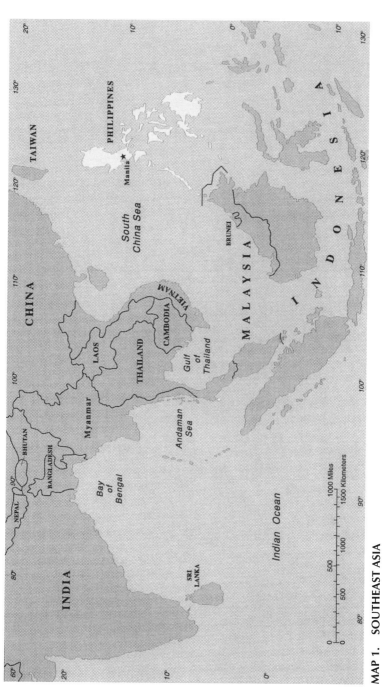

MAP 1. SOUTHEAST ASIA

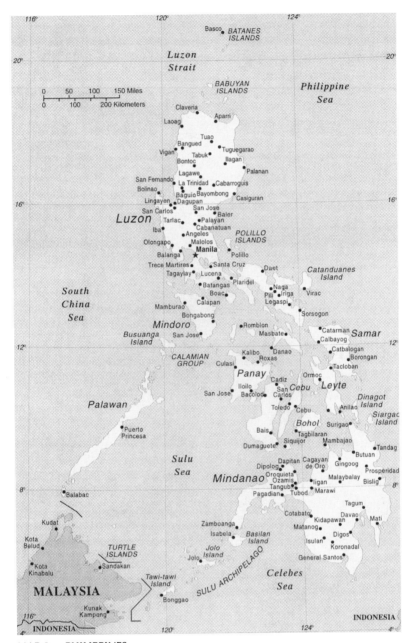

MAP 2. PHILIPPINES

Introduction

LAND AND PEOPLE

The Philippines is a quintessential amalgam of islands spread out on the Orient seas. Four cultural influences and three major religions have molded a distinctive administrative unity among disparate entities and ancient island fiefdoms. Philippine history is the story of 380 arduous years of struggle to throw off the oppressive yoke of Spanish colonizers, only to be replaced by another predatory but benevolent invader that enlightened the people to the rudiments of the democratic process and led them eventually to the tortuous path of their cherished dream of freedom. Over the years, the country weathered massive political and economic upheavals without significantly harming the basic foundation of the republic. During World War II, the foundation was severely strained by the brief and brutal occupation of the country by an Asian power. Although its economy and infrastructure were in shambles, the Philippines kept its rendezvous with destiny to be an independent nation in 1946. In the ensuing years the experiment in democracy has proven its endurance by its stalwart public institutions, progressive educational system, and vibrant mass media.

The Republic of the Philippines is situated approximately 400 miles off the Asian mainland. It is flanked by the South China Sea to the north and west, the Sulu Sea and Celebes Sea to the southwest, and the Philippine Sea to the east. Malaysia and Indonesia are the nearest land neighbors to the south and west along with Taiwan to the north. Geographically, ethnically, and culturally, the Philippines lie within the realm of Southeast Asia. The Philippine archipelago comprises approximately 7,100 islands and islets covering a total land area of 300,780 square kilometers and extending 1,843 kilometers from north to south. The main island belt is generally less than 400 kilometers wide. Luzon with 104,607 square kilometers and Mindanao with 945,532 square kilometers, the two largest islands, comprise nearly three-quarters of the land area. Palawan, Mindoro, and seven of the larger islands in the Visayan group—Masbate, Samar, Leyte, Bohol, Cebu, Negros, and Panay—account for most of the remainder. The islands are separated by inland seas at their farthest points and by channels and straits at their nearest. The Philippines' total coastline is 15,500 kilometers. Lowlands are found in the river valleys of the larger islands and on scattered coastal areas of the smaller ones. The largest freshwater lake in the Philippines is Laguna de Bay located on Luzon. There are 22 active and inactive volcanoes, the highest being Mt. Apo (2,954 meters) in Mindanao. Mt. Pinatubo in Luzon, which has been dormant for 600 years, erupted in 1991 and 1994.

Anthropologists believe that the islands may have been inhabited for 250,000 years. First arrivals were the Aetas or pygmies, who crossed the land bridge from Asia about 30,500 years ago. After the disappearance of the land bridge, the early Malays, who came by barangays from the Indonesian Islands, accomplished human migrations via sea. Hence, the majority of the Filipinos are of Malay descent. The tropical maritime climate is marked by high temperatures, high relative humidity, heavy precipitation, and light winds. The northeast monsoon months are December to February while the southwest monsoon season is from May to October. Typhoons normally occur during the monsoon seasons. In most areas, maximum daily temperatures at sea level range from the mid-80s Fahrenheit (27 degrees Celsius) to the mid-90s Fahrenheit (28 degrees Celsius), dropping to the mid-60s Fahrenheit (19 degrees Celsius) at night. Mean relative humidity varies from 75–90 percent. The average annual rainfall registers between 42 inches in the extreme southwestern portion of Mindanao to 180 inches in the mountains of northern Luzon. The two distinct seasons are wet and dry. The wet season is usually the time for rice planting.

The population as of the 2000 census stands at 76.5 million concentrated in 12 major islands, which constitute 95 percent of the available land space. This represents an increase of 11.5 percent or 7.9 million over the 1995 census count of 68.6 persons. The population grew at the rate of 2.36 percent annually between 1995 and 2000. If the annual growth rate continues at 2.36 percent, then the Philippines population is expected to double in approximately 29 years. Life expectancy at birth for the total population is estimated at 68.12 years. The population is made up of 86 percent Christian Malay, 6 percent Muslim Malay, 5 percent Chinese, and three percent indigenous groups. Manila, the principal city, has about 8 percent of the national population. The greater portion, just over 63 percent, live in or near villages (barrios) of less than 5,000 residents. Almost 37 percent of the populace is under 14 years of age.

Philippine society is the product of eastern and western cultural influences, which blend into a distinctive entity. Four cultures and two major religions have shaped the modern Philippines. Early exposure to Chinese cultural and commercial influence, more than three centuries of Spanish colonial rule, and almost 50 years of American tutelage have appreciably altered, but not obscured, the Malayan character of Philippine society. Its basic unit is the nuclear family with the father as the head; the family includes extended relatives of both husband and wife. Social stratification is governed by wealth and education, a byproduct of Spanish and American influence. The upper class constitutes 11 percent (professionals, civil servants, teachers, and business people) and a lower class, comprises 89 percent (farmers, laborers, fishermen, merchants, etc.).

Literacy is substantially higher in the Philippines than in other countries in Southeast Asia. According to the 2002 census, 95 percent of the total population 15 years of age and over can read and write in at least one language. Literacy ranges from a high of 91.5 percent in the Greater Manila area to a low of 55–65 percent in the rural countryside. A large proportion of the nation's population therefore uses some form of mass communication. In 2003, there were 26 broadsheets (newspapers and tabloids), 12 of them in the English language, 366 AM and 290 FM radio stations, and 75 television and broadcasts stations. The Philippine press is described as one of the freest in the world, mainly because of its propensity for muckraking, a legacy of American journalism.

Filipino, a derivative of Tagalog, is the officially designated language spoken by 46 percent of the population, while English is understood by some 40 percent and serves as the lingua franca in government, business, mass media, and academia. There are no less than 87 indigenous dialects. However, 86 percent of the people belong to eight linguistic groups, namely: Tagalog, Cebuano, Ilocano, Ilongo, Bicolano, Waray-waray, Pangasinan, and Pampango. All eight belong to the Malay-Polynesian language family. Each has impressive literary traditions, especially Tagalog.

HISTORY

Prehistoric Period

Long before the Europeans came to what is now the Philippines, the Chinese were among the early group of Asian traders who had direct contacts with the ancient Filipinos. Sino-Philippine contacts became extensive probably at the turn of the 10th century A.D. and reached its peak by the middle of the 14th and the 15th centuries. During these periods, thousands of trade items—mostly porcelain wares—reached the country. The earliest Chinese traders to reach the Philippines were those who belong to the T'ang Dynasty. Evidence of T'ang wares was found in gravesites by archaeologists. After the decline of the T'ang in China, another group of Chinese merchants came to trade with the early Filipinos. These were the Sung peoples. Archeologists have identified artifacts from various excavations as belonging to the early and late Sung period and kilned in South China. Chinese junks brought their business to the known port, Tondo, which is the present location of Manila. Aside from porcelain, the Sung merchants also traded with the ancient Filipinos nonceramic items, such as mirrors, scales, coins, and jade. Chinese influence on Filipino life is considerable.

Following the Chinese were the Arab traders, missionaries, and teachers who brought Islam from the Malay Peninsula in the latter part of the 13th century. They entered the Philippines by way of Borneo and to the Sulu archipelago and the southern coast of Mindanao. It is in these areas that early Arab teachers such as Rajah Baginda and Sharif Kabungsuan firmly established Islam. The latter was able to set up a sultanate in Sulu, and from there he succeeded in spreading the faith in southern Philippines. Those who accepted the faith became converts, and those who refused Islam went to the interior parts of the mountains (their descendants are known today as Bilaans, Tagabilis, Subanons, Bagobos, Mandayas, and Manobos). These Muslim sultanates challenged the intrusion of the Spanish as they tried to spread the Christian religion in southern Philippines.

What was the nature of prehistoric Filipino life and society? Filipino historian Jose V. Abueva described this briefly: "The early Filipinos developed their own cultures and social and economic organizations. They were governed by their own leaders under their own laws. Their implements, pottery, jewelry, and graveyard markings indicate remarkable craftsmanship and artistry. Filipinos lived in scattered barangays, or communities of some 30–100 households based largely on kinship. Each barangay was an independent social, economic, and political unit. As its head, the datu was paternal protector and a political leader. Like other peoples of Southeast Asia before their conquest by Western imperialist, the Filipinos had developed indigenously their free village communities, tilling their own land, governing themselves according to their own customs and traditions, fighting each other on occasions, and combining in loose confederation under the always-precarious suzerainty of feudal princes. For Southeast Asian, freedom—*kalayaan, merdeka*—is neither an imported word nor an imported thing."[1]

Colonial

Spanish Period

Ferdinand Magellan, a Portuguese navigator, who commanded a fleet of five ships flying the flag of Spain, claimed the islands for Spain when he landed in Samar on April 16, 1521. Natives provided food for his starving crew. His chaplain planted the cross of Christianity and baptized the local chief and his followers. Magellan proceeded to Cebu Island, where he met violent resistance from Chief Lapu-lapu of nearby Mactan Island. In the battle, the Portuguese explorer was killed. Subsequent expeditions, such as the one led by Miguel Lopez de Legaspi, initiated the establishment of Spanish colonial rule, which was primarily commercial and secondarily religious. The latter became a more enduring legacy, and today Roman Catholicism is the predominant religion of Philippine society. Spanish churches built on a colossal scale to impress the natives with power of the Christian God dominate the Filipino landscape. After vanquishing the ruler, Rajah Sulayman, Legaspi founded Manila.

Spain treated the islands as a feudal agrarian estate for 333 years. The harshness of the Spanish rule led to more than 300 revolts and uprisings throughout the islands. Spanish rule had two lasting effects on Philippine society: the near universal conversion of the population to Roman Catholicism and the creation of a landed elite—the encomienda system. Although under the direct order of Philip II that the conversion of the Philippines to Christianity was not be accomplished by force, the monastic orders set to their missionary duties with purpose. Unable to extirpate the indigenous beliefs by coercion and fear, Philippine Catholicism incorporates a deep substratus of native customs and ritual. While the missionaries spread through the colony to found parishes and estates in the barangays, the officials of the civil administration preferred to stay in Manila and govern indirectly through the traditional barangay datu or village chief. The creation of a privileged landed-holding elite on whom most of the rural population was dependent as landless tenants introduced a class division in Philippine society that has been the perennial source of social discontent and political strife ever since. Spanish rule ended when the United States took over the islands after a short war with Spain and the Philippines became an American colony.

American Period

The Philippines was ceded to the United States in 1898 by the terms of the Treaty of Paris, which ended the Spanish–American War. There was vigorous resistance to the United States takeover by the Filipino people led by General Emilio Aguinaldo, who had declared the independence of the Philippines from Spanish colonial rule on June 12, 1898. The Philippine–American Revolution lasted for three years until Aguinaldo was captured in 1901 by American troops. Aguinaldo had to sign an oath of allegiance, which squelched active resistance in most of the islands. General Miguel Malvar continued to fight until his surrender in 1902 finally ended the war. An estimated half million Filipinos were killed during that brief revolution. The establishment of a military government marked the occupation of the Philippines. A civilian government in 1900 following directives from U.S. President William McKinley replaced it. William Howard Taft was appointed the first American governor-general. His administration was highlighted by an astute benevolence, yet a guarded attitude toward the Filipinos, whom he considered still unfit for self-rule. As a result, he introduced policies designed to guide the Filipinos to self-government.

As Filipinos readily began to learn the rudiments of social and political democracy, they realized how limited their power was. Municipal governments functioned under Filipino officials, but they were under the supervision of provincial governments made up of Americans, who maintained final control over political life. When the Filipinization program of Governor-General Francis Burton Harrison began to take effect, however, more Filipinos won civil service positions. By 1916, the Filipinos had obtained complete control of the legislative branch of government. In the ensuing years, their overwhelming cry was for complete self-government.

Commonwealth Period

In 1935, a commonwealth government was instituted. Full independence came in 1946 by an enabling act of the U.S. Congress. American colonization of the Philippines was strongly influenced by economic interests. Taft's agenda and those of succeeding governors-general were based on one central policy: to make the new colony dependent upon the United States. The policy was implemented by creating a U.S. market for Philippine export goods, with the United States as a source of manufactured goods and investment capital. The policy constituted the framework of the special relationship between the Philippines and the United States for the next 50 years.

In establishing control of the Philippines, America did not rely on its regulation of the economic base alone, but used popular education as an indirect tool for political domination. Nevertheless, the organization of a public school system is perhaps America's greatest single achievement in the Philippines. Spain made little effort to educate the "Indios," as Filipinos were then called. The few *ilustrados* (rich intelligentsia), notably the Filipino hero Jose Rizal, came from wealthy families and went to Europe for higher education. The American program of free and universal public education resulted in the widespread enlightenment of the populace and the rise of many new leaders. Foremost among these were Manuel L. Quezon and Sergio Osmeña, who owed their careers to American political mentors. They were imbued with ideas of democracy and self-government, which in turn made them ardent nationalists with national independence as their main political objective.

American Legacy

Between 1901 and 1902, more than 1,000 American teachers, known as Thomasites after the vessel USS *Thomas* on which they arrived, taught in the public schools. These teachers, who were the precursors of the Peace Corps, were assigned throughout the archipelago. Most of them taught English and served with dedication. Their pioneering work instilled in the Filipinos a deep faith in the general value of education, a faith that continues to this day. In the early 1920s, many private and public institutions of higher learning were founded. The first of the publicly funded universities was the University of the Philippines established in

1908. Its curricula and structure were patterned after American universities. The university is the alma mater of many leaders in government, industry, and business. Currently, there are 1,675 institutions of higher education with approximately 56,380 instructors.

One other legacy of the Americans was the press, which the Filipinos used so effectively to gain their independence and build a nation. In the postwar years, the Philippine press became the "fourth estate," which assumed its role as a tool of the democratic process so much so that the Philippine press was dubbed the "freest press" in Asia. There were prices to pay like its suspension during the martial law years of the dictator Ferdinand Marcos, and many Supreme Court decisions that went against violators, but the freedom of the press remained firmly anchored in the Constitution. It learned a lesson by balancing its role as the disseminator of information and watchdog on government while serving its entertainment function with great fanfare.

World War II

World War II briefly interrupted the democratization process. Japan invaded the Philippines on December 8, 1941, after its perfidious attack on Pearl Harbor on December 7. Faced by a superior invading force, the defending United States Armed Forces in the Far East (USAFFE), under the command of General Douglas MacArthur, withdrew to the Bataan Peninsula and the island of Corregidor. Military advisors of President Franklin D. Roosevelt informed MacArthur of the futility of continued resistance and ordered him to leave his beleaguered forces. On March 11, 1942, a submarine was sent to rescue MacArthur together with President Manuel L. Quezon and his family. They were taken to Australia so MacArthur could organize a liberation force. The Filipino people, although gravely disillusioned by his departure, were greatly heartened by MacArthur's famous parting words: "I shall return." Quezon subsequently organized a government-in-exile in Washington, D.C.

For three and a half years, Japanese imperial forces occupied the Philippines under conditions of brutality and total disregard for human rights and life. Japan introduced the Greater East Asia Co-Prosperity Sphere, which was an attempt to transform Philippine society and link its economy to Japan. The invaders began by granting the Philippines its independence, which the Filipinos had sought from the Americans, but even though they feared their occupiers, the Filipinos remained loyal to America. Throughout the Japanese occupation was an organized resistance to the puppet government of President Jose P. Laurel. Eventually, MacArthur returned with a powerful armada of naval, air, and army forces and led the first U.S. landing in Leyte Gulf on October 21, 1944. Other landings followed in Luzon in order to encircle and annihilate the main Japanese occupation army. Although the Japanese fought to the bitter end, the American armed forces, with the help of Filipino guerrillas, liberated the Philippines in August 1945. During the war, an estimated million Filipinos lost their lives at the hands of the Japanese. After the Allied victory, Japanese Army Generals Masaharu Homma and Tomoyuki Yamashita were tried for war crimes by a military court. Both were hanged on April 3, 1946, in Los Baños, Laguna.

Independence

The Philippine Congress met on June 9, 1945, for the first time since its election in 1941 with the surviving political leaders. It faced enormous problems—a devastated economy, institutions, and infrastructure. Nevertheless, the United States kept its promise of independence, which was granted on July 4, 1946. President Manuel Roxas hoisted the Philippine flag in ceremonies held at Luneta Park in front of the monument of Jose Rizal, the national martyr. The U.S. Congress subsequently provided $800 million to rehabilitate the country. In later years, Japan furnished $800 million as reparations, which was used in rebuilding the infrastructure. The enormous task of reconstructing the war-torn country was complicated by the destabilizing activities in central Luzon of the Communist-dominated Hukbalahaps (Huks) who resorted to terror and violence in their efforts to achieve land reform and gain political power. They were largely brought under control after a vigorous attack launched by the minister of national defense, Ramon Magsaysay. The Huks continued to function, however, until 1970, and other Communist guerrilla groups have persisted in their oppostion to the Philippine government. They terrorized the countryside and caused untold miseries to the people.

When Ramon Magsaysay took office as president in 1953 succeeding Elpidio Quirino, his first concern was to restore law and order. He provided leadership in agrarian reform and self-government at the barrio level. These measures helped reduce the insurgent base of the Huks and many of their commanders, like Luis Taruc, gave up their arms and accepted the government's amnesty. Huk soldiers were subsequently resettled on new farmlands in Mindanao. After Magsaysay was killed in an airplane crash, his successor, Carlos P. Garcia, stressed Filipino nationalism and economic independence. Lands reserved for American military bases were reclaimed and given to the landless. Diosdado Macapagal, who ran as a candidate of the Liberal party and was elected president in 1961, followed Garcia. His administration was fairly successful in restoring economic stability in part through abolishing sharecropping by tenant farmers and eliminating economic controls.

On matters of foreign relations, relations with the United States in the early 1960s were severely rocked by the issue of Philippine sovereignty over the several military bases that had the 99-year lease period. Furthermore, the jurisdiction over service personnel stationed in the Philippines aroused considerable anti-American feelings and led to widespread demonstrations, particularly in Manila, before the huge U.S. Embassy. This necessitated new base negotiations and resulted in an August 1965 agreement to adopt provisions similar to the Status of Forces agreement of the North Atlantic Treaty Organization (NATO) regarding criminal jurisdiction. Meantime, the Philippines became aware of its relations with its Asian neighbors. In 1954, the Philippines joined the short-lived Southeast Asia Treaty Organization (SEATO). It was replaced with the Association of Southeast Asian Nations (ASEAN) in 1967, in whose formation the Philippines played a major role and kept up friendly and constructive relations with its Asian neighbors.

The Marcos Era

Ferdinand Marcos, who succeeded to the presidency after defeating Diosdado Macapagal, came to power in 1965 on a platform of land reform. Although this platform was attractive to the majority of the people, it alienated the politically powerful landowner elites, sometimes referred to as *oligarchs* and thus was not carried out. He tried to improve the quality of life by building roads, bridges, schools, health centers, and irrigation facilities, and promoted urban beautification projects. However, many of these programs deteriorated during his second term as president as he faced new and grave problems, which included the mounting Communist insurgency, particularly the New Peoples' Army and the insurrection of the Moro National Liberation Front (MNLF) in Mindanao. These insurgencies contributed immensely to the disintegration of law and order in the country.

Bombings, student demonstrations, spiraling crime, and rampant graft and corruption of government officials added to the discontent of the people. Their outrage was vented in violent street demonstrations in front of Malacañang Palace. Marcos reacted by blaming leftists and eventually suspended habeas corpus, followed by a declaration of martial law in 1972. This unilateral move made him a virtual dictator. Opposition figures were arrested and thrown in jail. A total of 30,000 detainees were kept in military compounds, including Senator Benigno Aquino Jr., an archrival of Marcos and a potential presidential candidate. To further consolidate his power, Marcos initiated a move to rewrite the constitution. He claimed that the 1935 constitution, written during the American period, was no longer viable in the face of new political and economic developments. He subsequently abolished Congress and ruled by presidential decrees. A new constitution, drafted and ratified in 1973, provided for a parliamentary form of government. Under this system, in force for 12 years, Marcos exercised the powers of both the president and the prime minister.

On January 17, 1981, Marcos lifted martial law and, in June, ran for re-election and won overwhelmingly. His opponents, though allowed some freedom, boycotted the elections. His chief opponent, Benigno Aquino Jr., after spending seven years in detention, was also allowed to go to the United States in May 1980 for medical treatment. Pressure from the United States played a major role in his release. Arrangements were made for him to serve as a lecturer at Harvard University. At Harvard, he took on the role of opposition leader-in-exile. He blasted Marcos on every public occasion. The deterioration of the economic and political situation in the Philippines and Marcos' worsening health persuaded Aquino to return. He intended to appeal to Marcos' altruism to relinquish power voluntarily and, if not, to help build a responsible opposition. However, when he landed at Manila International Airport, Aquino was assassinated before a huge throng of people, who were waiting to welcome him. A subsequent investigation into the assassination revealed that the military escort who met Aquino on the plane was responsible for his death. Aquino was shot in the head and his body was left on the tarmac. His widow Corazon "Cory" Aquino buried him in his bloody clothes.

The Aquino Era

Despite Marcos' denial of involvement in the assassination, public opinion laid Aquino's death at the door of Malacañang Palace. To bolster his credibility, both domestically and abroad, Marcos announced he would hold a "snap election" on February 7, 1986, a year before his six-year presidential term expired. Corazon Aquino ran as the opposition presidential candidate with Salvador Laurel as her running mate. The election was marred by gross fraud, intimidation, ballot box stuffing, and falsified tabulation. However, Aquino won based on the ballot count of NAMFRE, an independent monitor. Marcos claimed he won, according to the tabulation of COMELEC, the official commission on elections. Members of a team of U.S. observers, led by Senator Richard Lugar, expressed shock and indignation at the fraud and irregularities of the election. Consequently, there was a political standoff between the avid supporters of Aquino and the military-backed forces of Marcos.

The impasse changed dramatically when Juan Ponce Enrile, Marcos' secretary of defense, and General Fidel Ramos, chief of the Philippine Constabulary, joined forces and issued a statement demanding Marcos' resignation and recognizing Aquino as the election winner. They seized a military compound near Manila for their headquarters, and they led 200 armed men. Marcos ordered loyal military units to crush the mutineers by force. Before the order was carried out, Jaime Cardinal Sin, Roman Catholic archbishop of Manila, took to the airwaves and appealed to the people to bring food and supplies to the rebels and to use nonviolent methods to block Marcos' troops. Within hours thousands of people swarmed around the headquarters. Disaffected troops joined the rebels. Soon civilians faced the tanks and machine guns of government troops, who held their fire at the "human sea," popularly called "People Power." Marcos finally realized that he had lost the support of the Philippine people and the United States. Advised by U.S. Senator Paul Laxalt "to cut and cut cleanly," Marcos complied, packed his family onto a U.S. aircraft, and flew to Hawaii, where he died in exile two years later. An almost-bloodless revolution brought Corazon Aquino into office as the seventh president of the Republic of the Philippines. Aquino faced the daunting task of restoring law and order in a demoralized nation. A new constitution returned the Philippines to a presidential system. One of its provisions was a bill of rights similar to that contained in the U.S. Constitution. It included other clauses intended to preclude the repetition of abuses, which occurred under the Marcos regime. The new constitution was ratified in a plebiscite and took effect on February 11, 1987. Corazon Aquino's term of office was plagued by major problems: six coup attempts, controversy over U.S. military base rights, agrarian reform, renewed insurgency of the New Peoples' Army and the Muslim separatists, corruption in public office, and a heavy foreign debt of $28 billion incurred during the Marcos regime. As Aquino's term drew to a close and her inability to deliver on her election promises became evident, her popularity declined considerably. However, she has been credited for restoring the democratic process, which had been severely damaged during the Marcos dictatorship. Her term of office was concluded amid protest marches to Malacañang Palace in Manila, and riots and wild demonstrations in major cities. In the national presidential elections of 1992, there were six candidates, including Marcos' wife, Imelda Marcos.

The Ramos Era

Fidel Ramos, handpicked by Aquino to succeed her, was elected president. The Ramos administration's most pressing task, besides the gargantuan political and domestic problems inherited from the profligate regime of Marcos, was to rejuvenate the crippled economy, which had been the root cause of political and social unrest in Philippine society. Under his sound management, Ramos devised a new plan called "Philippines 2002." The plan's primary goal was the industrialization of the country and its transformation into a "tiger economy" of Asia by the next millennium. Trade liberalization and industry deregulation were just some of the reform policies that Ramos adopted to fulfill the goal. Development in technology and infrastructure were the hallmarks of Ramos' term. Roads, bridges, and flyovers were built to ease the increasing traffic problems in Metro Manila. Despite the reversal of fortunes experienced in Asia since late 1995 and 1997, Ramos managed to keep the local economy buoyant and left the presidency with optimistic hopes for the continued recovery in the hands of a new administration.

The Estrada Era

Joseph Ejercito Estrada rode on the wings of his popularity as a successful movie actor and his promises of improving the lot of the poor and downtrodden. He became the 13th president on May 11, 1998, and immediately swore to fight corruption within the government and continue the economic reforms initiated by his predecessor. He came into his position with a lot of experience as municipal mayor of a progressive suburban city, congressman, and senator. However, he brought in his inefficient management style when it came to handling pressing domestic problems facing the nation. Added to this were his poor lifestyle and his greed for wealth. However, his mailed fist policy in dealing with the separatist Muslim rebel group earned him plaudits from the press.

Unfortunately, his administration crashed when a governor revealed that Estrada and his son were gathering untold amounts of money from the illegal numbers game of jueteng. The public caught on to his corruption and the massive demonstrations, known as EDSA II, forced him to reluctantly resign after only 31 months in office. Then Congress impeached him for the crime of plunder, but the Senate, which was controlled by his friends, exonerated him. Nevertheless, he remained incarcerated awaiting final judgment from the court. His vice president, Gloria Macapagal Arroyo, was sworn in as president of the republic to continue the remaining three and a half years of the Estrada presidency.

The Arroyo Era

Gloria Macapagal Arroyo inherited an administration in disarray. The country was faced with a huge deficit, poor revenues, restive population, and Muslim rebellion in Mindanao. But being a trained economist she focused her sights on issues that matter: poverty, employment, development, investments, social services, and law and order. Her macroeconomic stabilization program returned the economy to the path of long-term growth. As a result, gross domestic product expanded by 4.1 percent in the 2002, employment grew by an additional million jobs, and the inflation rate went down to 2.5 percent, the lowest in the last three decades. The Muslim rebellion was neutralized with the help of American forces. In dealing with the resurgent MILF, Arroyo adopted a policy of calibrated reciprocity, while a parallel peace initiative was carried out. In the social sphere, more than half a million farmer families became agrarian-reform beneficiaries, and a million more poor people were given health insurance coverage—an important step in the elimination of poverty. Arroyo fired and prosecuted corrupt government officials and replaced them with men and women of integrity. She mended frayed foreign relations with ASEAN nations by her state visits and also strengthened relations with the United States and European nations.

Arroyo's vigorous style of leadership did not sit well with her political opponents, and the liberal media focused more on her negative traits rather than on her achievements. In 2003, Arroyo survived attempts by military mutineers to unseat her. She has allied herself closely to U.S. President George W. Bush's "war on terror." The road ahead for a possible reelection appeared bumpy, and rather than face political annihilation she decided to withdraw from the presidential election in 2004 to concentrate on her agenda of political reform, economic recovery, and poverty alleviation. However, she changed her mind in October 2003, and decided to run. In her political bid for office, she emphasized her crusade for the eradication of poverty and corruption as well as continuance of the successful programs and farm policies that had launched the economic recovery. She won a fresh mandate in the May 10, 2004, presidential elections. Her victory was greeted with relief by the Philippine business community. On her inauguration, she pledged to bring a pro-poor agenda, expand the economy, and create six million jobs in the ensuing six years of her mandate. Meanwhile, the burgeoning population—growing at 2.36 percent annually—will have a major impact on President Arroyo's economic reform package. Unless, a population program is implemented, any increase in economic growth would be irrelevant and problems of food production, health, and education will continue to bedevil the country.

NOTE

1. Abueva, Jose V. ed. *The Making of the Filipino Nation and Republic: From Barangays, Tribes, Sultanates, and Colony.* Manila: University of the Philippines Press, 1998.

The Dictionary

– A –

ABACA (MUSA TEXTILES). A plant known as Manila hemp, abaca belongs to the banana family and is grown commercially in Mindanao for the manufacture of marine cordage. Because the natural fiber of the plant is strong, durable, and resistant to seawater, the production of Manila hemp has become the major industry in the Philippines, the world's largest supplier of the product. Abaca pulp is exported to China. In 2004, China bought 640 metric tons worth $1.92 million. The Philippines also exports abaca fiber and abaca forms to the United States, Japan, and Europe. *See also* ABEL; PIÑA.

ABAD SANTOS, JOSE (1886–1942). Chief justice of the Supreme Court. Educated in the United States, where he obtained law degrees from Northwestern and George Washington Universities, Jose Abad Santos started his public career as a clerk and quickly rose through the ranks from assistant attorney to become undersecretary of justice under the American administration. He resigned this position together with many Filipino government officials to protest the harsh administrative rule by American Governor-General **Leonard Wood**, who was unsympathetic to the independence campaign of the Filipino officials. When Governor-General **Henry Stimson** arrived, Abad Santos was appointed secretary of justice, rising three years later to the position of associate justice of the Supreme Court. When the Pacific War broke out President **Manuel Quezon** appointed him chief justice. He chose to stay behind when Quezon evacuated to Australia and, later, the United States. Since Abad Santos was the highest ranking official remaining in the Philippines, Quezon appointed him as the president's delegate and virtual head of the commonwealth government. The

Japanese captured him while he and his son were traveling in **Cebu**. Despite promises of a high position in the puppet government, he refused to take an oath of allegiance and was consequently executed in Lanao del Sur on May 7, 1942.

ABAD SANTOS, PEDRO. *See* SOCIALIST PARTY.

ABADIANO, BENJAMIN (1965–). A 2004 **Ramon Magsaysay awardee**. Abadiano was recognized for his steadfast commitment for indigenous Filipinos and their hopes for peace and a better life consonant with their distinctive tradition and hallowed ways of life. In 1988, Abadiano started a school for **Mangyan** school children in Tugdaan, Mindoro. With the help of funds from abroad, Abadiano built a school on land donated by the Mangyan community. The Tugdaan school started as nonformal education, but after Abadiano took a crash course in agriculture from the University of the Philippines, the school curriculum was expanded to include formal courses including subjects like environment and resource management, Mangyan culture, income generating programs, and human resource management. As more Mangyan students enrolled, the school increased its program to include a herbal and vegetable garden, fishpond, food laboratory, and carpentry. *Tugdaan*—Mangyan word for seedbed—is now a major hub where Mangyan's produce are tested and developed. Under Abadiano's direction, the first Mangyan dictionary was published, a result of 13 years of living with the Mangyans. In 1995, the *Tugdaan* school was awarded the "Best Education Program" in Southern Tagalog region. *See also* INDIGENOUS PEOPLES' RIGHTS ACT.

ABEL. Native fabric made of cotton produced in the Northern Ilocos region and especially used as table covers, handicraft items, and dresses. Abel is the material for *camisa*, a popular costume that is usually dyed in indigo. The hand-loomed fabric is identified as a cultural handicraft of the Ilocanos. *See also* JUSI; PIÑA.

ABELARDO, NICANOR (1893–1934). Musician and composer. A native of **Bulacan**, Abelardo learned to play the guitar at the age of six and wrote his first composition at age eight. He moved to Manila to live with an uncle who taught him to play the piano. While a music student at the University of the Philippines, Abelardo won first prize for his "U.P. Beloved" song, and he was later appointed head of the conservatory's department of music. During his lifetime, he composed some 149 love songs called **kundimans**, which have become classics in Filipino music and have earned him the title of "father of kundiman." He died at the age of 41. The main theater of the Cultural Center of the Philippines, Manila, is named after him. *See also* CELERIO, LEVI.

ABLAN, ROQUE. *See* GUERRILLA.

ABRA. Located in northwest Luzon, Abra province is bordered by the Ilocos Mountains on the west and the central range of the **Cordillera** Mountains on the east. It occupies a land area of 3,976 square kilometers and is one of the more sparsely populated provinces of the Philippines. Its capital, Bangued the province's only urban center, was founded in 1598 by the Spanish. The province has a population of 200,000, composed mainly of **Ilocanos**, who outnumber the native **Tinggians** by more than three to one. Only one major highway crosses the province, and there is little tourism. This landlocked province is transected by the 160-kilometer long Abra River, which meanders across a broad fertile plain before emptying into the South China Sea. The main agricultural products are corn, rice, and tobacco.

ABSENTEE VOTING. Overseas foreign workers of voting age including permanent residents of other countries are allowed to vote in national elections for president, vice president, and the 24-seat Senate under a law signed by President **Gloria Macapagal Arroyo** in 2003. Balloting is done at Philippine embassies or can be arranged by mail.

ABU BAKR. *See* ISLAM.

ABU SAYYAF. This is a terrorist group, which claims to fight for an Islamic state in Southern Philippines. Its name means "bearer of the sword." The founder, Abduragak Abubakar Jajalani, who led the group in many firefights with police and army, was killed in Basilan. His brother, Khadafy Jajalani, took over and has carried on its nefarious work of bombings, assassination, and piracy. Its finances used to come from Usama Bin Ladin but since his fall they have obtained their resources through ransom kidnappings—usually of foreigners and wealthy locals. Abu Sayyaf has ties to Al-Qaeda and **Darul Islamiyah Nusantra.** Government intelligence claims that there are only about a hundred fighters left who are on the run, and probably decimated by the relentless military campaigns of the Philippine armed forces with the help of the U.S. army. In 2003, one of the key leaders—Ghalib Andang—was captured by the Armed Forces. Andang and his cohorts were responsible for kidnapping 21 foreign tourists in the Malaysian resort island of Sipadan. Lately, Abu Sayaff has changed its name to *Al-Harakatul Al-Islamaya* (Islamic Movement).

ACOHIDO, BYRON. *See* TIZON, ALEX.

ACTION WITHOUT BORDERS. This is a global network that is independent of any government, political ideology, or religious creed. Its work in the Philippines is to foster the idea "to build a world where all people can live free and dignified lives in a healthy environment." And its work is guided by the common desire of its members and supporters to find practical solutions to social and environmental problems, in a spirit of generosity and mutual respect.

ADAT. *See* TAGBANUA.

ADOBO. A popular Filipino dish of chicken or pork cooked in vinegar and soy sauce, spiced with garlic and black peppercorns. This dish is Spanish in origin. *See also* BALUT; LECHON; SUMAN.

AETA. Also called *Agtas*, *Dumagats*, and *Negritoes*. They are the original people of the Philippines who came to the islands by using the land bridges from the south. The migration took place about 12,000 years ago. They are an Australo-Melanesian people with dark skin and tight, curly brown hair, short of stature and small in build. They live in small clans and are a nomadic people—hunting and gathering—who inhabit the rain forests and mountain regions. They were once found all over the islands but their environment has been reduced due to the spread of the Philippine population. Now they are found only in the highlands of Palawan, Luzon, Panay, Negros, and Mindanao. Philippine Negritoes are similar in physical characteristics to the aborigines of Peninsular Malaysia and Thailand. *See also* AUSTRONESIANS.

AGA KHAN MUSEUM. *See* LANAO DEL SUR.

AGILE. This is an acronym for Accelerated Growth Investment and Liberalization with Equity, which is the umbrella name for a project funded by the United States Agency for International Development (USAID) and supported by the Philippine government. Its function is to provide policy analysis, formulate advocacy and technical assistance in support of liberalization and competition, including monitoring and assessment of monetary aid requested—and received—from America. Agile was formed in 1997 during the **Fidel Ramos** presidency as an authorized activity of the economic development component of the Philippine Assistance Program Support. Staffed by academic experts in various fields, Agile has produced vital policy papers and information, which have assisted lawmakers in developing legislation for improved governance, economic growth, and equity. In the government's goal of making institutions, policies, and practices transparent and accountable and less prone to corruption, Agile has assisted by pushing for the strengthening and enforcement of commercial law.

Agile provided technical assistance in the development of the country's capital markets—a crucial issue required for sustained and rapid economic growth. It assisted the country's efforts to achieve pension reform by recommending legislation, which provided tax incentives for long-term retirement savings. The project has been involved in helping the Bureau of Internal Revenue achieve more transparency and efficiency by modernizing customs procedures and improving the ability of customs authorities to facilitate trade and audit and manage risk. It also helped government units to access funds for their development programs. Agile's main assistance to government in strengthening the management of expenditures has been in helping to reengineer the bureaucracy. It aided the government's ability to manage its contingent liabilities while making investment incentives more transparent. To spur competition in infrastructure and trade, Agile served in researching policy and regulatory infrastructure to promote competitive investments in public utilities and basic industries.

AGLIPAY, GREGORIO LABAYAN (1860–1940). Supreme bishop of the **Iglesia Filipina Independiente (IFI)** (Philippine Independent Church). Ordained as a Roman Catholic priest, Aglipay led the schism from the Roman Catholic Church to establish the Iglesia Filipina Independiente. With the encouragement of General **Emilio Aguinaldo**, who appointed him chaplain-general of the revolutionary forces, Aglipay sent out manifestoes to all Filipino priests to unite and take over the government of the church. This act and his participation in the establishment of a revolutionary government led to his excommunication. In the ensuing conflict, Aglipay donned a soldier's uniform and led his own guerrilla attacks against the Spanish. When the Americans arrived, he continued his guerrilla activities.

After his surrender, Aglipay returned to his priestly duties and to his earlier efforts to Filipinize the Roman Catholic clergy. Thus, in 1902, having gathered sufficient followers and, with the help of laymen **Isabelo de los Reyes** and Pascual Poblete, Aglipay formalized the breakaway from the Vatican and founded the Iglesia Filipina Independiente. He became the first church supreme bishop. His dynamic personality became so well known throughout the country that soon the IFI was attracting hundreds of thousands of followers. Although, having split from the Roman Catholic Church, Aglipay still followed most of the rituals of the church. In later years he modified rituals and also became attracted to the theology of Unitarianism, which led to a division of his followers. The other group stayed in the church and claimed to be the true followers of Aglipay. Most of the Aglipayans today are found in the northern provinces of the Philippines. *See also* BARLIN, JORGE IMPERIAL; MANALO, FELIX; REYES, IS-ABELO DE LOS; SECULARIZATION; ZAMORA, NICOLAS.

AGONCILLO, FELIPE (1859–1941). Philippine–Spanish revolutionary leader. A native of Batangas, Agoncillo obtained his law degree from the University of Santo Tomas in 1879. He practiced law in his hometown and gave free legal services to the poor; this displeased the Spanish parish priest who accused him of preaching nationalistic ideas and he was recommended for deportation. However, he left the country on his own for Hong Kong where he helped Emilio **Aguinaldo** as a propaganda officer. When the **Philippine–American Revolution** broke out in 1898, Aguinaldo sent him to Washington to secure recognition of Philippine independence, and then to Paris to present the cause at the American–Spanish Peace Conference. Both of these efforts failed. Agoncillio rejoined Aguinaldo in Hong Kong, and while waiting for their return to the Philippines, his wife Marcela was commissioned by Aguinaldo to design the national **flag**, which was unfurled in Kawit, Cavite, during the declaration of Philippine independence on June 12, 1898. After the end of the revolution, Agoncillo took the oath of allegiance and served his province as representative to the Philippine Assembly in 1907. He fought for the **Filipinization** of the government service. *See also* BONIFACIO, ANDRES.

AGONCILLO, TEODORO (1912–1985). He is considered to be the country's preeminent historian by virtue of his voluminous writings—books and articles—all of which were written from the Filipino perspective as against those written by Western-oriented historians who merely chronicle events and dates. His most popular books are the "Revolt of the Masses" (a biography of the hero of Manila **Andres Bonifacio**) and the "History of the Filipino People." Agoncillo was a prize-winning essayist and fictionist writing in English and Tagalog. His story *Sa Kamatayan Lamang* (Only in Death) won the top prize in the 1953–1954 Palanca contest. He was also a Republic Cultural Heritage awardee in 1967, which he refused to accept. A native of historic **Batangas** province, Agoncillo studied at the University of the Philippines, later worked as technical assistant at the Institute of National Language, and taught Tagalog Literature at Far Eastern University (Manila). He retired as a professor of history at the University of the Philippines.

AGONG. A knobbed metal gong used in various communal rituals, more prominently in Muslim regions as a musical instrument in their festal celebrations. Suspended in the air by rope or metal chains, the agong is also employed by some indigenous groups as a means to announce community events and an indicator of the passage of time. *See also* GAMELAN.

AGRICULTURE. Agriculture maintains a major role in the country's **economy**. A significant number of Filipinos live and work in the rural areas. Almost half of the working population—45 percent—and 45.1 percent of all employed in the household earned the bulk of their income directly through agricultural activities. In the past three decades, faster and wider inroads were noticeable in agricultural production. This was seen in the agribusiness or cash crop production. Philippine agricultural produce includes crops such as food crops (rice, corn, tubers) spices, traditional export crops (such as sugar, **coconut**, bananas, and tobacco), nontraditional export crops (such as asparagus and mango) fruits, nuts, vegetables, and fibers. Four crops—rice, corn, coconut, and sugar—are of major significance to the country's agriculture. These crops alone utilize some 10 million hectares or 79 percent of the total land devoted to agriculture.

Until the **International Rice Research Institute (IRRI)** introduced modern rice varieties in 1996, the average yield per hectare was 1.3 metric tons and annual production on 3.1 million hectares of rice land amounted to 4.1 metric tons. The introduction of **hybrid rice** established a record of 3.09 metric tons per hectare. Since then rice hectarage has increased by about seven percent to 3.6 million. Regions that are primarily devoted to rice production are Luzon (50 percent), Western Visayas (13 percent), Mindanao (23 percent). Corn production is concentrated in Mindanao, contributing a total of 68 percent to national production. Production of basic food crops is costly, labor intensive, and highly dependent on chemical inputs such as fertilizers and pesticide. Nontraditional exports command higher prices than traditional export crops. Asparagus produced in Mindanao stands out as the highest performer. Bananas and pineapples are considered major agricultural exports with significant earnings. The production of nontraditional export crops and high-value crops is gaining importance in the country's agriculture. This is influenced by the present policy environment that gradually puts a premium on the latter rather than the production of basic food crops. Attaining "global competitiveness" and "comparative advantage" by putting commercial concerns and operational principles in the forefront are guiding the **Gloria Macapagal Arroyo** government. Although biotech crops contribute to sustainability by enabling technologies that can improve soil and water, the introduction of

Genetically Modified Organisms (GMO)—like a new variety of corn—has become a controversial issue to farmers. The controversy is based on the risk that genetically modified corn can cause allergies, or even be toxic—an issue raised by a number of **Non-Governmental Organizations**. (NGOs). However, the influential **Roman Catholic Church** has come out in support of GMOs, with the proviso that all the risks must be minimized. The church sees the new agricultural technology as an answer to combating hunger, poverty, and disease. *See also* AQUACULTURE; FISHING INDUSTRY; SUSTAINABLE DEVELOPMENT.

AGUINALDO, EMILIO (1869–1964). Emilio Aguinaldo was president of the first Republic of the Philippines and leader of the revolution against Spain and America. At age 17, he was appointed by the Spanish government *cabeza de barangay*, for example, the head of a governmental unit. As he proved to be a capable official, he was promoted to *capitan* municipal (mayor) in 1895. When the Spanish–American War broke in 1896, he led the uprising in his home province of Cavite. In a political dispute with **Andres Bonifacio**, founder of **Katipunan**, he led his own armed force against the Spaniards. He formed a revolutionary government and, at age 29, he was elected president. With the war in Cuba, the Spanish government negotiated the **Pact of Biak-na-Bato** on December 15, 1897, with Aguinaldo, who agreed to accept $800,000 from the Spanish government and to go with his officers into exile to Hong Kong. There he met Commodore **George Dewey**, American commander of a naval fleet, who was waiting for his orders to proceed to the Philippines following the outbreak of the Spanish–American Revolution. Aguinaldo agreed to an alliance with the Americans to destroy the Spanish army and navy. Aguinaldo returned to the Philippines to lead the Filipino forces.

After the destruction of the Spanish Navy by Dewey, Aguinaldo organized a provisional revolutionary government and proclaimed independence on June 12, 1898, in Kawit, Cavite. However, the Americans refused to recognize the Aguinaldo government and hostilities began when an American sentry shot three Filipino soldiers who were crossing the San Juan Bridge in Rizal province. This incident sparked the **Philippine–American Revolution**. Aguinaldo and his forces fought a protracted guerrilla war against the Americans. The war ended when the

Americans captured him on March 23, 1901, in Palanan, Isabela. *See also* PAUA, JOSE.; RICARTE, ARTEMIO.

AGUSAN DEL NORTE. Located in northeastern Mindanao, Agusan del Norte consists of the northern section of what was formerly Agusan province, the southern section now comprises the separate province of **Agusan del Sur.** Agusan del Norte covers 2,590 square kilometers and has a population of 440,000, mostly Cebuano-speaking Visayan, although several indigenous ethnic tribes, such as the Mamanwa, Manobo, and Higaonon are also present. Vast timber resources support the large-scale production of plywood and veneer, which is the primary industry. Butuan City, the provincial capital, is both a sea and river port, making it the commercial center of the Agusan Valley. The city is the site of an annual fluvial procession and municipal charter day, both of which are celebrated simultaneously with cultural programs, competitions, a beauty pageant, and boat races. The province is also the location of an important archeological site where the fossil remains of a **barangay** were found. The chief towns are Buenavista, Cabadbaran, and Nasipit.

AGUSAN DEL SUR. Located in the Agusan Valley in northeastern Mindanao, Agusan del Sur was formed in 1968 when the former Agusan province was divided into the two separate provinces of **Agusan del Norte** and Agusan del Sur. The provincial capital is Prosperidad, a market town in the valley situated on the Davao-Agusan highway. This province, with a population of about 265,000 people and a land area of 8,966 square kilometers, is one of the most sparsely populated regions in the country. Cebuano is the major language, but there are also a number of sizable non-Cebuano ethnic groups, such as the Higaonon, Manobos, Barwaons, Magahats, and Talandigs, who live in settlements among the hills and along the riverbanks where they raise the staple crops of rice, corn, and taro. Many of the province's inhabitants are also employed in logging, which is the main industry. The chief towns are Esperanza, San Luis, Talacogon, and San Francisco.

AGUSTIN, MARCOS VILLA. *See* GUERRILLA.

AGYU. This is the folk epic of the Ilianon people of **Cotabato del Norte** province. This epic consists of 1,279 lines, which narrate seven distinct episodes in the lives of the hero Agyu. Narration is done by a village shaman during important occasions such weddings, anniversary celebrations, and harvest time. *See also* BANNA; SUMAKWEL; *SANDAYO.*

AKBAYAN CITIZENS' ACTION PARTY. Akbayan was established on January 1998 by various groups—labor, peasants, youth, women, gay and lesbians—as a political party. Calling itself a prodemocracy group, Akbayan is the most vigorous to break the hold of "**trapo**" traditional politicians and **political dynasties** on Philippine politics. In Akbayan's analysis, members of the elite who join government to further vested economic interests have undermined public welfare. Akbayan claims that it is nonideological in Marxist terms and its organizational approach is instilling transformational governance that directly addresses the interests of marginalized groups like **women** or workers in the informal sector of the community. Thus, the party is trying to contribute to building a participatory democracy from the village level upward. The party tested its strength in 2001 by participating in the first local **party-list** elections and won two seats in congress. Although the party is relatively young, many of its members have been active in the armed antidictatorship struggle in the 1970s and 1980s under the **National Democratic Front** (NDF) and the **Communist Party of the Philippines** (CPP). Akbayan's base has been fast growing in the past four years and it now claims an estimated 100,000 members. Akbayan is a member of the Socialist International. *See also* BUKLURAN NG MANGAGAWANG PILIPINO.

AKLAN. This province, formed when **Capiz** province was subdivided in 1956, consists of 17 municipalities, 312 barrios (rural villages), and a total population of 395,00 people. The province occupies 1,818 square kilometers in the northwestern part of Panay Island. The people speak a distinct Aklanon dialect and are closely related to the Ilonggos. Aklan is noted for its cottage textile industry, there being a loom in almost every home. Aklan is also noted for its famous weeklong *ati-atihan* festival held in January in honor of the Christ child.

This is a major event in the capital Kalibo, and the province's most colorful celebration, akin to the Mardi Gras of New Orleans. Participants in the procession wear multicolored papier-mache masks and dress in Roman-style costumes. Those without masks paint their faces and bodies with soot or black color, which alludes to the early inhabitants, the Aetas. Throwing caution to the wind, participants representing high and low position shout, sing, and dance in the streets to the tune of orchestras, school bands, and combos. The festivities end on a Sunday with a religious torch procession. Principal towns are Ibajay, Altavas, Numancia, New Washington, and Pandan.

AKSYON DEMOKRATIKO PARTY (ADP). Founded in Pasig City by former senator **Raul Roco** and 168 other political leaders from several small parties, Aksyon Demokratiko presented a full slate of candidates in the 1998 national elections from president—Roco as the standard bearer—to provincial governors and city mayors. The party came in sixth place with **Joseph Ejercito Estrada's** *Partido Ng Masang Pilipino* as the top vote getter. The party's basic platform was to establish a government that ensures access to resources and opportunities for the Filipino people and removes the obstacles for participatory governance. After the 1998 elections, ADP and three other parties formed the People's Power Coalition (PPC). Their objective was to present a united opposition against the ruling Lakas-CMD party of President **Gloria Macapagal Arroyo**. However, the PPC was dissolved due to intraparty wrangling and the ADP reverted to its original structure and, in the May 2004 election, nominated its leader **Raul Roco** as the presidential candidate.

ALABASTRO, ESTRELLA (1941–). A cabinet member of the **Gloria Macapagal Arroyo** administration. Estrella Alabastro is a chemical engineer who distinguished herself in food technology and research. She obtained her chemical degree from the University of the Philippines and earned her master's and doctorate degrees in chemical engineering from Rice University in Houston, Texas. She served her alma mater (UP) as dean of the college of home economics and chaired the department of food science and nutrition. Her numerous research papers on food technology and processes earned the prestigious achievement award from the National Research Council of the

Philippines and a fellow in food research from the Philippine Association of Nutrition. *See also* SCIENTISTS.

ALABEL. *See* SARANGANI.

AL-AZHAR UNIVERSITY. *See* ALONTO, DOMOCAO.

ALBAY. Located in the southern part of Luzon. Albay province covers a land area of 2,553 square kilometers, part of which is occupied by Mt. **Mayon**, an active volcano acclaimed as the world's most perfect cone. The mountain is one of the main **tourist** attractions in the region. The rich volcanic soil in the plains and valleys make these excellent places for the farming of **rice** as well as cash crops such as **coconuts**, sugarcane, and **abaca**. Legaspi, the capital city, and the port city of Tabaco are the province's major commercial centers. Albay is densely populated, and its 950,000 inhabitants are known as Bicolanos, all of whom share a common culture. Bicol is the language spoken here as well as in the other Bicol provinces of **Camarines Norte**, **Camarines Sur**, and **Sorsogon**.

ALBERT, DELIA DOMINGO (1943–). A career diplomat, Delia Domingo-Albert was appointed foreign affairs secretary in 2003 replacing the late **Blas Ople**. The first female to head the diplomatic corps of the country, Domingo-Albert has served the foreign office for 36 years in various capacities both in the Philippines and abroad—Switzerland, Romania, Hungary, Germany, and Australia. Having attended language courses in Tokyo, Geneva, Bucharest, and Bonn, Domingo-Albert speaks seven languages. In the home office, she served as director-general of the **ASEAN** national secretariat. A graduate of the University of the Philippines and Harvard University, Delia Domingo-Albert announced that she would continue the clear vision and direction of Philippine foreign policy of her predecessor. She comes from **Baguio City**. *See also* DEL ROSARIO, ALBERT.

ALCALA, ANGEL C. (1929–). Known as the Filipino international authority on community ecology, biogeography, and systematic of amphibians and reptiles. He established the first marine reserve designed to enhance fishery yields and to protect **biodiversity** in the

Philippines in 1974, which is now emulated as the premier model for community fisheries development in the region. He was instrumental in the creation of the Apo and Sumilon marine reserves as well as the establishment of the Carbin and Pamilacan reserves. He set up the Silliman Research and Development Center, Dumaguete City, and currently serves as director. Alcala's main research interests are herpetology and marine biology, and he has published extensively (130 papers and books) in both fields. The Guggenheim Foundation and the Pew Fellowship in Marine Conservation have supported his work. Alcala has more than 30 years of experience in tropical marine resource conservation throughout Southeast Asia in academic, government, and consultant positions.

ALCALDE MAYOR. Provincial governor. In the Spanish colonial period, the *alcalde mayor* was the provincial chief appointed by the governor-general. The Spanish divided the country into 12 provinces or *alcalde mayors*. The *alcalde mayor* was appointed as the authority who would exercise all the functions of the government within his jurisdiction. His duties involved running the civil government, administering justice, collecting taxes, and defending the province against attacks by hostile forces. *Alcalde mayors* held office from three to six years. They had to be of Spanish blood and be lawyers, who had been in practice for the past two years. The office was subject to purchase and royal patronage. There were considerable changes in the duties of the *alcalde mayor* during the Spanish colonial administration due to wanton abuse and corruption of the officeholders. One of these changes required the nominee to post a bond, which became necessary because he was the treasurer, accountant, and revenue collector. Prior to 1844, the provincial chiefs were actually merchant governors, who used their office to amass a great deal of money, but after 1844 the privilege of engaging in business was abolished. Toward the end of the Spanish administration the *alcalde mayors* became full-time judges. *See also* PUEBLO; PUEBLO OFFICIALS.

ALEJANDRINO, CASTO. *See* HUKBALAHAP.

ALIBATA. *See* SYLLABARY.

ALIGUYON. This is the epic tale of the Ifugao people, famous for their legendary **rice terraces** in the mountain provinces of North Luzon. The original song known as *Hudhud* or harvest song was translated by Amador T. Daguio into English. The life and soul of the Ifugao people revolved around the cultivation of **rice** in their ancient rice terraces, which figure prominently in the epic. The story is about the fierce rivalry between equally matched tribal heroes who fought valiantly for days, months, and years, with neither of them slain, because they possessed supernatural powers. *See also* ANTING-ANTING; BANNA; LUMAWIG.

ALIMUD DIN. Muslim statesman. He succeeded his brother as sultan of Jolo and Mindanao in the 16th century when the Spanish were extending their rule in the archipelago. The Sulu sultanate was the main center of Muslim power and religion. Many expeditions of Spanish soldiers and mercenaries failed to subjugate the redoubtable **Moros**. The disastrous war forced Alimud Din, who came to power in 1647, to seek a peaceful rapprochement with the Spanish. He negotiated a treaty of friendship, navigation, and commerce with his adversaries. By the treaty, the Spanish government recognized the sultanate of **Jolo** and its sovereignty over the region while the Spanish were allowed to establish a mission in Jolo. However, peace in the region was short-lived for Alimud Din was deposed and sought sanctuary in Manila. When the British occupied Manila in 1762 Alimud Din signed a treaty of territorial cession of North Borneo (known as **Sabah**) and he was restored to his sultanate. During his rule, he revised the Sulu code of laws and system of justice, translated into Sulu parts of the Koran, and promoted the Arabic language. *See also* JAMALUL, KIRAM.

ALIWAGWAG FALLS. This falls is the highest waterfall in the country—388 meters high—in Cateel town, **Davao Oriental** province. The cascade has 13 rapids and looks like a stairway with 85 steps of varying heights. *See also* MARIA CRISTINA FALLS; PAGSANJAN FALLS.

ALONTO, DOMOCAO AHMAD (1914–2002). Alonto was known as the father of the bill, which created the Mindanao State University in Marawi City, the largest state institution in Mindanao, with campuses in major cities in the southern island. During his term as the only Maranao Muslim senator, Alonto championed the struggle of Muslim Filipinos by authoring bills that protected their rights and development agencies and promoted economic growth in Muslim communities. In a meeting with the late Gamal Abdel Nasser in Bandung, Indonesia, in 1950, Alonto requested the Egyptian leader to sponsor Filipino youth to study at Al-Azhar University in Cairo. Today many of the graduates are leaders in their communities. It was his advocacy for the recognition of Muslim rights that inspired Muslim leaders in the 1970s, which led eventually to the creation of the **Autonomous Region of Muslim Mindanao**. (ARMM) Alonto founded his own school, the Kamilol Islam Colleges in Marawi City, which later became the Jamatul Philippine al-Islamia, which has offered Islamic studies since 1968. He initiated the first translation of the Koran into the Maranao language. *See also* HUSSIN, PAROUK; RASUL, SANTANINA.

AL-QAEDA. *See* MORO ISLAMIC LIBERATION FRONT.

ALSA MASA (MASSES ARISE). This is a vigilante group supported by the military, which originated in Davao, Mindanao, in 1986. The **Corazon Aquino** government promoted the spread of **vigilantes** and similar civilian armed groups throughout much of the country as an alternative to containing the insurgent **New People's Army**. Their efforts at pacification in the rural areas resulted in brutal violations of human rights through their method of "salvaging," summary executions of even suspected sympathizers of the insurgents. According to **Amnesty International (AI)**, which has documented numerous cases of executions and torture, the salvagings were committed by vigilantes under the command or with the sanction of the regular armed forces. Because of the intervention of the AI, President Aquino ordered the disbanding of the vigilante group. *See also* SPARROW SQUADS; VIGILANTES.

AMADORE, LEONCIO. *See* SCIENTISTS.

AMAI MINGKA. *See* DATU PIANG.

AMAN DANGAT. A datu of Sabtang Island, **Batanes**, also known as *Kenan*, who led an uprising to defend his people's native rights and freedom in 1791. Upon the establishment of Spanish rule in Batanes on June 26, 1783, he continued to govern his people in accordance with indigenous customary laws. Ordered by Spanish agents of the new regime to follow Spanish policies, he asked for an explanation of why he should, but he received none. When non-Batanes Filipino agents demanded supplies and timber from his people without just compensation in 1791, he protested, but his men were put in chains instead. Under his leadership, over a hundred leading men from all over Sabtang joined him in a revolt and killed seven Spanish government officials. In the ensuing conflict, Aman Dangat and his men were overpowered by superior Spanish arms, and were subsequently killed. To commemorate this valiant warrior of Batanes, a statute stands in front of the provincial capitol in Basco, **Batanes**. *See also* DAGOHOY, FRANCISCO; SUMUROY; TAMBLOT.

AMERICAN REGIME (1900–1946). American rule over the Philippines covers a period of 47 years (1899–1946) starting with Commodore George Dewey's destruction of the Spanish navy at the **battle of Manila Bay** (May 1, 1899) and ending with the grant of full independence on July 4, 1946. Initial efforts to occupy the country were met with strong resistance by General **Emilio Aguinaldo** in the **Philippine–American Revolution**, but eventually dissipated with his surrender in 1901. A period of benevolent assimilation followed. The Americans gradually introduced institutional changes in the educational, religious, and political fields. Most notable was the introduction of the democratic form of government, a secular educational system, English language as a means of communication, and principles of religious freedom and separation of church and state. These changes were accepted reluctantly but peaceably by leaders such as **Manuel L. Quezon** and **Sergio Osmeña** whose careers developed out of the new educational system.

Once these leaders mastered the rudiments of democracy their ensuing crusade was for full independence for the country. The cry for political autonomy was greeted with ambivalence by the various political parties in the United States. The Republicans sought to grant the islands a greater measure of self-government short of complete sovereignty, while the Democrats were committed to full independence. The passage of the **Tydings-McDuffie Act** by the United States Congress finally satisfied the wishes of Filipino leaders. The act pledged independence after a 10-year transition under a commonwealth government. This transition was interrupted by the devastating three-year occupation of the Philippines by the Japanese, after which the United States fulfilled its pledge, conferring complete independence on the islands on July 4, 1946. *See also* BELL TRADE ACT.

AMNESTY. President **Fidel Ramos** signed into law (May 31, 1994) two proclamations, which granted amnesty to Communist insurgents, military rebels, and culpable policemen and soldiers. This peaceful gesture was designed to bolster the reconciliation program in his administration. To implement this program, a national amnesty commission was created composed of a chairman and six members. The amnesty applied only to persons who had committed politically-related crimes such as participation in a coup d'état, rebellion, seditious activities, illegal assembly, or illegal possession of firearms. Amnesty was also granted to personnel of the Armed Forces of the Philippines. One condition of amnesty was that any person who wanted it should apply for it. Some 6,000 rebels subsequently applied for amnesty.

AMNESTY INTERNATIONAL (AI). An international agency that monitors human rights abuses. This agency was partially responsible for bringing to the attention of the international community the human rights abuses committed by the military during the **Ferdinand Marcos** and **Corazon Aquino** administrations. AI reported that between 1988 and 1991 there were approximately 550 unarmed victims killed. It also reported patterns of extra-judicial executions, "disappearances," and other civil rights violations. After the government admitted these violations, many cases were brought before the courts for redress and resolution. As a result of these reports, the Aquino administration issued new guidelines for procedures to protect civilians. *See also* SPARROW SQUADS; VIGILANTES.

AMORSOLO, FERNANDO (1892–1972). As a painter of landmark canvases, Amorsolo was honored as the first National **Artist** of the Philippines. Born in Paco, Manila, he was the first fine arts graduate of the University of the Philippines in 1919. His first important painting, *Rice Planting*, became one of the most popular images of the

Commonwealth period. During his peak years (1930–1940), he produced portraits, landscapes, and genre scenes. In his canvases, Amorsolo popularized the quintessential image of the beautiful Filipina maiden in her traditional domestic role. He portrayed Filipino customs and manners, fiestas, and occupations. Amorsolo also did a series of historical canvases on precolonial scenes. The Amorsolo paintings—idyllic genre scenes—dominated for at least three decades. *See also* ARTISTS; TOLENTINO, GUILLERMO.

ANCHETA, CELEDONIO. *See* REVOLTS.

ANCIENT MAN. The greatest number of large fossil remains that could shed light on the past environment during the Ice Ages are located in **Cagayan** Valley, which includes the provinces of **Nueva Vizcaya**, **Kalinga-Apayao**, and **Isabela**. Stone tools recovered from archaeological sites in the Cagayan Valley area could provide evidences of early man's activities. Based on fossil records, the area was generally forested with a subtropical moderate climate, cooler than the present-day climate. Elephants, stegodons, rhinoceros, primitive bovines, pig and deer, crocodiles, and giant turtles roamed in its wilderness. Food gathering and trapping were the basic survival methods at that time. People gathered shells in streams and rivers while scavenging or hunting took place in open areas or on the edges of forest. Stones were worked on to make tools. *See also* PALEOLITHIC CULTURE.

ANGARA, EDGARDO (1934–). Edgardo Angara is one of the country's top public leader who was born to middle-class parents in Baler, **Aurora**. He gained prominence during his stint as president of the University of the Philippines from 1981 to 1987. During the turbulent years of stewardship he defended not only the state university's tradition of dissent but also significantly improved its financial and human resources. Angara helped draft the 1973 constitution, authoring landmark constitutional provisions such as the democratization of ownership of public utilities and the protection of public domain from undue exploitation by developers. In 1993, he was elected to the Senate where he used his legal talents as an activist and reformer. He pushed hard for the passage of over 100 laws that turned around the economy and created the environment for economic dynamism and growth. A new Philippine Central Bank was created, the banking system was liberalized, and the infrastructure build-up boosted the economy with the massive entry of foreign investments. Angara was the principal author of the law granting free high school education to all Filipinos. He authored the Magna Carta for public health workers. Two laws sponsored by Angara created the Commission on Higher Education and Technical Education and Skills Development Authority and this enabled the Education Department to focus on its main concern—basic **education**. As secretary of agriculture, Angara directed agricultural research and development. He was the voice in the fight for fair trading rules in global trade. He coined the phrase "fair trade in a free trade context" to dramatize the resolve of developing countries to end the protectionist and unfair trade policies of developed countries.

ANGLICANS. *See* SAGADA.

ANTIFOREIGNISM. *See* FILIPINO FIRST POLICY.

ANTI-GRAFT COVENANT. The Philippines was a signatory to this United Nations Anti-Graft Covenant signed in Mexico City in December 2003. This global agreement was designed to fight **graft and corruption** among the signatory countries. Like other countries, the Philippines is concerned about the problems and threats graft and corruption pose to its stability and security and how they undermine the institutions and values of democracy. One of the major contributions of the Philippines to the covenant was the provision compelling governments to return stolen assets to the countries that owned them. The Philippines was also a signatory to a United Nations treaty on Transnational Organized Crime. Under this covenant, the Philippine government can pursue international criminals. The government has its Anti-Graft and Corruption Act (Republic Act 3019) to handle local violations of the law. *See also* PLUNDER WATCH.

ANTING-ANTING. Filipino amulet or talisman believed to have magical powers—invincibility against blade or bullet—or a harbinger of success and victory. Other names of *anting-anting* are *jikiri, galing, agimat, mutya,* and *virtud*. The amulet is often in the shape of small rings, bracelets, medallions, and necklaces and acquisition of any of these items is by bestowal or as an inheritance. Belief in the power of an amulet is often observed in the rural and mountainous regions; however, its use is shrouded in religious mystery. Many Filipinos who participated in the fight against Spain and the United States used *anting-anting* of all types for personal protection. *See also* BABAYLANISM.

ANTIPIRACY. This refers to the illegal reproduction and distribution of intellectual property such as movies, printed matter, music, video and similar materials. The Philippines is signatory to all major intellectual property rights conventions, with the exception of the area of cable piracy. The government has adequate legislations in place to address intellectual property piracy issues. However, enforcement actions to prevent both illegal reproduction and distribution are inadequate. Approximately 70 percent of the music and home video market are dominated by pirated products, which are sold openly, and undermine legitimate business while reducing government revenues. Piracy of broadcast signals by some cable operations is also a problem. A cable bill has been introduced in the Senate and House of Representatives to make illegal the unauthorized retransmission of cable signals and would open the cable industry to foreign investment. *See also* ANTI-TRAFFICKING ACT.

ANTIQUE. This province is located on the west coast of Panay with the city of San Jose as its capital. It occupies 2,522 square kilometers of fertile valleys planted in rice, corn, and coconuts. A mountain range on the west isolates Antique from the neighboring provinces. It is a relatively undeveloped province lacking good harbors and roads. The 424,000 inhabitants are called Antiqueños and speak the Kinaray-a dialect. This province is the site of the first Malay settlement, which was established according to legend when Bornean datus landed and bought the land from the Negritos in exchange for a golden native hat (*sadu*k). Principal towns are Barbaza, Bugasong, Caluya, Hamtic, San Remegio, Semirara, and Valderama. *See also* AKLAN; PANAY.

ANTITERRORISM. The terrorist attacks on America and the abduction of three Americans and 15 Filipinos by the **Abu Sayyaf** in 2001 have secured Philippine–U.S. military ties even more firmly. Since then the Philippine government has toughened its war against terrorism. In the pursuit of terrorists, military forces were able to rescue most of the hostages, except for two Americans and one Filipino. **Balikatan**, the joint military exercises of the Philippine and American military forces in **Basilan** Island, has effectively pacified the depredations of Abu Sayyaff and other terrorist elements. The government has aligned its policy of participation in the global campaign against terrorism with the United States by adopting four multilateral treaties. These treaties are the suppression of the financing of terrorism, suppression of terrorist bombings, suppression of unlawful acts or violence in airports, and suppression of unlawful acts against the safety of fixed platform intercontinental shelves. U.S. assistance helped the Philippine military shift the focus from insurgents to terrorists, but maintained the war being waged against the same enemy—the **New People's Army** and Muslim guerrillas. *See also* BALIKATAN.

ANTI-TRAFFICKING ACT. The Anti-Trafficking Act of 2003 was signed into law by President **Gloria Macapagal-Arroyo**. This is a landmark measure that will criminalize the act of trafficking of **women** and children, locally or internationally, and includes penalties. Trafficking is defined as the recruitment, transfer, provision, harboring, receipt, or deployment of persons for the purpose of forced servitude, slavery, sexual exploitation, involuntary servitude, debt bondage, physical and other forms of abuse, removal or sale of organs or involvement in armed activities, or other similar acts. *See also* ANTIPIRACY: BIOPIRACY.

APAYAO. This province in Northern Luzon was created by virtue of Republic Act No. 7878 on February 14, 1995, and is a part of the **Cordillera Autonomous Region** (CAR). It was formerly a sub-province (Kalinga-Apayao) of the old Mountain Province, which was divided into four provinces. Apayao is bounded to the north and east by Cagayan, to the west by Ilocos Norte and Abra, and to the south by Kalinga. Apayao has a population of 93,000 with seven municipalities. The major dialects are **Ilocano**, **Isneg**, and Kalinga. Its capital is Kabugao. Nineteen percent of the land is agricultural. The province has rich natural resources, namely copper, manganese, gold, and phosphates. *See also* KALINGA.

APO ANNO. A 500-year-old mummy found in a burial cave in Buguias, Benguet province, in 1918, which was reportedly stolen and eventually returned to the Kankan-ey tribe. The mummy is that of a man, about 5'8" in height, and his body was preserved in a squatting position. His skin is heavily tattooed—a symbol of his rank as a high priest, hunter, and leader. According to Kankan-ey legend, Apo Anno was the son of a goddess. Mummification was a traditional burial ritual in Benguet before the Spaniards came to the region; however, they discouraged the custom in their efforts to Christianize the tribe. Unlike the mummification in ancient Egypt, the internal organs of Benguet mummies are not removed. The body was preserved by covering it with many kinds of herbs and being smoked slowly for several days. Then the mummy was placed inside a cave. *See also* TABON CAVES.

APOSTOL, CECILIO (1877–1938). Spanish-language poet. A graduate of Ateneo Municipal de Manila, he was taking law courses at the **University of Santo Tomas** when the **Philippine–Spanish Revolution** broke out. He joined the revolutionaries in Manila as a propagandist using his skill in the Spanish language. When the revolution was over he went on to finish his law degree and passed the bar exam in 1903. He became a staff member of *La Independencia* and *El Renacimiento* newspapers, which had nationalist persuasions. Apostol's forte was patriotic poems. Two of his masterpieces were *A' Rizal* (To Rizal) and *Mi Raza* (My Race). They placed first in a national contest.

AQUACULTURE. Fish farming started with the cultivation of *bangus* or milkfish, the popular table fare of Filipino cooking. Due to the declining catch from the seas, the industry has expanded to the production for export of other financially lucrative species such as prawns, **tilapia**, carp, grouper, and mud crab. In 1998, the Philippines became the world's biggest aquaculture producer. Aquaculture is projected to contribute 42 percent of total fishery production in the country. This dramatic growth, however, is turning some places into environmental disaster areas. Many of the country's mangrove resources have been converted into fishponds. As a result, the country's mangrove has shrunk from 450,000 hectares to 300,000. Fish production from aquaculture increased from 8 to 12 percent of all fish produced from 1951 to present, with milkfish (*bangus*) constituting 90 percent of all aquaculture production. Milkfish farming throughout the country includes gathering and distribution, nursery and rearing pond production, and marketing. These activities generated slightly less than 0.5 percent of the GNP. The Philippines has increased aquaculture production over the past decade, with the help of foreign agencies, which have invested in aquaculture projects in Mindanao. *See also* AGRICULTURE; FISHING INDUSTRY; FLORA AND FAUNA.

AQUINO, BENIGNO "NINOY" JR. (1932–1983). Opposition politician. Aquino started his career as a war correspondent in the Korean War and served in the government as special assistant to three presidents: **Ramon Magsaysay**, **Carlos P. Garcia**, and **Diosdado Macapagal**. His service to Ramon Magsaysay was remarkably distinguished, in particular the negotiation with Huk leader **Luis Taruc**, who eventually surrendered to the government. In 1955, at age 22, Aquino was the youngest elected mayor, but he was disqualified from assuming office because of his age. However, he ran for governor and was elected at age 28 and, finally in 1967, he was elected senator at age 35. A member of the opposition, he was known for his unrelenting and incisive probing of public revenues, which made him the bitterest political foe of **Ferdinand Marcos**. His great popularity and charisma caused him to be widely regarded as the next **Liberal Party** candidate for the presidential elections in 1973. Ferdinand Marcos had already noted his rising star and considered him a potential threat to his power.

When **martial law** was declared in 1972, Aquino was among the first to be arrested. He was detained for seven years and held mostly in solitary confinement. During those years, Aquino brushed up on his reading. Even while he was in prison he became the symbol of opposition to the dictatorial regime. He was tried on trumped up charges of murder, illegal possession of firearms, and subversion. A military tribunal sentenced him to die by firing squad. The sentence was not carried out for fear that his death would make him a martyr and result in adverse world opinion toward the Marcos regime. However,

Marcos granted him permission to seek medical treatment in the United States for a heart condition. Although he promised Marcos to return after his surgery Aquino decided to stay in the United States with his family. During his three years in exile, he was granted a research fellowship at Harvard University and the Massachusetts Institute of Technology.

In August 1983, Aquino decided to return to the Philippines, spurning the warnings of First Lady **Imelda Marcos** to delay his return to Manila, because of alleged plots against him. He was assassinated at the Manila International Airport on August 21, 1983, as he disembarked from his aircraft in the company of a security detail of military officers. The assassination set in motion a train of events, which ultimately proved uncontrollable and resulted in the fall of the Marcos regime.

AQUINO, CORAZON C. (1933–). Corazon Aquino was the seventh president and first woman president of the Philippines. Maria Corazon Sumulong Cojuangco was born on January 25, 1933, in Manila, the sixth child of Jose **Cojuangco** and Demetria Sumulong. Her father, a lawyer, owned one of the largest sugar plantations in the province of Tarlac. Cory, her nickname, finished her bachelor's degree with a major in French language and a minor in mathematics from Mount St. Vincent College in New York. Following her graduation, she returned to the Philippines and enrolled as a law student at Far Eastern University in Manila. After a semester of course work, she met and married **Benigno "Ninoy" Aquino, Jr**. on October 11, 1954. They had five children.

The popular indignation that followed the assassination of her husband in August 21, 1983, immediately catapulted Cory Aquino into the limelight. She became a strong opponent of **Ferdinand Marcos** and a leading contender for the presidency. In the 1986 "snap" presidential elections, Marcos was declared the winner by the government "Commission on Elections" in a delayed count, but Aquino led earlier in the tally of the **National Citizens Movement for Free Elections** (NAMFREL). A stalemate in the proclamation of a winner followed. Meanwhile, Aquino led a nationwide protest against the widespread election fraud. The stalemate was broken when a faction of the military led by Minister of Defense **Juan Ponce Enrile** and

Vice-Chief of Staff of the Armed Forces General **Fidel Ramos** came to her support. They seized two military camps for their headquarters. Hundreds of thousands of people rallied to the side of the mutineers and faced the guns and tanks of the administration. Although approximately 15 people were killed, the Epifanio de los Santos Avenue revolution succeeded in stopping the government troops from crushing the Ramos-Enrile faction.

Aquino was installed as president on February 25, 1986. Marcos, his family, and 60 followers went into exile in Hawaii. She served as president for six years (1986–1992) and her term was punctuated by six coup attempts, domestic insurgency, and disagreements with the United States over military bases, and huge foreign debts. Her administration has been described as a transition government and her most pronounced success was restoring democracy to the Philippines.

AQUINO, FRANCISCA REYES (1899–1984). A leader in folk dancing and a National **Artist**, Aquino started her career as a physical education instructor at the University of the Philippines. The president of the university, **Jorge Bocobo,** recognized her talent in folk dancing and sent her to the provinces to study and collect the native folk dances, songs, and other forms of music. Her research included collecting regional costumes, musical instruments, and compiling information on folk practices and traditions. Aquino's work made her an authority on the subject and an important resource for school and civic group presentations of folk dances. At a time when the art of folk dancing was being overwhelmed by the heavy influx of Western music and other dance forms, Aquino's work constituted a refreshing wind on the cultural landscape. Her students at the University of the Philippines accepted her research with enthusiasm and became her strong supporters in the spread of the art of folk dancing. Due to her enthusiastic interest, folk dance instruction has been included in the programs of many private and public schools. In 1973, President **Ferdinand Marcos** conferred upon Aquino the National Artist Award for her contribution to the preservation and propagation of the folk dances of the Philippines. *See* SINGKIL; TINIKLING; URTULA, LUCRECIA REYES.

AQUINO, MELCHORA (1812–1919). A heroine of the Philippine–Spanish Revolution, Melchora Aquino born to a poor peasant couple in

Kalookan (now part of Quezon City). Aquino grew up with a gift for curing wounds and blurred vision. She was married to Fulgencio Ramos with whom she had six children. Her husband died early and so she was forced to support her children on the produce of rice and sugarcane from their 25-acres of land. The widow was affectionately called *Tandang Sora* (old Sora). It was on her land where the Katipuneros of **Andres Bonifacio** declared war in 1896 against their Spanish overlords. She opened her house for the underground meetings of members of the Katipunans. She also provided food for the underground army and nursed the sick and wounded. For her acts of kindness and valor, she was called the "Mother of the Philippine Revolution." Her house was put to the torch by the Spaniards who learned of the clandestine meetings and her role in supplying the needs of the incipient revolutionaries. In 1896, Aquino was captured by Spanish soldiers and deported to Guam together with 171 Filipinos charged with sedition and rebellion. She was released in 1903 when the Americans defeated the Spanish in the **Battle of Manila Bay**. She died on March 2, 1919, at the age of 107.

ARBULARYO. This is the **barrio** herbal medicine man also called *herbolario*. In most barrios and townships in the Philippines, the *arbularyo* serves as the local source of first aid. Well-versed in the healing power of herbs, the arbularyo uses his knowledge to treat common health maladies like stomach ache, injuries, indigestion, mumps, insect and snake bites, and headaches. Leaves of herbs are crushed together between the palms of his hands and the inky juice is squeezed on the affected area. For indigestion, a mixture of crushed ginger and water is boiled and sugar to taste is guaranteed to nullify indigestion. *See also* FLAVIER, JUAN; HERBAL MEDICINE.

ARELLANO, CAYETANO S. (1847–1920). He was the first Filipino justice of the Supreme Court. Born in Bataan, Cayetano Arellano was educated by the Dominican fathers of San Juan de Letran College, where he served as a house boy to earn his keep. He earned his law degree from the **University of Santo Tomas** at the age of 15. After passing the bar, he practiced law and taught at his alma mater. He also served as corporate counsel to various religious corporations as well as banking and other commercial institutions. During the last two decades of the Spanish regime, Arellano was the country's leading civil lawyer. The American authorities recognized his legal acumen by appointing him one of the six Filipino members of the Supreme Court. Arellano and his colleagues assisted the transition from Spanish to American government by harmonizing systems of legislation and other juridical matters. When the Philippine Commission reorganized the Supreme Court, Cayetano was the logical choice for chief justice. His opinions on a wide range of legal matters were highly respected by his colleagues on the court. He resigned his office on April 1, 1920, due to advancing age. The Philippine legislature awarded him a life-time pension for his long and meritorious services to the government and to the people of the Philippines. *See also* PENAL LAW.

ARMED FORCES OF THE PHILIPPINES (AFP). In 1947, the AFP was formed with three major commands: the Philippine Ground Forces, Philippine Air Force, and Naval Patrols. Then in 1970, the AFP was reorganized into four services: the Philippine Army, Philippine Constabulary, the Philippine Air Force, and the Philippine Navy. In 1980, the Regional Unified Command (RUC) was established to respond to emerging communist insurgency all over the country. As the AFP shifted its forces from internal security to national defense in the 1990s, the Philippine Constabulary was removed from the AFP and became the core of the Philippine National Police (PNP). Today, the AFP's three major branches—Philippine Army, Philippine Air Force, and Philippine Navy—are directly under the control and supervision of the president of the Philippines.

ARNIS. Originally a method of self-defense, *arnis* is more of a sport and an entertainment that involves dexterity and skill in the use of wooden staffs. *Arnis* predates the Spanish conquest of the Philippines, and was known as *kali* or *kabaroan* in Ilocos, *pagkalikali* in **Cagayan**, or *kalirongan* in Pangasinan. It is similar to European sword play and requires alertness, agility, and concentration. The sport has drawn worldwide attention by the presence of *arnis* clubs in the United States and Canada and its international competition. *See also* SIPA; SPORTS.

ARROYO, GLORIA MACAPAGAL (1947–). She is the 14th president of the Philippines—elected in the 2004 presidential national elections. Macapagal Arroyo became president on January 20, 2001, following the ouster of **Joseph Ejercito Estrada**. A daughter of the late President **Diosdado Macapagal**, she is the second **woman**— after Corazon Aquino—to be thrust into power through extraordinary means—**people power**—in the political history of the country. Arroyo began her career in academics teaching economics in which she has a doctorate degree. During the administration of President **Corazon Aquino**, she served as an undersecretary of trade and industry. She was elected senator in 1992 and authored 55 laws on economic and social reform. The people in the 1998 elections rewarded her successful work in the Senate when she was elected vice president with an unprecedented majority. In that national election Joseph Estrada won the presidency, but because Arroyo came from the opposition party she was appointed as concurrent secretary of the department of social welfare and development.

Her service was cut short when she took over the presidency and a government that was in disarray with a negative credit rating and a sluggish economic growth. After 24 months in office she was able to bring some stability and integrity—soiled by her immediate predecessor—to her office in spite of a vociferous, well-funded opposition and threats of coups. A first-class economist she focused on the issues that mattered—development, employment, investment, social services, law, and order. Muslim and communist insurgencies were neutralized—with the help of U.S. military forces—during her attempts to consolidate power and head the nation. Under her macroeconomic program the country's gross domestic product grew by 3.4 percent beating government expectations of a 3.3 per cent growth. **Foreign investments** generated a million jobs. The inflation rate went down to 2.5 percent in the last three decades. Her goal— like that of her father President **Diosdado Macapagal**—was to crush poverty with programs such as new land reforms—half a million farmer families became agrarian reform beneficiaries and poor people were given health insurance coverage.

The turning point of her presidency came in December 2002 when Arroyo fired inept cabinet secretaries and abolished scandal-ridden departments to highlight her administration's determination to curb corruption and strengthen the state's authority. *Time* headlined the president as the "Iron Lady of Asia" and aptly so since she was a workaholic who pursued her implementation programs and brooked no compromises and poor performance. In December 2002, Arroyo decided not to run for president during the election of 2004, a decision she and her family made to liberate her and the nation from the quicksand of politics and so she could direct her leadership to the promotion of economic, social, and political reforms. She changed her mind in October 2003 and campaigned largely on her track record and her movie actor opponent **Fernando Poe Jr.'s** inexperience. She won the presidency by a convincing margin of over 1.2 million votes or 42 percent majority against her opponent.

ART GALLERIES. Paintings and other objets d' art are mostly found in private galleries, like the **Ayala Museum** in Metro Manila and in other capital cities. Some of these galleries like the Casa San Miguel Center for the Arts include halls designed for concerts, plays, and ballet performances and an outdoor theater and garden. Works of the modernist/genre painter Anita Magsaysay-Ho are exhibited in Casa San Miguel, San Antonio, Zambales. In Luzon there are 10 art galleries, four of them are situated in Angono, Rizal. Casa Gorordo, the oldest gallery, is found in Cebu City, where the famous battle of Mactan painting is shown. Cebu City has three art galleries. Davao City has the Genuina Art Gallery, which exhibits the work of Emiliano Lo and Abdul Imao. Most paintings feature contemporary art and local artists use materials and elements that are indigenous to their region. Examples are the use of vista-inspired colors in ethnic art, and the use of ash glaze in pottery/sculptures of Luzon, particularly those from the Pampanga area. *See also* LOPEZ MEMORIAL MUSEUM.

ARTIAGA, JOSE. *See* PEFTOK.

ARTISTS. The highest honor given to artists is the National Artist Award, Republic Cultural Heritage. The awardees receive a cash prize and a monthly pension, medical benefits, a place of honor in state functions, and a state funeral. The first award was given posthumously in 1972 to painter **Fernando Amorsolo**. Since then the following artists have received this prestigious award: Architecture: Juan Nakpil 1973, Pablo Antonio 1976, and **Leandro V. Locsin** 1990; Dance: **Francisca Reyes Aquino** 1973, Leonor Orosa Goquinco 1976, and **Lucrecia Reyes Urtulo** 1988; Drama and Film: Lamberto Avellana 1976 and Gerardo de Leon 1982; Literature: Amado V. Hernandez 1973, **Jose Garcia Villa** 1973, **Nick Joaquin** 1976, **Carlos P. Romulo** 1982, and Francisco Arcellana 1990; Music: Antonio Molina 1973, Jovita Fuentes 1976, Antonio Buenaventura 1988, and **Lucrecia R. Kasilag** 1989; Painting: Carlos V. Francisco 1973, Victoria Edades 1976, Vicente Manansala 1981, and Cesar Legaspi 1990; Sculpture: **Guillermo Tolentino** 1973 and Napoleon Abueva 1976; Theater and Music: Atang de la Rama Hernandez 1987. *See also* SAPRID, SOLOMON.

ASEAN FREE TRADE AREA (AFTA). A historic trade agreement of the **Association of South East Asian Nations (ASEAN)**, which is also called the *Common Effective Preferential Tariff (CEPT),* signed in Singapore in 1999. The agreement called for a gradual tariff reduction mechanism by which tariffs on goods traded within the ASEAN region, which meet a 40 percent ASEAN content requirement, will be reduced to 0 to 5 percent by the year 2003 (2006 for Vietnam, and 2008 for Laos and Myanmar). These goods include manufactured items, capital goods, and processed and nonprocessed agricultural products.

ASSOCIATION OF SOUTHEAST ASIAN NATIONS (ASEAN). A regional association formed in August 1967 by the Philippines, Indonesia, Malaysia, Singapore, and Thailand. It has since expanded to 10 members after accepting Brunei, Laos, Cambodia, Myanmar (Burma), and **Vietnam**. Its objective is to pursue economic, social, cultural, and technical cooperation. Since its founding, these Asian nations have found common ground to discuss and resolve some of their regional problems, such as territorial disputes between the Philippines and Indonesia concerning the **Spratly** Islands and between the Philippines and Malaysia over **Sabah**. Unlike the defunct South East Asian Treaty Organization (SEATO), ASEAN has no defense function, but its members are committed to establishing a "zone of peace, freedom, and neutrality." President **Fidel Ramos** and Indonesian President Soeharto signed an agreement in 1993 creating the **Asian Free Trade Area** (AFTA), which expanded trade and investments between the two countries. In the ninth summit meeting held on October 2, 2003, in Bali, Indonesia, the 10 members signed the Declaration of Asian Concord II, also known as the Bali Concord II, which called for the establishment of an Asian community comprising three pillars: political and security cooperation, economic cooperation, and sociocultural cooperation. Concord II is the realization of the ASEAN Concord I adopted in Bali in 1976. A Commemorative Summit meeting was held in Japan in December 2003 in which the ASEAN members signed the Treaty of Amity and Cooperation following the Bali conference. The treaty enhanced the ties and mutual cooperation in economic, financial, and monetary issues.

ATI-ATIHAN. *See* AKLAN; MORIONES.

ATO. *See* BONTOC.

AUGUSTINIANS. *See* SAN AGUSTIN CHURCH.

AURORA. What is now Aurora province was formerly the two municipalities of Baler and Casiguran, then a part of Quezon (formerly Tayabas). It was created as a subprovince on June 14, 1961, by virtue of Republic Act No. 648. The province is named after Aurora Quezon, wife of President **Manuel Quezon**. It has eight towns with Baler as the capital, which is situated along the Pacific coast. The province has a population of 173,000 and a land area of 3,089 square kilometers. The dialects spoken are Ilocano, Casiguran, and Dumagat. Aurora's indigenous people are Dumagat, **Aeta**, and Ilongot. More than 70 percent of the land is still rain forest, and the remaining portion is devoted to agriculture.

AUSTRALIA. This land down-under is strongly involved in Philippine programs of **sustainable and equitable development** through the Australian Agency for International Development. Funds are coursed through the Philippine–Australian Community Assistance Program (PACAP), in poverty reduction, forest and ecological projects, and livelihood opportunities. Thanks to Australia, a cable car system in Talisay, Negros Occidental, has enabled farmers to transport livestock, vegetables, fruits, and other agricultural produce to marketing centers. Financial and technical support from the Australian government contributed to the success of the Philippine agriculture project of controlling foot-and-mouth disease of cattle. Australia is among the top five donors of grant aid to the Philippines. Over the past 10 years, the Australian government, through PACAP, has worked with some 500 partner **nongovernmental organizations** providing a total of 700 million pesos to support more than 900 projects benefiting many poor communities. While this partnership appears to be going on smoothly, the two countries are engaged in trade disputes involving exportation of Philippine fruits—bananas and pineapples—and the importation of Australian milk and dairy products.

AUSTRONESIAN. This term refers to the root language of almost all Southeast Asian languages, including most of the languages of the Philippines. Scholars differ in the actual definition of the term, although most of them use it mainly as a linguistic construct, while others use it to include the speakers of the language. However, the prevailing view is that Austronesian was a trade language, which was spread by seafarers in the area of northern Luzon, Taiwan, and south China.

AUTONOMOUS REGION IN MUSLIM MINDANAO (ARMM). A regional arrangement of Muslim Filipinos in self-government (Republic Act 6743 or the Organic act for the creation of the Autonomous Region for Muslim Mindanao). This arrangement was a concession made by the Corazon Aquino government to the **Moro** movement. In a referendum on November 19, 1989, only five provinces elected to join the autonomous region; namely, **Tawi-Tawi**, **Sulu**, **Maguindanao**, **Basilan**, and **Lanao del Sur**. Marawi City and Isabela City joined later. Disagreement continued over the location of the seat of government and the supervisory powers of the autonomous government over local government officials. Under this agreement the Muslims were given control over some aspects of government but not over national security and foreign affairs. Muslim customary laws (**sharia**) and Philippine laws were harmonized, including exemption of Muslims from the illegal practice of polygamy. These changes led to greater assimilation. Nevertheless, Muslims and Christians generally remained distinct societies. The rebellious **Moro National Liberation Front** (MNLF), which is divided along tribal lines, remained unsatisfied with the limited autonomy over a specific area embodied in the autonomous region.

When President **Fidel Ramos** assumed office, he sought a peaceful resolution with the MNLF of their demands for autonomy and other grievances with the government. After many negotiations between representatives of the government and the MNLF, taking place in Tripoli, Libya, **Jeddah**, Saudi Arabia, and Jakarta, Indonesia, a peace agreement was forged that became the Southern Philippines Council for Peace and Development (SPCPD). This document was signed in Manila by representatives of both sides and witnessed by President Ramos. Under this peace accord, elected leaders will administer and supervise development projects designed to foster economic growth in Muslim Mindanao. In the ensuing four years, the ARMM under the leadership of **Nur Misuari**, failed poorly in the implementation of the accord and the monies provided were used in rampant **graft and corruption**. When the government turned down his request for reelection, Misuari led a rebellion that was quelled by the government. He fled to Malaysia to seek political asylum but the Malaysian government turned him down and eventually extradited him to the Philippines, where he was charged with the crime of rebellion.

A new leader was elected, **Parouk Hussin**, a physician, to lead the poverty-stricken region, which has a population of three million Moros. Saddled with violence and lawless elements, Hussin's initial objective was to restore stability in the strife-torn region so that development could proceed. Thus, to hasten the development of the ARMM, the Regional Economic Zone Authority (REZA) was created by congress in 2003 to provide foreign traders with investment incentives, tax holidays, and tariff privileges. REZA was passed to complement President **Gloria Macapagal Arroyo's** effort in fostering normalcy in areas devastated by hostilities between government forces and **Moro Islamic Liberation Front** (MILF) rebels. In addition, the United States Aid For International Development (USAID) has approved a $33 million five-year grant to be used in **education** programs for the ARMM. *See also* MUSLIM SEPARATISM.

AVANCEÑA, RAMON (1872–1957). During the Philippine Spanish Revolution, Avanceña formed a committee whose main objective was to drive the Spaniards out of Panay Island and the neighboring islands. He also organized a provincial revolutionary government in Santa Barbara, Iloilo. In their first encounter with the American troops, Avanceña and his comrades were taken prisoners. They were later set free in March 1901. He worked on his profession as a lawyer for several years, until President **Manuel Quezon** appointed him a Supreme Court justice during the Commonwealth period.

AVES DE RAPINA. This is the famous title of an editorial, which appeared in the *El Renacimiento*. The Spanish-language nationalist paper was edited by Teodoro Kalaw and was published during the early period of the American colonial administration. The editorial, which appeared on October 30, 1908, satirized **Dean C. Worcester**, then secretary of interior in the colonial government. He felt that the "bird of prey," portrayed in the title, alluded to him and sued the paper. The suit became a celebrated libel case when the issue of nationalism was in ferment. In the trial the editor and publisher were found guilty and the paper was sold to satisfy the financial damages claimed by Worcester. American Governor-General **Francis Burton Harrison** later pardoned the defendants.

AWIDON MESA. *See* PALEOLITHIC CULTURE.

AYALA MUSEUM. A private museum in Makati founded by **Fernando Zobel**. It was established in 1967. The museum exhibits dioramas of historical events interpreted in three-dimensional forms by Filipino artists and carvers from Paete, Laguna. Sixty-three handcrafted dioramas, portraying Philippine history from 30,000 B.C. to the 20th century form the core of the museum's archaeological, ethnographic, and numismatic and art collections. Rare 19th century paintings by Damian Domingo, Jose Lozano, and **Juan Luna** are exhibited as well as gold jewelry and religious icons from the Spanish colonial period. The museum also houses an array of model boats, historical paintings, and photographs. Two significant collections of 20th century art are the work of **Fernando Amorsolo** and the abstract painter **Fernando Zobel**. *See also* ART GALLERIES; LOPEZ MUSEUM.

– B –

BABAYLAN (PHILIPPINE WOMEN'S NETWORK). A Filipina network of 20 migrant organizations from nine European countries, which hold conferences on economic empowerment. Organized in

1991 in Rome, the conference provides an opportunity for Filipinas to formulate new strategies to fight unfair labor practices and exploitation—two of the many issues faced by Filipino overseas' workers—in their places of employment. Caritas di Roma, a Catholic social service that works with migrants, estimates that there are about 40,000 Filipina domestics in Italy alone. Many of these Filipinas who have higher education opted for the better rewards of domestic work overseas; however, the negative effect of their work situations and long separation from their families are problems that are being addressed by Babaylan. Its advocacy has brought about better working conditions for Filipina domestics in some European nations. A similar advocacy union in Hong Kong greatly aided Filipina domestics to secure better pay and labor contracts. *See also* ABSENTEE VOTING RIGHTS; OVERSEAS FOREIGN WORKERS.

BABAYLANISM. This is a religio-political movement on Negros Island. The name was derived from *babaylan*, the title given to traditional shamans or religious functionaries in the **Visayas**. With the coming of the Spaniards the *babaylan* tradition survived on Negros Island, which has many rugged mountains and hills to serve as hiding places. These *babaylanes* served as intermediaries between *diwatas* (nature gods) and the people. Central to the traditional ceremony of nature worship is the sacrifice of a pig to the *diwata*s, accompanied by drinking, dancing, and eating. The *babayl*an confers to his followers **anting-anting** (amulets), which protect them from the harm of swords or bullets. Babaylanism was quite widespread on Negros and Panay islands in the 1870s. By that time, the followers were also called *babaylanes*. By 1896, the number of adherents had increased and were well-entrenched in the mountains of Negros. Their ceremonies have become a mixture of indigenous and **Roman Catholic** elements. The *babaylanes* were involved in the **Philippine–Spanish Revolution** and the subsequent **Philippine–American Revolution**. Following an incessant military campaign against the *babaylanes*, their charismatic leader, Isio, was forced to surrender, thus effectively bringing the cult to an end.

BACOLOD. *See* NEGROS OCCIDENTAL.

BAGOBO. The Bagobo is an ethnic tribe found in **Davao del Norte** province. They inhabit mountainous regions and generally practice swidden agriculture to produce their main food staples of rice, maize, sweet potatoes, and other root crops. The Bagobos are divided into three language groups, which are geographically separate and culturally distinct from one another. The coastal Bagobos have been influenced by Christianity and reside in plantations and settlements. Their villages are governed by datus, who practice kinship reckoning and enforce strict incest laws. *See also* LUMADS.

BAGONG ALYASANG MAKABAYAN (NEW PATRIOTIC ALLIANCE). This party was established in May 1985 and indicated its political color by its commitment to "our people's struggle for national freedom and democracy." The founding chairman was the nationalist **Lorenzo Tañada.** The umbrella organization brought together small grassroots groups representing different classes and sectors. In the 2002 national elections two of their candidates for congressmen were elected.

BAGUIO CITY. The Philippines' resort and summer capital is located in **Benguet** in the mountains of northern Luzon province. The city rests on a plateau, 1,520 meters above sea level and enjoys an average temperature of 18 degrees centigrade, making it the coolest spot in the country and a popular vacation place especially during the hot summer months of March to June when its population swells to half a million people. The Spaniards explored the area for its **gold** but American governors-general who transferred their administration to this city to escape the stifling heat of Manila primarily developed it as a resort. Since then, the Philippine government has established offices and residences for its officials. As a local and foreign **tourist** retreat, Baguio offers many attractions, such as tours of gold mining towns, crystal caves, and the Lourdes grotto. *See also* CORDILLERA.

BAHALÀ NA. Idiomatic expression among the Tagalogs, which means to leave things in the hands of *Bathalà* (God), or "Come what may." *See also* KA; PO.

BAHAY KUBO. Tagalog word for small hut. This is the traditional hand-built dwelling of rural folks. It is called *payag* in the Visayan Islands. *Bahay Kubo* is usually made from bamboo (*kawayan*) for the framework and **nipa** palms (*anahaw*) for the roofing and sidings.

Flooring is also made from lattice bamboo. Posts are **narra** wood. The one-level house consists of a wide room, which converts into a bedroom at night, a kitchen, and a side room for storing clothes, beddings, and accessories. The hut is airy and cool with its wide windows. The typical *bahay kubo* is often seen today more as a summer house. It has also inspired the popular *Bahay Kubo* song that praises the cultural qualities of this humble abode.

BAJA JR., LAURO LIBOON (1938–). As the Philippines' permanent representative to the United Nations, Lauro Liboon Baja Jr. was elected president of the UN Security Council in June 2004, the fourth time the Philippines has assumed the post of the world organization. The presidency of the council has always been an event to its members, and the Philippines is the first among the five newly elected members to be president of the council. It will again assume the presidency during the first quarter of 2005. Baja and his Philippine delegation bring to the presidency comprehensive knowledge of issues in the council. Baja's presidency came at a crucial time when the UN was confronted with the controversial question on the post occupation of **Iraq**.

In the international area, Baja has served in various ambassadorial posts—Italy, Brazil, and London—until his appointment as head of the Philippine mission to the United Nations. He started his career as an undersecretary of the department of foreign affairs and worked for the **Association of Southeast Asian Nations** (ASEAN) as the legal expert in drafting and negotiation of statements on regional cooperation. He has represented his country at diplomatic conferences, including the Rome conference establishing the International Criminal Court. He also participated in UN meetings, such as the Commission on International Trade Law and served as senior official in ASEAN forums and meetings of the Non-aligned Movement. Baja received his bachelor's degree in jurisprudence from the University of the Philippines.

BAJAU. The Bajau is a Muslim ethnolinguistic group and known as the "sea-gypsies" of the Sulu archipelago. Some Bajaus are found along the sea coasts of Zamboanga, but most are concentrated around the island of **Tawi-tawi**. The Bajaus, with their distinctive boats, lead a nomadic lifestyle close to the sea. Traditionally, they are born and live on their boats but many have now settled in houses built on stilts over coral reefs. They are mostly fishermen who thrive on seafood, although those who live on the coasts have taken to cultivating seaweed for sale to chemical and pharmaceutical companies. *See also* BATAK; TAUSOG.

BALAGTAS, FRANCISCO BALTAZAR (1788–1862). To the Tagalog-speaking people, Francisco Baltazar Balagtas is considered the "Prince of Tagalog Poets" for his epic masterpiece "**Florante At Laura**," which was composed in 1838 in the stately Tagalog language. Written as a metrical romance, the poem contains some 400 quatrains of four lines each of perfect vowel rhymes. "Florante At Laura" depicts the evils that beset the Filipinos during the Spanish regime. While Albania was the setting and the characters had foreign names, the heroes and heroines stood for his countrymen, and the conditions described were the very ones existing in the Philippines. The book contains passages on upright living and lessons in justice, love, respect for elders, industry, and patriotism. Balagtas articulated the idea of a Filipino nation by allegory in the early 18th century. Balagtas was born in **Bulacan.** *See also* BUKANEG, PEDRO.

BALAGTASAN. A popular debate in verse form conducted in **Tagalog** by well-known poets in honor of Francisco Balagtas. The first balagtasan was held on October 18, 1925, between Jose Corazon de Jesus and Florentino Collantes. De Jesus, who won the contest, was crowned *Hari ng Balagtasan* (King of Balagtasan).

BALANGA. *See* BATAAN.

BALER. *See* AURORA.

BALIKATAN (SHOULDERING THE LOAD). Joint military exercises (war games) between the **Philippine armed forces** and American military conducted in Basilan Island and Luzon during January to June. The U.S. contingent of 660 combat troops trained Filipino soldiers to fight **Abu Sayyaf** rebels while 300 U.S. engineers were engaged in civic action—building landing strips, paving roads, and digging wells in impoverished areas as part of the rehabilitation of **Basilan** Island—the hotbed of terrorism. Philippine soldiers were also provided with sorely needed military hardware—helicopters, heavy guns, and electronic detection equipment. Under the provisions of the **Visiting Forces Agreement** U.S. troops are not allowed to fight directly, unless fired upon, and serve under the command of a Filipino general. The war exercises have been held annually since 1981 under the previous Philippine Mutual Defense Treaty—the last one was held in 1995. It was suspended in 1996 in the absence of an agreement. It was revived in 1997 following the signing of the **Visiting Forces Agreement**. The objective was to enhance the Philippine armed forces' capability to combat terrorists and communist guerrillas.

BALIKBAYAN. A *balikbayan* is an immigrant Filipino primarily from North America who periodically visits the motherland. It was the **Ferdinand Marcos** regime in the mid-70s that coined the term *balikbayan* by joining the Tagalog word *balik*, to return, with *bayan*, meaning town and nation. The balikbayan was planned as a **tourist** program to encourage dollar-earning Filipinos to visit the country. Thus, the government passed a law (Balikbayan Act), which provides a visa-free entry for foreign nationals for one year and the extension of generous shopping privileges in duty-free shops. Added to the privilege is the ability to own land and other business. In 2003, another bill was also passed allowing overseas Filipinos to vote (**absentee ballot**) in local and national elections. Since the *balikbayan* started, some 400,000 families have visited annually and their spending has enhanced the country's dollar-starved economy. *See also* OVERSEAS FOREIGN WORKERS.

BALIK ISLAM. This means, "revert" referring to former Christians who "reverted" to Islam. Reverts as they like to be called, live in traditionally Catholic Luzon, but the Balik Islam movement—propagation of the faith—has since spread all over the Philippines. An indication of the success of Balik Islam is the number of mosques recorded as of 2003 by the Office of Muslim Affairs: 33 in Metro Manila, 29 in Northern Luzon, 15 in Central Luzon, 56 in Southern Luzon, and 38 in the Visayas. The office has also estimated that there are some 20,000 reverts. What started as a public curiosity about **Islam**—following the Muslim insurgency in Mindanao—has become a serious movement, which has been drawing many Roman Catholics to the Muslim faith. The first Filipino reverts were the overseas workers in Middle Eastern countries, especially in **Saudi Arabia**, where **sharia** law is enforced. When these overseas workers came back, they impressed many with their piety that their family, relatives, and friends followed suit. The reverts became the most effective teachers of *da'wah* (propagation) because they spoke with the background of other more popular religions.

Their zeal, however, triggered suspicion that their groups were being used as fronts for terrorist operations and avenues for laundering money to finance training and the acquisition of weapons and ammunition so the Philippine government monitored their activities. This suspicion was also an extension of the distrust of organizations established in Manila in the 1990s by Osama bin Laden's brother-in-law Jamaal al-Khaliffa, who was later deported by the Philippine government for his subversive activities. So far the Balik Islam movement and its allied organization—Islamic Call and Guidance-Philippines–has kept within the parameters laid down by the Philippine government.

BALITAO. Visayan romantic folk song. Like the Tagalogs who have the **kundiman**, the Visayans have their own folk song called *balitao*, which is a popular form of entertainment at social gatherings. In a *balitao* presentation a man and a woman engage in sentimental debate, usually about love and courtship, while dancing to the music of a *subing* (a native flute) or a *sista* (a guitar made out of coconut shell). As in a debate one party prevails, usually the man. *See also* KUNDIMAN.

BALMACEDA, JULIAN CRUZ. *See* NATIONAL ANTHEM.

BALUT. A popular delicacy, especially among the Tagalogs. It is duck egg that has been artificially incubated for 14 days in heated rice husks and hard-cooked. It is usually eaten as an afternoon repast accompanied with beer. Pateros, **Rizal**, where duck raising is an industry, supplies the balut sold in Metro Manila. Balut is also known in China, Vietnam, and other Southeast Asian countries. *See also* CUISINE; LECHON; SUMAN.

BAMBOO. Its scientific name is *bambusa*, the giant of the grass family. Growing wild bamboo is found on almost all of the islands in the Philippine archipelago and is so versatile a product that it can be used as a building material, especially for the quintessential *bahay kubo*, in handicrafts, fish traps, storage and cooking vessels, canoe outriggers, and as food when its young shoots are tender. One of its more famous uses, however, is in the fabrication of musical instruments. The bamboo organ constructed by a Spanish priest for his church of Las Pinas is an example. Many tribes utilize the bamboo as a flute or as a string instrument. Its most recent adaptation is the *musikong bumbong,* which is the bamboo version of the brass band. This bamboo orchestra is composed of children playing folk tunes on 100 or more instruments made of bamboo.

BANANA. It is one of the country's major export crops and an important earner of foreign exchange. The banana, locally called *saguing,* grown for export is the cavendish (dwarf) variety. Banana production is handled by three transnational corporations, Del Monte, Dole, and United Brands, which export the produce exclusively to Japan. Most of the banana plantations are found in Mindanao.

BANATAO, DIOSDADO (1946–). Computer guru. A native of Iguig, **Cagayan**, Diosdao Banatao obtained his engineering degree from Mapua Institute of Technology, Manila. He came to the United States and worked for various electronic companies. With his scientific knowledge he is credited for eight major contributions to information technology, one of which is the first single-chip graphical user interface accelerator that made computers work a lot faster and another is the Ethernet controller chip that made the Internet possible. In 1989, he pioneered the local bus concept for personal computers and in the following year developed the first windows accelerator chip. Intel is now using chips and technologies developed by Banatao. In recognition of his technological innovations, the University of the Philippines honored him with a doctor of science (*honoris causa*) degree in March 2000. *See also* SCIENTISTS.

BANAUE. *See* IFUGAO; RICE TERRACES; SAGADA.

BANDALA. *See* TRIBUTES.

BANGKO SENTRAL. *See* MONETARY SYSTEM.

BANGON PARTY. A multisectoral party organized in November 2003 by Vice President **Teofisto Guingona** in response to calls from his supporters to run for the presidency. However, he declined the challenge and instead vowed to fight what he claimed the widespread corruption in the bureaucracy. Guingona said there was a need of a "third force" in Philippine politics to serve as the watchdog against **graft and corruption** during the next presidency.

BANGSAMORO. *See* MUSLIM SEPARATISM; TRIPOLI AGREEMENT.

BANGUED. *See* ABRA.

BANGUS (MILKFISH). *See* CAPIZ.

BANKING. *See* MONETARY SYSTEM.

BANNA. An epic tale of the Kalinga tribe. Like most tribes in the Philippines the **Kalingas** kept their cultural heritage in the form of *ullalim* (ballads), which bards chanted during harvest festivals and peace pact assemblies. The *ullalim* is a romantic and lively account of heroic battles in which the hero Banna is involved in the process of winning the hand of his lady love. Major episodes of the epic depict many customs and traditions of the people. *See also* HUDHUD.

BAPTISTS. *See* PROTESTANTISM.

BARANGAY. Basic unit of local administration. Throughout the Spanish occupation, from 1565 to 1898, the *barangay* was the basic unit of local government. The word *barangay*, also *balangay*, is a Malay term for a large sail boat, which was the means of transport for the early Malay immigrants to the Philippines. A *barangay* was also essentially a group of extended families who arrived on the *barangay* boat and settled on coastal areas and riverine sites forming a community. The settlers were headed by a datu who was usually an elder and the wisest of the group. Large *barangays* were ruled by a rajah. When a datu died the community elected a new datu from among the elders. The post was not hereditary.

The Spanish, who saw the stability provided by the *barangay* system, sought to preserve it as the basic unit of local administration by appointing the datu as the *cabeza de barangay* (chief). Since *barangays* were widely scattered, the Spanish had to consolidate cognate villages to form a **pueblo** for better political control and economic exploitation. In addition the Spanish considered the consolidation as a better way to teach the inhabitants the dogmas of **Roman Catholicism**. This strategy, called *reducciones*, was carried out with the sword and the cross, and it was strongly and forcibly resisted by the early datus. Such resistance did not totally stop throughout the Spanish colonial period for there were datus who took their people to the highlands to avoid Spanish rule.

Today, the term *barangay* refers to communities consisting of 1,000 inhabitants residing within the territorial limit of a city or municipality and administered by a group of elective officials. The *barangay* is the administrative arm of the government and functions as part of the delivery system of goods and services at the community level, such as assisting the national and local government units in the maintenance of law and order, engaging in cleanliness and beautification campaigns, or regulating urban traffic. A number of *barangays* make up a municipality. *See also* PUEBLO; PUROK.

BARASOAIN CHURCH. A **baroque church** in the historic town of Malolos, **Bulacan**, where the first congress of the Philippine Republic was held on September 15, 1898. Before an assembly of delegates representing various sectors of the Philippines, President **Emilio Aguinaldo** read his message in Tagalog and later in Spanish. Then he announced that the ceremonies were over and that the congress should elect its officers. Elected president was **Pedro Paterno**. Barasoain church today houses the Bulacan ecclesiastical museum. It has an invaluable collection of religious artifacts, mementos, articles, documents, and handicrafts from Bulacan during the period of the **Philippine–Spanish Revolution**.

BARLIN, JORGE IMPERIAL (1850–1909). At a time when **friarocracy** was in practice during the Spanish ecclesiastical rule in the Philippines, Jorge Imperial Barlin was the exception. Ordained a priest in 1875 in **Albay**, where his piety and talent became known, he was promoted in 1898 to **Sorsogon** province and became the first clergyman to become civil governor until the coming of the Americans in

1900. Subsequently, he was appointed the first full-blooded Filipino—**Indio** as the Spaniards called the natives then—bishop in the **Roman Catholic** hierarchy. Bishop Barlin's name is historically linked to a landmark Supreme Court ruling regarding possession of church properties in the Bicol region seized by the fledgling Philippine Independent Church (**Iglesia Filipina Independiente**), also known as the Aglipayans. The decision to return the properties—buildings and land—was an irreparable blow to the Aglipayan movement. He was later appointed archbishop of Nueva Caceres diocese, which earned him again the distinction as the first Bicolano to achieve the highest level in the episcopacy. *See also* GOMBURZA.

BARONG. A heavy blade wielded for combat or used for domestic chores by Muslims in Southern Philippines. Barong and its twin weapon—the double-edge serpentine *kampilan*—brandished by rampaging **juramentados** struck fear in the American soldiers who were engaged in pacifying recalcitrant **Moros** in the early 1900s. *See also* MASSACRES.

BARONG-BARONG. Squatter's shack made of flimsy building materials—discarded wood, cardboard, bamboo, and corrugated roofing—constructed by the urban poor and usually found in the fringes of cities. *See also* BAHAY KUBO.

BARONG TAGALOG. A square cut, richly embroidered, nearly transparent shirt, usually made of finely woven **jusi** cloth or **piña** from the fibers of the pineapple plant *Barong Tagalog* became very popular when **Ramon Magsaysay** was inaugurated president of the Philippines in 1953 wearing this dress shirt. It has become de rigueur in Philippine society for men. *See also* RAMIE.

BAROQUE CHURCHES. Baroque architecture was brought by Spanish priests to the Philippines in the 17th century. The grandeur of the baroque is illustrated by the surviving models of massive church buildings that played significant roles in the Christianization of the country. Among the best examples are **San Agustin Church** built in Manila in 1587 by the Augustinian order, the Church of San Agustin in Paoay, **Ilocos Norte**, the Church of Nuestra Señora de la Asuncion in Santa Maria, **Ilocos Sur**, and the Church of Santo Tomas de Villanueva in **Miagao** in **Iloilo**.

BARRIOS. This is a **nongovernmental organization** that is devoted to deliver mass quantities of educational materials procured from donor individuals and discards of U. S. public schools. Its volunteers bring the books to remote and disadvantaged schools. In 1999, BARRIOS distributed 400,000 pounds of educational materials to eight public schools designated by the Philippine Department of Education as deprived, depressed sites that severely lacked classroom resources and reference learning materials.

BARTOLOME, JUAN. *See* MORO-MORO.

BARWANAOS. *See* AGUSAN DEL SUR

BASA, MOUNT. *See* SARANGANI.

BASCO. *See* BATANES.

BASCO, JOSE. *See* TRIBUTE.

BASE CONVERSION DEVELOPMENT AUTHORITY. Authorized agency to develop the American military bases. In February 1992, with the closure of the United States bases in the Philippines the government established this interim agency, which created five special economic zones at the vacated United States bases. Its function was to sell the land connected with the bases with half of the proceeds to be used to convert the bases to civilian use. The former **Subic Bay** Naval Base has since been converted into a tourist center, industrial zone, container port, and commercial shipyard.

BASI. Ilocano wine made from sugarcane juice. The sugarcane is crushed in wooden mills, and the juice is cooked in vats and then transferred to earthen jars called *burnay*. A flavoring mixture made of powdered rice, fruits, and sumac leaves is added. The jars are sealed with banana leaves and stored underground in a cool, dry place where the mixture is allowed to ferment for one to three years. During the Spanish colonial period, the Spaniards imposed a monopoly on *basi*, but the hardy Ilocanos rose up in revolt to retain control over the manufacture of their favorite drink. *See also* TUBA.

BASILAN. Located southwest of Mindanao in the northern most group of the Sulu archipelago, Basilan is an island province with a land area of 1,372 square kilometers and a population of more than 200,000, most of whom are **Yakans**, a Muslim ethnic group. The capital city of Isabela was named after Queen Isabela II of Spain in 1845 after the Spanish defeated the reigning sultan. The province is composed of seven municipalities. Basilan produces world-class rubber and exportable quantities of copra and coffee. Yakan women are famous weavers of colorful dress fabrics. Basilan is heavily forested, which provided the home base of the terrorist group **Abu Sayyaf**. The major provincial towns are Lamitan, Maluso, and Tuburan. *See also* BALIKATAN.

BASKETBALL. *See* SPORTS.

BATAAN. This province occupies a peninsula in western Luzon, the land area of which is 1,373 square kilometers. Most of the approximately 500,000 inhabitants are ethnic **Tagalogs**. The capital city of Balanga is centrally located and functions as the commercial hub of the province. Much of the fruit and fish sold in the markets of Manila comes from Bataan, where plantations produce large quantities of mangoes, star apples, bananas, and pineapples, and the coastal waters yield catches of tuna, red snapper, squid, mackerel, and sardines. The city of Mariveles, on the tip of the peninsula, is an export processing zone and a major center of heavy industry. Bataan Peninsula is also the site where the defending Philippine–American troops under the command of General **Douglas MacArthur** made their last-ditch stand against the invading Japanese forces. Japan's surprise attack on the Philippines on December 8, 1941, began with aerial bombardment followed by the landing of troops, which overwhelmed the defenders and forced them to withdraw on April 1942 to Bataan Peninsula and on May 1942 to **Corregidor** Island. *See also* HOMMA, MASAHARU; YAMASHITA, TOMOYUKI.

BATAK. Indigenous people of **Palawan** who live along the coastal villages near Puerto Princesa. They are the smallest of three Palawan groups, numbering about 400 people, and speaking the Binatak language. Their physical characteristics—small in stature, kinky hair, hirsute faces and bodies—relate them to **Aetas**, but anthropologists classify them as more related to the Semang and Sakai of the Malay Peninsula. Despite contacts with other Palawan groups and settlers, Batak material culture has not changed from its semi-nomadic character. Some members still continue their hunting and gathering way of life. Batak society has been severely affected by disease and malnutrition due to poverty. The Batak are an animist society. A distinctive feature of the men is the colorful tattoos on their arms and chest. *See also* BAJAU; TAGBANUA.

BATANES. This is the Philippines' smallest province, located on the north coast of Luzon. Batanes province, consisting of 10 small islands in the Luzon Strait, has a total land area of 209 square kilometers and a population of 12,200. The three largest islands are Batan, (where the provincial capital Basco is located), Itbayat, and Sabtang. The natives of Batan speak the Ivatan language, and the natives of Itbayat speak the Itbayaten dialect. Since the islands are often struck by typhoons, houses and other buildings are built low to the ground, with meter-thick stone walls and heavy thatched roofs. There is not much arable land, so the natives raise fast-growing crops such as garlic, the economic staple, and various kinds of root vegetables. Two of the interesting towns in this island province are Mayan on Itbayat Island and San Vicente on Sabtang Island. *See also* AMAN DANGAT; FUGA ISLAND.

BATANGAS. This province lies southwest of Manila and is the site of famous **Taal Lake** and volcano. Its capital city is also named Batangas. With a land area of 3,166 square kilometers and a population of 1.4 million people, Batangas is one of the principal provinces of the **Tagalog** culture, together with **Cavite**, **Laguna**, and **Rizal**. Evidence from archeological excavations shows that a thriving and stratified society has existed in the region for centuries. This is the homeland of such famous Filipino heroes as **Apolinario Mabini**, **Miguel Malvar**, and **Jose P. Laurel**. Batangas is known as a major producer of mandarin oranges, papayas, mangoes, bananas, and pineapples. The chief towns are Batangas, Tanauan, Lipa, Lemery, Tanauan, and Balayan.

BATASANG PAMBANSA. National Assembly. The unicameral legislative body was created by President Ferdinand Marcos in 1978 to replace the bicameral system, which he claimed was no longer an effective forum to meet the political and economic requirements of the nation. The Batasang Pambansa provided Marcos with an excuse to perpetuate his presidency, which was due to end under the 1935 constitution. His declaration of **martial law** in 1972 suspended the constitution and gave him absolute powers to govern the country. The Batasang Pambansa provided for a parliamentary form of government and a prime minister as head of government. It was composed of 200 elected members whose duty was to pass legislation and forego opposition and obstructionism. The new system was a political experiment since the Filipino people had no experience with a parliamentary government and relatively few in the Batasang Pambansa possessed the political skills necessary in a unicameral system. As for Marcos, he took the office of prime minister and retained his title of president. He also had the power to dissolve the assembly and issue presidential decrees that had the effect of law.

At its first assembly on June 10, 1978, Marcos addressed the members about the four major principles of government; namely, survival of the public order and of individual rights, articulation of the interests of the poor and participation in government, development of rural areas, and eradication of poverty and inequality in society. Using these priorities, Marcos appointed his wife **Imelda Marcos** to the newly created positions of minister of human settlement and governor of Metro Manila to implement the president's sweeping objectives. In this capacity, the First Lady pursued her work with vigor by using government funds for her projects at the cost of other ministries and their activities. Since the majority of the congressmen were elected under the banner of the president's party Kilusang Bagong Lipunan (New Society Movement) the Batasang Pambansa turned out to be a rubber stamp for presidential directives that were designed to keep Marcos in power. This body was dismantled by President **Corazon Aquino** when she assumed office in February 1986 and the bicameral system was restored when the new constitution was approved in a national referendum in 1987. *See also* CONSTITUTION OF THE PHILIPPINES and FREEDOM CONSTTUTION.

BATES TREATY. When the Americans learned that the Muslims in the south had not been completely subjugated, they tried to neutralize their initial resistance with the use of diplomacy. General John Bates tried to win their friendship by negotiating with them on the basis of equality. The Sultan of Jolo—having been informed of the superior firepower of the American military—was amenable and laid down some conditions, such as no Americans must be allowed to occupy any part of Sulu except the town proper of Jolo, the right to collect customs duties in places not occupied by the Americans, respect the rights and dignities of the Sultan and his datus and their religion. On the part of the Americans, they expressed the sovereignty of the United States over the whole archipelago of Jolo and its dependence. The sultan agreed to the blanket statement while the Americans accepted the sultan's conditions. To sweeten the deal, the Americans agreed also to pay the sultan and his datus monthly salaries. General Gates and the Sultan signed the so-called Bates Treaty in Jolo on August 20, 1899. With the neutralization of the Muslims, the Americans proceeded in the pacification of Mindanao.

BATHALA. *See* DIWATA.

BAUTISTA, AMBROSIO RIANZARES (1830–1903). Author of the declaration of Philippine independence. A lawyer by profession, Bautista was involved in the movement to free the Philippines from the Spanish yoke of tyranny and oppression. He helped finance *La Solidaridad*, the organ of the **propaganda movement** in Spain. Named as a political adviser to Emilio Aguinaldo, Bautista wrote the declaration of Philippine independence, which he read during the proclamation in Kawit, Cavite, on June 12, 1898. He succeeded **Pedro Paterno** as president of the revolutionary congress when it reconvened in **Tarlac** in 1899. When the **Philippine–American Revolution** ended, he was appointed a judge of the court of first instance.

BAYAN BAGONG ALYASANG MAKABAYAN (NEW NATIONALIST ALLIANCE). Bayan was formed in the early 1980s as an affiliate of the left-wing underground **National Democratic Front**. Its platform was based on nationalist themes to attract people who were disenchanted with the established political parties. It succeeded in drawing many well-known non-Communists into its membership. By 1986, it claimed a membership of over two million, which made its members feel ready for political action. They created the Alliance for

New Politics (ANP) and fielded a senatorial slate in the 1986 elections. However, none of their candidates won any seats. *See also* SECTORAL PARTIES.

BAYANIHAN. A Filipino cultural trait, which means group spirit or teamwork. It denotes an atmosphere of unselfish cooperation in a communal activity, such as the sharing of labor for the common good. This is mostly demonstrated when farmers help out their neighbors in rice planting, in harvest, and in other community endeavors that require immediate action or effort to alleviate the distress of an individual in trouble.

BAYANIHAN CENTER. *See* SINGAPORE.

BAYANIHAN DANCE COMPANY. The people of the Philippines through the 10th Congress enacted Republic Act 8626 declaring Bayanihan Philippine National Dance Company (BPNDC) as the Philippines' National Folk Dance Company. Since its inception in 1957, the Company, which was founded by Helen Z. Benitez, chairperson of the Philippine Women's University, Manila, has mounted 14 major world tours and more than 100 short trips. Adjudged top among 13 countries during its debut at the Brussels World Fair in 1958, the Bayanihan has earned many "firsts" including the first Filipino group to perform at the Winter Garden Theater of the Lincoln Center for the Performing Arts, Washington, D.C. Bayanihan was also the first cultural group to perform in Russia and the People's Republic of China; the first to make an in-depth tour of South America, and the first Filipino dance company to perform at the World Showcase Millennium Village EPCOT, Disneyland, Florida. In 2003, the BPNDC won the Gold Temple Award and the Absolute Gold Award in the 47th International Folk Festival in Sicily, Italy. In 2004, the company embarked on a series of performance tours in Europe. The dance company is the only Filipino cultural group to receive the **Ramon Magsaysay award** for international understanding. *See also* SINGKIL; TINIKLING.

BAYAN MUNA. Its name "People First" embodies its core idea and ideals as a militant organization. Bayan Muna was established on

September 25, 1999, as a progressive political party. Its purpose was to push the people's agenda for basic reform and expose government policies that disadvantage the people. In the first party-list elections of May 2001, Bayan Muna garnered the highest number of votes cast for **party-list** group—1,078,000 representing 11.31 percent of the total, which netted the party three seats in congress. Bayan Muna bested 161 other parties. The party attracted voters because its candidates claimed they were not engaged in traditional politics of personalities and patronage. *See also* SECTORAL PARTIES; TRAPO.

BAYBAYIN. *See* SYLLABARY.

BAYOMBONG. *See* NUEVA VIZCAYA.

BELL TRADE ACT. United States legislation that defined post-war economic relations between the Philippines and the United States. This act, passed by the U.S. Congress in 1946, restored economic control of the Philippines to the United States. The act had five important provisions: reciprocal free trade for eight years until 1954, after which gradually increasing duties would be imposed on both sides until 1973, when full duties would be imposed; the Philippines could not impose taxes on exports to the United States; absolute quotas on exports to the United States of seven Philippine products, including sugar, coconut oil, hemp, and tobacco; a pegged rate of exchange between the Philippine peso and the dollar in such a way that the Philippines could not alter the exchange rate of the peso or impose restrictions on the transfer of funds from the Philippines to the United States without the agreement of the U.S. president; and a grant of authority to the U.S. president to suspend all or parts of the act if he should find the Philippines to be discriminating in any manner against U.S. citizens or business interests. The Bell Trade Act was tied to another piece of legislation, the Philippine Rehabilitation Act, which provided $620 million in war damage payments on condition that payments for claims in excess of $500 would not be released until the Philippines accepted the Bell Act.

There was also a rider in the Bell Trade Act, which required the Philippines to extend **parity rights** to U. S. nationals in the development of natural resources. The parity rights provoked a contentious national debate. Supporters, mostly prewar elites or the **oligarchy**, wanted the economic rehabilitation of the devastated country to be expedited as quickly as possible. Opponents argued that the act compromised the sovereignty and dignity of the country. The debate fell along party lines between the ruling **Nacionalista party** and the **Liberal** party led by the President **Manuel Roxas**, who influenced the Philippine Congress to accept the onerous provisions. In 1954, the Bell Trade Act was replaced by the more amenable **Laurel-Langley** Agreement. *See also* LAUREL, JOSE P.; PAYNE-ALDRICH TARIFF ACT.

BELMONTE, FELICIANO JR. (1936–). As the chief executive of **Quezon City**, Belmonte was adjudged one of the most outstanding city mayors by the local government leadership foundation in 2003. During his tenure he made dramatic changes in solving the city's major problems—garbage collection, traffic congestion, lack of housing, and lack of access to education. His housing and urban renewal authority was an effective mechanism to address the housing requirement of informal settlers (squatters) and low-income groups. Belmonte used the participatory style of management that had resulted in enhanced governance as demonstrated through multisectoral and **barangay** consultations. One of his successful projects was the Muslim consultative council that provided a voice for the city's Muslim population. Known as "Mr. Country Service" to his constituents, Belmonte never forgot the poor and disadvantaged. He initiated and completed the Project TEST (Technology Enriched Schools for Tomorrow) where students and teachers were provided with computer aided education. Before he became mayor, Belmonte was a thrice-elected congressman of the fourth district of Quezon City. It was during his term that he led the prosecution panel in the successful impeachment case of President **Joseph Ejercito Estrada**.

BENEDICTO, ROBERTO. *See* CRONIES.

BENGUET. Located in north central Luzon, Benguet province has a population of 450,000 and an area of 2,592 square kilometers. **Baguio**, its most famous city, is well known as the summer capital of the Philippines. Benguet was partitioned off from the larger Mountain

Province in 1968 with La Trinidad as the new provincial capital. The extremely mountainous terrain is home to a number of ethnic tribes like the Ibaloi and the Kankanai, who are skilled woodcarvers, basket makers, and back loom weavers. The province is the site of many gold and copper mines, of which the former were heavily exploited by the Spanish. Benguet is the country's main producer of temperate vegetables, most of which are sold in Baguio and Manila. Chief towns are Tublay, Natubleng, Itogon, and Buguias. *See also* CORDILLERA AUTONOMOUS REGION.

BENITEZ, CONRADO (1889–1971). Educator. Benitez was one of the *pensionados* (government scholars) sent to the United States for training in higher education. He obtained a master's degree from the University of Chicago, and he later received a law degree from the University of the Philippines (UP). He was the first dean of the UP College of Liberal Arts and first Filipino to head the department of economics. He authored several textbooks that were used in colleges and public high schools, including *Economic Development of the Philippines* and *Stories of Great Filipinos.*

BENITEZ, HELEN Z. *See* BAYANIHAN DANCE COMPANY.

BERNALES, FELIX. *See* COLORUM.

BEYER, HENRY OTLEY (1883–1966). H. Otley Beyer came to the Philippines in 1905 as a young man armed with an M.A. degree to work as an ethnologist of the American colonial government. He was assigned to the Mountain Provinces to do field work among the **Ifugaos**, **Igorots**, **Apayaos**, and **Kalingas**. In the course of five years, he compiled an impressive record of his research that became the 150-volume Philippine Ethnographic Series. In 1925, he was appointed head of the new anthropology department of the University of the Philippines and established a strong faculty that made anthropology a major course. Beyer became archaeologically and prehistorically oriented after the 1926 discovery of the Novaliches dam site where he discovered stoneware, prehistoric tools, jewelry, Chinese ceramics, and tektites. Between 1910 and 1959, Beyer wrote and published a large number of scientific papers and books on Philippine archaeology, ethnology, and history. After World War II, Beyer completed two important works, which remain to this day his main contribution in the field of archaeology and prehistory. These are the *Outline Review of Philippine Archaeology by Islands and Province* and the *Philippine and East Asian Archaeology and Its Relation to the Origin of the Pacific Islands Population*. The Filipiniana collections that he built for 50 years are the largest of its kind in the world and are on displayed at the **National Museum** of the Philippines. *See also* BUGAN; TABON CAVES.

BHAVE, VINOBA. *See* RAMON MAGSAYSAY AWARD.

BICOL. Language spoken in the southeastern provinces of Luzon in **Camarines Norte**, **Camarines Sur**, **Albay**, **Sorsogon**, and on the islands of **Catanduanes** and **Masbate**.

BILAAN. A tribe of people found in south-central Mindanao (Davao and Cotabato provinces). Bilaan villages are ruled by chiefs called datus. Most Bilaans are agriculturists who raise domestic animals and such crops as rice, maize, and root crops. *See also* LUMADS.

BILIRAN. An island province north of Leyte in Eastern Visayas. Formerly a subprovince of Leyte, it became an independent province in 1992 following the division of Leyte into two provinces. It is surrounded by the Visayan Sea on the North, Samar Sea on the east, Strait of Biliran on the west and Carigara Bay on the south. The island is 32 kilometers long and 18 kilometers wide, and linked to Leyte by a bridge across the narrow Biliran strait. It has a population of 118,012—a mixture of Boholanos, Samareños, and Leyteñeos—living in eight towns with Naval as its capital. Its mountainous interior is dominated by Mt. Suiro.

BILOG, GINAW. *See* LIVING TREASURES.

BIOCERAMIC ORBITAL PLATE IMPLANT. Filipino scientists of the Department of Science and Technology developed an artificial bone that can be used in the treatment of orbital bone fracture in cases of bone injuries. Composition of the orbital plate is 77 percent B-tricalcium phosphate and 23 percent hydroxyapatite, which are similar to the human bone. The first human transplantation was successfully carried out on August 28, 2001, at the **University of Santo Tomas** Medical Hospital, Manila. *See also* SCIENTISTS.

BIODIVERSITY. Biological diversity or biodiversity includes all genes, species, and ecosystems. The Philippines has been regarded as one of the highest priority countries in the world for conservation concern. There are three reasons for this: the enormous biological diversity among both animal and plant species within the archipelago, which bridges two major biogeographical regions; the extraordinarily high percentage of uniqueness or endemicity among the species—about 67 percent of the species among the major groups of animals and plants occur nowhere else in the world; and the high rate of **deforestation** and other forms of habitat destruction, and the serious inadequacies in the existing environmental protection measures and the protected areas network.

In June 1992, the Philippines undertook an assessment of its biodiversity through a grant from the United Nations Environment Program. Based on the comprehensive assessment of the current status of the country's biodiversity problems, threats, issues, and gaps were identified: marine, forest, wetlands, protected areas, and agriculture. In the marine ecosystem 4,951 species of marine animals are found in Philippine coastal and marine habitats. Fishes, noncoral invertebrates, and seaweeds constitute the greatest numbers. Some 1,390 or 28 percent are economically important, 403 or 10 percent are flagship species, while 145 species or 2.4 percent are under threat. Fifteen species are listed as endangered. Coral reefs are by far the most diverse or species rich with 3,967 species. The Philippine coral reef ranks the country second to the great Barrier Reef and the 16 taxa of seagrasses recorded in the Philippines make the country the second highest in terms of seagrass species richness in the world. In the area of floral diversity in Philippine forests—the flora is composed of at least 13,500 species that represent 5 percent of the world's flora. The ferns and fern allies, gymnosperms and angiosperms constitute 22.5 percent of the Malesian and 3.88 percent of the world's vascular flora. Twenty-five percent of the plants are endemic to the Philippines. In the area of wetlands, there are 1,616 species of flora and 3,308 species of fauna. A total of 1,200 species of plants are relevant to **agriculture** with a variety of uses and values.

Some have food values (477 species), feed values (363 species), medicinal/herbal values (627), and ornamental values (201 species). During the decade of the 1990s, there was a substantial increase in the population of 61 economically important crops such as coconut, coffee, fiber crops particularly **abaca**, kenaf, piña, and ramie, and mulberry, while banana, cacao, rubber, and ipil-ipil dramatically increased in population. And during the same period domestic animal population has also increased with the exception of **carabaos**—the work animals of farmers—which decreased in numbers.

BIODIVERSITY CONSERVATION CENTRE (BCC). A wildlife rescue and captive center located in Bacolod City, **Negros Occidental**. **Australia** provides grant assistance to the center through its partner the Negros Forest and Ecological Foundation, a **nongovernmental organization**, committed to protect and conserve the environment. Negros Island is biologically the most important region, in terms of threatened endemic species, including the Philippine spotted deer (*cervus alfredi*), tarictic hornbill (*penelopides panini*), and Visayan warty pig (*sus cebifrons*). The BCC was founded in 1997 mainly as a breeding station for endangered species as well as a mini-zoo, rescue, and information center. Today the center is home for 15 different species, among them the Philippine hawk eagle (*spizaetus philippensis*), leopard cat (*prionailurus bengalensis rabori*), serpent eagle (*spilornis holospimus*), sailfin lizard (*hydrosaurus pustulatus),* and more than 60 captive individuals. *See also* FLORA and FAUNA.

BIOPIRACY. Since the discovery of the use of herbs as alternative medicine, many foreign pharmaceutical companies have taken advantage of the commercial value of Philippine medicinal plants by acquiring patents for a number of these herbal remedies. To prevent this exploitation the government enacted the anti-biopiracy law. Biopiracy is the exploration, extraction, and screening of biological diversity and indigenous knowledge for commercial, genetic, and biochemical purposes. However, the loosely worded and inadequate provisions did not prevent some multinational firms from obtaining patents for a pain-killing snail (*conus magnus*), a cancer-curing tree (*taxus matrana*), and several vegetables and fruits, which are remedies for diabetes. The most common biopiracy in the Philippines is the theft of an antibiotic extract from a soil in the province of **Iloilo** that became the world-known antibiotic erythromycin. Moreover, many Filipino **scientists** are now protesting against the onslaught of biopirates on biodiversity, traditional lore, and indigenous systems. *See also* HERBAL MEDICINE.

BIYO, JOSETTE (1960–). A Filipino science teacher who won the grand award for "Excellence in Teaching" in an international science competition sponsored by Intel International Science and Engineering Fair (Intel ISEF). In addition to this, Massachusetts Institute of Technology even named a minor planet located in the asteroid belt in her honor. A high school science and math teacher from **Iloilo**, Biyo submitted her winning proposal of teaching science research methods to Filipino high school students. Four of her students demonstrated their science projects before 2,000 students coming from 39 countries and the 51 states of the United States. They won cash prizes. Biyo taught for eight years in a rural community in her home province. Using her science training, she tutored students and rural folks primary health care, such as how to make cough syrup from plant extracts and soap from coconut oil. In 1995, the Philippine Science High School Western Visayas hired her as a special science teacher and in three years of dedicated teaching developed its science research curriculum and introduced innovations for teaching the course. While teaching her biology classes, Biyo often took her students on scientific adventures to study the diversity of sea grass or explore the community structure of mangrove forests. She also organized workshops for science teachers in the island of Panay. Third world countries, such as Laos and Cambodia, invited her to share her world-class science teaching methods. For Biyo, the award and accompanying grant has enabled her to share with other educators the benefits of steeping a community in what she calls "the culture of science." In the 2004 Intel ISEF competition seven Filipino students won four research awards for works in medicine, health, chemistry, and environmental science. *See also* SCIENTISTS.

BLACK NAZARENE. A religious procession of a 200-year-old statue of Jesus Christ bearing a crucifix known as the Black Nazarene held in downtown Manila on Good Friday (Holy Week) that draws enormous crowds and devotees. The celebration—one of the largest in the Philippines—Asia's only predominantly Roman Catholic country—has its roots in 17th century Mexico, from where a priest brought the life-size statue, which claimed miraculous powers to Manila in 1787. Devotees, mostly men, clad in white and maroon shirts, throng to the annual event to seek its special favors or give thanks. *See also* FESTIVALS; FIESTAS; QUIAPO.

BLOOD COMPACT. A native custom of the 16th century in which the participants drew two or three drops of blood from their arms and then mixed it in the same cup with wine. This mixture was then divided equally into two cups and drunk to seal eternal amity. The first known international treaty of friendship between a Spaniard and a native chief took place on March 16, 1565, between Datu Sikatuna of Bohol Island and Miguel Lopez de Legaspi. A painting of Juan Luna made this unique ritual famous. *See also* MARINDUQUE.

BLUMENTRITT, FERDINAND (1853–1913). **Jose Rizal's** famous Austrian friend who translated his books—"*Noli Me Tangere*" and "*El Filibusterismo*"—into German, and thus spread word of the infamous Spanish colonization of the Philippines in Europe. Blumentritt was a professor in Leitmeritz, Austria, but later directed his academic interest toward the study of the Philippine archipelago. He became an authority in **Tagalog**. Because of his defense of the Philippines struggle for justice, freedom, and independence, the Spanish authorities vehemently denounced Blumentritt.

His friendship with Jose Rizal resulted in many long letters indicating their mutual respect for each other's intellect. It was Blumentritt who encouraged Rizal to finish his two social tract novels when the latter was becoming discouraged. Blumentritt singled out Rizal among his distinguished peers in the Philippine **propaganda movement** and recognized Rizal as the greatest man the Malay race has produced. Blumentritt castigated the Americans for their forced colonization of the Philippines and staunchly defended the new republic of General **Emilio Aguinaldo**.

BOCOBO, JORGE (1886–1965). Educator, jurist, and author. A native son of Tarlac, Bocobo was one of the **pensionados** (government scholars) sent to the United States for training in higher education. In 1907, he obtained his law degree from Indiana University and passed the bar in 1910. He started his career as an instructor in the College of Law at the University of the Philippines, and in a few years rose to full professor and dean. In 1934, he was appointed president of the university. During the independence movement, Bocobo helped the cause by writing two books and by translating into English **Jose Rizal's** novels, and the **National Anthem**. In 1939, he served as secretary of public instruction and then became a justice of the **Supreme Court**. He was the principal author of the Civil Code of the Philippines for which he received the Presidential Award of Merit in 1949.

BOHOL. An island province southeast of **Cebu**, occupying a land area of 3,865 square kilometers and containing a population of 875,000 people, most of whom are Cebuano-speaking Visayans. Long before the Spanish colonizers arrived in Bohol, the island already had contact with traders from **China** and other older civilizations. Excavations in ancient burial grounds on the island have unearthed Tang dynasty porcelain, Sung and Ming vases. Boat-shaped coffins dating as far back as 500 years were discovered wedged into cliff sides. Bohol is notable as the site of an 85-year long rebellion against the Spanish by **Francisco Dagohoy**, and also of the famous **blood compact** between Datu Sikatuna and Miguel Lopez de Legaspi. The main commercial crop is coconut; iron, steel, and manganese are also produced. The capital city is Tagbilaran. Chief provincial towns are Jagna, Tubigon, Ubay, Talibon, and Valencia. *See also* GARCIA, CARLOS P.

BOLINAO ARCHAEOLOGY. A feature of the archeological materials recovered from 14th–15th century burial site in Balingasay, Bolinao, **Pangasinan**, is a beautiful and ornate method of decorating the teeth with gold. Dental gold ornamentations have been encountered in various Philippine archaeological sites like Santa Ana, Manila; Calatagan, Batangas; Samar; and Marinduque. The original specimen is presently stored at the **National Museum** in Manila. The dental ornamentation of the Bolinao specimen differs from the other sites. They are like tiny nails with flat rounded tops or heads and once the body is placed in a bored hole on the tooth it looks like "fish scales" especially if there are more than one placed in a tooth. Pegging varies from one up to eight pegs in a single tooth, the two upper and lower teeth usually have more pegs than the rest of the teeth. Other materials on display at the museum are contact period ceramics, stone tools, metal implements, earthenware materials, bone implements, and shell objects recovered from the Bolinao excavation. *See also* GOLD ARTIFACTS.

BONCAYO, ALEX. *See* LAGMAN, FILEMON.

BONGGAO. *See* TAWI-TAWI.

BONIFACIO, ANDRES (1863–1897). Founder of the **Katipunan** revolutionary society and known as the Great Plebeian. He was born to poor parents and by dint of hard work and self-education, rose from poverty to found the resistance movement known as **Katipunan** against the ruthless Spanish rule in the Philippines. In collaboration with **Emilio Jacinto**, who became known as the brains of the revolution, he issued stirring literature to arouse the people to revolt against the Spanish. On August 23, 1896, Bonifacio assembled his men at Balintawak and tore their *cedulas* (head tax) to symbolize the start of the resistance. Inspired by his action, the flame of resistance spread to other provinces. Spanish garrisons were stormed and seized by Katipuneros. However, a conflict of leadership developed between Bonifacio and **Emilio Aguinaldo**, who was leading the struggle in his home province of Cavite. In the subsequent power struggle, Bonifacio lost and was killed together with his brother on May 10, 1897. But the revolution against the Spanish continued unabated under the leadership of Aguinaldo. *See also* CRY OF BALINTAWAK.

BONTOC. An ethnic tribe found in Mountain Province in northern Luzon. The Bontocs till the famous rice terraces, where they raise their staple crops of **rice**, and *camotes* or sweet potatoes. Bontoc villages (called *ato*) are governed by councils of elders, and most villages feature the characteristic *ulogs*, or dormitories for unmarried girls and boys. When the rice planting and harvesting season is over, the people turn to cloth weaving, wood carving, and basketry. The Bontocs are famous for their stone **rice terraces** and cone-shaped, one-room thatched houses. The people practice a monotheistic form of religion with male shamans who preside over ancestral rites marked by pig sacrifice. *See also* CORDILLERA.

BORACAY. One of the 7,100 islands of the Philippine archipelago, this butterfly-shaped island is located at the northwestern tip of **Panay** across **Palawan** in the West Visayan region, off the Sibuyan Sea. Boracay is made up of three little communities: Yapak in the north, Balabag in the middle, and Manoc-manoc in the south. Noted as a resort, the palm-studded island has crystal waters, powder white sand, coconut trees, and rich marine life. The island offers a variety of tourist sports like kayaking, sailboating, scuba-diving, trekking, mountain climbing, golf, and beach bumming.

BOSTON-C. *See* HERBAL MEDICINE.

BRACKEN, JOSEPHINE (1876–1902). Wife of **Jose Rizal**. Josephine was born in Hong Kong on August 9, 1876, of Irish parents, James Brown and Elizabeth MacBride, but took the family name Bracken from her adopted father. In 1865, she was in Manila accompanying George Edward Taufer, a 63-year-old blind widower and her foster father, to consult **Jose Rizal**, a well-known ophthalmologist, for an operation on his cataracts. They visited Rizal in Dapitan, **Zamboanga**, where he was deported by the Spanish authorities for his subversive activities. During the treatment of her foster father, Josephine became Rizal's sweetheart. After bringing her foster father to Hong Kong, she returned to Dapitan and lived with Rizal. Their liaison produced a still-born son. Earlier, their application for a marriage license was denied by church authorities. It was only on the eve of December 30, 1896, that they were married, two hours before Rizal was executed by a firing squad at Bagumbayan (now Rizal Park). Josephine was taken in by the family of Rizal. In the ensuing revolution Josephine took care of sick and wounded Filipino soldiers.

BRAID, FLORANGEL ROSARIO (1931–). A writer and investigative reporter. Florangel Rosario Braid holds a Ph.D. in Communication degrees from Syracuse University. Upon her return to the Philippines she put her research and administrative expertise to good use in the production of in-depth studies—books, papers, and monographs—which covered a variety of subjects, including education, social problems, literacy, broadcast journalism, column-writing, megatrends, marginalized communities, and communication strategies for urban and rural communities. Braid started her academic career as a senior researcher at the University of Hawaii East West Communication Institute and later moved to the Philippines to be involved in the burgeoning field of information and communication technology development.

Together with *Manila Times* editor Jose Luna Castro they founded the Asian Institute of Journalism and Communication and from this base she and her staff produced innovative scholarly studies designed for planners and policy makers in government and industry, communication scholars and educators. Braid was one of the founding directors of the **Philippine Center for Investigative Journalism** and the *Philippine Daily Inquirer* where she initiated and wrote reports on the malfeasance of government agencies and personnel. In 1986, President Corazon Aquino appointed Braid and five other women as members of the Constitutional Commission that drafted the 1987 Constitution. They were responsible for writing the provisions on communication, education, cooperatives, science and technology, **nongovernmental organizations**, and **human rights**. *See also* CORONEL, SHEILA.

BRAIN DRAIN. Migration of Filipino professionals to the United States and Europe. A major change in the United States immigration laws in the 1950s permitted thousands of Filipino professionals, including doctors, nurses, teachers, engineers, and medical technicians, to emigrate to the U.S. Many of these professionals found lucrative employment in the private and public sectors where they distinguished themselves in their lines of work. For example, the lunar vehicle used by the astronauts was designed by a Filipino engineer. The exodus of Filipino professionals to the United States has been described as "reverse migration." This dispersion also referred to as diaspora abroad reached its peak during the Ferdinand Marcos era when hundreds of thousands of Filipinos, including blue-collar workers, emigrated from the Philippines making the two million Filipinos one of the largest Asian-American groups in the United States. The brain drain is still flowing with thousands of Filipino university-educated workers going to European, Middle Eastern, and Asian countries. *See also* BANATAO, DIOSDADO; OVERSEAS FOREIGN WORKERS.

BRIGANDAGE ACT. *See* NATIONALISM.

BRITISH NORTH BORNEO COMPANY. When the British restored **Alimud Din** to power in 1762, he signed a treaty in which he gave territorial cession of parts of North Borneo (known as **Sabah**), which was then ruled by the Sultanate of Sulu. Over a hundred years later, this territorial cession was followed by an agreement between Sultan **Jamalul Kiram** and the British North Borneo Company, which agreed to pay the sultan and his heirs an annual fee. The company, represented by Baron Von Overbeck, was granted "absolute ownership and dominion over the large territory." However, the United States contested the territorial cession by the sultan or his heirs since an American company had preceded the British North Borneo Company in acquiring the territory from the sultan of Brunei and since Overbeck also acquired the American rights. Spain protested these "cessions" on the grounds that the sultan of Sulu, being a Spanish subject, could not cede territories to foreign powers without Spain's consent. However, in 1885, Britain and Germany concluded a treaty with Spain recognizing her full sovereignty over the Sulu archipelago and relinquishing all claims to northeastern Borneo, which was formerly ruled by sultans of Sulu. Thus, northeastern Borneo fell under the administration of the British North Borneo Company.

The sultan of Sulu disputed the claim of Spain. He affirmed that it had no right to dispose of a territory over which it had no effective control, and he further disputed the claim by the sultan of Brunei that North Borneo (**Sabah**) was not a part of his sultanate. This controversy over whether North Borneo was part of the Sulu Sultanate, which in turn was part of the Philippines when Spain ceded the country to the United States, remains unresolved. During the conflict waged by the Moro National Liberation Front (MNLF) against the Philippine government, Sabah was a conduit for Libyan aid to the MNLF. The Philippine government still has a pending claim to North Borneo. *See also* JABIDAH.

BRITISH OCCUPATION OF MANILA. The British presence in the Philippines was an aspect of the Seven Years War between Britain and France (1756–1763) in which the Spanish king, who belonged to the house of Bourbon, sided with his fellow Bourbon king of France.

During that war, the British seized all the French colonies in North America and the West Indies. Since war was also declared between Britain and Spain, the British sent Admiral William Draper with an expeditionary force to capture Manila and the Spanish colonial possessions in the Philippines. Draper's army consisted of 2,000 European and Indian soldiers, the latter called Sepoys, which landed in Manila on September 22, 1762, without any opposition from the Spanish, who fled to the hills. The acting governor-general Archbishop Manuel Antonio Rojo formally surrendered the city on October 2 and thus opened Manila to plunder by the invading army. The Spaniards rallied the natives to drive the enemy out, but their weapons were no match for the superior armament of the British. While the British occupied Manila, the surrounding provinces were held by the Spanish who employed native soldiers to defend them.

With the British occupation of Manila, Filipino rebels saw an opportunity to expel their Spanish overlords. One of these rebels was **Diego Silang** who, with the help of the British, spearheaded the revolt in the Ilocos region. This was followed by another revolt led by **Juan de la Cruz Palaris** in **Pangasinan.** Meanwhile, the British restored Sultan **Alimud Din** to his throne in Sulu for the price of a territorial concession in Borneo (now called Sabah). The Chinese population in Manila supported the British and formed military units to fight the Spaniards. The occupation ended in March 1764 following the end of the Seven Years War and the signing of the **Treaty of Paris**. Manila was returned to Spain and a new governor-general was appointed to take over from the British. The British fleet sailed back to India, but many of the Sepoy soldiers chose to stay behind and settled in Cainta and Taytay, **Rizal**, where to this day physical evidence of their unions with the native women is shown by the swarthy complexion of their descendants. The two-year British occupation of Manila left a residue of smoldering resentment against Spain, and the resultant minor **revolts** in the provinces led to wider uprisings throughout the islands.

BUDONG. *See* KALINGA.

BUENCAMINO, FELIPE SR. (1848–1929). Felipe Buencamino studied law at the **University of Santo Tomas** and later served as judge and registrar of deeds in the colonial administration. Siding with the Spaniards in the 1896 revolution he went over to the insurgents after being accused of being a spy, becoming General Emilio Aguinaldo's secretary of war in 1898. He was taken prisoner by the Americans in 1900. He was one of the framers of the Malolos Constitution, founded the **Federal Party** in 1900, and was a cofounder of the Philippine Independent Church (**Iglesia Filipina Independiente**).

BUGAN. This is the folk epic of the Ifugao people. The original story was taken down by **H. Otley Beyer**, the noted anthropologist of the Mountain Province, who mastered the **Ifugao** language. The Bugan character is famous in the mythology of the Ifugaos. This story has a peculiar motif in that a goddess from the skyworld found and married a destitute Ifugao trapper. The villagers found her eating habits disagreeable so they drove her out of her home. In return the goddess wrecked havoc on the community by creating pests and diseases to torment the people. *See also* LUMAWIG.

BUKANEG, PEDRO. To the **Ilocanos**, Pedro Bukaneg is regarded as the "father of Iloco Literature," for his epic poem *Biag ni Lam-ang* (Life of **Lam-ang**), which is considered his greatest achievement. Born blind, his parents abandoned him but he was rescued by Augustinian friars who raised and tutored him in the convent. Early on the Augustinians became aware of his special talent. He mastered Latin and the Spanish language in addition to his Ilocano and **Isneg** languages. He was sent on missions to convert the natives to Christianity. His translation of *Doctrina Cristiana* to Iloko in 1606 facilitated their conversion. Before he died, he left many Spanish translations of native songs, poems, and other folkways depicting native culture. Besides his works, *bukanegan*, a literary joust similar to the Tagalog **balagtasan** owes its origin to him. Unfortunately, there is no record of his birth.

BUKIDNON. A landlocked province located in Northern Mindanao. The name means "People of the Mountains," which pertains to the early settlers. It has the largest pineapple plantation in the Far East—the Del Monte farms. The province is noted for its National Park Kitanglad which is the home of the serpentine eagle, red harrier, sparrow hawk, and the famous **Philippine eagle**. It has an area of 829,378 hectares of rural and agricultural land. The Polangui river system provides the power for industrial, agricultural, and household use. It also drives the National Power Corporation's 255 megawatt hydroelectric power plant in Maramag. The Kitanglad range—2,880 meters—is the telecommunication hub of Northern Mindanao. Malaybalay is the capital. The province has an estimated population of one million living in 22 towns.

BUKLURAN NG MANGAGAWANG PILIPINO (BMP) (SOLIDARITY OF FILIPINO WORKERS). This is a revolutionary socialist mass organization of the working class, aspiring to develop itself as a driving force within the **trade union** movement in organizing the class struggle along socialist lines. The BMP traces its origin to the split within the pro-Maoist **Kilusang Mayo Uno** (KMU) May First Movement, when the entire regional chapter in Metro Manila broke away in 1993. The chapter accounted for more than half the total membership of the KMU. This was also the period in which a major split took place in the underground **Communist Party of the Philippines**, when almost half of the membership rejected its Stalinist-Maoist politics. The establishment of the BMP was also in response to the failure of established national labor organizations to unify the labor movement in the country and to effectively advance the struggle of the Filipino working class. *See also* LAGMAN, FILEMON.

BUKLURAN SA IKAUUNLAD NG SOSYALISTANG ISIP AT GAWA (BISIG) (MOVEMENT FOR THE ADVANCEMENT OF SOCIALIST IDEAS AND ACTION). This political action group was organized after the fall of **Ferdinand Marcos** in 1986 by two University of the Philippines professors—Francisco Nemenzo and Randy David—as an alternative to the **Communist Party of the Philippines (CPP)**. The founders believed that the Philippines' dependency on capitalism was wrong and proposed that socialism would better serve the country because workers would govern and utilize various forms of public and cooperative ownership of economic enterprises. BISIG emphasized the formation of cooperatives for the business sector and small commodity producers rather than resorting to the imposition of socialized systems. It also encouraged the presence of multiple political parties with each having its own perspective on the correct path to socialism. BISIG provided an intellectual alternative to communism and courted other progressive groups. Contrary to the expectations of its leaders, BISIG failed to enlist mass support from the Philippine left but retained its influence on **labor** and farmers' groups. BISIG remained a viable influence and critique throughout the **Corazon Aquino** administration.

BULACAN. Bulacan is a densely populated province north of Manila. It has an area of 2,637 square kilometers and a population of 1.4 million, mostly speaking Tagalog. Its name derives from *bulak*, the Tagalog word for cotton, which was the principal crop. The main products are rice, fruits, poultry, pigs, fish, and leather, which are mostly sold in Manila. Several of the rivers that crisscross the province, flow into Manila Bay. The Ipo Angat dam provides power and irrigation. Industries, such as textiles, sawmills, pulp and paper, cement, poultry, and feed plants abound in the province, along with numerous small-scale garment industries and handicraft enterprises. Because of its proximity to Manila, many of its towns are highly urbanized bedroom communities. Besides its famous festivals, Bulacan is noted for having produced many notable revolutionary poets, propagandists, and journalists, such as **Marcelo H. Del Pilar**. The main towns are Obando, Bucaue, Baliuag, Plaridel, and Pulilan. Malolos is the capital and principal trading center. *See also* DEL PILAR, GREGORIO.

BULOSAN, CARLOS (1914–1956). Noted Filipino-American author. He was born on November 24, 1914, in the town of Binalonan, **Pangasinan**, to a peasant family of five brothers and two sisters. After several years of secondary schooling, he left for the United States in 1930 to join his older brother Aurelio. In the U.S. he worked in Alaskan fish canneries and as a fruit and vegetable picker in Washington and California, and eventually became an activist in the labor movement. The horrendous conditions of Filipino laborers was fictionalized in his most famous autobiographical novel, *America Is In the Heart* (1946). Excerpts of his 1944 book, *Laughter of My Father*, were published in *The New Yorker* and *Harper's Bazaar*. Bulosan was commissioned by President Franklin Roosevelt in 1945 to write "Four Freedoms," an essay for the Federal Building in San Francisco.

Because of his radical activism, Bulosan was blacklisted by Senator Joseph McCarthy during the anti-Communist movement of the 1950s. His other books include the poetry collections *Letter From America* (1942), *Chorus from America* (1942), and the *Voice of Bataan.* Two of his novels—*Cry and Dedication* and *Sound of Falling Light*—were published posthumously in 1995.

BUNDOK. A **Tagalog** word for mountain. This word is entered as boondocks in the English dictionary. American soldiers, who fought in the Philippines during World War II, picked up the term bundok to describe a remote countryside, rough country, or an out-of-the-way place.

BUTU, HADJI ABDUL BAQUI (1865–1938). Muslim legislator. A precocious child, he mastered the Koran at age six and the Arabic language at age 10. At 15 he was named prime minister of Sultan Badarudin of Jolo and upon the death of the Sultan Butu was given the same position by the new Sultan **Jamalul Kiram**. When the Americans arrived in 1899, Butu led his people to a peaceful settlement with the new colonizers, and he advocated amity with his Christian brothers. In 1904, he became governor of the new province of Sulu and later served as senator (1923–1931), representing Mindanao and **Sulu**.

BUTUAN. *See* AGUSAN DEL NORTE.

BUTUAN ARCHAEOLOGY. Butuan, **Agusan del Norte**, boasts its wooden boats excavated in the area, which predates European boat construction. These boats were constructed using a very ancient technique. Carbon-14 dates of 320 A.D., 900 A.D., and 1250 A.D. were obtained from samples taken from parts of the three excavated boats. The *balangay* (referring to the smallest political unit *barangay* in Philippine society whose organization is similar to what existed in the boat), as the Butuan boats were called, were constructed using the edge-pegged, plank-built technique. The planks were secured using dowels or wooden pegs. They are round bottomed and were propelled by sail and steered by a rudder. These characteristics are similar to other Southeast Asian boats. So far nine *balangays* have been documented to exist. The National Museum excavated three boats while the rest are still waterlogged in specific sites in Butuan City until such time that personnel and finances permit their scientific excavation and conservation.

The archaeological investigations conducted between 1975 and 1977 in Butuan revealed a settlement with large domiciles built similar to the traditional houses still found in Butuan. The kitchen midden underneath the house gave evidence of their subsistence and economic patterns. The population subsisted on marine life such as sea shells and fish, wildlife like wild boar and domesticated fowls, animals (dogs and pigs), root crops, and rice. Cultural remains of this prehistoric habitation included not only utilitarian wares, but also the metal working industry (gold and iron) and foreign trade items such as porcelain ware coming from China and Southeast Asia. When did the Butuan settlement exist? In 1977, samples from the burials (coffins) were sent to Scripps Institute of Oceanography at La Jolla, San Diego, California for dating. The date obtained was 1297 A.D. and another item was dated 1430 A.D.

– C –

CABALLERO, FEDERICO. *See* LIVING TREASURES.

CABANATUAN. *See* NUEVA ECIJA.

CABARROGUIS. *See* QUIRINO.

CABEZA DE BARANGAY. Each barrio or **barangay** during the Spanish colonial regime was headed by a *cabeza de barangay*, an administrative functionary, who reported to the friar-curate and whose chief responsibility was to collect the levies, called *tributos* (**tributes**), from each adult member of the barangay, and to see to it that the personal labor services—called *polos y servicio*, a system of forced labor for supposed public purposes—were rendered. Each Filipino, above 16 years and those below 60, was compelled to pay tribute. In recognition of his service, the *cabeza* was exempted from the *tributo*, including his first son. The position was hereditary and the tributes were used to finance the colonial administration, construction of churches, government buildings, roads, and bridges. When it was introduced in 1570, the tribute was small. Then it was gradually increased and became so onerous to the people that it was one of the causes of the more than 300 uprisings during the colonial period. The King of Spain eventually abolished it in 1884 and replaced it with the *cedula* (head tax).

CACIQUE (CACIQUISM). A hierarchical system of quasi slavery developed during the Spanish colonial period in which rich landlords (*caciques*) exercised absolute economic and political power in the community. Under the *caciques* the tenants tilled the land for a pittance and become heavily indebted for the purchase of seeds and cash advances. These debts were often inherited by subsequent generations of tenants, thereby resulting in a form of quasi enslavement of the entire family. *See also* BARANGAY.

CAGAYAN. Located on the northeastern tip of Luzon, Cagayan province is densely populated by almost a million people who live on 9,003 square kilometers of land. Vast forests cover half of the province, and extensive swamplands drain the 80 kilometer-long Cagayan River. Cagayan is a major producer of rice and tobacco. Logging is a third major industry. The native population is made up of the **Gaddangs**, who are also found in Nueva Vizcaya, the Ibanags, reputed to be the tallest Filipino tribe, and a substantial **Negrito** population. Tuguegarao, the provincial capital and commercial center, is located in the south of the province. Near Tuguegarao is the Callao Caves National Park, whose limestone caves are of wide renown. The city of Aparri is located at the mouth of the Cagayan River in the north and is a fishing and trading port. The other important towns are Gattaran, Solano, Sanchez Mira, Claveria, and Camalanuigan.

CAGAYAN DE ORO. *See* MISAMIS ORIENTAL.

CALAPAN. *See* MINDORO.

CALATAGAN POT. An ancient clay pot excavated in **Batangas** in the early 1960s. Archaeologists claimed this artifact was the earliest pre-Hispanic item to be found. The writing goes around the neck and the letters look similar to those of classic Philippine scripts (**Tagalog** and **Tagbanua**). However, paleographers still have to decipher the writing. The clay pot is displayed at the **National Museum**, Manila. *See also* LAGUNA COPPER PLATE INSCRIPTION; POTTERIES.

CALAUIT ISLAND. This island, located northwest of Palawan, is a 3,700-hectare wild life sanctuary that serves as a host to African and Philippine wildlife. The government developed the sanctuary in response to an appeal by the International Union of Conservation of Nature (IUCN) to save endangered animals. The only one of its kind in the Philippines, Calauit is home to over 600 species of giraffe, impala, topi, gazelles, eland, and zebra and Philippine endangered species such as the Calamian deer, Palawan bearcat, mouse deer, tarsier, pheasant peacock, scaly anteater, and monitor lizard. The island also provides a refuge to sea turtles (*pawikan*), giant clams, and the rare sea cow or dugong. *See also* MALAMPAYA SOUND; TUBBATAHA REEFS.

CALDERON, FELIPE (1868–1908). Lawyer, journalist, and cowriter of the first Philippine Republic Constitution. A lawyer who obtained his degree from the **University of Santo Tomas**, Calderon grew wealthy in his profession. He also wrote journalistic articles promoting the cause of Filipino nationalism. When the revolution broke out he identified himself with **Emilio Aguinaldo**, who invited him to help form the first Republic of the Philippines. With the help of **Apolinario Mabini**, he drafted a constitution that provided for a three-branched republic and a unicameral legislature. One of the salient provisions of the constitution guaranteed freedom of religion. With major amendments, the **Malolos Constitution**, as it became known, was adopted and proclaimed law on January 20, 1899, by President Emilio Aguinaldo.

CAMACHO, JOSE ISIDRO (1955–). He is the former secretary of finance under the Gloria Macapagal Arroyo administration. Camacho presided over the worst budget deficit in history in 2002 but he was able to reverse the crisis by speeding up tax collections to put the 2003 budget on track to show its first deficit decline in five years. Camacho resigned his post in November 2003 following the government's failure to support his efforts to reform the financial sector, an agenda that was put on hold when President Arroyo decided to run in 2004. Before he went into government service, Camacho honed his business skills in the field of banking by serving as assistant treasurer and Asia international officer of Bankers Trust Company in New York. After the debt crises in 1983, Camacho helped develop the first debt-for-equity transactions in the country. He moved to Deutsche Bank AG in 1999 as a managing director and head of Country Coverage Function for Investment Banking for the Asia Region. Prior to his appointment to the Department of Finance post, he was the bank's managing director and chief country officer for the Philippines. Camacho has a master of business major in finance from the Harvard Business School.

CAMARINES NORTE. Located on the southern arm of Luzon, Camarines Norte occupies 2,112 square kilometers of land area and is the gateway to the Bicol Peninsula, that part of Luzon composed of the provinces of Camarines Norte, **Camarines Sur**, **Albay**, and **Sorsogon**. Camarines Norte has a population of 390,000. The city of Daet is the provincial capital. Since Spanish times, the province has been known for its gold-mining industry, although rich **forests** support an important logging industry as well. **Abaca** and pineapple are grown extensively. Mercedes, one of its major cities, has a large fishing fleet, which is a major supplier of fish and shrimp to Manila.

CAMARINES SUR. Located on the Bicol Peninsula on the southern arm of Luzon, Camarines Sur province, occupying a land area of 5,267 square kilometers, is the most populated region (more than a million) of the Bicol provinces. Its capital is Naga City. This anvil-shaped province is hilly and mountainous in places, but the fertile plains produce large quantities of rice. The name Camarines derives from the Spanish word meaning "food warehouse," a reference to the many rice granaries that were found in the area in 1573. Cash crops include coconuts, abaca, sugarcane, coffee, citrus fruits, and bananas.

CAMIGUIN. An island province located in the Mindanao Sea. Camiguin was formerly a part of **Misamis Oriental** province but became independent in 1968. With a land area of 230 square kilometers, the island is noted for its seven volcanoes. Its fields are fertile with volcanic ash. Its 62,000 inhabitants, mostly farmers and fishermen, live in constant fear of devastating eruptions, the last being that of Mt. Hibok-hibok in 1951. Cebuano is the main language. Its capital, Mambajao, is the island's trading center and an old town whose former inhabitants were already trading with foreign merchants before the Spanish came in 1521. The important towns are Catarman, Guinsiliban, and Mahinog.

CAMPOS, PAULO (1921–). A health scientist well-known for his work in nuclear medicine, Paulo Campos established the first radio isotope laboratory at the UP Philippine General Hospital, Manila. He is also credited with establishing the thyroid clinic at the Philippine General Hospital. After obtaining his medical degree from the University of the Philippines in 1946 he interned at the Harvard School of Medicine and at Oakridge Institute of Nuclear Medicine. During his active practice he produced 75 scientific publications on subjects such as red cell studies, genetic factors in endemic goiter, and insulin action. These achievements won him the honor of National Scientist awarded by the Philippine Association for the Advancement of Science. In 1973, Campos founded a school in Manila that initially offered undergraduate courses in nursing, medical technology, and midwifery. Eventually, the school developed into a full-fledged institution of higher education with campuses in Manila and Cavite. Its college of radiologic technology is rated as among the top three colleges in the Philippines. *See also* NUCLEAR ENERGY.

CANO, SEBASTIAN DEL. *See* MAGELLAN, FERDINAND.

CAPITAN CAVE. Capitan Cave, located in Nueva Vizcaya, is the fifth largest cave in the country—considered a geologist's paradise due to its varying rare calcite arrangements and unique stalagmite and stalactite formations. With its four kilometers length is a subterranean river that doubles as a passage way to a multichambered cave. Part of the cave network are the Lion and Alayan caves, measuring four and a half kilometers and along the caves are hot springs.

CAPIZ. This province occupies 2,633 square kilometers in the northwestern part of the island of Panay. Capiz is densely populated with

613,751 Capizeños who speak the Hiligaynon language. The province produces rice, coconuts, and sugarcane. Sugar mills are found in the towns of Pilar and Dumalag. The countryside is dotted with fishponds where *bangus* (milkfish) are raised for export to Manila. Roxas City, the capital, was named after its native son, **Manuel Roxas**, Philippine president from 1946–1948. The province has many mountain peaks and is still heavily forested. Principal towns are Pontevedra, Cuartero, Dao, and Manbusao.

CARABAO. Carabao is the Spanish adaptation of the Tagalog *kalabao*, the word for the water buffalo (*Bubalis bubalis*). Carabao resembles the Indonesian name *kerbau* for the buffalo. The water buffalo is primarily used as a draft animal in plowing the rice fields. Because the animal has no sweat glands, it can be used only during the early mornings and late afternoons. After each use, the animal is allowed to wallow or soak in a pond or river to cool off. The buffalo produces excellent milk that is highly fatty, its hide is utilized for shoe leather, and its meat is served at wedding parties and fiestas in rural areas. *See also* TAMARAW.

CARABAO TEST TUBE TWINS. Filipino **scientists** induced the birth of the world's first twin test-tube buffalo (carabao) using embryo technology (ET). The calves—both male—were born on March 21, 2003, at the Philippine Carabao Center, Muñoz, **Nueva Ecija**. The births were the result of the test-tube and freezing technology or in-vitro fertilization developed by the scientists. Until the twins came, only single-buffalo births have been done through ET anywhere around the globe. With this scientific breakthrough, Filipino **scientists** claim that it is possible to propagate high genetic buffalo in a shorter period of time and produce buffalo that can help supply the need for meat and milk of the burgeoning population. Research on the genetic makeup of the native buffalo is also going on at the Philippine Carabao Gene Pool at the Cagayan State University.

CARAGA REGION. Identified by government economists as one of the growth areas for agro-business and agro-forest ventures. This region is the newest geopolitical subdivision that is comprised of two cities (Butuan and Surigao) and four provinces located on the northeastern portion of Mindanao. The area possesses large deposits of gold, nickel, and iron. Presently, it produces the country's export crops of **banana** and palm oil. In addition, the region's major agricultural products are palay, corn, mango, rubber, prawns, milkfish, and seaweeds. Nasipit, strategically located on the mouth of the Agus River, handles international shipping. The region is sparsely populated—two million inhabitants, or 103 persons per square kilometer. In addition to its rich mineral resources, the region is also a **tourist** paradise with its natural caves and crystal clear waters. *See also* SOCSKSARGEN.

CARILLO. A shadow puppet theater. Carillo figures are made of wood or cardboard representing persons or animals, which are tied to fine strings and manipulated by expert hands. The figures are projected onto a screen for the entertainment of the audience seated on the opposite side in a darkened room. The performance may be either silent or narrated. Shadow plays were introduced in the 1870s in Manila and were popular for the remainder of the Spanish colonial period. With the coming of the Americans and the introduction of the cinema interest in the shadow puppet theater declined. Carillo is known as *teatro anino* in Tagalog. *See also* MORO-MORO; RONDALLA; ZARZUELA.

CARITAS DI ROMA. *See* BABAYLAN.

CASTRO, JOSE LUNA. *See* BRAID, FLORANGEL ROSARIO.

CATANDUANES. Formerly a subprovince of Albay, from which it was separated in 1968, this island province is located off southeastern Luzon. It has 19,000 inhabitants who speak the Bicol language. It occupies 1,511 square kilometers of land and is located on the Pacific Ocean side of Luzon. Catanduanes is subject to frequent typhoons, especially between June and October, thus earning the nickname "Land of the Howling Wind." Vicar is the capital and principal commercial center.

CATARMAN. *See* SAMAR, NORTHERN.

CATBALOGAN. *See* SAMAR, WESTERN.

CAVAN. A weight measure of palay (unhusked rice). One cavan is approximately 44 kilograms (97 pounds). Rice production is measured by cavans. *See also* RICE; WEIGHTS and MEASURES.

CAVITE. This province, southwest of Metro Manila, is densely populated with about 800,000 people, mostly Tagalogs, living on 1,288 square kilometers of land. There are four cities: Cavite, Tagaytay, **Trece Martires**, and Imus, the last being the provincial capital. Over half of the people live in urban areas with many employed in manufacturing and commerce. Cavite is Manila's leading supplier of vegetables, fish, fruits, and flowers. It was the center of revolutionary activity during the wars against Spain and America. Other towns are Bacoor, Noveleta, Kawit, Silang, Ternate, Indang, and Naic. *See also* PHILIPPINE-AMERICAN REVOLUTION; PHILIPPINE SPANISH REVOLUTION.

CAVITE MUTINY. On January 20, 1872, a regiment of artillery soldiers, led by a Filipino sergeant, staged a coup and killed the governor. They seized the arsenal of Fort Felipe and held it overnight. Government forces promptly quelled the mutiny. In the ensuing investigation of the incident, several prominent citizens were wrongly implicated, most significantly three Filipino priests—Mariano Gomez, Jose Burgos, and Jacinto Zamora—all of whom were later cruelly executed by garrote (strangulation). Those who were not executed were imprisoned or exiled to the Marianas. The ring leaders were denounced by the Spanish friars whose word was law and obeyed by their archbishops and the governor-general. The Cavite mutiny of 1872 was a turning point in the burgeoning resentment against the friars and it pushed the Filipinos and Spaniards to a fork in the road that they had traveled for centuries. The unjust execution furthered the cause of the Filipino revolutionaries. A historical marker was erected by the **National Historical Institute** on the site in Rizal Park. *See also* FRIARCROCY; GOMBURZA.

CAYETANO, BENJAMIN (1939–). Cayetano is the first and only American of Filipino ancestry who became a state governor in the United States. He was first elected as governor of Hawaii in 1994 and was reelected in 1998. A Democrat and a lawyer by profession,

Cayetano had served as a congressman of Hawaii, a state senator, and lieutenant governor. In a state where Filipinos make up 13 percent of the population, Cayetano, while highlighting his ethnic identity, has stressed a no-nonsense style of leadership in his political career. *See also* FILIPINO AMERICAN GENERALS.

CEBU. This historic province is the hub of the Visayan Islands and sits in the center of the Philippine archipelago. Long before the Spanish came in 1521 Cebu was a prosperous and well-populated trading center. The Spanish conquistador Miguel Lopez de Legaspi made Cebu the first capital of the emerging Spanish colony in 1565. Its capital, Cebu City, also called Sugbu by the residents, is the oldest and the second largest metropolitan area in the Philippines. It is the commercial, industrial, cultural, religious, and educational center for the central Visayas and northern Mindanao. Its land area of 5,088 square kilometers is densely populated with almost two million Cebuano-speaking people. There are five cities and 53 municipalities. The province, which includes the adjacent islands of Mactan, Bantayan, and Camotes, is noted for its export-quality mangoes and huge copra processing factories. Corn is the main food staple of the Cebuanos. Across the bay from Cebu City is historic Mactan Island, where the Portuguese explorer **Ferdinand Magellan** was killed in an engagement with the forces of chief **Lapu-lapu.** Lapu-lapu City was named in his honor for being the first Filipino to resist the Spanish. The five cities are Cebu, Danao, Lapu-lapu, Mandaue, and Toledo. Other towns are Carcar, Argao, Santander, Dumanjug, Toledo, Balamban, Tuburan, and Bogo. *See also* SINULOG.

CEBUANO. Language spoken principally in the Visayan Islands of Cebu, Bohol, Siquijor, Negros Oriental, Leyte, southern Leyte, and parts of Mindanao.

CEDULA. *See* CABEZA DE BARANGAY; TRIBUTES.

CELERIO, LEVI (1910–2002). A 1997 national **artist** in music and literature. Celerio was the acknowledged dean of Filipino lyricists and known for writing the words to classic songs that tugged at the Filipino heartstrings and resonated in the collective memory—*"Ang*

Pipit" (A Bird), "*Dahil Sa Isang Bulaklak*" (Because of a Flower), *Saan Kaman Naroroon*" (Wherever You Are), and "*Dalagang Bukid*" (Farm Maiden). During his lifetime he composed an estimated 4,000 songs, which earned him a spot in the Guinness Book of World Records and listed him as the only man who could play music on a leaf. The maestro was born in Manila and started his musical career as a violinist and became the youngest member of the Manila Symphony Orchestra. Unfortunately his dreams of becoming a professional violinist ended when he fell from a tree and broke his wrist. Instead he turned his talents to writing songs many of which were adopted in movies and received numerous citations and awards. For his significant contributions to the development of Philippine arts and to the cultural heritage of the country, Celerio was conferred a doctorate in humanities *honoris causa* by the University of the Philippines.

CENTRAL BANK (BANGKO SENTRAL). Established in June 1948, the Central Bank of the Philippines is charged with maintaining monetary stability, preserving the value and convertibility of the peso, and fostering credit and exchange conducive to the economic growth of the country. From the time it began operation until the early 1980s, the Central Bank intervened extensively in the country's financial life. It set interest rates on both bank deposits and loans. However, interest rates ceilings were deregulated by 1983 which affected the ratio of the country's money supply—savings and time deposits—to Gross National Product, just above 0.2—the lowest in Southeast Asia. To reduce capital flight, interest rates of time deposits were bid up even though commercial banks offered significantly variable rates for deposits of different amounts. The dependence of the banking system on funds from the Central Bank at low interest rates contributed to the financial chaos in the 1980s. Increased borrowings of the government-owned Development Bank of the Philippines from the Central Bank added to the crises. The Central Bank had to renegotiate its existing loans with the International Monetary Fund (IMF) to stabilize the financial situation. The interest paid on this debt necessitated even greater borrowing. High inflation was abated after the Central Bank met IMF requirements.

CEPEDES, DARIO. *See* ZARZUELA.

CHA-CHA. *See* CONSTITUTIONAL AMENDMENT.

CHAMPS. *See* OCAMPOS, LORETO.

CHARTERED CITIES. These are independent administrative units separate from the provincial government. The mayor and vice mayor are elected. Department heads are appointed and serve at the pleasure of the incumbent mayor. As of 2004, there are 61 chartered cities in the Philippines. *See also* PROVINCES.

CHAVACANO. A Spanish Creole spoken in and around Zamboanga City in the southwestern part of Mindanao. *See also* LANGUAGE; ZAMBOANGA DEL SUR.

CHINA. The Philippines adheres to a one-China policy. Diplomatic relations between the Philippines and the People's Republic of China were opened in 1973 ending years of hostile feelings. Filipinos have been suspicious of Chinese aid to the **New Peoples' Army**, which was unfounded, and the Chinese disliked Manila's support of **Taiwan**. Mutual feelings of goodwill were strengthened in 1988 when President Corazon Aquino visited Beijing and met Chinese Prime Minister Deng Xiaoping, and made a ceremonial pilgrimage to her ancestral home and temple in Fujian province. Other presidential visits followed—Fidel Ramos and Gloria Macapagal Arroyo—both of whom reaffirmed the one-China policy, although Manila continued its trade and economic ties with Taiwan. China, however, continues its huge exports to the Philippines and visits of Chinese premiers have cemented cordial relations in spite of some differences such as their dispute over the ownership of the **Spratly Islands**. **Chinese** Filipinos **(Tsinoys)** constitute about 12 percent of the total Philippine population.

China is the Philippines' sixth largest trading partner, the eighth largest export market, and sixth biggest import supplier. The Philippine government and China have agreed to reinforce its trade and economic cooperation, specifically on cement and coal supply to help in local industry requirements. Total bilateral trade in 2002 amounted to $2.58 billion with exports at $1.35 billion and imports at $1.23 billion. More than half of the country's exports to China in 2002 consisted of semiconductor devices and components while major imports consisted of motor gasoline, parts and accessories of automatic data processing machines and electrical machinery, cellular phones, fabrics, and compact discs. In 2004, the Chinese and Philippine governments signed a $400 million loan agreement for the development and rehabilitation of the Philippine National Railways. In 2004, the Philippines celebrated the Philippines–China Friendship Day to commemorate more than 400 years of friendship between the Filipinos and Chinese that dates back even before Spanish colonization of the Philippines. This is the third time the two countries have celebrated the friendship day that was set on June 9 of each year by proclamation by President **Gloria Macapagal Arroyo**, and also marks the 29th year of diplomatic relations between the two countries.

CHINESE. The presence of Chinese in the Philippines dates back to the 13th century when the Ming Emperor Yung Lo established trading posts on Luzon Island. Chinese junks brought ceramic wares, which they bartered with the natives for forest products such as wax. Later trading goods brought to Manila included silk and porcelain jars, vases, plates, and bowls. Chinese settlements began to appear in the 14th century, particularly in the Manila area. By the time the Spanish had consolidated their position in Manila, the number of Chinese merchants and the junk trade had increased. The Chinese population in Manila in 1603 was approximately 2,000. Though the Spanish depended on the Chinese for silk, which made up the bulk of goods in their galleon trade with Mexico, they were fearful of the growing dominance of the Chinese. Their repressive measures against the Chinese community led to bloody uprisings.

However, the Chinese population continued to grow. By 1876, there were over 30,000 Chinese living in scattered towns throughout the Philippines, most of them in the pariah district in Manila. The word pariah stems from **parian**, which is a segregated enclave strictly for Chinese. Throughout the Spanish period and the subsequent American regime, the Chinese population in the country significantly increased as the Filipinos accepted their role in society and the economy. Their skills have influenced Filipino cuisine, customs, and business practices. Their intermarriage with Filipinos has produced a substantial number of **tsinoys** in the country. Estimates of Chinese in the Philippines show that five percent of the population is concentrated mainly in the more developed provinces of central Luzon, and in Manila and its environs. Hokkien, Cantonese, and Mandarin are spoken by older members of the Filipino–Chinese community.

Although a small minority, the Chinese have been very active and successful in business and own a disproportionately large share of wealth, which has created some friction between the Chinese and the Filipinos. One enduring Chinese contribution is the presence of **sari-sari** or small stores found in most busy street corners in towns and cities where the Filipinos, called *suki* or favorite customer, buy their daily food needs. *See* Gokongwei, John Jr.

CHRISTIANS FOR NATIONAL LIBERATION. Front of the Communist party. A Roman Catholic priest, Father **Edicio de la Torre**, who was deeply influenced by **liberation theology**, founded this organization in 1972. He started with a small following of militant priests and nuns. This group initiated an embarrassing schism within the church hierarchy. As early as 1960, Father Luis Jalandoni, son of a wealthy family in Negros, became a Communist because he could not accept the stark socioeconomic inequalities in his parish. This action sparked the formation of a left-wing group, Christians for National Liberation, which was affiliated with the **Communist Party of the Philippines** (CPP). Its members felt that drastic change in society was needed in the face of the futile government attempts at land reform and the wanton disregard of human rights by the military. Although they denied that they were communists, several priests actually joined and even led armed guerrilla bands. In 1986, they had a clandestine membership of over 3,000 clergy and lay workers. The visit of Pope John Paul II, who appealed to the movement to disband, did not dampen the spirit of these militant clerics who were guided by **liberation theology** as a moral and religious justification for their sociopolitical actions.

CHUA, QUEENA LEE. She distinguished herself with her gifted teaching of mathematics—dreaded subject to most Filipino students. She graduated with a mathematics degree (summa cum laude) from Ateneo de Manila University and later on earned a doctorate in clinical psychology. Although her forte was English she got into teaching on the prodding of her professor who recognized her talent. Her initial teaching of the theory of probability excited her students because she made it simple and challenging. Chua taught game theory and applied it to Philippine politics—people power and **Spratly** Islands—to determine pure strategies and locate equilibrium points. Her objective was to bridge the gap between the classroom and the real world. She passed on to the public her passion for teaching mathematics through her inspired newspaper columns (Mind Games) and math textbooks. Her creative seminars on math and science education inspired new curricula in Philippine public schools. Her extensive research work on math education, business, and clinical psychology were published in international journals. In 2002, she was voted one of the 10 outstanding women of the Philippines. For her innovative teaching methods Chua won the prestigious Jose Rizal Award of Excellence.

CHURCH AND STATE. Under the constitution of 1986, the church and state are officially separate. This principle was first embodied in the **Malolos Constitution** and remained in the various constitutions that followed. During the Spanish period, church and state were inseparable, and in most cases, the Spanish friar had more power than the *gobernadorcillo*. This situation led to abuses and consequently sparked numerous **revolts** against the Spanish authorities. Thus, to avoid future conflicts, the framers of the constitutions wrote into law the basic principle of the separation of church and state. *See also* FRIAROCRACY; RELIGION; POLITICS.

CLARK INTERNATIONAL AIRPORT. This was formerly the historic Clark Air Force Base, the largest overseas U.S. military base in the world—63,262 hectares—that was leveled in the eruption of **Mount Pinatubo** in April 1991. The base was the subject of protests and demonstrations by activist and nationalist groups during the administration of President Corazon Aquino. After its destruction the Air Force transferred Clark to the Philippines. The military base was converted into a modern airport, which could accommodate large aircrafts, as an alternate international airport to the Ninoy Aquino International Airport (NAIA) in Manila. In 2003, Clark International Airport was renamed **Diosdado Macapagal** Airport by President Gloria Macapagal Arroyo. Airports are under the authority of the Bureau of Air Transportation. There are 87 airports in the Philippines.

CLOMA, TOMAS. *See* SPRATLY ISLANDS.

COCKFIGHT. *See* SABONG.

COCO LEVY. Under the Ferdinand Marcos administration (1986–1972), **coconut** was a monopolized industry. A coconut levy was imposed via a presidential decree (P.D. 276) which imposed "a levy, initially, of 15 pesos per 100 kilograms of **copra** resecada or its equivalent in oilier coconut products." The levy was initially intended to subsidize domestic consumption of coconut-based commodities premised on a crisis brought about by an abnormally high price in the world for fats and oils. However, through the issuance of a series of other presidential decrees, the original purpose was soon changed to "investment for coconut farmers" and made to appear as "private" funds even though it was exacted from millions of coconut farmers. The original levy of 15 pesos ballooned to 100 pesos per 100 kilograms of copra during the nine-year period, depending largely on its export price, or 60 pesos on the average. The small coconut farmers shouldered the burden for the coco levy as it was deducted from the actual price of the copra they sold in accordance with the levy rates. This significantly reduced their income, and very few farmers dared to protest due to **martial rule**.

After the ouster of Marcos, the Commission on Audit investigated the coco levy funds at the instigation of the Philippine Coconut Authority and found that the total collection reached an astronomical figure of 9.6 billion pesos. There were misappropriations of some funds to the Miss Universe Pageant, World Chess Championship, and coconut palace. Huge expenditures from the levy funds were not necessarily connected to its purpose and intent. Some were invested in banks owned by **cronies** and shares of stocks under questionable names of individuals and business entities. After Marcos fled the country in 1986, the **Corazon Aquino** administration placed under sequestration most of the stocks of companies acquired through the levy funds, and attempts were made to recover the multimillion levy fund and assets. Currently, the sequestered assets are under the control of the **Philippine Commission on Good Government (PCGG)**.

COCONUT. Sometimes called the "tree of life" because it provides food, shelter, and an energy source for the people. Its meat is eaten unripened and the dried meat (**copra**) is the source of oil widely used in many food preparations. Its tender shoots are used for food and are the source of a local alcoholic beverage called *tuba*. The dried shells are made into charcoal for cooking, and the husk fibers are woven into hats, doormats, and household decorations. Coconut leaves are also woven for use as roof and wall materials. The midribs of the dried leaves are made into brooms, baskets, and handicrafts. The Philippines is the second largest producer of coconut products, after Indonesia. Copra is one of the major export products. In 2001, the country exported $582 million worth of coconut products. Total coconut production in 2002 was 3.3 million metric tons. The top three coconut producing regions are southern Tagalog, northern Mindanao, and Bicol.

Copra, the dried, oil-bearing meat of a coconut, is one of the major export products of the Philippines, which supplies 60 percent of the world's requirements. It earns more than $353 million in foreign trade and accounts for more than 40 percent of the country's dollar income. Copra export for the year 2002 was 15,675 metric tons. The United States remained the leading importer of Philippine copra— buying 40 percent or 373,000 metric tons annually. The second biggest market was the Netherlands with 38 percent share. Total coconut production in 2002 was 13 million metric tons from a production area of 3.11 million hectares (7.7 million acres).

COJUANGCO. A wealthy politically powerful family, which owned vast interests in agricultural, land, banks, manufacturing companies, educational institutions, transportation, and import and export businesses. The origins of the wealth of this family date from the Spanish period to a **Chinese** forebear named Jose Cojuangco who started a prosperous dry goods business in Tarlac, which eventually expanded to sugar lands and mills. The family's prime asset was the **Hacienda Luisita**, considered the largest and most profitable sugar plantation on Luzon. Under the management of the heirs, which included **Corazon Aquino**, the Cojuangco family fortunes further increased in value when the family diversified into other business enterprises and the Cojuangco men and their cohorts strengthened their political control over the province. The Cojuangco fortunes bankrolled the political adventures of **Benigno Aquino Jr.**, who became the most articulate critic and possible challenger to **Ferdinand Marcos**. During the **martial law** period, the Cojuangcos suffered a tremendous setback when Marcos tried to wipe out the family businesses through a government takeover of the enterprises and their distribution to his **cronies**.

COJUANGCO, EDUARDO. *See* FILIPINO PARTY; NATIONALIST PEOPLE'S COALITION; SAN MIGUEL.

COJUANGCO, MARGARITO. *See* KABALIKAT NG MALAYANG PILIPINO (KAMPI).

COLLABORATION ISSUE. Collaboration with the **Japanese occupation** forces during World War II was one of the hottest issues that confronted the postwar Philippines. Following the instructions of President Franklin D. Roosevelt regarding those who assisted the enemy, the United States Army arrested and detained more than 5,600 persons for collaboration with the Japanese. They included high government officials, such as **Jose P. Laurel** and **Manuel Roxas**, who served in the Japanese-sponsored republic (1942–1944). A People's Court and an Office of Special Prosecutors were created to try alleged collaborators. A few prominent personalities were convicted, such as Teofilo Sison, secretary of the interior during the war. However, when Manuel Roxas was elected president, he proclaimed an amnesty on January 28, 1948, putting an end to an issue that had created considerable discord. *See also* KALIBAPI.

COLLANTES, FLORENTINO. *See* BALAGTASAN.

COLORUM. Colorum is a commune of believers and followers of Felix Bernales, who was known as Lantayug, the incarnation of Jose Rizal. This movement started in the Surigao region and spread rapidly in the early 1920s. According to their beliefs, Jose Rizal would return from the dead and bring social equity. His coming would be preceded by calamitous events, such as **earthquakes**, and only Colorum members would be saved. Their lifestyle caused misunderstanding with the government and, in 1924, led to an armed uprising by the colorums and attacks on constabulary troopers. The ensuing Pamosaligan massacre resulted in 54 colorums killed and many wounded, among them Lantayug, who was forced to surrender. *See also* SAKDALISTA.

COMEDIA (KUMEDYA). *See* MORO-MORO.

COMMISSION ON ELECTIONS (COMELEC). This government agency is mandated by the constitution to enforce and administer all election laws and regulations. It is composed of a chairperson and six commissioners, who have not been candidates for any position in the immediately preceding elections. A majority of the members must be lawyers and all must be university educated. They are appointed by the president, with the consent of the Commission on Appointments, and they serve a single term. Although COMELIC has broad powers and an apparently independent position, **Ferdinand Marcos** during his time was able to influence its decisions. However, under the 1987 constitution, COMELEC has been provided with powers to counter unwholesome influence and to call upon law enforcement agencies to assist in carrying out its mandate. *See also* NATIONAL MOVE-MENT FOR FREE ELECTIONS.

COMMONWEALTH. As provided for in the **Tydings-McDuffie Act (TM)** that was passed by the American Congress in 1934, a transition government called the Commonwealth was established in 1936 as training for Filipinos in self-government. The transition period was set for 10 years, after which the Philippines would be granted independence. The conditions asked for by **Manuel Quezon** were incorporated in the TM law and were fully implemented in the new government. Filipinos replaced American administrators and new political leaders were elected to the National Assembly. In the national elections, Manuel Quezon was chosen president of the Commonwealth government, with **Sergio Osmeña** as vice president. Under the TM law, qualified Filipinos were elected to offices in the municipal and provincial administrations. All of these developments happened in the next five years and were heady stuff to the Filipino people. The Commonwealth government was on the way to success when the war in the Pacific broke out. On December 7, 1941, Japanese bombers attacked Pearl Harbor in Hawaii and the Philippines. The subsequent three-year Japanese occupation left the country in total economic ruins, but nevertheless the Filipinos kept their date with destiny in 1946, when they finally obtained their independence. The

Commonwealth government had indeed well prepared the Filipino officials to take over the reins of the Republic of the Philippines.

COMMUNICATIONS. *See* MASS MEDIA.

COMMUNIST PARTY OF THE PHILIPPINES (CPP). The communist insurgency—it began in the 1930s—is one of the world's longest insurrections: divided, relatively weak but still formidable. The conditions that gave rise to the Marxist insurgency—poverty, landlessness, government neglect, and the stranglehold elite families and businesses have on the economy and political power—remain as real as ever to breed another generation of resistance fighters. In the early 1930s, agrarian unrest in **Pampanga** province, with its vast rice and sugar haciendas, triggered the emergence of militant peasant organizations, such as the *Aguman Ding Maldang Talagobra* (League of Poor Workers) and the Socialist Party, its political arm. The armed clashes between the private armies of the landlords and organized farmers were described as a class struggle. The events in Pampanga were not isolated developments since the wave of organizational activity among workers had spread to other provinces. Among its leaders were Communists who had links to the Communist leadership in China, the United States, Indonesia, and Russia.

One of these peasant leaders was Crisanto Evangelista, who founded the *Partidong Komunistang Pilipinas* (Communist Party of the Philippines) in 1930. Class conflict in the countryside became more visible as the leaders whipped up a mass frenzy of revolutionary zeal promoting the overthrow of American imperialism and capitalism and the establishment of a labor dictatorship. The party was outlawed in 1931 and its leader imprisoned on orders of Senate President **Manuel L. Quezon**. Alongside the Communists were the Socialists known as **Sakdalistas** led by Benigno Ramos whose slogans were "down with the oppressors, remove land taxes and corrupt officials." The government crushed the abortive uprising in 1935 and Ramos fled to Japan, where he stayed until the beginning of World War II. The leadership was taken over by a wealthy lawyer in Pampanga, Pedro Abad Santos, who reorganized the Socialist Party (SP) and made it proactive in politics rather than confrontational. Since the CPP and SP were both peasant movements and quite similar in their political agenda, the two organizations merged in 1938 and thus eased the CPP into legal status.

Quezon pardoned CPP leaders as an indication of his new policy of social justice. Under the new CPP banner, the labor and peasant movement continued to mount militant protest and strikes. The Japanese occupation (1942–1945) forced the CPP to go underground as an anti-Japanese guerilla group calling itself **Hukbo ng Bayan Laban sa Hapon or Hukbalahap** (People's Army Against the Japanese). Widely known as "Huks," they waged an effective harassing battle against the Japanese invaders while fighting periodically against the non-Communist guerrillas of General Douglas MacArthur. After the end of the war, the CPP resurfaced as a political entity called *Pambansang Kaisahan ng mga Magbubukid* (National Peasants' Union) and fielded candidates for political offices in the national elections of 1946. **Luis Taruc**, who led the "Huks" during the guerrilla war with the Japanese, won a seat in Congress, but he was denied his seat, alongside with his five successful colleagues who were charged with fraud and terrorism. This move infuriated the "Huks," who again went underground to wage a guerrilla war against the government in order to gain land reform and a fair share of the harvest.

In 1950, the Huks expanded their bases in Central Luzon to **Panay** Island. In turn, President Manuel Roxas responded with a mailed fist policy and outlawed the organization. The uprising was suppressed only after **Ramon Magsaysay**, an ex-guerrilla leader, was appointed defense minister. He introduced the **EDCOR** program offering land to surrendering "Huks"; many Huk fighters took advantage of the offer. Communist insurgency resurfaced during the **Ferdinand Marcos** administration when the New Peoples' Army (NPA) was organized as the military arm of the CPP, which had now adopted the tenets of **Maoism** (Mao Zedong). NPA soldiers were called Maoists, although there was no evidence that they received material support from their Red Chinese counterparts.

It was this threat of a Communist takeover that prompted Ferdinand Marcos to declare **martial law** in 1972. Like their former Huk antecedents, the NPAs were driven to militancy due to problems of tenancy, inadequate sharing of harvests, absentee landlordism, and dashed expectations. Other grievances raised by the NPAs were American imperialism and **neocolonialism**. Despite his large army, Marcos was unsuccessful in containing the NPAs. The task of dealing with the NPA was left to Corazon Aquino. By offering a program of land reform and amnesty, she was able to coax the major NPA leaders to come to the peace talks, which led to cease-fire agreements. President **Fidel Ramos** further upped the ante by offering **amnesty** to Communist insurgents and military rebels.

The Gloria Macapagal Arroyo administration pursued a slightly different approach—talk and fight strategy—to keep the insurgents off balance while offering them the olive branch of peace. President Macapagal Arroyo has stressed that poverty has bred many of the decades-old insurrections she inherited and pledged to bring development to far-flung areas. Thus, Arroyo has proceeded with negotiations with rebel factions, including the Mindanao **Muslim separatists**, hoping that a peaceful détente would be achieved. Yet in the often-convoluted turn of events in the Philippines, the two forces have found a common path and are helping each other wage a war that has outlived four presidents. *See also* AMNESTY; BAYAN; CHRISTIANS FOR NATIONAL LIBERATION; MAYO UNO; NATIONAL FEDERATION OF SUGAR WORKERS; NATIONAL UNIFICATON COMMISSION; PARTIDO NG BAYAN.

COMPOSTELA VALLEY. This valley is an extensive flat alluvial plain hemmed in by mountains along the boundaries between **Davao Oriental** and **Davao** provinces. It became a province in 1998 by virtue of R.A. 8470. The province has 11 towns with a population of 580,244 of which a majority are Cebuanos and Boholanos. Because the valley enjoys a typhoon-free climate and even rainfall throughout the year, its main products are corn, rice, bananas, coffee, and coconuts. The biggest town is Monkayo, which has 85,830 people.

CONSTITUTIONAL AMENDMENT. The charter of 1987—the prevailing law of the land—is the third **constitution** of the postwar Philippines. Like its two predecessors, these were amended on the self-serving initiative of strong presidents in the mould of **Manuel Quezon** and **Ferdinand Marcos**. Today there are current moves to amend the 1987 constitution in view of the fact that it was hurriedly adopted—as claimed by its supporters—during a time of crises when President Corazon Aquino took office. In regaining democracy after a decade of martial law, the people were euphoric over a new charter that had no vestiges of the hated Marcos regime. In their hurry, the framers—mostly persons with insufficient experience in government—incorporated some flawed remedies for the martial law anomalies, and slashed the allowable terms of office of elective officials, including the president. These provisions were intended to prevent the reemergence of **political dynasties**, private armies, and the accumulation of illegal wealth by those in power.

However, it is the three-year term limits that aroused the ire of those holding elective office since they claim that their term was insufficient to show their efforts and develop new constituencies. They felt the need to scrap the term limits from the charter. The clamor for charter change (popularly called *cha-cha*) reemerged shortly after the 1992 general elections but it was not the removal of term limitations that the people objected to. It was the presidency because of its abuse by Marcos. Thus, the immediate reaction of the citizenry to the "cha-cha" was negative. President Fidel Ramos told supporters to back off, following massive protest demonstrations nationwide. Even Joseph Ejercito Estrada was forced to withdraw his interest for an extended term; although he was elected with the largest ever margin of victory in presidential elections. Thus, plans for a charter change are still up in the air since proponents have not yet proposed definite amendments to further identify flaws in the charter.

CONSTITUTIONS OF THE PHILIPPINES. Since the Philippines declared its independence first from the Spanish and second from the Americans, there have been seven historic documents. These are the Biak-na-bato constitution of 1897; **Malolos Constitution** of 1898 under Emilio Aguinaldo; Commonwealth Constitution of 1935; 1943 Constitution during the Japanese occupation; Constitution of 1973 under the regime of Ferdinand Marcos; **Freedom Constitution** of 1986; and 1987 Constitution under the Corazon Aquino presidency.

CORDILLERA. This is a long mountain range in northern Luzon, which is the homeland of nine ethnolinguistic groups: Kankanai, Ibaloi, Bonito, Kalinga, Isneg, Itneg, Kalanguya, Iwak, and Gaddang. Like the Muslims in the south, these people have a history of resisting the invaders—Spanish and Americans—who were unable to pacify them even by their superior armament. What attracted the conquistadors to this region was **gold**, which was found in abundance in the region, but they were denied access to the mineral wealth by the indigenes' staunch defense of their domain. While Spain failed to subdue the Igorots (generic term to refer to the mountain people), the American colonizers drew a more systematic design for pacification by conducting a census in 1903 in which the population was categorized into two: wild and civilized. The Igorots were classified as wild. Thus, the Americans created the Mountain Province, which consists of Benguet, Amburayan, Bontoc, Apayao, Ifugao, Kalinga, and Lepanto. American lieutenant governors administered each of these subprovinces. To keep the peace among the warring tribes, the governors adopted the divide-and-rule strategy. However, with the entrance of the Catholic and Protestant missionary groups, the missionaries became instruments of change in the region. They filled the void left by the early Spanish missions that collapsed along with the end of the Spanish colonial regime. On the other hand, the Episcopal Church, which was the most influential religious institution during the early American administration, established stations in **Bontoc** and **Sagada**. The establishment of schools all over the Cordillera drew out the people from the isolated village to the colonial mainstream. Since Philippine political independence in 1946, several attempts were made by the government to integrate the Cordillera into the mainstream. The Commission on National Integration was created in 1957. In 1964, the Mountain Province Development Authority (patterned after the Tennessee Valley Authority) was established to facilitate developmental efforts in the region. By the 1970s, the Cordillera was the haven of many foreign-funded infrastructure programs like the **San Roque Dam**. Unfortunately, the Cordillera people, who continued to experience not only geographic but also social dislocation, opposed all these efforts. However, intensified military operations suppressed the local resistance. The 1987 Philippine constitution recognized the need for the establishment of a Cordillera Autonomous Region.

CORDILLERA AUTONOMOUS REGION (CAR). A regional arrangement in self-government. Like the **Autonomous Region in Muslim Mindanao**, this region was created by a presidential executive order (R.A. 6766 October 23, 1988) and is governed by special laws. The CAR consists of the provinces of Abra, Benguet, Ifugao, Kalinga,

Apayao, Mountain Province, and the chartered City of **Baguio**. As an autonomous region, these provinces administer the affairs of government and promote socioeconomic advancement through the maintenance of schools, operation of health facilities, legislation, and implementation of development plans. Their powers do not include national defense, security, banking, trade, and foreign affairs. Members of the law-making body, the *Sangguniang Pampook* are duly elected and meet in **Baguio City**. As of this time (2004), however, the CAR is still in the process of organization.

CORDILLERA MOUNTAINS. Mountain ranges in the northwestern Luzon highlands that rise to between 2,500 and 2,750 meters. Running parallel on the northeastern side of Luzon is the Sierra Madre mountain range, which has a slightly lower elevation. The Sierra Madre Mountains have been used by dissident elements from Spanish times to the present as a hiding place and sanctuary from pursuing government troops.

CORN (MAIZE). Corn is the second major staple crop of the Philippines. Agricultural land devoted to corn in 1991 was 3.59 million hectares (nine million acres), which produced a harvest of 4.85 metric tons. Corn is planted mostly in rice deficient areas. In 1991, southern Mindanao harvested 26.89 percent (1,251.69 billion metric tons) of the country's total corn production. Central Mindanao harvested 1.3 billion metric tons of corn in 2003. *See also* AGRICULTURE.

CORONEL, SHEILA (1958–). A 2003 **Ramon Magsaysay awardee** for journalism, literature, and creative communication, Coronel was recognized for leading a groundbreaking collaborative effort to develop investigative journalism as a critical component of democratic discourse in the Philippines. Coronel was only 14 when President Ferdinand Marcos declared martial law in 1972 and gagged the country's free press. She studied political science at the University of the Philippines, but instead she began writing for a popular Manila magazine. And when, in 1983, the assassination of **Benigno Aquino Jr**, cracked the edifice of Marcos' power and the Philippine press stirred tentatively back to life, Coronel became a compelling journalist. She covered the movement to bring Marcos down and emerged as one of the young chroniclers of the **EDSA** revolution. Afterward, she sealed her reputation at the *Manila Chronicle* with probing stories. Her work appeared in the *New York Times* and the *Manchester Guardian*.

Growing frustrated with the constraints of a conventional newsroom, in 1989, Coronel and eight like-minded reporters founded the **Philippine Center for Investigative Journalism** (PCIJ). She became the executive director. Finding its stride under Coronel, PCIJ plumbed the state of the nation. It probed attempts by military power-grabbers and their political allies to overthrow President Corazon Aquino. PCIJ's scrupulous reporting played a key role in scrutinizing the anomalies of Joseph Ejercito Estrada's presidency. At the center, Coronel applied herself tirelessly to the work. Its production of hundreds of articles, books, and documentary films reflect her commitment to Philippine democracy. For the past 12 years, the PCIJ has become a source of the country's most reliable and incisive studies on some of the most serious ills that plague Philippine society. *See also* BRAID, FLORANGEL ROSARIO.

CORREGIDOR. This is a small tadpole-shaped island—two square miles—strategically located and heavily fortified before World War II at the entrance of Manila Bay. Corregidor, also called the Rock, was the scene of the last battle between the defending Filipino–American forces and the invading Japanese army. The island fortress was protected by batteries of heavy 12-inch guns and stocked with supplies and ammunition in tunnels dug deep in the mountains and defended by 11,000 U.S and Filipino forces. Corregidor became the headquarters of General **Douglas MacArthur** during the battle of **Bataan** where he led a delaying action in hope that American aid would come, which it never did. After the fall of Bataan (April 9, 1942) MacArthur and President **Manuel Quezon** and their staff were rescued by submarine and taken to Australia. Twenty-seven days later on May 6, 1942, the embattled Filipino–American forces depleted of rations surrendered to General **Masaharu Homma.**

On January 22, 1945, American paratroopers retook Corregidor after a bloody battle. A shrine—the Pacific War Memorial—and a museum were erected in 1968 on Corregidor in honor of the Filipino and American servicemen to commemorate their courage and heroism. Inside the

rotunda structure designed by a Filipino sculptor Aristides Demetrios is
the Flame of Freedom burning eternally. Because of its fame Corregidor is visited not only by Filipinos but also Japanese tourists.

CORRUPTION. *See* GRAFT AND CORRUPTION.

**COUNCIL OF PHILIPPINE AFFAIRS. A nongovernmental organ-
ization**, which was one of the major groups behind the **EDSA 2** revolution. The group galvanized the peaceful uprising, which led to the
toppling of President Joseph Ejercito Estrada and the establishment
of Vice President **Gloria Macapagal Arroyo** as president. This militant group also led protests against President Arroyo for some of her
controversial decisions, one of which was the forced resignation of
Vice President **Teofisto Guingona** as foreign affairs secretary over
his disagreement regarding the presence of American troops in Basilan to train the Philippine Army to fight the **Abu Sayyaf.** *See also*
BASILAN.

COUP D'ÉTAT (KUDETA). Coups d'état plagued the presidency of
Corazon Aquino. There were six attempts to destabilize the administration staged by military officers and persons loyal to the exiled Ferdinand Marcos. All of these coups d'état failed because the country's
political leaders and the armed forces remained supportive of Aquino
and the 1986 constitution.

One of the biggest and bloodiest attempts against the Aquino government occurred on December 1, 1989. A combined force of 3,000
rebels seized Villamor Air Base and Camp Bonifacio, closed Manila
International Airport, and launched attacks on the presidential palace.
Other rebel contingents took over a TV station and occupied key positions in Metro Manila while another group controlled Sangley
Point, an airbase in Cavite. Planes from Sangley Point strafed Malacañang Palace. At this juncture, United States jet fighters, at the request of President Aquino, flew over rebel-controlled air bases and
sent a clear message to the dissidents that America stood behind the
Aquino government. Meanwhile, other rebel troops were in control
of military installations and communications in the provinces.

In the face of an imminent debacle, AFP Chief of Staff General Renato de Villa was able to rally the uncommitted regional commands

to close ranks. Loyal troops came from the nearby provinces to bolster the Aquino forces in Metro Manila. After three days of combat in Manila, government troops defeated the rebels. Their comrades in the provinces quickly surrendered when they heard of the failure of their Manila counterparts. By December 7, all pockets of resistance had been suppressed. These coups considerably weakened the administration of President Corazon Aquino and greatly overshadowed her significant accomplishments.

CRISOLOGO, MENA PECSON. *See* ZARZUELA.

CRONIES. Friends of Ferdinand Marcos. During the Marcos regime, the word referred to friends, relatives, and sycophants who were rewarded by Marcos with lucrative businesses, high government positions, and political offices. These cronies in turn channeled part of their profits to Malacañang Palace. When Marcos ordered the break up of the businesses and enterprises of the **oligarchs** during the period of martial law, the families of Ferdinand and Imelda Marcos and their friends (cronies) took over control of banks, mining firms, and finance and investment companies. One of his closest cronies was Roberto Benedicto, a fraternity brother during their college days, who became the head of the sugar monopoly, which controlled procurement, financing, and both domestic and foreign marketing. Additionally, Benedicto controlled two banks, his own Traders Royal Bank and the sugar industry's Republic Planters Bank. When Marcos fled to Hawaii on February 26, 1986, Benedicto was in the United States and later fled to Venezuela to seek political asylum.

Among others, the Lopez family business conglomerate, which included major newspapers, a broadcast network, and the country's largest electric power company, had been broken up and its management was distributed to Marcos loyalists, including Imelda Marcos' brother. There were cronies in banking, department stores, and the production of tobacco and bananas, textiles, and construction electronics. Most of these activities profited from presidential decrees and received favored loan approvals and marketing arrangements. The modus operandi was to take cuts up front, or cronies could vie for tax laws, which helped them underwrite their operations. The net effect of the crony system, or **kleptocracy**, was to siphon much-needed funds from the economy, consequently increasing the country's debt to as much as $22 billion. *See also* COJUANGCO.

CRUZ, APOLINARIO DE LA. Better known as *Hermano Pule* in history, he was one of the early revolutionaries who fought for his religious beliefs against the entrenched **Roman Catholic Church**. As a devout Roman Catholic, Pule wanted to join a religious congregation in Manila. He was refused admission for being an "Indio" by the Spanish curate. So in 1832, he and 19 other province mates established their own order and called it the Hermanidad de la Archi-Confradia del Glorioso Señor San Jose y de la Virgen del Rosario, or Confradia de San Jose. The confradia conducted its own masses, prayed the rosary, and partook of common meal. The idea of a confradia was not new as there were many of them in those times—1832 to 1840—but they were ignored by religious authorities. However, the Confradia de San Jose attracted some 5,000 members, which alarmed the church hierarchy and civil authorities. The Spanish vicar branded the group subversive and ordered its arrest. Pule and his followers took to the hills where the Spanish forces attacked them. The result was a massacre and among the dead was Pule. His revolt laid the groundwork for the **Philippine–Spanish Revolution,** which started in 1896. *See also* FRIAROCRACY.

CRUZ, JUAN MATAPANG. *See* ZARZUELA.

CRY OF BALINTAWAK (PUGAD LAWIN). Balitanwak, a small hamlet north of Manila, is the site of the first stirrings of revolt against the Spanish. **Andres Bonifacio** and his followers gathered at the site and tore up their personal *cedulas* (head tax) to symbolize the termination of their subservience to Spain, while shouting the battle cry "Long Live the Philippines." The event went down in history as the "Cry of Balintawak" in Pugad Lawin and is regarded as the starting signal of the **Philippine–Spanish Revolution.** Today, a monument created by **Guillermo Tolentino** marks this site, which shows a Filipino peasant brandishing the bolo. It is in Balintawak where Bonifacio issued the call for a general revolt in the whole country. The first encounter between the revolutionaries and the Spanish troops was staged in **Pinaglabanan** (San Juan Del Monte). Faced with superior firepower, Bonifacio had to retreat but the revolution could no longer be controlled. One city after the other rose in revolt under the banner of the **Katipunan** and later by the forces of General **Emilio Aguinaldo**.

CUISINE. Filipino cuisine is as diverse as the different cultural groups that make up the Filipino people. It is flavored by a rich variety of herbs and spices found all over the islands. Aside from the many tropical fruits and vegetables grown in the lowlands and the mountains, fish, meat and poultry are also a major part of the diet. **Rice** is a staple food. Contact with foreign cultures—Chinese, Spanish and American—resulted in delicious blends of flavors. However, prior to their contact with other cultures through trade and conquest, the various indigenous ethnolinguistic groups share certain cooking techniques and flavor preferences, many of which are still found today. Early Filipinos cooked their food minimally by roasting, steaming, or boiling on clay pots over charcoal or firewood stoves. The freshest of fish was made into *kinilaw*, "cooked" by immersion in vinegar and salt with ginger, onions, and red peppers. Most Filipinos, including expatriates, still show a distinct preference for sour and salty cuisine, such *as sinigang* (lightly boiled fish, usually milkfish or *bangus*), in a sour fish sauce. For salty flavoring, **Pinoy** cooks rely on *patis*, *bagoong* (shrimp paste). Chinese influences on Filipino cuisine are stir-frying and deep-frying, noodles (*pancit*) and soy products. The Spaniards introduced thick, rich stews, sausages, and dishes emphasizing meat and dairy products. Pork and chicken **adobo** is the best-known Filipino dish. Americans introduced the burger that Filipinos eat with chopped onions, garlic, and soy sauce. Fried chicken is a favorite but marinated in soy sauce, vinegar, and garlic before it is fried. *See also* BALUT; LECHON; SUMAN.

CULION. Infamously called *Culion lepers' colony*, this tiny island— 12 kilometers long and 6 kilometers wide and located north of **Palawan**—was the haven of people who were called the "living dead" because of their affliction of the ancient disease of leprosy. Leprosy was discovered in the late 1900s by American troops during their pursuit of General Emilio Aguinaldo's holdouts in remote villages in various islands. Governor-General **Leonard Wood** then ordered that all known cases—200 were found—of leprosy should be isolated and brought to Culion Island. A modern leprosarium was built and the government provided all the medical care. Eventually, the Philippine Leprosy Mission took charge of the care of the patients. Since the lepers brought their families the community has grown over the years to some 7,500 people (lepers and nonlepers). Culion leper colony has become a place not only to treat lepers but also to conduct medical researches and find a cure for the disease. It also became the *de facto* international laboratory for the study of leprosy by local and foreign doctors and scientists. Today, the disease has been stopped from spreading because of multidrug therapy.

CULTURAL CENTER OF THE PHILIPPINES (CCP). One of the most significant and historic landmarks of the Philippines is the Cultural Center of the Philippines in Metro Manila. Built during the time of the Ferdinand Marcos regime on 21-hectares of reclaimed land along Roxas Boulevard, the CCP was created to promote and preserve Filipino arts and culture. It was formally inaugurated on September 8, 1969, with a three-month long inaugural festival that was opened by the epic musical drama *Dularawan*. Over the years, the CCP has sought to embody its logo *Katotohanan* (truth), *Kagandahan* (beauty), and *Kabutihan* (goodness). The CCP exemplifies the Filipino value of **bayanihan** (teamwork). National Artist **Leandro Locsin** designed its buildings; the magnificent **capiz** chandelier in the foyer; and National Artist Carlos Francisco, the CCP logo. The design of the curtain in the foyer of the main theater was based on "Genesis," a painting by National Artist H. R. Ocampo. Visual artist and first director of the CCP Museum Roberto Chabet designed the curtain of the little theater. From Vicente Manansala, another National Artist, came the commanding bronze relief sculpture "A Tribute to the Seven Arts" at the main theater's entrance. Arturo Luz, National Artist Oscar Legaspi, and Eduardo Castrillo created murals for the little theater lobby. Today, several companies representing dance, music, and theater reside within the CCP, which also houses the major venues for the performing arts: Tanghalang **Nicanor Abelardo** (main theater), the Tanghalang Aurelio Tolentino (little theater), the Tanghalang Huseng Batute. The CCP has a museum that features paintings of

Juan Luna, **Fernando Amorsolo**, Victorio Edades, and many other contemporary artists. Its library offers extensive facilities and services for research, readings, viewing, and listening.

CULTURE. Historians researching Filipino culture prior to the 16th century possess no dynastic histories or wealth of annals such as other Southeast Asian countries have. The Filipinos had not attained the political administrative integration that existed in Siam (now Thailand). The inhabitants of the archipelago lived in widely scattered and almost isolated communities. To subjugate the islanders the Spaniards entered into separate treaties and **blood compacts** with various chiefs and *datus*. The different languages of the people also attested to this isolation, although they were descended predominantly from Malay stock. However, there was one common trait they shared and that was the **barangay**. Each barangay was an independent self-governing unit that was ruled by a datu. There was very little contact between or among the barangays, except probably in minimal trade-barter transactions or in petty skirmishes.

The Spanish adopted this basic administrative unit when they started their colonization of the country. The Spanish meticulously superimposed their culture on the already existing culture of the Filipinos. The Filipino traditional way of life was overlaid by the culture of their conquerors, which accounts for many of the Spanish customs and traditions that exist in Filipino life today. In time, the Filipinos considered the Spanish way of life as de rigueur, which was best exemplified by the *ilustrados*. Spain's imprint was evident in the institutions Spaniards left behind, most importantly the **Roman Catholic** religion, which had a lasting impact on the life of the Filipinos. Subsequently, the Americans arrived with a different brand of culture. Although their rule lasted only about 50 years, they left a legacy that was more pervasive than the Spanish. This legacy included the introduction of public education and, more significantly, the development of the democratic process—freedom of the press— which the Filipinos adopted with alacrity. Today, these institutions form the bedrock of a thriving society. The Chinese, the Indians, and the Japanese, who left a patina of their unique cultures on the **literature**, business, and **cuisine** of the Philippines, have also influenced Philippine life and culture. *See also* SOCIAL VALUES.

– D –

DAET. *See* CAMARINES NORTE.

DAGDAG-BAWAS. Vote padding and shaving scheme. An illicit operation of adding (*dagdag*) or subtracting (*bawas)* of votes to ensure the victory or defeat of political candidates. This poll fraud is usually committed at the municipal level. The way *dagdag-bawas* works is for the operators to disrupt the canvassing of votes by violent incidents such as grenade throwing, strafing, and ballot-snatching. As poll-watchers scamper for safety, the operators are given the chance to tamper with the election results. Thus, it would be difficult for volunteers of the poll watchdog **NAMFREL** to detect on the spot any discrepancies in the certificate of canvass. Opposition candidates used *dagdag-bawas* scheme in the 1995 senatorial elections. It was tried again in the 2001 national elections but the scheme was foiled by the introduction of electronic voting machines (Operation Quick Count), which counted votes accurately and speedily. NAMFREL also mobilized half a million more volunteers to monitor the election.

DAGOHOY, FRANCISCO (ca. 1744). A famous rebel leader in **Bohol**. Dagohoy was given the Christian name Francisco by Jesuit friars. He is famous for the **revolt** he led that lasted 85 years (1744–1829)—the longest revolt in Philippine history against Spain. The revolt had its origin in the refusal of a Spanish priest to give a Christian burial to Dagohoy's brother, who was killed on a mission to capture a renegade. For this affront Dagohoy incited about 3,000 people to revolt, plunder the prosperous Jesuit estates, and kill the friars. Dagohoy led his followers to the rugged mountains of Bohol to establish fortifications to defend themselves against the Spanish. Several government expeditions failed to dislodge him and in the ensuing years Dagohoy carried out successful raids against churches and government properties seeking to drive all Spaniards out of the island. In its effort to pacify him, the government offered to allow secular priests to officiate in the churches and proposed a general amnesty, but these concessions only encouraged the rebels to continue their armed defiance of Spanish authority. Dagohoy set up his own government and declared the island of Bohol to be an independent nation. Twenty governors-general from Gaspar de la Torre

(1739–1745) to Juan Antonio Ramirez (1822–1824) failed to subdue Dagohoy in his island bastion. Meanwhile, Dagohoy died and his followers continued the resistance. They kept Bohol free from the Spanish. In 1829, the Dagohoy rebellion was finally suppressed by Governor-General Mariano Ricafort (1825–1830) who led a contingent of 5,000 troops and overwhelmed the last remaining strongholds of the insurgents. *See also* PALARIS, JUAN DE LA CRUZ; SILANG, DIEGO; SUMUROY; TAMBLOT.

DAGUIO, AMADOR. *See* ALIGUYON.

DALTON PASS. This strategic pass in **Nueva Vizcaya** was the site of a major battle during World War II. During the final stages of the war, Japanese troops under General **Tomoyuki Yamashita** unsuccessfully resisted the advancing Philippine–American forces under General Charles Dalton, and in the end some 17,000 Japanese, Americans, and Filipinos were killed. One of the casualties was General Dalton for whom the pass was named. At 3,000 feet above sea level, Dalton pass is the gateway to the Cagayan Valley and the Ifugao rice terraces. *See also* TIRAD PASS.

DAMIAN DOMINGO. *See* AYALA MUSEUM.

DANGWA, BADO (1905–1976). Bado Dangwa is a household word in the Mountain provinces for the transportation company, which still bears his name, and for being the first native—an Igorot—to serve as provincial governor of Benguet. Born poor, he was tutored by American teachers who discovered his knack for mechanical objects, particularly motor vehicles. When he graduated from the American-run Trinidad Agricultural School in Benguet, his American teachers encouraged him to go into the transportation business. He was practically penniless then, but with the help of his friends, he converted junk cars into jeepneys plying the route between Trinidad Valley and Baguio city. By 1928, his transportation company became a fleet of buses called Dangwa Transport, and soon became also the major transport in all mountain provinces and employing mostly his native people. The war destroyed much of his transportation business but again with the help of his friends, Dangwa was able to rebuild his bus company. Dangwa's reputation for integrity, honesty, and efficiency earned him the respect of President **Elpidio Quirino** who appointed him governor of the Mountain Provinces. And later on, **Ramon Magsaysay**, who succeeded Quirino, reappointed him to the post.

DANSALAN. *See* MARAWI CITY.

DAPITAN. *See* ZAMBOANGA DEL SUR.

DAR, WILLIAM DOLLENTE (1954–). Director general of the International Crop Research Institute for the Semi-Arid Tropics (ICRISAT). The first Filipino to head an international agency based in Andhra Pradesh, India, William Dar distinguished himself in agricultural research as minister of agriculture during the administration of President **Joseph Ejercito Estrada**. It was during his stewardship that **agriculture** gained a positive 2.7 percent growth, with rice and corn registering 35 percent and 62 percent growth respectively, the highest in six years. Growing up as a poor boy from Santa Maria, **Ilocos Sur**, Dar worked his way through college and ultimately obtained his Ph.D. in horticulture from the University of the Philippines at Los Baños, **Laguna**. He helped set up the Bureau of Agricultural Research of the Philippines, and served as its first director. In 1994, he became executive director of the Los Baños-based Philippine Council of Agriculture, Forestry, and Natural Resources Research and Development, which is the top agricultural research institution of the country. As the ICRISAT chief executive, he directs several scientists in the research of five mandate crops: sorghum, millet, groundnut, chickpea, and pigeon pea—highly nutritious crops needed to improve the life and health of the poor in Asia.

DARANGEN. *Darangen* is one of the best-preserved pre-Spanish folk epics of the Maranao people of the lake region of **Lanao del Sur** province. The *Darangen* is an extremely long oral poem composed of about 25 songs rendered in 72,000 lines. So far scholars have recorded 18 of the songs, each of which comprises an autonomous narrative of the adventures of the principal character, Bantugan, who is endowed with supernatural powers and who subdues his enemies with his magic *kampilan*, or sword. Bantugan is handsome, skillful, and bold, qualities that make him very popular with numerous princesses. He marries many of them in the course of his travels. Besides Bantugan, the epic contains many other characters, all involved in some kind of conflict, plot, or undertaking. The epic also contains elaborate comments on the nature and practice of kinship, love, war, and other topics of social concern. *See also* FRANCISCO, JUAN; LAUBACH, FRANK.

DARUL ISLAMIYAH NUSANTARA. A confederation of Islamic followers in Mindanao, Malaysia, and Indonesia. The Philippine government has listed this organization as a terrorist group, which has connection with al-Qaeda and the **Abu Sayyaf**—which was held responsible for many kidnappings of Americans and Filipinos. Hostages were held for ransom and in many cases their lives ended in tragedy.

DATU SIKATUNA. *See* BLOOD COMPACT.

DATUMANONG, SIMEON AMPATUAN (1947–). First Muslim legislator appointed to a cabinet level position—secretary of the department of justice—by President **Gloria Macapagal Arroyo.** Before his appointment he served as secretary of public works and highways where he distinguished himself by cleaning the department of corrupt employees. Though critics had earlier questioned his qualifications for the justice post, Arroyo recognized his aggressive leadership in rooting out malefactors in government positions. Born in Shariff Aguak, **Maguindanao**, a descendant of Moro royalty, Datumanong was an honor student in high school. He graduated from the University of the Philippines with a bachelor of laws degree, and passed the bar in 1959. He entered politics in Cotabato and got elected as governor, followed by another term as governor of the newly created Maguindanao province. He was instrumental in the creation of the **Autonomous Region of Muslim Mindanao**. Then he went on to serve as congressman representing Maguindanao. During his three terms he was voted one of the outstanding legislators and received many awards and citations. *See also* MUSLIM SEPARATISM.

DATU UTO (1860–1888). Datu Uto, a Muslim leader, distinguished himself in his many battles against the Spaniards for his defense of his capital Buayan in Cotabato. He was defeated in his last battle, and eventually signed a peace treaty with the Spaniards in 1887. *See also* JIKIRI.

DATU PIANG (1846–1933). From the time the Spaniards, with their Catholic faith, set foot on Mindanao, where Islam held sway over much of the island, the *kris* and the cross would be locked in mortal combat. For the Moros, there is no separation of church and state, since Islam encompasses all of life. To fight for their religion, is to fight for freedom and life. Many Moro warriors epitomized such a fight, for which they are now venerated as heroes. One of them was Datu Piang, known also as Amai Mingka. He was the powerful datu of Cotabato who forged an alliance with other datus to resist the encroachment of Spanish troops in Mindanao. Under the Americans, he was recognized as a unifier of his people, preaching the importance of education and the art of government. The Christians, whom he encouraged to live peacefully with the Moros, praised him. He was a friend to the Americans, who let Moros preserve their religion as long as they they paid their taxes. The town of Datu Piang was named in his honor.

DAVAO DEL NORTE. This is the northern portion of the former Davao province, which was divided into three provinces in 1968, the other provinces being Davao del Sur and Davao Oriental. These provinces are all located in the southeastern part of Mindanao. Davao del Norte is the largest of the three with an area of 8,130 square kilometers, mostly low agricultural lands, which produce large quantities of bananas, the major export crop. The province has a population of 750,000, mainly migrants from Luzon and Visayas, although the Mansaka, Mandaya, Dibabawons, Mangguangans, and Atas ethnic tribes are also found here. Part of the province consists of the large **Samal** Island in the Davao Gulf, across from Davao City. The island is the home of the Isamal, a Muslim minority tribe who live in fishing villages. The provincial capital is Tagum, and the chief towns are Babak, San Jose, Kaputian, Compostela, and Asuncion.

DAVAO DEL SUR. The southern portion of the former Davao province, which was divided into three provinces in 1968, the other provinces being Davao del Norte and Davao Oriental. Davao del Sur province is located along the coastline of the Davao Gulf in the southeastern part of

Mindanao. The province covers a land area of 6,378 square kilometers and has a population of 600,000, who are mostly Visayan immigrants. The province is also the homeland of several indigenous ethnic groups: **Bagobo**, **Bilaan**, Tagakalao, Mangguangans, Matigsalug, Kalagan, and Sangil. Its capital, Digos, is built on seven hills and is surrounded by fertile rice fields. The legendary Mt. Apo, the highest mountain peak in the Philippines (3,144 meters above sea level), is in this province. Wood processing and fishing are the major industries. The chief towns are Padada, Santa Cruz, Malalag, Malita, and Jose Abad Santos.

DAVAO ORIENTAL. One of three provinces formed when the former Davao province was divided into Davao Oriental, Davao del Norte, and Davao del Sur in 1968. This province is in the southeast corner of Mindanao. It covers 5,164 square kilometers of land with shorelines facing the Pacific Ocean. The Pacific Cordillera Mountains dominate the rugged terrain. The province has limited arable lands but extensive timberlands, which support logging and wood processing industries. It has a population of 330,000, who are mostly Visayan immigrants. Davao Oriental is the homeland of the Mandaya tribe, who are famous for their colorful handwoven clothes. Mati is the provincial capital and main seaport. The chief towns are Baganga, Boston, Cateel, and Caraga.

DAVID, RANDY. *See* BUKLURAN SA IKAUUNLAD NG SOSYALISTANG ISIP AT GAWA (BISIG).

DAVIDE, HILARIO JR. (1935–). Supreme Court chief justice. Appointed to his office in 1991 by the then President Joseph Estrada, Davide served as presiding officer of the impeachment tribunal that brought the indictment on his benefactor. A law graduate of the University of the Philippines, Davide started a successful law practice in his native Cebu and entered politics as an assemblyman of his district. President Corazon Aquino appointed him commissioner of the 1987 Constitutional Commission—the group that drafted the present charter. He holds the record of having presented the largest number of resolutions and has played a significant role in restoring the democratic system of government. As chief justice he reorganized the judiciaries by weeding out corruption, incompetent judges, and crooked lawyers in a decisive effort to preserve the integrity of the courts. Davide made his mark as a hardworking jurist noted for meticulously argued opinions and interpretation of the law. He wrote decisions strengthening the hand of the state against violators of the environment and, in one landmark case, asserted the right of children to sue for a healthy habitat both for themselves and for "generations yet unborn"—a decision that helped to save 800,000 hectares of the country's virgin rain forests. Davide was a recipient of the **Ramon Magsaysay award** in 2002 for government service in recognition of his life of principled citizenship in profound service to democracy and the role of law in the Philippines. In 2003, Davide faced impeachment filed by 87 congressmen based on alleged charges of **graft and corruption**, but the Supreme Court justices later ruled that the charges were unconstitutional.

DAVIS, DWIGHT (1879–1945). American governor-general in the Philippines in 1929–1931. He was a native of St. Louis, Missouri, where his affluent and civic-minded forebears established successful businesses. Davis was a lawyer by profession, but his political career started as a parks commissioner. During World War I, he served in France, where he rose to the rank of lieutenant colonel. An active Republican, he was appointed an assistant secretary of war and rose to become the youngest member of the cabinet following the resignation of the secretary. President Herbert Hoover appointed him governor-general in the Philippines to succeed **Henry L. Stimson**. During his brief two-year tenure, Davis was well liked and did much to improve relations between his office and aggressive Filipino cabinet ministers. His policy of having Americans do the work while Filipinos got the credit added to a smooth working relationship with Filipino legislators. *See also* WILLIAM HOWARD TAFT.

DEATH MARCH. The infamous forced march of the defeated Filipino and American soldiers. After the fall of **Bataan** and **Corregidor**, 80,000 Filipinos and American soldiers who surrendered were herded together at Mariveles airfield in Bataan province. The death march began on April 10, 1942, under a blistering summer sun. Soldiers who fell behind were executed and stripped of their valuables. Japanese soldiers randomly beat the POWs and denied them food and water for many days. Only on the ninth day were the prisoners given food, and it was only a handful of contaminated rice. Of the original marchers, only about 54,000 reached Camp O'Donnell prison camp. Of the 32,020 American POWs 12,526 died during the nine-day march. Thousands more died in the concentration camp due to disease, starvation, and brutality. After the war, the American forces arrested 5,000 Japanese officers and soldiers suspected of brutalities. At the Allied war crimes trial held in Tokyo, 800 were acquitted, 2,400 went to prison, and 800 were executed by firing squad, and eight were hanged, including Hideki Tojo, **Masaharu Homma**, and **Tomoyuki Yamashita**.

DA'WAH. See BALIK ISLAM.

DEBT STOCK. The country's total foreign exchange liability as of December 2002 was about $54 billion and growing. The debt buildup is a legacy of four decades of trade deficits and foreign borrowings. This mounting debt stock, according to Finance Secretary **Jose Isidro Camacho**, could not be stopped without improving the borrowing efficiency of the government and unless Congress would be able to pass immediately pending economic reforms that are expected to generate revenues. Over the past few years, the government has been borrowing largely to finance its obligations. Interest payments are estimated to amount to 231 billion pesos as the country's debt stock was seen to rise to almost 80 percent of gross domestic product in 2002. However, improved tax collection in 2002 kept the government deficit in check with the shortfall staying below 15 billion pesos. The deficit as of October 2002 stood at 215 billion pesos or the equivalent to about 4.7 percent of gross domestic product. The government's huge fiscal gap had prompted credit rating firms Standard & Poor and Fitch Ratings to downgrade their outlook on the Philippines to negative from stable.

DE CASTRO, NOLI (1949–). De Castro was a popular radio broadcaster for 25 years before he entered into politics. He was an anchorman of a highly rated radio/TV program, *Kabayan*, which also became his radio persona to his nationwide listeners. As a broadcaster, Noli de Castro, who hails from **Oriental Mindoro**, triggered investigations and enhanced his image as "Mr. Clean," an image that registered with 16 million voters and made him the topnotcher in the May

2001 senatorial elections. As a junior senator, De Castro authored the Local Government Transparency Act, which aims to end **graft and corruption** through transparency measures in the local government. He pursued issues such as environment protection, public service, and public safety, which Filipino voters consider essential to good government. In December 2003, President Gloria Macapagal Arroyo chose him for her running mate in the 2004 national elections. They won the elections with huge majorities. Since the office of vice president is a ceremonial position, De Castro was appointed as secretary of the department of social welfare.

DE LEON, MEDINA LACSON (1914–1990). A native of **Bataan**, where Philippine–American forces met defeat at the hands of the Japanese, Lacson De Leon was in the infamous **Death March** but escaped with several officers and men, who eventually formed guerrilla groups. She spent the war years as an undercover agent with the rank of a lieutenant colonel, frequently supplying food to the guerrillas. In 1949, De Leon was elected congresswoman for the lone district of Bataan. During her four-year term, she introduced bills to establish the Bataan National School of Arts and Trades and the Mindanao Institute of Technology, which upgraded the nursing profession. She was later appointed undersecretary of commerce and industry and headed delegations to international conferences. A lawyer by profession, she was active in such civic organizations as the Women Lawyers Association of the Philippines and the Community Chest. The Civic Assembly of Women in the Philippines recommended her for a Presidential Award of Merit for her distinguished contribution to the economic development of the Philippines and the Asian region.

DECENTRALIZATION. The Philippines politico-administrative system was highly centralized. Under the various constitutions, which the republic had adopted, centralization had always been deeply entrenched as the basic law of the land. A case in point was the disbursement of public funds: only 10 percent were under the control of local officials. The national government controlled as much as 87 percent of government programs. On April 24, 1991, the Supreme Court decided that for cases in which the law is capable of two interpretations, one in favor of centralized power and the other advantageous to local autonomy, the scales must be weighed in favor of local autonomy. This decision was a clear ruling mandating a bias for local autonomy.

President Corazon Aquino, who made decentralization a hallmark of her administration, utilized this decision in many of her decentralization projects. Many of the targeted provinces used their fund allocations for high priority programs directly related to the socioeconomic benefit of the people. The **nongovernmental organizations** (NGOs) often came into play by influencing local officials on the expenditure of their allocations.

One major impact of the decentralization program of Aquino was the establishment of the autonomous regions in Mindanao and Mountain Provinces. Under this arrangement, the executive department acts by intervening between the provinces and the national government. Control of infrastructure projects will be in the hands of the local government. *See also* AUTONOMOUS REGION IN MUSLIM MINDANAO; CORDILLERA AUTONOMOUS REGION.

DEEP SPOT. The world's second deepest underwater spot, known as Philippine Deep, is in the Philippines. This place found on the coast of Surigao del Sur has a recorded depth of 10, 430 meters (34,419 feet) below sea level. Also called the Mindanao Deep, this spot runs on the floor of the Philippine Sea. The world's deepest part of the ocean is the Marianas Trench, which is over 11,000 meters below sea level.

DEFORESTATION. A few hundred years ago, before the coming of the Spaniards, the Philippine archipelago was covered almost entirely by rain forests. By the time the Spanish arrived in the 16th century, scattered coastal areas had been cleared for agriculture and villages. Some forest had been cleared in the interior as well—particularly the terraced rice lands of the Central Cordillera of northern Luzon—but most coastal areas and the richest of the lowlands remained completely forested. At the end of more than 300 years of Spanish colonial rule, rain forests still covered about 70 percent of the land. Some islands had been heavily deforested, while others remained nearly untouched. Cebu Island was so badly deforested that ornithologists visiting the island in the 1890s reported that they could find no old-growth forest, and the neighboring islands of Bohol and Panay had less than half of their original forest. By 1992, the date of the most recent forest survey, old growth rain forests had declined to a shocking 9 percent. The extent of old-forest destruction, from 70 to less than 9 percent is considered the most rapid and severe in the world. Thus, the country is ranked as having the most severely endangered mammal and bird faunas—one of them the **Philippine eagle.** The degradation of the land has also contributed to increased floods and droughts as well as massive erosion and ground water depletion. Reforestation projects have already been going on in many areas under government initiative and aided by privately funded programs like **Project Good Roots**. *See also* FORESTRY; SUSTAINABLE DEVELOPMENT.

DE JESUS, GREGORIA (1875–1943). Heroine of the Philippine–Spanish Revolution. She was one of the first **women** members of the Katipunan, initiated on the night of her marriage to Supremeo **Andres Bonifacio** under the nome de guerre *Lakangbini* (princess). She was elected president of the Katipunan's women's chapter entrusted with keeping the society's secret papers, arms, and seal. She learned to ride a horse, shoot a rifle, and manipulate weapons. Her skills used in battle, Gregoria was a shining example to other patriotic women in the revolution. She helped create the first Katipunan flag. Widowed at 22 with the death of Bonifacio on May 10, 1897, Gregoria sought refuge in the hills of Pasig where she met the revolutionary composer Julio Nakpil, deputy to the ill-fated supremo. She bore Julio eight children, and discovered an artistic nature expressed in her wood carvings and hand-hammered kitchen utensils, cooking, embroidery, and poetry.

DE JESUS, JOSE CORAZON. *See* BALAGTASAN.

DEL CANO, SEBASTIAN. *See* FERDINAND MAGELLAN.

DEL MUNDO, FE (1911–). Known as the foremost pediatrician in the Philippines, Del Mundo was born in the island of **Marinduque**. She dedicated her life to the cause of pediatrics after observing children dying of diseases in her hometown. She finished her medical degree at the University of the Philippines, and went on to get a master's degree in bacteriology at Boston University. She concentrated her studies on the diseases of children, and devoted her research to immunization. Her work led to the invention of the incubator and the jaundice-relieving device, which was recognized as a major contribution to the world of medical technology. The incubator saved many prematurely born babies. Later on she established the Children's Medical Center and the Institute of Maternal and Child Health in Quezon City, which became a major pediatric training center for physicians, paramedics, and lay health workers in childcare.

Del Mundo also went to rural areas doing extension work. Because of her initiative the government started training rural medical workers in maternal, child health, and family planning. While actively pursuing her medical work, she wrote books, newspaper columns, and research papers on pediatrics. Her book entitled *Textbook of Pediatrics and Child Health* was used extensively in two medical schools in the Philippines. Her untiring devotion to childcare earned her the 1977 **Ramon Magsaysay award** for public service by a private citizen, and in 1980 the National Science Technology Authority proclaimed her the first Filipina National Scientist.

DEL PILAR, GREGORIO (1875–1899). Gregorio del Pilar, born in San Jose, Bulacan, considered the hero of **Tirad Pass** and one of the most romantic figures in Philippine history wrote these valiant words before he died: "I am surrounded by fearful odds that will overcome me and my gallant men, but I am pleased to die fighting for my beloved country." He was commanding **Emilio Aguinaldo's** rear guard with 60 poorly armed soldiers who faced a far better armed American battalion. The 24-year-old general and his men were annihilated, and the victorious invaders looted the corpses of the fallen. A chivalric American officer gave the hero an honorable burial with these words inscribed on his tombstone: "An officer and a gentleman."

DEL PILAR, MARCELO (1850–1896). Journalist and patriot. A lawyer by profession, Marcelo Del Pilar was an early participant in the revolutionary movement through his readings of Jose Rizal's novels. He founded the ***Diariong Tagalog*** and in its columns agitated for reforms. He denounced the "**friarocracy**" or government of friars and was consequently blacklisted by the Spanish friars. Forced to flee to Spain, he continued to denounce the abusive policies of the civil government in the Philippines. With anticlerical ferment brewing at home, Del Pilar in Spain stoked the fires of the revolution with his fiery articles in *La Solidaridad*, which he took over after its first editor, **Graciano Lopez Jaena**, resigned. During his six-year editorship, he wrote numerous editorials, articles, and pamphlets on the theme of liberty and equality for the Filipinos. Copies of the pamphlets written in simple Tagalog were smuggled into the Philippines and read by the revolutionists with great interest. He was preparing to return home when his life was cut short by tuberculosis. Del Pilar died in Barcelona, a pauper, just weeks before the revolution began. Historians described Del Pilar as the most intelligent and indefatigable leader of the Filipino separatists in the 1880s, and the real soul of the **propaganda movement**, which preceded the Philippine revolution of 1896.

DEL ROSARIO, ALBERT (1941–). Appointed Philippine ambassador to the United States by President Gloria Macapagal Arroyo, he brought strong business expertise and diplomatic skills to his post. Del Rosario, who graduated from New York University with a B.S. degree in economics, started his four-decade business career in the Philippines by working in the field of insurance, banking, real estate, shipping, telecommunications, consumer products, pharmaceutical, and food industries. In between his many corporate chairmanships, Del Rosario was actively involved in promoting social and civic causes—fund drives for cancer, rural eye clinics, and education. He was also a keen supporter of sports and was the chair of the martial arts association. In recognition of his civic works, he received the Philippine Army Award, and for his efforts in promoting democracy President Gloria Macapagal Arroyo honored him with the EDSA II Heroes Award. Well-regarded by American officials, Del Rosario has successfully promoted his country's interests—investments, trade, and economic aid—in the United States. In 2004, he resigned his post to return to private life. *See also* FOREIGN RELATIONS.

DEMETRIOS, ARISTEDES. *See* CORREGIDOR.

DE VILLA, RENATO. *See* COUP D'ETAT.

DEWEY, GEORGE (1837–1917). Victor of the **battle of Manila Bay**. He commanded the Asiatic Squadron of seven cruisers, which were lying at anchor in Hong Kong Bay and waiting for orders to engage the Spanish fleet at Manila. Upon receiving the orders, Dewey led the American warships on his flagship, USS *Olympia*, into Manila Bay and attacked the Spanish fleet, which was caught by surprise. All Spanish vessels were sunk or destroyed. The casualties included 381 seamen. Dewey was hailed as the "hero of Manila Bay" and was given a hero's welcome when he returned to New York City. Dewey was born in Montpelier, Vermont, and he studied at the U.S. Naval Academy at Annapolis. He was an executive officer of the USS *Mississippi* during the Civil War. The *Olympia* is permanently docked at the Philadelphia naval shipyard as a tourist attraction.

DIARIONG TAGALOG. First Tagalog newspaper published in Manila in 1882 by its founder **Marcelo Del Pilar**, who had his own press. The newspaper launched the first propaganda movement asking for reforms in the Spanish colonial government. Because of its anti-Spanish slant—exposing the abuses and tyranny of the Spanish clergy and civil officials—the authorities ordered its closure and the arrest of Del Pilar, who had to flee the country. The paper had only six months of life. Its closure did not stop other Filipino journalists from starting other papers with the same anti-Spanish sentiment. Some of these were *Patnubay*, *Ang Pliegong Tagalog*, and *Kalayaan*, which also had brief publication lives. They planted the seeds of protest that blossomed into a full-scale revolution in 1896. *See also* MASS MEDIA.

DIGOS. *See* DAVAO DEL SUR.

DIOKNO, JOSE W. (1922–1987). A zealous **human rights** advocate, Jose W. Diokno was one of the hundreds of political, civic, and social leaders—incarcerated during the **martial law** period of President **Ferdinand Marcos**. For lambasting the unlawful arrests of citizens who opposed martial law, Diokno was jailed and languished there for two years together with **Benigno Aquino Jr**. As a senator, twice re-elected, Diokno was considered "pro-people" in the senate for championing the rights of the masses by introducing legislation, which humanized the system of taxation. He was against the imposition of more taxes on the poor and believed that the rich should carry more of the burden of taxation by increasing taxes on their real estate and private automobiles. He also introduced laws that regulated the petroleum industry, which was fully controlled by four refineries and set the high price, which were a burden on thousands of **jeepney** drivers. For four consecutive years—1967–1970—he was voted outstanding senator by the prestigious *Philippine Free Press.*

Marcos released Diokno from prison in 1974. He immediately organized the Free Legal Assistance Group, which provided free legal services for the victims of military oppression under martial law. From the time he was released from prison, Diokno fearlessly fought for the restoration of Philippine democracy together with **Jovito Salonga** and **Lorenzo Tañada** who were the towering figures in opposition rallies denouncing the Marcos regime from 1974 up to the **EDSA** revolution in February 1986.

After the ouster of Marcos and the accession of Corazon **Aquino** to the presidency, Diokno was appointed chairman of the presidential committee on human rights. He tried to negotiate the return of rebel forces to the folds of the law. However, after the "**Mendiola Massacre**" of January 22, 1987, where 19 farmers died during an otherwise peaceful rally, Diokno resigned from his two government posts in protest at what he called "wanton disregard" of human lives by an administration he had helped install. As a crusading senator he brought his legal expertise and brilliant mind to bear on issues such as the nuclear arms race and American intervention in Philippine affairs. He was the driving force behind the nationalist and democratic movement in the country.

DIPOLOG. *See* ZAMBOANGA DEL NORTE.

DIWA, LADISLAO (1863–1930). A native of Cavite, Diwa obtained a B.A. degree from the Colegio de San Juan de Letran, Manila. He met **Andres Bonifacio** and joined him in the founding of the revolutionary society Katipunan. Diwa, Bonifacio, and Teodoro Plata formed the first triangle of the secret association. His responsibility was to propagate Katipunan revolutionary teachings in central Luzon. In 1901, when Emilio Aguinaldo was captured, effectively ending the

Philippine–American Revolution, Diwa settled down as a court clerk in Cavite.

DIWATA. In ancient Filipino culture, the *diwata* or *anito* was the dominant concept in the religion. The *anito* concept was pervasive in Luzon, while the *diwata* prevailed in Visayas and Mindanao. According to anthropologist F. Landa Jocano, the *diwata* or *anito* refer to an ancient spirit, a deity or groups of deities, sculptured objects, a body of shared ideas and symbols, and to events associated with religious phenomena. The terms were used by ancient Filipinos to emphasize the existence of a body of beliefs and practices associated with supernatural beings. In the structure of precolonial cosmology, some deities were perceived to be very close to men and participated actively in their affairs. Others took an interest in human affairs only when invoked during proper ceremonies that compelled them to come down to earth. Most of the deities did not have any definite rank or power at all. The deity considered the most powerful by the **Tagalogs** was *Bathala*. *Bathala* is considered the creator, protector, and keeper of the people. *See also* BABAYLAN; SINGKIL.

DOCTORS WITHOUT BORDERS (DWB). Volunteer doctors from the United States and Europe who visit the Philippines to deliver emergency aid to victims of armed conflict, epidemics, and natural and man-made disasters, and to others who lack health care due to social or geographical isolation. DWB, also known as *Médecins Sans Frontiéres (MSF)*, was founded in 1971 by a group of French doctors who believed that all people have the right to medical care and that the needs of these people supersede respect for national borders. It was the first **nongovernmental organization** to provide emergency medical assistance and publicly assist in the plight of the poor, mostly in remote **barrios**, unreached by health providers. One of their popular medical services is the work with children who were born with harelips—congenital fissure of the upper lips. Many children received emergency repair and thus enhanced their esteem among their peers.

DRILON, FRANKLIN (1945–). Drilon was the Senate president of the Philippine legislative when he was drafted by the **Liberal Party** as their standard-bearer in the May 2004 elections. Before he was elected senator in 1995, Drilon served in the cabinets of presidents **Corazon Aquino** and **Fidel Ramos** in various capacities—labor, justice, and executive secretary. In his first senatorial campaign, he ran on the slogan *"Kontra sa Krimin, Justicia Agad"* (Against Crime, Justice Now) that resonated with the voters and elected him, placing fourth in the slate of 12 elected solons. In keeping with his political platform, he introduced legislations to improve the justice system. He not only concentrated on the country's justice system, he also drafted and submitted bills for the benefit of the working class: on banking, housing, and electoral reforms. Drilon's political base is the Western Visayas.

DULA, LANG. *See* LIVING TREASURES.

DUMAGAT. *See* AURORA.

DUMAGUETE. *See* NEGROS ISLAND.

DUNGEON. *See* FORT SANTIAGO.

DUTCH. Dutch interest in the Philippines was of a commercial nature. The competition with Spain over the profitable spice trade in the East Indies (now Indonesia) in the 17th century led to fierce naval battles between the two nations. The Dutch learned from the Chinese about heavy trading going on in Manila, and they wanted to have a share in the profits. Because the two nations were engaged in the Dutch–Spanish War (1567–1648), Spain denied the entry of Dutch merchant ships to Manila. In 1600, a Dutch fleet under the command of Admiral Oliver Van Noordt was sent to Manila, which the Spanish met with their own fleet under Captain General Antonio de Morga. A six-hour naval battle took place off the coast of Bataan on December 14, 1600. Morga's flagship was sunk, but the Dutch warships were also heavily damaged. Van Noordt and his remaining crew managed to escape to Borneo. In 1607, another Dutch fleet blockaded Manila Bay but was repelled by a force under Governor Juan de Silva. The Dutch continued their harassment of Manila and other Spanish settlements in the Visayan Islands, but they later gave up their attacks when they captured Malacca in 1640 and concentrated their military and naval power on the colonization of the East Indies. *See also* BRITISH OCCUPATION OF MANILA; *SAN DIEGO* WARSHIP.

– E –

EARTHQUAKES. The country is crisscrossed by large geological fractures along which any dislocation can produce a tectonic earthquake. The government compiles and publishes data on significant earthquakes. Earthquakes of a severe nature have been experienced in the Philippines. The Lanao earthquake of 1955 was one of several quakes that hit the country. In August 1968, the quake in Luzon killed more than 300 persons. In 1970, a main shock was felt in Luzon and Visayas but there were no casualties. On August 17, 1983, the worst earthquake in 52 years hit northern Luzon. On July 16, 1990, Luzon was hit by a severe quake of a magnitude of 7.7 with the epicenter near Cabanatuan City, **Nueva Ecija**. A second killer quake with the same magnitude wrought havoc in the **Baguio**-Benguet area. Together, these quakes killed 1,283 persons and left 120,021 homeless.

ECONOMIC DEVELOPMENT CORPS (EDCOR). A land settlement program to rehabilitate former members of the **Hukbalahaps**, EDCOR was the successful answer to communism developed in 1950 by **Ramon Magsaysay**, defense secretary of President **Elpidio Quirino**. Under this program, former Huks who had surrendered were each given a 10 hectare (25 acre) plot of land in Mindanao. With the help of army engineers forest lands in the Kapatagan Valley in Lanao were cleared and divided into plots. Former Huk soldiers and their families were brought over to the project and given tools and provisions with which to start their new lives. In the Kapatagan project, 1,680 hectares (4,150 acres) were awarded to some thousand former Huks. Another project was opened in 1951 in Cotabato province to accommodate additional surrendering Huks and another in Isabela province in 1954. The attainment of these projects effectively counteracted the Communist slogan "Land for the Landless."

ECONOMY. Despite the economic and political shocks, both internal and external, in the past administrations (**Ramos, Estrada**, and

Arroyo), the Philippine economy proved to be resilient and posted growth in real Gross Domestic Product (GPD) of 3.2 percent in 2002, one of the highest in Southeast Asia. This growth was evident during the stewardship of President **Gloria Macapagal Arroyo** when the GDP grew by 4.1 percent compared to 3.0 percent in 2002. On the supply side, the three major sectors of the economy and their corresponding increase are services 5.1 percent, industry 3.8 percent, and **agriculture** 2.3 percent. The strength of services owes a great deal to the innovation-inducing liberalization and deregulation measures pursued over the past few years. **Telecommunications**, following the opening up of long-distance service and mandatory interconnection, continues to grow. The growth of private services—including call centers, backroom operations, and software design—owes a lot to the acceleration of the development of the information and communication technology sector. Thanks to the government's agriculture and **fisheries** modernization program, the sector is getting diversified. The vagaries of weather have slightly slowed production. However, bumper crop **rice** came through in 2002 that gave the economy the biggest kick to growth. Domestic demand continues to be lifted by low inflation. The slowdown in exports in 2002 appeared to be a blip as a result of the U.S. performance. Imports for the same period were strong and indicated also a strong production. Manufacturing and processing of textiles, furniture, and handicrafts are industries that employ a large number of people. Most of the manufactured goods are exported to the United States, European countries, **Japan**, and **Taiwan**. Although it has heavy debts the Philippines is far from defaulting on its loans from the International Monetary Fund (IMF) and the World Bank, in spite of drastically devaluing its currency, suffering from hyperinflation, and shutting its financial operations so that its reserve is not depleted. The government has improved its tax collection and revenue from other sources to stem the tide of budgetary deficits. The unemployment rate was 11 percent in 2002. Tensions in the Middle East have affected exports and dampened domestic demand. High poverty incidence and joblessness—products of long years of neglect and inappropriate policies—will continue to be major economic problems. *See also* AGRICULTURE; DEBT STOCK; INVESTMENT.

EDSA I. Acronym for Epifanio de los Santos avenue, Manila, which was the scene of the four-day (February 22–25, 1986) revolution against the Ferdinand Marcos regime. This avenue skirts Camps Crame and Aguinaldo, where Minister of Defense **Juan Ponce Enrile** and General **Fidel Ramos** and their forces took their stand and demanded the resignation of President Marcos. Under Marcos' orders the military surrounded the army camps with tanks and combat equipped soldiers. Their supporters were threatened with annihilation and Enrile and Ramos appealed to Manila's Archbishop **Jaime Cardinal Sin**, who went on the radio and rallied the people to provide help and food to the beleaguered forces. Hundreds of thousands of people went to EDSA to form human barricades against Marcos' tanks and soldiers who, fearful of a massacre, disobeyed commands to attack the camps and thus averted a tragedy. This event, known as "People Power," became the rallying force for **Corazon Aquino**, who claimed victory in the presidential election. "People Power" quickly spread throughout the country. In Cebu City several military officers supporting Aquino seized Camp Osmeña. People heeded the appeal of the Roman Catholic bishop to form human barricades around the camp. Although some 15 people died in the EDSA revolution in Manila, the event marked the high point of the people's nationwide peaceful protest against the authoritarian rule of Marcos. Since Marcos lost the support of the United States, he was forced to relinquish power and had to flee to Hawaii.

EDSA II (PEOPLE POWER). A massive but nonviolent protest that took place on January 16–20, 2001, at the EDSA shrine, Quezon City, and in various plazas in the country that resulted in the ouster of **Joseph Ejercito Estrada** and brought **Gloria Macapagal Arroyo** to the presidency. Also called "**people power**" it was initiated and carried out openly by civilians, mostly students, their parents, business executives, private and public employees. **EDSA I** was the first mass peaceful and successful protest, which forced Ferdinand Marcos out of power in 1986. Since the movement started in the Epifanio de los Santos Avenue, Quezon City, marchers adopted the acronym EDSA. To commemorate the historic movement supporters raised money to build a shrine on the avenue. It has since become a symbol for People Power where protests are held and thus prevent huge traffic jams on Manila streets. EDSA II was a continuation of the process of restoration of democracy and its consolidation.

EDUCATION. The educational system of the Philippines is patterned after the American system of formal and nonformal education in public (government-owned) and private (nongovernment) schools. The Philippines is using a bilingual medium of instruction. Certain subjects are taught in English and the national language—**Filipino**—and local dialects, particularly in the lower grades.

Formal education is a sequential progression of academic schooling at three levels, namely elementary, secondary, and higher education. The first level, elementary or primary education involves compulsory and free six grades in public schools and seven grades in some private schools, in addition to optional preschool programs—kindergarten and nursery schooling. Children at the age of three or four may enter nursery school until five and at six years old enter grade one. The secondary level consists of four years of high school. The student starts high school at age 12 and graduates at 15. The third level is higher education where a student enters at age 16. As in the American system, higher education is divided into collegiate, master's, and doctorate levels in various disciplines. Medical and law schools takes as long as eight years. Graduate school is an additional two years. There is a postsecondary schooling that consists of two- or three-year non-degree technical or technician courses. The non-formal system of education is aimed at school dropouts and adult illiterates, who cannot avail themselves of formal education, like a functional literacy program for nonliterate and semiliterate adults that integrates basic **literacy** with livelihood skills training.

The Philippine Constitution has specific provisions that require education to be accorded the highest budgetary priority. The responsibility for administering, supervising, and regulating basic education (elementary and secondary) is vested in the Department of Education, Culture and Sports (DECS) while that of higher education is handled by the Commission on Higher Education. The postsecondary technical-vocational education is under the Technical Education and Skills Development Authority (TESDA) that is also in charge of skills orientation, training, and development of school dropouts and unemployed adults. There are more than 50,000 schools at all levels, of which 84 percent are public. The pupil-teacher ratio in primary education is 33:1 for the public sector and 35:1 for the private sector—the internationally accepted standard is 40:1. In the secondary level, there are over 6,000 schools, of which 59 percent are public. Of the more than 1,600 higher educational institutions, 80 percent are private. A majority of these institutions are sponsored by religious orders or church denominations. English is the language of instruction in higher education. Colleges and universities hold classes on the semestral system from the months of June through March, which coincides with the term of the public schools. *See also* LANGUAGE; LEGAL EDUCATION; LITERACY; MADRASAH; STATE COLLEGES AND UNIVERSITIES.

ELECTORAL SYSTEM. The electoral system was established in the 1987 Constitution. It set the positions and terms of offices of elected officials as follows: at the national level, the president and vice president are elected for six-year terms. The legislature consists of the Senate and the House of Representatives. The 24 members of the Senate serve for six years; half are selected every three years. The 200-member houses, plus **sectoral** representatives appointed by the president, serve three-year terms. Local government officials including governors, provincial councilors, municipal and city mayors, municipal and city councilors are elected to three-year terms. Senators, congressmen, and local government officials are elected in midterm elections, but during presidential election years, everyone is elected at the same time.

Elections in the Philippines are based on plurality. Whoever receives the largest number of votes wins. Voters are required to write down the names of individual candidates. Votes are counted by hand at the precinct level. Then precinct returns are canvassed at the municipal level, municipal returns at the provincial level, and only then added up at the **Commission on Elections** (COMELEC) in Manila. Elections are supervised by the COMELEC, a constitutionally mandated body. Political parties are required to register with the COMELEC with a verified petition with attachments including constitution, by-laws, and platform. *See also* DAGDAG-BAWAS; POLITICAL PARTIES; SECTORAL PARTIES.

EL FILIBUSTERISMO. This is Jose Rizal's second polemic novel written in Spanish and published in Belgium on September 1891. The title comes from the French form "filibuster," as derived from the word "flyboot" or the Dutch word "fileboot," or in short, the rebel. The book was dedicated to the three priests Mariano Gomez, Jose Burgos, and Jacinto Zamora (**GOMBURZA**)—who were unjustly and cruelly executed by the Spaniards. *El Filibusterismo* in its abbreviated form is a continuation of the *Noli Me Tangere* in its plot. Crisostomo Ibarra is obsessed with the overthrow of colonial rule. He points out the corruption of the ruling class, their arrogance toward the natives—who were called derisively **Indios**—and the oppression machinery. The *Fili* contains dramatic and romantic elements of the social novel of the late 19th century influenced by Alexander Dumas. It is essentially a call to revolution.

EL SHADDAI. *See* VELARDE, MARIANO.

ELIZALDE, MANUEL JR. *See* TASADAY HOAX.

ENCOMIENDA. Landed estates of the Spaniards. During the Spanish colonization of the Philippines, Spaniards were granted vast tracts of land by the Spanish king as a reward for their services in subjugating the country. Governor-General Miguel Lopez de Legaspi started this system in 1568 at the orders of King Philip II. The Philippines was parceled out and large allotments of land called *encomiendas* were given to Spanish soldiers, civilians, and religious orders. The people who lived in these *encomiendas* became tenants, and they had to pay an annual **tribute**, a kind of head tax, to Spain. The *encomienderos* made great fortunes in the collection of tributes. The tributes increased annually and the people hated the payments because of the humiliating manner of collection. The Spanish king abolished the *encomienda* system in 1674 due to the evils and abuses committed by the *encomiendero*. However, the vassalage to Spain continued in the form of forced labor. It was compulsory for all natives from 16 to 60 years of age to work without pay in the building and repair of roads and churches, cutting of timber, and working in shipyards. The exploitation and oppression led to sporadic uprisings against Spanish activities. Records have shown that there were 300 **revolts** during the 380 years of Spanish rule. *See also* CACIQUE; KASAMA.

ENERGY. The bulk of the country's energy is derived from oil-fired thermal plants powered by imported petroleum. Hydroelectric power and coal account for most of the remainder. Because of the burgeoning population and increasing energy needs, frequent and prolonged shortages (brownouts) occur in the cities. The Philippines has an energy plan to develop its own sources of supply to meet domestic needs. Prompted by the world oil crises in 1972 and 1978, the government issued policy reforms, which called for the centralization of all regulatory functions of the power industry under one government body. This Energy Regulatory Board was empowered with adjudicatory functions as well. A reversal in world crude oil prices between 1987 and 1989 increased the industrial energy requirements by 8 percent, which outstripped the 5.5 percent annual growth in gross domestic product. Much of the energy needs were met by oil.

In 1987, the government launched an intensive promotional campaign to increase investment in oil exploration. The resulting surge in exploration led to oil discoveries in **Palawan** the most significant of which are the Camago, west Linapacan, **Calauit**, and Octon oil and gas finds. **Malampaya** gasfield in northwest Palawan has a recoverable reserve of 2.4 to 4 trillion cubic feet of natural gas. The aggregate demand for petroleum products is projected to grow at a steady rate of 5 percent annually over the next ten years. In terms of energy, about 57,000 megawatt capacity will be required for 2005 to 2025. The share of indigenous energy increases significantly due to additional capacity from geothermal steam and natural gas reserves. Wider use of coal from the 293 megawatt mineable reserves will be undertaken. The window for local coal will start in 2006. The optimal utilization of these indigenous resources will result in about 50 percent of the expected capacity required for the the period 2005–2025.

ENRILE, JUAN PONCE (1924–). Juan Ponce Enrile played a vital role in the ouster of Ferdinand Marcos and the elevation of Corazon Aquino as president of the Philippines in the disputed snap elections of 1986. Together with General **Fidel Ramos**, then commander of the National Constabulary, he issued a joint statement demanding **Ferdi-**

nand Marcos' resignation. However, Marcos upstaged them by having himself sworn into office in **Malacañang** Palace on February 25. At the same time, Marcos ordered his troops to storm the rebel headquarters of Enrile and Ramos at Camp Aguinaldo. Only the timely intervention of **Jaime Cardinal Sin**, Roman Catholic archbishop of Manila, saved them from being crushed when he broadcast an appeal to the people to block the government troops. Marcos had lost the battle to stay in office and he went reluctantly into exile in Hawaii.

Enrile's checkered career as a politician was tainted by his involvement in a coup d' etat costing him his post as national defense minister. On February 27, 1990, he was accused of the high crimes of rebellion and murder for which there was no bail. Later the **Supreme Court** threw out the charges and Enrile was released from prison. His imprisonment boosted his popularity, which he capitalized on in winning election as senator in the 1992 general elections. He lost his reelection bid in 2002 for siding with the deposed **Joseph Ejercito Estrada**. He was reelected senator in the 2004 elections under the banner of **Fernando Poe Jr.**

EPISCOPAL CHURCH. *See* CORDILLERA; SAGADA.

ESPERANZA. *See* AGUSAN DEL SUR.

ESTRADA, JOSEPH EJERCITO (1937–). A successful movie actor turned politician who became the 13th president of the Philippines. Elected with the largest plurality in the 1998 presidential elections, Estrada served for only 31 months until he was ousted on January 19, 2001, by "people power" (**EDSA II**) following charges of allegedly amassing a huge amount of money—$64 million—received from illegal gambling payoffs (**jueteng**), tobacco tax kickbacks, and questionable government investments. In the impeachment charges, he was also accused of violating the Constitution by participating in real estate businesses controlled by his family. His ill-gotten assets, which were deposited in a number of Philippine banks, were frozen while he and his son faced trial for the crime of **plunder**—penalized under a law which he himself signed as a senator—that carries a maximum penalty of death. Estrada denied wrongdoing. During his brief tenure, prominent businessmen complained about his poor management style and his disinterest in the direction of the economy. Estrada was on the verge of resigning as early as November 3, 2000, when his government came under heavy siege with widespread demands for his resignation.

Estrada entered politics in 1969 as mayor of Manila's San Juan suburb and served for 16 years while continuing a successful acting role as a macho man in many Pilipino movies that won the hearts of the Filipino people and brought several best actor awards. In 1987, he was elected senator. One of the acts he authored was the creation of the Philippine Carabao Center for the propagation of the **carabao** to enable farmers to secure good quality stock. He became vice president in 1992 in a landslide vote. Since he belonged to a different party, President **Fidel Ramos** appointed him chairman of the Presidential Anti-Crime Commission. He successfully pursued leaders of organized crime. In 2004, the plunder trial of Estrada was still going on before the **Sandiganbayan** and he remains in detention in a police camp. His son Jose Estrada, who was free on bail as an accomplice in the plunder case, ran for senator in the May 10, 2004, elections under the party of **Fernando Poe Jr.** and got elected. However, government prosecutors vowed to pursue the corruption charges against the son and the deposed president.

ETHNIC MINORITIES. There are more than a hundred tribal groups that constitute approximately 3 percent of the population. Seven principal ethnic groups live in the Cordillera Mountains. These highlanders are the Ifugao, Bontoc, Kankanay, Ibaloi, Kalinga, Tinguian, and Isneg. Other minority groups consist of lowlanders such as the Gaddangs and the Ilongots. Negritos (Aetas), who lead nomadic lives, reside in scattered mountain ranges in central Luzon, Panay, and Negros Island. The other major concentration of ethnic minorities is in Mindanao, and consists of the Manobo, Bukidnon, Bagobo, Mandaya, Mansaka, Subanon, Mamanuas, Bilaan, Tiruray, and T'boli. All of these tribal groups are under the protection of the Office of Minority and Cultural Affairs, which has the responsibility of preserving the cultural and ethnic identities of tribal peoples and aiding them in adjusting to the problems of a changing society. The **Indigenous Peoples' Right Act** of 1997 has bolstered their territorial rights. *See also* LUMADS.

EUROPEAN UNION (EU). President Gloria Macapagal Arroyo received a major boost to her poverty programs when the European Union made a historic grant of 63 million Euros to the Philippine government. In 2004, the EU and the Philippine government signed three cooperation agreements aimed at eliminating poverty, promoting good governance, and supporting economic, social, and environmental development projects. The grant called the National Indicative Program (NIP) will be implemented up to 2006 in the poorest areas of the country and will focus on supporting government programs on poverty alleviation, trade, and investment promotion. These programs were planned to increase access to justice for the poor and vulnerable groups, and prevent corruption. By removing both grievances and the opportunities that contribute to terrorism and political violence, the programs will improve service delivery to the poor and enhance the country's standing as a partner for foreign investment and trade.

EVANGELISTA, CRISANTO. *See* COMMMUNIST PARTY.

– F –

FEDERAL PARTY (FEDERALISTAS). One of the short-lived political parties organized during the early 1900s, which advocated American sovereignty and the incorporation of the Philippines into the American statehood system. Its founders T. H. Pardo de Tavera, Benito Legarda, **Cayetano Arellano**, and **Felipe Buencamino Sr.** enjoyed only lukewarm support from the American governor-general. When support for the party waned in 1907, it was reorganized to become the Progressive Party. The statehood idea was abandoned, and support was given instead to the independence movement, for which there was much greater public approval. *See also* JONES LAW; TYDINGS-MCDUFFIE ACT.

FELIPE, JULIAN. *See* NATIONAL ANTHEM.

FERTIG, WENDELL. *See* GUERRILLA.

FESTIVALS. May is the month of religious festivals and **fiestas**, when folks in the countryside gather in their harvest, and when innumerable flowers and trees—the **sampaguita**, **ylang-ylang**, *cadena de amor, calachuchi*, and fire trees blossom with flowers. May is a month-long celebration of thanksgiving and offering. Named after Maia, the Roman goddess of spring and growth, the month signifies rejuvenation. May is harvest time in the rural areas when farm families hold their thanksgiving celebrations where the centerpiece is their offerings of the first fruits to their ancestors and gods. *Atang* or *alay* means "offerings" and *pasasalamat* means "thanksgiving." These folk rituals have many forms and faces in the provinces and everyone—young and old—is involved. In Samar, the festival is called *pahoy-pahoy;* in Quezon, *aranya't balwarte* and *pahiyas*; in Bulacan, *aurorahan*, and the famous *Santakrusan* reliving Queen Helena's search and discovery of the cross. Fishermen also have their thanksgiving celebration—*pintakasi.* In Dagupan City, **Pangasinan**, they celebrate their famed *bangus* fish festival (*kalutan*), which won a Guinness World Record in 2003 for the longest barbeque (1,008 meters). For Filipino Catholics, Flores de Mayo tops all May celebrations for its colorful pageantry and religious procession. *See also* MORO-MORO.

FIESTA (PISTA). To most Filipinos, the celebration of the annual town fiesta—feast-day of the patron saint—has deep religious and historic significance. Most towns and cities have patron saints, which were introduced by early Spanish friars to replace *diwatas* (spirits) worshipped by the natives. The celebration is traditionally held on the birthday of the saint and is observed with a religious procession and high mass. Over the years, the traditional *pista* has evolved in varying shapes and forms, and for different reasons. In Manila, the Feast of the **Black Nazarene** is held in marked contrast to the revelry of the **ati-atihan** of Kalibo, Aklan. The fiesta of Obando, **Bulacan**, is known for the intense dancing—a celebration of fertility. A special feature in fiestas, however, is the culinary and gustatory delights that are lavishly served to guests. It is during fiestas when the town or local food—special **cuisine**—is featured. Of course, the main *piece de resistance* is often the **lechon**. One regular fare of prewar town fiestas was the **zarzuela** that enthralled audiences with its musicality and dramatic action. In most towns, fiestas are observed for two to three days, with well-to-do families serving as hosts—providing the wherewithal—for the entire celebration. Today, the Philippine fiesta, while it still preserves its religious roots, has become more of a cultural and entertainment festival with its profusion of colors, revelry, and pageantry. *See also* FESTIVALS.

FILIPINIZATION. A nationalist movement, which started during the time of **Gregorio Aglipay**, founder of the Philippine Independent Church (*Iglesia Filipina Independiente*) (IFI). During the revolution against Spain, he advocated the placement of Filipino priests in all Roman Catholic Churches. This movement led to the establishment of the IFI Church. **Francis Burton Harrison** started appointing Filipinos to cabinet positions during his term (1913–1921) as governor-general. Eventually Filipinos held a majority of civil service positions, much to the anger and distress of American bureaucrats in the islands. Toward the end of the Harrison term, the government was almost completely in the hands of capable Filipinos. Many of them were **pensionados** who had been trained in the United States. The statistics for 1921 showed a total of 13,240 Filipinos and 614 American administrators. Critics accused the governor-general of transforming a colonial government of Americans aided by Filipinos into a government of Filipinos aided by Americans.

FILIPINO. This is the generic name of people of the Philippines. It is derived from Filipinas, which was the name given by Miguel Lopez de Legaspi after his benefactor King Felipe II of Spain. The name Filipino was originally ascribed to those of Spanish descent who were born in the islands. The native people were called by the pejorative term *Indios*. Filipino came into use only when the Americans took over the islands and kept the name Philippines. The word Pilipino refers to the language, which is another name for **Tagalog**, the prevalent language in the provinces of Rizal, Batangas, Cavite, Bulacan, Nueva Ecija, and Quezon. Another name for Filipino is **Pinoy.** *See also* TSINOY.

FILIPINO–AMERICAN GENERALS. Three Filipino–Americans have the distinction of becoming U.S. Army generals. They are Major General Edward Soriano, Brigadier General Archine Laano, and Major General **Antonio M. Taguba**. Soriano and Taguba are so far the only Filipino–Americans to have attained the rank of major general in the

U.S. Armed Forces. Soriano was born in **Pangasinan** and migrated to the United States with his family at an early age. In 2001, he was the director of operations, readiness, and mobilization at the office of America's Deputy Chief of Staff for Operations and Plans. Laano, on the other hand, is a physician by profession and a 1963 graduate of the University of the Philippines College of Medicine. President Ronald Reagan appointed him brigadier general in 1988. Taguba received his appointment as major general from President George W. Bush in May 2003. He was born in Manila, and moved to Hawaii at age 11. He is a graduate of Idaho State University with a B.A. degree in history and the United States College of Naval Command and Staff with an M.A. degree in national security and strategic studies.

FILIPINO FIRST POLICY. When **Carlos P. Garcia** became president in 1957, he enunciated his twin policies of austerity and Filipino first. These policies were promulgated as a resolution of the National Economic Council on August 28, 1958. Under this policy priority was given to Filipinos engaging in enterprises and industries vital to the economic growth, stability, and security of the country. In joint venture enterprises of foreigners and Filipinos, Filipinos should own 60 percent of stock. This policy led to pained cries of "anti-foreignism" from powerful alien interests, specifically American and Chinese. *See also* NEOCOLONIALISM.

FILIPINO MIGRATION TO THE UNITED STATES. Even prior to the U.S. annexation of the Philippines, there was already a Filipino community in Louisiana. However, it was the American colonization of the Philippines that paved the way for an exodus of Filipinos to the United States. There were two types of Filipino migrants who went to the United States. One type was comprised of the educated and, initially, middle class Filipinos who came as **pensionados**, or government scholars, for the purpose of furthering their education and training in the U.S. The second type were poor Filipinos who came as a cheap migrating labor supply for the Hawaii plantations, California farms, and Alaska fishing industry. While most of the pensionados went home after several years of schooling, most of the Filipino migrant workers eventually made the U.S. their new homeland. The civil rights legislation in the United States in the 1950s, which included a drastic change in immigration laws, further increased Filipino migration. Today, there are more than two million Filipinos in the U.S. and they constitute the second biggest Asian community in the country. *See also* BALIKBAYAN; BRAIN DRAIN; OVERSEAS FOREIGN WORKERS.

FILIPINO PARTY/PARTIDO FILIPINO. Formed in 1991 by Eduardo Cojuangco, the estranged cousin of President **Corazon Aquino**, as a vehicle to launch his presidential candidacy in the 1992 elections. Cojuangco was one of Ferdinand Marcos' close **cronies**, who were accused of graft and corruption before the **Presidential Commission on Good Government**. During the Marcos regime, he controlled the giant coconut and sugar industries and amassed a fortune. When the Marcos regime collapsed, he fled with Ferdinand Marcos to Hawaii. Cojuangco slipped back into the country during a coup d' état to face criminal charges and, at the same time, to seek the country's highest political office. With his millions he ran a well-oiled political machine, spending freely on advertising and personnel. In spite of his huge war chest, his party came in last in the seven-candidate race for the presidency.

FINANCE. *See* CENTRAL BANK; MONETARY SYSTEM.

FIRST PHILIPPINE COMMISSION (SCHURMAN COMMISSION). Appointed by President William McKinley to report on the extension of American authority in the Philippines at the end of the **Philippine–American Revolution** in 1901, Jacob Gould Schurman headed a commission to find the most effective way to facilitate American rule in the islands. His civilian team included **Dean Worcester** and Charles Denby. Their hearings, conducted in Manila, with only 60 mostly wealthy Filipinos and *ilustrados* as witnesses, produced a flawed report on the prevailing political and economic conditions of the country. The report supported America's supremacy throughout the archipelago and recommended that Filipinos be allowed limited self-government under U.S. supervision. The Schurman Commission's report was well received by President McKinley, who later sent a Second Philippine Commission headed by **William Howard Taft** to further implement his policies. *See also* MANIFEST DESTINY.

FISHING INDUSTRY. Fish and other seafood are a major source of protein for 60 percent of the people and provide a livelihood to about a million people. Fishery resources are divided broadly into marine and inland resources. As a result of the declaration of the 200-mile zone, the marine waters of the Philippines cover a total area of 2,200,000 square kilometers. Some of the richest fishing grounds are to be found in western and central **Visayas**. Inland water resources comprise about 20,000 hectares (49,000 acres) of lakes, 19,000 hectares (47,000 acres) of reservoirs, 31,000 hectares (77,000 acres) of rivers, and an aggregate area of 222,000 hectares (550,000 acres) of developed brackish water and freshwater fishponds. Recently developed **aquaculture** produces prawns, which are mostly exported to the United States.

A total of 2,157 fish species have already been identified in the country. The 10 major species of fish caught in Philippine waters are the following: round scad (*galunggong*), sardines (*tamban, tunsoy*), frigate tunas (*tulingan*), anchovies (*dilis*), slipmouth (*sapsap*), yellow fish (albacore), big-eyed scad (*matang baka, bisugo*), round herring (*tulis*), and skipjack (*gulayasan*). Other important species include mullet (*banak*), fusilier (*dalagang bukid*), bream, grouper (*lapu-lapu*), cavalla (*talakitok*), slipmouth (*hasa-hasa*), and mackerel (*alumahan*). Shellfish (crustaceans and mollusks), such as shrimps, prawns, crabs, and mussels abound in Philippine waters. Fish production has grown considerably since the 1970s. Fishponds are the source of the popular fish *bangus* (chanos) milkfish, and **tilapia**, found in Iloilo province, which leads the country in fishpond culture.

Total fish production in 1997 derived from commercial fisheries, aquaculture, and municipal fisheries reached 2.8 million metric tons valued at 83 billion pesos. About 300,000 metric tons were exported. Shrimps, prawns, and tuna are considered the top exports of the fishing sector and are mostly sold to Japan. The industry has been faced currently with low production because of a number of factors such as destruction of the marine environment, overfishing, and encroachment of commercial fishermen into shallow waters. *See also* AGRICULTURE; MALAMPAYA SOUND; TUBBATAHA REEFS.

FLAG. The national flag of red, white, and blue was officially presented on June 12, 1898, at the proclamation of Philippine independence at Kawit, Cavite. It consists of a white equilateral triangle at the left side with an eight-rayed sun in the center of the triangle. At each angle of the triangle is a five-pointed star symbolizing the three geographic areas of the Philippines: Luzon, Visayas, and Mindanao. The right side of the flag has an upper band of blue and a lower band of red. Emilio Aguinaldo designed the flag in Hong Kong with the help of Marcella de Agoncillo and her daughter Lorenza and Delfina Herbosa Natividad (niece of **Jose Rizal**). The design showed sunrays, which represent the original provinces that revolted against Spain, namely Rizal, Bulacan, Pampanga, Nueva Ecija, Laguna, Batangas, and Cavite. The colors red and blue symbolize war and peace, respectively. The flag received its first "baptism of fire" in Imus, Cavite, in a bloody confrontation between Aguinaldo's forces and Spanish marines on May 28, 1898. Aguinaldo raised the flag as a symbol of victory against Spain. The flag was raised again during the independence ceremonies on June 12, 1898, in Kawit, Cavite. In 1962, President **Diosdado Macapagal** declared June 12 as the official day of celebration of Philippines independence.

FLAGELLANTS. *See* PAMPANGA.

FLAVIER, JUAN (1935–). Dubbed "doctor of the **barrio**," Juan Flavier spent 30 years as a country doctor serving the poor in rural and urban areas. Born to a destitute couple—fourth among six children—Flavier was obsessed with education. He graduated valedictorian in high school and went to the University of the Philippines for his medical degree. He took advanced training at Johns Hopkins University where he obtained a master's in public **health**. His experience in serving the poor led him to the presidency of the **Philippine Rural Reconstruction Movement** (PRRM). Later Flavier became president of the International Institute of Rural Reconstruction. President Fidel Ramos appointed him secretary of health in 1992. In 1995, he was elected senator and during his first term he distinguished himself by the number of bills that he authored in the areas of health, environment, agrarian reform, **indigenous people's rights**, and conservation. Alarmed at the exploding **population** and the increasing incidence of AIDS (HIV virus), he promoted measures such as artificial family planning methods for which he was reviled by the hierarchy of the **Roman Catholic Church**. Flavier's views on health care have been reflected in his newspaper columns for the past 20 years. Since he was reelected for a second term in 2001 Flavier has sponsored new bills on nutrition for **women** and **indigenous people's rights**. *See also* AR-BOLARYO; HERBAL MEDICINE.

FLORA AND FAUNA. The Philippines is exceptionally rich in flora and fauna with a very high endemicity. There are over 15,000 species of plant life—edible grasses, medicinal herbs, ornamental vines, and sturdy trees for industrial and construction purposes. There are 3,000 catalogued species of trees found in most of the 7,100 islands. The **coconut** tree—dubbed the tree of life—is a common sight along the coastal regions. The national palm is the *anahaw*. Other palms are the **nipa** used as roof shingle and *buri* used in making handbags and light furniture. **Bamboo** is endemic and the source of basic building material of the picturesque *bahay kubo*. **Rattan**, a climbing plant, grows abundantly in Mindoro.

Philippine **cuisine** is vegetable heavy because of the abundance of vegetables. Fibrous plants include **abaca**, maguey, and pineapple. The **narra** tree is the country's national tree. Its wood is used for furniture and house posts. Mango is the most popular fruit tree, followed by banana. There are endemic fruits in some provinces. Davao has distinct fruits—*marang*, *mangosteen*, *rambutan*, and the controversial *durian* which "smells like hell but tastes like heaven." Other known indigenous fruits are jackfruit, *papaya*, *guyabano*, *casuy*, *pomelo*, *rimas*, *atis*, *guava*, and *anonas*. The succulent *lanzones* is found in Laguna. Some plants are a rich source of **herbal medicine**—*banaba* for diabetes, *luya* (ginger) as an antirheumatic, hibiscus for poultice, and *pandan* for stomach aches.

The flora consists of at least 13,500 species that represent 5 percent of the world's flora. The ferns and fern allies, gymnosperms and angiosperms constitute 22.5 percent of the Malesian and 3.88 percent of the world's vascular flora. Twenty genera of the plants are endemic. Among the 1,000 flowering plants and ferns, the most prized is the rare orchid *waling-waling* that thrives in Mt. Apo, which is also the home of the **Philippine eagle.** Other fragrant flowers are the **ylang-ylang**, *camia*, *champaca*, *rosal*, and *dama de noche*. Native species are used for ornamental and horticultural purposes, many of which are harvested and cultivated.

About fauna, the Philippines has a bounty of aves, mammalia, reptilia, and insecta. Two are native species—the Mindoro *tamaraw* and the Palawan tarsier. In Palawan also there are 105 species of birds among which are four species of hornbills, crested serpent eagle, falconet, and scoops owl. Labuyo, a wild species of ground fowl, is found in the forests of Quezon Memorial Park. Unfortunately many species are now endangered due to habitat destruction. There are 850 species of the fine-feathered creatures.

Being an archipelago, its marine and coastal habitat teem with 4,951 species of marine plants and animal life. Fishes, noncoral invertebrates, and seaweeds constitute the greatest numbers. Some 1,396 or 28 percent are economically important, 403 or 10 percent are flagship species, while 145 species or 2.4 percent are endangered. Favorite table fare are *tilapia, galunggong, banak* (mullet), *talakitok* (flatfish cavalla), *tanguingue* (mackerel), *labahita* (surgeon), and *bangus* (milkfish). Coral reefs are by far the most diverse or species rich with 3,968 species. The 381 coral species and 1,000 species of fish recorded in the Philippine coral ranks the country second to the Great Barrier Reef in coral and coral reef fish diversity. **Malampaya Sound** off the coast of Palawan is regarded as the "Fishing Bowl of the Philippines."

As for sea shells, Philippine waters have the largest number—about 2,000 shell varieties, some of which are edible. Prized shells are the golden cowrie (*conus gloria maris*), which are found in Leyte and Bohol. The biggest mollusks measuring as long as five feet are found in **Palawan** and **Sulu**. *See also* BIODIVERSITY; FISHING INDUSTRY, SOCSKSARGEN; TUBBATAHA REEFS.

FLORANTE AT LAURA. This is the romantic epic of the **Tagalog** people who live in the central plains of Luzon. Written as a metrical romance by **Francisco Baltazar Balagtas** in 1838 in the Tagalog language, there are some 400 quatrains of four lines each of perfect vowel rhymes. This vernacular masterpiece has been translated into English poetry. The plot is based on the conflict between Christians, represented by the hero Florante, and the Muslims depicted by Aladdin. Court intrigues, treachery, and unrequited love fill much of the dialogue. *See also* AGYU; *LAM-ANG.*

FLORES, PEDRO. He was the Filipino who invented and introduced the yo-yo toy in the United States. Flores, a native of Vintar, Ilocos Norte, immigrated to the United States in 1915. Prior to Flores, the yo-yo was called *bandalore* in the United States He was credited with popularizing the Filipino word "yo-yo" in the late 1920s, after the centuries-old Filipino game of his youth. Flores opened the first yo-yo factory, and ran the first yo-yo contest held in 1928 in Santa Barbara, California. These contests made the "yo-yo" name wildly popular. In 1930, Flores sold the trademark rights to Duncan Company, while continuing to run the contests for Duncan through the early 1930s. Flores started the first yo-yo craze in America. Thanks to Pedro Flores and his yo-yo spinning contest, yo-yoing became immensely popular in the United States in the late 1920s and its resurgence is once again alive.

FOLK EPIC. Epic poetry was the highest form of ancient Filipino literary heritage. The epics are tribal folklores that have survived and remained unchanged in their oral form as they were narrated by local bards. From the mountain tribes of northern Luzon to the southern tribes of Mindanao, folk epics have entertained the natives for generations. Among the famous epic tales are *Lam-ang* of the Ilocanos, *Handyong* of the Bicol region, *Labaw Donggon* of Panay Island, *Indarapatra* of the Maguindanaos, *Tu-waang* of the Bagobo, and *Bantugan* of the Maranaos. The bards chanted or sang the epic tales of tribal heroes and heroines before the villagers during festive occasions, such as marriage ceremonies and at harvest time. These folk epics have provided historians evidence of pre-Hispanic Filipino culture, such as the tribal beliefs and practices, worldview of the inhabitants, religious rites, and methods of livelihood.

FORBES, WILLIAM CAMERON (1870–1959). American governor-general in the Philippines (1909–1913). When Secretary of War **William Howard Taft** was seeking a candidate with a business background to fill the position of commissioner for commerce and police on the Philippine Commission, Forbes was offered the job and came to the Philippines with ideas to shore up the country's economic foundation. Accordingly, he concentrated on infrastructure, extending and improving road, rail, and water transportation. In his capacity as police commissioner, he curbed the abuses of the constabulary and reduced the depredations of banditry in the country. Racial tensions, beyond his control, deepened divisions between Americans and Filipinos. Following the inauguration of Woodrow Wilson in 1913, Filipino leaders wanted a new governor-general who would be more sympathetic to independence. Forbes was removed from office and replaced by **Francis Burton Harrison**.

FOREIGN POLICY. The Philippines' foreign policy is based on its mission to advance the interests of the country and Filipino people in the world community. It has three main objectives, which are national security, development diplomacy, and the promotion of the welfare of Filipino overseas workers. In pursuing the policy objectives, the **Gloria Macapagal Arroyo** administration has outlined eight realities, which are 1. China, Japan, and the United States and their relationships will be the determining influence in the security situation and economic evolution of East Asia. 2. Philippine foreign policy decisions have to be made in the context of the **Association of Southeast Asian Nations** (ASEAN). 3. The international Islamic community will continue to be important for the Philippines. 4. The country's economic growth will continue to be heavily dependent on foreign investments. 5. The coming years will see the growing importance of multilateral and interregional organizations to promote common interests. 6. The defense of the nation's sovereignty and the protection of its environment and natural resources lie at the heart of foreign policy. 7. A country like the Philippines can benefit from international **tourism**. 8. Overseas Filipinos continue to play a critical role in the country's economic and social stability.

The Department of Foreign Affairs has been tasked to implement the foreign policy objectives by adopting cultural diplomacy and public diplomacy. The Philippines works closely with other countries to address threat to national security. Its relations with neighboring countries are dictated by its desire to achieve peace, prosperity, and stability within its borders. A significant focus of the Philippines' development diplomacy is the pursuit of bilateral, regional, and multilateral arrangements geared toward ensuring food security and the delivery of health and nutrition, housing, education, and other social development services. Several projects have been arranged in partnership with the German government, which include development projects. The long-term goal of the Philippines is to bring back overseas workers to an industrialized Philippines where employment opportunities abound. The Philippines works closely with the United Nations as part of the country's efforts to advance the call for development with a human face. The Philippines has been at the forefront of promoting human rights, particularly **women's** rights in various regional and international fora. The Philippine government remains firm in its commitment to conserve, protect, and develop the environment as an integral part of the country's pursuit of **sustainable development**. In the region, the Philippines has retained the chairmanship of the ASEAN Working Group on Nature Conservation and Biodiversity. The Philippines is home to ASEAN's Regional Center for **Biodiversity Conservation Center** found in Los Baños, Laguna.

The main focus of the Philippines economic relations with Europe is the promotion and support of Philippine tourism, export, and investments. Philippine involvement in the global fight against terrorism was based on the United Nations Security Council Resolution 1368, which mandates member countries to join the international coalition to combat terrorism. The Philippines has intensified friendly relations with individual members of the Organization of Islamic Conference (OIC) and with the organization itself. With regard to the **Sabah** issue, the Philippines' position is to continue diplomatic dialogue with Malaysia. It has also worked with Islamic countries to resolve the problem of **Muslim separatism**.

FOREIGN RELATIONS. The Philippines has diplomatic relations with virtually all member countries of the United Nations. It is a member of most international organizations, including the United Nations and its affiliated agencies, the **Association of Southeast Asian Nations** (ASEAN), and the Asian Development Bank. The 1987 Constitution requires that an independent **foreign policy** be undertaken in pursuit of the national interest. Diplomatic relations were established with the People's Republic of **China** in 1975, at which time the Philippine government recognized **Taiwan** as an "inalienable" part of the People's Republic. This position has led Presidents Corazon Aquino and Fidel Ramos to forge closer ties with the People's Republic. In 1988, the Philippines established relations with **Vietnam** in a treaty of amity and cooperation. Diplomatic missions have been opened in Oman, Qatar, and Bahrain, where there are thousands of Filipino **overseas workers**.

The secretary of foreign affairs has visited countries in Eastern Europe as well as Western Europe to project a new image of friendly relations. The Philippines is a member of the Non-Aligned Movement (NAM), since 1992, and has links with the Organization of Islamic Conference (OIC). Philippine soldiers and police have participated in a number of multilateral civilian police and peacekeeping operations, and a Philippine Army general served as the first commander of the UN Peacekeeping Operation in East Timor.

The close ties that for decades characterized the relations between the United States and the Philippines were destabilized in 1991 following the Philippine Senate's rejection of the U.S. air and naval bases in the Philippines. President George W. Bush's visit to the country in October 2003 in reciprocation of President Gloria Macapagal Arroyo's state visit to the United States in May 2003 reaffirmed the political, economic, and cultural climate. The close ties were further strengthened by the **Visiting Forces Agreement** which formed the basis for greater security cooperation and added support to the existing U.S.–Philippine Mutual Defense Treaty. Today, Philippine diplomatic thrusts combine old conservatism rooted in new democratic ideals based on progressive nationalism and pragmatic internationalism. *See also* BAJA JR., LAURO; CHINA; INDONESIA; JAPAN; MALAYSIA; SABAH; SAUDI ARABIA; SOUTH KOREA, SINGAPORE; UNITED STATES; VIETNAM.

FORESTRY. More than 20 percent of the Philippines are forested land. In 1995, the country's forest areas consists of 5.6 million hectares of which 0.805 million hectares were old growth or virgin forests. The forestry sector plays an important role in the socioeconomic development of the country. Forest-based export reached its peak in the 1960s and early 1970s when about $212 million worth of logs and lumber were sold to Japan and some European countries. Commercial hardwood exported included **narra**, *tindalo*, *camagong*, *molave*, *ipil*, and *yakal*. Mahoganies included *lauan, tanguile*, *mayapis*, and *guijo*. Forest-based industries provided employment to over 200,000 workers involved in logging and wood processing activities.

The country's forests are now fast diminishing due to indiscriminate activities of illegal loggers and firewood gatherers. In the late 1970s, the government became aware of the dangers of **deforestation** and began to impose restrictions. Illegal logging and charcoal making have been major problems in forest maintenance. Caused by the deforestation of the surrounding mountains, the devastating Ormoc flood in Leyte in 1991 killed 10,000 people. Since then, the government has intensified its reforestation program to replant 100,000 hectares (247,000 acres) per year. The Department of Environment and Natural Resources is the primary government agency responsible for the conservation, management, development, and proper use of the country's environment and natural resources. *See also* SUSTAINABLE DEVELOPMENT.

FORT DEL PILAR. *See* PHILIPPINE MILITARY ACADEMY.

FORT SANTIAGO. Infamous dungeon. It was built in 1582 by the Spanish on the ruins of **Rajah Sulayman's** fortification at the mouth of Pasig River to protect Manila from marauding privateers, such as the Portuguese, Chinese, and Dutch. The fort was given the name of Fuerza de Santiago by the Spanish and made a part of the walled city of Manila, which became a staging area for the colonization of the Philippines. The fort served as the headquarters for the Spanish military and, until the end of Spanish rule, its cells became dungeons for prisoners. Many Filipinos, who were suspected of being revolutionaries, died of torture and starvation in this fort. The place has become a landmark and a shrine to the national hero **Jose Rizal**, who was unjustly imprisoned in this dungeon before his execution. The Japanese used its dungeons for political prisoners and captured Filipino and American guerrillas, many of whom died due to inhuman treatment. Today, the government has converted Fort Santiago into a museum, which houses exhibits of memorabilia of national heroes and an open-air theater for performing artists. *See also* JAPANESE OCCUPATION.

FOX, ROBERT. *See* TABON CAVES.

FRANCISCO, JUAN R. (1929–). Juan Francisco is an academician whose prodigious research work and expertise in Indology firmly established the extent of Indian influence in Philippine life and culture. Francisco obtained his Ph.D. at the University of Madras, India, on an

Indian government fellowship. His work on extant sources—epigraphy and paleography—revealed that Indian material culture reached the Philippines during the period that **Sri Vijaya** (686 A.D. through 13th century) played a major role in the trade and commerce of the Southeast Asian region. His well-documented scholarly work confirmed that Philippine societies had a fully organized society as well as a highly developed system of writing that belied what the Spaniards made Filipinos believe, namely that their real history commenced only at the coming of the West. Part of Francisco's evidence is Sanskrit elements embedded in ancient **Tagalog** epigraphs discovered in the **Laguna Copperplate Inscription** (A.D. 900). The most significant part of his contribution is his extensive research on Indian values, themes, and symbols found in *Maharadia Lawana*, the Philippine **Maranao** version of the Indian epic, *Ramayana*. Francisco's works can be found in the Asian Center at the University of the Philippines, Diliman. *See also* INDIA.

FREEDOM CONSTITUTION. A provisional constitution put into effect when President Corazon Aquino assumed office in 1986 and intended to supersede the 1973 constitution of the Ferdinand Marcos administration. Under the Freedom Constitution, all of the agencies created under the Marcos regime were abolished. President Aquino was to assume all the powers of government until a new constitution was ratified by the people. She subsequently called a constitutional convention and the new constitution, which restored the presidential form of government, was ratified in a national plebiscite in 1986. *See also* CONSTITUTIONS OF THE PHILIPPINES.

FRIAROCRACY. Power of religious orders. Spanish colonial rule was noted for the power wielded by members of the various religious orders who came with the Spanish soldiers. By the turn of the 16th century, there were already five religious orders in place in the Philippines. The Augustinians, Dominicans, Franciscans, Recollects, and Jesuits each had their own territories. Along with the civil authorities, the religious orders conducted many of the executive and control functions of the government on the local level, including administration of education and educational measures, keeping census and tax records, conscription of laborers for road and shipbuilding, supervising the selection of local and police officers, and surveillance of individuals suspected of seditious influences. The friars had such a thorough hold on the life of a **barangay** that their presence has been labeled "friarocracy." Their most questionable activity was reporting incidents of sedition to the authorities; since the information to identify troublemakers was obtained in confessions. The orders also gained a powerful foothold on the land by their extensive estates granted to them under the *encomienda* system, which provided vast incomes that enabled the friars to live like princes. While the friars conducted their principal duty of Christianizing the **Indios**, as the Filipinos were called, their other activities included the enslavement of the people by the onerous **tribute** and labor levies. Their wanton abuses were reported to the king of Spain but seldom resulted in an improvement for the Indios because of the powerful intervention of their representatives in the king's court. Unable to seek relief of their grievances, the Indios fomented **revolts** and uprisings against the friars that culminated in the **Philippine–Spanish Revolution** started by **Andres Bonifacio**. *See also* BARLIN, JORGE IMPERIAL; GOMBURZA; FILIPINIZATION.

FUGA ISLAND. A pristine island located in the northernmost tip of the Philippines. Geographers consider Fuga and Babuyan islands as the missing link in the island bridges that connected the Philippine archipelago to the Asian mainland. As a municipality of **Cagayan** province, Fuga Island has a land area of 10,000 hectares, surrounded by 70 kilometers of fine white beaches, and has numerous sites for scuba diving, snorkeling, and game fishing. Inhabitants of the island are mostly Ilocanos. Archaeologists have discovered prehistoric artifacts such as fossils of extinct mammals and stone tools as old as five million years. The island has a network of caves—considered sacred by the natives—that contained hundreds of prehistoric terra cotta burial jars. *See also* BORACAY; MAITUM ANTHROPOMORPHIC POTTERIES; MANUNGGUL JAR.

FULBRIGHT-HAYS SCHOLARS. *See* PENSIONADO.

– G –

GABRIELA. An acronym for General Assembly Binding Women for Reforms, Integrity, Equality, Leadership, and Action. Founded in March

1984, this **women's** activist movement was formed from a coalition of several militant middle-class-oriented women's groups. The coalition sought to reform Philippine society in the following areas: feudalism, patriarchy, colonialism, and United States imperialism. At their first general assembly in Manila, they staged a peaceful march to **Malacañang Palace** to protest the brutal killings of women labor leaders and activists by the military. GABRIELA also became politically involved following the assassination of **Benigno Aquino Jr**. because the **Ferdinand Marcos** government failed to address the root causes of prostitution at the U.S. naval and air force bases. GABRIELA believed that prostitution was an economic and political problem but not a moral one. Furthermore, the organization proclaimed that the struggle of the Filipino people and the liberation of women must go hand in hand. *See also* MAKIBAKA; BAYAN; NONGOVERNMENTAL ORGANIZATIONS; SECTORAL PARTIES.

GADDANG. An ethnic tribe inhabiting the Cagayan Valley (Cagayan province) in northern Luzon. Although a majority of the Gaddangs has become assimilated into Christian Ilocano society, there is still a considerable number who continue to practice the ancestral way of life in the villages. Female shamans are the recognized social leaders, healers of ailments, and protectors against evil spells. The Gaddangs practice swidden agriculture to raise their staple food crops of rice and camotes, or sweet potatoes.

GAJAH MADAH. *See* MAJAPAHIT.

GALLEON TRADE. Trade between Manila and Mexico. This trade was carried on between the Spanish government in Manila and its counterpart in Acapulco, Mexico, from 1593 to 1815. Galleons loaded with Chinese silk and wares left Manila and returned with silver bullion, which supported the Spanish government and the church. At the height of the trade, five huge vessels were involved annually. Thousands of Filipinos were engaged in forced labor in the construction of these huge ships, which were three or four-deckers. They manned the vessels as well. The galleon's cargo hold was divided into shares of a fixed size, which were allotted only to Spanish citizens. The church supplied most of the capital to buy the Chinese goods and outfit the galleon for which it received 30 to 50 percent interest when the galleon returned. Whenever a galleon left Manila for the year-long journey, it was sent off with the church's blessings, and its arrival was greeted by the ringing of the church bells. Many of these galleons were lost, captured, or shipwrecked and the colony sometimes suffered from the loss of their income. When a galleon arrived successfully in Manila, it brought not only silver bullion but also luxury European goods, mail for the Spanish colonists, personnel, supplies, and correspondence for the church and the government.

The galleon trade was abolished after the collapse of Spanish rule in Latin America. After the abolition of the galleon trade, Spain started developing programs to promote economic development in the Philippines. The economic programs were meant to make the colony self-sufficient so that it would no longer be an economic burden on Spain. Governor-General Jose Basco (1178–1789) was the first one to pay attention to the improvement of the Philippine economy. Basco made the colony produce export goods that were needed in Europe and America, such as cotton textiles, cinnamon, tobacco, and indigo. *See also* LOUISIANA COMMUNITY.

GAMAL ABDEL NASSER. *See* ALONTO, DOMOCAO.

GAMBOA, PATROCINIA (1875–1938). She was popularly known as the "Heroine of Jaro," **Iloilo**, where she was born to an **ilustrado** family. Since her heart burned with a longing of freedom from Spain, she secretly read the writings of **Jose Rizal**, **Graciano Lopez Jaena** (a province mate), and other revolutionary propagandists. She was among the first leaders and members of the secret conclaves of the revolutionary movement in Santa Barbara, Iloilo. Because of her gender and tie to wealth, Spaniards did not suspect her of revolutionary sympathies. This proved to be an asset as she acted as an intelligence agent and secretly raised funds for the revolution. When hostilities broke out, Patrocinia risked her life in battle as a Red Cross nurse attending to the comfort of the wounded and sick. Her famous role in the revolution was preparing a replica of the flag made by Marcela Agoncillo in Hong Kong, which she delivered on time—at a great risk to her life—for the inaugural ceremonies on November 17, 1898, of the revolutionary government of the Visayas.

GAMELAN. A musical ensemble of Muslims in Mindanao. The word gamelan is derived from Javanese "gamel" which means to hammer. Typically, a gamelan consists of percussion instruments such as gongs and drums of graduated sizes, wood and metal xylophones of varied timbre, flutes and whistles, assorted bamboo, wooden and metal percussion instrument, and voices for singing and for expressive vocals. In the Philippines a gamelan ensemble uses ideophones such as *kulintang*, *gangsa, tongalong*, and *kalutang*; chordophones like *hegalong*, *kulibet*, *gitgit*, and *kuritang*; aero phones such *diwdiw-as*, *tongali* and *suling*; membranophones like the *debakan*, *solibaw*, and Cordilleran drums of varying sizes and shapes. Gamelan has been widely promoted by the musical company KONTRA-GAP that performs with as many as 50 and as a few as five players. Their repertoire includes singing, dancing, mime and they play as many as 10 instruments. Their total-theater approach is like a tribe in primeval ritual.

GAMES. *See* ARNIS; SIPA; SPORTS.

GARCIA, CARLOS P. (1896–1971). Fourth president of the Republic of the Philippines. Garcia was born on November 4, 1896, in Talibon, Bohol province, to Policarpio Garcia, a municipal mayor, and Ambrosia Polestico. He completed his higher education at Silliman University and at Philippine Law School in Manila, where he earned a law degree in 1923. That same year, in the bar examinations, he finished among the top 10. Instead of practicing law, he taught for two years at the Bohol Provincial High School. In 1925, Garcia ran for Congress and won. In the local elections of 1931, he was elected governor of Bohol. In 1941, he was elected senator, but his tenure was interrupted by the Japanese invasion of the Philippines. He fought the Japanese as a guerrilla and when the country was liberated, in 1945, he ran for senator and was elected.

Garcia served until 1953 when he was drafted as the running mate of presidential candidate **Ramon Magsaysay**. The team won and Garcia was concurrently appointed secretary of foreign affairs. Garcia became president when Magsaysay was killed in a plane crash on March 17, 1957. In the subsequent national elections, he won the presidency by a 600,000 vote margin against four big-name opponents. He was a popular president because he articulated the nationalist theme, the **Filipino First policy**, which put the interests of Filipino people above those of foreigners and of the ruling party. Nevertheless, he lost in his reelection bid in 1961. After his defeat, Garcia retired to his native Bohol. However, he was called back to public service in 1971 to serve as president of the Constitutional Convention called by Ferdinand Marcos. Shortly after assuming the office, he died of a heart attack in Manila on June 14, 1971.

GENERAL SANTOS. *See* SOCSKSARGEN; SARANGANI.

GIDA OFONG (1975–). Her Christian name is Flor de la Cruz, but she is locally known as Gida Ofong, a Tiboli princess reknown for her spirited leadership of her so-called forgotten tribe. She is one of the daughters of a datu of the **T'boli** tribe that inhabit the mountains of South Cotabato and the region of Lake Sebu. A precocious child, she learned to speak Ilongo (Hilagayno) at the age of three, and then mastered the English language in her grade school. She finished high school at the head of her class, one of three Tiboli women out of the 58 who went to a Christian school in Koronadal, **South Cotabato**. Being a princess, she was ordered to be married to a cousin, but she broke their ancient tradition and told her father that she would rather find her own husband. By setting the example, her two aunts and several relatives followed suit. Gida found a job with the General Santos City Chamber of Commerce, and from her position she initiated programs that were designed to educate and elevate her Tiboli tribesmen in the eyes of mainstream Filipinos. Tiboli culture has been deteriorating in the past decades and no record of their history has been gathered. Gida Ofong's immediate goal is to preserve the culture and heirlooms of the Tiboli people by establishing the Tiboli Cultural Heritage Foundation.

GOKONGWEI, JOHN JR. (1927–). John Gokongwei is an industrialist whose business acumen made him one of the Philippine tycoons and a generous philanthropist. Born to impoverished parents in Cebu, he was thrust at age 15 into supporting his family due to the early demise of his father. He sold soap, thread, and candles to support his five siblings. Before World War II broke out his mother sent his siblings to China where relatives cared for them. During the Japanese occupation he eked out a livelihood by trading. When the war ended he was 19 and with his little business experience he started an import company. With the encouragement of the government he decided to go into manufacturing glucose and cornstarch—which turned out to be profitable. Then, with the capital loaned by a Chinese banker, he boldly launched into manufacturing household items such as coffee, toothpaste, chocolate, and candy. Meantime, he obtained an M.B.A. and went to Harvard for advanced management training. In the ensuing years he saw globalization on the horizon and therefore diversified his business into textiles, retail, real estate, telecommunications, aviation, banking, and petrochemicals. His companies faced tough competition with entrenched and powerful multinationals, but he prevailed with his aggressive marketing strategies. His companies grew from a one-man operation to a group of 30,000 employees. Gokongwei donated his wealth substantially to programs of higher education and many civic causes. *See also* TSINOY.

GOLD. Early gold miners were the Igorots of **Bontoc** province who used the precious metal to barter with the Ilocanos in the lowlands. As early as the 13th century, gold was already used in trade with Chinese merchants. When the Spanish came, they sent several unsuccessful expeditions to exploit the gold fields of the Igorots. It was left to the Americans, who brought in their gold mining technology, to exploit the gold fields of the mountain provinces and to successfully obtain the precious metal. *See also* MINING.

GOLD ARTIFACTS. The gold artifacts include gold ornaments from the **Central Bank** (Bangko Sentral) of the Philippines collection; Bolinao, **Pangasinan** gold teeth peggings; nose disc, and gold eye mask retrieved from an open grave in Barangay San Antonio, Oton, **Iloilo**, dating from the late 14th century or early 15th century A.D.; and gold artifacts from underwater archaeological sites. The gold facial orifice coverings are delicately worked sheets of gold that were used to cover the eyes, nose, and mouth of the dead. The southern Chinese and a limited group of Filipinos practiced this burial custom, which persisted through the early Spanish era.

GOLDEN BUDDHA. A three-foot golden statue rumored to have been buried by General **Tomoyuki Yamashita** somewhere in the Mountain

Province and found by Rogelio Roxas. Army men under orders from **Ferdinand Marcos** on the pretext that the golden figure was a national treasure forcibly took the statue from him. The Philippine government recovered this treasure when Marcos died in Hawaii.

GOMBURZA. Acronym formed by the names of three Filipino priests, Mariano Gomez, Jose Burgos, and Jacinto Zamora, executed by the Spaniards by garrote on February 17, 1872. Known as champions of the **secularization** movement, they were wrongly implicated in the **Cavite Mutiny**, and after a mock trial were sentenced to die before the public. GOMBURZA became a national symbol against Spain's tyrannical rule when the revolution broke out in 1896. *See also* FRIAROCRACY.

GOULD, JACOB. *See* FIRST PHILIPPINE COMMISSION.

GOVERNMENT. Organization of the Philippine government. Under the newly approved 1987 constitution, the government of the Philippines is republican in form and democratic in process. It has three separate and coequal branches: executive, legislative, and judicial. It mandates a number of independent commissions: the Commission on Elections, Commission on Audit, Commission on Human Rights, and Commission on Good Government. It has a bill of rights, which is similar to that found in the United States Constitution. The church and the state are separate. The president is elected by a direct vote of the people for a term of six years and is not eligible for reelection. The president's cabinet consists of the executive secretary, press secretary, cabinet secretary, national security adviser, and secretaries of the following departments: agrarian reform; agriculture; budget and management; economic planning; education, culture, and sports; environment and natural resources; finance; foreign affairs; health; interior and local government; justice; labor and employment; national defense; public works and highways; science and technology; social welfare and development; tourism; trade and industry; and transportation and communications. *See* FREEDOM CONSTITUTION; MALOLOS CONSTITUTION.

GRAFT AND CORRUPTION. Philippine newspapers use this phrase to describe embezzlement of government money, kickbacks, and *pay-*

ola. Newspapers vie with each other in reporting the juiciest details and the modus operandi of the suspected culprits. Graft and corruption did not come into fashion until the end of World War II, when some officials were caught selling surplus army goods and pocketing the funds. From the lowly clerk who accepted "fixes," called *pabagsak* or *lagay*, to facilitate the issuing of licenses, to high government officials who expect a percentage on the total award of public funding (pork barrel), all were engaged in graft and corruption. In an effort to curb crime in public office, Ferdinand Marcos created the **Sandiganbayan** to prosecute corruption cases. This court, with its poor record of convictions, proved to be just another example of form without substance. Embezzlement of public funds spiraled into the millions of pesos and reached its peak ironically during the Marcos regime. And, it was the Sandiganbayan that prosecuted the Marcos family for their ill-gotten wealth of $658 million, which was forfeited in favor of the government following a Supreme Court decision.

Graft and corruption also brought the downfall of **Joseph Ejercito Estrada** and is still the hottest issue in every election campaign. During the administration of President Gloria Macapagal Arroyo, she started a campaign—"Report-a-Mistress"—to nab officials living beyond their means. The campaign netted 500 high government employees. Most of them were prosecuted. *See* JUDICIAL SYSTEM; PENAL LAW; PRESIDENTIAL COMMISSION ON GOOD GOVERNMENT.

GUARDIA CIVIL. The local police force of Spaniards, whose duty was to maintain law and order in a community. They were the eyes and ears of the Spanish civil authorities and were aided by conniving friars in detecting any sign of subversion. As the Spanish regime was coming to its end; Spanish authorities became jittery of subversives. The Guardia Civil could make arrests on the basis of suspicion and enjoyed a de facto authority for the use of force to extort confessions. Aside from surveillance of suspected subversives, the Guardia Civil, through its auxiliary, the Guardia Civil Veterana, patrolled the streets, maintaining order and arresting prostitutes, thieves, and drunkards. The excesses of the Guardia Civil were immortalized in Jose Rizal's writings and the publication of the **Propaganda Movement**. The Guardia Civil became such despised symbols of Spanish authority that, at the outbreak of the **Philippine–Spanish Revolution**, the revolutionaries pounced upon the Guardia Civil with ferocity.

GUARDIA DE HONOR. The backdrop of many of the uprisings in the Philippines during the Spanish regime was that visionary leaders exploited the confused state of the natives' belief system. These leaders, who came from the lower ranks, had a moral and spiritual authority superior to that of the Spanish friars, not unlike the Christian God. These uprisings did not stop with the expulsion of Spain but extended well into America's involvement in the Philippines. One such uprising was that launched by the Guardia de Honor in the Ilocos region in the 1800s. Dominican friars in Manila founded this group to uphold Christian orthodoxy among the laity. Their basic doctrine was devotion to the Mother of God, thus the members were called Guardia de Honor de Nuestra Señora del Santa Rosario. Prayers, rallies, and procession held with much fanfare helped swell the roster. Outside Manila, where clerical control was less centralized, the movement started taking on a different form. Fearing a rapidly growing cultist movement on their hands, the Dominicans severed affiliations with the Ilocano chapters in 1882, but by then it was too late.

A local *anitero* (animist) named Julian Baltazar from Urdaneta arose as spiritual leader, consolidated the movement on Santa Ana Island in the Agno River, and prophesied judgment day. The Spanish authorities worked quickly to disperse them and Baltazar returned to Urdaneta, which became a center for endless pilgrimages by his followers. The best the Spaniards could do was to issue a stern warning to the group not to cause trouble. In 1897, Baltazar, reverently referred to as *Apo Lakay*, moved to a barrio called Cabaruan and set up a virtually autonomous state. During the **Philippine–Spanish Revolution**, General **Emilio Aguinaldo** courted Apo Lakay and his followers to join the revolution, but he demurred and instead organized his own guerrilla unit for war against all outsiders, whom he believed were undermining their cause. Led by *Apo Lakay*'s deputy Antonio Valdez, Guardia de Honor amassed weapons taken from Spanish garrisons and attacked nearby towns and haciendas. At this point, Guardia de Honor shifted its position from defenders of the church to defenders of the peasants, and they also changed their name to "Los Agraviados." After the defeat of the Spanish, Los Agraviados had to face the Americans, who did not allow the hostile group to exist with their strange religious devotion to their leaders. In June 1, 1901, the recalcitrant units were surrounded by American military forces and as a result all their leaders were captured and hanged

GUERRILLA. Resistance movement during **World War II**. Soon after the defeat of the Philippine–American armed forces in the battle of **Bataan** and **Corregidor**, some of the soldiers and officers, with their weapons and equipment, escaped to the mountains, while others blended in with the population to serve as undercover agents. The Allied defeat did not diminish the loyalty of the Filipinos to America. Thus, in the ensuing three years of Japanese occupation guerrillas carried on the war through hit-and-run tactics, disruption of enemy convoys, and destruction of supply depots. These activities dealt crippling blows to the enemy, but guerrillas paid a heavy price with their lives. The Japanese retaliated with brutal massacres of innocent civilians. Despite the costs to the guerrillas, who were supplied with arms and ammunition from General Douglas MacArthur's headquarters in **Australia**, they fought the Japanese all over the country with unrelenting attacks on their most vulnerable points.

During this protracted underground resistance, there were several outstanding Filipino and American officers whose feats were succinctly recorded by Major General Charles Willoughby in his book *Guerrilla Resistance Movement in the Philippines: 1941–1945*. They included **Macario Peralta** in Panay; **Ruperto Kangleon** in Samar; **Jesus Villamor**, intelligence officer; Roque Ablan in Ilocos Norte; Edwin Ramsey and Guillermo Nakar in Nueva Ecija; Marcos Villa Agustin in Rizal and Manila; and Wendell Fertig in Mindanao. While the guerrillas waged subversive operations, they tied up large contingents of Japanese military units, which otherwise could have been deployed in strategic areas. They also gathered vital information on enemy shipping and troop movements, which was relayed to MacArthur in Australia in preparation for the liberation of the country. *See also* JAPANESE OCCUPATION.

GUIMARAS. An island province located between the islands of Panay and Negros. It has an area of 604 square kilometers and a population of 117,990. There are three towns in the island and Jordan is the capital.

GUINGONA, TEOFISTO (1928–). Appointed vice president by President Gloria Macapagal Arroyo, Teofisto Guingona also concurrently served as secretary of foreign affairs. A three-time senator, Guingona was first elected to the Senate in 1987, appointed executive secretary in 1993, and then secretary of the Department of Justice in 1995. During his stint as senator he had been senate minority leader, senate majority leader, and senate president pro tempore. Before becoming a legislator, Guingona rose to prominence as the chief negotiator of the government panel during peace talks with the **New Peoples' Army** under the **Corazon Aquino** administration. Later he was chairman of the commission on audit from 1986–1986. His political bailiwick is Mindanao. He was relieved of his concurrent post of foreign affairs secretary in 2002 following a major policy difference over the issue of foreign troop presence and the **Visiting Forces Agreement**. A staunch nationalist and a civil libertarian, he claimed that the presence of American military violated the Constitution. *See also* BANGON PARTY.

GUINTING-GUINTING NATURAL PARK. Saw-toothed shaped Mt. Guiting-Guinting is at the heart of Sibuyan, one of the seven islands of **Romblon** province. *Guiting-Guiting* in the local dialect means jagged. Its highest peak is at 2,058 meters. The island is known for its unique chain of ecosystems that starts with grasslands at high altitudes followed by undisturbed mossy and montane forests, **biodiversity**-rich lowland forests, intact mangroves, and beautiful coral reefs. The core of the island is known as Mt. Guiting-Guiting Natural Park. Sibuyan Island is one of the richest spots in the world in terms of density, diversity, and endemism of **flora and fauna**. Some species exist only on the island, and nowhere else on earth. These include four mammals—the Greater Sibuyan and Lesser Sibuyan forest mice, Sibuyan pygmy fruit bat, Sibuyan stripped shrew rat, and some plants. The Philippine tube-nosed bat and the Philippine hawk-eagle, classified respectively as "endangered" and "vulnerable," are found in the park, while dugongs, dolphins, and whales are sighted in the municipal waters.

– H –

HACIENDA LUISITA. A vast 6,000-hectare sugar plantation owned by the **Cojuangco** family in **Tarlac** province, about 160 kilometers north of Manila. This hacienda, founded by a Chinese named Jose Cojuangco during the Spanish times, is the largest landed estate in central Luzon engaged in the production of sugar for export. When Jose Cojuangco, Cory Aquino's father, assumed management the hacienda encompassed 11 *barangays* where 20,000 people lived as farmers, migrant workers, managers, and caretakers. About 10 percent of the cane cutters are housed in squalid quarters and since they worked only three months of the year they often had inadequate income to tide them over until the next cutting season. The hacienda advances the needed cash and kind, which are deducted from their wages come next season. They survive amidst poverty and malnutrition. However, some of the hacienda's resident population live in better conditions with their small incomes from cottage industries, **sarisari** store, and home gardens. The better-to-do were the managers, skilled employees, and mill workers who live on fixed wages and in company houses. The collapse of sugar prices on the world market in the 1960s brought underemployment, indebtedness, and insecurity to the hacienda residents, many of whom joined the Huk movement that promised them a better deal.

When Cory Cojuangco Aquino became president she announced the family's intention to participate in the nation's agrarian reform program. Some 7,000 permanent farm workers received small plots to cultivate and became minority owners in a corporation of which the Cojuangco family controlled 67 percent. Although the farmers received small dividends they had no voice in the corporate practices, while the Cojuangco Corporation retained control of the profitable sugar mills. Hacienda employees were unionized and obtained minimal health and medical benefits. The farm workers, such as the cane cutters and migrant workers, were less fortunate. Their annual incomes and benefits offered little opportunity for the future. Like other haciendas in the country, Hacienda Luisita has its own private army, which enforces company rules and regulations in its domain. And like other haciendas it continues to be run in the same manner as in the past while landed classes and their representatives in Congress also continue to oppose attempts to redress the grievances of its impoverished population. *See also* KASAMA SYSTEM.

HAMLETTING. *See* SAKAY, MACARIO.

HANDYONG. An epic tale of the Bicol region of Southern Luzon. Also called *Ibalon*, which is the ancient name of Bicol, this narrative was translated from the Bicolano language to Spanish by a Roman Catholic priest. After World War II, Filipino scholars rendered the 400-page manuscript into English. In the story, the hero Handyong performed deeds of heroic proportions. Its three culture heroes, Baltog, Handyong, and Bantong, share glory in freeing Ibalon of predatory and ferocious beasts. *See also LABAW DONGGON.*

HARE-HAWES-CUTTING ACT. *See* OS-ROX MISSION.

HARRISON, FRANCIS BURTON (1873–1957). American governor-general in the Philippines (1913–1920). Compared to his predecessors, Harrison most clearly indicated his commitment to the cause of Philippine independence. The only congressman to be named governor-general, Harrison's legislative experience not only was a common bond between him and the rising Filipino politician **Manuel Quezon** but also influenced him in the passage of legislation that broadened Philippine autonomy. Although **William Howard Taft**, the first civilian governor-general, advocated the independence of the Philippines after a period of limited self-government, Harrison wanted the speedy transfer of authority to the Filipinos. Thus, he gradually set out to divest the American government of its authority by discharging American personnel and replacing them with qualified Filipino officials. Consequently, he incurred the enmity of resident Americans whose mercantile interests were increasingly threatened by the aggressiveness of Filipino businessmen. His two terms as governor-general were wracked by disagreements with American bureaucrats over the fitness of the Filipinos for independence. At the end of his time, Harrison wrote an excellent defense of his **Filipinization** policies, and he praised the capabilities of Filipinos for self-government.

HEALTH. Health care of Filipinos is served by a healthcare system of public and private hospitals and puericulture centers. Private hospitals outnumber government hospitals, although government hospitals have more bed capacity. Infant and maternal mortality rates remained high in the last decade. In addition, the threat from infectious diseases and the burden of degenerative conditions have also been rising. There is the large variation in health status across population groups, income classes, and geographic areas. Those who live in rural and isolated communities receive less and lower quality health services. To address these problems, the government has introduced the Health Sector Reform Agenda in 1990. This improved the health status of the people through greater and more effective coverage of national and local public health programs and increased access to health services especially by the poor. The government has been making a great effort to upgrade its healthcare system into one of world-class standing, such as the availability of freestanding surgical centers and renal care units that can provide services to far-flung hospitals. Already, a world-class hospital that costs approximately one billion pesos is under construction in Metro Manila by a Singapore–Filipino joint venture while a Korean group has built a modern 200-bed hospital in **Trece Martires**, Cavite.

HERBAL MEDICINE. An alternative therapy called *arbularyo*, *herbolario*, or *hilot* practiced by local medicine men or women who for generations have used wild-crafted herbs to treat a variety of illnesses. Filipino scientists have lately taken cognizance of the effectiveness of herbal medicine. Herbal medicinal research and development was started in 1992 by the then secretary of health **Juan Flavier**. His research team found 10 medicinal plants that had curative value for common health problems. These native plants and their use are *akapulko,* for skin antifungal; *ampalaya,* for diabetes mellitus; *bawang* (garlic), to lower cholesterol; *bayabas* (guava), for wound disinfection; *lagundi,* for cough and asthma; *niyog-niyogan,* for ascariasis (anthelminthic); *ulasimang-bato,* for arthritis and gout; *sambong,* as a diuretic; *tsaang-gubat,* for abdominal pain; and *yerba buena,* for fever and body aches. The latest research on herbal medicine shows that one of the byproducts of coconut—*nata-de-coco*—contains a herbal food supplement identified as Boston-C, that has been found effective against a number of serious diseases such as cancer, diabetes, and kidney trouble. With a better knowledge of herbal medicine, the government agency—Institute of Traditional and Alternative Health Care—is producing quality herbal medicines that are being made available through "rolling stores" to 55 rural areas of the National Capitol Region. Rural folks are also instructed in the use and preparation of herbal therapies. *See also* ARBULARYO.

HERMANO PULE. *See* CRUZ, APOLINARIO DE LA.

HIBOK-HIBOK VOLCANO. *See* CAMIGUIN.

HIDALGO, FELIX RESURRECION. *See* AYALA MUSEUM.

HIGAONON. *See* AGUSAN DEL SUR.

HILIGAYNON. People who live in the islands of Panay, Guimaras, and Negros who speak the language Hiligaynon also called Ilonggo. Its variant dialect is Kinaray-a. *See also* MIRIAM DEFENSOR SANTIAGO.

HINILAWOD. A folk epic of the western Visayan people, which forms the oral tradition of the mountain people of Panay Island. It is still chanted on social occasions in the Sulod language. This epic dates back to pre-Christian times and contains 2,230 long stanzas. The principal characters in the story are the brothers **Labaw Donggon**, Humadapnen, and Dumalapdap. According to the story these brothers became the rulers of the provinces of Iloilo, Capiz, and Antique on Panay Island. The hero Labaw Donggon is a skillful and fierce warrior and an amorous lover. Themes depicted in the epic are the evil of violating the unwritten laws that govern society, the curse that befalls one who defies kinship solidarity to satisfy a whim or caprice, the obligations of offspring to avenge a parent's disgrace, and the credulity of those who believe in magic and the supernatural.

HIROO ONODA (1922–1998). Famous Japanese straggler who holds the honor of being the last soldier to surrender to the Philippine army, 30 years after the formal surrender of Japan and 15 years after being declared legally dead in Japan. Hiroo carried out a one-man guerrilla warfare on Lubang Island and successfully evaded pursuing police and civilian guards. He lived on wild fruits and game and rice stolen from farmers. Attempts were made to persuade Hiroo to surrender, including appeals from his relatives. It took his former commanding officer to convince Hiroo that the war was over. He emerged from the jungle with his .25 caliber rifle, 500 rounds of ammunition, and several hand grenades. His surrender on March 9, 1974, to President Ferdinand Marcos at **Malacañang Palace** created an international media sensation. He returned to Japan to receive a hero's welcome, and later wrote his autobiography, which became a best-seller. Since he was unable to adapt to modern life, Hiroo moved to Brazil to raise cattle. *See also* JAPANESE OCCUPATION.

HO, ANITA MAGSAYSAY. *See* ART GALLERIES.

HOMMA, MASAHARU. This brilliant Japanese general defeated General Douglas MacArthur in the battle of **Bataan** and **Corregidor** during **World War II**. Some 11,000 American and 70,000 Filipino soldiers surrendered to the Japanese army. Unable to transport the captured soldiers by trucks or rail to Camp O'Donnell in Tarlac, a distance of 140 kilometers, Homma ordered the captives to walk the distance under blistering heat. The incident known as the **Death March** resulted in the death of more than 7,000 soldiers from diseases and the savagery of Japanese soldiers. After the victory of the United States Armed Forces in the Far East, MacArthur ordered the arrest of Homma, who was living in Japan. He was tried and convicted as a war criminal together with General **Tomoyuki Yamashita**, who was held responsible for the innumerable atrocities and killings of Filipino civilians. Both were executed in 1946 in Los Baños, **Laguna**.

HONASAN, GREGORIO. *See* NATIONALIST REVOLUTIONARY ALLIANCE.

HORNBILL. *See* VISAYAN WRINKLED HORNBILL.

HUDHUD. In May 2001, UNESCO designated 19 traditions as "Masterpieces of Oral and Intangible Heritage of Humanity" in an effort to save them from extinction. They include forms of popular and traditional expressions, such as the Hudhud chant of the Ifugao. Hudhud is a musical record of Ifugao myths, traditional beliefs passed down orally from as far back as the 15th century. Few know the Hudhud chants, which can last as long as three days, by heart. The vast majority of Ifugao people have given up their traditional way of dress, their religion, and many of their rituals and customs. The UNESCO proclamation gave Ifugao culture a much-needed boost. Thus, the Philippine government provided funds for a school in Kiangan where Ifugao students learn the Hudhud chants, and other traditional cultural traits such as loom weaving, rice wine making, dancing, and forms of myth narrating. *See also* ALIQUYON.

HUKBALAHAP (HUKBO NG BAYAN LABAN SA HAPON) (PEOPLES ARMY AGAINST THE JAPANESE).

Established in 1942 in central Luzon, the movement was led by **Luis Taruc** and Casto Alejandrino. The Huks were effective in harassing the Japanese army during the occupation. After liberation, the Huks changed their name to Hukbong Mapagpalaya ng Bayan (People's Liberation Army), converting from a military into a peasant movement. They turned their attention to tenant-landlord conflicts, such as the fair division of the harvest and the redistribution of lands. Most of their members and supporters were tenants who had long been under the heel of unscrupulous absentee landlords and had felt that the government was not on their side. Unable to have their grievances redressed, they reverted in the ensuing years to subversive tactics against the government. At the same time the Huks joined closely with the emerging National Peasant Union, a Communist organization that was active in the 1946 presidential elections.

Luis Taruc was one of the congressional winners in that election, but he was excluded from the legislature on charges of using terrorist methods during the campaign. This exclusion provoked the Huks to attempt an overthrow of the government. Great unrest ensued in the districts that had elected Taruc. To appease the Huks, President **Manuel Roxas** asked Congress to pass a law giving tenants 70 percent of the harvest, an extremely difficult measure to enforce in the countryside. Roxas followed this action, however, by outlawing the Huk organization and increasing counterinsurgency activities. This only generated more support for the Huks from the tenant farmers. The rebellion reached its height between 1949 and 1951. From central Luzon the insurgency spread to the Visayan Islands and Mindanao. After 1951, the Huk movement slowed down. The atrocities and wanton killings of innocent persons, such as the assassination of Aurora Quezon, widow of the late President Manuel Quezon, lost them the sympathy of the people.

The appointment of Ramon Magsaysay, a World War II veteran guerrilla, as defense secretary brought a vigorous campaign to defeat the Huks militarily and at the same time win popular support for the government. His strategy was effective and the Huk insurgency was defeated. His success, along with his charismatic personality, made him popular among the peasants and laborers, who formed the base of his support in his election as the third president of the republic of the Philippines.

HUMABON. The ruler of Cebu who welcomed Ferdinand Magellan when he landed in Cebu Island on April 17, 1521. As a price for landing, Humabon demanded tribute from Magellan, who refused and instead offered to help him conquer other chiefs so he could be made the king of Cebu. One chieftain, **Lapu-Lapu**, who disliked Humabon, attacked Magellan along with 48 Spanish soldiers. Magellan and 15 of his men were killed and the rest fled to their ships. Humabon then turned against the Spanish soldiers, who remained on the shore and slaughtered them. *See also* LIMASAWA; PIGAFETTA, ANTONIO.

HUMAN RIGHTS. The international image of the Philippines on human rights has been poor—a legacy of the Ferdinand Marcos regime. The imposition of martial law led the military forces to carry out extrajudicial killings, torture, disappearances, arbitrary arrest and detention, and other physical abuse of suspects and detainees. After the fall of Marcos, a new constitution was established (1987) and one of its provisions was the establishment of the Commission on Human Rights. The commission was granted broad powers to monitor the government's compliance with international treaty obligations on human rights. The commission pursued its mandate by charging members of the security forces, including police, soldiers, and local civilian militants, with human rights abuses, often in the context of counterinsurgency operations. Police officials at times appeared to sanction brutality and extralegal killings as expedient means of fighting crime. In its report, the commission described the civilian Philippine National Police (PNP) as the leading abuser of human rights, followed by the Communist **New Peoples' Army (NPA)**.

The government has taken few effective steps to stop military and police abuses, and the government has also been ineffective in reforming the police, military forces, or court system with its poorly paid, over-burdened judges and prosecutors. Furthermore, the court system remains susceptible to the influence of the wealthy and powerful, while failing to provide equal justice for others. An example is the 1987 Lupao massacre in which 17 villagers, including six children and octogenarians were killed but which did not result in any military or civilian convictions. An allied private organization helping monitor the government's work on human rights is KARAPATAN (Alliance for the Advancement of Human Rights)—a militant human rights alliance that is made up of 40 member organizations with a core consisting of Task Force Detainees of the Philippines (TFDP), KAPATID (Association of Relatives and Friends of Political Prisoners), Ecumenical Movement for Justice and Peace (EMJP), Desaparecidos, and SELDA (Society of Ex-Detainees for Liberation from Detention and for Amnesty). *See also* SPARROW SQUADS; VIGILANTES.

HUNDRED ISLANDS NATIONAL PARK. The Hundred Islands National Park was declared a National Geological Monument in September 14, 2001, because of its unique geological formation. The park covers a land area of 1,884 hectares with 123 islands. The Hundred Islands were shaped from uplifted coral deposits by the erosional actions of rainwater and ground water. These islands are clustered in the Lingayen Gulf northeast of Alaminos, **Pangasinan**, 250 kilometers from Manila.

HUSSIN, PAROUK (1944–). A Muslim physician, in 2001, Parouk Hussin took over the governorship of the **Autonomous Region in Muslim Mindanao (ARMM)** after the ouster of **Nur Misuari**, who faced charges of rebellion following the defeat of his forces in Jolo at the hands of the Philippine military forces. Hussin, of **Tausog** descent, faced the daunting task of resuscitating the failed administration of his predecessor over an embattled region, which has a high poverty incidence and the presence of lawless elements. The average head of a family in the autonomous provinces possesses a gun, which he is inclined to use to procure his family needs. Hussin's foremost problem, therefore, is the law-and-order situation that had to be addressed first before development of the land. With the support of President Gloria Macapagal Arroyo, he has made a good head start by obtaining the cooperation of the breakaway group, Moro Islamic Liberation Front (MILF), to join his Moro National Liberation Front (MNLF) in bringing stability to the region. Under Hussin's leadership the geographical coverage of the autonomous region was expanded with the passage of the New Organic Act 9054 to include Marawi City and the trouble-plagued **Basilan** province, the bailiwick of **Abu Sayyaf** and scene of the tragic kidnappings of two American missionaries and the **Balikatan** War games.

HYBRID RICE. Developed by the **International Rice Research Institute (IRRI)** super hybrid rice offers the Philippines self-sufficiency although experts cry caution. However, the Gloria Macapagal Arroyo administration had made the Hybrid Rice Commercialization Program (HRCP) the flagship program of its One Million Jobs Office. The objectives of the HRCP are to attain rice-sufficiency and food security for the country, increase job opportunities, and reduce poverty in rural areas through the used of hybrid rice technology. The hybrid rice PSB Rc72, a major improvement on the **Masagana 99** rice variety, yields at least 15 percent more than the best inbred varieties. The HRCP, however, does not intend to replace the inbred or certified seeds with hybrid rice but to complement them.

Hybrid rice is produced by cross-pollinating two genetically different rice plants with superior qualities. The offspring or seed inherits the superior qualities of the parents. This gives rise to strong and healthy seedlings with longer roots and wider leaves. This increase in growth, size, and yield over those of the parents is called heterosis or hybrid vigor. The hybrid rice technology was first used in China in 1976 and the ensuing large-scale production enabled the country to feed its 1.3 billion people. Since then, 17 countries have followed suit. To encourage Filipino farmers to plant the hybrid rice, the government subsidizes half the cost of 2,400 pesos for a 20-kilo bag, which is sufficient to plant a hectare of rice field. The Philippines has had to import about 625,000 tons of rice each year since 1983 to feed its exploding **population**. In the 1970s, the Philippines was one of the major rice-exporting countries but was later overtaken by Thailand and Vietnam. However, the days of importing would soon be over. Following from one million metric tons, the country now imports only half a million metric tons of rice since farmers began planning

"Gloria" hybrid rice. In 2003, the country harvested a record crop of 14.9 to 15.4 million metric tons of rice. The national **palay** requirement was estimated at 15.5 metric tons in 2004.

– I –

IBA. *See* ZAMBALES.

IBALOI. A tribe found in Benguet and western Nueva Vizcaya provinces in northern Luzon. The Ibalois are subsistence farmers who cultivate terraced fields to raise their staple food crops of rice, camotes or sweet potatoes, and maize. Their small, thatched-roof houses lie scattered among the fields and hillsides near their farms. The women are expert cloth weavers. During the past century, the Ibaloi culture has changed considerably under the influence of their neighboring predominantly Christian groups.

IBALON. Folk epic of the Bicol people. This epic of southern Luzon existed in oral form before the Spanish colonization. Like other major Philippine folk epics, the central figure is a superhero whose name in this case is Handyong. According to legend, Handyong was a great warrior and leader. He fought a one-eyed monster for 10 months, defeated a winged dragon, and won over a seductive snake. He then founded a settlement, which prospered under his rule. He made the first boat, and he invented the plow, the harrow, and other farm implements. *See also HANDYONG.*

IBARRA, CRISOSTOMO. *See NOLI ME TANGERE.*

IDE, HENRY CLAY (1844–1921). American governor-general in the Philippines (1906). Ide was a native of Vermont where he practiced law and was active in state politics. President Benjamin Harrison appointed him American Land Commissioner in Samoa, where he subsequently became chief justice of the Samoan Supreme Court. When the Second Philippine Commission was formed, President William McKinley called Ide to serve as a member. His work as a skilled tax expert and legislator led to a major reform of the Philippine Civil

Code, taxation, and currency. After the departure of **Luke Wright**, Ide became acting governor-general in which he served for a brief six months. When he resigned in September 1906, he had completed six years of service during the most constructive period in establishing a U.S.-based government in the islands.

IFUGAO. A province in northern Luzon, site of the world famous **rice terraces**, which are sometimes called the eighth wonder of the world and which constitute the number one tourist attraction of this rugged region. Partitioned from the larger Mountain province in 1968, Ifugao occupies roughly 2,518 square kilometers of mountainous territory and has 140,000 inhabitants, most of whom belong to the Ifugao tribal group. The capital is Lagawe, but Banaue and Batad are better known because of their proximity to the terraced mountainsides. The Ifugaos, who farm the rice terraces, are also recognized as skilled carvers and weavers. During the Spanish period, they were among the few mountain tribes that successfully resisted subjugation. Besides rice, they raise camotes or sweet potatoes, taro, cotton, beans, and a variety of vegetables. Ifugaos live in small villages consisting of approximately 10 houses built in close proximity to the terrace fields. The number of rice terraces and water buffaloes it owns typically determines a family's status. Ifugao society is monogamous and has strict incest prohibitions. The Ifugaos have a complex cosmology, which consists of a sky world and an underworld inhabited by a myriad of spirits. Shamans or priests treat illnesses through divination and curing rituals. The dead are seated on chairs and mourned for several days before being buried in wooden coffins. *See also* ALIGUYON; APO ANNO; BANNA.

IGLESIA FILIPINA INDEPENDIENTE (IFI). Philippine Independent Church. In 1902, in revolt against the authoritarian power of the Roman Catholic hierarchy, **Gregorio Aglipay**, a priest, founded the independent Roman Catholic Church for Filipinos. For his attempt to give the Filipinos control over their own religious institution, he was excommunicated by the Vatican. With the support of General Emilio Aguinaldo, who encouraged him to Filipinize the church, Aglipay continued his revolt. Most of the Filipino priests took control of their own parishes and joined the new movement. Within a few years, the number of Aglipayans, as the members were called, had increased rapidly. By 1905, the Filipino church claimed 1.5 million adherents or about 25 percent of the Christian population. Most of its adherents came from the north, the Ilocos region, and Aglipay's native area. By 1919, however, membership growth had declined because Aglipay changed his views on the interpretation of church doctrines and the divinity of Christ. In the initial stage of church growth, Aglipay himself had de-emphasized the doctrinal differences between his church and Roman Catholicism. His priests followed Roman Catholic ritual saying mass, hearing confession, and presiding over folk religious ceremonies. Later, Aglipay philosophically shifted closer to Unitarianism. In 1938, a crippling schism took place. One group, led by **Isabelo de los Reyes**, who protested the Unitarianism of Aglipay, separated and wrote its own constitution with a trinitarian theology. In 1955, in a decisive court case, the new group won the right to both the name and property of the *Iglesia Filipina Independiente*. Followers of Aglipay, who died in 1940, continued to argue that they represented true Aglipayanism. In 1955, the IFI established full communion with the Protestant Episcopal Church of the United States, which opened its seminaries for the training of Aglipayan priests. *See also* BARLIN, JORGE IMPERIAL.

IGLESIA NI CRISTO. *See* MANALO, FELIX.

IKALAHAN. *See* KALANGUYA.

ILIANON. *See* AGYU; MANUEL, E. ARSENIO.

ILOCANO. Language generally spoken in the northern Luzon provinces of Ilocos Norte, Ilocos Sur, Abra, La Union, parts of Pangasinan, Nueva Ecija, Tarlac, and the Cagayan Valley.

ILOCOS NORTE. A province on the northwestern coast of Luzon with a land area of 3,399 square kilometers and a population of 450,000. The capital, Laoag City, is the center of trade and education. Like its sister province of Ilocos Sur, Ilocos Norte figured in numerous revolts against the Spanish over abuses suffered under the tobacco monopoly (1782–1881). Many of its towns still have Spanish churches and vintage homes. In spite of the limited amount of agricultural land, the Ilocanos manage to raise significant crops of rice and Virginia tobacco. The latter is both exported and processed locally for cigarette manufacture. Corn, cotton, and garlic, an important cash crop, are also grown. Cottage industries include the weaving of cloth, baskets, and mats, the making of pottery, and the brewing of *basi*, a local alcoholic beverage. During the long annual drought from October to May, the rice land requires irrigation. This province is also noteworthy for being the bailiwick of former president **Ferdinand Marcos**. The chief towns are Paoay, Batac, San Nicolas, Bacarra, Burgos, and Bangui.

ILOCOS SUR. This northwest coastal province of Luzon Island shares a common geography and culture with the other Ilocos provinces of Ilocos Norte and La Union. Ilocano or Iloko is the predominant language spoken by a population of over 500,000 who live on 2,580 square kilometers of land. Ilocos Sur has the greatest population density of all Philippine provinces. Its capital, Vigan, is noted for its original Spanish colonial architecture. During the Spanish period, Vigan was the ecclesiastical capital of northern Luzon. Ilocos Sur was also the site of famous rebellions, including one led by **Diego Silang** and his wife Gabriela to protest the forced labor and **tributes** demanded by the Spanish regime. Although the land is relatively infertile, the Ilocanos rely on farming to produce staple crops of rice, corn, sugarcane, and cassava. Tobacco and cotton are the principal cash crops. An active cottage industry of loom weaving produces the durable Ilocano **abel**. Important towns are Narvacan, Candon, Cabugao, Tagudin, Cervantes, and Sevilla.

ILOILO. The largest province on Panay Island, occupying the southeast part of the island and including the province of **Guimaras**, with a total land area of 5,324 square kilometers and a population of 1.2 million. Hiligaynon is the main language. With its capital at Iloilo City, the province is the cultural, religious, educational, commercial, manufacturing, and transportation center of the western Visayas. It is rich in agricultural land and produces great volumes of rice and sugar, much of which is exported to other regions. The province is also known for the great variety of fish caught in the Guimaras Strait. Herring, sardines, anchovies, and mackerel are the most common catches. The fish are dried and preserved for distribution to markets throughout the Philippines. Most households are engaged in producing local styles of textile with such names as *jusi, piña*, *hablon*, and *sinamay*. Its principal towns are Ajuy, Barotac Viejo, Buenavista, Calinog, Dumangas, Janiuay, Miagao, Tigbauan, Guimbal, San Joaquin, and Pototan.

ILONGO. Also called *Hilagaynon*, the language is spoken in Panay Island, Negros Occidental province, and the southern portion of Mindoro.

ILONGOT. This tribe traditionally inhabited the interior regions of **Nueva Vizcaya** and **Quirino** provinces in north central Luzon. They live in groups or settlements of about 10 households near their fields, where they grow rice, maize, and taro. When the land becomes unproductive they clear new forest by the *kaingin* (slash and burn) method and establish new settlements. Warfare between tribes often results in a form of headhunting for which the tribe is famous. However, this practice has been abandoned under the influence of Protestant missionaries. Their belief system includes worship of supernatural beings that are believed to be the source of illness and bad luck.

ILUSTRADOS. The Philippine elite during the Spanish period. These wealthy and educated Filipinos, together with the muscle of peasants like **Andres Bonifacio**, brought about the end of Spanish rule. Foremost of these ilustrados was **Jose Rizal**, whose European education and polemical novels (*Noli Me Tangere* and *El Filibusterismo*) provided the early revolutionaries with a raison d'être for the revolution. Once committed to the struggle, they became the spokesmen and leaders for independence first against Spain, then against the United States. *See also* PROPAGANDA MOVEMENT.

IMAO, ABDUL. *See* ART GALLERIES.

IMUS. *See* CAVITE.

INDARAPATRA. This is the epic tale of the **Maguindanaon**, who were early converts to Islam. It was about the 14th century Arab traders succeeded in introducing Islam to the southern islands of Mindanao and the Sulu island chain. Hence, this epic tale is heavily influenced by Arabian night's mythical figures such as monsters, magic carpets, and genies. The name Sulayman, and other characters in Indarapatra, is definately Arabic. The scholar Nejeeb Saleeby translated the original Maranao story into English.

INDIA. India has a distinct cultural influence on the Philippines by way of language elements. The paleographic evidence is found in the **Laguna Copper Plate Inscription**, which was written in Kawi script. The latest discoveries of large sea-going vessels in archaeological sites in Butuan, **Agusan del Norte**, attest to the Sanskrit provenance. Research by Filipino Indologist, **Juan R. Francisco**, found that major Philippine languages—Tagalog, Iloko, Sugbahanon, Maranaw, Maguindanao, and Tausog—contain many Sanskrit words. As to how Sanskrit was introduced in the Philippines, Francisco postulates that the islands were in the ancient maritime trade and traffic routes during the existence of the **Sri Vijaya** (686 A.D. through 13th century). Sanskrit is found in the names of **flora and fauna**, terms pertaining to man and his works; to the human body, its parts, ailments, clothing, ornaments, scents; terms reflecting human society—god, religion, its practices, idols, beliefs, the natural phenomena—elements, the sun and other cosmic bodies, trade and the economy; the numerals, time, and seasons; terms relating to the government and its operations. The *Maharadia Lawana*, the Philippine version of the Indian epic, *Ramayana*, is replete with Sanskrit words. *See also* BUTUAN ARCHAEOLOGY.

INDIGENOUS PEOPLES' RIGHTS ACT (IPRA). This landmark law on tribal rights (Republic Act 8371) was signed by President Fidel Ramos on October 29, 1997. Also known as the Ancestral Domain Law, the law recognizes, protects, and promotes the territorial rights of indigenous peoples in the Philippines. It also seeks to stop prejudice against tribal peoples through the recognition of certain rights over their ancestral lands, and the right to live their lives in accordance with their traditions, religions, and customs. The Philippine Supreme Court upheld its constitutionality after it was challenged by vested interests. The IPRA potentially benefits an estimated 10 million indigenous peoples in the biodiversity-rich uplands of the Philippines. *See also* LUMADS.

INDIOS. A disdainful term given to natives of the Philippines by the Spaniards. When the Spaniards discovered the Philippines they believed that they had found India and called the inhabitants *Indios*. The term remained as a class label for all natives throughout the Spanish colonial regime. The terms *Filipinos* and *Peninsulares* were reserved for resident Spaniards who came directly from Spain. **Filipino** became the proper term after the advent of American administration.

INDONESIANS. The first known immigrants who came from mainland Asia to settle in the Philippines. Anthropologists have identified the first wave as "Indonesian A" arriving circa 7000 B.C. Essentially agriculturalists, their main crops were millet and cassava. The next group, "Indonesian B," came circa 1500 B.C. and settled in the coastal regions of Luzon. They too were agriculturalists who cultivated rice, taro, and cassava. In addition, overpopulation, scarce resources, and other economic hardships pushed Indonesians at the beginning of the Christian era to the southern Philippines. The term "Indonesia" came from the writings of Europeans, who called the East Indies "Ultra-India," the islands beyond the Indus River. Those who used the term called the peoples of the East Indies "Indonesians."

Indonesia is the Philippines' biggest and closest neighbor. They have many things in common: climate, geography, race, language, and culture. Both are founding members of the **Association of Southeast Asian Nations** (ASEAN). Bilateral relations with Indonesia are, at best, on friendly terms. When Indonesia became independent in 1949, the Philippines was one of the first nations to recognize Indonesia and to establish diplomatic relations. Soon after President Corazon Aquino assumed office in 1986, she made a visit to Indonesia to dispel the pro-Western image of the Philippines and to promote the idea that the Philippines' greatest interests lie in Asia. At that time, trade between the two countries was negligible, but since then the Philippines has sent economic missions to Indonesia and trade relations have significantly improved. One sensitive issue between the two countries is the presence of Indonesians, mostly illegal immigrants, in the southern islands, including Mindanao.

Indonesians started these migrations in the early 1900s in response to the **Dutch** presence in their homeland. These migrations were kinship based. However, of the approximately 10,000 Indonesians now residing in the southern Philippines, most are illegal entrants, especially those who entered the country after 1946, and most are Protestant Christians. They subsist mainly by farming, fishing, and trading. Migrations continue to occur into the provinces of south Cotabato, Davao del Sur, Davao Oriental, and Samal Island. In order to control and regulate these illegal immigrants, the Philippines and Indonesia entered into an agreement on immigration and illegal entry in 1956. Other agreements on border crossings, border patrol, and border trade followed. With illegal immigration under control, the Philippines does not consider the presence of illegal Indonesian immigrants a threat to national security, despite claims that they may be drawn to Muslim irredentism. Because the Indonesian settlers live very peacefully, few Filipinos are even aware of their presence.

In 2004, cross border trading with Indonesia was opened using the General Santos-Bitung sea route between Mindanao and North Sulawesi. The newly-opened route will cut cost and sailing time for East Indonesia exports to East Asia and the U.S. west coast by as much as 50 percent.

INFRASTRUCTURE. The Department of Public Works and Highways has the responsibility for the maintenance and construction of national highways, bridges, water wells, school buildings, flood control and seawalls, barangay roads, and multipurpose pavements. The 1990 progress report of the department showed that since 1986, a total of 36,530 meters of permanent bridges and 35,356 kilometers of highway and minor roads had been constructed, 28,011 school rooms had been built, and 72,623 wells had been installed. Metro Manila, which faces severe transport problems, is the premier project of the department. Infrastructure has been lagging behind the rapidly growing population and the increase in motor vehicles.

INQUILINOS. *See* KASAMA.

INSTITUTE FOR POPULAR DEMOCRACY. *See* TORRE, EDI-CIO DE LA.

INSULARES. A term used by the Spanish to refer to full-blooded Spaniards born in the Philippines but who were less well off than the Peninsulares. They constituted the second class in social status during the Spanish regime. *See also* ENCOMIENDA; INDIOS.

INTARAY, MASIMO. *See* LIVING TREASURES.

INTERNATIONAL RICE RESEARCH INSTITUTE (IRRI). Initially funded by the Rockefeller and Ford Foundations, the Institute was established in 1960 in Los Banos, Laguna, where a team of international scientists has conducted extensive research on **rice** culture. Their work has produced the Masagana 99 strain, which is a high-yielding, faster-growing, disease-resistant rice variety. Average productivity of Masagana 99 increased rice output to 99 *cavans* of *palay* (unmilled rice) for every hectare with the help of fertilizers and pesticides. *See also* HYBRID RICE.

INTRAMUROS. The original walled city of Manila. Miguel Lopez de Legaspi declared Manila the new capital of the archipelago in 1571 after his defeat of the local Muslim chieftain Rajah Sulayman. Legaspi planned a medieval port to be built on the site of the former Muslim stronghold at the mouth of the Pasig River. The resulting building complex included a fortification known as **Fort Santiago**, a large house for Legaspi, and a church for the Augustinian friars. Other structures, most of them made of stone, were added later as the number of residents and commercial establishments increased. In 1590, a stone wall was built around the city to protect it from invading **Dutch** and Portuguese privateers. Filipino and **Chinese** stonemasons supervised by Jesuit priests erected the construction. When completed in 1600, the massive four-kilometer-long pentagonal walls had seven gates. The city within the wall was called *intramuros*, and only Spaniards were allowed to live there. From *intramuros* emanated the powers of both church and state, and its walls became an intimidating symbol of Spanish rule throughout the archipelago. In 1762, the seemingly impenetrable walls fell to **British** invaders, who occupied the city until 1764. *Intramuros* was the last stronghold of the Spanish to fall to the Americans in 1899. It was reduced to rubble during the battle of Manila in 1945.

INVESTMENT. The Philippine economy has been dependent on foreign investment, especially American capital, which has flowed intermittently, depending on the prevailing political climate, since the country achieved its independence in 1946. Nationalist-inspired legislation has curtailed this flow but presidents Corazon Aquino, Fidel Ramos, and Gloria Macapagal Arroyo have considered foreign investment in a larger political context as a necessity for the economic survival of the nation. United States corporations followed by Japanese companies have been the largest foreign investors in the Philippines. These transnational corporations (TNCs) operate in the nonagricultural sectors of the economy: manufacturing, commerce, electricity, and mining.

The pattern of foreign direct investments flowing into the country showed a growing preference for labor-intensive services, since the Philippines has a labor surplus, as the key strength of the Philippine **economy**. The major centers of industrialization are the **Subic Bay Metropolitan Authority** and Clark Development Corporation. The manufacturing sector has obtained the bulk of foreign investments— 86 percent of 22.6 billion pesos—during the past two years (2001 and 2002), particularly in the information communication technology-enabled services. The Board of Investments reported total investments reached 4.53 billion pesos in 2002. The country's competitive edge is in information communication technology—customer service centers, business process outsourcing, software development, data transcription, and animation. **Taiwan** and **Japan** are the biggest foreign investors—each contributing some $11.3 billion and $9.2 billion, respectively—and making up over 75 percent of total investment. The Asian financial crisis in 1997 and the perceived political instability in the Philippines put a damper on foreign investment interest over the past year. *See also* ECONOMY.

IRAQ. The Philippines, a close ally of the **United States**, sent a peacemaking contingent of 200 soldiers, policemen, doctors, and social workers to Iraq in 2003 as part of the non-U.S. foreign troops engaged in peace keeping and humanitarian work. President Gloria Macapagal Arroyo was one of the Asian leaders to fully support the United States war in Iraq. Meanwhile, the United States also sent American military forces to the Philippines, not as combatants, but to train Filipino troops to fight the terrorist group **Abu Sayyaf** and undertake civic action work in **Basilan**. Apart from the Filipino humanitarian contingent, there are 3,000 civilian Filipino workers in Iraq, mostly employed in U.S. military installations. The relationship of the Philippines and the United States changed dramatically in July 2004 when the Philippines withdrew some 50 of its military contingent to save the life of a Filipino truck driver who was held hostage by the terrorists. This caused a rift in the relationship. President Arroyo justified the withdrawal as demanded by the terrorists by stating that her priority is protecting the national interest first rather than fulfilling its international commitments. *See also* BALIKATAN.

ISABELA. The largest province in the northern Luzon, Isabela is relatively prosperous with its farming and logging industries. It occupies 10,665 square kilometers of land and has a population of more than a million people who speak several languages, including Ilocano, Tagalog, Pangasinan, and Pampango. The Ibanags are the native people of this province, and tobacco is the major cash crop. The giant Magat Dam provides extensive irrigation, which helps the province produce two rice crops a year from its arable land. There are 39 towns in the province, the major ones being Santiago, Ilagan, Cauayan, Ramon, and Roxas. In 1995, Isabela province was divided into Isabela Del Norte and Isabela Sur. *See also* PADACA, MARIA GRACIANA; SAN ROQUE DAM.

ISABELA DEL NORTE AND ISABELA DEL SUR. These two provinces located in the middle of Cagayan valley were created out of the old Isabela province in 1995. Isabela Del Norte's capital is Ilagan and it has 21 municipalities. Isabela Del Sur's capital is Cauayan and it has 15 municipalities. Ilocanos constitute the majority of the population and there are also many natives—Ibanags, Yogada, and **Gaddangs**. The provinces' vast tracts of agricultural land have been used for the production of rice and tobacco.

ISAMAL. *See* DAVAO DEL NORTE.

ISIO. *See* BABAYLANISM.

ISLAM. Arab traders introduced the religion of Mohammed—Islam—in Old Malaysia in the latter part of the 13th century. Old Malaysia (Malacca) included the present Indonesia, the Malay Peninsula, Borneo, and what was later called the Philippines. These traders were called *mukhdumin* (missionaries trained in Islamic knowledge) and from Malacca proceeded to the southern islands of Sulu to spread their faith—belief in one God and the teaching of His prophet. They were followed in 1390 by Rajah Baguinda, one of the rulers of a state in Sumatra, who settled with his retinue in Buwansa, which became the first capital of the sultanate of Sulu. After Baguinda, Abu Bakr, who married one of Baguinda's daughters, continued the propagation of the Islamic faith in the Sulu Islands. Abu Bakr became a sultan and exercised his powers over the Sulu archipelago. In Mindanao, **Sharif Kabungsuan**, who came from Johore, led the spread of the faith in what is now **Cotabato** and **Lanao**. He met the local chieftains and converted them to the Islamic faith. And by marrying some of their daughters, Kabungsuan strengthened his base and firmly established Islam in southern Mindanao. Later on Muslim preachers and holy men carried their faith to Luzon Island where they found receptive villagers. So rapid was the spread of Islam that when the Spaniards first arrived in Luzon in 1570, they found Manila to be a thriving Muslim kingdom. *See also* BALIK ISLAM; RAJAH SULAYMAN; SRI VIJAYA.

ISNEGS. These are the indigenous people of Apayao province, and are interchangeably referred to as Apayaos. The term "Isneg" was derived from a combination of "*is*" meaning "recede" and "*uneg*" meaning "interior." Thus, it means people who have gone into the interior. Up until recently, the Isnegs practiced swidden agriculture, but have increasingly abandoned the practice and adapted intensive rice farming. The Isnegs are noted basket and mat weavers and the womenfolk trade their products for cloth, pots, and materials from Ilocano merchants. Women favor colorful garments for their traditional costumes, while the men are traditionally clothed in a dark-colored (often plain blue) G-string called *abag*, but presently most have adapted to the use of Western clothes. *See also* TINGGIAN.

IVATAN. *See* BATANES.

IWAHIG PENAL COLONY. This penal colony is found in **Palawan**, south of Puerto Princesa City. It was established by the United States Army in 1904 for hardcore criminals who resided in a "prison without bars" and worked in plantations on the 386 square kilometers of surrounding land. The colony encompasses a 37-hectare tract planted with coconuts, rice, and other crops. The prison has a population of about 4,000 and many inmates live with their families in so-called rehabilitation areas. Today, Iwahig is more like a picture of a modern farm rather than a prison. The prisoners toil in their farms unguarded and are allowed to earn an income by working in the many shops that make various handicrafts, most popular of which are the hand-carved items from mahogany (*kamagong*). Their products are sold mostly in tourist shops and curio stores in Manila.

– J –

JABIDAH. Code name of the paramilitary force President Ferdinand Marcos allegedly organized in 1967 and which he placed under the direct supervision of the Philippine Armed Forces. The Jabidah project was presumably organized to pursue the Philippine claim to the Malaysian state of **Sabah** (the Jabidah) and had enlisted Moro (Muslim) recruits. The Philippine Armed Forces trained the recruits in jungle warfare and guerrilla tactics on the island of Simumul in **Tawi-Tawi** and later shifted to **Corregidor**. Unfortunately, the trainees mutinied when they were not properly paid. The project became public after about 28 trainees had been summarily executed. The Jabidah incident offended the sensitivity of the Muslim Filipinos. The execution, which took place on March 18, 1968, was seen by many observers to be an important factor that gave rise to the founding of the Muslim Independence Movement (MIM) by Udtog Matalam. Matalam's MIM was directed at the creation of an Islamic state in Mindanao and Sulu. The idea of creating an Islamic state created waves because it constituted a significant political expression of the Muslims just about two months after the much-publicized Jabidah massacre. The emergence of the Moro National Liberation Front (MNLF) was also a political reaction to the Jabidah massacre.

JAENA, GRACIANO LOPEZ • 191

JACINTO, EMILIO (1875–1899). Youthful adviser of **Andres Bonifacio** and historically known as the "brains of the Katipunan," Emilio Jacinto was born on December 15, 1875, in Trozo, Manila, to Mariano Jacinto, a bookkeeper, and Josefa Dizon. As a boy, he learned the Spanish language by rote and also mastered his native tongue **Tagalog.** With his skill in languages, he helped Bonifacio write the primer of the Katipunan, the oath of pledges, and edited the revolutionary newspaper *Kalayaan* (Liberty). In addition, he served as Bonifacio's secretary and fiscal adviser, and later he became a general. In 1898, while leading his troops against the Spanish in the battle of Maimpis at Magdalena in **Laguna** province, he was severely wounded and captured. He was saved by an identity pass, which belonged to another man, identifying him as a spy for the Spanish. His wounds were treated, and he was able to escape. While Jacinto was establishing his headquarters in the hills, he contracted malaria, which caused his death on April 9, 1899, at the age of 23. *See also* VALENZUELA, PIO.

JAENA, GRACIANO LOPEZ (1856–1896). Propagandist of the **Philippine–Spanish Revolution.** Born in Iloilo of poor parents, Graciano Lopez Jaena started his education at the age of six under Spanish friars. Pursuing his ambition to be a physician, he went to Manila and apprenticed to a doctor. Although he did not have a license to practice, he went back to his home province to minister to the health problems of the people. He did not limit his activities to medical work, but also started writing about his ideas of equality and freedom. His articles lambasted the friars for their indifference, greed, lust, and indolence. For these writings he was persecuted and had to flee to Europe in 1880. Residing in Spain under the protection of a friend, he continued his crusade for reform in the Philippines, not only in his writings but also in his speeches, which he delivered with notable eloquence. In Barcelona in 1889, he and **Marcelo H. Del Pilar** founded *La Solidaridad* as an organ of the **Propaganda Movement**. Other Filipinos, Jose Rizal and Antonio Luna, among them, contributed articles advocating political reforms in the Philippines. Rizal's writings became the cannon balls of the publication. The paper ceased publication when financial support dried up and Jaena, having become persona non grata in Spain, returned to the Philippines under an assumed name. From there he fled again to Hong Kong where he continued his propaganda activities. He died in exile in that city in 1896 of tuberculosis.

JALANDONI, LUIS. *See* CHRISTIANS FOR NATIONAL LIBER-ATION.

JAMA MAPUN. *See* TAWI-TAWI.

JAMAL al-KHALIFFA. *See* BALIK ISLAM.

JAMALUL KIRAM. The last Sultan of Sulu. After the Moro Wars, he was forced to sign the Carpenter-Sultan agreement in 1899 establishing a mutual alliance of convenience between the sultanate and the United States. Kiram agreed to renounce his sovereignty over the Sulu archipelago and reduced his status to that of religious head of the Moro people. He was supported by the annual rental of $5,000 from **British North Borneo** (**Sabah**) and a subsidy from the U.S. government. The rental fee ended upon his death in 1936. And since he had no legitimate heir, the sultanate ceased to exist.

JAPAN. Despite years of bitter feelings toward this Land of the Rising Sun—an aftermath of World War II—most second-generation Filipinos appear to have forgotten the brutal regime and now consider Japan as a good trade and economic partner. Japan paid reparations money to rehabilitate the devastated country, which eased the ill feelings. In the postwar years Japan has become the major source of development funds, trade, investment, and tourism. In 1986, President Corazon Aquino visited Tokyo and met with Emperor Hirohito, who offered apologies for the wrongs committed by Japan during World War II, and this laid a foundation of goodwill between the two countries. Presidents Fidel Ramos and Gloria Macapagal Arroyo made other presidential visits. Japanese prime ministers reciprocated those visits. Japan has also been generous with its wealth. President Joseph Estrada secured $372 million in soft loans for **infrastructure** projects under Japan's special yen loan package. This was the result of Estrada's request during his meeting with Prime Minister Keizo Obuchi. Japan also committed over $3 billion in 10 years to fund food security and poor program initiatives. *See also* TREATY OF AMITY, COMMERCE AND NAVIGATION.

JAPANESE OCCUPATION (1942–1945). Japan occupied the Philippines after successfully destroying the United States Armed Forces in the Far East (**USAFFE**) and capturing the defending

Philippine–American forces, who were trapped in **Bataan** and **Corregidor**. The Japanese established their occupation government in 1942 by setting up a military administration headed mostly by Japanese officers with a civilian counterpart—the Philippine Council of State composed of former high officials of the commonwealth government. This council was replaced by an Executive Commission, which governed the Philippines under the Japanese Military Administration.

The Filipinos were given token independence and the second republic was inaugurated with **Jose P. Laurel** as president. To encourage the Filipinos to accept their rule, the Japanese abolished all political parties and replaced them with **KALIBAPI**, short for *Kapisanan sa Paglilingkod sa Bagong Pilipinas*. Strict press censorship was established with the creation of the *Manila Shimbunsha* as the only newspaper allowed to publish news. The *kempetai* (military police) arrested all who were known to be opposed to their rule. Hundreds of thousands of Filipinos were tortured and many executed on the mere suspicion of being subversives or **guerrillas**. Every major town and city had Japanese detachments to implement control over civilian life. The occupying Japanese Army, having meager supplies, appropriated people's resources like rice and livestock, which caused untold miseries and deep resentment to the people. Not only that, people were forced to do public work like repairing roads and building bridges and were paid with Japanese-issued paper currency, which the people called "Mickey Mouse" and practically had little value in the market place. Life and living was at a standstill during the three and half years of Japanese occupation of the Philippines.

Toward the end of Japanese rule guerrilla attacks increased when American forces under General **Douglas MacArthur** began the battle for liberation with landings in Leyte on October 17, 1944. The Japanese occupation ended on March 3, 1945, with the surrender of General **Tomoyuki Yamashita**. *See also* FORT SANTIAGO.

JAVELLANA, STEVAN (1918–1977). Filipino novelist, who wrote in English. Born in La Paz, Iloilo, Javellana was a practicing lawyer at the outbreak of World War II. A record of his experiences during the Japanese occupation resulted in his first novel, *Without Seeing the Dawn*, which was published in the United States in 1947, and later translated into a television play in Filipino with the title *Malayo Pa Ang Umaga. See also* VILLA, JOSE GARCIA.

JAWI. A documentary of indigenous written material of the Muslim faith written in the distinct form of writing locally known as *jawi* (*jawa* in Brunei, Malaysia, and Indonesia). As the only extant indigenous literature of the Filipino Muslim, the *Jawi* materials are indispensable to historians seeking to correct misinterpretations or distortions of Filipino Muslim history. *Jawi* is a generic term covering correspondence and other forms of discourse that express personal opinions and sentiments of official policies and recommendations directly written by or scribed on behalf of individuals comprising the Sulu sultanate. The bulk of *Jawi* sources located during the research of Samuel K. Tan, professor of history at the University of the Philippines, are addressed to top ranking officials of successive colonial governments in the Muslim South. The first volume of the series puts together 22 **Maguindanao** documents copied from originals in the archives. The first volume was written by Tan and translated by Samier Bakuladon.

JEDDAH ACCORD (1987). Since the **Tripoli Agreement** failed to settle the contentious demand for a separate state of the Muslim National Liberation Front (MNLF), representatives of the Philippine government and the MNLF agreed to meet in Jeddah, Saudi Arabia, on January 3, 1987, to continue the discussion of the proposal for the grant of full autonomy to Mindanao, Basilan, Sulu, Tawi-Tawi, and Palawan subject to the democratic process. The document that was signed stated that the Philippine panel would convey to then President **Corazon Aquino** the MNLF's request for the suspension of provisions on autonomy as contained in the draft of the 1987 Constitution. However, Aquino turned down the request citing the opinion of the Constitutional Commission that the Constitution should be submitted as a whole for approval in the February 2, 1987, plebiscite. In Mindanao, some 70 percent voted for the Constitution while Sulu, where the majority of the population is Muslim, garnered the highest votes at 95 percent.

JEEPNEY. The Filipino's common and unique mode of transportation in urban and provincial areas. This is a converted U.S. army jeep stretched to accommodate 12 closely packed passengers. After World War II, the United States Army left hundreds of thousands of jeeps in depots, which were sold to civilians and ingeniously reconstructed by Filipino rebuilders. These vehicles, artfully and colorfully painted with Filipino indigenous motifs, were christened "jeepneys" and became a means of cheap transportation replacing the prewar horse-drawn *carratela*. The jeepney is found only in the Philippines and nowhere else in the world. It was featured in the Seattle World Expo in 1962 as a tourist attraction.

JEMAAH ISLAMIYAH (JI). Al-Qaeda's arm in Southeast Asia. A militant **Indonesian**-based group that is active in Southeast Asian countries, including the Philippines, which is seeking to establish a Muslim fundamentalist state in the region. The United States has added JI to the list of foreign terrorists organizations, which also includes the **Abu Sayyaf**. The group has its roots in Darul Islam, a violent radical movement that advocated Islamic law in Indonesia, where it was held responsible for the 2002 Bali bombing, which killed 202 people, most of them Australian tourists. In 2004 the Australian Embassy in Jakarta was bombed and caused many fatalities. Some leaders were arrested and convicted by Indonesian authorities. In the Philippines, the military arrested 40 Indonesian JI operatives, who were training Muslim rebels in bomb-making and terrorist techniques. One of these operatives, Father Rothman al-Ghozi, was killed in Mindanao by the Philippine military for master-minding the December 2002 Metro Manila bombings that killed more than 20 people and injured hundreds of others. Since then Philippine military intelligence has kept a tight surveillance of suspected operatives.

JIKIRI (1869–1906). Jikiri was a valiant Isamal chieftain who led a group of Moro warriors in an attack against the American Constabulary during the American occupation of his bailiwick in Mindanao. His rebellion was a protest against the abolition of native leaders. Later, he captured the Borneans tasked to pursue him. He took a last stand, together with his warriors and their families, in a mountain redoubt on Patian Island near Jolo. American troops annihilated them. *See also* DATU UTO.

JOAQUIN, NICK (1917–2004). One of the country's most distinguished writers and the best postwar author in English, Nick Joaquin was born in Manila to professional parents (lawyer and school teacher). After he finished three years of high school education, Joaquin dropped out to work in odd jobs, while he discovered he could learn more by reading widely English literature—short stories—at the National Library. English had become the official medium of instruction in 1898 after the Spanish–American War. Starting as a proofreader at the *Philippine Free Press* he rose to contributing editor and essayist under the pen name *Quijano de Manila.* Joaquin's best known work is the play *A Portrait of the Artist as Filipino: An Elegy in three scenes*, which has been performed in **Intramuros** and by professional thespians. Joaquin's first novel, *The Woman Who Had Two Navels*, won the first Harry Stonehill Novel Award. He was declared a National **Artist** in 1976 and a **Ramon Magsaysay Awardee** in 1996 "for exploring the mysteries of the Filipino body and soul in his inspired novels." As a poet, short story writer, novelist, playwright, historian, journalist, editor and biographer, Joaquin has been the supreme exemplar for Filipino writers and a literary father to several generations.

JOCANO, F. LANDA. *See* DIWATA; *LABAW DONGGON.*

JOLO. See SULU.

JOLOANOS. *See* TAUSOG.

JONES LAW. This was a Philippine independence act passed by the U.S. Congress during the early years of the American colonial administration. The bill known as the Jones Act of 1916 expressly granted independence to the Filipinos with the proviso "as soon as a stable government could be established." Aside from a promise of independence, the Jones Law also provided for a government patterned after that of the United States with three branches: executive, legislative, and judicial. The important provision was the bill of rights. In consonance with this law, the Philippine legislature was inaugurated in Manila on October 16, 1916. By the time Governor General **Fran-**

cis **Burton Harrison** left in 1921, the Filipinos were administering their government. The **Filipinization** program, which Harrison fully supported, was well-received and fully implemented by the trained Filipino administrators.

JOURNALISM. *See* MASS MEDIA.

JUDICIAL SYSTEM. Spanish and Anglo-American law heavily influences the civil law system of the Philippines. An independent judiciary headed by the Supreme Court is made up of 14 associate justices and a chief justice. The court sits *en banc*, or in divisions of three, five, or seven members. Justices of the Supreme Court are appointed by the president from a list of a minimum of three nominees prepared by a Judicial and Bar Council. Other courts comprise the court of appeals, regional trial courts, metropolitan trial courts, municipal courts in cities, and municipal and municipal circuit trial courts. There is also a special court for trying cases of **graft and corruption**: the **Sandiganbayan**. The Office of the Ombudsman (*Tanod Bayan)* investigates complaints concerning the actions of public officials. Muslim Filipinos have their own judicial system. Islamic Shari'a courts were established in the southern Philippines in July 1985, under a presidential decree issued in February 1977. They are presided over by three district magistrates and six circuit judges. *See also* PENAL LAW.

JUETENG. A prewar illegal numbers game which mushroomed into a national operation in 2000 that triggered the downfall of the then president **Joseph Ejercito Estrada** in January 2001. Estrada allegedly collected through his cohorts millions of pesos of kickbacks from this nationwide gambling network. This illicit gambling—betting on three numbers called "*masiao*" in the Visayas—is funded by lords (financiers) who employ thousands of collectors (*cabos*), mostly unemployed people, who distribute tip sheets and collect 7 percent take on the winning numbers. Gambling lords have their jueteng system and exercise control by bribes of politicians, police, and the military. Anti-*jueteng* drives have failed because of the tolerance of public officials who look for easy sources of dole-outs for baptismal, marriage, and burial expenses of their constituents. *Jueteng* is a bailable offense—10,000 pesos—a minor dent in the pockets of jueteng lords who earn millions of pesos a month. Police sources claim that the areas where *jueteng* is widely operated are in Southern Luzon and the Visayan Islands. *See also* GRAFT AND CORRUPTION.

JURAMENTADO. The Moro *juramentado*, brandishing his evil-looking **barong**, was the most fearsome and dreaded opponent faced by American soldiers during the pacification campaign (1899–1910) of the Sulu islands. Among the Moro warriors, the *juramentado* commits the ultimate act of self-sacrifice and his wish to kill the enemy at the expense of his life is like that of the Kamikazes of Japan and the Palestinian "suicide bombers." The ferocity of the attack by a bunch of *juramentados* failed to stop some in their tracks even with the superior 38-caliber Krag rifle of American soldiers. Thus, a 45-caliber was introduced and successfully stopped the rampaging enemy. The *juramentado*—the root word is the Spanish *juramentar*—did not attack at random. His attack was planned, premeditated, and aimed at Christian soldiers—during the so-called Moro Wars—this meant Spanish soldiers and Filipinos. *See also* MASSACRES.

JUSI. Also called *sinamay* in Iloilo, where weaving is a cottage industry. This is the other traditional fabric of **Barong Tagalog**. *Jusi* is derived from banana stalk. Extracting the fiber and weaving the material is a tedious and complicated process, which is usually done by highly skilled women, who inherit the skill from their parents. The gossamer pale ecru fabric is durable and heavily embroidered for barong shirts or women's garments. *Jusi* weaving is also done in **Aklan** and Negros Occidental. *See also* PIÑA; RAMIE; WEAVING.

– K –

KA. A respectful word, which precedes a name. Commonly used in the Tagalog provinces, ka is the abbreviated form of *kasama*, or companion. The Communists adopted *ka* as an honorific title to mean comrade. *See also* PO.

KAAKBAY (KILUSAN SA KAPANGYARIHAN AT KARAPATAN NG BAYAN) (MOVEMENT FOR THE POWER AND RIGHTS OF THE NATION). A nationalist organization to the left of center, led by former Senator **Jose Diokno**. In the February 1986 snap elections, KAAKBAY was an anti-Marcos group, which threw its support to Cory Aquino in return for her support of the KAAKBAY's political agenda. Number one on its agenda was the removal of all U.S. military installations in the Philippines, which Aquino supported but later changed her mind when she was elected president. Number two was the release of all prisoners and the grant of general amnesty to those charged with political offenses under the Ferdinand Marcos regime. Aquino acquiesced to this request and freed political prisoners, including such prominent leaders of the left as Jose Maria Sison and Bernabe Buscayno. Aquino established a Presidential Committee on Human Rights headed by Jose Diokno. Number three was the drafting of a new **constitution** to replace the Marcos constitution, which was promptly done when Aquino issued the Freedom Constitution as a transitional document until the new constitution was approved in a referendum. Diokno had been imprisoned during the martial law period and released when the law was lifted. The experience made him a bitter anti-Marcos critic.

KABALIKAT NG MALAYANG PILIPINO (KAMPI). A political party founded in 1997 by Margarito Cojuangco, a former governor of Tarlac. This was the original party of Gloria Macapagal Arroyo until she decided to run for vice president under the Lakas-United Christian and Muslim Democrats (LAKAS-UCMD) banner in the 1998 presidential elections. She won her post but the standard bearer **Jose De Venecia** lost to Joseph Ejercito Estrada, who won the presidency. Arroyo served as his vice president and was later appointed as secretary of the department of social welfare and development.

KABATAANG MAKABAYAN (PATRIOTIC YOUTH). An activist youth organization established in 1964. The group led the violent demonstrations against the Vietnam War and the United States bases in the Philippines. Ferdinand Marcos outlawed it in 1972 and its members went underground and joined the New Peoples' Army.

KABISIG. A Pilipino term loosely translated as "arm in arm," which was the name of the movement founded by **Corazon Aquino** in 1990 in an effort to revive the spirit of "People Power" and mobilize public pressure on Congress for it to act on her agenda of economic and political reforms. *Kabisig* was also an attempt to shore up Aquino's dwindling base of political support after the *Laban* party, that had elected her to power, turned against her on issues of political patronage and unfulfilled promises. Although she endorsed political candidates, she refused to form a political party of her own, relying instead on her personal probity, spirituality, and simple living to maintain popular support. *Kabisig* failed to catch fire and made no difference in the people's perception of a failed presidency.

KADAKLAN. *See* TINGGIAN.

KAHABAGAN, AGUEDA. A native of Santa, Cruz, Laguna, Agueda Kahabagan was listed as the only woman in the roster of generals of the Army of the Filipino Republic under Emilio Aguinaldo. Kahabagan was already a member of the Katipunan even before its discovery by the Spaniards in August 1896. She was commissioned by General Miguel Malvar to head a detachment of Filipino fighters sometime in May 1897 and fought in a battle against the Spanish forces in Cavite. Her manlike fighting prowess became legendary. She was reportedly seen in the battlefield, armed with a rifle, brandishing a bolo and jumping over trenches. Because of her bravery in battle, General Pio Del Pilar recommended that she be granted the honorary title of *Henerala* (General). She was appointed on January 1, 1899. During the Philippine–American Revolution, she was an undercover agent for the Filipino forces for which she was imprisoned. She was later released and met General **Artemio Ricarte** in Hong Kong. They got married in May 1911 and when the British government removed all political exiles from Hong Kong after the outbreak of World War I, the Ricartes went to Japan. They lived there for 20 years together with their children and grandchildren. During the Japanese occupation of the Philippines, the Ricartes returned in 1943. Ill-health claimed the life of our heroine.

KAHAYAG FOUNDATION. *See* SANTIAGO, IRENE.

KAINGIN. Slash and burn **agriculture** or swidden agriculture—clearing forest or bush by wanton cutting and burning. Although the government had curbed swidden agriculture through stringent laws and enforcement, it is still practiced by isolated mountain tribes in northern Luzon and Mindanao. Utilizing this method, a small plot is cleared by the "slash and burn" technique and then planted with a quick growing dry rice variety or root crops such as cassava, taro, or yams, which require little water. The clearing is dry-farmed for several seasons. When the soil is depleted, the farmer moves to another site and repeats the technique. As evidenced by artifacts found in the Duyong Cave in Mindanao, Filipinos have practiced *kaingin* as far back as the Neolithic period (circa 8000 to 4000 B.C.). However, when valley lowlands for irrigated rice farming became available and settlements became established, the *kaingin* method of growing rice was abandoned. Early swidden farming contributed to the premature destruction of virgin forests in central Luzon, Cebu, and Mindanao.

KAISA (KAISA PARA SA KAUNLARAN) (UNITED FOR PROGRESS). This is a **nongovernmental organization** aimed at promoting the integration of the Chinese–Filipinos in the mainstream of Philippine society. It was established on August 28, 1987, by Chinese and Filipino businessmen, academicians, and professionals who shared a common belief that they do not want to be bystanders in the challenge of rebuilding the nation, which had been wrecked by the mismanagement of the Ferdinand Marcos administration. Thus, their first task was to bring Chinese–Filipinos into meaningful participation in national concerns. Kaisa also devoted its efforts to enhancing the Filipino's understanding and awareness of the ethnic Chinese minority (**Tsinoy**) who comprise about 15 percent of the population.

KAKAMPI (KAPISANAN NG MGA KAMAG-ANAK NG MIGRANTENG MANGAGAWANG PILIPINO) (ORGANIZATION OF RELATIVES OF MIGRANT WORKERS). A **nongovernmental organization** (**NGO**) that is involved in information, advocacy, and campaigns on specific and general issues related to overseas migration. It also works with other groups in lobbying for legislative measures and policies that promote the rights and welfare of the migrant sector—Vietnamese, Indonesians, and Chinese—and operate programs for the family and children of overseas workers. Kakampi coanchors a regular radio program that provides information and assistance to distressed migrants and documents cases of abuses and provides legal assistance, representation, claims processing, counseling, and medical services. *See also* HUMAN RIGHTS.

KALANGUYA. A subgroup of the Ifugao tribe, the Kalanguya are also known as "Ikalahan" or people from the forest. In spite of their association with lowland neighbors the Kalanguya have maintained a unique cultural identity in language, customs, and traditions, even though they are separated into several provinces. There are about 35,000 Kalanguya living in the mountain range of Nueva Ecija, Nueva Vizcaya, Pangasinan, and Benguet. The Kalanguya live in midaltitude tropical forests and practice a variant of the standard Cordillera culture, especially as regards the importance of pigs and meat sharing and the *padit* prestige feast. Taro is a preferred food. Rice is raised in low terrace fields and valleys. An important basketry industry exists in Imugan and Santa Fe area, Nueva Vizcaya. *See also* PULAG NATIONAL PARK.

KALANTIAO (ca. 1410–1433). According to historian **Teodoro Agoncillo**, Datu Kalantiao is the only son of Rajah Gulah, ruler of one of the three kingdoms of pre-Hispanic Panay. Kalantiao was said to be the author of the legendary code of conduct that has been acclaimed for its pragmatic wisdom and rigid justice. This is a disputed ancient penal code of rights, conduct, and governance written in the antique Visayan script that was discovered (circa 1614) by Francisco Deza, a Jesuit priest, who was stationed in Ilog, Negros Occidental. The code was found in the possession of a native **cacique**. It was eventually translated into Spanish. Another priest, Jose Maria Pavon, had access to the code and included the material in his writings about the life of the inhabitants of the island during that time. Dr. James A. Robertson, former director of the Philippine National Library and co-author of the 55-volume *The Philippine Islands*, has noted that Pavon was a historian first and a priest only second. Pavon believed that the code was promulgated in 1433. The original of this code is supposed to be in Spain and was last known to be in the possession of Don Marcelino Orfila of Zaragoza.

The 18 articles have been translated into old English. Article I states: "Ye shall not kill; neither shall ye steal; neither shall ye do harm to the aged, lest ye incur the danger of death. All those who infringe this order shall be condemned to death by being drowned in the river, or in boiling water." With the Spanish conquest and the imposition of the white man's religion on the inhabitants of the islands, the code slowly lost its influence until it was totally superseded by Catholicism and the Spanish laws. However, this controversial code was invalidated by **William Henry Scott**, a American historian, who found no evidence in his research (dissertation) to prove its existence. Nevertheless, Filipinos are still fascinated by this ancient code and historians still include Kalantiao in stories and researches. *See also* SUMAKWEL.

KALAW. *See* VISAYAN WRINKLED HORNBILL.

KALAW, TEODORO. *See* AVES DE RAPINA.

KALAYAAN. This is the Tagalog word for liberty and the name of the newspaper of the **Katipunan**. It was edited and published in 1896 by **Pio Valenzuela** and **Emilio Jacinto**, secretary to Andres Bonifacio. To keep its place of publication a secret from the Spanish, the masthead falsely bore Yokohama as its source and used a pseudonym instead of Jacinto. Only one issue of the paper appeared and the second was being prepared when the Spanish authorities discovered and destroyed the printing press in Manila.

KALIBAPI. A pro-Japanese political organization during World War II. As soon as the Japanese army occupied the Philippines in 1942, it abolished all political parties and introduced a mass party called *KALIBAPI*, an acronym for *Kapisanan sa Paglilingkod sa Bagong Pilipinas* (Association for Service to the New Philippines) to solidify the political power of all the parties under one banner. Benigno Ramos, the founder of **Sakdalista**, became director-general of the KALIBAPI and used the organization to solicit the cooperation of

Filipinos and promote the Greater East Asia Co-Prosperity Sphere. Membership in the KALIBAPI was limited primarily to Filipinos appointed to government positions. Most Filipino politicians stayed away from the KALIBAPI, knowing the organization to be merely a front for the Japanese military to expose **guerrilla** sympathizers. After the end of the war, KALIBAPI members were charged with collaboration and sequestered for a year, at which time they were granted amnesty by President Manuel Roxas. *See also* JAPANESE OCCUPATION.

KALIBO. *See* AKLAN.

KALINAW MINDANAW. A peace movement composed of Christians. Muslims, and **Lumads** in Mindanao, which was organized in 1996 by leaders representing the three core groups. Its main thrust was peace education through self-transformation, which its members conduct in collaboration with other **nongovernmental organizations** in the region. With financial support of the government and United Nations Children's Fund, Kalinaw Mindanaw held its first successful seminar in Cagayan de Oro drawing delegates from its tri-people constituents. It has been holding peace culture seminars in several institutions of higher education in Mindanao. Its manual for peace education, which has been translated into several languages, has become the textbook for propagating the culture of peace all over Mindanao. Participants in the seminars are involved in self-transformation modules, which provide them with the skills as leaders in the peace process in their communities in Central Mindanao. *See also* Rodil, Rudy.

KALINGA. This province was formerly a subprovince of the Old Mountain Province and is now a part of the **Cordillera Autonomous Region**. There are eight municipalities with Tabuk as the capital. This is the homeland of the Kalinga and the Isneg peoples, who have maintained their unique culture, traditions, and customs to the present day with little change. The Kalingas had been described by early American scholars as headhunters. However, during the American colonial administration the people were slowly assimilated into more civilized practices. Kalinga villages consist of 10 to 25 single-room dwellings and are usually located on ridges for easy defense. A council of elders makes all sociopolitical decisions, each village being a politically sovereign entity. The *budong* (peace pact) keeps the peace among the tribes. The staple food crops are rice and a variety of tubers, which are grown on communal plots in the mountains. Protein is obtained from the meat of home-raised pigs and water buffaloes. Kalinga society is patriarchal. Kalinga cosmology is characterized by a sky world ruled by the creator-god Kabunian. *See also* BUGAN.

KAMILOL ISLAM COLLEGES. *See* ALONTO, DOMOCAO AHMAD.

KAMPILAN. *See* BARONG.

KANGLEON, RUPERTO. He was the leader of guerrilla forces in Leyte, who provided military intelligence to General Douglas MacArthur to land the liberation forces at Palo, Leyte. Thus on October 20, 1944, U.S. armed forces landed at the designated site after Kangleon's guerrilla force cleared the area of Japanese defenders. For his role in the liberation of Leyte, General MacArthur, who also decorated him with the Distinguished Service Cross of the United States, promoted Kangleon to a full colonel. Kangleon became Leyte's civil governor upon the reestablishment of the Philippine Commonwealth under President Sergio Osmeña. When the Republic of the Philippines was proclaimed in 1946, President Manuel Roxas appointed Kangleon as the first defense secretary of the republic. He ran for senator in the election of 1952 and was elected. He championed the cause of Filipino veterans by filing bills and resolutions for their welfare and advancement. *See also* GUERRILLA; JAPANESE OCCUPATION.

KANKANAI. *See* BENGUET.

KANLAON, MT. *See* NEGROS ISLAND.

KAPAMPANGAN (PAMPANGO). Kapampangan is the language spoken principally in the province of Pampanga and parts of Tarlac and Zambales in western central Luzon.

KAPATAGAN VALLEY. *See* Economic Development Corps (EDCOR).

KAPIS. (*PLACUNA PLACENTA*). A valuable bivalve mollusk also called windowpane oyster whose translucent shell and small body is more prized than its delicious meat. The shell—known locally as "*lampiong*"—is used in windowpanes, lampshades, chandeliers, glass covers, wind chimes, wall panels, and flower vases, among other items. The shells can also be pounded and used as components for making glue, chalk, varnish, soldering lead, and paint. The creatures abound in the coastal towns along the gulf of **Panay**. From the 1960s to early 1990, *kapis* served the country's export-oriented shell craft industry. Unfortunately, indiscriminate harvesting—use of commercial compressors or dredges—caused the destruction of young (recruits) and old mollusk (breed stock). The *kapis* harvest has declined considerably and has led to the demise of the *kapis* industry, although the *kapis* is a highly prolific breeder. Massive harvesting occurred in the late 1970s and the late 1990s following the increased demand for *kapis* shells in Europe and Japan. Since the government ban on the use of dredges, the *kapis* has made a remarkable comeback.

KARAPATAN. *See* HUMAN RIGHTS.

KASAMA. Sharecroppers. The agreement of the landlord (*haciendero*) and tenant (*kasama*), which defines the share of the two parties in the production of rice, especially in rice producing regions of central Luzon and the Visayan Islands. The *kasama* system was started during the *encomienda* system of the Spanish period and continued with the haciendas. The landlords represented by religious orders or friars managed the land through *inquilinos* (hired managers) who had the estates worked by *kasamas*. Under the *kasama* system the landlords supplied seed and cash necessary to the *kasama*, who in turn provided the tools and work animals. Each party was responsible for one-half the expense of the crop production and theoretically each would receive half of the harvest. However, in the final accounting, the share of each turned out to be 70 percent for the landlord and 30 percent for the tenant, after the former had deducted a portion for advances of cash at steep rates before the planting season. This diminished share made tenants more indebted to the landlord as the principal and interest accumulated rapidly, making the debt an impossible burden. Furthermore, the landlords would ask their *kasamas* for personal services beyond those required in rice production, which were not often compensated for and thus bred resentment.

In 1933, the Rice Share Tenancy Act was enacted, which guaranteed larger shares for tenants, but its implementation was sabotaged by landlords and conniving municipal officials. Rapacious landowners evicted thousands of tenant farmers in 1939 and 1940 because they insisted on the enforcement of the tenancy law. Later, it was the *kasama* system and its inherent unfairness that became the principal issue raised by the **Huks** in their conflict with the government. *See also* HACIENDA LUISITA; SAKDALISTA; TAYUG UPRISING.

KASILAG, LUCRECIA R. (1918–). A leader in music education, Kasilag obtained her music education from Philippine and American institutions of higher learning. Her career has been distinguished by 200 original compositions that range from folk song arrangements, art songs, and choral numbers to orchestral works, which have been published and performed in the Philippines and abroad. She pioneered research of traditional Asian musical instruments and their use juxtaposed with orthodox Western instruments in compositions with an East-West flavor. For many years, she led Philippine cultural delegations to Asian and European countries. In October 1975 she was voted chairperson of the Asian Composers' League, and in 1989 the Philippine government honored her with the prestigious National Artists Award. *See also* URTULA, LUCRECIA.

KATIGBAG, EVA KALAW. *See* UNITED NATIONALIST DEMOCRATIC ORGANIZATION.

KATIPUNAN. A secret revolutionary society founded by Andres Bonifacio on July 7, 1892. Its main purpose was to drive away the hated Spanish colonizers from the Philippines. Its full name was *Kataastaasan Kagalanggalangang Katipunan ng Mga Anak ng Bayan* (Highest and Most Respected Association of the Sons of the Country), and was known by its initials K.K.K. or Katipunan. By the time the Spanish authorities discovered its existence in 1896, the organization had already enlisted 100,000 members. Bonifacio assembled a military force at Balintawak on August 23, 1896, told his men to tear up their *cedulas* (poll tax), the symbols of Spanish tyranny, and declared the start of the rebellion. The "**Cry of Balintawak**" signaled the beginning of the **Philippine–Spanish Revolution.** *See also* PINAGLABANAN.

KATIPUNANG MANGAGAWANG PILIPINO. *See* TRADE UNION CONGRESS OF THE PHILIPPINES.

KENAN. *See* AMAN DANGAT.

KIDAPAWAN. *See* NORTH COTABATO.

KIGOSHI, KUNIHIKO. *See* PANHUTONGAN ARCHAEOLOGICAL DISCOVERY.

KILUSANG MAGBUBUKID NG PILIPINAS (KMP) (PEASANT MOVEMENT OF THE PHILIPPINES). This is a movement that is made up of landless peasants, small farmers, farm workers, subsistence fisher folks, peasant women, and rural youth. Recognized as the most militant peasant federation in the Philippines, KMP advocates for revolutionary agrarian land reform programs, economic nationalism, and promotion of sustainable agriculture. KMP has 55 provincial and six regional chapters nationwide. Its militancy has been demonstrated by numerous protests and demonstrations against the government land reform program. It is also against the liberal trade policies of the World Trade Organization. This group has staged mass marches, demonstrations, and land occupations to obtain land reform. One of its noteworthy marches was held on January 22, 1987, at Malacañang Palace, which resulted in tragedy when government troops indiscriminately fired at the farmers. The incident became known as the **Mendiola Massacre**. The government regarded the KMP as one of several Communist fronts. *See also* HACIENDA LUISITA.

KILUSANG MAYO UNO (KMU) (MAY FIRST MOVEMENT). Formed in the 1980s, this small but influential union is the most militant left wing labor organization to emerge from the struggle against

Ferdinand Marcos. The KMU led many violent general strikes during the Aquino administration. The KMU grew in membership and influence so that by 1989 it controlled 19 affiliated labor federations and hundreds of unions. It claimed 500,000 members. As one of the country's largest labor groups, it played a prominent role in the anti-Marcos movement, and served as a funnel for funds donated to support the Communist Party of the Philippines (CPP). Non-Leninist in its approach, the KMU has preferred to work as much as possible within the existing system. It developed the tactic of the people's strike in which the larger, nonmember populations are brought out into the streets over political battles. These actions have brought cities, provinces, and even (in 1987) the entire nation to a standstill and won victories in matters such as reversing fuel price hikes. The KMU has a chapter for women — *Kilusang Manggagawang Kababaihan* (KMK) — that has addressed concerns such as sexual harassment on the job. The KMK is an independent organization within the KMU federation. *See also* LABOR.

KIMOD. *Kimod* is the epic tale of the Mansaka people, who live in the mountain regions of Davao province. This epic is about the adventures of one celestial maiden who married a mortal. Critics claim that the story of Kimod is similar to the ballet classic of Tchaikovsky "Swan Lake." *See also* PAILALAM RI BORAK.

KINARAY-A. *See* ANTIQUE.

KLEPTOCRACY. A word coined by former U.S. Congressman Stephen Solarz (D-NY) to describe the Marcos regime's practice of diverting huge government funds from programs and projects to the pockets of **Ferdinand Marcos** and his **cronies**. The extensive looting of the public treasury and the flight of millions of dollars to Switzerland led to a tottering economy and the eventual bankruptcy of the Marcos government and his demise as a leader. Appalled by the methods used by Marcos and his wife in siphoning off public money to their Swiss bank accounts, Solarz testified about the Marcos' modus operandi before the U.S. Congress, and he recommended cutting U.S. economic and military aid to the Philippine government. Solarz's assessment of the Marcos government, which was supported by U.S. Ambassador Michael Armacost and the State Department, produced letters from high U.S. officials condemning the Marcos administration and demanding changes in the U.S–Philippine relationship. One of these high officials was Admiral William Crowe, then chairman of the Joint Chiefs of Staff, who wrote to Marcos. He urged him to effect immediate changes and reforms in his administration. Certain that Marcos would not comply, Crowe sent a copy of his letter to President Ronald Reagan with a note that Marcos should leave office. Marcos failed to heed the warning sign and continued his dictatorial ways that led eventually to his downfall. *See also* GRAFT AND CORRUPTION; SANDIGANBAYAN.

KOIRALA, BHARAT. *See* RAMON MAGSAYSAY AWARD.

KOLAMBU. *See* LIMASAWA ISLAND.

KONGRESO NG MAMAMAYANG PILIPINO (KOMPI) (COUNCIL OF PHILIPPINE AFFAIRS). This is a political party, one of several parties that helped Gloria Macapagal Arroyo to wrest the presidency from **Joseph Ejercito Estrada**. Kompi mobilized a massive demonstration—**EDSA 2**—on January 16, 2001, of youth, labor, urban poor, peasants, business, and religious groups that ousted Estrada from Malacañang in a bloodless revolution. They marched to the EDSA shrine after Estrada supporters in the senate voted down a motion to open an envelope containing alleged evidence of Estrada's ill-gotten wealth.

KORAN. *See* ALIMUD DIN; ALONTO, DOMOCAO AHMAD.

KORONADAL. *See* SOUTH COTABATO.

KOROSAWA, AKIRO. *See* RAMON MAGSAYSAY AWARD.

KUNDIMAN. Favorite Filipino love songs. These songs have a haunting melody and harmony and they symbolize Filipino sentimentality. The love songs became thematic in Filipino orchestral work and folk melodies. During the American colonization period, *kundiman* became a medium to express the Filipino sentiment for nationalism and independence. *See also* BALITAO; CELERIO, LEVI.

– L –

LAANO, ARCHINE. *See* FILIPINO-AMERICAN GENERALS.

LABAN NG DEMOKRATIKONG PILIPINO (*LABAN*). A political party formed in 1988 to support Corazon Aquino's presidency. Its political shibboleth was *Laban* (fight) and was symbolized by raising the thumb and forefinger to portray the letter L which was popularized by Aquino during her political fight against Ferdinand Marcos in the 1986 snap elections. During the Aquino administration, it was the largest party in the House of Representatives, but it soon collapsed owing to defections to the new administration party, **Lakas National Union of Christian and Muslim Democrats (LAKAS-CMD).** The May 1995 poll left it with only 27 members in the lower house, while its majority in the Senate split into progovernment and opposition blocs. The party backed Joseph Ejercito Estrada in the 1998 elections after its leader, **Edgardo Angara**, abandoned his own presidential ambitions to run for the vicepresidency. He failed in his quest for the position. And the party also failed to recover lost seats in the lower house. Laban is now considered an opposition party and fielded a slate of candidates in the 2004 elections. In the senatorial elections, it won 5 of 12 seats, with 7 going to the Lakas-CMD.

LABAN NG MASANG PILIPINO (*LAMP*). Laban is a coalition of three parties that supported **Joseph Ejercito Estrada** in 1998 in his bid for the presidency, which he won. But the coalition unraveled and the parties went their separate ways following his removal. The smallest of the three, Partido ng Masang Pilipino (PMP), was formed specifically to back the Estrada candidacy and won no seats in the lower house in May 1998. However, the coalition of which it was the focal point had reached a membership of 195 in the lower house by the end of 1998. Its following in the Senate peaked at 12 in early 2000. But the downfall of Estrada resulted in the evaporation of Estrada's supporters in the Senate and the House of Representatives.

LABAN PARTY/LAKAS NG BAYAN (STRENGTH OF THE NATION). A political party organized in 1978 by **Benigno Aquino Jr**. and **Lorenzo Tañada**. During the martial law period, when Aquino and Tañada were in prison, Ferdinand Marcos allowed his opponents to form opposition parties under the strict scrutiny of his military. The Laban party fielded a slate of candidates for the 1978 National Assembly elections. Aquino campaigned for its slate of candidates from his prison cell. The Laban candidates lost nationally, but the party garnered 40 percent of the votes in Metro Manila. In 1979, Laban was reorganized as the **Laban ng Demokratikong Pilipino (LDP)** and successfully participated in the 1986 snap elections that resulted in the election of Corazon Aquino as president.

LABAW DONGGON. This is an epic tale of the people of **Panay** Island. Anthropologist F. Landa Jocano recorded the original in the Kinaray-a language. The epic ran into 2,325 lines, which he translated into English. *Labaw Donggon* is part of the oral tradition of the Sulod people who live in the mountains of Panay. In its original format *Labaw Donggon*, the tale of an amorous lover and fierce warrior, takes about three days to perform, including breaks for food and sleep, thus making it one of the longest epics in the Philippines. *See also* HINILAWOD.

LABOR. Most Filipinos are young—35 percent are below 15 years of age. The Philippine population of 15 years and over in 2000 was 49 million. According to the Bureau of Labor and Employment Statistics, there is an increasing feminization of the labor force as the number of **women** joining the country's workforce of 24 million or 49 percent is catching up with the men's headcount of 25 million or 50 percent. The entry of female labor en masse started in the 1970s as a result of the export-oriented economic development policy that employed young women in industries like garments, food processing, and electronics. In terms of employment, the bureau noted that of the population 15 years or above only 11 percent or 5 million are skilled. Seventy percent of the skilled workforce (3.2 million) are males and 1.4 million are females. Most of the skilled workers are concentrated in a few developed regions—Metro Manila, Southern Tagalog, Central Luzon, and Central Visayas. The high unemployment rate of 14 percent in 2000 was the result of foreign debt crisis brought about by the defective borrowings made during the decade-long **martial law** regime of President Ferdinand Marcos.

The private sector—mostly family-owned—is the biggest employer in the Philippines. It employed 10 million workers in 2000, or 38 percent of the total employed; the government, on the other hand, employed only two million workers (8 percent). The rural-based **agriculture**, **fishing industry**, and **forestry** sector remained the biggest employer accounting for 39 percent of employment in 2000. *See also* GOKONGKWEI, JOHN.

LACSON, PANFILO (1948–). Lacson is among the most controversial politicians in the Philippines. Identified with ousted President Joseph Ejercito Estrada, the former chief of the Philippine National Police (PNP) and Presidential Anti-Organized Crime Task Force (PAOCTF) allegedly planned two destabilization plots against the Macapagal-Arroyo administration. His political life has been dogged by allegations of conducting summary executions, kidnappings, bribery, and rebellion—for all of which he denied any wrongdoing. He was elected senator in the 2002 senatorial elections garnering 10th place in the slate of 12 successful candidates—among them was Loida Estrada, wife of ousted President Estrada—who drew the sympathy votes from among her husband's political party. In congress Lacson was a vociferous critic of President Gloria Macapagal Arroyo and her policies. A graduate of the Philippine Military Academy in 1971, Lacson followed a career in police and crime work. As junior senator he introduced bills on law enforcement and criminality, one of which was the **antiterrorism** bill. During his term as PNP chief, he led his force in the successful assault on the stronghold of the Muslim Islamic Liberation Front in Mindanao. He was an unsuccessful candidate for president in the 2004 national elections. *See also* POE JR., FERNANDO.

LAGAWE. *See* IFUGAO.

LAGMAN, FILEMON (1954–2001). Filemon Lagman made history by turning his revolutionary character to an aggressive supporter of the democratic way of life. Lagman was a freshman and journalism major at the University of the Philippines when Ferdinand Marcos declared martial law in September 1972. He dropped out and became an **urban guerrilla** of the **New Peoples' Army.** Under his leadership,

Lagman devised new and creative ways of making life difficult for the dictator, while he established and cultivated ties with the above-ground political opposition and other anti-Marcos groups. He helped put together the original *Lakas Ng Bayan* (Laban) ticket in the capital region for the interim **Batasang Pambansa** elections on April 8, 1978. Among the candidates were Benigno Aquino Jr, Aquilino Pimentel Jr, and Alex Boncayo. As expected all of the opposition candidates lost and only Marcos' **cronies** won. Lagman and his cohorts went underground again and declared urban warfare on the Marcos dictatorship.

After the downfall of Marcos, Lagman had a change of conviction about the theory of protracted people's war. Thus, he led his group to dissociate the revolutionary movement from the political opposition that began to gather strength following Benigno Aquino's assassination in 1983. By the 1990s, Lagman broke away from the mainstream communist party after a bitter war of words with the party orthodoxy. Henceforth, Lagman and his group, as well as other splinter groups, were called rejectionists. Lagman launched the **Bukluran ng Mangagagawang Pilipino (BMP)** and **Sanlakas** in 1995. They were no longer fixated on **guerrilla** warfare. The organization of labor unions and squatter communities became their main preoccupation. Despite being neophytes in parliamentary politics, they were able to win a **party-list** seat in Congress. Lagman continued to organize scores of labor unions and led numerous campaigns for higher wages and other working class causes. When Joseph Ejercito Estrada failed to fulfill his promises to the poor, Lagman led his BMP in the EDSA II and ousted the ex-matinee idol. By choosing to turn away from the armed struggle to the parliamentary way through legal yet militant means Lagman made his mark. *See also* KABATAANG MAKABAYAN; STUDENT MOVEMENT.

LAGUNA. This province, which is south of Manila, is the cultural homeland of the **Tagalogs** and birthplace of Filipino national hero **Jose Rizal**. It is densely populated with more than a million inhabitants living on 1,760 square kilometers of land. Santa Cruz, the capital, is located on the scenic Laguna de Bay. Laguna is the country's second largest **coconut** producer after Quezon province. The University of the Philippines (Los Baños) and the **International Rice Research Institute** are located in Laguna. **Pagsanjan**

Falls and various hot springs are star attractions. Among the historic towns are Calamba, Pakil, Paete, Kalayaan, Lumbang, Majayjay, Nagcarlan, Liliw, Rizal, and San Pablo.

LAGUNA COPPER PLATE INSCRIPTION (LCI). This is a thin strip of copper plate scooped out of the river in the process of quarrying in the Lumbang River area in Laguna province. It was acquired by the National Museum of the Philippines. The copper plate is inscribed with epigraphs, which were recognized to be scripts employed in inscriptions found in Java, Indonesia (A.D. 750–950). The date of the inscription is *Saka* year 822, which is A.D. 900. The language has been identified by **Juan R. Francisco**, an Indologist, to be Old Tagalog with a sprinkling of Sanskrit and is related to Old Malay and Old Javanese languages. The LCI is a legal document, a judicial decision regarding the acquittal of a substantial debt in gold, which may have been incurred by a person in high office. However, the inscription is incomplete as the document stops at midsentence, which implied there is a continuation in another copper plate, which is yet to be found. However, this plate confirms the existence of a highly sophisticated as well as literate precolonial Filipino society. *See also* CALATAGAN POT; MANUNGGUL JAR.

LAGUNA LAKE (LAGUNA DE BAY). This is Southeast Asia's second largest—after Indonesia's Lake Toba—located between the provinces of Laguna and Rizal, east of Manila. Global Nature Fund, a German-based group that monitors the preservation of international lakes, named this 90,000-hectare fresh water lake the 18th Living Lakes partner. The lake is a major supplier of water to the provinces of Cavite, Laguna, Batangas, Rizal, and Quezon (Calbarzon area). It has an average depth of 2.8 meters and a shoreline of 220 kilometers long, and a watershed area of 382,000 hectares. The lake is a multipurpose aquatic resource—fisheries and transport route. The water is also used for cooling of industrial plants and irrigation. Since the lake serves as a virtual "catch basin" for the effluents originating from domestic, agricultural, and industrial sources, marine species living in the lake are endangered, including aquatic plants.

LAKANDULA (ca. 1575). One of the most illustrious ancient Filipinos. He was the chief of **Tondo** when Miguel Lopez de Legaspi came to Manila. Rajah Lakandula became a Christian and took the name of Carlos, after the King of Spain. He entered into a **blood compact** with Martin de Goiti and fought alongside the Spaniards against the Chinese pirate, **Limahong**. When he died in 1575 the Spaniards gave him a fitting tribute. Church bells tolled and cannons fired. His coffin was borne by Spanish army captains. As a further token of Spanish appreciation, all the descendants of Rajah Lakandula were exempted from *tributos* or the taxes exacted by the Spaniards from the natives. *See also* RAJAH SULAYMAN.

LAKAS NG EDSA (NATIONAL UNION OF CHRISTIAN DEMO- CRATS AND MUSLIMS) (LAKAS-CMD). Jose de Venecia formed this political party in 1992 in order to support the presidential candidacy of **Fidel Ramos**. Ramos was helped by the National Union of Christian Democrats (NUCD). The coalition led to the victory of Ramos, who became the 12th president of the Philippines. However, its strength in the House of Representatives eroded rapidly after May 1998, falling from 112 members following the vote to fewer than 20 by the year-end. In the Senate—where party political labels have little significance—it had always been a small minority, with its representation in 2000 down to three of the 24 senators. In February 2001, Lakas joined with six small parties—**Reforma**, Probinsya Muna Development Initiative (PROMDI), **Aksyon Demokratiko**, **Liberal Party**, Partido Demokratiko, and Sosyalista ng Pilipinas, in the People's Power Coalition. The coalition presented a slate of candidates in the 2002 senatorial elections. The party succeeded in electing 8 senators, making Lakas a majority in the Senate. Lakas is the party of President **Gloria Macapagal Arroyo**. In the 2004 national elections, the party wrested 7 of the 12 senatorial seats and also won the presidency.

LAM-ANG. A folk epic of the Ilocanos of northern Luzon, originally written in Ilocano with the full title *Biag Ni Lam-ang* (Life of Lam-ang). *Lam-ang* is a long poem of 305 stanzas sung to the accompaniment of a guitar for entertainment as practiced by Ilocano peasantry. The narration is about the exploits of Lam-ang, who is endowed with superhuman qualities, and in his earthly life he reflects the culture and ideals of the ancient Ilocanos. This mythic warrior manages to vanquish his enemies, which include dragons, serpents, and barbarians. His magical powers also win for him the favor of his ladylove, Kanoyan. Although the poem is pre-Christian, the presence of Hispanized names and many Spanish words and customs bespeak a strong Spanish influence. It is the only Ilocano epic that has been translated and rendered into Spanish by **Isabelo de Los Reyes** and into English in two separate translations by Reyes and Leopoldo Yabes. *See also* ALIGUYON; BANNA; BUKANEG, PEDRO.

LANAO. Collective name of the two provinces in Mindanao, Lanao del Norte and Lanao del Sur. *See also* ALONTO DOMOCAO, AHMAD.

LANAO DEL NORTE. Province in northern Mindanao bordered by Iligan Bay on the west. It has a total land area of 3,092 square kilometers and a population of more than half a million, mostly Cebuano-speaking people. A large hydroelectric plant at **Maria Cristina Falls** on the Agus River supplies energy to a wide area of Mindanao, including a number of industrial complexes producing steel, tin plate, fertilizer, plastic, chemicals, and cement. Tubod, the capital, is a bustling port city. There are 22 towns in the province.

LANAO DEL SUR. Located southeast of Lanao del Norte in northern Mindanao, Lanao del Sur occupies a land area of 3,872 square kilometers and has a population of 550,000, 92 percent of whom are Muslim. Most of the towns are situated around the shores of Lake Lanao, the deepest and second-largest lake in the Philippines. The province's rolling hills and fertile soil support an agricultural economy with rice as the main crop. Marawi, the capital city, is the center of **Maranao** culture. Mosques are found throughout the city and Maranao handicrafts, including cloth and brassware, are sold in the bustling marketplace. The Maranaos, whose name means "People of the Lake," are one of the three major Muslim groups that converted to Islam in the 14th century. The other two are the **Maguindanaos** and the **Tausogs** of the Sulu archipelago. In spite of the intrusions by the Spanish and Americans, the Maranaos have preserved their cultural identity, with much of their Islamic heritage perpetuated through the **madrasah** system of religious education. Marawi City, known as Dansalan until 1956, is the site of Mindanao

State University (founded 1972), a showcase of Muslim culture, intellect, and aspirations. MSU's Aga Khan Museum displays Maranao and other Muslim and tribal artifacts, textiles, and Chinese pottery. The chief provincial towns are Tugaya, Malabang, Bacolod Grande, Kapatagan, and Wao.

LAND REFORM. Land distribution program. Haciendas are a legacy of the Spanish period, which allowed the concentration of land in the hands of a few, such as Spanish grandees, the church, favored individuals, and institutions. Since the early Filipinos had no legal means to establish ownership of their land, the Spanish were able to appropriate it and to force the inhabitants into the *encomienda* system to serve the new masters. The local inhabitants farmed the land and paid **tribute** as well. During the **galleon trade**, these *encomienda*s produced tobacco for export to Mexico. Tobacco production was exacted at a heavy price of forced labor and injustice, the root cause of the early **revolts** against the *encomienda* system. When the Americans came, they tried to break up the vast *encomiendas* and start a program of land redistribution. Some of the lands owned by the religious orders, which were the largest landholders, were purchased and subdivided among the tenants. However, many of the heirs of the *encomienderos* were able to keep their land and convert it to smaller estates called haciendas.

Several Philippine presidential administrations have launched land reform programs to maintain social stability in the countryside. Dissatisfied tenant farmers, who demanded the equitable distribution of the land and harvest, spearheaded the **Hukbalahap** insurgency. During the **martial law** period, President Ferdinand Marcos issued a decree on land reform particularly directed at breaking up many of the large haciendas in central Luzon, the major site of the Huk rebellion. The effect of this program was minimal, since the decree covered only certain areas and exempted the rest of the region.

An attempt to solve the vexing problem of the fair distribution of agricultural land, which previous administrations had tried and failed to solve, President Corazon Aquino, whose family owned the vast **Hacienda Luisita**, signed into law the Comprehensive Agrarian Reform Program of 1988. This was followed by the formation of a land reform commission. The objective was to create voluntary land sharing between landowners and farmers and to provide just compensation to the landowners. However, legislators emasculated the implementation of reform by inserting legal loopholes, which allowed landowners to continue to hold most of their acreage. The majority of the members of Congress were big landowners themselves, particularly the bloc of landowning legislators led by Aquino's brother Jose Cojuangco, that resisted efforts to pass more agrarian reform measures. In spite of the exceptions, the Comprehensive Agrarian Reform Program was considered a success as shown by statistics. Between July 1987 and March 1990, a total of 430,730 hectares (1,064,000 acres) were distributed to the landless. President Gloria Macapagal Arroyo was able to push agrarian reforms and health insurance coverage that benefited half a million farmer families. *See also* CACIQUE; INDIGENOUS PEOPLES' RIGHTS; KASAMA.

LANGUAGE. Filipino languages belong to the Malayo-Polynesian or **Austronesian** linguistic family. According to the **Summer Institute of Linguistics**, there are 172 languages in the Philippines. Of those, 169 are living/spoken languages and three are extinct. There are eight major ethnolinguistic groups and the estimated numbers of speakers are Tagalog (17 million), Cebuano (14 million), Ilocano (8 million), Hilagaynon (7 million), Bicolano (6 million), Waray-waray (2.4 million), Pampango (1.8 million), and Pangasinan (1.2 million). Each of these groups shares some elements of grammatical structure, phonology, and vocabulary, while others differ. For many years, **Tagalog**—the national language—was known as Pilipino. But in 1987, by act of the Philippine congress, "Pilipino" was changed to "Filipino." Tagalog words are widely used among the 87 languages of the people, including the so-called cultural minorities.

Basically, Tagalog is the predominant language in Luzon—Batangas, Cavite, Bulacan, Laguna, Rizal, and Nueva Ecija. It is the lingua franca in Metro Manila and of Filipinos anywhere in the world. It is the medium of instruction in the elementary starting with grade 1 and also in higher grades. English, which is also the official language, is still the language of academe, government, business, and politics. Radio and television newscasters popularly employ a combination of English and Tagalog called **Taglish**. Spanish is still spoken by many Spanish families and the upper class, while a variation of Spanish called **Chavacano** is spoken in Zamboanga, Davao, and Cotabato. *See also* SYLLABARY; ZAMBOANGA DEL SUR.

LAOAG. *See* ILOCOS NORTE.

LAPU-LAPU. Chieftain of Mactan Island who successfully led his warriors to repel the Spanish who tried to dominate the island. When **Ferdinand Magellan** landed in Cebu he demanded that the natives pay tribute to the king of Spain. Chief Lapu-lapu refused this demand. Magellan, leading 48 soldiers, met Lapu-lapu on the shore of Mactan Island. In the ensuing battle, Magellan and 18 of his men were killed. The rest fled to their waiting ships offshore. Chief Humabon of Cebu later killed Magellan's remaining soldiers. Lapu-lapu is acclaimed in Philippine history as a hero and the first Filipino to stand up against Western aggression. The scene of battle, which took place on April 27, 1521, today has a historical marker and cites Lapu-lapu for his bravery and as the first champion of native rights. The huge wooden *alho* (pestle) with which he killed Magellan is preserved in the **National Museum** in Manila.

LA SOLIDARIDAD. Organ of the Filipino propaganda movement in Spain. This periodical's first issue appeared on February 15, 1889, in Barcelona. Issued fortnightly, *La Solidaridad* published editorials and articles attacking Spanish policies and the friar-dominated regime. The editor and chief propagandist, **Marcelo Del Pilar**, had hoped that by his propaganda activities he could bring much needed reforms and spread the ideals of democracy in the Philippines. The paper generated an unstoppable nationalist current, which influenced the **ilustrados** to lead the fight for freedom. However, six years later, on November 15, 1895, *La Solidaridad* ceased publication due to lack of financial support. *See also* FRIAROCRACY; LOPEZ JAENA, GRACIANO; PROPAGANDA MOVEMENT.

LA UNION. This province covers 1,493 square kilometers of land along the northwest coast of Luzon. Its name was derived from the union of the southernmost towns of Ilocos Sur and the northernmost towns of Pangasinan in 1850. The capital of San Fernando, a commercial port and export processing zone, is the largest urban center in this province of 556,552 people. The fertile alluvial coastal plains and valleys support an extensive system of wet rice cultivation. Virginia tobacco is the major cash crop. Other crops include corn, vegetables, root crops, sugarcane, bananas, mangoes, and papayas. Cotton is also grown in commercial quantities, and the province has well-developed tourist areas. Chief towns are Bauang, Naguilian, Agoo, and Aringay.

LAUBACH, FRANK CHARLES (1884–1970). World literacy pioneer who started a unique method of language learning in the Philippines. In 1930, he adapted the Roman alphabet to the Maranao language spoken by the Muslims in Lanao del Sur province. He devised a picture-word-syllable method of teaching adults to read in their own language. The Maranao people began teaching one another, thus giving birth to the "Each One Teach One" literacy method. He was the first to attempt translating the Maranao epic *Darangen* into English. Laubach spent the final 35 years of his life establishing literacy programs abroad, visiting 105 countries, and helping to develop literacy materials in 315 languages. His method continues to be used around the world enabling tens of thousands of men and women each year to become literate. His son, Robert Laubach, established Laubach International, headquartered in Syracuse, New York, to promote the literacy program worldwide, and also established a graduate program in literacy journalism at Syracuse University.

LAUREL, JOSE P. (1891–1959). President of the Philippines during the Japanese-sponsored Philippine Republic (1943–1945). During his lifetime, he distinguished himself as a jurist, legislator, administrator, writer, lawyer, educator, and statesman. Jose P. Laurel was born on March 9, 1891, in Tanauan, **Batangas**. His father was Sotero Laurel, who served as undersecretary of the interior in Emilio Aguinaldo's revolutionary government. His higher education started in Manila, where he earned a BA at the **University of Santo Tomas**, and a law degree in 1915 at the University of the Philippines. As a government **pensionado** at Yale University, he acquired the doctorate of civil laws degree in 1920. Laurel served as the first secretary of interior in the cabinet of Governor-General **Leonard Wood.** He was elected senator in 1925 and was the majority floor leader until the end of his term in 1931. At the Philippine Constitutional Convention held in 1934, he was the delegate from his province and was instrumental in including a bill of rights in the new constitution. When the **Commonwealth** of the Philippines was established in 1935, President Manuel Quezon appointed him associate justice of the Supreme Court. Just before the outbreak of World War II, Quezon appointed him secretary of justice.

When Quezon fled to the United States in 1942 after the fall of **Bataan** and **Corregidor**, he asked Laurel to serve as the intermediary for the government with the Japanese military authorities. A national assembly organized by the Japanese elected Laurel president of the puppet republic. In 1945, after the Americans liberated the Philippines, Laurel was charged with the crime of **collaboration**. Indicted by the People's Court in Manila, Laurel and hundreds of others languished in jail until 1948, when President **Manuel Roxas** declared amnesty for all political and economic collaborators. Laurel ran for the presidency in the national elections of 1949 but lost to **Elpidio Quirino**, who became the second president of the republic. However, in the 1951 national elections Laurel topped the eight winning senatorial candidates. After serving in the Senate from 1951–1957, he retired from partisan politics and devoted his time to writing, teaching, and his law practice. He also founded the Lyceum of the Philippines, Manila.

LAUREL-LANGLEY TRADE AGREEMENT. A commercial agreement between the Philippines (Jose P. Laurel) and the United States (James M. Langley) signed on September 6, 1955, in Washington D.C., which amended the onerous **Bell Trade Act** of 1946. One of its provisions mandated ending the free American market for Philippine sugar. Since 1934 when the Philippines possessed commonwealth status, sugar was exported duty free to the United States Exports during the 1960s increased after the United States severed relations with Cuba. This agreement expired in 1974 and Philippine sugar was placed on a quota basis as it entered the United States and into the highly competitive world market. Other exports were also placed on a progressive application of tariffs. The new agreement abolished the authority of the United States to control the exchange rate of the peso, which was then pegged to the American dollar at the rate of two pesos to one U.S. dollar, and it made parity privileges reciprocal. **Parity**

rights were one of the unequal provisions in the Bell Trade Act, which the Filipinos called residual neocolonialism. The U.S. was the Philippines' largest trading partner since independence with an annual trade valued at $3.28 million, or 26 percent of Philippine foreign trade.

LAUREL, SALVADOR. *See* UNITED NATIONAL ALLIANCE.

LAVA, VICENTE. A U.S.-educated Filipino with a Ph.D. in chemistry. Lava, an early convert to communism, was one of the organizers of the **Communist Party of the Philippines** before the outbreak of World War II. He united the warring factions of the Communist party and during the Japanese occupation the Communist party became a guerrilla movement known as **Hukbo ng Bayan Laban Sa Hapon** (Hukbalahap) People's Army Against the Japanese. Lava was killed in 1950 in a gun battle with government troops and his brother Jose Lava, a lawyer, took over the leadership of the **Communist party**.

LECHON. A roast suckling pig, slowly roasted over a pit of charcoals. It is a very popular dish on such social occasions as baptisms, weddings, and fiestas. *See also* BALUT; CUISINE; SUMAN.

LEE, LILIAN. See SCIENTISTS.

LEGAL EDUCATION. Following the defeat of the Spanish colonial government in Manila, the Revolutionary government of 1898, during its brief existence, established a national university. A faculty of law was created, patterned after the Continental European law schools. It had a six-year curriculum, which combined, on the one hand, philosophy and political economy, and on the other, traditional law courses: civil code, penal code, political and administrative law, commercial law, procedural law, and public international law. America's takeover of the Philippine Islands in 1899 brought the first American-style law school, which was established on June 11, 1911, at the University of the Philippines. It used the case-method devised in American universities, and consequently, the common law reliance on decided cases. The law course also became a postbaccalaureate degree, following American practice, instead of a first university degree as practiced in many European jurisdictions. However, huge chunks of laws inherited from the Spanish remained, governing mainly **penal law** and civil law, together with the civil law reliance on annotators. Today, there are 77 law schools all over the country. The annual bar examination is the ultimate test of excellence for students and for law schools. Each year, on four Sundays in September, around 4,000 law graduates take the bar examinations; about 20 percent pass each year, or 800 new lawyers. There are 45,000 practicing attorneys in the Philippines today. *See also* SUPREME COURT.

LEYTE ISLAND. One of the principal islands in the Visayan Islands made up of the provinces of Leyte and southern Leyte. **Biliran** Island is linked to Leyte by a bridge across the narrow Biliran Strait. Leyte Island's 1.8 million inhabitants are divided between Waray-waray speakers (1.5 million) in the north and Cebuano speakers (310,000) in the south. The island has a land area of 7,214 square kilometers. *See also* LANGUAGE.

LIBERAL PARTY. The Liberal Party was formed in 1946 by **Manuel Roxas**, who was running for president against President **Sergio Osmeña** of the Nacionalista party. With the election of Roxas, the Liberal party became the dominant political party until 1953, when Ramon Magsaysay became president under the banner of the **Nacionalista** party. During the regime of Ferdinand Marcos, the Liberal party was in abeyance, putting up only token candidates in the sham elections of the 1960s. Like the **Nacionalista** party, the Liberal party underwent breakups, not because of ideological differences but rather because of personality conflicts among its leaders. Each leader joined with his own followers to form coalitions with other parties. Its main core remained intact, however, under the leadership of **Jovito Salonga**, who maintained the party's position as the loyal opposition against the Nacionalista party of Ferdinand Marcos. The party selected Salonga as a presidential contender in the 1986 elections, which Corazon Aquino won. She was backed by a loose alliance of the **Lakas ng Bayan** party, formed by her late husband Benigno Aquino Jr. when he was still in prison, and the United Nationalist Democratic Organization of Salvador Laurel, who ran as vicepresident. The Liberal party is still in existence and continues to function as the loyal opposition. *See also* LAKAS NG EDSA CMD.

LIBERATION OF THE PHILIPPINES. The return of General **Douglas MacArthur** leading a powerful American armed forces in the Leyte landing with President **Sergio Osmeña** on October 20, 1944. The Japanese made a ferocious defense at the Leyte landing, but it was futile in the face of massive American air, naval, and military might. The liberation of Luzon was followed by the **Lingayen Gulf** landing on January 9, 1945, which was unopposed by the Japanese, who had withdrawn to mountainous strongholds in northern Luzon. In their retreat, the Japanese left a path of total destruction by blowing up bridges and massacring thousands of innocent civilians. The battle to dislodge the Japanese, who decided to fight to the last man, cost thousands of American casualties. The liberation of Manila was probably the costliest engagement of all because the defending Japanese naval forces, which were not under the command of General **Tomoyuki Yamashita**, fought the Americans in a last-ditch stand. To demolish Japanese positions, the Americans had to use heavy artillery that left Manila in total ruins. The battle of Manila resulted in the deaths of 100,000 Filipino civilians, 16,000 Japanese soldiers, and 1,000 Americans. The battle in the northern Luzon was still going on when Emperor Hirohito accepted the terms of unconditional surrender on August 14, 1945. During the three years of occupation, Filipino historians estimated that a million Filipinos lost their lives at the hands of the Japanese. *See also* DALTON PASS; JAPANESE OCCUPATION.

LIBERATION THEOLOGY. A religious activist movement led by some Roman Catholic clergy and Protestant ministers who trace their inspiration to Vatican Council II (1963–1965), where some church views were liberalized, and the second Latin American Bishops' Conference in Medellin, Columbia (1968), which endorsed greater direct efforts to improve the lot of the poor. Advocates of liberation theology have introduced a radical interpretation of the Bible, one that employs Marxist terminology to analyze and condemn the wide disparities between the wealthy elite and the impoverished masses, *See also* CHRISTIANS FOR NATIONAL LIBERATION; TORRE, EDICIO DE LA.

LIGA FILIPINA. Reformist society founded by **Jose Rizal**. Without wanting an open break with Spain, Jose Rizal, on his return from Europe, founded in 1892 *La Liga Filipina* as a forum for Filipinos to express their aspirations for reform and freedom from the oppressive Spanish colonial administration. He believed that there was still a peaceful way to stop the grave injustices committed by the Spanish government. This effort was considered a last resort of the propaganda movement carried on earlier by **Graciano Lopez Jaena** and **Marcelo Del Pilar** in Spain. It served to warn the Spaniards about the violent consequences that might follow if the advocacy of reform was ignored or punished. The Spanish authorities chose the latter course and branded the newly formed society subversive and its activity seditious. Rizal was arrested and exiled to Dapitan. *La Liga Filipina* was disbanded, and its officers were arrested and imprisoned. Rizal's deportation led **Andres Bonifacio** to found the **Katipunan**, a revolutionary society, as the only alternative to Spain's refusal to negotiate with the Filipinos.

LIM, VICENTE (1888–1945). Filipino general and a hero of Bataan. A brigadier general when the war broke out, Vicente Lim obtained his military training at the Infantry School at Fort Benning, Georgia, the General Staff and Command School at Fort Leavenworth, Kansas, and finally the War College, in Washington, D.C., where he became the first Filipino to graduate. When the Philippine–American armed forces retreated to Bataan, he was assigned as commander of the 41st Division to defend the perimeter of Abucay, Pilar, and Bagac against the advancing forces of General **Masaharu Homma.** The heroic three-month stand made by his troops enabled General **Douglas MacArthur** and President **Manuel Quezon** to escape to Australia. Finally outnumbered and overpowered, this line of defense fell and General Lim and his men surrendered. He survived the **Death March** and was later released. However, the Japanese kept close watch over his activities, and he was eventually recaptured off the coast of Mindoro while attempting to contact a submarine for his escape to Australia. He was taken to **Fort Santiago** where he was tortured and executed. *See also* CORREGIDOR.

LIMAHONG. 16th-century Chinese privateer. His Chinese name was Lin-Fung or Dim-Mhon, but historians gave him the name Limahong as the Chinese privateer who almost succeeded in stopping the colonization of the Philippine archipelago. He led an invasion of Manila and carried out depredations of coastal towns in 1574. Limahong was born during the rule of Emperor Chia-Ching (1522–1567) and grew up to become a leader of petty gangs. His life as a pirate began when his gang seized ships and sailed them on the high seas, robbing merchants of their precious cargo. In 1574, Limahong set sail for Manila with a hundred armed junks and 6,000 soldiers and their families. The fleet arrived in Manila Bay at dawn and caught the defending Spanish forces by surprise. The invaders set the city on fire and killed the Spanish commander Martin de Goiti, but they failed to capture the city due to the fierce resistance of the defenders and the native soldiers. Reinforcements led by Captain Juan de Salcedo arrived in time to save the city and drove the Chinese invaders to their waiting ships. Limahong and his remaining 2,000 corsairs went to Corregidor and stayed there for a short period. Later Limahong took his men to Agno River on **Lingayen** Gulf where they established their kingdom. He built a fort and tried to settle down peacefully among the native population. The Chinese occupied the Lingayen Gulf area for almost a year until a large force of Spanish and native soldiers routed the pirates from their stronghold. The Chinese escaped annihilation by digging a channel, now known as Limahong Channel, to enable their ships to sail out from their beleaguered base on the Agno River to the safety of the South China Sea. Some of Limahong's warriors fled to the nearby Cordillera Mountains where they married women of the **Tinggian** tribe. *See also* PANGASINAN.

LIMASAWA ISLAND. This small island of Limasawa—known then as Mazaua to the Spaniards—off the southern coast of Leyte is historically significant as the site where **Ferdinand Magellan** celebrated the first Catholic mass on March 31, 1521, in the Philippines. The chieftain of Limasawa, Kolambu, and his men attended the mass officiated by Father Pedro Valderrama. The stop at Limasawa provided Magellan and his crew of 237 men a much-needed respite and afforded them time to replenish provision. Before leaving the island, Magellan arranged to have a Christian cross erected on the site. Then Magellan's flotilla of three ships proceeded to Cebu where he met **King Humabon**. And again a religious milestone occurred with the Christian baptism of the king and his wife Queen Juana. This signaled the spread of Christianity all over the island of Cebu. *See also* PIGAFETTA, ANTONIO.

LIMESTONE URNS. These are hollow limestone cylinders with vertical fluting. A variety of quaintly carved lids of soft stones were recovered from the caves and rock shelters of Salangsang, Salaman-Lebak, and Menteng, Kulaman plateau in **South Cotabato**. These limestone urns were also recovered from the Seminoho Cave with a high percentage of anthropomorphic covers. A radio carbon date of 585 A.D. +/− 85 was taken from the collagen extracted from human bone found inside the carved limestone urn. See also MAITUM ANTHROPOMORPHIC POTTERIES; MANUNGGUL JAR.

LINGAYEN GULF LANDING (JANUARY 9–13, 1945). After Japan lost the naval battle of Leyte; the ensuing American landing on Lingayen Gulf marks the beginning of the end of the three-year Japanese occupation of the Philippines. General Douglas MacArthur's Sixth Army landed on January 9, 1945, on Lingayen Gulf supported by the Seventh Fleet and the Royal Australian Navy. After the battleships had laid a heavy shore bombardment, 68,000 GIs landed unopposed and raced to Lingayen and Dagupan cities, which were abandoned by the Japanese defenders. General **Tomoyuki Yamashita's** forces retreated to the Mountain Province where they made their last ditch and futile stand against a powerful American army and avenging Filipino guerrillas. While the Sixth Army armor columns pursued the retreating Japanese to the north, another secondary landing was made on January 31 at Bataan Peninsula to keep the Japanese from falling back there as General MacArthur did in 1942. To halt the American juggernaut, Japan used Kamikaze planes to inflict damage on the landing ships anchored on Lingayen Gulf. The suicide pilots sank three ships and heavily damaged 10 others, but the price they paid was loss of all their operational planes. This gave the American forces total air superiority that led quickly to the destruction of the Japanese troops in Northern Luzon. To the south Filipino guerrillas and American troops cornered and annihilated some 16,000 Japanese troops in Manila who fought to the death and inflicted untold casualties on Filipino civilians and wanton destruction of property. *See also* DALTON PASS.

LITERACY. Literacy in the Philippines is classified into two categories: simple literacy (10 years and over) or people who can read, write, and understand a simple message in English, Pilipino, or any of the 120 languages and dialects and functional literacy (10 to 64 years) or people who can read write and have arithmetic skills. The Philippines basic literacy rate is high for a developing country: simple literates are 93.9 percent (47.3 million out of 50.4 million) or roughly 9 out of 10 Filipinos aged 10 years old and over and functional literates are 96.6 percent for 15–24 years old. The National Capital Region posted the highest proportion (98 percent) of literates among the country's 15 regions. The **Autonomous Region in Muslim Mindanao** (ARMM) had the lowest rate of 73.5 percent. Southern Tagalog has 96.4 percent.

Studies have revealed that a symbiotic relationship exists between **education** and economic growth; the progress of one makes possible the development of the other. The five regions with the lowest literacy rates were Central Mindanao 78.3 percent, Western Mindanao 80.4 percent, Eastern Visayas 81.7 percent, **Cordillera Autonomous Region** 86.4 percent, and Bicol region 87.3 percent. These are also among the economically depressed regions. Poverty is at the root of illiteracy. A relatively small percentage of 4.6 percent who are basically illiterate translates into at least 2.8 million Filipinos who can not read or write and about 7.4 million are functionally illiterate. The urban-rural disparity at the national level was marked at 9.2 percentage points—95.4 percent and 86.2 percent in urban and rural areas, respectively.

The Literacy Coordinating Council (LCC) is the government's overall advisory and coordinating body that provides policy and program directions for literacy endeavors in the country. One of its main functions is to recommend strategies in combating illiteracy with the help of several **nongovernmental agencies** and the private sector. The antiliteracy campaign is affected by the dropout rate in the formal school system—out of every 1,000 children who enroll in grade 1, only 70 manage to finish grade 6. This rate is increasing as budgetary problems are hampering programs such as nonformal education, including the perennial shortage of teachers, classrooms, and books. *See also* LANGUAGE.

LITERATURE. Filipinos have repeatedly adopted the language of their colonizers. Jose Rizal wrote his two novels—*El Filibusterismo* and *Noli Me Tangere*—in Spanish. Poets such as Cecilio Apostol, Jesus Balmori, Fernando Ma. Guerrero, and Claro M. Recto used Spanish to express their ideas in a literary form. After the end of the Spanish colonial government, the use of Spanish declined as a new generation learned English under the tutelage of the Americans. After a few years of apprenticeship, Filipinos were able to produce literary works in English. Some of the early writers in English were Paz Marquez Benitez, Angela Manalang Gloria, Arturo B. Rotor, Federico Mangahas, and I. V. Mallari. One of the outstanding English writers was the poet and novelist **Jose Garcia Villa**. Alongside the English writers were the Tagalog writers such as **Lope K. Santos**, Pedro Gatmaitan, Iñigo Ed. Regalado, Julian Cruz Balmaceda, Patricio Mariano, Severino Reyes, and Amado V. Hernandez. They wrote the first novels and modern stories in Tagalog and popularized the **zarzuela** and *balagtasan*.

During the Spanish period, regional literature developed and continued into the modern period. Fiction, epic poems, and serialized novels were produced by writers in the following languages: Ilocano, Pampango (Kapampangan), Bicol, Cebuano, and Ilongo. Regional writers have formed their own literary circles and associations to preserve and further the cause of native language literature. English and Tagalog writers still account for the biggest number of literary works.

LIVING TREASURES (NATIONAL). In April 1992, the *Gawad Sa Manlilikha ng Bayan* or the National Living Treasures Award was institutionalized through Republic Act No. 7355. Tasked with the administration and implementation of the Award is the **National Commission for Culture and Arts** (NCCA), the highest policy-making and coordinating body for culture and arts of the state. NCCA conducts the search for the finest traditional arts of the land, adopts a program that will ensure the transfer of these skills to others, and undertakes measures to promote a genuine appreciation of and pride in the genius of the Filipino people of the *Manlilikha ng Bayan*. These are some of the recently declared National Living Treasures and their forte:

> **Masimo Intaray** of Makagwa Valley, Brooke's Point, Palawan, is a gifted poet, musician, epic chanter, and storyteller, and has been promoting and preserving the musical and literary tradition of the Palawan people.

Samaon Sulaiman of Maganoy, Maguindanao, is known for his unwavering dedication and commitment in his art of *kudyapi* playing at a time when this instrument no longer exists in many parts of Mindanao.

Ginaw Bilog of Panaytayan, Mansalay, Oriental Mindoro, faithfully preserved the Mangyan script and poetry by writing it on bamboo, and by promoting it on every occasion, hence, preserving it for posterity.

Lang Dula, a T'boli of Lake Sebu, South Cotabato, was awarded for producing creations that remain faithful to the Tiboli tradition as manifested in the complexity of her designs, fineness of workmanship, and quality of finish.

Alonzo Saclag of Lubuagan, **Kalinga**, has nurtured Kalinga culture through constant research on traditional rituals involving the performing arts, dance patterns and movements, and Kalinga musical instruments. He formed the Bodong Dance Troupe that has represented and promoted Kalinga performing arts and rituals in countless performances nationwide.

Salinta Monon, a Tagbanua-Bagobo of Bansalan, Davao del Sur, is awarded for fully demonstrating the creative and expressive possibilities of *abaca-ikat* weaving at a time when this art is threatened with extinction.

Federico Caballero is a Sulod-Bukidnon chanter from Kalinog, Iloilo, who possesses an encyclopedic repertoire of more than 10 major epics of Panay, rendered in highly poetic, mythic language called *Ligboc*. The language though related to *Kiniray-a*, is no longer spoken. Among the epics that he has memorized are *Sinagnayan*, *Nagbuhis*, *Tikung Kadlum*, *Pahagunong*, *Amburukay*, *Kalampay*, and *Derikaryong Pada*.

Uwang Abadas is a **Yakan** master of instrumental music from Lamitan, Basilan, Sulu. He is the undisputed master of the *kulintang* (five gongs laid in a row*), kwitangan kayu* (five horizontally suspended log beams), *gabbang* (bamboo xylophone), *agung* (three large suspended gongs), and *tuntungan* (wooden platform). He has been teaching Yakan music for decades and is the acknowledged teacher of accomplished Yakan instrumentalists.

LO, EMILIANO. *See* ART GALLERIES.

LOCSIN, LEANDRO. Known as Manila's master builder, Locsin was the architect of famous edifices—churches, business, hotels—which earned him many awards, one of which was the prestigious Ten Outstanding Young Men. After obtaining his architecture degree from the **University of Santo Tomas** in 1969, he designed the Chapel of the Holy Sacrifice at the University of the Philippines and a chapel in Fabrica, Negros Occidental. These two structures drew the attention of builders for their boldness in the use of forms and elements suggestive of traditional architecture. He was the designer of the **Philippine Cultural Center** and the Folk Arts Theater, which set an unprecedented record of having been completed in less than three months. His work personifies the triumphant emergence of modern Filipino architecture distinctive in style and quality. His use of brown turf (locally called adobe), dark pebbles on the walls and floors, the revival of the traditionally large Filipino roof, use of lattices in the arches, buffers or ramps, the wide two-meter eaves, and the meticulous treatment of the under-the-eaves for maximizing ventilation—all these he introduced and popularized. They have become integral parts of contemporary architecture of the Philippines. *See also* NATIONAL ARTISTS.

LOPEZ MEMORIAL MUSEUM. The Lopez Memorial Museum in Pasay City, Metro Manila, is an artist's and researcher's paradise. Established in 1960 by the philanthropists brothers Don Eugenio and Fernando Lopez, the remarkable building designed by Filipino architect Angel Nakpil houses a collection of rare book, maps, artwork, and Jose Rizal memorabilia. For years, Don Eugenio had collected old and rare books and maps, gathered from the finest antiquarian shops and booksellers in Europe and America. The rare books include such explorer's volumes as James Burney's *A Chronological History of the Voyages and Discoveries in the South Sea or Pacific Ocean* (London 1803–1817); Bartolome Juan Leonardo y Argensola's *The Discovery and Conquest of the Molucco and Philippine Islands* (London 1708), one of few extant copies; Pedro Chirino S. J.'s *Relacion de las Islas Filipinas* (Rome 1604), and a rare gem, the institution's oldest Filipiniana work, the first edition of Belarmino's *Doctrina Cristiana* (Manila 1620), translated into Ilocano by Fr. Lopez and printed by Antonio Damha and Miguel Saixo. The museum's collection currently counts some 16,000 Filipiniana titles by 12,000 authors, rare books, manuscripts, and literary works in various languages.

During his lifetime, Don Eugenio Lopez acquired a priceless collection of works of **Juan Luna**, Felix Resurrecion Hidalgo, and **Fernando Amorsolo**. The museum now counts, as the anchor of its collection, a dazzling 38 Lunas, including the allegorical *España y Filipinas* (oil on wood 1886) and the dreamy oil on wood *Ensueños de Amor* that picture Luna's wife Paz sleeping. Among the 182 Hidalgo's are two oil studies of the stunning *La Barca de Aqueronte*, considered by many to be Hidalgo's masterpiece, and the lyrical 1885 oil *En El Jardin*. Among the Amorsolo is an important early work, the 1942 oil on canvass *Burning of the Intendencia*. At present the museum art collection also includes 20th century art work—contemporary Filipino artists—whose works encompass the length and breath of Philppine art history. *See also* AYALA MUSEUM.

LOUISIANA COMMUNITY. The earliest Filipino settlement in the United States was the Manila men of the Saint Malo village, Louisiana. Called the Louisiana community, the settlers were Filipino sailors who jumped ship from the Spanish **galleons** plying the famous Manila-Acapulco trade during the Spanish colonization of the Philippines. While the galleon was docked in the west coast of Mexico, many Filipinos escaped the oppressive colonial conditions and traveled east to Vera Cruz, where they boarded another ship or traveled by land until Louisiana. An 1883 *Harper's Weekly* report on the Louisiana community noted the presence of this Manila community, which it dated at that time to over 50 years, and which was comprised of about a dozen small huts raised above the swamps. Almost entirely men, these Filipinos lived by fishing and catching alligators. They were said to speak Spanish and a Philippine language, most probably Tagalog since they were referred to in the report as Tagalas from the Philippine islands. They were believed to have eventually assimilated and at present the Saint Malo village is no longer in existence.

LOZANO, JOSE. See AYALA MUSEUM.

LUBANG ISLAND. See HIROO ONODA.

LUCENA. *See* QUEZON.

LUMADS. A Visayan term meaning "native" or "indigenous," it is the generic name of a group of 19 Mindanao ethnic groups that was adopted in their Cotabato Congress in June 1986 to differentiate them from other Mindanaons—Moro or Christians. Lumad was accepted by the Corazon Aquino administration when the word was used in R.A. 6734 to identify their communities from the **Autonomous Region of Muslim Mindanao**. Mindanao Lumadnon account for 2.1 million out of the total 6.5 million indigenous people nationally. These 19 tribes are the following: Ata, Subanon, Bilaan, Bukidnon, Mamanwa, Mandaya, Higaonon, Banwaon, Talaandig, Ubo, Manobo, Tiboli, Tiruray, Bagobo, Tagakaolo, Dibabawon, Manguwangan, Matigsalug, and Mansaka. Lumads are found in Cotabato, Davao, Zamboanga del Sur, Surigao, Bukidnon, Agusan, and Sarangani.

Economically, Lumadnon practiced **kaingin** (swidden) agriculture depending on the land's productivity. Their sociopolitical arrangements are varied. Their *bagani* or warrior is the leader of some groups while the Bagobos, Manobo as well as most of the Lumadnon, is led by their *datu*. Since the early 1930s, they have remained isolated and withdrawn from the hills and forest due to the incursion of Christian groups into their domains. Lately the government has taken interest in their welfare since foreign agribusiness bought some of their ancestral lands for pineapple plantations. The concern for the Lumadnon is focused on **sustainable development** projects, like reforestation and conservation, and return of their ancestral lands. Since the introduction of the **Indigenous Peoples' Rights**, which spelled out their rights, many educated Lumadnon are articulating their demand for political representation in the autonomous government of Mindanao.

LUMAWIG. This is the well-known epic of the **Bontoc** people who are also called Igorots. Bontocs are famous for their stone **rice terraces** and cone-shaped, one-room houses. In their cosmology Lumawig is the greatest and most powerful of all deities in the sky world. The motif in this tale is the marriage of Lumawig and a mortal. The people practiced a monotheistic form of religion with male shamans who preside over ancestral rites marked by hog sacrifice. *See also* ALIGUYON; BANNA; BUGAN.

LUNA, ANTONIO (1866–1899). Revolutionary general. A pharmacist by profession, he became a nationalist in Europe after he met and associated with **Jose Rizal**. He wrote satirical essays on the Spanish colonial administration in the Philippines. Having studied military strategy, Luna was appointed a brigadier general by **Emilio Aguinaldo** when the **Philippine–Spanish Revolution** broke out in 1896. He trained the officers who fought in the revolution and led many successful attacks against the Spanish forces. Considered an aggressive general, he was also abrasive in his relationships with other generals. Soldiers loyal to Emilio Aguinaldo killed him with his adjutant in Cabanatuan, Nueva Ecija.

LUNA, JUAN (1857–1899). Painter. He was born in Badoc, **Ilocos Norte**, on October 23, 1857. An **ilustrado** like his brother Antonio Luna, he studied painting under a Spanish painter and went to the Academy of Fine Arts in Madrid. His forte was historical painting and his canvas *Spolarium*, which depicted gladiators in combat, won first prize (gold medal) in the National Exposition of Fine Arts in Madrid in 1884. Another famous historical painting *The Battle of Lepanto* won a gold medal in the Barcelona Exposition of 1888. *See also* LOPEZ MUSEUM.

LUPAO MASSACRE. *See* HUMAN RIGHTS.

LUUK. *See* SULU.

– M –

MAASIN. See LEYTE, SOUTHERN.

MABINI, APOLINARIO (1864–1903). The "sublime paralytic" and "brains of the Katipunan." In spite of his disability, he ably served General Emilio Aquinaldo as secretary of foreign affairs and president of the cabinet. He wrote the proposed constitution for the Philippine Republic in order to instill the ideals of the revolution among the people. He also wrote most of the decrees of the revolutionary government. The Americans captured him shortly before the end of the **Philippine–American Revolution** and exiled him to Guam, where he wrote his memoirs, *La Revolucion Filipina* (The Philippine Revolution). He died in Manila of cholera on May 13, 1903, at the age of 39. *See also* EMILIO JACINTO.

MABUHAY (MA-BOO-HIGH). This is a popular Filipino greeting and a wish, meaning "may you live and have a long life." It is both a blessing and a lusty cheer. It is also used as a word for welcome, congratulations, Godspeed, and good luck. Often this greeting is expressed in public rallies and political gatherings.

MACABEBES. For nearly two centuries, the province of Pampanga had supplied Spain with its Macabebes, the most trusted mercenaries, for its garrisons in the islands and foreign expeditions. During the Spanish–Philippine Revolution, the Macabebes inflicted heavy casualties upon the revolutionaries. When Spain ceded the Philippines to America, the Macabebes were abandoned and left to fend for themselves. Instead they offered their services to the American forces. They were employed as boatmen and *cargadores* (dock workers). Since they proved themselves reliable, the Americans organized a regiment of Macabebes who attacked Aguinaldo's elite Manila Battalion and captured their entrenched position. They were later instrumental in the capture of Aguinaldo in Palanan, **Isabela**. After the end of the Philippine–American Revolution, the Macabebes were integrated into the Philippine Constabulary, the peace-keeping force in the provinces.

MACAPAGAL, DIOSDADO (1910–1997). Fifth president of the Republic of the Philippines. He was born on September 28, 1910, in San Nicolas, Lubao, Pampanga to Urbano Macapagal, a tenant farmer, and his wife Romana Pangan. Early in his youth, Macapagal showed his talent by graduating as the valedictorian in his elementary school class and salutatorian in his high school class of 1929. In college he excelled in debate and oratory. He obtained his law degree from the **University of Santo Tomas**, and he placed first in the bar examinations in 1935. He joined a law firm and practiced law until the outbreak of World War II. Macapagal served briefly in the Department of Foreign Affairs, and was head of a panel, which negotiated the transfer of the Turtle Islands from Great Britain to the Philippines. He ran for Congress from his native **Pampanga** province and was elected in 1949, then reelected in 1953. During his term as a congressman, he sponsored the successful passage of laws benefiting the farmers, which earned him the honor of the "Best Lawmaker" for 1954–1957.

In the national elections of 1958, he was elected vice president, but his **Liberal party's** standard-bearer, Jose Yulo, was defeated. Carlos P. Garcia of the **Nacionalista** party won. Macapagal served under Garcia and in the presidential elections of 1961 he won the presidency. His accomplishments during his administration include land reform, which freed many farmers from virtual slavery as tenant farmers, and major improvements in infrastructure. During his term, he declared June 12 as the national independence day in honor of General Emilio Aguinaldo's declaration of freedom from Spain in 1898. *See also* ARROYO, GLORIA MACAPAGAL; CLARK INTERNATIONAL AIRPORT.

MACARTHUR, ARTHUR. *See* WILLIAM HOWARD TAFT.

MACARTHUR, DOUGLAS (1880–1964). General of the United States Army Force in the Far East (USAFFE) Philippine-American forces in Bataan and Corregidor. MacArthur was appointed by President **Manuel L. Quezon** as Field Marshal of the Philippine Army before the outbreak of World War II, in which capacity he planned for the defense of the Philippines against the Japanese. Due to their inferior military strength, however, the Philippine–American forces capitulated in their last-ditch stand in the **Bataan** and **Corregidor** perimeter. MacArthur was ordered by President Franklin D. Roosevelt to evacuate to Australia. Three and a half years later, he returned to the Philippines with the massive force of the army, navy, and air force. This time, the Japanese army commanded by General Tomoyuki Yamashita were at the receiving end of a superiorly armed force that totally crushed the defending Japanese military and navy. MacArthur declared complete liberation of the Philippines on July 4, 1945, in Manila. *See also* LIBERATION OF THE PHILIPPINES; MASAHURO HOMMA.

MADRASAH. A parochial private school providing Islamic religious education to Muslim Filipinos. Arabic is the language of instruction and the curriculum is one used by similar schools in the Middle East.

Muslims who pass through the *madrasah* become the religio-social class of *pandita* or the Arabic-educated intelligentsia. The root word of *madrasah* is *darsh*, signifying rote lessons, which was the traditional method of instruction. The system has in modern times undergone some major changes, such as replacement of the tutorial method with more modern instructional techniques. *See also* SHARIA.

MAGAHATS. *See* AGUSAN DEL SUR.

MAGAT SALAMAT (1550–1589). Magat Salamat was the son of Rajah Matanda, chief of **Tondo** when the Spanish arrived. Salamat endeavored to recover his heritage by participating in the Tondo conspiracy (1587–1588), designed to overthrow the Spanish sovereignty in the Philippines. Magat Salamat planned the movement in cooperation with two other Tondo chieftains. He also obtained the help of chieftains of Bulacan, Cavite, Laguna, and Batangas. Just when they were ready to strike, a Spanish agent learned of the plot. Magat Salamat and his conspirators were arrested and subsequently executed. And so the first rebels of **Tondo** were annihilated. The significance of this conspiracy is that it was proof that early Filipinos were capable of united action. Several centuries later Magat Salamat's martyrdom was duplicated by two of his district mates, **Andres Bonifacio** and **Macario Sakay**.

MAGBANUA, TERESA (1871–1947). This little-known heroine of the **Philippine–Spanish Revolution** was the first woman in **Panay** to respond to the call to arms by the Katipunan. As a young girl, she learned farm work and developed skills in handling firearms. Her well-to-do parents sent her to school in Manila, where she enrolled in teacher education. However, her plan to teach school was cut short when she joined the revolutionary force of General Martin Delgado in Jara, Iloilo. She fought bravely with men in the battle of Sap-ong near Jara. For her feat, General Delgado promoted her to a brigade captain. She led her brigade in several successful skirmishes against the Spaniards. When the revolution ended, she continued her command and fought the American occupiers of her province. Eventually, it became obvious that the fight against the superiorly armed Americans was futile, so she disbanded her men and returned to civilian life.

MAGDALO. A name adopted by a group of Philippine Armed Forces junior officers who staged a mutiny on July 27, 2003, to express their grievances against **graft and corruption** in the military service. The rebellious soldiers barricaded themselves in a posh hotel in **Makati** and waited for government forces to take them. The encounter failed to materialize when the mutineers agreed to a peaceful negotiation. They were arrested and charged with the crime of coup d' etat.

MAGELLAN, FERDINAND (1480–1521). Portuguese explorer and navigator. Under the sponsorship of King Philip II of Spain, Magellan led an expedition of five ships and 265 men to find a trade route to the Moluccas. He left Spain on September 20, 1519, and landed on Homonhon, Samar in the Philippines on March 16, 1521, with three ships. Two of his ships were wrecked in the Pacific Ocean. He made a **blood compact** with Chief Kulambo and proceeded to Cebu, where Chief Humabon demanded tribute. Although Magellan refused to comply, the chief allowed him to land. Having established good relations with the chief, Magellan ordered other chieftains of Cebu and neighboring islands to recognize Chief Humabon as their king. Chief **Lapu-lapu** of Mactan Island spurned this demand. Magellan, along with 48 men, went to Mactan to punish Lapu-lapu. Lapu-lapu and his warriors routed the Spaniards and killed Magellan and 18 of his men on April 18, 1521. The survivors fled to Cebu, where some were massacred. Only one of Magellan's ships, the *Victoria* with 18 men under the command of Sebastian del Cano, was able to return to Spain to complete the first circumnavigation of the earth. For all its losses, the voyage was a huge financial success. The *Victoria*'s 26 ton cargo of cloves sold for 41,000 ducats. This returned the 20,000 ducats the venture had cost plus a 105 percent profit. *See also* LIMASAWA ISLAND.

MAGSAYSAY, RAMON F. (1907–1957). Seventh president of the Republic of the Philippines and well-known champion of the common man. He was born on August 31, 1907, in Iba, Zambales. His parents were Exequiel Magsaysay, a trade school teacher, and Perfecta del Fierro. He obtained a B.S. degree in commerce from Jose Rizal College in Manila. When the Japanese invaded the Philippines in 1942, he was working as a manager of a bus company. During the occupation, he was a guerrilla fighter in Zambales. The United States

Army subsequently recognized his unit as Magsaysay's **Guerrillas**. After the liberation, General **Douglas MacArthur** promoted him to major. He was elected twice, in 1946 and 1949, as a representative of his province. In 1950 President Quirino appointed him secretary of national defense. As secretary, he broke the back of the Communist-led **Hukbalahaps** by effective military action and attractive economic reforms. For this feat, his popularity rose dramatically, and he ran for president in the 1953 national elections. He won by a landslide victory and took the oath of office wearing the **barong tagalog**, which became popular as a dress shirt for Filipino men. He also opened the **Malacañang** Palace to the people. Although Magsaysay served for only two years, he was instrumental in acquiring land settlements for the landless people, lowering the price of consumer goods, and breaking up the big landed estates. He died at the age of 50 in a plane crash on March 17, 1957, on Mt. Manunggal in Cebu. *See also* EDCOR; RAMON MAGSAYSAY AWARDS.

MAGUINDANAO. Homeland of the "people of the flood plain," who inhabit the broad riverbanks and valleys of the great Mindanao River, which meanders through the province and annually floods its banks, leaving fertile deposits of soil on the adjacent land. Maguindanao province was sectioned off from the former Cotabato province in 1972 in deference to the need for a separate Muslim province for the Maguindanao people, who now constitute 70 percent of Maguindanao province's 750,000 inhabitants. The province covers a land area of 6,565 square kilometers in the southwestern part of Mindanao. **Rice** and **coconuts** are the major crops. Maguindanao province is also the homeland of another ethnic group, the **Tirurays**, who live in the hills of the Cotabato Cordillera as subsistence farmers. Although Matanog is the provincial capital, the trading center is Cotabato City, the former capital of Cotabato province before 1972. Other chief towns are Datu Piang, Buluan, Parang, South Upi, Sultan Barongis, and Pagalungan.

MAGUINDANAO TRIBE. Name of an ethnic tribe and province located in south-central Mindanao. The Maguindanaos comprise the largest ethnic group of Muslim Filipinos and are spread throughout Lanao del Sur province, Maguindanao, and Cotabato provinces. The

Maguindanaos were early converts to Islam in the 14th century. Spanish colonial governors tried to subjugate them but were unsuccessful. The conflict known as the Moro Wars continued until the defeat of the Spanish by the Americans in 1898. Early Maguindanao settlements were located along the myriad waterways of the interior regions. These waterways facilitated transportation and communication, enabling the Maguindanaos to conduct profitable commerce with neighboring tribes. The datu is the ruling head of a community, which is usually composed of closely related families. The Maguindanao people are related culturally to the **Maranaos**, although there are characteristic distinctions in dress styles, art works, and literary traditions between the two groups. Sultans are the recognized authority figures in a Maranao society in which most people are farmers and fishermen. Disagreements between families sometimes result in serious and bloody feuds. Since their conversion to Islam, the practice of the Faith has been mixed with animism and folk beliefs. The *imam* and *pandita* (local priests) preside over the religious life of the people. Traditional Maguindanao attire consists of a colorful, long tubular skirt (*malong*) and a long-sleeved shirt reaching to the knees (*bargula).* They are also known for their exotic folk dances. *See also* SHARIF KABUNGSUAN and SINGKIL.

MAITUM ANTHROPOMORPHIC POTTERIES. Filipino archaeologists of the National Musem excavated a site in Pinol, Maitum, **Sarangani** province, and found anthropomorphic burial jars that date back to the Metal Age. The site had been dated to 830 $+/-$ 60 B.P. (calibrated date of A.D. 701 to 370) and 1920 $+/-$ 50 B.P. (calibrated date of 5 B.C. to A.D. 225). The radiocarbon dates were obtained from the soot samples taken from small earthenware vessels found inside one of the anthropomorphic burial jars. These burial jars are made of earthenware design and formed like human figures with complete facial characteristics. These were associated with metal implements: glass beads and bracelets, shell spoons, scoops, bracelets and pendants, earthenware potteries with incised designs and cut-out footings, and non-anthropomorphic burial jars. *See also* FUGA ISLAND; POTTERIES; TABON CAVES.

MAIZE. *See* CORN.

MAJAPAHIT (1292–1478). Singhasari king who founded the successor state of **Sri Vijaya**, Majapahit, in 1292. The Javanese Majapahit Empire's life was relatively short. It was founded just as the penetration of Muslim traders and proselytizers into the Philippine archipelago was gaining in strength. Majapahit was fortunate in having the services of Gajah Madah, an ambitious and determined prime minister and regent. In his long career from 1331 to 1364, Gajah Madah brought Bali, Java, and Sumatra effectively under Majapahit control. A few years later, the Majapahit navy took Palembang, the Sri Vijaya capital, and thus put the former empire to an end in 1377. The imperial ambitions of the Hindu kingdoms of Java, Malaya, and Sumatra concentrated mainly on gaining from their rivals a larger share of the commercial traffic that passed through the archipelago and the straits. Territorial aggrandizement does not seem to have been the object of their rivalries. From time to time new settlements from Java (985, 1280, and 1387) were founded in Borneo. Unlike the rapid spread of Islam in Asia, the influence of Hindic-Buddhist culture in the archipelago remained localized in the vicinity of the Straits.

MAKAR PORT. *See* SOCSKSARGEN.

MAKATI. The Philippines' premier financial and business center located in Metro Manila. Initially the site of a bedroom community, the place has been transformed into the Wall Street of the Philippines, where major business firms, insurance companies, international hotels, banks, and foreign embassies are located. Offices of the top 1,000 corporations and stock market are in the Makati district. The **Zobel** de Ayala family started the development of the area following the end of World War II by laying out sites for business enterprises and residential sections and calling it the new city of Makati, which is a city within a city (**Metro Manila**). In time, the city became the site of vast shopping centers, high rise buildings, and luxurious homes. During the Ferdinand Marcos regime, Makati became a symbol of affluence, a place where many of the anti-Marcos demonstrations were held, and where the failed coups against the Corazon Aquino administration were staged.

MAKATUNAW. *See* PANAY ISLAND.

MAKIBAKA (MALAYANG KILUSAN NG BAGONG KABA-BAIHAN) (FREE MOVEMENT OF NEW WOMEN). Established in the early 1970s during the height of the student activism, MAKIBAKA—a militant **women's** organization—espoused the development of women's consciousness among women workers, urban poor, the religious, the middle class, women artist, and peasants. MAKIBAKA claimed to be better organized than the suffragette movement in the early 1920s. However, this women's movement was nipped in the bud with the declaration of martial law in 1972. MAKIBAKA was declared illegal and the members joined the revolutionary underground. *See also* GABRIELA.

MALACAÑANG PALACE. Official residence of the president of the Philippines. A rich Spanish gentleman who sold it to the Spanish government as the summer residence of the Spanish governor-general owned the original two-story building by the Pasig River. It was renovated to make it look like a palace and the grounds were landscaped. In 1847, it became the official residence of the highest Spanish official and the place for entertainment of guests and where official dignitaries are received. American governors-general also made the palace their official residence and further improved its exterior and interior trappings by enlarging various rooms to accommodate more guests. **Manuel L. Quezon** was the first Filipino president to live in the palace and gave it the name Malacañang from the **Tagalog** word *may lakan diyan* (a nobleman lives there) and since then it has become the official word to refer to the residence of Philippine presidents. When President **Ferdinand Marcos** lived there, his wife Imelda made major renovations inside the palace to make the halls more spacious and to furnish the premises with ornate chandeliers. It was also during the Marcos regime that Malacañang became the target of many violent demonstrations against the government. Rampaging demonstrators sacked the place when Marcos fled to Hawaii with his family. President Corazon Aquino, when she took office in February 1986, turned Malacañang Palace into a museum and office where she worked and received her guests. She chose to live in a house near Malacañang Palace on Arlegui street. *See also* MENDIOLA MASSACRE.

MALAMPAYA SOUND. This is a seascape-protected area located at the northwestern part of **Palawan** and made up of terrestrial and coastal/marine areas. It is dubbed the "Fishbowl of the Philippines" for its rich marine resources with more than 156 species of fish (60 species have high commercial value). It is made up of a number of habitats and eco-systems such as tropical lowland forests, old growth mangroves, coral reefs, sea grass beds, and coastal beaches. The area abounds with **flora and fauna** including species endemic to Palawan. It is also known as the habitat of the bottle-nosed and Irrawady dolphins, attesting to its rich **biodiversity**. *See also* TUBBATAHA REEFS.

MALAYS. Third and largest group of immigrants who came in several waves to the Philippines between 200 and 1500 B.C. Sailing on their long boats, called *balangay* or **barangay**, they arrived from the Malay Peninsula and settled in various islands. Some of them went to northern Luzon and are considered the ancestors of the Igorots, **Bontocs**, **Tinguians**, and other mountain tribes. Some inhabited the lowlands and riverine sites of Luzon. A later wave of Malays settled in the Sulu Islands and Mindanao and are the ancestors of the Moro people. The Malay immigrants brought with them their traditional systems of government and laws, in addition to their religion, arts, and culture. They had a highly developed system of writing, which they used on **bamboo** bark. They were farmers, fishermen, and herdsmen, who were skilled in cloth, mat, and basket weaving, and jewelry making. The lowland Malays are the ancestors of the eight major linguistic groups in the Philippines today. *See also* LAGUNA COOPERPLATE INSCRIPTION.

MALAYSIA. Relations with Malaysia are friendly but guarded because of lingering disputes on the questions of **Sabah**, **Spratly Island**, and immigration. The first two problems are at best on the back burner, but the immigration of a thousand Filipinos working without permits in Sabah has pushed the countries to the negotiating table. Prime Minister Mahatir Mohammed stopped their deportation following a call from President Gloria Macapagal Arroyo. Malaysia had declared that it would welcome back the Filipinos it had earlier deported once their legal papers to work there are complete. The expansion of economic activities in Malaysia opened windows of opportunities for Filipino workers in the manufacturing, plantation, and construction industries. Philippine exports to Malaysia amounted to $1.6 billion in 2003.

MALOLOS. *See* BULACAN.

MALOLOS CONSTITUTION. Document, which formally established the first Republic of the Philippines, adopted in Malolos, Bulacan, on January 21, 1899. Drafted by **Felipe Calderon**, a lawyer,
and approved by the Malolos Congress, the constitution was in effect
until the downfall of Emilio Aguinaldo in 1901. One of its salient features was the separation of church and state, which formed a combined institution during the Spanish colonial period and was considered one of the root causes of the Filipino revolution against Spain.
See also CONSTITUTIONS OF THE PHILIPPINES.

MALONG. *See* OKIR.

MALVAR, MIGUEL (1865–1911). Revolutionary general. A *gobernadorcillo* (town head) in his hometown in Santo Tomas, Batangas,
Miguel Malvar joined Emilio Aguinaldo's army when the **Philippine–
Spanish Revolution** broke out. He became the commanding general
of Batangas and led his forces against the Spanish army. With the
signing of the **Pact of Biak-na-Bato**, the war ended, and Malvar
joined Aguinaldo in Hong Kong as an exile. However, he returned to
the Philippines at the start of the **Philippine–American Revolution**
and resumed the armed resistance against the new colonialists. Never
captured and successful in many battles, Malvar was the last Filipino
general to surrender to the Americans on April 16, 1902, which
marked the end of the war. *See also* DEL PILAR, GREGORIO.

MAMANWA. *See* SURIGAO DEL NORTE.

MAMBAJAO. *See* CAMIGUIN.

MAMBORAO. *See* MINDORO.

MANALO, FELIX (1886–1963). Founder of *Iglesia Ni Cristo*
(Church of Christ). Born to poor, devout Catholic parents in Rizal
province, Felix Manalo earned his living as a photographer, barber,
and hat-maker. The decade of the 1900s was a period of religious ferment, particularly in Manila, when evangelists of various Protestant

denominations vied with each other for converts. Manalo was one of those people attracted to the new teachings and attended the evangelistic meetings of the Methodists, Presbyterians, and the Seventh Day Adventists. None of these religious groups satisfied his inquiring mind. He decided to establish the *Iglesia Ni Cristo* (INC) on July 17, 1914, and he became its first bishop. His own evangelistic campaigns and Bible-based preaching drew many followers to his church. In the ensuing decade the membership grew into thousands. Contributions from the members enabled Manalo to build impressive churches and cathedrals around Manila and all over central Luzon. He died in 1963 a year short of INC's golden jubilee. His son Eraño Manalo assumed leadership of the thriving church. *See also* VELARDE, MARIANO.

MANDAYA. *See* DAVAO ORIENTAL.

MANGGOB. This is an epic tale of the Mansaka people who live in the hinterlands of **Davao** province. This Mansaka epic poem consists of 15 episodes. The hero Manggob, who has superhuman powers, battles storms, giants, and ferocious reptiles. The tale gives an amazing description of the customs and traditions of the tribe. *See also* AGYU.

MANGYANS. The Mangyans are the native inhabitants of **Mindoro** Island. With the coming of lowlanders and settlers, they experienced social and political isolation. Their basic rights to their ancestral domain, to maintain a distinct identity, and to be heard and enjoy basic services have been to call their domain. Pasture leases, mining, and other commercial operations have encroached upon their lives.

The Mangyans comprise 10 percent of the Mindoro population. They number approximately 60,000. About 200 have finished college education. They currently have 0.6 percent of the elective positions at the provincial and municipal levels. The Kapulungan Para sa Lupaing Ninuno (KPLN), founded in 1994, brought together organizations from seven Mangyan tribes. It addresses the ancestral domain issue. The passage of the Indigenous Peoples' Rights Act of 1997, which the Mangyans lobbied for, gave marginal indigenous groups great hope. The Mangyans belong to seven major tribes—Alangan, Bangon, Buhid, Iraya, Hanunuo, Tagyawan, and Taubuid. They speak a language of their own, aside from Filipino. The Mangyans of Mindoro and the **Tagbanua** of Palawan are the only indigenous groups in the Philippines that have preserved their own way of writing based on a **syllabary** (a set of written characters, each one of which represents the sound of a syllable). In the past, Mangyans' writings were etched on bamboo with a sharp blade. *See also* POSTMA, ANTOON.

MANIAGO, FRANCISCO. The armed revolt led by Maniago in **Pampanga** is considered by Filipino historian **Teodoro Agoncillo** as one of the most successful in the history of uprisings against the Spaniards. In 1660, the Pampangos, under the leadership of Francisco Maniago, declared "war" against the Spaniards. Their revolt was caused by the abuses of Spanish officials who refused to pay for the food they had taken from the Filipinos. The angry Pampangos set fire to their houses and drove out the abusive friar-curates. Then they tried to stop commerce between Manila and Central Luzon towns by setting up stakes along the rivers. At the same time, they issued an appeal to the Filipinos of neighboring provinces to join them in their battle for freedom. The governor-general—fearing other towns might follow—rushed troops to the affected areas. Before hostilities could start, the governor-general sent a courier to find the cause of their revolt. In order to make peace, Maniago listed his people's grievances to the governor-general. Some of Maniago's demands were payment for their labor in cutting timber, payment for provisions taken from his people, and pardon for all of his men. Surprisingly, the governor-general accepted these demands and Maniago and his men laid down their arms. The revolt was a success since Maniago was able to air his people's grievances and to get what they wanted. Diplomacy worked and bloodshed was avoided. *See also* REVOLTS.

MANIFEST DESTINY. This is the political principle of President William McKinley that America had the moral and political rights to free the Filipinos from the grasp of the Spanish monarchy. McKinley is a key figure in Philippine history because he was the first American president to put expansionism and imperialism into practice. In 1899, Americans were divided sharply over whether to annex the Philippines. Annexationists and antiannexationists, despite their differences, generally agreed that the United States needed opportunities for commercial expansion but disagreed over how to achieve that goal. Few believed that the Philippines themselves offered a crucial commercial advantage to the United States, but many saw them as a crucial way station in Asia. Before the signing of the **Treaty of Paris** (December 10, 1898), McKinley did not know what to do with the Philippines. However, men who saw the Philippines not only as a market for American products but also as a stepping-stone to Asia's markets surrounded him. In addition, the military and naval pressure groups wanted the Philippines as a base for American warships and as a first line of defense. These factors gave McKinley the basis for his decision to make the Philippines an American colony. After the signing of the treaty, which officially ended the Spanish–American War, McKinley issued the so-called "Benevolent Assimilation" proclamation. It clearly indicated the intention of the United States to exercise sovereignty over the entire Philippines.

MANILA. Major city and capital of the Philippines. Located on the east shore of Manila Bay, Manila has one of the finest harbors in the country. Before it was captured by Miguel Lopez de Legaspi in 1571, it was a bustling Muslim settlement on the Pasig River ruled by **Rajah Sulayman**. Under Spanish rule, the settlement became the hub of colonial power as well as an important commercial center during the galleon trade. The Americans seized Manila in 1899 and developed it into a cosmopolitan center and modern port. Throughout the 50 years of American colonization of the Philippines, Manila was the seat of government, center of commerce, and the site of major educational institutions. During World War II, the invading Japanese, who occupied the city as well as its environs for three years, plundered the city. Manila was retaken by the Americans in the battle of Manila with a frightful loss of life and property. More than 100,000 Filipinos perished in the battle and most public buildings were razed. War-damage funds from the United States Congress helped rebuild Manila. Japan also provided $550 million in reparations, which the government used to rebuild the infrastructure.

Today, Manila sports modern structures, which include hotels and banks, supermarkets, malls, **art galleries**, and **museums**. In addition to being the political, judicial, and educational capital, Manila is the major entertainment and arts center of the Philippines. It is also the hub of the communications and media industry. The city limits have been enlarged to include outlying towns creating a vast, ever-increasing sprawl that is the current **Metropolitan Manila**, a metropolis of 15 million people. *See also* MAKATI; MALACAÑANG PALACE; QUEZON CITY; INTRAMUROS; TONDO.

MANILA BAY, BATTLE OF (May 1, 1898). American and Spanish naval battle. At the outbreak of the Spanish–American War, Commodore **George Dewey** and his Asiatic Squadron of seven steel battleships and two transports were in Hong Kong Bay awaiting orders from under-secretary of the navy Theodore Roosevelt. On April 27, 1898, Dewey received orders to proceed to Manila Bay and capture or destroy the Spanish fleet under Admiral Patricio Montojo who had 10 cruisers and gunboats. At dawn on May 1, 1898, the American fleet reached Manila Bay and immediately fired on the Spanish warships, which were anchored in the Cavite Naval Yard under the protection of Cavite shore batteries. In a span of six hours the superiorly armed American battleships destroyed the Spanish fleet and killed 381 seamen. The Americans suffered no losses of either men or ships. This naval victory made the United States an important maritime power in the Pacific Ocean.

MANOBO. The eight Manobo tribes are scattered in **Agusan del Sur**, Bukidnon, Davao, North and South Cotabato. Each of these tribes has its own language. The population estimate in 2000 was 250,000 people. They are primarily agriculturists; many use the "slash and burn" method. Social life is patriarchal, or male-dominated. The political structures of the Manobo groups are all quite similar. A ruler, called datu, is the head of the group. The religious beliefs of the Manobos revolved around the concept of the "Great Spirit," usually viewed as the creator figure. The traditional fabric for clothes is the **abaca**, or hemp. The women wear armlets made of black coral. The Manobos are considered one of the most literate tribal groups since they have their folklore, myths, and epics. *See also* BAGOBO; *TUWA-ANG*.

MANO PO. A show of respect. Some Filipino customs have survived in spite of generations of change, and are still being practiced today. The most tenacious of these customs is the *pagmamano*, or laying an elder's hand on the forehead to show respect, and observed anytime when young people approach their elders by saying "*Mano Po*," during various occasions, such as baptisms, weddings, and Christmas. This custom appears to be a carryover of the practice of Spanish priests who placed their hands on the foreheads of their parishioners to pass on their blessings. *See also* MABUHAY.

MANUEL, E. ARSENIO (1920–). Considered the Philippines' foremost and best folklorist, E. Arsenio Manuel is responsible for bringing to the attention of the Filipino people the rich heritage of folk epics of many unknown tribes. His pioneering work with the peoples of Central Mindanao as well as his striving to provide clear-cut guidelines and principles by which such a study is to be undertaken earned him the title "Father of Modern Filipino Folklore Studies." However, even this designation fails to capture the essence of his work, one that spans more than half a century of painstaking and careful research and documentation. He worked with and studied the **Manobos** in detail, summarizing his findings and insights in a comprehensive volume called "Manobo Social Organization." Before his investigation, the community had not attracted the attention of scholars. For that reason, its social system and language remained largely unexplored and undocumented. Immersing himself in the study, Manuel set forth to describe in detail how the system and its various aspects—economic, ritualistic, legal, and political—functioned across time. Unfortunately, his was the first and last study of the Manobo culture. The society disappeared, its people most likely scattered all across Mindanao in the wake of logging companies, ranchers, and land-grabbers. What many consider the most important result of his anthropological fieldwork is the discovery of three ethno epics from three different ethnic groups: *Manobo*, *Matigsalug*, and *Ilianon*. He recorded all three and published them in book form. All three are recognized as significant contributions to the wealth of Philippine literature.

MANUNGGUL JAR. The Mannunggul jar was recovered at Chamber A of Manunggul cave in Palawan. It is an elaborately designed burial jar with anthropomorphic figures on top of the cover that represent souls sailing to the afterworld in a *prao* (death boat). The figure on the rear is holding a steering paddle with both hands; the blade of the paddle is missing. Both figures appear to be wearing a band tied over the crown of the head and under the jaw. The manner in which the hands of the front figure are folded across the chest is a widespread practice in the Philippines and Southeast Asia when arranging the corpse. The *prao* is carved like a head with eyes, nose, and mouth. This motif of carving is still found on the traditional sea vessels of the Sulu archipelago, Borneo, and Malaysia. The execution of the ears, eyes, and nose has similarities with the contemporary woodcarvings of Taiwan, and many areas in Southeast Asia. It is dated to as early as 710–890 B.C. The Manunggul jar was declared a National Treasure and its portrait is on the 1,000 Philippine peso bill. *See also* MAITUM ANTHROPOMORPHIC POTTERIES; TABON CAVES.

MAOISM. Ideology of the Communist party. The **Communist Party of the Philippines (CPP)** had identified itself closely with the tenets of Mao Zedong; hence the armed forces of their New Peoples' Army have been called Maoists. China's support of the Philippine insurgents was more ideological than material. The Maoists obtained their support from sympathizers in the countryside, although much of this support came through intimidation and terrorism. The height of the Maoist insurgency was reached during the martial law period when Ferdinand Marcos' military troops were tied up in innumerable battles and skirmishes. When martial law was lifted, the Maoists surfaced as a political group and ran their senatorial candidates in national elections. Although the voters rejected the candidates, the Maoists were successful in infiltrating student activist groups, labor unions, and church institutions. However, a schism in the leadership divided the Maoist guerrillas and weakened their armed struggle against the government. Rather than face incarceration, their leader Jose Maria Sison chose to live in exile in the Netherlands. The U.S. government has branded him a terrorist and this has made him a fugitive. *See also* NEW PEOPLES' ARMY.

MARAGTAS. *See* SUMAKWEL.

MARANAO. A group of people inhabiting the shores of Lake Lanao, an inland body of water, in the province of Lanao del Sur in Mindanao. They are descendants of the wave of Malays who came to the

Philippines circa 12th century B.C. The word Maranao is derived from *ranao*, meaning "lake." Therefore, the word means "people of the lake." Centuries before Islam was introduced in the region, the Maranaos were in contact with the Indians and the Chinese. The influence of the former is reflected in the popular epic *Darangen*, a 72,000-line poem, which has Sanskrit origins. *Darangen* stands side by side with the Koran as the basic foundation of Maranao life and culture. *See also* FRANCISCO, JUAN; MAGUINDANAO.

MARAWI CITY. Center of Muslim culture in Mindanao. Marawi City, capital of the **Lanao del Sur** province formerly called Dansalan, is located on the north end of Lake Lanao and considered the center of Muslim culture of Maranao society. Like the whole province, Marawi is predominantly Muslim (92 percent), and powerful families who have engaged in political strife since the American occupation dominate political life. The city mirrors the life and culture of the Maranao people. Minarets pierce the skyline of Marawi and Maranaos in their splendid clothes throng this city by the lake. Artifacts of brass and the colorful finery of Maranao weavings are on display in the many shops that abound in the city. *See also* ALONTO, DOMOCAO.

MARBEL. *See* SOUTH COTABATO.

MARBLE. *See* ROMBLON.

MARCOPPER SPILL. A major environmental disaster that occurred on the island of Marinduque when a copper mine drainage tunnel collapsed and spilled 34 million tons of copper-bearing mine waste (tailings) into the Boac River and Calancan Bay damaging local crops, fish life, and the ecosystem. Placer Dome, a Canadian-owned company, which started mining operations in 1975, shut down the mine and admitted responsibility for the accident and immediately initiated cleanup operations and provided compensation for the local community. Since the mid-1970s, Marcopper had used Calancan Bay for the disposal of mine waste and tailings. The dumping continued despite orders by the government environmental authorities to construct a submerged disposal system that would place the tailings out to sea where corrals and seagrasses would be less affected. Because then a dredged channel had been constructed and the tailings outflow has been controlled. After the accident, mining officials raised concerns over Placer's mining credentials. At the time, the Marcopper case symbolized the government's new commitment to the environment. *See also* MINING.

MARCOS, FERDINAND (1917–1989). Ferdinand Marcos was the 10th president of the Philippines and president-prime minister under a parliamentary form of government that he created in 1972. A declaration of **martial law** on September 21, 1972, invested him with dictatorial powers to arrest his political opponents. After a reign of 20 years, he was ousted from power in 1986 by a peaceful revolution led by **Corazon Aquino**. During World War II, Marcos had fought in Bataan and survived the Death March. He was a guerrilla during the Japanese occupation and led his unit in sporadic ambushes against the enemy. After liberation, he served as a technical assistant to President **Manuel Roxas** (1946–1947); member of the House of Representatives (1949–1959); member of the Senate (1959–1965); and Senate president (1963–1965). He became president in 1965 and was reelected in 1969, the first Philippine president to serve a second term. His first term was marked by progress in agriculture, industry, and education. However, his second term was wracked by student demonstrations and violent **urban guerrilla** activities perpetrated by the **New Peoples' Army (NPA)**.

Claiming that the Communists and subversive forces had caused the deterioration of law and order in the country, Marcos declared martial law on September 21, 1972. The army made mass arrests of political enemies and imprisoned thousands without due process. Among them was **Benigno Aquino Jr.**, Marcos's bitter political enemy, who remained in detention for almost eight years. Meantime, a new constitution, which provided for a parliamentary form of government, was ratified, making Marcos president and prime minister with vast powers and extending his rule indefinitely. When he lifted martial law on January 17, 1981, hundreds of political prisoners were released. However, the economic conditions of the Philippines had worsened, forcing the government to borrow huge sums from the World Bank to shore up the economy. Adding to the economic woes was the rampant **graft and corruption** committed by his **cronies**. Student activism and violent demonstrations mounted in 1983 while the NPA continued its depredations in the countryside.

A **snap election** that Marcos called in 1986, in a vain attempt to show that he was still popular, indicated he had miscalculated the strength of Corazon Aquino, who defeated him by a plurality of votes. Army officers led by General **Fidel Ramos** and National Defense Secretary **Juan Ponce Enrile**, convinced of massive voting frauds by Marcos followers, gave their support to Cory Aquino. Already suffering from a debilitating disease, Marcos realized that the verdict of the people was against him. He fled with his family and some 60 loyal followers into exile in Honolulu, where he died on September 28, 1989. His widow Imelda Romualdez Marcos was left to fend for herself before the courts in the Philippines against allegations that the Marcos family salted away billions of dollars in Swiss banks allegedly earned from investments in real estate abroad. **The Presidential Commission on Good Government** has recovered $700 million of the monies and assets, but they are still on the trail of several ill-gotten millions stashed in European banks. *See also* PANBANSANG BATASAN; URBAN GUERRILLA.

MARCOS, IMELDA (1929–). Imelda Marcos was once the "Steel Butterfly," the beautiful wife and confidante of **Ferdinand Marcos**, whose regime (1963–1986) was regrettably marked by corruption, political repression, and gross financial shenanigans. Such acts were also attributed to Imelda, who was privy to most of them. The Marcoses were finally deposed in 1986 and fled to Hawaii, where Ferdinand died in 1989. Imelda Marcos later returned to the Philippines and, in spite of everything, was elected congresswoman from her district of Leyte. After her term, she made another bid for the presidency, but was trounced. In 2001, she was arrested on charges of **graft and corruption** committed during her husband's tenure. She had previously been found guilty of similar charges in 1995, but was acquitted on some of them. Also, in 2001, her fabulous jewelry collection was auctioned with the proceeds going to the government.

To her great credit, while she was the First Lady, she advocated the construction of hospitals, schools, and museums. She also instituted many social welfare programs throughout the nation and also cultural programs, as well as the "green revolution," a successful beautification campaign. Furthermore, she initiated the establishment of new homes for wayward children and the aged. During national disasters, such as fires, typhoons, floods, volcanic eruptions, and earthquakes, people turned to her for relief and assistance. This was not only because they believed she had a compassionate heart, but also because they were confident she would take action immediately. Meanwhile, although she is in quiet retirement, her **graft and corruption** case relating to the millions of pesos and dollars allegedly stashed in foreign banks remains with the **Sandiganbayan** and awaiting final judgment. *See also* CULTURAL CENTER OF THE PHILPPINES; PRESIDENTIAL COMMISSION ON GOOD GOVERNMENT.

MARIA CRISTINA FALLS. This is the better known waterfall in the Philippines located in Iligan City, also known as the city of waterfalls. Maria Cristina is one of the 20 waterfalls in **Lanao del Norte**. Although it has lost its role as a tourist attraction since the falls had been converted into a hydroelectric power plant in 1952, the falls still holds its pristine tropical beauty. Maria Cristina Falls is an indispensable source of electrical power—90 percent of the waters are diverted to six hydroelectric power plants. Its 300-megawatt provides power to the Mindanao grid. Recently, the government had plans of selling the Maria Cristina hydroelectric plants to a foreign investment company in exchange for $1.37 billion loan. The sale is awaiting enactment of the proposed Omnibus Electric Power Industry Act into law. *See also* ALIWAGWAG FALLS; LANAO DEL SUR.

MARIANO, ELEANOR (1955–). A Filipino physician who served in the White House and a top-ranking officer of the U.S. navy. Mariano was the director of the White House medical unit attending to the health of former President Bill Clinton. In 1992, she became the first military woman to serve as a White House physician under President George H. W. Bush. When Clinton got elected he asked her to stay and even promoted her as senior White House physician in 1994. By attending to two American presidents for more than eight years, Mariano had the longest service as a White House physician in American history. When Clinton left the White House in 2000, she was promoted as rear admiral of the U.S. Navy. Her father served in the U.S.

navy as a steward and retired as a master chef. She earned her medical degree from the Uniformed Services University of Medicine in Bethesda, Maryland, in 1981. *See also* FILIPINO–AMERICAN GENERALS.

MARIKUDO. *See* PANAY.

MARINDUQUE. A small island province of 959 square kilometers located in the Sibuyan Sea just south of Luzon and east of Mindoro Island. It has a population of less than 200,000, mostly Tagalogs, who live in six municipalities. Boac is the provincial capital. The island is noted for its cattle ranches and for its colorful pageant, the **Moriones** Festival, held during Holy Week. During Spanish times, galleons were built in its shipyards by the **Indios** who were forced to do the job. The chief municipalities are Buenavista, Gasan, Mogpog, and Santa Cruz. *See also* AKLAN; FESTIVALS; MARCOPPER SPILL; MORA, IRENE.

MARTIAL LAW. The declaration of martial law by President Ferdinand Marcos on September 21, 1972, suspended the democratic process and made the president a virtual dictator. Under martial law, the Philippines entered a grim period of human rights abuses. Several suspicious bombing incidents, most notably the grenade explosion at a **Liberal party** rally in Plaza Miranda, which Marcos claimed to be the work of Communist insurgents, furnished the final excuse to declare martial law. Within hours after the declaration, government troops seized control of all communications and public facilities and closed the schools. The military arrested more than 40 opposition politicians, including members of Congress, outspoken journalists and publishers, student leaders, intellectuals, and labor union leaders. Marcos dismissed the members of Congress and assumed all powers of government—executive, legislative, and judicial. An estimated 6,000 people were arrested during the early years. In the ensuing period, Marcos issued decrees, proclamations, and orders, which had the effect of law. Meanwhile thousands of people, accused of insurrection, subversion, and conspiracy, languished in jails and army detention camps. A new term, "salvaging," came into use to euphemize the torture, disappearance, and death of ordinary citizens.

Initially, the Roman Catholic Church bishops and the middle class supported martial law, for they felt it would mean the end of the domination of the economy by family oligarchies. Even the American business community welcomed martial law because they believed that it would restore discipline in the military by solving problems of civil disorder and crime. Eventually it dawned on them that Marcos had used martial law as an excuse to dismantle the opposition and consolidate his power. The Armed Forces of the Philippines (AFP) rose dramatically from a force of 50,000 troops to over 200,000. With the military acting at the behest of Marcos, "criminals" were tried and convicted by military courts. Further, he used martial law to divest his opponents of their businesses. The Lopezes, owners of the Manila Electric Company and its media network, lost their corporation to the patronage system, which Marcos used to reward his **cronies**. Yet, the greatest wrongs wrought by martial law were the thousands of cases of sordid violations of **human rights** later documented by **Amnesty International** and the church hierarchy. On January 16, 1981, martial law was lifted in time for the visit of Pope John Paul II. Thousands of prisoners, except those who were charged with capital crimes, were released.

MARY JOHNSTON HOSPITAL. *See* TONDO.

MASAGANA. A variety of rice. This new high-yielding variety of rice was developed at the **International Rice Research Institute (IRRI)** and introduced in the early 1970s. To encourage farmers to adopt the new rice, the government offered collateral and low interest loans through the Masagana 99 program. The new variety was designed to increase the yield per hectare (2.47 acres) to 100 **cavans**. In 2000, A new **hybrid rice** variety has been developed by IRRI with the cooperation of the Chinese, and is grown in several rice-producing provinces.

MASBATE. This province is located southwest of Luzon, and is comprised of Masbate, Ticao, and Burias and numerous other small islands. Masbate province has a total area of 4,048 square kilometers and a population of 700,000 representing various linguistic groups, including **Tagalog**, **Hiligaynon**, **Cebuano**, and Waray-waray. Its capital is the city of Masbate, the main port of entry into the province. Cattle raised in Masbate supply Manila's slaughterhouses, while copra is processed for export on the neighboring islands. There are also gold mines, and the waters around the islands are rich with fish. Other important towns are Aroroy, Milagros, Mandaon, Dimasalang, and Placer.

MASSACRES. Committed during the **Philippine–American Revolution** (1899–1906) by American soldiers. There are three major incidents recorded by Filipino historians and were not isolated atrocities in view of the magnitude of the war crime.

1. **Lonoy**. This atrocity took place March 10, 1901, in Lonoy, Jagna, Bohol. The bolo-wielding *insurrectors*—as the Americans called the revolutionists—under the command of Capitan Gregorio Caseñas were ambushed by heavily armed American troops and 406 were slaughtered. Some survivors claimed that they were raising their arms in surrender but the soldiers kept on firing at them. Their commander, Captain Andrew Rowan, was ordered not to take any prisoners. The Americans entered Jagna and burned the whole town sparing only the Catholic church. The Philippine Historical Society placed a marker in Jagna to commemorate the tragic event.

2. **Balangiga**. The atrocity took place on September. 27, 1901, in the little town of Balangiga, Samar. Filipino rebels led by General Vicente Lukban and Mayor Eugenio Daza slipped into town early in the morning disguised as mourners in a funeral procession. The rebels attacked and killed 54 American soldiers while they were asleep. In retaliation General Jack Smith ordered a punitive expedition in which most of the inhabitants (5,000)—men, women, and children—were killed in a mass massacre, including all the work animals **(carabao)**. The whole town was razed, excluding the Catholic Church. The bells of the church that were used to warn the inhabitants were taken by American troops as war prizes and today those bells are displayed at Warren Air Force base in Cheyenne, Wyoming.

3. **Bud Dajo.** The atrocity took place March 5–7, 1906, during the American occupation of Jolo, Sulu. The Americans required the Moros to pay a poll tax of two pesos per head, an onerous

amount to them. The **Tausogs** refused to pay the tax. Some 1,000 of them—men, women, and children—fled to Mt. Bud Dajo, a 2,100-foot extinct volcano, which served as a natural fortress. Governor-General **Leonard Wood** ordered the U.S. Army to hunt down the renegades. Their superior firepower was no match against the *kris*, **barongs**, and spears of the Moros. The result was a massacre. No one was spared. The massacre caught the attention of the American press (*New Orleans Times*), which called it a "frightful atrocity." Editorials, letters, pamphlets, and poems were written denouncing the incident. Nevertheless, President Theodore Roosevelt congratulated General Wood for a successful mission. *See also* MENDIOLA MASSACRE.

MASS MEDIA. The mass media include print and electronic means of communication. The roots of Philippine journalism go back to the publication of *Doctrina Christina* in the early part of the 17th century. The first book to be printed in the Philippines, *Doctrina Christina* was a primer on Christian doctrines produced by Chinese craftsmen using the xylograph method under the direction of friars. Throughout the Spanish colonial period, various types of **newspapers** appeared, among them *Del Superior Gobierno*, and other short-lived publications. Their appearance depended on the pleasure of the Spanish governor-general, who would often close down publications that publicly attacked the administration. Early in the American administration, Philippine journalism began to blossom with the appearance of Spanish, Tagalog, and English-language newspapers. A number of these led precarious lives because of their political overtones and minimal financial resources. A major setback in Philippine journalism occurred with the closure of *El Renacimiento*, which lost a libel suit for maligning an American public official. Other than that, Philippine journalism flourished with many Filipinos starting their own publications. The commonwealth period saw the proliferation of newspapers, magazines, and books. The broadcast medium, for example, radio, was introduced in Manila in 1928 and became the principal medium of communication before the outbreak of World War II. The broadcast industry was in both private and government hands, with the former having more stations in most of the principal cities. Radio was widely used for entertainment and information.

During the war years, 1942–1945, the Japanese military took complete control of all means of communication and imposed tight censorship on what could be printed or broadcast. The mass media industry suffered a severe decline, but after liberation, the industry quickly recovered as private entrepreneurs established their own newspapers and radio stations in most of the principal cities. In the first year, 20 dailies appeared and 22 broadcasting stations began operation. The business of reaching the public with entertainment and information became disastrously competitive. Within 10 years, many of the new newspapers and radio stations had disappeared. With the introduction of commercial television in 1953, media owners began merging their radio and newspaper operations with this new medium.

By the early 1960s, television had replaced radio as the main medium of communication. There were seven TV stations in Manila, including those owned by the government. Their affiliates are found in the key cities of the archipelago. By 1970, there were 15 television stations located in Manila, Cebu, Davao, Bacolod, Dagupan, and Baguio. In a little over a decade, television has become a powerful new medium for information, education, entertainment, and advertising. Statistics on the mass communication industry for 2002 showed that there were 300 radio stations (commercial and noncommercial) and five major television networks with 25 carrier and 10 relay stations. TV has replaced radio as the dominant form of mass media followed by newspapers, and video. Up to now, the bulk of the circulation of national newspapers has been sold in Manila, and the major audiences of TV and radio shows are in the cities. In addition, there are 402 radio and 156 television stations throughout the country, many times more than there were 15 years ago. The media audience swelled during the economic growth of the 1990s. During this period, appliance dealers were selling as many as 500,000 new TV sets a year and cable television experienced unprecedented growth. Because there were virtually no constraints on the press, such rapid growth brought about unbridled competition and a race for the sensational. News, in both television and print, became increasingly tabloid politics. The tabloidization of the news came side by side with the tabloidization of politics.

The politics of the new democracy are increasingly being played out in the media: in the endless number of newspaper columns, talk shows, live news coverages, and public affairs shows. TV is the new kingmaker as evidenced in the 2004 national elections when the major competing parties used television extensively to deliver their message. As many as 80 percent of Filipinos have access to a TV set. Some 52 percent of TV viewers, according to a survey, said they tried not to miss news and public affairs programs. Constant TV exposure is a sure-fire guarantee of electoral success as proven in the election of four TV talk show hosts in the 2004 senatorial elections. *See also* DE CASTRO, NOLI.

MATABAGKA. This is the epic tale of the Bukidnon people. The epic narrates the adventures of a remarkable warrior princess, full of high spirits and independent-minded. There are 10 parts of the ballad, of which summaries are only mentioned in the story. Filipino feminists claim that *Matabagka* is the ancient model of the liberated Filipina today. *See also* AGYU; SILANG, JOSEFA GABRIELA.

MATANOG. *See* MAGUINDANAO.

MATI. *See* DAVAO ORIENTAL.

MAUNG, CYNTHIA. *See* RAMON MAGSAYSAY AWARD.

MAYON VOLCANO. This is the most active and quintessential volcano in the Philippines. Located southwest of Manila in **Albay**, this 2,462-meter high mountain is famous for its near-perfect cone—some say more majestic than Mt. Fuji of Japan—and historic for its 50 eruptions in the past four centuries. The deadliest recorded eruption was on February 11, 1814, when it buried the entire town of Cagsawa and the barrio of Budiao killing more than 1,300 people. Only the church bell of the town remained. Volcanologists classify Mayon as a stratovolcano (composite volcano). Its symmetric cone was formed through alternate pyroclastic and lava flows. *See also* TAAL VOLCANO; VOLCANOES.

MCKINLEY, WILLIAM. *See* MANIFEST DESTINY.

MCNUTT, PAUL VORIES (1891–1955). U.S. High Commissioner to the Philippine Commonwealth (1937–1938). President Franklin Delano

Roosevelt appointed him high commissioner to the commonwealth government in the Philippines. While in the Philippines, he suggested that the American policy of rapid independence for the islands merited reexamination. McNutt tried to effect a smooth transition with Filipino officials in the new relationship between the two governments. He believed that the U.S. had sovereignty over Philippine foreign policy and that the Philippine government had jurisdiction over the collection of taxes in the archipelago. McNutt sympathized with Filipino politicians, such as **Manuel L. Quezon**, in their desire for early independence. During his one-year term, he tried to convince Filipino high officials that it was in their best interests to keep U.S. military power for political and strategic purposes. Before his departure for the U.S. in search of a higher political office, McNutt laid the groundwork for the effective military presence of the U.S.

MENDIOLA MASSACRE. On January 22, 1987, the **Kilusang Magbukukid ng Pilipinas** (Farmers Movement of the Philippines) and their supporters led a peaceful march to **Malacañang Palace** to protest the lack of government action on land reform. The demonstrators had to cross Mendiola Bridge where violence erupted. In the disturbance, 19 were killed and Palace guards, who fired at the demonstrators intent on scaling the gates, injured 100. The event became known as the Mendiola Massacre. *See* LAND REFORM; MASSACRES.

METHODISTS. *See* PROTESTANISM.

METRO MANILA DEVELOPMENT AUTHORITY (MMDA). Formerly called *Metro Manila Commission* under the Marcos administration, the MMDA is in charge of the urbanization of Metro Manila, which has blossomed into 15 million metropolises encompassing several suburban towns. Its authority includes the formulation and implementation of programs and projects regarding transport operations, traffic enforcement, engineering services, and infrastructure of greater Manila. Some of the major improvements have been the Metro Rail Transit that has relatively eased the travel of commuters and traffic jams caused by too many vehicles. Because of undirected growth the MMDA has developed a master plan of effective metropolitan governance to address problems such as urban pollution, garbage disposal, and transport infrastructure.

METROPOLITAN MANILA. The Metropolitan Manila Authority, established on November 7, 1975. Metro Manila consists of four cities—Manila, Quezon City, Pasay, and Kalookan—and the 13 municipalities of **Makati**, Malabon, Mandaluyong, Marikina, Muntinlupa, Navotas, Las Piñas, Parañaque, Pasig, Pateros, San Juan, Taguig, and **Valenzuela**. The combined population of these cities and municipalities was 15 million (2002 Census).

METROPOLITAN MUSEUM. This museum in Manila exhibits the money collection, which shows the evolution of Philippine currency from ancient barter rings and gold nuggets to the "Mickey Mouse" money of the Japanese occupation and the Bagong Lipunan notes. Commemorative coins and coins from all over the world are also on exhibit. The museum is also a popular venue of exhibits on baroque and modern prints. *See also* AYALA MUSEUM; LOPEZ MUSEUM.

MIAGAO CHURCH. Church fortress in the coastal town of Miagao, Iloilo. The Spanish Augustinian missionaries originally built the church fortress as a protection against Moro raiders, who often pillaged coastal towns in the Visayan area. The architecture is Philippine baroque with a mixture of medieval and plateresque styles. Carbonaceous limestone of soft yellow ocher, quarried from the Igbaras Mountains, was the basic building material. Records show that the present church is the third one on the site, the earlier church buildings having been burned down by Moro pirates. The uniqueness of the Miagao church lies in its facade, the surface of which is almost entirely embellished with varied relief sculptures of diverse period styles, all done by local artists and artisans. *See also* BAROQUE CHURCHES; SAN AGUSTIN CHURCH.

MINDANAO INSTITUTE OF TECHNOLOGY. *See* NORTH COTABATO.

MINDANAO STATE UNIVERSITY. *See* LANAO DEL SUR.

MINDORO. A mountainous island southwest of Luzon with a total land area of 9,735 square kilometers. Mt. Halcon, a rugged, heavily forested mountain range, provides a natural boundary between two provinces: **Occidental Mindoro** and **Oriental Mindoro**. The island was formerly called Mait by Chinese traders even before the coming of the Spaniards. In 1520, the Spanish began to explore the island and named it *"Mina de Oro"* (gold mine) after finding some of the precious metal, though no major gold discoveries were ever made. During the Spanish regime, Mindoro was administered as part of **Batangas**. In 1902, during the American administration, Lubang Island, which was formerly part of **Cavite**, was annexed to Mindoro. On June 12, 1950, Mindoro was divided into two provinces.

MINING. The mining industry has suffered in recent years from lack of capital, depressed world metal prices, and onerous regulations. However, conditions had brightened with the passage of the Philippine Mining Act of 1995, which liberalized the laws governing domestic mining industry. Under the provisions of the Philippine **constitution**, foreign ownership of the country's mineral resources is limited to 40 percent. The new act has opened the industry to foreign investment and provided a more competitive system of mineral resources exploration, development, utilization, and conservation. The act also allows 100 percent foreign-owned firms to operate large-scale mining activity for 25 years; lifts the 40 percent limit on the amount of profit a foreign partner can take; and exempts from duty and taxes all imported equipment and parts. Over 40 foreign firms have filed applications to mine copper, silver, zinc, and gold in Luzon and Mindanao. The passage of this act was not without stiff opposition from **nongovernmental organizations**, environmental and interest groups. Most vocal were indigenous peoples like the **Lumads**, whose mineral-rich ancestral lands and livelihoods would be unduly affected by mining exploration. *See also* MARCOPPER SPILL.

MISAMIS OCCIDENTAL. Province forming the eastern tip of Zamboanga Peninsula in northern Mindanao and covering an area of 2,077 square kilometers. The population of 465,000 is composed mostly of Cebuano-speakers, although there are concentrations of native Subanon people in the interior uplands. The capital is at Oroquieta, a port city and center for coconut processing. **Coconut** is the main product and coir-making the main industry. A more important port and commercial center is Ozamiz City, an early Spanish fortified settlement. The Ozamiz Cathedral is noted for its fine German-built pipe organ. The principal towns are Aloran, Tangub, Baliangao, Clarin, and Tudela. *See also* OCAMPOS, LORETO.

MISAMIS ORIENTAL. Province located on the north coast of Mindanao, with a land area of 3,570 square kilometers and a population of 700,000, mostly descendants of Visayan immigrants, living in 26 municipalities. The capital city is Cagayan de Oro, a name given by the Spanish after they discovered gold in the Cagayan River, that is, River of Gold. The city is the main transportation center of northern Mindanao. Visayan is the major language. The primarily agricultural economy is based on the production of copra. Corn is the staple food crop of the people. Early pottery, ornaments, stone and metal implements, dating back to 2500 B.C., have been found in the province. These artifacts, which also include skeletal remains and Chinese pottery shards, are on exhibit in the Xavier University Folk Museum. The chief provincial towns are Gingoog City, Balingasag, and Initao.

MISUARI, NURULADJI (1935–). He was the first elected governor of the **Autonomous Region in Muslim Mindanao**, which he helped forge in 1996 as a peaceful settlement for his separatist cause—ending more than two decades of violent struggle for an autonomous Muslim state in the southern Philippines. The peace agreement ended the 24-year war that has claimed the lives of 120,000 people in the region. When his six-year term was over he wanted to run for reelection, which President Gloria Macapagal Arroyo denied. Misuari's administration was marred with mismanagement of government funds allocated for public works and programs designed to improve impoverished areas. Instead government auditors found that funds were used to strengthen his **Muslim Liberation National Front**. With his reelection bid turned down, he renewed his separatist fight by leading his armed followers in a showdown with government troops who promptly routed his forces. Misuari fled to **Malaysia** where he sought political asylum that was rejected by the prime minister. He was sent back to the Philippines under custody where he faced charges of rebellion.

MI ULTIMO ADIOS **(MY LAST FAREWELL).** This is Jose Rizal's renowned poem that he composed on the eve of his execution on the morning of December 29, 1896. Imprisoned at **Fort Santiago** on charges of subversion, Rizal was formally notified of his death sentence, which was approved by Camilo Polovieja, governor general of the Philippines. Then he wrote his valedictory poem on a piece of scrap paper, which he hid in an alcohol cooking stove and gave to this visiting sister. The sister upon discovering the poem immediately made copies and mailed it to all their friends in the Philippines and abroad. Since then the amazing poem has been translated into 50 languages all over the world. In the 14-stanza poem Rizal devoted 12 stanzas to his agapic love for his "adored country, region loved by the sun, pearl of the Orient seas, our Eden lost." The poem, a masterpiece in Philippine literature in Spanish, has five alexandrine lines and perfect rhyme.

MONCADO, HILARIO CAMINO (1898–1956). Born in **Cebu**, Moncado was a charismatic leader who organized Filipino laborers in the sugar and pineapple plantations in Hawaii and the U.S. mainland. His unions—Filipino Federation of America and Filipino Crusaders World Army—gave the Filipinos political clout that he used successfully to gain benefits for its members. He also used his wealth to improve the economic and social conditions of his countrymen. He returned to the Philippines before the war and was elected a delegate to the Commonwealth's Constitutional Convention in 1934. He later unsuccessfully run for president of the Philippines.

MONETARY SYSTEM. Monetary policies are supervised by the **Central Bank (*Bangko Sentral*)** of the Philippines, which is charged with maintaining monetary stability, preserving the value and convertibility of the peso, and fostering monetary, credit, and exchange conditions. The Monetary Board is composed of the governor of the Central Bank acting as chairman, the secretary of finance, the director general of the National Economic and Development Authority, the chairman of the Board of Investment, and three members from the private sector. The Central Bank also supervises the commercial banking system and manages the country's foreign exchange system. Since it began operation, the Central Bank has set interest rates on both bank deposits and loans. The dependence of the banking system on funds from the Central Bank at low interest rates has been cited as one of the contributing factors to the financial chaos that occurred in the 1980s. Interest rates were deregulated, and by January 1983 all interest rate ceilings had been abolished. The monetary unit is the peso, which has undergone several devaluations in the past decade.

MONEY LAUNDERING LAW. Since 2000, the Philippines was among 11 nations placed under financial sanctions by the Paris-based Financial Action Task Force (FATF)—the international antimoney laundering watchdog—a group of 29 industrialized countries that coalesced to curb money laundering in Asia. Being placed under sanctions made financial transactions difficult and increased the cost of remittances and trade. Offshore banks refused transactions from the Philippines. With the urging of FATF, the Philippine Congress passed in 2003 the Anti-money Laundering Law (AMLA) that effectively lifted the sanctions and granted the Central Bank authority to monitor deposits without the need for a court order. There was a caveat; however, the Philippines will still remain in the blacklist of countries considered to be money-laundering havens by international community until mid-2005 when the new presidential administration will have proven its commitment to fighting dirty money. The stiff half-century Philippine bank secrecy law, which required judicial approval for inspecting accounts, had been a sticking point with the FATF. Now all banks would be required to report suspicious accounts to the Central Bank. Suspicious accounts are monies realized from predicate crimes, which include kidnapping, illegal drugs, hijacking, murder, terrorist activities, graft and corruption, smuggling, and illegal trafficking of women and children.

MONON, SALINTA. *See* LIVING TREASURES.

MONTOJO, PATRICIO. *See* MANILA BAY, BATTLE OF.

MONTECLARO, PEDRO. *See* SUMAKWEL.

MORGA, ANTONIO. *See* DUTCH

MORIONES. A dramatic mime with a religious theme. Moriones is performed on open stages during Lent wherein the townsfolk reenact the legend of the martyr Longinus based on the gospel of St. John. In the Philippine version, Longinus is a Roman centurion blind in one eye. His spear pierces the side of Christ and the spurting blood restores his sight. When he proclaims the divinity of Christ, his men turn against him. The resulting conflict, vigorously acted in silence, gives the moriones its tension. Participants wear masks and the uniforms of Roman legionnaires. Before the mime is staged, the colorful costumed participants join in a procession to attract people to the evening presentation. There are several towns in the Philippines that stage this spectacular festival. However, the Marinduque version is the most famous. The audience's attention is drawn to the fanciful masks, colorful costumes, and dramatic dialogue. *See also* AKLAN; QUIAPO.

MORO. Name given to Muslim Filipinos by the Spanish (from the word Moor) who inhabit the southern islands of Mindanao, the eastern islands of Palawan, and the Sulu Island chain. There are 10 subgroups, which are identified on the basis of language. Three of these subgroups make up the majority of Moros and include the **Maguindanaos** of North Cotabato, Sultan Kudarat, and Maguindanao provinces; the **Maranaos** of Lanao del Norte and Lanao del Sur provinces; and the **Tausogs** of Sulu Island. Throughout the 400 years of Spanish rule, the Moros successfully resisted the military expeditions sent to subjugate them. After converting to Islam in the early 14th century, these people of **Malay** stock were ruled by sultans and datus who had absolute authority over their subjects. The Tansogs, a seafaring people, often called pirates, controlled the southern seas as they carried on their jihad or religious wars until the American colonization period. The Americans, with their superior military technology and new economic incentives, eventually pacified and brought under control the Moro region. However, the Moros remained a restive sector of Philippine society throughout the various periods of Philippine political life and until the present day. *See also* MUSLIM SEPARATISM; MORO ISLAMIC LIBERATION FRONT.

MORO-MORO. A Philippine version of the operetta. Moro-moro, sometimes called *kumedya* or comedy, is a form of stylized folk drama with musical accompaniment. It is a scripted folk play, written in octosyllabic verse with eight lines to a stanza and performed by young adults of a town or church parish during the **fiesta** honoring a saint's day. As in an opera, the background music is played during entrances, exits, duels, and fight scenes. The theme of the moro-moro revolves around the Moro–Christian wars, which took place during the early part of the 18th century. The word "moro" was coined by the Spaniards to refer to the Muslim Moors of northern Africa, and was later extended to include Muslim Filipinos. In a moro-moro drama, the actors wear costumes and armaments. The climax is often a mock battle, complete with clashing blades, which arises over disputes of love and religion. In a moro-moro, the Christians are always victorious. Moro-moro plays (which often last for hours and sometimes days) together with the **zarzuela** are popular forms for nightly entertainment during town fiestas. Filipino playwrights, like Juan Bartolome, have mastered this genre.

MORO ISLAMIC LIBERATION FRONT (MILF). This is a Muslim militant armed movement in Southern Philippines. It was founded in 1977 as a splinter group from the **Moro National Liberation Front** that signed a peace treaty with the Philippine government in 1996. The MILF has been fighting for an independent Islamic state in Mindanao. Supported by funds coming from al-Qaeda, it was able to establish fortified encampments in Central Mindanao and mounted guerrilla warfare against the Philippine government. In its bailiwicks the MILF functioned as a quasi government—collecting taxes, practicing **sharia** law, and declaring foreign policies. Government intelligence found that the MILF had international connections with Libya's Muammar Qadafi. Some of its leaders had trained in al-Qaeda camps in Afghanistan.

Though they disclaimed connection with the kidnap-for-ransom **Abu Sayyaf** group, their acts of violence against civilian and military targets have met the full force of the Philippine military. In 2003 their strongholds in Mindanao were overrun and destroyed by Philippine military forces. Their ragtag units continue their hit-and-run warfare and destruction of infrastructure. *See also* MISUARI, NUR.

MOTHER TERESA. *See* RAMON MAGSAYSAY AWARD.

MOUNT APO. *See* DAVAO DEL SUR.

MOUNT BULUSAN. *See* SORSOGON.

MOUNT HALCON. *See* ORIENTAL MINDORO.

MOUNT MATUTUM. *See* SOUTH COTABATO.

MOUNTAIN PROVINCE. This large region on north Luzon was subdivided in 1968 into four provinces: Mountain, **Kalinga-Apayao**, **Benguet**, and **Ifugao** provinces. Mountain Province covers 2,097 square kilometers and has a population of 140,000. The capital is Bontoc. Its inhabitants, Bontoc Igorots, are mostly farmers tending plots of millet, vegetables, and rice. Because of the rugged topography, the province remains largely underdeveloped, which has made it possible for the Igorots to preserve their traditional culture. One of their more picturesque customs is the celebration of *canyao*, or feast, which is held on occasions of marriage and death and to celebrate planting and harvesting seasons. The host of a *canyao* prepares a delicious entree of chicken, pork, or carabao meat sufficient to feed the entire village. Mountain Province boasts some rice terraces and 10 municipalities. *See also* HUDHUD.

MUAMMAR QADAFI. *See* MORO ISLAMIC LIBERATION FRONT.

MUKHDUMIN. *See* ISLAM.

MUNICIPALITY. A unit of local government. A town is a municipality and several municipalities make up the provincial government. In 1991, there were 1,538 municipalities. The town is headed by a mayor and a vice-mayor who are elected and usually serve a term of three years. Under each municipality are the **barangays**, sometimes also called **barrios** or rural villages. The barangays constitute the municipality. In 2002, there were about 50,000 barangays. A barangay is headed by a *teniente del barrio* (village lieutenant) who is appointed by the mayor.

MURPHY, FRANK (1890–1949). American governor-general in the Philippines (1933–1935). In 1933, Murphy, an ex-mayor of Detroit was named governor-general by the newly elected president Franklin Delano Roosevelt. With the enactment of the **Tydings-McDuffie Act**, which provided for a transitional government before the grant of independence, the office of the governor-general was abolished on the inauguration of the commonwealth on November 15, 1935. Murphy was the last American colonial proconsul in the Philippines. Murphy's administration, staffed by able officials, was successful in meeting such issues as the sugar quota, gold devaluation claims, and trade concessions, which had been left unresolved by his predecessor. In his three-year term, Murphy improved the social welfare, revised the penal code, and balanced the budget of the Philippine government. One of his notable contributions was the signing of the **women's** suffrage bill, which enfranchised Filipino women. *See also* MCNUTT, PAUL V.

MUSIC, DANCE AND SONGS OF PREHISPANIC FILIPINOS. Prehispanic Filipinos had their own music, dances and songs. This fact was observed and attested in writing by **Antonio Pigafetta**, the official historian of the Magellan expedition. When Magellan landed in Cebu, Pigafetta witnessed four young women harmoniously playing with the native cymbals, which they called *platiles*. Ancient Filipino dances and songs were previously engaged in as a serious occupation by the people. Each tribe had its own musical instruments, songs and dances. The natives of Northern Luzon had nose flutes, bamboo mouth organs, and harps called *subbing*, *gansa* or brass gongs. The Visayans had the *lontoy* or flute, and *kudyapi* or guitar. The Tagalogs used the *barimbaw* and *kalutang,* guitar. The Ilocanos had the *kutibeng*, guitar. The Moros from Mindanao played the *gabbang*, similar to a xylophone, *agong*. The songs were usually melancholic and about themes of love, woman, and war. They were highly spiced with romance and poetry. The natives had war songs, festival songs, religious songs, and folk songs. They also had songs for harvests, for catching fish, animals, and building homes. The **kundiman** and **balitao** were among the more popular songs. The Ilocanos had a ballad-epic song called *dallot*, depicting the life and heroism of *Lam-ang*.

In precolonial Philippines, songs were closely associated with dances, so that the singer was also the dancer and vice versa. Natives performed the dances primarily to please the god or *anito*. In religious dances, the dancer or the priestess danced to exhaustion, until she fell to the floor and was believed to be possessed by the spirits. Prehispanic Filipinos also danced to please themselves during their **festivals**. *See also* GAMELAN.

MUSICAL TRADITIONS. Early Philippine musical traditions date from the Spanish colonial period of roughly 300 years (1521–1898). The creation of a colonial state and economic system as well as the influence of Roman Catholicism shaped what was to be the mainstream—lowland Filipino society. A major part of the cultural experience of the people centered on religion or Christian subjects. At the beginning, Western music was introduced by way of the Spanish friars who taught Gregorian chant for masses and other Christian services. Paraliturgical rituals and folk rites developed as indigenous traditions were transformed to utilize Christian symbols. Music in the rites progressed to dialectically combined Western forms with native/indigenous style—the *sanghiyang* of Cavite, *subli* of Batangas, *turumba* of Laguna exemplify the syncretism of folk religion and Catholicism. Probably, the most widespread is the *pasyon*, a chanted epiclike singing of the life of Christ performed during the Lenten season. Secular entertainment and technical forms would also have Christian elements. These include the **moro-moro**, which depicts the Muslim–Christian wars, *cenaculo*, a play on the passion of Christ, *duplo*, a literary musical form associated with a nine-day series of prayers, and the *carillo*, a shadow play. Filipino dance music was patterned after Spanish and European dance form. These include the *cariñosa*, *balitao*, *pandanggo*, *polka*, *dansa*, and *rigodon*. Perhaps connected to these is the development of the **rondalla**, an ensemble of plucked string instruments that include the *banduria*, *laud*, *octavina*, *gitara*, and the *bajo*. These instruments are adaptations of European equipment. *See also* BALITAO*;* KUNDIMAN.

MUSIKONG BUMBONG. *See* BAMBOO.

MUSLIM SEPARATISM. Since the Spanish and American colonization of the Philippines the Moros or Muslims have never considered themselves part of the Philippine republic. In spite of several punitive expeditions, the Spaniards were unable to subdue or occupy Moroland, particularly the stronghold of Jolo, **Sulu**. It was the Americans with their superior ordnance who brought the recalcitrant Moros, poorly armed with their fearsome kampilans and **barongs**, to their knees in a huge battle that ended in a **massacre** (Bud Dajo). They regrouped after the **Commonwealth** stabilized and were reluctantly bought into the new republic. The Moros kept their indigenous culture expressed in dress, music, and political traditions and lived peaceably with their Christian neighbors. But government efforts to integrate Muslims into the political and economic fabric of the country met with only limited success.

   Christian Filipinos have often tended to view the Moros as socially backward and untrustworthy, and these concepts date back to their history of resistance. In turn the Moros, who constitute 7 percent of the population, have entertained deep suspicions of the intentions of the Philippine government and are generally wary of the large-scale migration of Christian Filipinos into their homeland of Mindanao. Many Muslims claimed that they continue to be underrepresented in civilian and military positions. Provinces in Mindanao that are predominantly Muslim lagged behind the rest of the island in almost all aspects of socioeconomic development. Thus, the seeds of separatism began to sprout just after World War II following the worldwide resurgence of Islam and stirring the Moros to the idea of a Bangsa Moro identity, which became a full-blown separatist movement in the 1960s. The movement, which was both Islamic and anti-colonial—against the government—developed into an armed resistance prominently led by the **Moro Nationalist Liberation Front** whose leader **Nur Misuari** advocated a separate state of all Moroland. However, only the **Maranaos** and **Maguindanaos**—of the five major Muslim groups—are involved in this Muslim separatism. *See also* BALIK ISLAM; HUSSIN, PAROUK.

MUTUAL MILITARY LOGISTICS AND SUPPORT AGREE-MENT. An executive agreement, which allowed U.S. forces to use the Philippines as a supply center for antiterrorism and other military operations. This gave the United States authority to set up storage centers for supplies such as ammunition, food, water, and fuel as well as support and services such as billeting, transportation, communications, and medical services. The agreement will remain in force for five years subject to review in case the fight against terrorism continues. *See also* BALIKATAN.

– N –

NACIONALISTA PARTY. The grand old party of the Philippines. Organized in 1907 by **Manuel L. Quezon** and Sergio Osmeña. The party was a vehicle to support their campaign for Philippine independence from American rule. As the majority party, it controlled national politics during the commonwealth period. In 1920 and 1934, the party split primarily because of personal and ideological differences between Quezon and Osmeña. After the death of Quezon, Osmeña revived the party and was its standard bearer in the postwar presidential elections of 1946. In spite of a coalition with the Democratic Alliance, an anticollaboration party formed before the elections, and Osmeña and the Nacionalista candidates went down in defeat. The party's fortunes were revived in 1953, when **Ramon Magsaysay** took over the leadership and successfully won the presidency and majorities in the upper and lower houses of Congress. In 1965, when Ferdinand Marcos became president, the Nacionalista party was once more in the majority. Under Marcos's leadership the party dominated the political scene for two decades. *See also* LIBERAL PARTY.

NAGA. *See* CAMARINES SUR.

NAKAR, GUILLERMO. *See* GUERRILLA.

NAKPIL, ANGEL. *See* LOPEZ MUSEUM.

NARRA. National tree (*pterocarpus indicus*) of the Philippines since 1934. This deciduous hardwood is known for its strength and durability and is often used as a building material, especially for house posts. The sap is used for dyeing clothes and for medicinal purposes. More importantly, *narra* is widely used for woodcarving, furniture, and cabinet making. *See also* RATTAN.

NATIONAL ANTHEM. The Philippine National Anthem, then known as *Marcha Nacional Filipinas*, was played on June 12, 1898, without words during the proclamation of Philippine independence by Emilio Aguinaldo. Julian Felipe composed the martial music. In 1899, Jose Palma wrote the first lyrics in Spanish and titled it *Filipinas*. With the presence of the Americans it became necessary to translate the lyrics into English. A Filipino writer, **Camilo Osias**, and an American made the translation. The **Philippine Commonwealth** officially adopted the English translation of the National Anthem in 1934. An entire prewar generation of Filipinos thus grew up singing the National Anthem in English. Finally, during the term of **Ramon Magsaysay**, a new national anthem in Filipino, *Lupang Hinirang*, was composed by Julian Cruz Balmaceda and Ildefonso Santos. On May 26, 1956, the new anthem was sung in Filipino. Minor revisions were made in 1962, and it is this final version that is in use today. *See also* FLAG.

NATIONAL BUREAU OF INVESTIGATION (NBI). An intelligence agency of the government. The NBI was formed in 1936 as a division of the Department of Justice and patterned after the United States Federal Bureau of Investigation. The Bureau's principal mission was to assist the Philippine Constabulary and police in crime detection and investigation and the collection of intelligence on internal security threats. It cooperates with the Department of National Defense in maintaining an extensive intelligence apparatus. During the Ferdinand

Marcos regime, this agency had 4,000 operatives in Metro Manila under the control of Marcos. He used them and the National Intelligence and Security Authority to gather intelligence on and track down his political opponents. Some of its operatives have been linked to underworld contacts such as the Yakuzas of Japan, who are believed to control some businesses in Manila. With the election of President Fidel Ramos, the NBI has been cleaned of corrupt officials and its integrity has been restored.

NATIONAL COMMISSION FOR CULTURE AND ARTS (NCCA). This is a governmental body, which is charged with policy making and coordination for culture and the arts. It conducts research for the finest traditional artists, adopts a program that will ensure the transfer of their skills to others, and undertakes measures to promote a genuine appreciation of pride in arts and culture among the people. Awardees are called **National Living Treasures**, and are given a monthly stipend for life.

NATIONAL DEMOCRATIC FRONT (NDF). This leftwing group is the principal political front of the Communist Party of the Philippines. It controls and operates many of the party's other fronts, such as the **Christians for National Liberation Front** and **Bayan**. Since its founding in 1973, the Communist party participated in many anti-government demonstrations against the Ferdinand Marcos regime and Corazon Aquino administrations. Government efforts to reach a peace settlement have been stymied by excessive demands of its leaders. Since the party went underground, some of its officers have been living in exile in the Netherlands. *See also* BAYAN MUNA.

NATIONAL FEDERATION OF SUGAR WORKERS (NFSW). Founded in 1971 under the auspices of the Catholic Church, the NFSW is the largest labor union of combined mill and plantation sugarcane workers. It is affiliated with the Kilusang **Mayo Uno**, a leftwing group. Most of its members are in **Negros Occidental** province where the largest sugar plantations are located. *See also* TRADE UNIONS.

NATIONAL HISTORICAL INSTITUTE (NHI). This is an agency mandated by the Constitution of the Philippines and created in 1972. The NHI is responsible for the conservation and preservation of the country's historical legacies. Its major thrusts encompass a cultural program, historical studies, curatorial works, architectural conservation, heraldry, historical information, and preservation of relics and memorabilia of heroes and other renowned Filipinos. The NHI building is located in Manila.

NATIONAL LIBRARY. The National Library is located in Manila and is the repository of the recorded cultural heritage, which consists of intellectual, literary, and information sources. Its collections, facilities, and resources are available to scholars, researchers, students, and the general reading public. Its Filipiniana collection of books and reference materials is one of the best in the country. Besides the National Library, there are 545 public libraries scattered throughout the provinces.

NATIONAL MOVEMENT FOR FREE ELECTIONS (NAMFREL). A private group established in the 1950s, to serve as a watchdog to keep elections honest and clean. Accredited as a citizens' arm of the official government **Commission on Elections** (COMELEC), it proved instrumental in the election of **Ramon Magsaysay** in 1953. It then lapsed into inactivity during the martial law years, reviving to play an important role in Corazon Aquino's 1986 victory. NAMFREL recruited public spirited citizens as volunteers to watch the voting and monitor ballot counting, guard ballot boxes, and prepare a "quick count," based mostly on urban returns, to publicize the election results immediately. Since the Commission on Elections can take weeks or even months to certify official returns, NAMFREL made it harder for unscrupulous politicians to distort the results. With financial support provided by private individuals and foundations, NAMFREL played a major role in the 1986 presidential elections by reporting Marcos-instigated irregularities. Based on "Operation Quick Count" reports, initial returns of the 1986 presidential contests showed that Corazon Aquino was ahead by half-a-million votes, while a week later Marcos overtook Aquino's lead and claimed to be the winner by COMELEC count. The obvious fraud provoked violent citizens' demonstrations and protests that finally led to the declaration of Aquino as the winner. NAMFREL continues as a private group and plays a vital role in preserving clean and honest elections. *See also* DAGDAG BAWAS.

NATIONAL MUSEUM. The main repository of the country's historical and cultural artifacts is the National Museum located in Manila. Its activities include collecting, identifying, and preserving anthropological, archaeological, botanical, geological, and zoological specimens. Its other programs are basic research in the social sciences, the natural history of the Philippines, and the conservation and restoration of cultural landmarks. There are branch museums scattered across the country, such as the Aga Khan Museum at Mindanao State University, Bohol Museum, Silliman University Anthropology Museum, University Museum of Anthropology at University of San Carlos. *See also* AYALA MUSEUM; LOPEZ MUSEUM.

NATIONAL SECRETARIAT FOR SOCIAL ACTION, JUSTICE AND PEACE. The social and political arm of the Catholic Bishop's Conference of the Philippines. It had led protests against anomalous government contracts and claims as the protector of public interest. Its protests in the form of peaceful street demonstrations have obliged government leaders to heed their grievances. Their involvement in political matters has raised questions of the separation of church and state but nevertheless they have been doing this for years since they are the predominant religious majority. Other smaller groups have also made their political impact on national elections— **Iglesia Ni Cristo** headed by Eraño Manalo and El Shaddai by **Mariano Velarde**.

NATIONAL SECURITY. Armed forces of the Philippines. National security is provided by the armed forces, which is comprised of 68,000 soldiers, the navy with 23,000, including 8,500 marines and 2,000 coast guardsmen, and an air force of 15,500. The total active duty strength is 106,500. The country is divided into six unified area commands, six naval districts, and 13 air force squadrons. The Philippines and the U.S. have a **Mutual Defense Treaty** signed in 1951. The president is the commander-in-chief. The armed forces' chiefs of staff report to the minister of national defense. The Philippine National Police (PNP) is responsible for maintaining internal law and order. *See also* VISITING FORCES AGREEMENT.

NATIONAL UNIFICATION COMMISSION. On June 30, 1992, newly elected President Fidel V. Ramos assumed office. In a move to reestablish political stability and social order, which were badly shaken by various coups d'état, he constituted a National Unification Commission. The purpose of this ad hoc body was to make contacts with all rebel elements, whether rightists or leftists, and the **Moro National Liberation Front** (MNLF). He followed this move by calling on Congress to lift its 35-year ban on the **Communist Party of the Philippines** (CPP). His goal was part of a larger strategy of reconciliation to allow the party to function peacefully. Among the first to take advantage of this strategy was the **National Revolutionary Alliance** (RAM) leader Gregorio Honasan and his officers, who had led two ill-fated coups. A cease-fire agreement was reached with the **New Peoples Army** (NPA) and some of its leaders, including leaders of the CPP, who came out of hiding and surrendered peacefully to government troops. The friendly overtures of Ramos broke the central leadership of the insurgents and gave the president the respite he needed to attend to the daunting task of reviving the national economy. *See also* MAGDALO.

NATIONALISM. In the early years of American colonial rule, the American administrators tried to suppress Filipino nationalist feelings. The Philippine Commission, the law-making body, most of whose members were Americans, enacted laws whose purpose was to discourage any act that did not favor the American rule. The Sedition Law passed in 1901 was one of these acts. The act made it unlawful to advocate independence and violators would be punished severely. The following year, the Brigandage Act was passed imposing severe penalties on those found in company with or who were members of armed groups. Another law of 1903 provided for the reconcentration of the inhabitants of a town known to have thieves and outlaws. Nationalism under these circumstances was totally curtailed. However, the Americans allowed the Filipinos some measure of freedom and that was through the formation of political parties whose platform was not based on independence. Thus, the political gateway was opened for enterprising Filipinos to organize their own parties. The first party to be founded was the **Federal Party** (Federalists) whose platform was based on making the Philippines a state of the United States. Many Filipinos who opposed this platform founded the first **Nacionalista Party** (1901), the **Liberal Party** (1902), the first Democrata Party (1902), and others. Despite the ban, these early political parties led the resurgent struggle for independence that became an unstoppable movement in the ensuing years.

NATIONALIST PEOPLE'S COALITION (NPC). A political party established by Eduardo Cojuangco in 1992 to support his presidential candidacy. It initially teamed up with **Lakas CMD** in support of President **Fidel Ramos**, but became the official opposition after **Laban** agreed on an electoral pact with the proadministration party, **Lakas**, in 1994. It backed Joseph Ejercito. Estrada's presidential candidacy in 1998 and its former leader in the lower house, Ronaldo Zamora, was given the key post of executive secretary in his administration.

NATIONALIST REVOLUTIONARY ALLIANCE/REBOLUS YONARYONG ALYASANG MAKABAYAN (RAM). Military reformist organization. After the assassination of Benigno Aquino Jr. in 1983, a faction of young officers fed up with the personalization and manipulation of the military by Ferdinand Marcos, secretly formed RAM with the tacit support of National Defense Minister **Juan Ponce Enrile**. Its objective was to restore "professionalism" in the armed service. Its leader was Colonel Gregorio Honasan, who was Enrile's chief of security. Their first demonstration in 1985 was in protest at the undeserved promotion of officers, incompetence of senior officers, and domination by General Fabian Ver, who was Marcos' chief of staff. In the 1986 presidential elections, RAM threw its support behind Enrile and General Fidel Ramos, who were instrumental in forcing Marcos out of power and installing Corazon Aquino as president. RAM leaders had hoped, with Aquino in power, that their reform movement of depoliticizing the military would be implemented. Their hopes were dashed when Aquino appointed left-leaning lawyers to her cabinet, released political prisoners, including Communist leaders, and promoted favorite officers. Angered by this seeming betrayal of their hopes,

RAM flexed its military muscles by staging a coup d'état on August 28, 1987.

Its intention was to install **Juan Ponce Enrile** as prime minister and Aquino as a figurehead. Leading a force of 1,200 men, Honasan led an assault on Malacañang Palace, but presidential guards under orders of General Fidel Ramos repulsed his men. Fifty-three civilians and soldiers died in this encounter. Coup leader Honasan was captured, but he eventually escaped. The next attempt to dislodge Aquino was in December 1988 and this time another group of younger RAM leaders led the coup. The rebels launched a series of attacks in Manila and bombed the presidential palace grounds. Their confederates in the provinces launched simultaneous attacks on army bases. Again General Ramos coordinated the defense of Malacañang and rallied loyal troops to defend the constituted authorities. With the aid of United States warplanes from Clark Air Base, which flew over Manila, the rebels were clearly made to understand that the United States stood behind the Aquino government. This unequivocal display of support inspired government troops to fight and to encircle the rebel positions. The rebellion collapsed after eight days of fighting. Nearly 100 people died in the coup attempt and more than 600 people were injured. A presidential panel, appointed to investigate the coups, revealed that although many of the complaints from the military were legitimate it was a desire to return to the power and privileges that officers had enjoyed under Marcos that had animated the rebel movement. *See also* MAGDALO.

NEGRITOS. *See* AETAS.

NEGROS ISLAND. The fourth largest island in the Philippine archipelago, divided into two provinces: Negros Oriental, with the provincial capital at Dumaguete City, and Negros Occidental, with the provincial capital at Bacolod City. The major language spoken in Negros Oriental is Cebuano, a fact reflecting the province's nearness to Cebu, while in Negros Occidental the close proximity to Panay makes **Hiligaynon** the preferred language. The whole island has a total land area of 12,705 square kilometers and is characterized by a varied topography. The northern part of the island is pockmarked with volcanic peaks, of which the highest is the dormant Mt. Kanlaon (2,465 meters). The other four peaks are in various stages of activity.

Negritos inhabit the heavily forested interior. Negros Occidental has a land area of 7,926 square kilometers with a population of 2.2 million, while Negros Oriental covers 5,402 square kilometers of land with a population of about one million. The west side of the island is planted mostly with sugarcane, making Negros Occidental the sugar bowl of the country. The west side is planted with coconut, some sugar cane, and corn, which is the staple food of the people. Dumaguete City is the site of Silliman University, famous for its anthropology museum and marine laboratory. The six cities on Negros Occidental are Bacolod, Bago, Cadiz, La Carlota, San Carlos, and Silay. The three cities on Negros Oriental are Bais, Canlaon, and Dumaguete. *See also* ALCALA, ANGEL.

NEOCOLONIALISM. Filipino nationalists used this term to describe the infringement on Philippine sovereignty by the presence of American naval and air force bases. In the 1980s, their presence was the primary cause of the often violent demonstrations in front of the United States Embassy in Manila and on the streets of major cities of the country. These bases were obtained on a 99-year lease, which was denounced by militant nationalists. Later negotiations (**Laurel-Langley Agreement**) reduced the time of the lease to 25 years and released the tremendous acreage occupied by the bases. The United States wanted to continue the lease, but the Philippine Senate rejected the agreement. In 1992, the departure of the American military presence marked the end of neocolonialism or the neoimperialist era of Philippines history. *See also* NATIONALISM.

NEW PEOPLES' ARMY (NPA). A guerrilla force formed in 1968 in **Tarlac** province, north of Manila, by the newly established **Communist Party of the Philippines** (CPP), which spread to other parts of Luzon and throughout the archipelago. A successor to the Huk movement, the NPA's main grievance was based on economic discontent, particularly the extreme polarization of wealth and power. The NPA carried its subversive activities to the cities by the assassinations of public officials as well as Americans. In Plaza Miranda, during a political rally on August 21, 1971, a grenade exploded and killed nine people and wounded 100. NPA was blamed for the attacks, which prompted Ferdinand Marcos to suspend habeas corpus. The Communist insurgency plagued the Marcos administration and continued its subversive activities during Corazon Aquino's government. Since the NPA has not been eradicated, it still poses a threat of destabilization of the government. A kink in the insurgency armor has developed due to age and attrition.

However, the firebrands who founded the communist party are getting on in years. Several of them have died in combat, of natural causes or by assassination. Some have gone above ground and have chosen to follow the path of least resistance. In 1993, a schism pitted major personalities in the left against each and brought about various methods of advancing the revolution. A major leader like Satur Ocampo was forced to go above ground due to age, and brought his battle to the halls of congress. He was elected as a sectoral representative. Another example was **Filemon Lagman**, an urban guerrilla, who chose to get involved in the organization of trade unions. Still the government regard the CPP and the NPA as the most serious security threats in the country, besides Muslim groups waging a long-running separatist campaign in Mindanao. The guerrillas have shown extraordinary resilience. Battered by logistical shortage, battle setbacks, and loss of outside support owing to China's free-market reforms and the collapse of communist Eastern Europe, the rebels have managed to continue with sporadic attacks, like daring raids on armories in provincial camps in recent years. The military estimates that the guerillas now number about 10,000 and have infiltrated at least 500 of the country's 50,000 barangays. The NPA and the CPP are listed as terrorist organizations by the U.S. government.

NEWSPAPERS. Early Philippine newspapers were either pro-Spanish or had a Spanish orientation. The first of this genre was *Del Superior Gobierno*, which came out in 1811 and was clearly a Spanish government mouthpiece. After 15 issues, the paper was discontinued. Other short-lived newspapers, *La Esperanza*, *Diario de Manila*, and *El Comercio* followed. A new era in Philippine journalism arrived when *La Opinion* appeared. In its first issue, anti-Spanish in tone, it attacked the friars for their abuses, and it urged the ouster of the archbishop. In 1890, a nationalist newspaper, *El Resumen*, was published. The most famous newspaper of the prerevolutionary period was *La Solidaridad*, published in Spain. Its basic premise was to advance the cause—freedom—of the Filipino revolutionaries. In Manila, **Emilio Jacinto**, a colleague of **Andres Bonifacio**, founder of the Katipunan, published the *Kalayaan* in Tagalog. Considered the first truly Filipino newspaper, it only published one issue before the Spanish authorities discovered it and shut it down. Another famous newspaper was *El Renacimiento*, which figured in a libel case brought by an American public official. The newspaper lost its case and ended publication.

Meanwhile, English-language newspapers flourished in Manila. Carson Taylor published the *Manila Daily Bulletin* in 1900. Although the newspaper has undergone changes in its format, it continues to be published, making it the oldest existing newspaper in the Philippines. Another English daily was the *Manila Times*, which was started by George Fairchild. Over the years, the newspaper changed ownership. After World War II, Rafael Roces acquired the newspaper. Following a successful history of excellent journalism, it stopped operations in 1972 when Ferdinand Marcos declared **martial law**. In 1986 when Corazon Aquino became president, the *Manila Times* resumed publication. Another notable publication was the *Philippine Free Press*, a weekly magazine, which first appeared in 1906. This magazine has a history of muckraking and public exposure of chicanery by public officials. Marcos shut it down in 1972, but it resumed publication after his fall from power.

The most popular prewar **Tagalog** newspaper was *Taliba*, which was first issued in 1915. *Taliba*, now defunct, was the pioneer in the use of **Taglish** and other tabloid newspapers, one of which is the Metro News, a weekly tabloid that enjoys a large readership, copied its style of language. Tabloid journalism started in the 1950s and continues to be the best-seller in Manila and other cities. The media expansion since 1986—and the advent of the Aquino administration—has been dramatic. There are currently 25 newspapers publishing in Manila; there were less than 10 before Marcos fell. *See also* MASS MEDIA; PHILIPPINE CENTER FOR INVESTIGATIVE JOURNALISM. (PCIJ).

NIPA. A palm tree that thrives in marshy areas and produces large quantities of tough leaves, which are used for thatch roofs and walls of village houses and shelters. The sap is also made into vinegar and wine. *See also* BAHAY KUBO.

NOLI ME TANGERE. This is **Jose Rizal's** first novel written in Spanish and published in 1897 with the help of **Maximo Viola**, a close friend and a fellow medical student in Madrid. Rizal named his book *Noli Me Tangere in Brom Ruhre nicht an* or *Beruhre mich nicht* (in English, Touch Me Not). Rizal wanted to express with the novel, that for the first time he was dealing with problems and conditions, which up to then no one dared to touch on—the political, religious, and economic oppression of the Filipino people by their Spanish overlords (government officials and friars). Vivid descriptions of the oppressors are clearly depicted by the principal character—Crisostomo Ibarra. Rizal wrote *Noli* as a social novel in the genre of Dickens, Zola, and Daudet. *Noli* had a profound effect on the incipient Philippine revolution and the **Katipunan** as *Uncle Tom's Cabin* had for the liberation of the African-American slaves in North America. *See also* EL FILIBUSTERISMO.

NONGOVERNMENTAL ORGANIZATIONS (NGO). "People Power" gave rise to this grass roots democratic movement to empower people through private sector organizations. Under the Ferdinand Marcos administration, people had become so jaded with the unfulfilled government promises of socioeconomic development that they began to take the initiative through civic groups, such as Rotary Clubs, Jaycees, Zonta, and various religious organizations. Some of these NGOs are politically oriented and some are politically neutral. NGOs also differ in terms of size and programs. Some are small with about 10 to 20 people. Others, like Philippine Business for Social Progress, have more than 100 members. The rest are medium-sized, with about 30 to 70 people. In terms of programs, some NGOs address agrarian issues and rural development while others specialize in urban issues (e.g., urban poverty, squatters). Many of these NGOs tend to cooperate with each other through interlocking directorates and networks and help members to obtain access to funds and training. Funding for the NGOs is acquired from international agencies in Europe and America. NGOs are allocated seats on local development councils and with organizations fostering peace and order. The NGOs reject the traditional view of the left that socioeconomic reforms are mere palliatives to strong political and economic organizations built at the grass roots level. *See also* BARRIOS; GABRIELA; PEPE; PROJECT GOOD ROOTS.

NORTH BORNEO. *See* SABAH.

NORTH COTABATO. Province in southern Mindanao formed when
the former Cotabato province was subdivided in 1968. North Cotabato was renamed Cotabao by virtue of *Batas Pambansang* (Presidential Decree) 1983. The province has an area of 6,565 square kilometers of mostly fertile valleys and lowlands. The province has vast
acreage of rubber plantations, which supply a local rubber-processing
industry. This province is the homeland of the **Manobo** people, who
number about 250,000 and are ruled by datus. Kidapawan, the capital, is the seat of Manobo culture, and native handicrafts are sold in
many of the city's retail stores. The other important town of Kabacan,
situated on the Mindanao River, is the site of the Mindanao Institute
of Technology, a government institute of higher learning. Cotabato
has 18 municipalities and a population of close to a million people,
70 percent are migrants from Luzon and Visayas. Chief towns are
Midsayap, Kidapawan, M'lang, Pikit, and Pigkawayan. *See also*
SULTAN KUDARAT.

NUCLEAR ENERGY. The development of nuclear science and technology officially started in 1958 with the passage of the Republic Act
2067 creating the Philippine Atomic Energy Commission (PAEC),
the precursor of the Philippine Nuclear Research Institute (PNRI),
which is the regulatory agency in charge of research and development. The Philippines' first nuclear facility, located in Quezon City,
is the PRR-1, which became critical for the first time in 1963. From
the early 1960s to the 1970s, research and manpower training activities in nuclear energy applications became the main thrust of the
PRR-1. The PRR-1 became the principal facility for many research
and manpower activities in the field of radio isotopic production,
neutron spectrometry, neutron activation analysis, and reactor
physics. Routine production of some 30 radioisotopes and labeled
compounds was undertaken. The PRR-1 became the training ground
for students and new graduates in the natural sciences and engineering and the operators. The reactor conversion into a TRIGA type was
initiated in March 1982 and the TRIGA Converted Reactor became
critical in February 1988. Soon after the same year, the PRR-1 has
been mothballed when the reactor lining developed a leak. In March

1999, the 51 fuel assemblies of mixed enrichment from the PRR-1, consisting of 50 spent and one fresh were shipped to the United States. Notwithstanding the developments surrounding the Philippine Nuclear Power Plant, the Nuclear Power Steering Committee was created in May 1995 by President Fidel Ramos to provide polices, directions, monitoring, evaluation, and other necessary functions to attain the overall nuclear power program.

Nuclear energy was first used in the Philippines in the field of medicine in the 1970s when the first radio isotope laboratory was established by **Paulo Campos**, the first Filipino nuclear medical scientist. A tissue bank is now in existence at the UP-PGH. Although there has been some resistance and controversy by some groups (**NGOs**) to nuclear power generation, nuclear energy has nevertheless been widely used to improve food products and other agricultural resources, help in the diagnosis and treatment of diseases, enhance industrial productivity, and help protect the environment.

NUEVA ECIJA. This province in the heartland of central Luzon occupies 5,284 square kilometers and has a population of 1.26 million people. Nueva Ecija is the nation's leading rice producer, with poultry and cattle as secondary products. Scientific farming and irrigation enable the farmers to produce high rice yields. Cabanatuan City is the capital and major commercial center. During World War II, the city was the site of a huge concentration camp operated by the Japanese military for the detention of American civilian prisoners and other Allied nationals. The major towns are Palayan, Guimba, San Jose, Gapan, and Cuyapo.

NUEVA VIZCAYA. Named after a Spanish province, Nueva Vizcaya is hemmed in by three mountain ranges in northeastern Luzon. The province is sparsely populated with 320,000 inhabitants, mostly migrant Ilocanos and hill people such as the Gaddangs, Ikalahans, Iwaks, Isinais, Ilongots, and Negritos. Bayombong is the provincial capital, while Solano is the biggest town and main commercial center. Logging is a major industry, and salt springs are found in Salinas. The province occupies 3,094 square kilometers and has 16 towns. The major ones are Bagabag, Bambang, and Dupax.

– O –

OBLATION. *See* TOLENTINO, GUILLERMO.

OCAMPO, SATUR. *See* NEW PEOPLES' ARMY.

OCAMPOS, LORETO (1957–). As a provincial governor, Ocampos was cited as one of the most outstanding government executives by the local government leadership foundation in 2003. Ocampos received the award for his successful implementation of the provincial executive program, CHAMPS—competence, health, agricultural productivity, maintenance of peace and order preservation of the environment, and social services—that was created to oversee and ensure that all projects, basic services, and program thrusts of the provincial government are delivered efficiently according to the prime needs and priorities of the constituents. A strong advocate of environmental protection and **sustainable development**, Governor Ocampos authored the Misamis Occidental Environment Code, the first in the province since 1992. He then created systems and structures in support of goals in this code by creating the Baywide Enforcement Task Force that safeguards the coastal resources of Panguil Bay. The governor had also been recognized for his successful law enforcement program through the Provincial Anti-Crime Team. This is the 24-hour "Text Mo C Governor" facility, which is an online complaint desk where drug activities are reported. Among the other winning projects, which have been replicated by other provincial executives, are a provincial rehabilitation center, water system, health and environmental preservation. Ocampos worked closely with **NAMFREL** in the execution of free and honest elections in his province. *See also* MISAMIS OCCIDENTAL.

OCCIDENTAL MINDORO. This province is the western part of the island of **Mindoro**, south of **Batangas**. It is bounded on the south by Calavite Passage, on the east by Oriental Mindoro, on the west by Apo East Pass, and on the south by the Mindoro Strait. Occidental Mindoro consists of high rolling mountains in the east. It has an area of 5,879 square kilometers and a population of 282,593. To the west are coastal plains where 11 towns are situated. The plains are inhabited by Tagalogs and the remote forested interior by **Mangyans**. The province is basically agricultural. Its capital is Mamburao. *See also* MORA, IRENE.

OKIR (OKIL). A unique folk motif of **Maranao** art. Geometric forms of plants, chickens, and serpents, which most often appear imprinted or etched on brass or other metal objects, characterize okir. A distinctive feature is the *sari-manok* motif of a chicken carrying a fish in its beak. The Maranao brassware center is in Tugaya, Lanao del Sur province, where okir art is a cottage industry. Okir art is also expressed in the distinctive architecture and multicolored dress of the Maranaos. The spires and carved beams that protrude from the front of their homes and the designs on their *malongs* (woven Maranao cloth) are adorned with okir motifs. *See also* MARAWI.

OLIGARCHS. A small, almost all-powerful elite, which has shaped much of the history and the social and economic life of the Philippines. These oligarchies trace their roots to the **ilustrados**, whose claim to status was based on wealth and aristocratic lineage. During the Spanish period, they were instrumental in defining government policies as well as setting the social values of society. Under American colonial administration, the elite class expanded rapidly with a new group of recently rich, highly educated individuals made up of **technocrats**, bureaucrats, and functionaries. This new oligarchy wielded political control when World War II broke out. After the end of the war, economic conditions enabled the oligarchs to increase and consolidate their power over the political and economic life of the nation. There were oligarchs who controlled sugar industry, **mass media**, energy, and vast landed estates.

A new elite was further developed by the cronyism of **Ferdinand Marcos**, whose friends and relatives amassed great wealth and resources from government contracts and business. These **cronies** formed the core of Marcos' political and economic support during his administration. The traditional oligarchs, the rich and powerful families, were systematically destroyed by Ferdinand Marcos for their failure to assist him. Their businesses were expropriated and transferred to cronies and dummy companies. After Marcos' downfall, the oligarchs were able to retrieve their properties with the exception of

• OLONGAPO

some collaborators, who were charged with unlawful enrichment before the **Sandiganbayan**, a special court created to investigate **graft and corruption**. *See also* CRONIES; PATRONAGE POLITICS; SAN MIGUEL; TRAPO.

OLONGAPO. This bustling city is located on **Subic Bay** where a huge naval base was built by the U.S. government after the end of World War II. This was also the headquarters of the Seventh Pacific fleet. The base and other presence of American military power (Clark Air Base) became the source of numerous confrontational anti-American protests fueled by communists and leftist elements. The bases employed some 40,000 Filipinos and provided lucrative business enterprises. The operation of the bases, of which there were 23, was part of the 1947 Military Bases Agreement, which was to run for 99 years. However, the continued protests and the action of the Philippine Senate ended the operation of the bases in 1992. The naval equipment was moved to Honolulu, and the base facilities were turned over to the Philippine government. Subic Bay is now the site of the Subic Bay Metropolitan Authority, a free-trade zone and a bustling hub for commerce and **tourism**. *See also* PINATUBO.

OPLE, BLAS (1927–2003). A distinguished senator, Ople took over the office of the secretary of foreign affairs after the resignation of Vice President and concurrent Secretary of Foreign Affairs **Teofisto Guingona**. Considered the country's foremost foreign policy specialists and chair of the Senate committee on foreign relations, Ople left his Senate post to join the Gloria Macapagal Arroyo cabinet and, although he was in the opposition party **Laban ng Demokratikong Pilipino** (LDP), he defended the **Visiting Forces Agreement** (VFA) and bilateral treaties on the Senate floor. The accord eventually led to the deployment of hundreds of American forces to help train Filipino soldiers against the **Abu Sayyaf** as part of an emerging global war on terrorism. He represented the Philippines in many international pacts, which were approved by the Senate, such as General Agreement on Tariff and Trade (GATT). Ople was widely known for his friendly attitude toward the United States and as an admirer of its great political and civil institutions; he was also a great friend of China, Japan, and the European Union.

Ople spent 48 years as a newspaperman and a politician—labor leader, serving as labor secretary of President Ferdinand Marcos, a post he held for 17 years. He later served as congressman of his province **Bulacan**. Ople framed the country's labor code and worked to promote labor rights. He became the first Filipino president of the International Labor Organization (ILO). Elected to the Senate in 1992 and reelected in 1998, he worked on the approval and ratification of 37 international and bilateral treaties. *See also* FOREIGN RELATIONS.

ORIENTAL MINDORO. This province occupies the eastern part of the island of Mindoro. It is bounded in the north by Verde Passage, on the east Tablas Strait, on the west by Occidental Mindoro, and on the south by Semerata Island. The province has an area of 4,364 square kilometers and a population of 550,049. Its capital is Calapan, and the province has 15 towns. Oriental Mindoro has a varied topography dominated by rugged mountain ranges on the west and fertile valleys on the eastern coast. The plains stretch from Baco, Calapan, Naujan, and Victoria on the north, Pinamalayan and Bongabong in the middle, and Roxas to Mansalay in the south. The predominant language is Tagalog. **Mangyans**, the earliest inhabitants, also live in the province. Agriculture is the major economic activity and fishing is a lucrative industry.

OSIAS, CAMILO (1889–1976). Writer, educator, and legislator. A product of the public schools, Osias was sent to the United States as a **pensionado** (government scholar). He studied at the University of Chicago and Columbia University. Osias began his career as a public school teacher and rose to become president of National University in Manila. During his educational stint, he authored the popular "Philippine Readers," a textbook widely used in primary and intermediate schools. In 1928, Osias was elected senator and was instrumental in legislation that improved the quality of the educational system. He was reelected senator several times and made educational legislation his priority. Osias was known also as an avid writer on **Jose Rizal**. He translated the hero's novels into English and wrote numerous books and essays on Rizal. *See also* NATIONAL ANTHEM.

OSMEÑA, LITO. *See* PROGRESSIVE MOVEMENT FOR DEVOLUTION INITIATIVE.

OSMEÑA, SERGIO (1878–1961). Second president of the Philippine **Commonwealth** (1944–1946) and fourth president of the Philippines. He was born on September 9, 1878, in Cebu City. Osmeña served on the staff of General Emilio Aguinaldo as a courier and a journalist. At the close of the war he went home to Cebu and married Estefania Chiong Veloso. His wealthy father-in-law gave him the capital to start a newspaper *El Nuevo Dia*, which first appeared on April 16, 1900. This paper lasted for three years. Although he did not finished his law course he was allowed to take the bar examinations in l903. He placed second among the top national students, and went home to Cebu to serve as legal assistant to the governor. He was appointed fiscal officer of Cebu at the age of 25. When the governor retired, Osmeña served as acting governor and then became governor in 1906. He gave up his position that same year to run for election to the first National Assembly. His colleagues unanimously elected him speaker, a position he held from 1917 to 1922. This was followed by his service as a senator from 1923–1935. When the Philippine Commonwealth was established in 1935, he was elected vice president with Manuel L. Quezon as president. When the Philippines was invaded by Japan in 1942, Osmeña and Quezon were evacuated to the United States where they formed a government in exile. He succeeded Quezon upon his death in 1944 and returned to the Philippines in 1945. In the national elections of 1946, he was defeated by **Manuel Roxas** for the presidency. Osmeña retired as an elder statesman to his native Cebu City.

OS-ROX MISSION. The promise of independence made in the **Jones Law** and the slow implementation of its provisions were not satisfactory to the Filipinos. In order to hasten the action, Filipino political leaders organized an independence commission whose purpose was to negotiate for immediate independence of the Philippines. Two missions were sent to the United States but both met with failure due to the strong objection of American trading firms that were then enjoying a booming business. In 1931, a third mission was sent under the leadership of Senator **Sergio Osmeña** and Speaker **Manuel Roxas**, known as the OS-ROX mission. This time, there were factors favorable to Philippine independence. The American farm group and the labor unions endorsed the early independence of the country. As a result of the intensive campaign of the OS-ROX mission, the American Congress passed the Hare-

Hawes-Cutting Act. The law provided a 10-year transition period, to be known as the Commonwealth, after that, independence would be granted. President Herbert Hoover vetoed the law, but the Congress repassed it over his veto. However, Manuel Quezon, then the president of the Philippine Senate, considered the Hare-Hawes-Cutting Law unfavorable to the interest of the Filipino people. The law was rejected by the Philippine legislature, and in 1933 Quezon organized another mission, which he headed. The Hare-Hawes-Cutting was reenacted as the **Tydings-McDuffie law** with minor changes. President Franklin Roosevelt signed the bill on March 24, 1934.

OVERSEAS FOREIGN WORKERS (OFW). These Filipino overseas contract workers are employed on a contractual basis in such places as the Middle East, Europe, East and Southeast Asia. Financial straits drove many Filipinos to seek job opportunities in foreign countries. Many of them are professionals—nurses, medical technicians, teachers, and engineers. Poverty and low wages added impetus to the mass exodus (BRAIN DRAIN), including an estimated half a million Filipinos who fled to Sabah as refugees from the Muslim separatist rebellion in Southern Philippines. It is estimated that there are about seven million Filipinos working overseas and sending annual remittances of $6 billion dollars to their families. The money has been keeping the Philippine economy afloat in the past two decades. Unlike the **Balikbayans**, who generally are assimilated as professionals in America, OFWs rarely expect to remain permanently in their host country, because of their positions of relative subservience and marginality as sheer labor power. Most of them eventually return to the Philippines, or emigrate to Canada or America. *See also* BALIK ISLAM; FILIPINO MIGRATION TO THE U.S.

OZAMIZ. *See* MISAMIS OCCIDENTAL.

– P –

PABAGSAK (FIXES). *See* GRAFT AND CORRUPTION.

PABALAN, PROCESO. *See* ZARZUELA.

PACT, BIAK-NA-BATO. The pact signed between the Spanish Governor-General Primo de Rivera and General Emilio Aguinaldo on December 15, 1897, at Biak-na-Bato. As agreed, Aguinaldo and his military officers were to go into exile in Hong Kong, a general amnesty was to be granted to Filipino soldiers who surrendered their weapons, and payment of an indemnity of $800,000 was to be made to Aguinaldo and his forces. Half of the indemnity money was given to Aguinaldo and his officers when they landed in Hong Kong. The other half was never paid by the Spanish. Thus, neither of the parties lived up to the agreement and the rebellion revived when Aguinaldo returned to Manila on May 19, 1898. *See also* MANILA BAY, BATTLE OF.

PADACA, MARIA GRACIANA (1963–). Grace Padaca, a polio-stricken former radio broadcaster, won the bitterly fought **Isabela** gubernatorial contest in the May 10, 2004, against an incumbent— Faustino Dy—whose family has dominated the province for three decades. Her victory struck a blow against ruling **political dynasties** in the Philippines. As a radio broadcaster for 14 years, she became an influential figure not only in Isabela, one of the country's largest provinces, but also in Cagayan Valley. Following calls from her supporters to run for public office, she resigned from her job and ran against Faustino Dy III in Isabela's third congressional district race. She lost by a slim margin—48 votes—against Dy in 2001. The **Commission on Elections** junked her protest for a recount of disputed votes. Despite her physical handicap and a meager campaign chest of half a million pesos raised by supporters, Padaca returned in 2004 to challenge the Dy dynasty for the governorship of the province. This time she won by over 44,000 votes that were ironically contested by the defeated governor claiming that the communist-led **New Peoples' Army** allegedly supported Padaca's candidacy. This time the COMELIC ruled in her favor.

Padaca's election scored the biggest upset in the nationwide general elections that won her the press' accolade as the "giant slayer" in Philippine politics and a symbol of democratic reform. She attributed the overwhelming support—from religious, civic groups, and farmers–to their exasperation with the Dy political clan—which still holds sway in the province with a congressman and two mayors. Padaca, who ran under the banner of **Raul Roco's** Aksyon

Demokratica, campaigned on the hot button issues of graft and corruption and need to reform the system. Her parents are retired school teachers in Naguilian, Isabela, where she was born. Stricken with polio at the age of three, Padaca excelled in school and graduated valedictorian in her high school class. She earned a business administration degree, *magna cum laude*, at the Lyceum of the Philippines, Manila, in 1984. She became a public accountant in 1985, but later switched to radio broadcasting in her home province.

PAGADIAN. *See* ZAMBOANGA DEL SUR.

PAGSANJAN FALLS. One of the famous tourist spots 60 kilometers south-east from Manila located in Pagsanjan, which calls itself the "tourist capital of Laguna province." Its main attraction to local and foreign visitors is "shooting the rapids," which is a three-hour upstream *banca* (boat) ride along the Pagsanjan River passing through magnificent scenery of rain forest and river wildlife and ending at the cascading falls—a miniature Niagara Falls. Besides the falls, another attractive offering is the annual *bangkero* (boat) festival, an upstream race of excellent *bangkero*s (boatmen) paddling 20-foot dugout canoes and speeding toward the waterfall. Since Pagsanjan was the capital of the province during the Spanish period, it still maintains much colonial architecture from private houses to **baroque churches**. *See also* ALIWAGWAG FALLS; MARIA CRISTINA FALLS.

PAILALAM RI BORAK. An epic tale of the **Subanon** people who inhabit the mountainous regions of northwestern Zamboanga provinces. The epic narrates battles fought to defend peace loving kingdoms against invaders. The heroine is the warrior princess *Pailalam ri Borak* who—with her supernatural powers—slays countless enemies with her magic *kampilan* (sword). *See also* BANTU-GAN; MATABAGKA.

PALABRICA-GO, RAMONA (1958–). She became the first Filipina battalion commander who rose through the ranks in the male-dominated Armed Forces of the Philippines. Appointed by President Gloria Macapagal Arroyo in Janaury 2003, Palabrica-Go was given command of the Light Armor Brigade based in Fort Magsaysay, Laur, **Nueva Ecija**. A graduate of the **Philippine Military Academy**, she was the head of her graduating class. *See also* REGALADO, GEORGIA.

PALARIS, JUAN DE LA CRUZ (1733–1765). Palaris was the legendary **Pangasinan** revolutionary hero who led successful **revolts** against the Spaniards during the Spanish occupation in the Philippines. Palaris was born in Binalatongan (now San Carlos), Pangasinan, to prominent parents—his father was the *cabeza de barangay* (head man). As a boy, he was extraordinarily big, thus earning the sobriquet, "the giant's son." The town priest taught him the rudiments of reading and writing in Spanish. He was 22 years old when he witnessed an incident that rankled him and made him lose his respect for the Spanish authorities. It was that of a priest slapping and kicking a poor native boy for not having kissed his hand. He started the insurrection in Binalatongan by defying the **tribute** collectors on the ground that because of the **British occupation of Manila**, the colonial government no longer existed. With the help of his brother and the support of his town mates, Palaris started the Pangasinan revolt on November 3, 1762, by successfully seizing an abandoned armory in Lingayen. With their artillery pieces, the rebels were able to repulse the onslaughts of Spanish troops. Between 1762 and 1763, Palaris and his 3,000 fighters occupied Binalatongan as their capital. The fighting was marked by much cruelty and ruthlessness on both sides. Eventually, the combined forces of Spanish and **Ilocano** routed the rebels. In desperation Palaris burned down the church and convent and his fighters retreated into the forest, but were hunted down and publicly hanged. *See also* SILANG, DIEGO.

PALAWAN. The largest province in the Philippines, Palawan consists of 1,769 islands and a combined land area of 14,896 square kilometers. Some 80 percent of the land area consists of the main island of Palawan, the fifth largest island in the Philippine archipelago. The province stretches north to south over 650 kilometers from Busuanga Island to the Balabac Islands. The area is rich in natural resources, including wildlife. Vast virgin forests still exists in this relatively underdeveloped land. Palawan's rich fishing grounds supply about 65 percent of the national catch. Southern Palawan Island is the site of the **Tabon Caves** National Park. The capital city is Puerto Princesa, and the island's population is made up mostly of Muslims, Chinese, Tagalogs, Ilocanos, and **Tagbanuas**. North of Puerto Princesa is the **Iwahig Penal Colony**. Chief towns are Aborlan, Balabac, Brooke's Point, Coron, El Nido, Magsaysay, and Quezon.

PALAY. Unmilled **rice**. Agricultural land planted in palay totals 3.42 million hectares (8.45 million acres), which produce 9.67 million metric tons. The top three rice-producing regions are central Luzon, western Visayas, and southern Luzon. Central Luzon reported the highest yield per hectare of 3.50 metric tons, southern Mindanao was second with 3.35 metric tons per hectare, followed by Cagayan Valley with 3.18 metric tons per hectare. Due to major calamities that struck the country in 1990, rice production took a slump, which forced the country to import rice from Thailand. With the introduction of a new high-yielding **hybrid** variety, rice production has significantly increased in the past few years. *See also* AGRICULTURE.

PALAYAN. *See* NUEVA ECIJA.

PALEOLITHIC CULTURE. The earliest evidence of the presence of the *homo erectus* species in the Philippine archipelago appeared in Cagayan Valley. In the plains of Liwan Filipino paleontologists found fossil remains of large animals now extinct in the Philippines. These animals include elephas (a kind of ancient elephant), rhinoceros, stegodon, crocodile, and tortoise. The presence of these animals indicates that the islands were connected during the Ice Age with mainland Asia. The scientists estimate that these animals last roamed in the islands some 250,000 years ago. Although scientists have not found proof of early man in the valley they discovered evidence of his existence in caves in which he lived, such as fragments of stone tools, animal bones, and shells of fish. Flake tools and the fossils were uncovered in the same layer of rock, named Awidon Mesa Formation, which was formed over the western Cagayan Valley floor during the Ice Ages. *See also* ANCIENT MAN; FUGA ISLAND; TABON CAVES.

PALMA, JOSE. *See* NATIONAL ANTHEM.

PAMPANGA. A densely populated province, with a total land area of 2,181 square kilometers and a population of 1.5 million. During the Spanish rule, Pampanga province figured prominently as a source of timber and slave labor for the **galleons** that plied the Manila-Acapulco route. The province has a long history of rebellion against the Spanish taskmasters. Its rich, fertile plains produce rice and sugarcane and its extensive swamp and mangrove areas, which have been converted into fishponds, supply fish for the Manila market. San Fernando, the capital city, is noted for its flagellants and lantern festivals. People speak the Pampango language and retain a distinctive cultural identity. Some of its major towns are San Fernando, Angeles, Lubao, Arayat, Mexico, and Apalit. *See also* MACABEBES; MANIAGO, FRANCISCO; YUZON, AMADO.

PANAY. A major island in the Visayan region. Panay was one of the islands settled by Malay immigrants circa A.D. 1212 coming from Borneo. According to legend, 10 Bornean datus (chiefs) were fleeing from oppression by their overlord, the tyrant Datu Makatunaw. The 10 datus, led by Datu Puti, sailed in their barangays, loaded with their families, and landed at the present site of Aklan in Panay Island. They were met by aboriginal **Aetas** (Negritos), who were in control of the island. For the price of settling in their region, Chief Marikudo of the Negritos agreed to trade parts of the island of Panay for a golden *salakot* (hat) and a basin. Maniwantiwan, Marikudo's wife, also demanded an ankle-length necklace of gold belonging to the wife of the Bornean datu. The Negritos in return gave the Borneans a bushel of live crabs, a long-tusked boar, and a full-antlered white deer. Then the Negritos withdrew to other parts of the island. *See also* SUMAKWEL.

PANDAY, SANDEEP. *See* RAMON MAGSAYSAY AWARD.

PANG-ALAY. A **Tagalog** word for offering and it refers to ritual pottery in ancient Philippines. Early Filipinos used pottery as containers of food offerings placed on the surface of gravesites during burial or during ritual revisits to the dead. As grave goods (*paba-on*) or offerings (*pang-alay*), these clay products were intended to ease the journey of the departed. The earthen vessels provided the deceased with pots they could use as they continued their existence in the hereafter. Jars were also used to contain the body of the dead or to keep their bones after ritual cleansing. *See also* FESTIVALS; MANUNGGUL JAR.

PANGASINAN. A language spoken principally in the province of Pangasinan in the Lingayen Gulf region in west central Luzon. The natives like to call themselves *Pangalatoks*.

PANHUTONGAN ARCHAEOLOGICAL DISCOVERY. Panhutongan is a **barangay** of Placer in **Surigao**, where Filipino archaeologists found a formal burial site of ancient inhabitants. Unearthed were dugout coffins, with trade ceramics placed upside down on the faces of the human remains. Associated with these human remains were cultural materials like white and blue Chinese trade ceramics in perfect condition, as well as metal tools, spear points, metal ornaments, iron slags, charcoal, a medallion, and a smoking pipe. In another excavation, the archaeologists found plank-type coffins that revealed another prehistoric burial practice. In the context of Philippine prehistoric culture and society, the archaeologists estimate that the site was in continuous habitation from 140 A.D. to 1770 A.D.—a period of 1,630 years. The carbon-14 dating, made by Professor Kunihiko Kigoshi of Gaku-shuin University Radiocarbon Laboratory of the wood sample dated at 1260 A.D., indicated that a structure once existed on the same ground 261 years prior to the coming of Ferdinand Magellan in 1521. *See also* BUTUAN ARCHAEOLOGY.

PARDO, T. H. de. *See* FEDERAL PARTY.

PARIAN. Old Chinese enclave in Manila. Chinese traders had been regularly visiting Ma-i (Chinese name for Manila) even before the coming of the Spaniards in 1521. **Chinese** trading junks brought goods such as iron needles, porcelain, silk, and glass beads, which were bartered for Filipino products such as tortoise shells, cotton, betel nuts, and pearls. Early Spanish governors-general encouraged the trade, especially for the much-valued Chinese silk and porcelain ware that were brought to Mexico during the **galleon** trade. In 1580 the Spanish built a Chinese trading center in Manila where the Chinese merchants, called Sangleys, lived and had their own shops. The burgeoning trade made the center inadequate and another center was built outside the walls of the **intramuros**, which was called Parian or marketplace. There the Chinese merchants prospered and their numbers increased, to the alarm of the Spanish, who began to persecute them. In 1603, the Chinese staged an uprising under the leadership of Eng-Kang, who was caught and executed by the Spanish. When the persecutions became severe the Chinese carried out revolts against the Spanish during the years 1639, 1662, 1686, and 1762. All of these uprisings were put down by the Spanish with the help of mercenaries at a cost of 20,000 Chinese lives. Because the Parian had been a hotbed of restiveness, it was demolished by the Spanish in 1860 and the Chinese population, greatly reduced in number, was dispersed to other parts of the city Quiapo, Santa Cruz, and San Nicolas. Today, Chinatown is known as Binondo. *See also* TONDO TSINOY.

PARITY RIGHTS. A controversial provision of the **Bell Trade Act,** also known as the Philippine Rehabilitation Act. It was passed by the United States Congress in 1946. The act granted U.S. citizens equal economic rights with Filipinos in the development of natural resources. Payment of war damages amounting to $620 million, as stipulated in the act, was made contingent on Philippine acceptance of the parity clause, which enraged Philippine legislators, many of whom believed that the clause was an "inexcusable surrender of national sovereignty." The issue of the clause, submitted to a national plebiscite in March, 1957, was approved by a majority of the 40 percent who voted. The parity rights expired in 1976. *See also* LAUREL-LANGLEY.

PARTIDO NG BAYAN (PARTY OF THE NATION). A leftist political party formed by the Communist Party of the Philippines in September 1986 to contest the congressional elections. It fielded a slate of senatorial and congressional candidates, but failed to elect any of them. As a consequence, the party dropped out of the electoral scene and later reverted to guerrilla warfare. *See also* BUKLURAN NG MANGAGAWANG PILIPINO; COMMUNIST PARTY OF THE PHILIPPINES.

PARTY-LIST SYSTEM. Under the 1987 Constitution, there is a provision that mandates that 20 percent of the total seats in the House of Representatives are reserved for marginalized and underrepresented sectors such as **women**, labor, peasants, fisherfolk, urban poor, indigenous cultural communities, disabled, youth, elderly, veterans, **overseas workers**, and professionals. To implement this constitutional provision, Congress passed Republic Act 7941 on March 3, 1995, or the Party-List System. Registered national, regional, and **sectoral parties**, organizations or coalitions can nominate a maximum of five names. A party is entitled to a maximum of three seats and to get one seat, it must obtain at least 2 percent of the total votes for all participating parties. Of the 257 seats in the House, 52 seats were hotly contested by small and new political parties and sectoral organizations. The 1990s saw a notable increase in the number of women and winning decisive elective posts particularly at the local legislative councils in the barangays and municipalities. The May 11, 2002, party-list elections gave women and other minority parties an opportunity to mainstream in the legislative process and transform personality-based politics—**political dynasties**—into issue oriented politics. Under the party-list system, voters chose political parties rather than individual candidates. Thus, the stress is on party programs, issues, and platforms rather than the popularity of candidates.

PASYON. A popular book whose text is sung during the Lenten season. *Pasyon* comes from the Spanish word meaning "passion" and refers to the passion of Christ. The book narrates in verse form the story of Christ from nativity to the crucifixion and resurrection. It consists of rhyming stanzas of five lines, each line composed of eight syllables. The public reading of the *pasyon*, called *pabasa*, begins on Ash Wednesday and ends on the evening of Good Friday. The *pasyon* is chanted or sung either solo or in groups in front of well-decorated altars inside barrio chapels, houses, or specially prepared public places. The *pasyon* has been read in Tagalog since 1704, although other vernacular versions have since come into use in various major regions of the country.

PATERNO, PEDRO A. (1857–1911). Patriot and lawyer. Paterno was born to a wealthy Manila family, which was able to send him to schools of higher education in the Philippines and Spain. He obtained his law degree in Spain and returned to the Philippines to establish his practice. He was a famous **illustrado** who dabbled in political journalism by writing articles on reform and nationalism. When the **Philippine–Spanish Revolution** broke out he served as an aide to Emilio Aguinaldo and was instrumental in negotiating the so-called Pact of **Biak-na-Bato**, which technically ended the hostilities with the Spanish but was broken later by both sides. When Aguinaldo returned to the Philippines he called a revolutionary congress to draft a constitution for a republic. Paterno served as president of the constitutional convention, and, through his adroitness and knowledge of parliamentary procedures, the Malolos Constitution was approved by the delegates and subsequently signed into law by Aguinaldo. *See also* BARASOAIN CHURCH.

PATRONAGE POLITICS. This system of politics revolves around a continuing bond between the landed elite and the clients who depend on them. Underneath this relationship is *utang na loob* (debt of gratitude) in which the landlord is the patron who bestows favor upon his subordinates who in turn must reciprocate in kind or give their devotion to the cause of their patron. Patronage politics has been the bedrock of political life and in the Philippines and it can be traced to the **encomienda** system of the Spanish period. *See also* CRONIES; POLITICAL DYNASTIES; SOCIAL VALUES.

PAUA, JOSE IGNACIO (1872–1926). As a Chinese general in the Philippine–American revolution, Paua was the only high ranking pure-blooded Chinese to join **Emilio Aguinaldo's** army in the short-lived struggle against the American colonizers. His knowledge as a blacksmith and expertise in native canons called *lantakas* and gunpowder earned him Aguinaldo's confidence and made him a colonel. After the Battle of Binakayan—where he proved his valor by leading his bolo-wielding Tagalog troops and successfully stopped Spanish riflemen—Paua was raised to a full general. Paua was born on April 29, 1872, in an impoverished village of Lao-na in Fujian province, China. In 1890, he accompanied his uncle to seek his fortune in the Philippines. He served first as an apprentice blacksmith in a shop in Manila—a job he held for several years until he became an expert. Aware of the shortage of arms, he suggested to Aguinaldo to set up an ammunition factory in Imus, Cavite. Under his skillful supervision, old canons and broken Mausers (rifles) captured from the enemy were repaired; large bamboo canons taped with wires were manufactured and numerous *paltiks* (crude firearms) were made. In spite of his being a Chinese—he wore his pigtails—he never hesitated risking his life for his beloved country. Paua proved himself in attacks on Spanish garrisons and confrontations against the enemy. After the end of the war Paua was tasked with raising funds for the empty coffers of the newly established Republic. He raised a staggering sum in Bicolandia alone—mostly from the Chinese. He retired in Albay and was once elected mayor of Manito, Albay. On Independence Day June 12, 1989, General Paua was fittingly honored with a monument at the Aguinaldo shrine in Kawit, Cavite, as a tribute to this unknown and unsung hero of the Philippine revolution. *See also* CHINESE; TSINOY.

PAYNE-ALDRICH TARIFF ACT. A law passed by the U.S. Congress in 1909 that provided for free entry of all Philippine products except rice, sugar, and tobacco. Rice imports were subjected to regular tariffs, while quotas were established for sugar and tobacco. Later in 1913 the Underwood Tariff Act abolished all restrictions and thus made the Philippines more dependent on the American market. The net effect of this new trade law was that it enabled wealthy landowners such as the sugar, tobacco, hemp, and coconut planters to sell more and therefore to prosper in the tariff-free U. S. markets. By 1939, the Philippines exported 85 percent of its goods to the United States, and 65 percent of its imports came from the United States When the Philippines achieved its independence, the **Bell Trade Act** of 1946 corrected the trade imbalance. *See also* LAUREL-LANGLEY TRADE AGREEMENT.

PEACE CORPS. Since the first group of Peace Corps volunteers arrived in 1961, more than 8,500 American volunteers have shared their expertise with Filipino nongovernmental organizations and communities. Up until 1990, when the Peace Corps was suspended, some 6,500 volunteers had served in the Philippines, the largest group to serve in any single Peace Corps country. Two years later in 1992 when the operations resumed, the Peace Corps designed the small island development that featured PCVs assigned to island provinces of **Catanduanes**, **Romblon**, and **Batanes**. At present, some 100 volunteers are working throughout the country, from Batanes to Mindanao, in the areas of environmental education, coastal resources management, English teacher training, water sanitation and waste management, and protected area management.

PEACE TALKS (PHILIPPINE GOVERNMENT AND COMMUNISTS). President Gloria Macapagal Arroyo, during her administration, adopted a policy of keeping "open lines of communications" with the leadership of the **Communist Party of the Philippines (CPP)** and its military arm, the **New Peoples' Army (NPA)**. Unlike the mailed fist policy of previous administrations, the Arroyo government tried to keep the door open for a peaceful settlement not only with the communists but also with the separatist Muslim elements in Mindanao. Although these organizations have been included in Washington's blacklist of "foreign terrorist organizations," formal peace talks were conducted with CPP leader Jose Maria Sison—who fled to the Netherlands in 1987 after being pardoned and freed from prison—and his surrogates. However, the U.S. move blocking the flow of funds to the CPP imperiled the fate of the negotiations for peace. Government officials estimated that the NPA raises more than 100 hundred million pesos from extortion and other illegal activities on Philippine territory as well as from contributions from leftist and other parties and groups in Europe. Cutting off the flow of funds appeared to have affected the terrorist activities of **Abu Sayyaf** that had been linked to Al-Qaeda. Nevertheless, some progress was achieved. While peace negotiations were suspended, the government panel has submitted its draft of a comprehensive peace agreement on three major agenda items: socioeconomic, political, and economic reforms, the end to hostilities, and demobilization of forces. *See also* MORO ISLAMIC LIBERATION FRONT; MUSLIM SEPARATISM.

PELAEZ, PEDRO. See SECULARIZATION.

PENAL LAW. The Philippine penal code used to be based on the Spanish penal code of 1870, but this was replaced when the Americans colonized the Philippines and a new penal code was adopted on January 1, 1932. The penal code set forth the basic principles affecting criminal liabilities, established a system of penalties, and defined classes of crimes. It also provided for aggravating and mitigating circumstances. Under the code, penalties were classified as capital (requiring a death sentence), afflictive (six years to life imprisonment), correctional (one month to six years), and light (up to 30 days). The 1987 constitution, however, outlaws the death penalty unless provided for by subsequent legislation. In the Muslim areas of the south, Islamic law (**sharia**) is employed with Philippine law still the basis of litigation.

PENINSULARES. A term used by the Spanish to distinguish Spaniards residing in the Philippines who were born in Spain. The Peninsulares, who constituted the elite class, were mostly the rich and powerful high government officials and friars of the various religious orders. *See also* INDIOS; INSULARES.

PENSIONADO. A term applied to Filipino scholars sent to the United States to study in institutions of higher education during the years 1903–1928 of the American regime in the Philippines. These were talented students selected from all over the islands whose educational expenses were paid for by the U.S. government, hence the name pensionado, after the Spanish term pension. Recipients who came back successfully with a degree from a U.S. college or university were assured of teaching or government positions. Many of the early Filipino leaders in education, business, and politics were pensionados. They were active in the independence movement. This educational program was followed after the end of World War II with the introduction of the Fulbright-Hays Scholarships, which sent thousands of Filipinos to study for higher degrees in U.S. colleges and universities. Many who held Ph.D.'s became the "**technocrats**" or second echelon personnel who provided managerial and technical competence in science, economics, education, and government at a time when the country was recovering from the devastation of World War II. *See also* BENITEZ, CONRADO; BOCOBO, JORGE; OSIAS, CAMILO.

PEOPLE POWER. Part of a coup d'état staged on February 22, 1986, and known as the EDSA revolution. It toppled the government of Ferdinand Macros and led to the assumption of power by Corazon Aquino. Hundreds of thousands of people were summoned to the streets by

Archbishop of Manila Jaime Cardinal Sin. They barricaded themselves on Epifanio de los Santos Avenue (EDSA) in front of Camps Aguinaldo and Crame to prevent government troops from crushing coup leaders **Fidel Ramos** and **Juan Ponce Enrile** and their followers. This "People Power" provided the strength for Aquino to push through her economic and social programs. *See also* COUP D' ETAT.

PEPE (POPULAR EDUCATION FOR PEOPLE'S EMPOWER-MENT). This is a **nongovernmental organization (NGO)**, which was formed in 1986 by several development-oriented organizations to serve as a center for their various popular education activities known as "pop-ed." PEPE is dedicated to the promotion of "pop-ed" programs and practices as tools for people's empowerment. It provides services to diverse sets of people: urban poor, farmers, fisher folk, profession-als, **women**, and indigenous peoples. Its services are focused on en-hancing these sector's capacities, knowledge, skills, and attitudes as community educators. This key function has brought PEPE into close contact with numerous developmental organizations, in the process strengthening its advocacy and networking efforts at the community, national, and global level. *See also* PROJECT GOOD ROOTS.

PERALTA, MACARIO. A noted guerrilla leader during the Japanese occupation, Peralta and his group are credited with saving the Amer-ican invasion fleet off the coast of Leyte from disaster by the timely radio encryption of the whereabouts of Japanese battleships to Gen-eral **Douglas MacArthur**. A powerful Japanese naval fleet was spot-ted by Peralta's coast watchers winding their way through the Suri-gao and San Bernardino strait seeking to intercept the flotilla of American landing forces approaching Leyte. Unaware of the ap-proaching enemy ships, the landing on Leyte without air cover pro-ceeded without opposition from the Japanese. Peralta's decisive warning sent hundreds of American fighter planes to intercept the fleet of Admiral Kurita. What ensued was the largest naval battle in history—Battle for Leyte Gulf. After the fall of **Bataan**, Peralta went into **guerrilla** warfare in his native province of Panay, where he or-ganized a military command. During the **Japanese occupation** of Panay, Peralta's guerrillas harassed and destroyed military convoys. After the end of the war, MacArthur awarded Peralta with medals and made him a permanent colonel in the U.S. Army. He was later appointed secretary of defense in the postwar government of President **Manuel Roxas**.

PEREZ, ASUNCION A. (1895–1967). A leader in community service. A graduate of the University of the Philippines, Perez entered government service in 1941 as chief of the Division of Public Assistance, and three months later President Manuel L. Quezon appointed her director of the Bureau of Public Welfare. Her service was interrupted by the Japanese occupation, whereupon she became a **guerrilla**. Perez was caught by the Japanese and subsequently imprisoned in dreaded the **Fort Santiago**. After the war President Sergio Osmeña reappointed her as director of public welfare. Her position was elevated to commissioner and later administrator of the Social Welfare Administration. She was the first woman to hold a cabinet rank in the **Manuel Roxas** and **Elpidio Quirino** administrations. During her term of office, she organized a number of associations devoted to alleviating the woes of children. She founded and organized the Children's Garden in Taytay, Rizal, one of the country's most modern child-rearing institutions. Her institution set the example for the proper care, education, and training of destitute, abandoned, and orphaned children. Perez also formed the Philippine Foundation for the Crippled and served as its president. She created the Poliomyelitis Association as well as the government's national welfare program, which helped in the fight against communism during the administration of four Philippine presidents. *See also* DE LEON, MEDINA LACSON.

PFAU, RUTH. *See* RAMON MAGSAYSAY AWARD.

PHILIPPINE–AMERICAN REVOLUTION (1899–1901). When the promised independence from the U.S. was not granted after the destruction of the Spanish fleet in Manila Bay, **Emilio Aguinaldo** declared a free Philippine republic on June 12, 1898. A bloody three-year war followed during which the Filipinos suffered heavy casualties in the face of superior firepower of the Americans. Betrayal assisted the Americans in their ruthless pursuit of Aguinaldo, whose capture in 1901 effectively ended the revolution. According to Philippine historian **Teodoro Agoncillo**, the death toll of Filipinos at the hands of American soldiers was 500,000. However, American historians claimed that 200,000 civilians died in the war from starvation, disease, and brutality. *See also* MACABEBES; PHILIPPINE–SPANISH REVOLUTION.

PHILIPPINE ATOMIC ENERGY COMMISSION. *See* NUCLEAR ENERGY.

PHILIPPINE CENTER FOR INVESTIGATIVE JOURNALISM (PCIJ). The Philippine press is the envy of many Southeast Asian countries. Free, bold, and hard-hitting, the press makes politicians quake and has succeeded in catalyzing important reforms in government. But while the press in the Philippines revels in its freedom, it also suffers from sensationalism, sloppy reporting, and breaches of professional and ethical standards. There is a great deal of influence peddling and it is widely accepted that a **newspaper** might slant a story to favor a candidate or the publisher's business associate. Part of the problem is the extreme competitiveness of the newspaper industry: there are two dozens dailies publishing out of Metro Manila alone. Many of the newspapers were set up by businessmen who see the press as an extension of their business empire. With the pressure to compete—the standards imposed by conservative publishers and budgetary constraints—it was difficult to expect journalist to do more than routine reporting.

When the Philippine Center for Investigative Journalism (PCIJ) was founded in 1989, three years after the fall of Ferdinand Marcos, many of the shortcomings of a free and rambunctious press were already becoming apparent. The center, an independent, nonprofit news organization, was set up to address some of these shortcomings. Nine Filipino journalists who realized the need to hone journalistic skills—to go beyond day-to-day reportage, and provide more depth and content to news reports—founded the center. The PCIJ began by offering fellowships to print and broadcast reporters who wished to do investigative projects. The center funded their research and field expenses, offered editorial and research support, and sold their stories to mainstream newspapers and television stations. In the last decade or so, the center has published 250 stories in major newspapers, aired about four dozen short features on primetime news programs, and produced five full-length documentaries. It also published 10 books on politics, health, the environment, and the military. The PCIJ expanded into radio, which reaches more households in the Philippines than newspapers and television. Besides the modest income obtained from selling books and stories, PCIJ center receives foundation support for its activities. The PCIJ sees itself as playing a developmental role while creating a culture for it within the Philippine media. *See also* BRAID, FLOR-ANGEL ROSARIO; CORONEL, SHEILA; MASS MEDIA.

PHILIPPINE CONSTABULARY. *See* NATIONAL SECURITY.

PHILIPPINE EAGLE (*Pithecophaga Jefferyi*). The Philippine eagle—local name *Haribon*—is one of the largest eagles in the world, with a wing span approaching two meters. Its favorite prey is the monkey, which it snatches from treetops in its native habitat of **Mt. Apo**, Mindanao. This bird is not found elsewhere in the world and has become the national symbol of the Philippines. Since 1981 the eagle population has declined from an estimated total of 500 to just 70 today, thus making it a critically endangered species. A breeding pair will only produce a single young every other year. Widespread destruction of its habitat—logging and mining—and illegal trade and trophy hunting is driving this rare species to extinction. The eagle's natural habitat has also been depleted by the economic needs of the millions of Filipinos who sell forest products or farm using slash-and-burn techniques. To save and preserve the eagle, a private foundation, Philippine Eagle Foundation (PEF), a captive breeding program, has been developed in Davao. Since 1998, the PEP has successfully bred new birds and released them to their habitat. Regarding the dilemma of the farmers, PEF has introduced programs to improve their economic life while preserving the habitat of the eagle. In 2004, the Philippine government declared June 4–10 as Philippine Eagle Week each year to generate awareness of the eagle's importance in the ecosystem. *See also* BIODIVERSITY.

PHILIPPINE–EUROPEAN SOLIDARITY CENTER (PESC). The work of this **nongovernmental organization** (NGO) is to build a "just and sustainable society" in the Philippines, and thus it cooperates in the programs of other NGOs. The PESC also is active in the fields of **human rights**, agrarian reform, environment, overseas Filipino rights, economic reforms, and **women**. It supports these causes by distributing news on their activities, announcements, and analyses; helping them get in contact with their counterparts in Europe and other parts of the world; calling for solidarity actions in their support and linking the various Philippine solidarity efforts with each other. *See also* SUSTAINABLE DEVELOPMENT.

PHILIPPINE EXPEDITIONARY FORCE TO KOREA (PEFTOK) (1950–1955). On September 19, 1950, the first Filipino combat team of the Philippine Expeditionary Force to Korea landed in the southeastern Korean port of Pusan as the Philippine government contribution to the United Nation's defense of South Korea. There were five-battalion combat teams that had combat strength of 7,000 officers and soldiers who served under the United Nations Command (UNC) during the four-year conflict. The PEFTOK proved its mettle in the battle of Yultong, one of the biggest battles of the Korean War. Fighting side by side with the Puerto Rican and Turkish brigades, the Filipino soldiers held their three-mile sector against the Chinese People's Volunteer Army troops. Although heavily outnumbered the Filipino soldiers resisted ferociously and repelled the enemy advance. In the four-year combat, the PEFTOK suffered some 400 casualties. Two officers earned medals: Captain Conrado Yap, Medal of Valor, the Philippine's highest award for heroism, and Lt. Jose Artiaga, Distinguished Service Cross. *See also* PHILIPPINE SCOUTS*;* USAFFE.

PHILIPPINE MILITARY ACADEMY (PMA). This is the premier institution of learning for future officers in the Armed Forces of the Philippines. Established on December 21, 1936, by President **Manuel L. Quezon**, the PMA was patterned after the U.S. Military Academy. Its sprawling 373-hectare campus located near **Baguio City** is called Fort Del Pilar after **Gregorio del Pilar**, the young hero of **Tirad Pass**. Cadets are chosen through a rigorous entrance examination, and successful cadets are enrolled in a four-year bachelor of science course in military science and tactics. After graduation, cadets are formally inducted as second lieutenants. In 1972, the PMA curriculum was changed for a set of courses balanced between the techno-scientific and sociohumanistic—to provide functional officers for the three branches of service of the armed forces. In 1995, the Academy admitted the first batch of female cadets. *See also* PALABRICA-GO, RA-MONA; REGALADO, GEORGIA.

PHILIPPINE RURAL RECONSTRUCTION MOVEMENT (PRRM). A **nongovernmental organization** agency started in 1953 by James Yen who brought his idea of rural construction from China to the Philippines. Funded by U.S. philanthropic foundations and private sources, the movement started in **Nueva Ecija** and **Rizal** provinces by deploying 200 trained rural reconstruction workers. The centerpieces of their work are empowerment, poverty eradication, and self-government—organizing barrio councils, later adopted by the government as a basic unit of administration, and cooperative development programs. In cooperation with the government, the PRRM expanded its work in 95 barrios in the provinces of **Quirino**, **Kalinga-Apayao**, **Cagayan**, **Isabela,** and **Nueva Vizcaya**. The PRRM now operates in 15 provinces with 300 development workers. Some of its projects include the Lagawe Highland Rural Bank in Ifugao, Save the Rice Terraces Movement, Marinduque **Sustainable Development** Program, Responsible Parenthood Program, and Integrated Protected Area System. Its professional consultants have developed survey reports on natural resource management that have helped the government enact legislation to stop **deforestation**, overfishing, and the destruction of habitat. *See also* FLAVIER, JUAN.

PHILIPPINE–SPANISH REVOLUTION (1896–1899). Started in mid-1896 when Spanish authorities discovered the **Katipunan**, a secret society dedicated to ending Spanish rule. Upon discovery its founder **Andres Bonifacio** in Balintawak immediately made a call to arms. Skirmishes and pitched battles ensued with heavy casualties on both sides, with the poorly armed Filipinos sustaining the bulk of the losses. In 1897, an armistice was declared with the Spanish authorities, but neither side followed its provisions. Hostilities were resumed in May 1898, and on June 12 **Emilio Aguinaldo** proclaimed the independence of the Philippines. He followed this act with the declaration of the Philippine Republic on June 12, 1898, when the Spanish military forces were almost crushed. The short-lived republic disappeared with the declaration of the Spanish–American War and the subsequent arrival of the Americans. *See also* PINAGLABANAN.

PHILIPPINE SCOUTS. At the end of the Philippine–American Revolution, the U.S. Congress authorized the recruitment of Filipinos in the U.S. Army. They were called Philippine Scouts and officered by Americans. The scouts were involved in local campaigns in the interior Philippines. When World War II came, the well-trained Philippine Scouts made up the backbone of the regular American forces. It had a prewar strength of 7,000 men composed of two infantry divisions, one cavalry regiment, and two coastal artillery. At the battle of Bataan, the scouts provided coverage to the withdrawal of the **USAFFE** forces on Luzon to Bataan. In one of the major skirmishes with the Japanese, the cavalry regiment participated in the last organized horse-cavalry actions. The scouts fought in two separate engagements, at the "the Battle of the Points" that slaughtered all but 50 of the 1,200 Japanese attackers, and at the Abucay-Cabcaben perimeter, where it successfully delayed the advance of the Japanese forces. Their defense earned the respect of the Japanese, who came out with a larger force of tanks and artillery to defeat the defending scouts. The U.S. Army showered the Filipino scouts with its highest decorations. The soldiers earned nine Distinguished Service Crosses, 74 Silver Stars, and at least 2,000 Bronze Stars. For nearly four months, the USAFFE, stiffened by the scout regiments, held the Bataan Peninsula until disease and dwindling supplies exhausted their units. *See also* DEATH MARCH.

PHILIPPINES. Name given to the archipelago by conquistador **Ruy Lopez de Villalobos** in 1543. When he claimed the island of Tandaya (Leyte or Samar), he called it Filipinas for his future sovereign King Felipe (Philip) II of Spain. Later the name was applied to all the islands even though the Spaniards had no effective military or political control. Before the Spaniards arrived, the islands were known by various names. To the Chinese, who already carried on a lucrative trade with the island kingdoms, the islands were *ma-i* (land of barbarians), *chin-san* (mountain of gold), *lui-sung* (land adjacent to the mainland), and *san-tao* (three islands). The Japanese used the terms Luzon Island, Luzones, or Lucanes.

PIGAFETTA, ANTONIO (1491–1535). Pigaffeta was the historian of **Ferdinand Magellan** in his famous voyage in 1521 in search of a trade route to the Spice Island for the king of Spain. Pigaffeta diligently kept a diary of events and places on that historic journey. Of the five ships and 270 men who set out, only one ship *Victoria* and 17 men returned to Spain. Pigafetta was one of the survivors. He presented his journal to the king for which he was handsomely compensated. His travel chronicle is the fullest and most valuable geographical document known. In addition to naval and military battles, Pigafetta faithfully documented plants and animals and manners and customs of people. His eyewitness account of the battle of **Mactan** and description of the people provide an interesting insight into the pre-Hispanic life and culture of the islands later to be called Filipinas. His work even included a dictionary of dialects of inhabitants of **Cebu**. *See also* LIMASAWA.

PILIPINO DEMOCRATIC PARTY (PDP). A regional political party. Its major followers are located in the Visayas and Mindanao regions. The party was organized by Aquilino Pimentel Jr, mayor of Cagayan de Oro City, Misamis Oriental province, as a political force in the southern region. In the 1986 snap elections, PDP combined with **Laban** and, along with **United Nationalist Democratic Organization** (UNIDO)**,** supported Corazon Aquino's successful presidential campaign against **Ferdinand Marcos**. Pimentel, who is a senator, is an ardent opponent of the Gloria Macapagal Arroyo administration.

PIÑA. A silky fabric made from delicately woven pineapple fibers and used especially for the elegant Filipino shirt **barong** or the graceful women's dress *terno*. The Philippine formal national dress was made popular by **Imelda Marcos**. *See also* JUSI; PINEAPPLE; RAMIE.

PINAGLABANAN. The first battle of the **Philippine–Spanish Revolution** was fought in Pinaglabanan on August 30, 1896, in what is now San Juan, Rizal. During that time, the Katipuneros who had joined **Andres Bonifacio** and his small band of fighters knew the town. Since the Spanish authorities had discovered the Katipunan secret society on August 19, 1896, Bonifacio quickly assembled his fighters for a general assault on the Spanish garrison in Manila. On August 29, Bonifacio decided to launch the revolt by leading some 800 men poorly armed with obsolete rifles, homemade guns, bolos, and bamboo lances. The Katipuneros with no military skills bravely attacked and fought the Spaniards. Although outnumbered, the Spaniards with their superior weaponry repulsed the Katipuneros who fled in disorder. Some 150 were killed in the clash. The significance of this battle was that it inflamed the revolution of 1896 and it soon spread to the nearby eight provinces. *See also* CRY OF BALINTAWAK.

PINATUBO. One of the 13 active volcanoes in the Philippines and located in **Pampanga** province. After being dormant for 600 years, Pinatubo erupted in June 1991. The eruption covered the surrounding countryside with six feet of *lahar* (molten ash) and devastated rich rice lands and the infrastructure in four provinces. The government reported that 400 people were killed. The base of the mountain had been the home of the **Aetas**. One of the casualties of the eruption was the sprawling United States military facility at Clark Air Base. The volcano had its second eruption on September 29, 1994. *See also* MAYON VOLCANO; TAAL VOLCANO.

PINEAPPLE. Major export product. Pineapple plantations and production are controlled by three transnational corporations, which export canned pineapples mostly to the U.S. and Japan. In 1990, the Philippines earned $200 million in foreign exchange from pineapple exports, but in 2000 production reports indicated a downward trend. Major pineapple plantations are found in Mindanao. Pineapple is the source of **piña**, the fiber used for barong shirts.

PINPIN, TOMAS. Regarded as the first Filipino printer whose work was discovered in the Vatican Library by Fray Jose Gonzales of the Dominican Order. He was born in Abucay, Bataan, but records about his birth were lost after the **Dutch** invaders destroyed his town in 1646. Pinpin learned the art of printing from Chinese artisans when he worked in the shop of a Filipino–Chinese printer, Luis Beltran. Pinpin published *Successos Felices* (Happenings Events) in 1637, a 14-page newsletter in Spanish that is now widely regarded as the first Filipino newsletter. *See also* DIARIONG TAGALOG.

PINOY. An idiomatic term for Filipino. *See also* TSINOY.

PIRA, PANDAY (1488–1576). Cannon maker. A Portuguese black-smith taught Pira the art of cannon making before the arrival of the Spaniards, in 1521. Panday Pira and his relatives had a foundry shop in Maynilad (now Manila). The Tagalog word *panday* means black-smith. According to legend he fabricated 12 large cannons for **Rajah Sulayman** in the futile defense of his stronghold. The Spaniards, who knew of his expertise, invited Panday Pira to make artillery cannons and balls. The quality of his cannons won the praise of the Spaniards so that when he died they could not find a single person to take his place. *See also* PAUA, JOSE IGNACIO.

PLATA, TEODORO (1866–1896). Cofounder of **Katipunan**. Plata was a clerk in Manila, when he became acquainted with **Andres Bonifacio**, who was then in the process of forming a revolutionary society. Together with Bonifacio, and **Ladislao Diwa** and Plata, they founded the revolutionary society **Katipunan** on July 7, 1892. Plata was chosen secretary and his job was to recruit members. When the revolution started Plata was named secretary of war. On August 23, 1896, when the Katipunan was discovered, Bonifacio and his men fled to Caloocan where they declared a general uprising against Spain. Plata was captured and brought to **Fort Santiago** and later ex-ecuted in Bagumbayan Field (now Rizal Park), the day after Jose Rizal was shot by a firing squad.

PLUNDER. Republic Act 7080 or the antiplunder law defines plunder as a series of criminal acts to amass at least 50 million pesos (One mil-lion U.S. dollars) in illegally acquired wealth. The law is a nonbailable offense and punishable by life imprisonment or death. Since the law came into effect, President **Joseph Ejercito Estrada** is so far the highest ranking official to be prosecuted for this capital offense and following his arrest on April 25, 2001, challenged its constitutionality arguing through his lawyers that some of its provisions were vague and defective. Estrada had hopes that the court would rule in his favor since some of the justices were his appointees, including the chief jus-tice. But the Supreme Court voted—with 10 justices to four against—to uphold the country's antiplunder law stating in its decision that the law was constitutional. The High Court stressed that the plunder law contains ascertainable standards and well-defined parameters that would consider the accused (Estrada) to determine the nature of his vi-olation. The court further ordered the **Sandiganbayan** to proceed with the prosecution and trial of Estrada and his son Jose, a former mayor of San Juan, Rizal. The son was later released on bail and in the 2004 national elections run for senator under the banner of **Fernando Poe Jr.** and won a seat. The plunder case against him is still pending be-fore the Sandiganbayan while the former president meantime is in prison and awaiting trial. *See also* GRAFT AND CORRUPTION.

PLUNDER WATCH. This is a loose network of individuals and or-ganizations that are united in the pursuit of truth and justice, partic-ularly cases against former president Joseph Ejercito Estrada and others. It monitors the development in the **Sandiganbayan** and serves as a watchdog to the entire process in order to help prevent any whitewash or compromise. In particular Plunder Watchers are able to launch popular action and organize activities to get the pub-lic involved on the trial of malefactors. One of its major accom-plishments to date was the favorable verdict against 27 officials who violated the Anti-Graft and Corruption Practice Act (Republic Act 3019) in connection with the over one billion pesos illegally used in the construction of the President Diosdado Macapagal International Airport (formerly Clark Air Base) in Pampanga. *See also* ANTI-GRAFT COVENANT.

PO. Tagalog honorific word for "Sir" or "Madam." The particle "po" is usually used to express respect to an older person or a stranger. *See also* KA; MANO PO.

POE JR., FERNANDO (1939–2004). Dubbed the "king of Philippine movies," Poe entered the 2004 presidential ring as the standard bearer of the *Koalisyon Ng Magkakaisang Pilipino* (Coalition of United Pilipinos), a merger of three small parties that coalesced to form the opposition against the ruling party of President Gloria Macapagal Arroyo. Poe's real name is Ronald Allan Kelly, son of the late actor–producer Fernando Poe Sr., who was best known for his prewar macho roles in movies. After dropping out of high school, Poe Jr. joined the show business of his father and worked his way up from messenger to stunt man. His first movie was decidedly a flop, but he finally made it in 1957 with five star-rated films. His movie persona is that of a good leading actor who is slow to anger but relentless when roused, a favorite character in Filipino Tagalog movies.

Despite his avowed disinterest in politics, a signature campaign and a high rating among the presidential hopefuls convinced him to run for president. His supporters turned his initials—FPJ—into freedom, peace, and justice that became his campaign platform. Unlike Joseph Ejercito Estrada, who had held extensive government elective positions, Poe Jr., a high school dropout, had no such experience and so entered the 2004 presidential derby as a neophyte. Nevertheless his followers—mostly movie fans—relied on his charisma and integrity to carry on their political platform, which included the perennial hot button issue of **graft and corruption.** Poe avoided political debates and made no significant political statements on any issue, a shortcoming that his opponents hammered at relentlessly during the political campaign. He and his vice presidential candidate—Loren Leviste—lost in the elections.

POET LAUREATE. *See* YUZON, AMADO.

POLITICAL DYNASTY. Political dynasties are established clans of elite families in various regions in the Philippines and wield a great deal of political clout in most aspects of government, business, and society. These power clans are active in every election whether local or national—where many of the same family names appear as candidates. Their political and business power feed on each other—the more influence, the more wealth. Hence, any enterprising candidate would find it difficult to dislodge the opponents who belong to the clan. Although there are restriction terms, these are only good on paper but seldom enforced. Incumbents whose terms are up skirt them by fielding their spouses, children, and seemingly endless names of other relatives to ensure plum posts remain within control of the clans. Leading clans keep their power because of the multifarious nature of the political system in which the parties coalesce or merge for convenience to strengthen their base during presidential elections. As their main weapons to maintain tight political control, the political dynasties have used the so-called "goons, guns, and gold" in their bailiwicks with the connivance of police agencies. This hierarchal political culture poses a major obstacle to the maintenance of democracy. *See also* OLIGARCHS; PADACA. MARIA GRACIANA.

POLITICAL PARTIES. Unlike the two-party political system in the United States, Philippine political life is multifarious. In the 2002 elections there were 85 separate political parties, which fielded more than 200,000 candidates for 20,000 positions. Most political parties are not ideological. They are mainly organized around a personality and his or her political ambition. Political leaders frequently derive their following from their charisma and popularity. One such individual was **Ramon Magsaysay**, who had been elected chiefly for his charismatic personality. Another characteristic of Philippine politics is the patron-client relationship or **patronage politics**. Leaders bestow favors or rewards on their followers, who repay them with fierce loyalty. This interpersonal relationship is related to the Filipino **social value** system of *utang na loob* (debt of gratitude or honor) and *compadrazgo* (fraternal kinship). Political parties in the Philippines are based on personalities and family wealth. Where no principles are at stake, elections are mere popularity contests. There is little distinction of the ideologies and platforms of the myriad parties called coalitions that emerge come election time, particularly during presidential contests.

The parties are described by Joel Rocamora, a Filipino political scientist, as "unabashed old boys clubs." Their followers are mainly men and women who identify with one or another party, but most of them are related by family and ritual kinship—godfathers, wedding, and baptismal sponsors. At the core of these parties are wealthy families that are related with dominant families. In electoral battles, these political families risk their fortune and fame to win elections. There is also another distinct characteristic of Philippine political parties— the shifting character of membership and leadership and the absence of ideological or programmatic differences among them. The Filipino voter goes to the party that has the largesse and not because of what the candidate promises to do for them. Money flows freely from the coffers of candidates who are determined to win the election. Election laws on spending are openly flaunted since the enforcers are not around to implement them. Most local politics is a competition of local elites and the winning party gets choice jobs in municipal and city administration. Election fraud—inflated vote counting—is a well-developed practice. Local politicians are adept in manipulating the process from beginning to end. During the 1995 national elections, a leading senatorial candidate was edged out of the slate due to the **dag-dag bawas** (add-subtract) scheme. Election protests take years to litigate, and the losing politician might as well forget it. The structure of major parties is the municipal level. Party units then go up the ladder to the provincial party committee, then the national convention. These bodies are made up of prominent leaders of the party. Within these bodies, there are executive committees made up of a smaller number of top party leaders.

Most political parties do not have permanent party headquarters or paid staff. In between elections, party headquarters are usually at the party leader's home or office. In the selection of the slate, the party candidate for president and his power group make the decision. Candidates are selected on the basis of their performance, political machinery, popularity, and adequate financial resources. For national candidates, it is generally accepted that if the presidential candidate comes from Luzon and its Tagalog-speaking population, the vice presidential candidate has to come from the Visayas and its Cebuano-speaking people. **Sectoral parties** do not play an important role within political parties. They are perceived to be important for rallying votes especially for national positions. Patronage politics demands that the winning politician using the powers of his office must reward supporters. A politician has to deliver what he has agreed to produce for political support. Joseph Estrada who ran on a poverty platform failed to deliver and this added to his woes as a leader and caused him to lose the support of the so-called "*masa*" (poor people).

To win Philippine elections, candidates have to spend enormous amounts of money. The party itself is rarely a source of electoral funds. Every candidate must raise his own funds, usually from family, friends, business associates, and from political allies. The ruling party has a distinct advantage in campaign fund raising. It can tap government resources—financial, human, and institutional. In addition, the ruling party is also better able to secure contributions from business sources because of the party's control over government contracts, licenses, and favors. Elections funds are either legitimate or illegitimate. Legitimate ones come from businesses, especially from Chinese businessmen and corporate contributions. Illegitimate money comes from operators of illegal activities, gambling, **jueteng,** smuggling, prostitution, and drugs. **Political dynasties** or clans invest a good share of the family fortune to back the candidacy of a kinsman. Still, as unpopular as political parties are, they continue to be the main political instruments of a democratic government. *See also* TRAPO.

POLO. *See* TRIBUTES.

POPULATION. Demographers of the National Statistics Office (NSO) are projecting that the population by 2016 would reach the 100 million mark with half of the population at 21 years old or below. The NSO based its projection on the results of the 2000 census, which placed the annual **population growth** rate at 2.36 percent described as one of the highest in the world. The 2002 total population stood at 76.5 million. Males outnumbered their female counterparts with a sex ratio of 101.43 males for every female or an estimated 38.5 million (50.36 percent) were males while 38 million (49.64 percent) were females. Luzon was identified as the most populous region comprising more than half (56 percent) of the country's population. It was followed by Mindanao with 24 percent and the Visayas with 20 percent.

POPULATION DENSITY. In 1990, when the population was 61 million, the national population density was 202.3 persons per square kilometer, an increase of 42 percent over that of 1980. This upward trend has existed since 1903, when the first census was undertaken. From a population density of 25.5 persons per square kilometer, the density rose to 34.4 persons per square kilometer in 1918, 53.3 in 1939, 90.3 in 1960, 122.3 in 1970, and 228 in 1995. Metropolitan Manila is the most densely populated area with 12,497 persons per square kilometer. *See also* TONDO.

POPULATION GROWTH. The Philippine government faces twin problems of population growth and poverty growth. Economists and foreign donors are concerned about runaway population that is predicted to reach 100 million by the year 2016 and the burgeoning poverty rate—40 percent or 32 million live below poverty line. The unemployment rate as of July 2002, according to the National Statistics Office (NSO), stands at 14 percent. At the current growth rate of 2.36 percent the population has ballooned to 80 million Filipinos in 2002. Among Southeast Asian nations, the Philippines has the highest birth rate of 31 per 1,000 population compared to the following countries: India at 27, Indonesia at 25, Malaysia at 29, and Vietnam at 29. Nongovernment organizations such as Employers Confederation of the Philippines (ECOP) and the Philippine Legislators Committee on Population and Development (PLCPD) warned of the dire consequences of the population explosion and advocated measures of family planning and reproductive health. But the politically influential **Roman Catholic Church** is against artificial birth control and President Gloria Macapagal Arroyo—a devout Catholic—has ordered an aggressive campaign to promote the traditional or natural method (withdrawal and rhythm)—with the church's blessings—to reduce the growth rate. With 40 percent of the population clustered around **Metro Manila** and the cities, the country faces the urban problems of congestion taxing the limits of the available infrastructure causing traffic jams, ghettos, crime, and degradation of the environment. *See also* FLAVIER, JUAN.

PORK BARREL. Public work funds. These are funds allocated to each congressman in a public appropriation bill. A quota or pork barrel is set up for each congressional district for the construction and maintenance of roads, bridges, and harbors and for community development projects. Since the president has the discretionary authority to withhold pork barrel funds, they constitute a form of political leverage by means of which the president can garner legislative support for legislative programs. This instrument enhances presidential power and is an important factor favoring presidential bids for reelection. *See also* SANTIAGO, MIRIAM DEFENSOR.

POSTMA, ANTOON (1935–). A Dutch expert on ancient Philippine script, Postma translated the famous **Laguna Copperplate Inscription** (LCI) by following the traditional method used by Indonesians. According to his translation, the LCI was an official document issued to clear a person, his family, and all their descendants of a debt. Postma lived most of his life with the **Mangyans** of Mindoro. He was director of the Mangyan Assistance and Research Center in Panay-tayan, Oriental Mindoro. His most remarkable contribution is the Mangyan bibliography (1570–1988). *See also* FRANCISCO, JUAN.

POTTERY. Prehistoric Filipinos have used pottery for various purposes from the common domestic earthenware *(palayok)* to ritual ware *(pang-alay)*. Pottery making is an ancient craft in the Philippines. Burial jars found in Huluga Caves, near Cagayan de Oro, contained skeletal remains that were carbon dated to the Neolithic Age. Ancient jars have also been found in Gasan, **Marinduque**. Ceramic pieces have been discovered in wooden coffins in the vicinity of Butuan dating back to the 14th century. Whole earthen jars are common in graves predating circa 1200 A.D. **Panay** Island is the prime source for kaolin and ball clay deposits. The Ilocos region is noted for its *burnay* (jars), which are used for storing grains, **basi**, and liquids. Extant examples of Philippine pottery show a wide variety of shapes and decorative techniques, such as incision, stippling, applique, and impression by rope and mat. *See also* MAITUM ANTHROPOMORPHIC POTTERIES; BUTUAN ARCHAEOLOGY; MANUNGGUL JAR.

PRESBYTERIANS. *See* PROTESTANTISM.

PRESIDENTIAL ANTI-CRIME COMMISSION. The rising crime rate in urban areas prompted President Fidel Ramos to form the Presidential Anti-Crime Commission to handle local and urban crime. He appointed Vice President **Joseph Ejercito Estrada** to head the commission. Estrada was a movie actor and former senator before he ran as the teammate of Eduardo Cojuangco in the 1992 presidential election. Cojuangco lost, but Estrada was elected. It was the second time a vicepresident from the opposition party was chosen. Estrada was successful in pursuing big-time crooks and prosecuting them. President Gloria Macapagal Arroyo later abolished the commission when she took office, and replaced it with a new agency called Philippine National Police headed by a retired general. *See also* NATIONAL BUREAU OF INVESTIGATION.

PRESIDENTIAL COMMISSION ON GOOD GOVERNMENT (PCGG). A special body with quasi-judicial functions created under

President Corazon Aquino's executive orders to recover the assets and properties illegally acquired or misappropriated by former president **Ferdinand Marcos**, his family, close relatives, **cronies**, and business associates. Its mandate includes investigation and prosecution of public officials involved in **graft and corruption**. Since its creation the commission has recovered $356 million in Swiss deposits made by the Marcos family and obtained favorable judgment in Hawaii for 27.7 million pesos in Philippine bills, $46.4 million in certificates of time deposits, and jewelry from the Marcoses when they fled to Hawaii. The PCGG scored a stunning victory when the Supreme Court upheld its July 2001 decision forfeiting in favor of the Philippine government the more than $683-million ill-gotten wealth of the Marcos family held in escrow at the Philippine National Bank. *See also* GOLDEN BUDDHA; YORAC, HAYDEE.

PRINCIPALIA. The local aristocracy during the Spanish colonial regime composed of the *cabezas de barangay* (barrio heads), *gobernadorcillos* (little governor), and *capitan municipal* (mayor) who served as buffers between the Filipino people and their Castillian overlords. The demands of Spanish officials and friars were transmitted to the masses of the Filipinos through the *principalia*. They in turn represented the native's difficulties to the rulers. To preserve their status with the mass below, the cabezas and *gobernadorcillos* sought in effect to moderate the regime's impositions. They were ill compensated for their onerous responsibilities and some of them succumbed to graft—from the *tributos* (tributes) and other sources. The ordinary people were of no consequence to the Spaniards except as a source of revenue. And the *principalia* were their petty collaborators in maintaining the economic and political structure of a decadent colonial order. However, some of the wealthy *principalia* were able to send their children abroad for higher education, which was not available to them in the Philippines. These educated Filipinos now called "**ilustrados**" returned to the Philippines with new ideas of liberty, fraternity, and equality. The ilustrados, like **Jose Rizal, Antonio Luna**, and others, dedicated their mental and physical energies to the developing **nationalism** of the Filipinos. *See also* DEL PILAR, MARCELO; LUNA, JUAN; JAENA, GRACIANO LOPEZ.

PROCUREMENT ACT. To curb **graft and corruption** in the procurement of materials and equipment for government use, the Procurement Act became law in 2002. Under this law contractors and service providers found it difficult to obtain fat sums through biddings. The law prohibited newspaper ads for scheduled government bids and bids are posted on government websites. Eligibility checks are conducted to make sure the government gets a fair share. For infrastructure projects, contractors are required to issue a five-year warranty to the government to make sure the project will not be substandard. A cap was also placed on charge orders and price adjustments, which have traditionally been the major infrastructure source of scams. *See also* PORK BARREL.

PROGRESSIVE MOVEMENT FOR DEVOLUTION INITIATIVE (PROMDI). This is a regional political party founded by former governor and presidential candidate Lito Osmeña of Cebu. One of its platforms is to spread and share the economic bounty currently concentrated in Metro Manila to all the provinces. As a **party-list** group it was able to elect one representative in the 2001 congressional elections. PROMDI united with the ruling **Lakas-CMD** party, but left following President Gloria Macapagal Arroyo's announcement to run in the 2004 national elections. The party was a staunch supporter of the president in the power struggle that ousted Joseph Ejercito Estrada. Although PROMDI has played a minor role in national politics, it decided to concentrate its political clout in the Central Visayas, its major bailiwick. *See also* AKBAYAN.

PROJECT GOOD ROOTS. Although **deforestation** continues, reforestation is progressing successfully in depleted regions because of Good Roots Project, **a nongovernmental agency**, started in 1991 by Ben Wallace, an anthropologist and former CEO of Caltex Philippines. Good Roots Project was designed to regenerate forests and provide a source of livelihood to people in rural communities. Unlike other reforestation projects where farmers were involved in a pay-for-plant scheme—when the money was gone, the project also ended—in the Good Roots Project farm families are not paid but instead own the project. The basic framework was successfully tried in Pagudpud, **Ilocos Norte**, where deforestation deprived the livelihood of surrounding towns. Farmers were convinced that they were investing in the future by making decisions about their environment. Technicians provided technology and skill to farm families and also supplied the seedlings. Once the project had taken root within the community in a span of five years, Good Roots turned over the project to the farm families. Seedlings distributed were not confined to the hardwood variety. There were short-term (vegetable), medium-term (fruit bearing trees), and long-term seedlings (teak or **narra**). Farm families had the opportunity to restore their forest and to earn a living. This methodology has been effective as evidenced by the 70 percent survival rate of the seedlings distributed. Similar results were reported in other sites of the Good Roots Project. *See also* SUSTAINABLE DEVELOPMENT.

PROPAGANDA MOVEMENT (1872–1894). The period of intense nationalism carried on by Filipinos living in Spain and France. By using **newspapers** and the printed word, they brought to the attention of the Spanish king the abuses, fraud, and corruption of Spanish officials in the Philippines. In their petitions, they asked the Spanish government to relax its iron rule, to correct abuses, and to respect human rights. Initial attempts to present their petitions in the Spanish Cortes were rejected, forcing the exiles to press their demands in peaceful ways such as publishing their grievances in *La Solidaridad*. Filipinos living in France also joined the movement by publishing nationalistic articles in *La Solidaridad*. This period is considered the golden age of Filipino nationalism, producing the best artists, poets, writers, and leaders. *See also* DEL PILAR, MARCELO; JAENA, GRACIANO, LOPEZ; RIZAL, JOSE.

PROSPERIDAD. *See* AGUSAN DEL SUR.

PROTESTANTISM. Roman Catholicism was the only Christian religion known to Filipinos until the end of the Spanish regime in the Philippines. After the end of the Spanish–American War in 1899, American army chaplains, who came with the American Expeditionary Forces, preached the first evangelical message to curious and receptive crowds in Manila, and thus planted the seeds of evangelical Protestantism. Then, in 1901, the mission boards of three Protestant denominations—Methodists, Presbyterians, and Baptists—started sending missionaries to Manila. To avoid duplication and competition, a comity agreement was signed in 1902 that divided the country into areas for their evangelistic work. Other Protestant denominations followed suit by sending missionaries to various islands. The evangelical faith "spread like wild fire" in Luzon, Visayas, and Mindanao—and before the Philippines received its independence in 1946 the denominations had already thriving churches, seminaries, and educational institutions in major towns and cities in the islands. *See also* MANALO, FELIX; ZAMORA, NICOLAS.

PROVINCE. Provincial government. In the 1987 constitution the province is the largest local administrative unit, headed by an elected governor and a vice-governor. Other officials are appointed to head departments concerned with finance, tax collection, audit, public works, agricultural services, health, and schools. These officials are subordinate to the governor, who appoints them. Whenever there is a change of governors, there is a corresponding turnover of department heads.

PROVINCES. There are 80 provinces of the Philippines as of the year 2004: 1. Abra 2. Agusan del Norte 3. Agusan del Sur 4. Aklan 5. Albay 6. Antique 7. Apayao 8. Aurora 9. Basilan 10. Bataan 11. Batanes 12. Batangas 13. Benguet 14. Biliran 15. Bohol 16. Bukidnon 17. Bulacan 18. Cagayan 19. Camarines Sur 20. Camarines Norte 21. Camiguin 22. Catanduanes 23. Capiz 24. Cavite 25. Cebu 26. Compostela Valley 27. Cotabato 28. Davao 29. Davao del Sur 30. Davao Oriental 31. Eastern Samar 32. Guimaras 33. Ifugao 34. Ilocos Norte 35. Ilocos Sur 36. Iloilo 37. Isabela del Norte 38. Isabela del Sur 39. Kalinga 40. La Union 41. Laguna 42. Lanao del Norte 43. Lanao del Sur 44. Leyte 45. Maguindanao 46. Marinduque 47. Masbate 48. Occidental Mindoro 49. Oriental Mindoro 50. Misamis Oriental 51. Misamis Occidental 52. Mountain Province 53. Negros Occidental 54. Negros Oriental 55. Northern Samar 56. Nueva Ecija 57. Nueva Vizcaya 58. Palawan 59. Pampanga 60. Pangasinan 61. Quezon 62. Quirino 63. Rizal 64. Romblon 65. Samar 66. Sarangani 67. Siquijor 68. Sorsogon 69. South Cotabao 70. Southern Leyte 71. Sultan Kudarat 72. Sulu 73. Surigao del Norte 74. Surigao del Sur 75. Tarlac 76. Tawi-tawi 77. Zambales 78. Zamboanga del Norte 79. Zamboanga del Sur 80. Zamboanga Sibugay.

PUEBLO. A compact settlement of **barangays**. A pueblo was composed of 10 or more barangays, a system that the Spanish adopted to recognize the ruling datus. To manage the pueblos, the Spanish forcibly resettled the inhabitants into more compact communities, a process that made the people's conversion to Christianity much easier. These compact communities or pueblos were governed by a *gobernadorcillo*, who was chosen from the datus (barangay heads or *cabezas de barangays*). Colonial laws enacted in Spain prescribed the physical layout of a pueblo. In the center was the plaza or town square; the streets formed a regular grid pattern. On one side of the plaza stood the *casa tribunal* or town hall, which was the seat of the pueblo government. The church occupied another side; the houses of the leading residents stood on the remaining sides. The rest of the pueblo inhabitants lived on the outskirts. *See also* REDUCCIONES.

PUEBLO OFFICIALS. The *gobernadorcillo* was the chief official of the pueblo. He had an *escribano* (clerk-secretary) and a number of *teniente mayors* (chief lieutenants) as assistants who took over the mayoral duties in the case of the *gobernadorcillo*'s illness or disability. The major functions of the chief lieutenants were the collection of taxes and enforcement of work on tobacco production. The government had a monopoly on the latter, tobacco being the chief export commodity during the **galleon trade**. Other pueblo officials were the *juez de policia* (chief of police), *juez de sementera* (superintendents of fields and harvest), and *juez de ganado* (superintendent of livestock). The electoral junta on the basis of their status and conduct in the community chose these officials. The endorsement of the local *cura* or priest was crucial to the selection of an individual. Nominees were sent to superior government officials in Manila for confirmation.

PUENTISPINA, CHARITO. *See* WALING-WALING.

PUERTO PRINCESA. *See* PALAWAN.

PUGAD LAWIN. *See* CRY OF BALINTAWAK.

PULAG NATIONAL PARK. This is the Philippines' second highest peak, 2,922 meters above sea level, located in the Grand Cordillera central mountain range in Luzon. Bonsai forests and grasslands with dwarf bamboos surround the peak. Mt. Pulag is home to rare plants like the pitcher plant and rare animals like the giant cloud rat, pygmy fruit bat, and the Philippine brown deer. The park provides resources to the indigenous **Kalanguya**, Ibaloi, Kankana-ey, and Karao tribes.

PULAHAN WARS (1902–1907). The year 1902 was supposed to be the end of the hostilities of the U.S. government and the Philippine Revolutionary troops of General **Emilio Aguinaldo**. But in **Leyte** a group called *Pulahan* (freedom fighters in red) carried on guerrilla warfare against the American troops for five years with devastating results. Led by two brothers, Juan and Felipe Tamayo, the bolo-wielding insurgents made many successful forays against American garrisons. In one encounter the *Pulahans* overran a constabulary force, killing the American captain, and recovered their rifles. For three years, the *Pulahans* were in control of several towns of Leyte. The *Pulahan* resistance ended on June 17, 1907, with the capture of their leaders.

PULONG BAYAN (TOWN HALL MEETING). Since President Gloria Macapagal Arroyo was elected into office, she started the first Pulong Bayan in July 2004 in Barangay Bosco, Paranaque, in a bid to sell her economic reform package to the people. Together with the president were Vice President **Noli de Castro** and other government officials who were present to help the president respond to the people's questions. Some 500 people crowded the gymnasium and bombarded the president with questions of social justice, **graft and corruption**, good governance, and basic needs. These town hall meetings will be continued in other places to give the administration a grassroots feeling of what ails and helps the people.

PUROK. A political subdivision of a barrio.

– Q –

QUEEN JUANA. *See* LIMASAWA; SINULOG.

QUEZON. This province, formerly known as Tayabas, was renamed Quezon in honor of **Manuel L. Quezon**, the first president of the

Philippines. Quezon province is located on the east central coast of Luzon and has an extremely long coastline on both the Pacific side and along the western interisland waters of Tayabas Bay and the Sibuyan Sea. The province, which includes Polillo Islands on the Pacific side, has a land area of 8,706 square kilometers and a population of 1.2 million people, mostly **Tagalogs.** It leads the country in **coconut** production. Cottage industries include food processing, woodcraft, basketry, buntal hat weaving, plus numerous products derived from coconut shells and husks. Lucena is the capital city, and the chief towns are Lukban, Sariaya, Infanta, and Lopez. *See also* AURORA; QUEZON NATIONAL PARK.

QUEZON CITY. Named after the late President Manuel L. Quezon, Quezon City used to be the national capital until it lost its title by virtue of Presidential Decree No. 940 on June 24, 1976. This city, 10 kilometers north of Manila, sprawls on 16,000 hectares and is populated by three million people. It still remains a residential community, a commercial center, and the educational capital of the Philippines. The Philippine Nuclear Research Center is in this city. Historically, Quezon City is the site of the first **Cry of Balintawak** that led to the downfall of the Spanish regime; and a monument of General Lawton—the highest-ranking officer of the American Expeditionary Army—killed by the **Katipuneros** during the Philippine–American Revolution. *See also* BELMONTE, FELICIANO.

QUEZON, MANUEL L. (1878–1944). President of the Philippine **Commonwealth** and leader of the fight for Philippine independence from American rule. When the **Philippine–American Revolution** broke out, he was commissioned as a second lieutenant in the revolutionary army. In the course of the war, Quezon was promoted to captain under General Miguel Mascardo. He and General Mascardo surrendered to the Americans when General Emilio Aguinaldo, leader of the Filipino forces, was captured. The American administration appointed him fiscal (chief provincial attorney) and later on was elected governor in 1905 at age 27. In 1907, he was elected to the Philippine Assembly and became the majority floor leader. Two years later, he was elected as resident commissioner to Washington, D.C., a post he held until 1916. During his term, he obtained the passage of the **Jones Act** in the United

States Congress, which granted Philippine independence. Elected senator in 1918, he eventually became the Senate president. Quezon was instrumental in enacting legislation on land reform, woman suffrage, and social justice. In 1934, he returned to the United States as chairman of the Philippine delegation in negotiations that secured passage of the **Tydings-McDuffie Act**, which set the date of independence in 1946. The law provided for a commonwealth government. Subsequently Quezon was elected first president, a position that he held until the outbreak of World War II. He fled and resided in Washington, D.C., where he set up the commonwealth government in exile with some of his cabinet members. He died on August 1, 1944, of tuberculosis in Saranac Lake, New York. *See also* HARE-HAWES-CUTTING ACT; OS-ROX MISSION.

QUEZON NATIONAL PARK. Just 180 kilometers southeast of Manila in Atimonan, Quezon province, lies one of the most beautiful mountains in Southern Luzon that has been declared a Game Refuge and Bird Sanctuary. The present area of the park is 984 hectares (4 square miles) with its highest point at 366 meters above sea level. Quezon National Park is a virgin forest that is teeming with wild life like monkeys, deer, wild pigs, and monitor lizard. Bird life is also prolific with parrots, *tarictic*, **kalaw**, doves, pigeons, and jungle fowl. The park is trekker-friendly. *See also* MOUNT PULAG.

QUIAPO. A famous place in Manila, Quiapo is the site of the annual procession, every January 9, of the **Black Nazarene**, patron saint of Quiapo district known as the *Nuestro Padre Jesus Nazareno*. The statue is paraded around the area followed by thousands of devotees, who jostle their way to the *carroza* (carriage), borne on the shoulders of devotees as they wend their way around the Plaza Miranda. The procession begins at three o'clock in the afternoon and ends about midnight. The Recollect friars brought the Black Nazarene, which the faithful believe holds miraculous powers, to the Philippines in the 18th century from Mexico. Since then, the Black Nazarene has been the object of devotion by Roman Catholics, who join the procession to express their gratitude for blessings or answered prayers. Besides being a religious Mecca for

Roman Catholics, during national elections Quiapo is a popular political grandstand where the political fortunes of the parties are made and unmade by the people. *See also* FESTIVALS; FIESTA; SINULOG.

QUIRINO. Named after President **Elpidio Quirino**, this province was partitioned off from Nueva Vizcaya in 1971. It covers a land area of 3,057 square kilometers and has a population of 115,000, mostly Ilocano migrants attracted by homesteads and rich natural resources. The capital is Cabarroguis. Quirino's five municipalities are found in the fertile Genano Valley, the site of vast rice fields. Logging is the main commercial activity. The province is the home of a number of ethnic tribes, including Ilongots, Negritos, and Ikalahans.

QUIRINO, ELPIDIO R. (1890–1956). Second president of the Republic of the Philippines (1948–1953)—sixth in the list of presidents of the country. Quirino was considered the father of industrialization. In his first attempt to run for public office in 1919, he staged a political upset by defeating the incumbent and was elected representative of his province. When his term expired he was elected to the Senate in 1925. As a senator, he pushed for successful legislation on taxation and tariffs. He was reelected senator in 1941, but at the outbreak of World War II, he was unable to take his seat. When that body reconvened in 1945, he was chosen Senate president pro tempore. In the 1946 national elections, he was the running mate of **Manuel Roxas**, who was elected president. Besides his post as vice president, Roxas designated him to serve as secretary of finance. Later, Roxas appointed him secretary of foreign affairs. When Roxas died of a heart attack on April 15, 1948, Quirino assumed the presidency. He was elected president in his own right on November 8, 1949. During his term, the economic conditions improved remarkably as indicated by the establishment of many light and heavy industries and the sharp rise in employment. Most notably, he succeeded in stabilizing the Philippine peso and balancing the national budget. In his bid for reelection in 1953 he lost to **Ramon Magsaysay**, the secretary of national defense. Quirino died on February 29, 1956, in Novaliches, Quezon City, at the age of 66.

QUISUMBING, EDUARDO (1895–1986). A world famous Filipino botanist, Eduardo Quisumbing is the sole acknowledged authority on Philippine orchids. He began studying at the college of agriculture of the University of the Philippines in Los Baños where his interest in botany was kindled by an American professor. He obtained his B.S. degree, and was sent to the University of Chicago as a scholar and acquired his doctorate degree. On his return to the Philippines, Quisumbing traveled to Europe to observe its outstanding herbaria. Back in the Philippines he was appointed botanist of the Bureau of Science, and later became director of the **National Museum**. One of his major accomplishments was the huge collection of plant samples, around 300,000. Quisumbing furnished Philippine taxonomy and botany with much valuable information. However, it was to orchidology that he devoted much of his research work, especially in the identification and classification of a huge number of Philippine orchids. Subsequently, he produced studies on the anatomy and morphology of the coconut, weed seed, rubber and the diospyros. One of his seminal works was "Naming of Orchids" which has since been used as a handy general science reference by orchid aficionados. In recognition of his signal accomplishments in the area of systematic botany, Quisumbing was honored by President Ramon Magsaysay with a distinguished service medal. In 1979, he was named a National Scientist. *See also* WALING-WALING; YLANG YLANG.

– R –

RACIAL LINEAGE OF FILIPINOS. A statistical survey conducted by the Social Weather Station in 1996 shows the following racial composition of some Filipinos. 1. Spanish. Over half of the estimated 3.5 million who call themselves Spanish–Filipinos are Visayans (1.9 million) with twice as many in rural Visayas as in urban Visayas. There are some 700,000 adult Kastiloyas in Mindanao, 500,000 in the Luzon provinces, and 400,00 in Metro Manila. 2. Chinese–Filipinos. There are some 400,00 adults in the Luzon provinces, over 300,000 in Mindanao, 200,000 in Visayas, and about 150,000 in Metro Manila. 3. Japanese. Most of the half-million Japanese–Filipinos are found in the Luzon provinces (over 300,000) with less than 100,000 in Mindanao, about 50,000 in the Visayas, and 40,000 in Metro Manila. *See also* POPULATION DENSITY; POPULATION GROWTH.

RAJAH HUMABON. *See* SINULOG.

RAJAH SULAYMAN (ca. 1571). The last native ruler of Maynilad (now known as Manila), then a Muslim kingdom on the southern end of the Pasig River. He was considered the "greatest king of Maynilad" and its most important native chief when the Spaniards landed there in 1570. He ruled Maynilad jointly with his uncle Rajah Matanda. When the Spaniards asked him to pay tribute to the king of Spain he spurned their demand and instead rallied his warriors to fight the invaders. He resisted the occupation of his city and was killed in the battle of Bangkusay, **Tondo**, on June 3. 1571. His realm was called Maynilad because of the abundance of the six-foot plant *nilad* along the Pasig River.

RAM. *See* NATIONALIST REVOLUTIONARY ALLIANCE.

RAMIE. A fiber extracted from the ramie plant, which is grown extensively in southern Mindanao and utilized as a textile for Philippine clothing such as the **barong** and women's dresses. Ramie is remarkably durable and is often used in combination with synthetic fibers. *See also* JUSI; PIÑA.

RAMIREZ, JUAN ANTONIO. *See* DAGOHOY, FRANCISCO.

RAMON MAGSAYSAY AWARD (RM). This award was conceived by John D. Rockefeller and established by the trustees of the Rockefeller Brothers Fund in April 1957 to commemorate the late president and perpetuate his example of integrity in government and pragmatic idealism within a democratic society by honoring individuals and organizations whose civic contributions exemplify his greatness of spirit and devotion to freedom. Often regarded as the Nobel Prize of Asia, these awards are presented in five categories: government service, public service, community leadership, international understanding and journalism, literature and creative communication arts. Up to

five awards of $50,000 each are given annually by the board of
trustees of the RM Foundation, which is headquartered in Manila.
The RM Center contains Magsaysay papers and memorabilia, a public library on contemporary Asia, and sponsors national and international symposia on subjects on vital current interest. Since 1958,
there have been 219 RM awardees. Some famous ones include the
Dalai Lama, Mother Teresa, Akira Korosawa, Vinoba Bhave, **Corazon Aquino, International Rice Research Institute**, and Operation
Brotherhood, U.S. **Peace Corps**.

RAMOS, AMELITA MARTINEZ (1930–). As the wife of the 12th
president of the Philippines—**Fidel Ramos**—Amelita Ramos
brought her stamp and character to her role as first lady. During the
six-year term of her husband she devoted her time to projects about
the environment, education, sports, and arts and culture. Her "Clean
and Green" campaign resulted in the Clean River Act, which made
the Pasig River clean and navigable. As an educator she spearheaded
programs for the gifted and handicapped children as well as transformed underprivileged Filipinos into self-sufficient and productive
individuals. **Sports** was another special area that she promoted in
public schools and drew many children into competitive games, including paraplegics and the disabled. Aided by government funding,
she arranged dwelling units for poor families. As an accomplished pi-
anist, the First Lady injected new life into the country's cultural life
by turning **Malacañang** into a showcase of musical events and indigenous arts and crafts.

RAMOS, BENIGNO. *See* SAKDALISTA.

RAMOS, FIDEL V. (1928–). Twelfth president of the Republic of the
Philippines. He was educated at West Point. After his graduation from
West Point in 1950, Fidel rose rapidly in the army, becoming a general and chief officer of the Philippine Constabulary before and during the martial law period of Ferdinand Marcos's presidency. He commanded Filipino troops in Vietnam. Unlike other generals, Ramos
remained uncorrupt during the Marcos dictatorship while his fellow
officers enriched themselves in business deals and by plundering the
public coffers. Together with **Juan Ponce Enrile**, he supported Cora-

zon Aquino in the controversial 1986 presidential election, an act that brought him into the limelight of Philippine political life.

When Corazon Aquino assumed power, she appointed Ramos as chief of staff of the armed forces, a position from which he immediately initiated reforms to professionalize a military that had been demoralized under the Marcos dictatorship. Ramos turned the military into an effective fighting force, which was able to deal with the **New Peoples' Army** and which nipped in the bud the rebellious military units. In the presidential elections of 1992, Roman Catholic Archbishop **Jaime Cardinal Sin** objected to Ramos, a Protestant, and he urged the faithful to vote for Catholic candidates. However, it was Ramos' image of incorruptibility that separated him from the other presidential competitors and endeared him to the electorate. Besides having the support of the outgoing president, Corazon Aquino, Ramos demonstrated his centrist positions in the middle of the political spectrum. In spite of his slender war chest, he beat his six well-heeled opponents, including **Imelda Marcos**, who finished fifth.

In his inaugural address he gave a straightforward response to the problems facing his administration and vowed to deal directly with poverty, unemployment, and inequalities of wealth. The United States government lent its support with increased military and economic aid to shore up the revitalized military and the spiraling economy, which had been saddled by a $29 billion debt. The debt was restructured, and in the ensuing year the Philippines had a favorable balance of trade with the United States. **Graft and corruption**, which had been endemic in the Marcos administration, was significantly curtailed by watchdog agencies, such as the **Presidential Commission on Good Government** and the self-policing efforts of public officials. Congress granted Ramos' request for emergency powers to prime the economy. He reorganized the National Power Corporation to increase electricity, which was in short supply during the Marcos and Aquino administrations. With the revitalized economic structure foreign investors from Taiwan, China, and Japan began to renew their investments in manufacturing and processing firms. Concerning the law and order problem, which had dogged the Aquino government, Ramos was able to restore some degree of stability by calling upon Congress to lift the 35-year ban on the Communist party, which resulted in the emergence of **New Peoples'**

Army leaders who had formerly been underground. As to the perennial problem of **Muslim separatism** in Mindanao, Ramos neutralized the rebellion by staunchly supporting the formation of the Southern Philippine Council for Peace and Development.

When the United States dismantled its air and naval bases on November 24, 1992, it marked the end of the **neocolonial** era of Philippine history and the beginning of a new partnership with the United States. Although dismantling the bases left much lingering bitterness between the Filipinos and the United States Congress, Ramos played a superb balancing act in assuring both sides of the benefits of the new relationship without hurting nationalist sensitivities or showing a patronizing attitude toward the country's former benefactor. Ramos' state visits to Southeast Asian nations, including China, renewed long-neglected ties of neighborliness, which were formerly overshadowed by issues raised by the United States presence. *See also* AUTONOMOUS REGION OF MUSLIM MINDANAO.

RAMSEY, EDWIN. *See* GUERRILLA.

RASUL, SANTANINA (1948–). In 1985, Santanina Rasul became the first and only Muslim woman senator of the Republic of the Philippines, a nationwide body composed of only 24 people. In 1992, she also became the only Muslim ever to be reelected to the senate. She was a member of the Philippine government panel, which successfully forged the peace agreement with the **Moro National Liberation Front** (**MNLF**) that ended almost 30 years of armed hostilities between the Armed Forces of the Philippines and the MNLF. Rasul's work reaches beyond her involvement with the government to local and national community activities. She worked from 1986–1989 as a member of the UNESCO Philippine Commission representing Muslims communities and as the chairperson of the Magbasa Kita Foundation. The *Magbasa Kita* (Let's Read) works to promote nationwide literacy programs, livelihood training for the marginalized in Mindanao, agricultural schools and the training for poor farmers, their children and the children of former MNLF rebels.

RATTAN. A Philippine palm tree that thrives in heavily forested areas. Its pliable branches are used in making wickerwork, baskets, and furniture. Farmers also use it as a fastening material in their homes, and fishermen utilize it in boat construction. Rattan is exported to Japan, the United States, and European countries. *See also* NARRA.

RECTO, CLARO M. (1890–1960). Filipino nationalist. In the early 1950s, **nationalism** resurfaced. Its foremost leader, Claro M. Recto, a senator, fired the first volley in a speech in 1951. He said that the Philippine government had a "mendicant foreign policy," and allowed Americans to continue their dominant prewar interests in the financial, commercial, and industrial life of the country. Recto's nationalist sentiments developed from his long-time experience as a congressman, for he had been twice elected to represent his home province of **Batangas**. In the 1935 Constitutional Convention, Recto served as president and was instrumental in advocating policies that protected the Philippine heritage and assured the safety of the democratic process. For a brief time, he served in the Supreme Court as an associate justice, a position that he gave up to go into private law practice. When World War II war broke out, he was a newly elected senator, garnering the highest number of votes among the 24 elected. During the Japanese occupation, he was recruited to serve in the Laurel War Cabinet and, after the war, he was accused of collaboration. He pleaded not guilty to the charge. Subsequently, he proved that he had had connections and had cooperated with the underground movement. In 1949, he ran for senator but was defeated. Since the elections were tainted with fraud and violence, he filed an election protest and won a seat. From his Senate seat, he denounced legislation that allowed the encroachment of American business and political elements upon the domestic and foreign affairs of the Philippines. One piece of legislation was the **parity rights** clause in the Bell Trade Act, which he described as a surrender of the Philippine birthright. In later years, his speeches continued to emphasize themes of political and economic nationalism for which he was branded anti-American. *See also* GARCIA, CARLOS P.

REDUCCION. Spanish word used for the process that the friars employed to bring the *Indios* (natives) "under the bell." To reduce meant to conquer, convert, and bring under the civil administration the natives to live within the sound of the church bell in a *poblacion*. *Reduccion* worked for people living in the lowlands, but not for those who live in the mountains, such as he Igorots, Bontocs, Ifugaos, and Kalingas who successfully resisted the *reduccion* for hundreds of years. The Moros of Mindanao were also an unconquered group and never fell under the yoke of the Spanish invaders. *See also* PUEBLO.

REFORMA. A political party that is an alliance of parties and civil societies that opposed former President **Joseph Ejercito Estrada**. It was formed after Estrada was ousted through the peaceful **EDSA** revolution in 2001. Its founding chief, Renato de Villa, ran for president in the 1998 elections. Reforma was formerly allied with the ruling **People's Power Coalition** (PPC), but it bolted the coalition soon after President **Gloria Macapagal Arroyo** announced her plans to run in the 2004 elections. The party decided to pursue its advocacy of good government and principled leadership. Reforma, **Aksyong-Demokratiko** and Promdi led the impeachment campaign against Estrada. *See also* KILUSANG MAGBUBUKID NG PILPINAS.

REGALADO, GEORGIA (1950–). A native of **Benguet**, Georgia Regalado is the country's first woman police chief superintendent—the equivalent to the rank of brigadier general in the military. Regalado distinguished herself in the field of medical services as the commanding officer of the Philippine Military Academy Hospital and chief of the Philippine National Police General Hospital. While in service, she received several awards such as the Most Outstanding Medical Officer and was nominated as one of the 10 Most Outstanding Police Women in 2002. *See also* PALABRICA-GO, RAMONA; PHILIPPINE MILITARY ACADEMY.

REGIDOR, ANTONIO MA. (1845–1910). Nationalist. Regidor received his early schooling at the Colegio de San Juan de Letran. He obtained a degree from the University of Santo Tomas in 1863, and a doctorate in canon law from the University of Madrid. He was secretary of the colonial Supreme Court, president of what was then the Board of Public Instruction. Regidor tried, but failed to procure a write of habeas corpus before a British colonial court to rescue **Jose Rizal**, who was returning to Manila as a prisoner.

REGIONALISM. This is a cultural characteristic in a country of many ethnic groupings. Regionalism is based on language like the Ilocanos of the North, Ilongos of Iloilo, and Bicolanos in Southern Luzon. Whenever people of these language groups find themselves in societal situations outside their domain they seek each other and form associations. This situation is obvious in the United States where this regionalism is represented in associations by calling themselves after their hometowns, provinces, for example, Ilocano Association of Los Angeles, Aklanon Association, etc.

RELIGION. Filipinos have a long tradition of religious beliefs and rituals going back into prehistory. Their cosmology involved animism and anthropomorphism, which even today is practiced by highland and lowland groups in Luzon, Visayas, and Mindanao. The introduction of **Islam** in the 15th century and Christianity in the mid-16th century considerably changed the belief system and economic activities of the Filipinos. Eventually, Islam became rooted in southern Mindanao and in the Sulu archipelago, which today remains its bailiwick with a majority of the people calling themselves Muslims. Christianity, in the form of **Roman Catholicism**, came with the Spanish conquerors, who spread their religion by the force of the sword and the cross. The **Indios**, as they were called, were compelled to adopt their conquerors' religion. Wherever the Spanish friars visited, they built massive churches using forced labor as symbols of the new religion. In due time, a majority of the people reconciled their animistic beliefs to the monotheism of Christian dogma. The Spanish labeled natives who refused to become Christians, *infieles* (pagan or heathen). While the Christian religion remained firmly in place during the 380 years of Spanish colonial rule, new doctrines of Christianity came to the Philippines in the 19th century brought by the Americans in the form of many branches of **Protestantism**. Many Filipinos became converts to this new expression of Christianity and during the 50 years of American administration membership in Protestant churches grew by leaps and bounds.

Religion has creatively shaped the life and culture of present day Filipinos. Roman Catholicism commands the highest number of adherents, approximately 85 percent of the population. Other religious groups—the Aglipayans, Muslims, and Protestants—each have about

5 percent. These religious groups have established educational insti-
tutions, of which the Roman Catholics have the greatest number. *See
also* AGLIPAY, GREGORIO; CHURCH AND STATE; FILIP-
INIZATION; FRIAROCRACY; IGLESIA FILIPINA INDEPIEN-
DENTE; MADRASAH; RELIGION AND POLITICS; UNIVER-
SITY OF SANTO TOMAS.

RELIGION AND POLITICS. Religion and politics have been in-
grained in Philippine life and society ever since the Spanish period.
Religion played a major role in the appointment of civil officials such
the *gobernadorcillo* (town head). During the American regime, the
Commonwealth Constitution tempered the role of religion. Earlier
the **Malolos Constitution** provided for the separation of church and
state. On occasion, the churches came out publicly on issues, which
they opposed or supported, though traditionally the Roman Catholic
Church exhibited a neutral role in the political life of the country.
Politicians, on the other hand, keep on friendly terms with religious
authorities and cultivate a close relationship with local priests by attending weddings, baptisms, and other important religious rites. The
church's so-called neutrality was broken when Archbishop of Manila
Jaime Cardinal Sin summoned the people to rally behind General
Fidel Ramos and **Juan Ponce Enrile** in their coup against Ferdinand
Marcos. Cardinal Sin again showed no neutrality in the presidential
elections of l986 when the bishop openly endorsed Corazon Aquino
for president against Ferdinand Marcos. Besides, the Roman Catholic
hierarchy and other indigenous religious groups have been major
players in the political arena, including the members of **Iglesia Ni
Cristo**, Church of Christ, whose leaders have shown partiality in
their support of candidates who favor their causes. *See also*
CHURCH AND STATE; FRIAROCRACY; NATIONAL SCRE-
TARIAT FOR SOCIAL ACTION, JUSTICE AND PEACE.

RELIGIOUS ORDERS. In the late 19th century, there were five religious orders working in the Philippines, namely the Augustinians,
Dominicans, Franciscans, Recollects, and Jesuits. Since the church
and state were in close alliance then, the friars were at the center of
the social and political organization of the country. Their civil and ecclesiastical power—called **friarocracy**—over the people was re-

markable. They conducted many of the executive and control functions of the government at the local level. They were responsible for educational and health programs, kept the census and tax records, reported on the character and behavior of individuals, supervised the selection of local police and town officers, and were also responsible for maintaining morals and reporting incidences of sedition to the police. The information was gained in confessions. The religious orders were regarded as the indispensable instruments of Spanish rule. Since the establishment of American rule, these religious orders have devoted their energies to institutions of higher education, and the practice of the faith. *See also* ROMAN CATHOLICISM; UNIVERSITY OF SANTO TOMAS.

REPARATIONS (PHILIPPINES–JAPAN). Under the terms of the Reparations Agreement, Japan paid the Philippine government $550 million ($500 million in capital goods, $30 million in services, and $20 million in cash) spread over a period of time ranging from five to 20 years. The granting of loans to the private sector amounted to $250 million. Hence, the total figure was $800 million. The agreement expired in July 1976. The government used most of the money to rebuild the infrastructure, which was heavily damaged during the war.

RETANA, WENCESLAO EMILIO (1862–1924). Retana is considered the foremost foreign Filipinologist for his published works on printing in the Philippines and a catalog of works on the general history of the Philippines. His *Aparata Bibliografica de la historia general de Filipinas* in 1906 in three volumes contain 2,623 entries on books about the Philippines regardless of the language of writing or publication; Philippine imprints regardless of subjects; and publications of Filipinos wherever published. The period covered was 1524 to 1905. There is also a listing of periodicals published in the Philippines from 1811 to 1905. Retana published *Origines de la imprenta Filipina; investigaciones, historicos, bibliograficas* in 1911, which discusses the historical development of Philippine printing with a list of Philippine incunabula from 1503 to 1640, chronologically and annotated.

REVOLTS (1571–1896). According to Filipino historian Alfredo Saulo, the Filipinos fought the largest number of revolts in world history.

Historians have recorded more than a hundred revolts, or roughly an average of one revolt every three years, from 1571—the beginning of the Spanish colonial rule in the archipelago—to June 12, 1896, when General **Emilio Aguinaldo** proclaimed Philippine independence from Spain—a time span of 325 years. The long string of armed uprisings is attributed to the Filipinos' consuming passion for freedom. The first revolt was fought in 1574, just three years after the Spanish conquistador Miguel Lopez de Legaspi took possession of Manila and proclaimed it the capital of the Philippines. This revolt was led by **Rajah Lakandula** (also known as Rajah Matanda), the ruler of **Tondo.** The cause of this revolt was the imposition by the Spaniards of the right to collect *tributos* (tribute) from the natives.

In the study of Philippine revolts fought during the Spanish regime, another Filipino historian Celedonio Ancheta noted that at least 12 of these revolts were political in nature, 16 religious, 23 socioeconomic, and 30 miscellaneous. Some of these political revolts aimed at the overthrow of the Spanish colonial rule were the Lakandula revolt of 1574; Pampanga revolt of 1585; Muslim–Filipino war of 1602; Gaddang revolt of 1621; Sulu revolt of 1628; Mindanao revolt of 1638; Ilocos revolt of 1661, and the **Katipunan** revolt of 1898. The religious revolts— aimed at driving out the abusive Spanish friars and **religious orders**—were the Muslim–Filipino skirmish in Cebu in 1569; Igorot–Filipino revolt in Northern Luzon; 1601; **Tamblot** revolt of 1621; Cagayan revolt in 1625; **Lanao** revolt in 1639; Ilocos Norte revolt in 1811; and **Apolinario de la Cruz** (Herman Pule) revolt of 1840–1841. Revolts due to social and economic causes were the Ilocos Norte revolt of 1589; **Caraga** revolt of 1630; Sultanbansa insurrection of 1639; Zambales revolt of 1645; **Maniego** revolt of 1660–1661; **Dagohoy** revolt of 1744–1829; **Diego Silang** revolt of 1762–1763; agrarian revolt in **Bulacan** of 1745; revolt of the Cebuanos of 1762–1763; **Kalinga** uprising of 1785; **Basi** revolt of 1807; and Cavite revolt of 1872. Coming under the rubric of "miscellaneous revolts" are the Magat revolt of 1596; Camarines revolt of 1649; **Pampanga** revolt of 1660; Muslim–Filipino war of 1752–1764; Laguna uprising of 1762–1794; **Samar** revolt of 1762–1764; Tayabas uprising of 1762–1764; **Panay** revolt of 1762–1764; Zamboanga revolt of 1762; Novales revolt (**Cavite mutiny**) of 1823; Cotabato uprising of 1861; and Cavite revolt of 1869.

Many of these revolts against the Spaniards failed because of the lack of unity among the natives and also because of the help of the natives recruited by the Spaniards and their superior force of musketry. When the Spaniards first arrived in the country early in the 16th century they found the natives divided into many independent little groups reflecting the mode of their arrival by **barangay** (boats) from the neighboring Malay areas of Southeast Asia. Coming in several waves of migrations, each boatload settled close to the seas in one locality or island not far from the others. In the course of time, their settlements expanded but retained their individual identities. This went on for centuries until the Spaniards arrived on the scene under the banner of "God, Gold, and Glory." To pursue their mission of conquest the Spaniards dealt individually with each settlement or village and with each province or island until the entire Philippine archipelago was brought under their imperial control. They saw to it that the people remained divided or compartmentalized, and with the minimum of contacts or communication. The Spaniards adopted the policy of *divide et impera* (divide and conquer). Thus for centuries the natives were unaware of their common destiny. However, when communication improved toward the 1800s with steamships, railroads, and roads the spirit of revolt was galvanized into a nationwide revolution. *See also* PUEBLO; REDUCCION.

REYES, ANGELO (1945–). He was the defense secretary of President Gloria Macapagal Arroyo. As the Armed Forces Chief of Staff, Reyes led the military withdrawal of support for his boss President Joseph Ejercito Estrada on January 19, 2001. His claim to fame as defense secretary was in leading the offensive against the **Moro Islamic Liberation Front** in 2000 that resulted in the recovery of Camp Abubakar, the largest MILF camp in Mindanao, and led to its disintegration as a fighting unit. Reyes was instrumental in preparing the terms of agreement on the **Balikatan** military exercises in the Philippines. Its essential feature was the role of the U.S. military in training Philippine soldiers how to fight the **Abu Sayyaf** and other terrorist organizations. A member of the Philippine Military Academy Class of 1966, Reyes served in the army for 39 years, rising as a young lieutenant to a four-star general.

REYES, ISABELO DE LOS (1864–1938). Religious and labor leader. De los Reyes was born in Vigan, Ilocos Sur, where he distinguished himself as a journalist. He edited the first Ilocano newspaper and produced books on Ilocano folklore. In 1898, he was exiled to Spain and confined at the Castillo de Montjuich. He used this time to translate the New Testament into **Ilocano**. He also continued his work in political journalism by exposing Spanish tyranny in the Philippines. On his return to the Philippines he resumed his advocacy for an independent Roman Catholic Church run by Filipino clergy. This led him to break with the Vatican in 1902 and to the founding of the Philippine Independent Church (**Iglesia Filipinas Independiente**). He, Pascual Poblete, Felipe Buencamino Sr., and Gregorio Aglipay were the founders. He later launched the first labor federation in the Philippines, the Democratic Labor Union, and he became its first president. Most of his life Reyes opposed the American administration, and for this sentiment he was elected to the Manila City Council and as a senator to the Philippine Assembly, where he served from 1910 to 1928. His introduction into the Senate of social legislation, which benefited Filipino farmers and laborers, earned him the title of Father of Philippine Socialism.

REYES, SEVERINO (1861–1942). Writer of **zarzuelas**. Born in Manila, Severino Reyes obtained a bachelor of philosophy degree from the **University of Santo Tomas**. He wrote his first zarzuela in 1901 and throughout his career composed a total of 25 one-act plays, four two-act plays, and 25 four-act plays. His popularity reached its peak in the early decades of American rule, after which the increasing popularity of movies put an end to the zarzuela theater. *See also* MORO MORO.

RICAFORT, MARIANO. *See* DAGOHOY, FRANCISCO.

RICARTE, ARTEMIO (1866–1945). Philippine–Spanish Revolution captain-general. A teacher by profession when the Philippine–Spanish Revolution broke out, Ricarte joined the Katipunan when the uprising began on August 31, 1896. He distinguished himself for his valor in the field of combat against Spanish forces for which he was dubbed *vibora* (viper). **Emilio Aguinaldo** named him captain-general in charge of supplies and manpower. He fought in pitched battles in Cavite, Laguna, and Batangas. In 1898, Ricarte joined Aguinaldo in exile in Hong Kong after the Pact of Biak-na-Bato, which temporarily halted the revolution against Spain. He returned with Aguinaldo to Manila in 1899 when the American forces occupied the city. At the outbreak of the Philippine–American Revolution, Ricarte was appointed chief of operations of the insurgent forces, but American soldiers subsequently captured him. He was banished to Guam together with **Apolinario Mabini**. He was released in June 1910 but again deported to Hong Kong for his refusal to take the oath of allegiance. From there he took his family to Tokyo, Japan, where he resided until 1943 when the Japanese brought him back to the Philippines to help in the pacification campaign. He died in 1945 in Mountain province where the Japanese forces had retreated in their last-ditch stand against the American liberation forces. *See also* KAHABAGAN, AGUEDA.

RICE. Rice is the staple food of about 85 percent of the population of the Philippines. Eleven percent of most household expenses are for purchasing rice. Rice also makes up about 35 percent of the total calorie intake of the average Filipino. A single Filipino consumes about 100–103 kilograms of rice a year. Rice is cultivated twice a year in 2.7 million hectares or 30 percent of the country's arable land. Rice farming is the primary livelihood of more than 2.5 million farmers. The rice industry has been performing well, except for some years when the *El Niño* phenomenon and other natural and man-made factors hit the country. Production in the year 2001 soared to 11.78 million metric tons, or 4.6 percent higher than the year 2000 output. Notwithstanding the steady increase in production, the Philippines have remained a net importer of rice. The import figure for 2004 was at 870,000 metric tons. This situation is primarily attributed to the yearly **population** increase of 2.36 percent. Seventy-five of every 100 farmers produce less than four metric tons per hectare owing to their inability to benefit from high-yielding technologies arising from high costs of production, uncertainties in production—insect pests, diseases, typhoons, drought—low or fluctuating prices, and inaccessible credit facilities. Based on the average yield (3.09 metric tons per hectare), an increase of 1.5 ton per hectare yield is needed from irrigated and rain-fed rice fields in the year 2030 to meet the increasing needs of the growing population.

Rice plays a major role in the country's economy and politics. Ensuring enough rice for the general public and the stability of the rice industry are used as measurements of political economy. Rice sufficiency has in recent years become synonymous with food security. As this is being written, the Philippine government Department of Agriculture announced that the country is well on its way to achieving self-sufficiency in rice production in 2005 by producing more than 15 million metric tons of paddy rice. *See also* HYBRID RICE; PALAY.

RICE TERRACES. Mountain rice fields found mainly in the Mountain provinces in northern Luzon. The rice terraces are stairlike structures carved out of the mountainsides by **Ifugaos**, one of the mountain tribes, without the benefit of iron tools. They have planted rice in such embankments over the last 2,000 years. An elaborate system of irrigation controls the flow of water from the highest to the lowest level allowing an even supply for the growing rice plants. The walls of stone are considered an engineering marvel. If stretched out, these walls would reach 21,000 kilometers or halfway around the globe. They are sometimes acclaimed as the eighth wonder of the world. *See also* BONTOC.

RIVERS. The most extensive river systems in Luzon are the Cagayan River in the Cagayan Valley, northeastern Luzon, which runs for 442 kilometers from its headwaters in the Sierra Madre through the valley floor to its mouth in Aparri; the Pampanga River, which flows from the Caraballo Mountains in central Luzon and empties into Manila Bay; and the Agno River, which rises from the Gran **Cordillera** Mountains and flows toward the Lingayen Gulf. In Mindanao, the second largest island, the Agusan River begins in the southwestern flank of the Pacific Cordillera and winds for more than 322 kilometers toward its mouth in Butuan Bay.

RIZAL. Located in western Luzon and named after the Filipino hero Jose Rizal. Rizal, adjacent to metropolitan Manila, is the country's most populous and commercially developed province. Local industries produce a wide variety of chemicals, pharmaceuticals, metal works, textiles, and processed food. The provincial capital of Pasig is a satellite community of Manila. The province's 15 municipalities, all close to Manila, contain two-thirds of the population of more than four million people, most of whom are Tagalogs. The total land area is 1,309 square kilometers. One of the province's towns, Antipolo, hosts each May a major religious pilgrimage and fiesta in honor of the patron saint. Several of the towns contain churches—built by Chinese craftsmen—exhibiting **baroque** architecture. Archaeological sites in Novaliches uncovered artifacts dating back to 300 B.C. Chief towns are Angono, Binangonan, Morong, Taytay, and Tanay. *See also* BEYER, H. OTLEY.

RIZAL, JOSE P. (1861–1896). National hero of the Filipinos. He was born on June 19, 1861, in Calamba, Laguna. His parents were Francisco Mercado Rizal and Teodora Alonso, well-to-do landowners. Educated in Europe and foremost of the **ilustrados**, Rizal used his cosmopolitan intellect to open the eyes of the Filipinos to the tyranny of Spain. In France he obtained his licentiate in medicine and a licentiate in philosophy and letters. In 1887, in Berlin, he published his first novel *Noli Me Tangere* (Touch Me Not) in which he described vividly the oppression of Spanish colonial rule. The Spanish banned the circulation of the book in the Philippines. Having been trained as an ophthalmologist, he returned to the Philippines to practice his profession and to lead a peaceful reformist movement. His first patient was his mother, whose failing eyesight was restored. He was forced to leave the country under pressure of the friars, who considered his novel heretical. He returned to Europe, where he continued his polemics against Spanish rule by publishing his second novel *El Filibusterismo* (The Rebel).

Upon his return to the Philippines in 1892, Rizal was arrested as a revolutionary agitator and banished to Dapitan in Mindanao. His reformist ideas caught on with Filipino leaders like **Andres Bonifacio**, who started a rebellion, which spread like wildfire. Although Rizal wanted a peaceful revolution, he was blamed for all the uprisings that had taken place. After a farcical trial he was imprisoned at **Fort Santiago** and later executed by a firing squad on December 30, 1896, at Bagumbayan, known today as Rizal Park in Luneta, Manila. *See also* BRACKEN, JOSEPHINE: LIGA FILIPINA; MI ULTIMO ADIOS.

ROBERTSON, JAMES. *See* KALANTIAO.

ROCO, RAUL (1941–). A former senator and secretary of education under President Gloria Macapagal Arroyo, Roco was an unsuccessful candidate for president in the May 2004 elections. Roco was president of **Aksyon Demokratiko** Party. As a senator, he authored several bills that benefited **women**, and these included Women in Nation Building (Republic Act 7192), the Nursing Act (RA 7164), the Anti-Rape Law (RA 7906) and the Child and Family Courts (RA 8369). He was considered the father of the **Central Bank** of the Philippines (Bangko Sentral). He was also the author of amendments to the tax laws, which avoided the double taxation on overseas Filipinos (RA 8424) and the bill allowing overseas Filipinos to vote.

RODIL, RUDY. A historian by profession, Rodil was one of the leaders who was instrumental in the successful peace talks between the Philippines government and the **Moro National Liberation Front (MNLF)** that resulted in the creation of the **Autonomous Region in Muslim Mindanao**. Appointed by President Fidel Ramos as a member of the negotiating team, he and his team completed the peace agreement with the MNLF in 1996. For this contribution to the peace process, the entire panel was awarded a special citation by the Aurora Aragon Quezon Peace Awards Foundation in 1997. President Ramos conferred upon him the Philippine Legion of Honor Degree in recognition of his valuable service in the peace negotiations. In academe, Rodil's expertise is Mindanao history, particularly Moro and **Lumad** affairs.

RODRIGO, FRANCISCO. *See* UNITED NATIONALIST DEMO-CRATIC ORGANIZATION.

RODRIGUEZ, BUENAVENTURA. *See* ZARZUELA.

ROJO, MANUEL ANTONIO. *See* BRITISH OCCUPATION OF MANILA.

ROMAN CATHOLIC CHURCH. Roman Catholicism is the historic religious faith of 85 percent of the Filipino people. The country claims itself as the only Christian nation in Asia. Since its introduction in the archipelago in 1565 by Miguel Lopez de Legaspi—by sword and the cross—Filipinos have practiced the faith with a distinctive folk-religious flavor. The religious system that the conquistadors and friars imported in the 16th century was superimposed on a polytheistic base—saints took primacy over spirits (*diwatas* and *anitos*), priests over shamans, and the mass over propitiation ceremonies. The mixing of different religious beliefs and practices marked Philippine Catholicism. It is similar to Latin American Catholicism in its social and theological conservatism.

Filipinos attend official church services, such as masses, novenas, baptisms, weddings, and funerals. They supplement these ceremonies with a number of folk-religious rituals basic to the community's social and religious calendar, such as the **fiesta**, which is celebrated on the special day of the patron saint of the town or **barangay**. Christmas is celebrated in a manner that blends Catholic, Chinese, and American customs. The people decorate their homes with lanterns, Christmas trees, and go out caroling. For nine days people attend the *misa de gallo* (early morning Christmas mass). During the Lenten season, most communities do a reading of the **pasyon** (passion) and a performance of a popular passion play. The custom of reading of the passion could be an adaptation of a pre-Hispanic practice of chanting lengthy epics. Indigenous ritual practices such as rice planting and harvesting and death anniversaries of departed ancestors have blended in meaning and timing with the Catholic rites such as *Fiesta de Mayo* and All Saint's Day.

The clergy is predominantly Filipino and an extensive network of parochial schools and institutions of higher learning support the church. Currently, due to the burgeoning **population** of the Philippines, the Catholic Bishops Conference has declared a serious shortage of priests and at least 25,000 are needed to serve some 68 million Filipino Catholics. There are only 10,000 priests nationwide and they are overworked. *See also* ATI-ATIHAN; BLACK NAZARENE; RELIGION; RELIGIOUS ORDERS; SIN, JAIME CARDINAL.

ROMBLON. The three main islands of this province Romblon, Tablas, and Sibuyan are situated southeast of Mindoro Island. Romblon, the smallest of the three, is the site of the provincial capital, also named

Romblon. Quarries on the islands of Romblon Alad, Cobrador, and Tablas are noted sources of marble, which is used for construction, gravestones, and monuments. Chief towns are Romblon, Odiongan, and Tablas.

ROMULO, CARLOS P. (1901–1985). Statesman, journalist, and foreign affairs secretary. One of the original framers of the Universal Declaration of Human Rights, Romulo was the first Asian president of the United Nations General Assembly, having been elected to that office in 1949. Romulo was born in Camiling, **Tarlac**, on January 14, 1901. He began his career in journalism in 1931, and by the time the war broke out in 1941 he had distinguished himself as the author of a series of articles on the political and military situation in East Asia, articles for which he won a Pulitzer Prize. While in the United States promoting the war effort against the Japanese, he wrote about his experiences in two books: *I Saw the Fall of the Philippines* and *I Saw the Philippines Rise*. As General MacArthur's aide de camp, he saw service in Bataan, Corregidor, and Australia, as well as in the invasion of Leyte and the liberation of Manila. He served eight Philippine presidents in various capacities, including as ambassador to the United States, envoy to the United Nations, and foreign secretary. He also became the ninth president of his alma mater, the University of the Philippines, while concurrently serving as the secretary of education. President Ferdinand Marcos recalled him from retirement to serve as foreign affairs secretary. He held the post from 1965 to l984. Romulo died in Manila on December 15, 1985.

RONDALLA. A musical ensemble using several multistringed guitars (*bandoria*) and mandolins. These instruments are usually used during town **fiestas**. Since most big towns have rondalla ensembles, rondalla contests are featured events during fiestas and help draw crowds to the annual events. Rondalla music is the popular accompaniment to folk dances and musical celebrations. *See also* MUSICAL TRADITIONS; ZARZUELA.

ROOSEVELT, THEODORE, JR. (1887–1944). American governor-general of the Philippines (1932–1933). Like his illustrious father President Theodore Roosevelt, Ted Jr. was elected Nassau county representative to the New York State legislature in 1920. A little over a year later, President Warren G. Harding appointed him assistant secretary of state. After three years of superb performance, Roosevelt ran for governor of New York but was defeated. In 1929, President Herbert Hoover appointed Roosevelt to the post of Governor-General of Puerto Rico, where he worked diligently and earned the goodwill of the Puerto Ricans. The next step in his political career was the governor-generalship in the Philippines. Although he served only for a year, Roosevelt initiated educational and land reforms and greatly improved health care, especially in the areas of child health and the control of tuberculosis and leprosy. Roosevelt was a brigadier general during World War II and served in France. *See also* CULION.

ROSALES, GAUDENCIO. (1932–). Archbishop of Manila. Pope John Paul II named Gaudencio Rosales archbishop of Lipa, Batangas, to succeed **Jaime Cardinal Sin**, who retired in 2003. The Archdiocese of Manila is one the largest and most active Catholic diocese in the Philippines. Archbishop Rosales brought with him an excellent record of pastoral supervision and a passion for the preservation of the environment. As the bishop of **Bukidnon**, he fought and won against illegal logging syndicates, for which he was cited as guardian of the forest. Rosales set a new style of governance with his extensive experience in training priests. The archbishop is known to be amiable and very low key. Unlike his feisty predecessor, who was a vigilant participant in local and national politics, Rosales has devoted his energies to the restoration of the faith and reformation of the clergy.

ROYAL AUDENCIA. The royal *audencia* was the supreme court of the Spanish regime in the Philippines, and also ran the government in case of a vacancy in the governmental office. The first royal *audencia* was created by the Spanish king in order to assist the governor-general and to protect the people from abuses of the officials. It was composed of the governor-general as the president, three justices, a prosecuting attorney, and other officials. It was abolished in 1589 when the governor-general and the justices had quarrels and misunderstandings. It was restored when the presidency was given to a regent instead of the governor. *See also* RELIGIOUS ORDERS.

ROXAS, GERARDO. *See* UNITED NATIONALIST DEMOCRATIC ORGANIZATION.

ROXAS, MANUEL A. (1892–1948). Last president of the Philippine Commonwealth and first president of the Republic of the Philippines. Roxas was born on January 1, 1892, in Roxas City, Capiz. His parents were Gerardo Roxas and Rosario Acuña. He began his political career in 1913 when he scored highest in the bar examinations. Starting as a law clerk of a Supreme Court justice, he became a municipal councilor and later governor in his home province. He was elected representative in 1922 to the National Assembly, where his colleagues chose him as speaker, a position he held for 11 years. During his term as congressman, he led several missions to the U.S. to secure the independence of the Philippines. In the 1934 Constitutional Convention, he was one of the seven members who drafted the 1935 charter. When World War II broke out, he was a senator, but he fought in **Bataan** and was captured by the Japanese. Roxas was forced to serve the Japanese-sponsored Philippine Republic. After the war, he was branded a **collaborator** together with President **Jose Laurel** and his whole cabinet. However, he was also a secret supporter of the guerrilla movement and the Filipino people exonerated him in 1946 by electing Roxas as president of the new Republic of the Philippines. He had served only two years when he died of a heart attack on April 15, 1948. *See also* OS-ROX MISSION.

– S –

SABAH (NORTH BORNEO). Territory in northeastern Borneo. This territory became a Malaysian state in 1963, but it has been claimed by the Philippines as a part of its jurisdiction. The Philippines based its case on a claim to territories that were part of the former Sultanate of Sulu, whose territory included Sabah during the 1800s. When the British took over the Malay Peninsula, they also acquired the island of Borneo. The Sultanate ceded the Sabah area to the British who paid the sultans and their descendants a stipend. Several Philippine presidents have revived the claim in meetings with Malaysia, which acquired the territory when it achieved independence from the British. Ferdinand Marcos tried to train a commando team for infiltration of Sabah, but due to public outcry against this clandestine operation, Marcos cancelled the plan as well as the claim to Malaysia. President **Corazon Aquino** tried to rush a bill through Congress in November 1987 to renounce the claim once and for all, but Congress failed to act on it. The issue of Sabah was revived more strongly by the secessionist **Moro National Liberation Front (MNLF)**, formed in 1970. The MNLF demanded a separate Muslim state, including Sabah as part of its territory. The then Sultan of Sulu **Jamalul Kiram** III took the Sabah issue directly to Malaysia and brought it also to the attention of the Organization of the Islamic Conference (OIC). The sultan claimed that the Philippine government had no authority to negotiate with Malaysia since Sabah was not part of the territory ceded by Spain in the Treaty of Paris in 1898. The sultan demanded 10 billion dollars in rent from Malaysia and a royalty of 5 percent of the income from Sabah's natural resources. Since the Sultan left no heirs the claim is now a moot issue. *See also* BRITISH NORTH BORNEO; JABIDAH.

SABATER, BENEDICTO. *See* ZARZUELA.

SABONG. This is game cockfighting, a favorite sport—and a form of gambling—held in most Philippine towns and cities. It is legally sanctioned by the government and a lucrative source of revenue. Cockfighting, which has been practiced by pre-Hispanic Filipinos, is observed Sundays in cockpit arenas called *sabongan.* Cocks are raised specially for their fighting abilities by aficionados. Before these "gladiators" are released a middleman (*kristo*) calls the bets by calling *lyamado* (cock on whom the majority have place their bets) or *dehado* (cock on whom the minority have placed their bets). The roosters are fitted with razor-sharp blades as spurs and duel with each other to death.

SACADAS. *See* SUGAR INDUSTRY.

SACLAG, ALONZO. *See* LIVING TREASURES.

SADUK. *See* ANTIQUE.

SAGADA. This is one of the picturesque towns of **Mountain Province** in the Cordillera region of Northern Luzon. The town, located about 100 kilometers from **Baguio**, is famous for its mountainous sceneries, ideal for trekkers, and many tourist attractions—pristine waterfalls, centuries-old burial caves, fantastic **rice terraces**, and hanging coffins. The forebears of the Igorots practiced an unusual burial practice by hanging and stacking coffins, hewed from tree trunks, in the limestone karst cliffs and caves near town. The locals speak the Kankana-ey dialect. Agriculture is the main source of income in Sagada, mostly vegetables that are sold in Baguio and Manila. Another source of income is the colorful Sagada cloth, one of the products of their famous weaving industry. Most of the people in the 19 towns of Mountain Province are Anglicans, the converts of early Episcopal Church missionaries who came to this remote region in the 1920s. *See also* APO ANO.

SAKAY, MACARIO (1870–1907). In the struggle for Philippine independence, Sakay was a controversial leader and historians often labeled him as a patriot or a *tulisan* (bandit). Before he joined the Katipunan, Sakay worked as tailor, a barber, and an actor in **moromoros**. In 1894, Sakay joined the Dapitan branch of the Katipunan, and due to his exemplary work, he became head of the branch. He fought alongside with Andres Bonifacio in several skirmishes with the Spaniards. After the surrender of Emilio Aguinnaldo in the ill-fated **Philippine–American Revolution**, he continued his struggle against the American occupiers until he was captured, but eventually granted amnesty in 1902.

Together with a group of Katipuneros he established the *Republika Ng Katagalugan* (Tagalog Republic) in the mountains of Southern Luzon. The republic had a constitution, and Sakay being the "generalissimo" issued a manifesto declaring that the Filipino people had a fundamental right to fight for independence, which was anathema to the Americans. The republic enjoyed the support of the Filipino masses in the provinces of Laguna, Batangas, and Cavite. In late 1904, Sakay and his men launched a military offensive against the enemy. They were successful in seizing ammunition and firearms in their raids in Cavite and Batangas. Using guerrilla warfare, Sakay attacked only at night. The effect of Sakay's depredations proved disastrous for the people. The U.S. Army started to employ "hamletting" or the reconcentration in areas where Sakay received strong assistance. The Sakay rebellion ended when Sakay took the bait of a promised amnesty and surrendered with his men on July 14, 1906. *See also* MALVAR, MIGUEL.

SAKDALISTA. Radical farmers' movement during the 1930s. During the early American colonial period the tenancy problem in the country had grown to such an extent that tenants, particularly in central Luzon, were becoming restive. Thousands labored under the harsh conditions imposed by their landlords. They complained that labor was insufficiently rewarded and that despite long servitude they had little prospect of ever being free. The American administration's effort to redistribute the big landed estates controlled by *encomienderos* and the friars were not enough to satisfy the farmers. The unrest soon spawned the radical farmers' movements known as the **Colorum** and the Sakdalista. Benigno Ramos, a labor leader, was the acknowledged founder of the Sakdalista in 1930 and under his leadership the Sakdalistas led uprisings in the provinces of Laguna, Rizal, Cavite, Quezon, and Bulacan. The movement flourished for five years until the government ultimately crushed the rebels in 1935, signaling the end of the Sakdalista. Ramos fled to Japan but returned during the Japanese occupation to organize the **KALIBAPI**, a pro-Japanese political movement, to support the Japanese military administration.

SALAS, QUINTIN (1870–1917). A famous Visayan general during the Philippine–American Revolution who waged guerrilla warfare in Iloilo even after the surrender of General Emilio Aguinaldo. He led his poorly armed fighters in nightly assaults and daytime ambushes and thus became a thorn to the American occupiers of his home province. The Salas guerrilla forays lasted for two years. He finally surrendered by laying down his arms on October 1901. In 1908, he went to school in Manila where he obtained a bachelor of laws degree from the Escuela de Derecho. He practiced law and aided his former comrades-in-arms in successful lawsuits. His only daughter became the first Ilonggo woman lawyer. *See also* KAHABAGAN, AGUEDA.

SALEEBY, NEJEEB. *See* INDARAPATRA.

SALONGA, JOVITO (1922–). Reputed as the "nation's fiscalizer," Jovito Salonga distinguished himself as a three-time senator under three different administrations—those of Diosdado Macapagal, Ferdinand Marcos, and Corazon Aquino. During his tenure as senator—senate president from 1987–1991—he introduced significant acts of legislation, many of which inspired public interest: the state scholarship law, disclosure of interest act, magna carta for public school teachers, code of conduct and ethical standards for public officials, and the crime of **plunder**. The son of a Presbyterian minister, Salonga has been fighting corruption and dictatorship since his youth. A lawyer by profession, Salonga topped the examinations and went to Harvard for his master's degree, and Yale University for his doctorate.

When **martial law** was declared in 1972, Salonga was one of its most outspoken opponents and defended political prisoners who challenged the Marcos regime. Severely injured in a grenade attack during a 1980 political rally in **Quiapo**, Manila, Salonga miraculously survived but Marcos had him arrested and detained without charges. Later he was released and returned to Yale University as a visiting scholar where he engaged in the revision of his book on international law. He returned to the Philippines when the Corazon Aquino government took over after the **People Power** revolution of February 1986. Aquino named him chairman of the **Presidential Commission on Good Government**, which was tasked with investigating and recovering the ill-gotten wealth of the members of the past regime. Salonga ran for president in 1991 on a platform of social equality that caused fear among the 81 families who control most of the nation's wealth. He lost but he continued as an active voice denouncing social ills in Philippine society. *See also* OLIGARCHS.

SALONGA, LEA (1971–). International stage performer-singer, Lea Salonga made history as the first Filipino to sing in the musical play *Les Miserables* and moved on to London, where she was involved in musicale groups performing before international audiences. Her stint in *Miss Saigon* paved the way to bigger roles. She sang in the Walt Disney animated production *Aladdin* and became also the first Filipino to have performed at the celebrated Oscar Awards when she rendered the Disney song "A Whole New World" before Hollywood celebrities. As a 10-year-old girl growing up in Manila, Lea started singing her favorite song "I Am But a Small Girl," and her sweet and tender voice caught the attention of talent scouts. She trained and sang until her voice was the most heard on radio and television shows in the Philippines.

SAMAHANG NAYON. Cooperative movement of small landowners. This cooperative movement was developed as part of the land reform program of President Ferdinand Marcos in the early 1970s and the goal of his *party Kilusang Bagong Lipunan* (New Society Movement). Under the program family-sized plots of three to five hectares were distributed to farmers who would pay for them over a 15-year period. In order for the farmers to acquire the title to the land they had to join the *Samahang Nayon* (cooperative). By 1982, there were 22,000 Samahang Nayons many of which operated as commercial enterprises involved in marketing activities such as buying produce in bulk and selling it at low cost to members. Farmers learned how to pool their assets and to develop new techniques of crop production. The cooperatives operated successfully for a time, but eventually many of them succumbed to mismanagement and **graft and corruption**. Their demise coincided with the end of the Ferdinand Marcos administration.

SAMAL. The Samals are the poorest and least independent of the five major Muslim groups. They serve as the "loyal commoners" in the hierarchy of Muslim minorities. They live literally over the sea, where the villages stand on stilts above the coastal waters of South Mindanao and the Sulu Islands. *See also* BAJAU; JIKIRI.

SAMAR. The third largest island in the Philippines with a land area of 13,429 square kilometers. Samar was divided into three provinces in 1968: northern, eastern, and western Samar. Homonhon, an islet south of Samar at the entrance of Leyte Gulf, was the site of the first landing of **Magellan** in 1521 and also the site of the first landing of General Douglas MacArthur's liberation forces in 1944. Waray-waray is the major language of the Samareños.

SAMAR, EASTERN. On the typhoon belt, typhoons are an annual problem for Samar Oriental's 325,000 people. Its capital, Borongan, lies on the east coast and is surrounded by forests and coconut plantations. Copra is the province's major product. Another major industry is logging while fishing provides the main livelihood of those living on Guiuan, where the Bureau of Fisheries and Aquatic Resources operates a pearl farm. The major towns are Borongan, Llorente, Taft, and Hernani.

SAMAR, NORTHERN. The smallest of the three Samar provinces, Northern Samar was created on June 9, 1995, by virtue of Republic Act No. 4221. It has a land area of 3,498 square kilometers, with a population of 454,195. Waray-waray is the spoken dialect. The capital, Catarman, is located on the seacoast of the northern plains and constitutes the commercial and educational center of the province. The Catubig Valley is the province's principal area of rice production. Archaeological excavations in the province have unearthed antique jewelry, which dates from 1804. The major towns are Catarman, Allen, Catubig, and Laoang.

SAMAR, WESTERN. The largest of the three Samar provinces, it occupies a land area of 5,591 square kilometers, with a population of 550,000. The capital is Catbalogan, an important port and fishing town and major commercial center. Another important town is Calbayog City, the principal port of Samar's northern region. Fishing is the principal means of livelihood for the people on the coastal areas of western Samar. The province's major tourist attraction is the famous Sohotan National Park, located near the town of Bassey, which features caves of various sizes with stalagmites and stalactites. Major towns are Almagro, Wright, Calbiga, Hinabangan, and Villareal.

SAMAT. A craggy mountain in **Bataan** province topped by a giant 95-foot cross, the "Shrine of Valor." The landmark commemorates the scene of the fierce battle that preceded the surrender of the Filipino and American forces to the Japanese in 1942, an account of which is inscribed on the monument. The Philippine government has declared April 2 as Bataan Day. World War II veterans, including Japanese survivors and their families, attend the annual wreath-laying ceremony, which takes place at the shrine. *See also* DEATH MARCH.

SAMIER BAKULADON. *See* JAWI.

SAMPAGUITA. The national flower of the Philippines (*jasminum sambac*). The blossoms have a sweet scent and are used in making beautiful garlands, which are worn by men and women over their **barongs** and mestiza dresses. The sampaguita bush blooms profusely in May, the **festival** month. *See also* WALING-WALING; YLANG-YLANG.

SAN AGUSTIN CHURCH. Church-monastery built in 1590 in **intramuros**, the walled city of Manila, by Augustinian friars. Although the original edifice no longer stands, the San Agustin Church is thought to be the oldest church retaining its 16th-century architecture. Through the centuries the Augustinians made additions, such as cloisters, quarters for the priests, offices, sacristy, library, and staircases. The walls are constructed of hewn stone, and the floor is paved with Chinese stone slabs and Spanish bricks. In 1762, British soldiers damaged the structure, necessitating extensive repairs during the course of which new annexes were built to accommodate a greater number of missionaries. Its solid base has withstood many earthquakes during the past centuries. During World War II, the Japanese military set up its headquarters in the church, and it suffered greatly from bombings and shellings during the **liberation** of Manila in 1945. Subsequent reconstruction has restored its pristine look. The facade is built along neoclassical lines and features Ionic and Corinthian columns supporting a triangular pediment. Its twin bell towers still house the 3,400 kilogram bell, and the main door is decorated with baroque bas-reliefs representing St. Augustine and St. Monica surrounded by the ecclesiastical symbols of the Augustinian Order. Inside the church the most highly artistic sculpture is the pulpit, which was carved from **narra** wood in 1627. The fully gilded altar is filled with finely carved statues and bas-reliefs, while the lectern features statuettes of griffins, sphinxes, and winged angels. *See also* BAROQUE CHURCHES.

SANCHEZ, PRISCILLA. *See* SCIENTISTS.

SANDAYO. An epic tale of the **Subanon** people who live in mountain communities in the two **Zamboanga** provinces. The recorded epic in the original poetic language of the Subanon had 7,590 long verses, which was translated into English. The epic portrays an aristocratic society composed of datus and their highborn ladies whose main concern is to fight off invaders of their traditional lands. *See also* BANTUGAN; PAILALIM RI BORAK.

SAN DIEGO **WARSHIP.** The *San Diego* was originally built as a trading ship. It was formerly known as the *San Antonio* before it was converted into a warship. It sank approximately 900 meters northeast of Fortune Island in Nasugbu, **Batangas**, after it engaged the Dutch warship *Mauritus* under the command of Admiral Oliver Van Noort on December 4, 1600. A total of 34,407 artifacts were recovered from the shipwreck. The artifacts include various forms of porcelain, stoneware, earthenware materials, and metals. The *San Diego* exhibition has been on tour around the globe before it was permanently displayed at the **National Museum** in Manila. *See also* DUTCH.

SANDIGANBAYAN. Anticorruption court. Set up in 1979 by order of President Ferdinand Marcos, the Sandiganbayan was the special court charged with handling graft and corruption cases, particularly those of public officials involved in malfeasance. The creation of this court was in response to the charges of graft and corruption by the mass media, which accused President Ferdinand Marcos of tolerating the egregious practice. In the course of its work, the court processed several thousand complaints, but prosecution and conviction of big name perpetrators were stymied by political pressure from above and by political patronage. Its record of convicting only small fry and letting the big fish go free undermined the credibility of the government. However, the appointment of new judges has given the Sandiganbayan a better image and improved its record of prosecution and conviction of malefactors in government service. Its biggest case so far is the **plunder** charge against former president **Joseph Ejercito Estrada** and his son Jose, a former mayor of San Juan, Rizal.

SANDIKO, TEODORO (1860–1939). Nationalist. Born in Manila, Sandiko completed his law degree in Madrid, Spain, where he was one of the leaders of the **propaganda movement** before the Philippine–Spanish Revolution. He returned to the Philippines to serve as secretary of the interior under Emilio Aguinaldo in the First Philippine Republic. He was not only a military leader but also one of the early Filipino statesmen. He conferred with U.S. General Wesley Merritt to avert a clash between the United States and the Philippines when the Americans refused to allow Filipinos to participate in the Battle of Manila in 1898. After the end of the revolution, Sandiko became active on the political front. He was twice governor of Bulacan and senator from 1919–1933. He served as the vice president of the Constitutional Convention in 1934. He was also a labor leader and founder of a school in Malolos, Bulacan. *See also* DEL PILAR, MARCELO.

SAN FERNANDO. *See* LA UNION.

SANGA-SANGA. *See* TAWI-TAWI.

SAN JOSE. *See* ANTIQUE.

SANTA CRUZ. *See* LAGUNA.

SANLAKAS. Sanlakas party was founded in 1994 as a broad coalition and mass movement of professionals, small entrepreneurs, and workers, urban poor residents, women, youth and students, and farmers, who are engaged in the struggle for social reforms in Philippine society. Sanlakas, which is leftist in orientation, utilizes various forms of political mobilization, such as rallies and marches. Thus, with its mass base of 200,000 it has led massive demonstrations over issues such as Philippine support of the U.S.-led **Iraq** war, globalization, human rights, and people's welfare. Sanlakas is included in the **party-list system** of proportional representation, and in the 2001 elections it was successful in electing one representative in congress. Through pressure politics Sanlakas has been prodding the government to address the people's fundamental concerns such as poverty, graft and corruption, and rights and welfare of marginalized voters. *See also* AKBAYAN.

SAN MIGUEL. A brewing company founded in 1893 by the Spanish in Manila, which was the subject of a political and financial brawl during President Gloria Macapagal Arroyo's administration. San Miguel has dominated the country's economy with its 90 percent profitable beer and soft-drink market and accounts for 4 percent of gross domestic product, pays 5 percent of national taxes, and employs about 15,000 people. During the Ferdinand Marcos dictatorship, Marcos seized the brewery firm and placed it under the management of his crony Eduardo Cojuangco. When Marcos fled the country in 1986, Cojuangco also fled and stayed abroad. Presidents Corazon Aquino—an estranged cousin of Cojuangco—and Fidel Ramos kept Cojuangco away from San Miguel for 12 years. But he returned to the Philippines when his friend **Joseph Ejercito Estrada** was elected president and took control of San Miguel on the basis of his 47 percent stake. **Haydee Yorac**, chair of the Presidential Commission on Good Government and chief crony buster, charged that Cojuangco's stocks were ill-gotten assets from the Marcos era. The government has a 20 percent uncontested share of San Miguel stocks owned by government pension funds. Yorac has waged a successful legal campaign and recovered the estimated $20 billion allegedly pillaged during the Marcos era. *See also* COJUANGCO.

SANTIAGO, IRENE (1950–). As a journalist in Mindanao, Irene Santiago's reporting and news analysis on the Muslim's war of secession in the 1970s brought to the nation's attention the dismal plight of Muslim **women**. With their men folk off to war, the women could hardly cope with family responsibilities as they lacked skills, education, capital, and opportunities. In her first foray into women's issues, Santiago organized the Kahayag Foundation in Davao to undertake literacy, income generating, and health and daycare services for the women. Her work led her to become a consumer rights activist and she was in the forefront of the fight against infant formula. She helped draft the Philippine Code of Breast Milk Substitutes that became the basis for the establishment of baby-friendly government hospitals that encourage rooming-in and breastfeeding. The legal rights of women, especially abused and battered wives, were addressed with the creation of the Pilipina Legal Resources Center in Davao, which she founded and headed. Santiago helped push into mainstream government policies such as gender issues, women's access to agricultural investments, and women's role in peace and environment.

SANTIAGO, MIRIAM DEFENSOR (1945–). As a senator (1995–2001) Miriam Defensor Santiago was known for her moral courage in fighting the culture of corruption, and thus has been acclaimed not only by the local but also by the foreign press worldwide. She was named recipient of the 1988 **Magsaysay Award** for government service. She was cited for her bold and moral leadership in cleaning up a corrupt agency—immigration service. As a senator from **Iloilo**, where she was born, her popularity surged after she exposed the **pork barrel** funds known as Congressional Initiative Allocation. Only she refused to get this pork barrel in 1996. She ran for president as an independent candidate in the 1992 election, and lost only by a very slim margin. She tried again in 1998 but could not afford election watchers to protect her votes. In the Senate trial of the then President **Joseph Ejercito Estrada** she voted with other senators who refused to open an envelope that contained evidence of Estrada's alleged money laundering. Because of this she lost her reelection bid for another term. In 1997, she won the landmark case of Santiago versus **COMELEC** in the Supreme Court. As a result, the court stopped a signature campaign for a people's initiative, and thus barred a controversial move to amend the constitution and lift term limits. In the 2004 national election she won her senate seat as a member of President Gloria Macapagal Arroyo's winning party.

SANTOS, ILDEFONSO. *See* NATIONAL ANTHEM.

SANTOS, EPIFANIO DE LOS (1871–1928). Epifanio de los Santos was the first Filipino member of the Spanish Royal Academy in Madrid, Spain. He started his career as a district attorney in **Nueva Ecija**, and was elected in 1902 as governor of the province. He left his post temporarily to become a member of the Philippine Honorary Commission for the Saint Louis Exposition, and from there he traveled through several European countries. During his travels, he spent his time in quest of rare Philippine documents and objects of arts in museums in the great European universities. In 1906, he was provincial fiscal for both provinces of Bulacan and Bataan. In the next 19 years that he held his position, he conducted extensive researches on Philippine history and literature and enriched his Filipiniana collection, thereby establishing his reputation as historian and bibliographer. Owing to his well-known scholarship, he was designated by Governor-General **Francis Burton Harrison** as technical director of the Philippine Census of 1918. He published a collection of stories and sketches, biographies of notable Filipinos, and translated **Francisco Balagtas'** *Florante at Laura* into Spanish. In 1925, he was appointed director of Philippine Library and Museum. *See also* EDSA; RETANA, WENCESLAO.

SANTOS, LOPE K. (1879–1963). Writer and grammarian. As director of the National Language Institute, Santos distinguished himself as a vigorous proponent of the use of **Tagalog** as the national language. He wrote the Tagalog grammar book *Balarila* that became a textbook in public schools and the basis for teaching the national language. In 1940, Commonwealth Act No. 570 was passed making Tagalog, designated as Pilipino, one of the official languages of the Philippines. Earlier in his political career, Santos served as governor of Rizal province, senator, and labor leader. He served also as editor of several Filipino magazines, and he wrote popular novels that have become classics in Filipino literature.

SANTOS, PEDRO ABAD. *See* SOCIALIST PARTY.

SAN ROQUE DAM. This is Southeast Asia's largest private hydropower project—financed by U.S. independent power producers and Japanese banks—along the Agno River, which traverses the provinces of Pangasinan, Benguet, Ifugao, and Nueva Vizcaya. Slated for completion in 2006, the multipurpose dam will be the 12th largest dam in the world and the tallest (200 meters) in Asia and will supply 345-megawatts of power to the burgeoning mining, agribusiness, export industry, and tourism centers of Northwestern Luzon. The dam will irrigate 87,000 hectares of farmland, reduce the perennial flooding of some 16 downstream towns during the rainy season, and provide clean water for communities. The dam project was approved during the administration of President **Fidel Ramos** and considered crucial to attracting foreign investment to the region. Although many countries have stopped building mega dams because of environmental and social costs, the Philippines is one of the few pursuing such infrastructure projects due to its dependence on oil-based power plants, which currently supply 47 percent of the country's electric power. San Roque is one of 22 dams planned for the **Cordillera** region. Presently, there are two existing 175-megawatt dams—Ambuklao and Binga—located upstream of the Agno River, which supply electric power to mining companies and cities as far as Manila. *See also* ENERGY; MARIA CRISTINA FALLS.

SAPRID, SOLOMON (1917–). A National Artist, Saprid engaged excellently in painting and sculpture, although he made his signature works in the latter. His early canvases portrayed religious themes, and some were surrealist in tones. But the subject that has become his virtual trademark is the figure "*Tikbalang*," the centaur of Philippine lower mythology symbolizing male power. One other signature work is the "*Penitensiya*," a monstrous steel statue that depicts a penitent in the act of atoning for his sin by whipping himself. Wielding strips of metal with a blowtorch, he produced a jagged effect along seams where the edges join that resemble ridges of scar tissue. His other masterpiece is the figure of the "Risen Christ" that stands today before the San Antonio Abad Church in Bacolod City. *See also* ARTISTS.

SARANGANI. This is the fifth province created on March 16, 1992, out of the old Cotabato province. The others are **North Cotabato**, **Maguindanao**, **Sultan Kudarat**, and **South Cotabato**. The province—at the southern tip of Mindanao—has seven towns and the capital is Alabel. It has an area of 2,980 square kilometers of rolling hills and mountains that dominate the landscape in the northern areas of coastal municipalities. Mt. Basa, at a height of 2,083 meters, is the highest peak. The estimated population of 400,000 is a mixture of people from various regions and tribes. Cebuano is the most widely spoken language. Ethnic groups represented are Bilaans, Tiboli, Tasgakaulo, and Maguindanao. The main sources of livelihood are farming and fishing. The surrounding waters, particularly Sarangani Bay, are rich fishing grounds. As many as 2,400 species of marine animals have been found in the bay. The dominant catch includes yellow fin tuna, skipjack, and mackerel. An **aquaculture** industry is producing commercial size prawns, **tilapia**, and milkfish that are exported and give the province its significant revenue. *See also* SOCSKSARGEN.

SARI MANOK. *See* OKIR.

SARI-SARI STORE. This is a small neighborhood variety store that sells personal and household items, such as soap, cigarettes, cooking oil, kerosene, salt, fish, vegetables, meat, and schools supplies. *Sari-sari* stores are found in most cities and towns and usually managed by Chinese merchants. *See also* TSINOY.

SAUDI ARABIA. The Philippines has more than 900,000 **Overseas Filipino Workers** in Saudi Arabia engaged in numerous types of jobs. The deployment of these workers has its accompanying problems— complaints ranged from workers' whereabouts to contract violations, including arbitrary arrests and summary executions. Recently, former overseas workers have strongly protested an unfavorable unified contract being imposed on new hires for being onerous to Filipinos. **Amnesty International** has called for the United Nations to break the "wall of silence" surrounding **human rights** abuses in Saudi Arabia. Philippine refineries import 60 percent of their crude oil from Saudi Arabia. The Philippines maintains an embassy in Riyadh. *See also* IRAQ.

SAULO, ALFREDO. *See* REVOLTS.

SAYRE, FRANCIS BOWES (1885–1972). American high commissioner in the Philippines (1939–1942). President Franklin Delano Roosevelt appointed him to succeed **Paul V. McNutt** as U.S. high commissioner to the Philippine commonwealth government. Sayre's appointment coincided with the rise of a militant Japan, which was expanding its economic interests in Southeast Asia, with the Philippines as one of its targets. Though he and General Douglas MacArthur directed considerable attention to the preparation of a national defense plan for the Philippines, Sayre's energies were largely spent on a political imbroglio with the mercurial **Manuel L. Quezon** who, as the president of the commonwealth government, exercised his executive powers with dictatorial abandon. His personal differences with Quezon and intrigues at home greatly handicapped his performance. He escaped from Corregidor with the Quezon family by submarine in February 1942 to Australia and then to the United States.

SCARBOROUGH SHOAL. *See* SPRATLY ISLANDS.

SCHURMAN COMMISSION. At the end of the Philippine–American Revolution in 1901, President William McKinley appointed Jacob Gould Schurman, president of Cornell University, to head a commission to find the most effective way to facilitate American rule in the islands. His civilian team included **Dean Worcester** and Charles Denby. Their hearings in Manila, which heard from only 60 witnesses, mostly wealthy Filipinos and **ilustrados**, produced a flawed report on the prevailing political and economic conditions of the country. The report supported America's supremacy throughout the archipelago, and recommended that Filipinos be allowed limited self-government under U.S. supervision. The Schurman Commission's report was well received by President McKinley, who later sent a Second Philippine Commission, headed by **William Howard Taft**, to further implement his administration's policies. *See also* AVES DE RAPINA.

SCIENCE AND TECHNOLOGY. When **Corazon Aquino** assumed the office of president, she issued orders reorganizing the Department of Science and Technology and made the secretary a member of the cabinet. This mandate provided a vigorous central direction and coordination of scientific and technological policies, plans, and programs to service the public and private sectors. The Technology Application and Promotion Institute was created to serve as the department's implementing arm. However, implementation was hampered by the lack of investment in science and technology programs in areas such as manpower training and research and development facilities. Therefore, the Philippines continued to rely on major industrial technologies imported from abroad. Under the new orders a presidential task force was created to formulate a science and technology master plan for development with the goal of attaining the status of a newly industrialized country. The plan identified 15 leading sectors by which to steer the country to industrial development. Among these sectors were **agriculture**, **aquaculture** and marine fisheries, electronics, forestry and natural resources, mining, and minerals. A performance report of the department showed major progress had been achieved, including marketing of seven new and 68 existing technologies and sharing of 110 new and 400 existing technologies with public and various end-users. Concerning science technology education and training, the report showed that more than 4,000 individuals had been trained and some 50,000 persons were participating in training sessions. Some of the breakthroughs achieved by Filipino **scientists** include development of a chemical to deter the spread of "red tide," a toxic element in shellfish, and extraction of essential oils in plants. *See also* SCIENTISTS; TELECOMMUNICATIONS.

SCIENTISTS. Scientific achievements contributed to the advancement of science and technology in the Philippines. More than 2,000 National Research Council of the Philippines (NRCP) members affirmed the significance of their colleague's scientific accomplishments toward the realization of the government's objective of developing a strong pool of R & D skilled human resource. Among the outstanding scientists who were recognized and their scientific contribution include the following: **Rosalinda C. Solevilla**, pharmaceutical science, for research on the anti-microbial activities, diuretic, analgesic, antipyretic, and anti-inflammatory properties of some Philippine medicinal plants. Her findings contributed significantly in the promotion of the use of medicinal plants as alternative medicines. **Leoncio A. Amadore**, earth science. The scientific works of this atmospheric scientists resulted in an empirical method of forecasting tropical cyclone movement, which has been internationally recognized as the Amadore Method. His technical and scientific articles enriched with scientific information from his meteorological researches on storm surges, tropical cyclones, disaster management cycle, and typhoon climatology were published in scientific journals. **Lilian Lee**, medical science, a neurologist who discovered the causes of a brain disorder known as recessive *dystonia parkinsonism* that became prevalent in the island of **Panay**. **Priscilla C. Sanchez**, biological science, for her two major scientific accomplishments as a parasitologist. First, she discovered two species of bacteria: *caldiverga maquiinensis* and *caldisphaera lagunensis*, that both inhabit the mud-spring in Mount Makiling, Los Baños, **Laguna**. Second, her research on microbial contents of fermented food products that play a vital role in the generation of novel technologies that are now used in the production of health fermented food products, free from disease causing parasites.

SCOTT, WILLIAM HENRY (1928–1993). A former American Episcopal lay missionary assigned in **Sagada**, William Henry Scott distinguished himself in the field of Philippine historiography. His
scholarly and well-documented book (dissertation) invalidated the
Kalantiao penal code as fabrications with no credible historical support. His thesis "Pre-Hispanic Source Materials" debunked well-
loved history myths like the barter trade of Panay and the wave migration theory. William Henry Scott obtained his doctorate in history
at the **University of Santo Tomas**. Later, he became the only non-
Filipino professor of Philippine history at the University of the
Philippines. During the **martial law** he was detained and later released. After his release, Scott went on to write 15 more significant
books on Philippine history and ethnography.

SEA GYPSIES. *See* BAJAU.

SECTORAL PARTIES. There are 77 sectoral parties accredited by the
COMELEC representing marginalized sectors such as fisher folk, urban poor, indigenous cultural communities, elderly, handicapped, veterans, youth, **overseas workers**, and professionals. In the 2004 elections seven sectoral parties fielded candidates, namely: 1. **ABANSE
PINAY** (Onward Filipina), comprised of educated and activist women.
This group believes that all issues are women's issues and women's
representation in politics is crucial for the promotion of women's human rights. Its agenda includes protection of women from violence and
discrimination, promotion of children's rights, and women's equal and
informed participation in governance. 2. **ANG BAGONG PILIPINA**
(The New Filipina). This group believed that educated and skilled
women leaders must take advantage of the new law that gives them the
opportunity to have their own representation in Congress. 3. **BABAYI**,
short for Babae at Bayan, Isulong! (Advocates for Women and Nation).
This group is a national alliance of grassroots, community, and sector-
based women's organizations and individuals. It advocates for a development program for rural women. 4. **GLOW** (Gloria's League of
Women). This group believes in the capability and integrity of the then
President Gloria Macapagal Arroyo and her concept of women-ori-
ented development. To them, she represented a model of political leadership by capable Filipinos. 5. **NATIONAL COUNCIL OF WOMEN**

IN THE PHILIPPINES (NCWP). This group has been representing women, youth, and the family. Its flagship issues ensure that women's programs are integrated in government plans, and communities enjoy the wholeness of life that includes access to basic services and protection of rights. 6. **WOMEN POWER, INC.** This group is composed of leaders of socio-civic groups with links to business. It believes that to advocate women's increased representation in legislature, one must join the realm of mainstream politics, not just through lobbying and advocacy but also through direct participation in the drawing up of laws. 7. **BAYAN MUNA** (Nation First). This is a progressive political party founded on September 25, 1999, to represent the nationalist and democratic aspirations of the Filipino people.

SECULARIZATION. Appointment of Filipino priests in parishes. This was an issue between the Spanish friars and the Filipino priests that had its root cause in a royal decree that gave the various religious orders the right to serve the parishes and thereby discriminated against native clergy. Throughout the period of the Spanish colonial regime, there had been a growing number of qualified Filipino priests who were denied church appointments because of the claim by the friars that they were not fit to take on parish duties. Their resistance to the appointment of Filipino priests was clearly based more on reasons of race than on their fitness for office. This resistance continued for centuries. Friars who held attitudes of overweening arrogance from positions of power preached the Roman Catholic religion to Filipinos. Father Pedro Pelaez, although Spanish, was the first champion of native clergy. He fought for the revocation of the royal decree in the Spanish Cortes, but he died in an earthquake in Manila in 1863. Although there were Filipino priests appointed to parishes, the Filipino clergy considered them as tokens and insufficient in number to satisfy their demands. The move for secularization turned into a nationwide issue when three priests became outspoken leaders: Mariano Gomez, Jose Burgos, and Jacinto Zamora. Spanish authorities accused them of seditious activities and implicated them as leaders of an army mutiny in Cavite. After a farcical trial they were executed by garrote in 1872. Their deaths did not diminish the secularization issue but inspired Filipinos to use the acronym GOMBURZA as a slogan to spark the movement. With its national and racial dimensions, the secularization question became a major factor in the revolution of 1896. *See also* FILIPINIZATION; FRIAROCRACY.

SEDITION LAW. *See* NATIONALISM.

SEGUNDO, FIDEL V. (1894–1944). General and World War II hero. Born in Laoag, **Ilocos Norte**, Segundo was a medical student at the University of the Philippines but left the course for a career in the military. In 1914, he went to West Point, and on his return to the Philippines he was appointed second lieutenant in the **Philippine Scouts**. Thereafter promotions followed: captain in 1920, commandant of cadets in 1932, chief of staff in 1936, and **Philippine Military Academy** superintendent in 1941. When the Japanese invaded the Philippines, Segundo was promoted to brigadier general and commanded a division that fought the Japanese landing forces in Tayabas, now Quezon province. His division was later deployed in Bataan where his troops kept the Japanese at bay until he was ordered to surrender on April 9, 1942. Segundo and his son were later captured by the Japanese and were executed barely two months before the **liberation** of Manila. *See also* LIM, VICENTE.

SHABU (*Methamphetamine Hydrochloride***, Chemical Ice, Crank, Crystal, Glass, Chalk).** Shabu, a powerfully addictive stimulant, is the drug of choice of over 90 percent of Filipino drug users. This illicit drug comes from China-based syndicates using Hong Kong and Taiwan as transshipment points. Shabu was mainly a drug used by the fringe literati, artists, and entertainment circle, but due to its easy availability it has filtered down to the masses and rural culture. A survey of youth aged 15–30 by the Social Weather Stations (SWS) showed 7 percent with drug use and 6 percent with drug pushing.

SHAFI MUSLIMS. *See* SHARIA.

SHAHANI, LETICIA RAMOS (1930–). A former senator, Ramos Shahani was a career ambassador. She was the first Philippine ambassador assigned to a communist country, Romania, the first Filipino assistant secretary of the United Nations, and secretary general of the Third World United Nations Conference on Women held in Nairobi, Kenya, in 1985. Throughout her career, Ramos Shahani has focused on foreign policy, social development, and the role of women. *See also* RAMOS, FIDEL.

SHARIA. In 1977, President Ferdinand Marcos decreed that Sharia Islamic Law should be part of the national law. A Code of Muslim Personal Law was promulgated that covered issues on family such as divorce, paternity, filiations, marriage registration, succession, and constitution. Sharia law applies only to Muslims, and applies regardless of their place of residence in the country. Muslims of the Philippines are Shafi. The national law handles conflicts between Muslims and non-Muslims. The Islamic court is under the supervision of the Philippine Supreme Court. *See also* PENAL LAW.

SHARIF KABUNGSUAN. A legendary Malay Muslim who brought precolonial Islamic civilization to mainland Mindanao. Coming to Mindanao around 1515 or about a decade after the fall of Malacca to the Portuguese, Sharif Kabungsuan landed first in Malabang (now Lanao del Sur) and proceeded to Cotabato. After converting the local chieftains to Islam, he continued to preach the faith to the known and inhabited areas of Mindanao. Out of his marital union with the Iranum and Maguindanao ruling class, he laid the foundations of the Maguindanao and Buayan sultanates. Kabungsuan's persona is clothed with an aura of mystery. Save for the firm claims of Maguindanaon indigenous tradition and hints from recorded history elsewhere, his origins and identity have bordered on anonymity. However, Sharif Kabungsuan's lineage is asserted by the Maguindanao *tarsila* (genealogy) and believed by generations of Maguindanaons as originating from a Sharif Zainal Abidin, who married into Malacca/Melaka or Johore royalty. Nevertheless, officials of Cotabato City in the mid-1970s honored Sharif Kabungsuan with a law designating every 19th of December as "Sharif Kabungsuan Day." Presently this is officially declared a holiday in the **Autonomous Region in Muslim Mindanao** and celebrated with cultural presentations, symposia, street-dancing, fluvial parade, and Koran-reading contest. *See also* SULTAN KUDARAT.

SIERRA MADRE. This is the Philippines' longest mountain range. It stretches from Cagayan province in northeastern Luzon to Aurora province in southern Tagalog.

SIKATUNA, DATU. *See* BLOOD COMPACT.

SILANG, DIEGO (1730–1763). Legendary revolutionary leader in Ilocos. Born in Aringay, La Union Silang was a *sacristan* (altar boy) in the church. He worked his way up to become a trusted courier between Vigan and Manila and was in the metropolis when the British occupied the city in October 1762. When he returned to Vigan he saw an opportunity to lead a revolt against the Spanish taskmasters. He told the people that they should stop paying tribute to the Spanish government and making contributions to and performing personal services for the friars. Many people responded and an army was raised. The revolt spread to Pangasinan and Cagayan provinces. His forces captured Vigan and held it for a short time when Silang was betrayed by a follower and subsequently killed. His widow **Gabriela**, who had accompanied him on the battlefield, took over command of the rebel forces. Diego Silang is remembered as a hero of the Ilocanos. *See also* PALARIS, JUAN DE LA CRUZ.

SILANG, JOSEFA GABRIELA (1731–1763). Widow of Diego Silang, who led the Ilocos uprising in 1763. Gabriela assumed leadership of the rebellion against Spain after the assassination of her husband. At 32, she led a force of 2,000 men armed only with *bolos* (machetes), head axes, and spears, and captured Vigan, Ilocos Sur. However, a more powerful force of Spanish and native soldiers defeated her ill-equipped army. She was captured and hanged with 80 of her men. In the history of revolts against Spain, Gabriela is the only woman to lead an uprising, and thus she has earned the title "Joan of Arc" of Ilocandia. *See also* REVOLTS.

SILLIMAN UNIVERSITY. *See* NEGROS ISLAND; SIQUIJOR.

SILVA, JUAN DE. *See* DUTCH.

SIMUNUL. *See* TAWI-TAWI.

SIN, JAIME CARDINAL (1928–). Archbishop of Manila. Sin played a key role in the downfall of President Ferdinand Marcos. Named a cardinal in 1976 by Pope Paul VI, Sin came into prominence in 1986, when he actively intervened in the presidential contest between Marcos and **Corazon Aquino** by his radio address urging hundreds of thousands of people to go to Camps Aguinaldo and Crame and physically prevent the Marcos forces from crushing the coup leaders, **Juan Ponce Enrile** and **Fidel Ramos** and their followers. What could have been a bloody encounter was averted. His intervention changed the outcome of the elections and led to the Aquino presidency. Later his influence also saved Aquino from being toppled from power in the 1989 coup attempt.

As a Roman Catholic prelate Sin was morally outraged by the manifold violations of human rights during the martial law years of the Marcos administration. He increasingly criticized the Marcos regime for its indifference to the plight of the poor. He also became vocal about the violence and cheating that characterized national elections. Thus, Sin caught the ire of President Marcos and First Lady **Imelda Marcos** that led to an open break in the 1986 **snap elections** and eventual defeat of Marcos. The Cardinal kept up his activism in political elections by urging the faithful to elect upright politicians. Due to ill health, he resigned as Archbishop of Manila in 2003 and was succeeded by Archbishop **Gaudencio Rosales** of **Batangas**. *See also* NATIONAL SECRETARIAT FOR SOCIAL ACTION; ROSALES, GAUDENCIO.

SINGAPORE. Diplomatic relations with Singapore were established in 1969. The Philippines enjoys warm and friendly relations with this city-state in the Malaysian peninsula and cooperates well on a range of issues at the international and regional level. Their bilateral ties are exceptionally strong on economic, arts and cultural matters. In 1998, the Philippine–Singapore Plan (PSP) was set up as a broad-based umbrella framework that covers co-operation in various areas including trade, investment, information technology, capital market development, education, culture, defense, and people-to-people exchanges. The Philippine–Singapore Air Pact has bolstered air travel between the two countries by more flights and increased passenger seats. A Bayanihan Center was built in Singapore with funds provided by the Singaporean government, which was inaugurated by

President Gloria Macapagal Arroyo while she was on state visit. The center serves as a place for vocational training and recreation of Filipino workers—about 130,000—in Singapore. As the major trading partner, Singapore is the leading investor in the Philippines with an investment of $55 million.

SINGKIL. This is the famous dance of Muslim Mindanao that is characterized by vivid colors and rhythmic movements, which reflect the influence of Indo–Malaysian culture. Singkil takes its name from the bells worn on the ankles of the Muslim princess. Considered one of the oldest of Filipino dances, Singkil recounts the epic legend of *"Darangen"* of the Maranao people. The epic recounts the fate of a princess who was caught in the middle of a forest during an earthquake caused by *diwatas* (fairies). The crisscrossed bamboo poles represent the trees that were falling, which she gracefully avoids. Her slave loyally accompanies her throughout the ordeal. Finally, a prince saves her. Dancers skillfully manipulate *apir* (fans), which represent the winds that prove to be auspicious. There are at least three versions of the singkil: one using two bamboo poles, one using four poles, and a complicated version with eight poles, all placed in criss-cross fashion. Singkil is the signature dance of the **Bayanihan Dance Company**. *See also* TINIKLING; URTULA, LUCRECIA.

SINGSON, LUIS CHAVIT (1941–). He is the **Ilocos Sur** governor who dropped a bombshell on President **Joseph Ejercito Estrada** in October 2000 that unraveled his presidency. Although a long-time buddy in politics, Singson revealed all in a sworn statement about the nationwide **jueteng** game in which Estrada and his son (Jose) were raking millions of pesos. Before Singson made his revelation he first obtained the blessings of Cardinal **Jaime Sin** who counseled him to bring the matter to the people. This led to the nationwide demonstrations for Estrada's resignation that prompted Congress to pass the impeachment bill. Estrada was charged with the crime of **plunder**, a nonbailable crime that carries the death penalty. Singson was granted immunity during his testimony in Congress. Estrada and his son have been incarcerated since 2002 and are awaiting the final verdict. Singson was reelected governor in the 2004 elections.

SINULOG. A lively annual festival held on the third Sunday of January by Cebuanos for the feast of their patron saint, the Señor Santo Niño, which draws thousands—including foreign tourists from 16 sister cities—to Cebu City, known as the "Queen City of the South." The tradition is deeply rooted in Cebuano culture and the weeklong mardigras-like celebration features dance contests, marching bands, costume competitions, beauty contests, pop music, street dancing, and fluvial procession. *Sinulog* kicks off with a holy mass at the Basilica Minore de Santo Niño, home to Cebu's celebrated Christ Child image that **Magellan** gave to Queen Juana (wife of **Rajah Humabon**) in 1521. *Sinulog*, the ritual dance evokes the movement of the river current "sulog" with a two-step forward and one-step backward in tune to the primal beat of native goatskin drums. When the Spaniards conquered Cebu, the dance evolved into an ethnic expression of thanksgiving and revelry. *See also* BLACK NAZARENE; MORIONES.

SIPA. An ancient Filipino game played with a *sapatilla* (rivet washer) gaily plumed with *papel de hapon* (thin colored paper) or a ball made of **rattan** or wicker. The ball is kicked (*sipa*) across a net by one or a team of players. Scoring is patterned after volleyball. Coordinated muscle work, discipline, timing, and a little flourish are the basic skills of the game. A variety of kicking styles is used to maneuver the ball over the net with carefully controlled speed and direction. *See also* ARNIS; SPORTS.

SIQUIJOR. The second smallest island province in the Philippines, it covers a land area of 343 square kilometers and is located 20 kilometers off the southeast tip of Negros. It is densely populated with approximately 80,970 people. The Cebuano language is the native tongue. This former subprovince of Negros Oriental is dubiously noted for its reputed witchcraft, **herbal medicine**, magic, and superstition. A collection of witch paraphernalia is exhibited at the Silliman University's Anthropology Museum in Dumaguete City, Negros Island. The island is hilly and replete with limestone, but the fertile soil in the valleys supports the production of rice, corn, and many root crops. The main occupations of the people are farming and fishing. The major towns are Siquijor, Maria, Larena, and Lazi. *See also* BATANES.

SISON, JOSE MARIA. *See* KAAKBAY; MAOISM; NEW PEOPLES' ARMY.

SISON, TEOFILO. *See* COLLABORATION ISSUE.

SMITH, JAMES F. (1859–1928). American governor-general in the Philippines (1906–1909). Smith was born in San Francisco and obtained his education in Roman Catholic schools. He earned his law degree from Hastings College of Law in San Francisco and became a partner of a law firm in the bay area. Smith came to the Philippines as a colonel of the California Volunteer Regiment, which fought the Spanish and Filipino forces in Manila. For his valor in leading his regiment, Smith was promoted to brigadier general and was appointed military governor of Negros Island. He distinguished himself with his tact and diplomacy in dealing with the restive hacienderos, who wanted to preserve their wealth and status. When the civil government was established, Smith was appointed an associate justice of the Philippine Supreme Court. After a year and a half, President **William Howard Taft** prevailed on him to serve as one of the Philippine commissioners with the responsibility for the portfolio of public instruction. He was appointed governor-general to replace **Henry Clay Ide**, who was sent to Spain as U.S. ambassador. During his three-year (1906–1909) tenure as the chief executive of the islands, Smith encouraged the presence of Filipino officials in elected and nonelected positions in the government. *See also* HARRISON, FRANCIS BURTON.

SNAP ELECTION. In early 1985 a number of American newsmen and two U.S. senators were in Manila to find out how **Ferdinand Marcos** was dealing with the worsening political imbroglio of his regime. George Will, an American political columnist, interviewing Marcos at Malacañang Palace, asked the president about his reported loss of mandate and what he planned to do. Marcos' response was that he was willing to move up the election date by calling a "snap" presidential election. He still had two years of his term to go but Marcos, confident of victory, figured he could use the election to bolster his sagging mandate and prove to President Ronald Reagan that he was still in charge. The snap election was held February 7, 1986, with Marcos as the candidate of his party *Kilusang Bagong Lipunan* (New Society Movement), and Cory Aquino, as the candidate of a united opposition. Because of his debilitating disease, Marcos was not actively involved in the campaign, which was waged by his trusted lieutenants. The election campaign was marred by charges of intimidation, massive vote buying, and killings. Observers from the United States led by Senator Richard Lugar confirmed rampant chicanery by Marcos' people. These charges were revealed in the counting of the ballots. While **NAMFREL**, an independent monitor, reported Cory ahead, COMELEC, the official Commission on Elections, delayed its count to enable Marcos political chiefs to manipulate the tally and went on to declare Marcos the winner. The Batasang Pambansa, which was held by Marcos supporters, promptly confirmed Marcos' election.

This ignited nationwide violent demonstrations by Aquino's followers. Aquino incited the boycott of all **crony** establishments, nonpayment of taxes, and other forms of civil disobedience. Two of the administration's highest officials deserted Marcos and joined Aquino's camp. Manila became a battleground of the two opposing sides. In spite of these developments, Marcos arranged the announcement of his proclamation to relinquish the presidency at Malacañang Palace on February 25, attended by his own family and a few political supporters. Having accepted an offer of safe transport by the United States that same day, Marcos, and his family, boarded an American helicopter and flew in the evening to Clark Air Base, where they took a U.S. transport plane for Hawaii and a life in exile.

SOCIAL CLASSES. Ancient Filipino society in the **Tagalog** region was divided into social classes—nobles, freemen, and serfs. The nobles were the ruling class, and they carried the title of *Gat* or *Lakan*. Membership in this class was hereditary. Next to the nobles were the freemen, people who achieved their status by purchase or grant from their masters. Below this class were the serfs or servants, people who were acquired by captivity in battle, by failing to pay debts, or by being pronounced guilty of a crime. The serfs composed the largest number in a community. They served their masters as household helps (*aliping namamahay*), or as farmers (*aliping sagigilid*) and their main job was planting and harvesting crops. The position of Filipino **women** before the arrival of the Spaniards was high. The custom of that period made women the equal of men. They could own and inherit property and sell it; they could engage in trade; and they could succeed to the chieftainship of the community or **barangay**. Wives also enjoyed the right to give names to their children. In most cases, woman of one class married into the same class. A man could marry as many women as he could support. *See also* WOMEN.

SOCIAL VALUES. Filipinos are bound together by traditional values or ethical rules that are deeply rooted in their Asian psyche, and distinctly Filipino in character. These values define personal alliances and ritual kinship violations, which cause perpetrators to incur the social disfavor of loss of face or being shunned. Loyalty, support, and trust begin first within the nuclear family and extend to persons who are connected by ceremonial affiliations of baptism, confirmation, and marriage. Persons who are within the bonds of a nuclear family and ceremonial affiliations are bound to observe *utang na loob*, literally translated as "debt of gratitude," by which a member who incurs a favor, whether big or small, from another member is expected to reciprocate in one form or another. *Utang na loob* governs a patron-client relationship, as in the case of a tenant-landlord or a ward politician to supporters. Closely connected with this concept is the value of *pakikisama*, group cooperation or camaraderie. Individuals who are members of a barangay, company, or club are expected to give their loyalty to the organization and sacrifice their personal interests or ambitions for its well-being and smooth interpersonal relationships. Overshadowing these values is the concept of *hiya*, i.e., shame or loss of face. Those who fail to observe *utang na loob* or *pakikisama* suffer society's sanction of *walang hiya* (no shame or loss of face.) The person is censured, expelled from the group, or totally shunned. *See also* PATRONAGE POLITICS; POLITICAL DYNASTY; POLITICAL PARTIES.

SOCIALIST PARTY/PARTIDO SOCIALISTA. Organized in 1929 by Pedro Abad Santos (1876–1948) in **Pampanga** province. Son of a landowning family, Abad Santos was a lawyer who served two terms as congressman of his district. The platform of the Socialist party was no different from that of the Communist party, which advocated the redistribution of lands (five hectares [12.4 acres] per farmer) and the abolition of capitalism. The socialists actively promoted class warfare, strikes, and the formation of a classless society. The socialists believed in the power of the ballot and encouraged labor unions to carry out party objectives. Through their representatives in Congress they secured the passage of legislation, which guaranteed better working conditions for sugar mill workers and farm tenants in central Luzon. The Socialist party merged with the **Communist Party** of the Philippines in 1938. *See also* KASAMA; SAKDALISTA.

SOCSKSARGEN. The acronym for the city and provinces that comprise it—**South Cotabato**, **Sultan Kudarat**, **Sarangani**, and General Santos. Government economic analysts have identified this region as one of the seven fastest growing economic zones in southern Mindanao. The area is a major agricultural and fisheries center that produces a wide variety of products for domestic and international consumption—**pineapple**, banana, asparagus, tuna, grains, and livestock. General Santos is the business hub with tuna canneries, livestock farms, meat and seafood processing plants. Large yellow fin tuna (sashimi grade) are landed and processed daily and quickly exported to Japan. Its international airport is one of the largest in the Philippines and is equipped to handle wide-body jets. Makar Port, which lies directly on international shipping routes, has a container-handling terminal, livestock-holding yards, and refrigeration facilities. *See also* CARAGA REGION.

SOHOTAN NATIONAL PARK. *See* SAMAR, WESTERN.

SOLANO. *See* NUEVA VIZCAYA.

SOLARZ, STEPHEN. *See* KLEPTOCRACY.

SOLEVILLA, ROSALINDA. *See* SCIENTISTS.

SORIANO, EDWARD. *See* FILIPINO–AMERICAN GENERALS.

SORSOGON. This province covers 2,141 square kilometers on the Bicol Peninsula at the southernmost tip of Luzon. Its capital city is also named Sorsogon. The population of 515,000 is composed of a mixture of Bicol, Waray-waray, and Visayan-speaking people. Its terrain is rugged, with Mt. Bulusan, an active volcano, and the highest point. **Abaca** is the main crop, but coconuts, corn, sugarcane, and pili nuts are also produced. The province lies at the heart of the typhoon belt, and typhoon damage is a major factor in the dynamics of the province's economy.

SOUTH COTABATO. A province situated in southern Mindanao, created by partitioning off the southern part of the former Cotabato province. South Cotabato covers 7,469 square kilometers and has a population of 775,000, mostly migrants from the Visayas and Luzon. The capital, Koronadal (formerly called Marbel), is situated in a fertile valley planted with **pineapples** and **bananas**, the province's chief export products. Plantations employ thousands of workers. South Cotabato province is the home of several ethnic tribes including the Tiboli, Ubo, B'laan, Tagabili, and **Tasaday** the most numerous being the **Tibolis** of whom there are about 200,000 inhabiting the Tiruray Highlands (Kematu mountain ranges). The Tibolis are noted for their colorful handwoven dresses and jackets made out of abaca fiber. The landscape of south Cotabato is dominated by Mt. Matutum (2,293 meters), an extinct volcano, around the base of which are extensive pineapple plantations. The province has 11 municipalities.

SOUTH KOREA. Relations with this Land of the Morning Calm was established in 1949 and since then the two countries have positively supported each other on the issues of politics, national security, and **foreign policy**. South Korea has been especially interested and involved in the development aspects of the Philippines. Over the years South Korea has especially offered its economic and technological support to the Philippines. It has lent funds for the construction of infrastructure projects, funded socioeconomic programs of a number of nongovernmental organizations, and set up training programs of Filipino medical personnel. One particular project that had caught national attention was the Philippine–Korean Friendship Hospital in

Trece Martires city, Cavite. South Korea provided $3.8 million to build the 160-bed hospital.

One area of heightened South Korea–Philippine cooperation is **energy** development. With the Philippines' Department of Energy (DoE) and the Korean Electric Power Corporation (KEPCO) taking the lead, South Korean expertise and technology has been deployed in the country to assist in the strategic electrification or energy development campaign of the administration. In 2004, a number of power plants were inaugurated by DoE and KEPCO in Batangas and Panay. Most recently, the DoE and KEPCO signed another deal to set up a 200-megawatt coal-fired plant in Cebu. A recent state visit of President Gloria Macapagal Arroyo netted $335 million in business agreements, which included the construction of a 100-megawatt power plant in Antique and $100 million for economic development and vocational training. The Philippines has diplomatic relations with both Koreas. During the Korean conflict (1950–1952) the Philippines sent three combat teams that served under the UN command. There are some 10,000 Filipino **Overseas Foreign Workers** in South Korea. *See also* PHILIPPINE EXPEDITIONARY FORCE TO KOREA (PEFTOK).

SOUTHERN LEYTE. A province in the eastern Visayas, which includes Limasawa and Panaon islands, has a combined land area of 1,735 square kilometers and a total population of 310,000. The capital of Maasin is the provincial trading center and port. The two islands are surrounded by fish-rich Sogod Bay. **Limasawa** Island is the site of a national shrine, which contains Magellan's cross and commemorates the celebration of the first Catholic mass in the Philippines in 1521. The main towns are Malitbog, Macrohon, Sogod, and Padre Burgos.

SPANISH COLONIAL REGIME. Spain ruled the Philippines as a colony from 1521 to 1899. At the head of this government was the governor-general who was appointed to and removed from office by the king and subject only to the **royal audencia** and Council of the Indies, which had legislative, executive, and judicial powers. The governor-general, who represented the crown, also had similar powers in the administration of the islands. He was charged with the defense of the colony against the Portuguese, Dutch, and English. Alongside the governor-general was the archbishop of Manila, an ecclesiastical leader who wielded tremendous political power, which in turn was also exercised by parish priests. For political administration the country was divided into provinces. A province had a *cabecera* (capital) and **pueblos** (municipalities), which were in turn made up of **barangays**. At each level of political administration there was a civilian official and a friar administrator. The functions of the *gobernadorcillo* (town head) basically entailed the collection of tributes or taxes, whereas the *cura* (priests) were in charge of the education and religious upbringing of the population. For law enforcement there was the **guardia civil** under the direct command of the governor-general. The *hacienda publica*, a central administrative body presided over by the governor-general, was responsible for the operational burdens of public administration, such as collection and accounting of all revenue due to the national treasury. The *hacienda publica* also approved and allocated monies for public works (roads and bridges). For over 333 years, the Philippines was a crown colony of Spain. Until 1821, when the Mexicans revolted and won independence from Spain, the Philippines was a dependency of Mexico, being administered by the viceroy in the name of the king. From 1821 to 1898, the country was a distinct government unit under the direct control of the home government in Madrid. There were important changes made before the Spanish colonial rule came to its end in 1899, but the basic framework remained the same. Although the Filipinos were given positions, they generally had little opportunity to participate in their own government, which was one of the major causes of the **Philippine–Spanish Revolution**. *See also* RELIGIOUS ORDERS; ROMAN CATHOLIC CHURCH.

SPANISH GOVERNOR-GENERAL. At the top of the centralized government established by Spain in the Philippines was the governor-general, who represented the king of Spain. He exercised great powers—executive, military, judicial, and religious. In his capacity as governor, he had the right to control and supervise administrative offices and appoint officials not named by the king. He was president of the **royal audiencia** or supreme court, and he was in charge of ecclesiastical matters, as he assumed ecclesiastical authority over the church, office and missions. During the 378 years of Spanish colonial rule, there were 63 governors-general. *See also* REVOLTS.

SPARROW SQUADS. These are the extremists within the New Peoples' Army who targeted prominent government officials, citizens, and Americans for assassination. Working in groups of three, they would hit their target in a lightning fashion and then disappear. One of their victims was U.S. Colonel James Rowe, chief of the ground forces division of the Joint U.S. Military Assistance Group (JUSMAG) killed in April 1989. The perpetrators were later apprehended by a joint force of Philippine military troops and American intelligence units. An offshoot of this incident was the formation of **vigilante** groups, which fought the sparrow squads. The vigilantes were civilians, who were provided armaments by the armed forces; most of them were actually private armies of politicians. Because of their rampant abuses of **human rights**, the armed forces disbanded many of the vigilante groups.

SPOLARIUM. Juan Luna's world famous painting, which depicts fallen gladiators being dragged to an unseen pile of corpses in a chamber beneath the Roman arena. "Spolarium" was painted in Madrid and won a gold medal at the Exposicion Nacional de Belles Artes in 1884, also in Spain. The oil on canvas painting measures four meters high by seven meters wide. Today, the Luna masterpiece hangs in the **National Museum**, Manila. One of the other Luna masterpieces was the "Death of Cleopatra" painted in 1880 that won second place in the Madrid Exposition, which is on exhibit at the Museo Nacional de Pinturas in Madrid. *See also* AYALA MUSEUM; LOPEZ MUSEUM.

SPORTS. The national unofficial sport of the Philippines is basketball. The game is so popular among the Filipinos that virtually every **barangay** in the community has at least one basketball court. **Sipa**, however, is considered the national sport. Among the sports where Filipinos have gained international recognition are billiards (notably nine ball), ten-pin, bowling, and chess. The *Palarong Pambansa*, a national sports event involving public and private tertiary schools, is held annually in various regions. It serves as a national Olympics for students with victors from competition at the provincial and regional levels. Competitive sports are archery, badminton, baseball, boxing, chess, gymnastics, tennis, soccer, softball, swimming, table tennis, taekwondo, track and field, volleyball, and sipa. Most modern sports in the Philippines were introduced by the Americans only in the 20th century. Filipinos for centuries have developed and perfected games like *arnis de mano* or *dumog* (wrestling), *sikaran* (martial arts), *patintero* (football), *siato* (baseball), *moro-moro* (long jump), *luksong baka* (high jump), *paligsahan kalabaw* (equestrian), *bato bato* (relay), and *dama* (chess). Other native sports in the country are *bunong braso* (arm wrestling), *luksong tinik* (jump the spine), *luksong lubid* (jump rope), and *sumpit* (blow gun).

SPRATLY ISLANDS. Since the discovery of oil on these islands in the South China Sea six countries have claimed the islands as part of their territories. The Philippines was the first claimant since it was found in 1956 by Tomas Cloma, a Filipino lawyer, who called it **Kalayaan Islands** (Freedom Islands). China contested the claim and other countries followed: Malaysia, Brunei, Vietnam, and Taiwan. Besides Spratly Islands, other disputed territories, mostly uninhabited, in the area include the Scarborough Shoal, claimed by the Philippines and China, and the Paracel Islands, also disputed by China and Vietnam. So far the battle of sovereign claims has been tempered by the landmark **Association of Southeast Nations (ASEAN)** agreement, although nonbinding and signed in Hanoi on November 2002 on the conduct of parties in the contested islands. Under the agreement, the six claimant-states pledged to exercise self-restraint and not to occupy uninhabited land features in the South China Sea and to resolve the territorial and jurisdictional disputes through peaceful means in accordance with international laws. The International Court of Justice awarded two tiny islands—Ligatan and Sipadan in the Celebes Sea—to Malaysia on the principle of "effectiveness" and not on sovereignty. Malaysia had effective control over these islands for over 80 years.

SRI VIJAYA (650–1377). For more than 600 years, the Buddhist kingdom of Sri Vijaya was the strongest of the Straits kingdoms. Sri Vijaya was located at Palembang in southern Sumatra facing out on the

Sunda Straits. The kingdom is first recorded in 650 A.D. as having conquered the west Java kingdom of Taruma. By 686, Sri Vijaya had asserted its dominance over the Sunda Straits and the adjacent Javanese kingdoms. A century later, in 775, it had similarly dominated the Straits of Malacca and commanded tribute from all the kingdoms along its shores. It attained monopoly control over the trade through the Straits and then imposed its demands by a special ruthlessness in suppressing rivals and discouraging interlopers. By the late 10th century, the Javanese kingdoms were mounting a serious challenge to Sri Vijaya's hegemony; so much so that in 992 it sent a mission to China seeking protection from its enemies. The India Chola states attacked Sri Vijaya in 1017, 1025, and again in 1068. By 1200, Sri Vijaya had lost control over several of its principal tributaries on the Malay Peninsula and Sumatra. From about this time in the Philippines comes the historical legend of the Ten Datus from **Sabah** who settled in the Visayas sometime around 1212. The Ten Datus were escaping from a tyrannical ruler of Borneo. *See also* MAJAPAHIT; SUMAKWEL.

STA. MARIA, FELICE PRUDENTE (1950 –). A tenacious advocate of cultural development for value education, Felice Prudente Sta. Maria was instrumental in intensifying people's understanding and appreciation of the museum as a learning center in the Philippines. She pioneered a distinct brand of museum pedagogy, focusing her efforts on conveying learning, skills, and value to allow Filipinos, especially school children, to fulfill their potential. In her view, museum education could serve as a support and viable alternative to the traditional educational structure. Accordingly, she developed guidelines geared toward these goals. So far-reaching were the goals that programs at the Metropolitan Museum, Manila, continue to conform to the same standards. Further, she began a bilingual approach in museum program, highlighting Filipino ideals for the public, convinced as she was of the merits of **Filipino** as a medium of communication and instruction. Again this strengthened her standing as a trailblazer in the field of museum management. She reiterated these same criteria and principles in the re-tooling of the National Centennial Committee Freedom Trail. A tireless champion of the need for professionalism in museum work, she accented the need for employees to continuously improve their skills as they maintain the highest of stan-

STATE COLLEGES AND UNIVERSITIES • 387

dards in the workplace. Her work with both the International Council of Museums (ICOM) Philippines, a UNESCO affiliate, and the National Committee on Museums (NCOM), gave her the latitude to achieve two important ends: restructure the NCOM to more closely parallel the ICOM and sustain its reinvigorated participation in the operation of the international council.

Along with her commitment to museum work, Sta. Maria Prudente stands as a multiawarded publisher and writer, having penned diverse works ranging from biographies to children's literature to cultural volumes. One of her outstanding works *In Excelsis* pays homage to the accomplishments of **Jose Rizal** through beautiful photographs and powerful narrative. Her book *Visions of the Possible: Legacies of Philippine Freedom* brings out unforgettable vignettes, rare photographs, and other symbols of patriotism, and celebrates how an awakened people learns to adapt new forms of democracy to its continually transforming needs and expectations. *See also* AYALA MUSEUM; LOPEZ MUSEUM.

ST. VINCENT FERRER CHURCH. One of the oldest and biggest churches in North Luzon found in Dupax del Sur, **Nueva Vizcaya**. The Augustinian friars constructed St. Vincent church in the 16th century. It features a bell tower that is among the well-preserved Spanish colonial monuments and an ecclesiastical museum. Beside the church is what is acclaimed as the oldest acacia tree (*semanea-saman*) in Luzon, planted by settlers from Nueva Ecija in 1880. *See also* MIAGAO CHURCH.

STATE COLLEGES AND UNIVERSITIES (SCU). A string of institutions of higher learning distributed in 80 provinces. There are 108 SCUs all over the Philippines, which is almost one college or university for every province. Most of these colleges were former agricultural schools. Their conversion into tertiary educational systems was primarily through the sponsorship of their congressmen. The government funds all of these converted institutions. The flagship of the state colleges and universities is the University of the Philippines, Diliman, which gets the lion's share of the total budget of higher **education**. As a result, the budget allocation for teaching materials and aids has become smaller and consequently affected the quality of education of some these provincial institutions. *See also* CAMPOS, PAULO.

STIMSON, HENRY L. (1867–1950). American governor-general in the Philippines (1928–1929). A Harvard law graduate, Stimson worked in Elihu Root's law office in Manhattan. During World War I, he served briefly in France as a colonel in the field artillery. As President **William Howard Taft's** secretary of war (1911–1912), he exercised general authority over the Philippines. When Leonard Wood died, Stimson was appointed governor-general and served only for a year. During his short tenure, he worked successfully with Filipino leaders, such as **Manuel L. Quezon** and **Sergio Osmeña**, for the passage of legislative bills that strengthened the executive branch in its control of public health, finance, and law and order. Early in 1929, Stimson went back to the U.S. to become secretary of state in the cabinet of President Herbert Hoover.

STUDENT MOVEMENT. The student protest movement in the early 1970s was directed against the United States, the war effort in Vietnam, and the worsening economic conditions of the Filipino workers in rural and urban areas. Led by student leaders from various private and public universities in Manila, the movement quickly spread across the country. For a time, **martial law** put a damper on the students, but their activities gained momentum as the martial law period came to an end. Then the protest movement came to life again during the **Corazon Aquino** administration. Aroused by wanton abuse of civil rights by the military, students led street demonstrations and strikes before the Malacañang Palace and the United States embassy. The protest before the United States embassy was against the continued presence of U.S. military bases. The student movement dissipated when they joined forces with the more militant labor unions and nongovernmental agencies. During the U.S-led Iraqi war student activism resurrected and protests and demonstrations were held before the U.S. embassy in Manila and other cities. As a consequence President Gloria Macapagal Arroyo was forced to withdrew the Philippine troops.

SUBANON. A tribe inhabiting the eastern portion of the Zamboanga Peninsula in Zamboanga del Sur province. The Subanons are swidden agriculturists and live in scattered villages near their small plots where they raise their main staple crop of rice plus a variety of root vegetables. They practice a dry-field method of agriculture in which no plow or hoe is used. Their society is governed by datus, but no effective political organization has developed to counter exploitation from outside. A peace-loving people, they seldom resist raids of marauding brigands on their villages. They are widely known for their feasts and rituals, which are marked by dancing, singing, gong playing, and story telling. At the core of Subanon life is a complex cosmology featuring supernatural beings that require frequent offerings, which always include food products and a betel chew. Subanon society is monogamous. Families generally arrange marriages. The influx of Christian missionaries has made profound changes in their lifestyle and religious orientation. *See also* PAILALAM RI BORAK; SANDAYO.

SUBIC BAY. Former site of the largest naval base of the United States in the Far East. It was located in southern **Zambales** province. The inlet has one of the finest harbors in the Philippines and was developed by the United States Navy to serve its fleet in the region. During the Vietnam War, Subic Bay Naval Base and Clark Air Base were staging areas for United States military activities. In 1966, the Philippine government renegotiated the 99-year lease to 25 years, which expired in 1991. The Subic Bay Naval Base became a hot political issue to the Filipinos, who saw the base as an infringement upon their sovereignty. The United States tried to negotiate an extension of the lease, but the Filipinos were in no mood to compromise. They indicated their displeasure by continuing demonstrations before the American Embassy. The Philippine Senate rejected the extension plan embodied in an earlier base agreement. The naval base dry dock and other facilities were dismantled and transported to Hawaii. The base previously had covered 13,000 hectares (32,110 acres) of virgin forest and employed 20,000 Filipino workers. Since the turnover of the base to the Philippine government, the facility has been converted to a free port, which has attracted some $2 billion worth of investments. Under the management of the Subic Bay Metropolitan Authority, the former naval base with its deepwater port has been converted into the new manufacturing center for Southeast Asia. *See also* BASE CONVERSION DEVELOPMENT AUTHORITY; OLONGAPO.

SUBING. *See* BALITAO.

SUFFRAGIST MOVEMENT (1898–1937). The active and prominent role of **women** in the revolution propelled the Filipina to a new role in the arena of politics and legislation during the American administration. The suffragist movement brought to the fore the activism of women who formed associations and organizations to advocate their cause. Members of these groups, who attended the public hearings of the Committee on suffrage of the Constitutional Convention of 1934, published informative articles in various native-language publications to spread their issues and formed the General Council of Women to coordinate their activities. The advocates succeeded in their campaign because Article V of the 1934 Constitution extended suffrage to women provided that 300,000 women qualified to vote would vote for the right. An intensive campaign ensued for the plebiscite on April 30, 1937. The result was that they managed to exceed the requirement— 447,725 yes against 44,307 no votes. On September 17, 1937, **Manuel Quezon** signed the law granting Filipino women universal suffrage.

SUGAR INDUSTRY. Sugarcane and coconuts are the leading commercial crops in the Philippines. The Spaniards introduced sugarcane as a subsistence crop to the Negros Occidental area in the 1800s. With the introduction of machinery by a British businessman the Spanish recognized its potential as an export crop. By the 1850s, Negros Occidental was the leading sugar producing province. Sugar production was built on the **hacienda** system where laborers are tied to the farm by means of sharecropping and debt relations. The rich sugar families, all with Spanish roots, created a classic *haciendero* system much like the Latin American model. This system prevailed until the American administration. From the mid-19th century to the mid-1970s, sugar was the most important agricultural export of the Philippines. The island of Negros was still the principal sugarcane growing region in the Western Visayas—the region accounted for half the area planted in cane and two-thirds of the production of sugar. Unlike the cultivation of rice, corn, and coconuts, sugarcane is typically grown on large farms or haciendas. Negros output came from farms 25 hectares or larger. Sugarcane workers are called *sacadas*, people who live in abject poverty and are subservient to their overlords.

In the early 1900s, American colonialists boosted the sugar industry in the form of the **Payne-Aldrich Act** (1909). This important law created a tariff wall that guaranteed easy export of sugar to the United States at prices held artificially well above the world norms. It also created a situation in which the gap between the rich and poor grew even greater, and ensured that there would be little economic incentive for modernization. Over the following decades, the Philippines produced and exported huge amounts of sugar to the American market. Later, in 1934, a quota system on sugar was enacted and remained in force until 1974. Philippine quotas for the United States market in the early 1970s accounted for between 25 and 30 percent of the total, double that of other significant suppliers such as the Dominican Republic, Mexico, and Brazil. Philippine sugar exports to the United States that had averaged just less than 1.3 million tons per year in 1968–1971 period averaged only 284,000 tons from 1983 to 1968. After the quota expired in 1974, Philippine sugar was sold on the open market, generally to unrestricted destinations. Consequently, shipments in the United States declined.

During the quota period, the Philippine producers enjoyed high profits, but operations were inefficient and lacking in mechanization. Sugar yields were among the lowest in the world. With falling prices and the end of the United States quota, attempts at raising productivity through mechanization increased yield, but caused a fall in labor requirements, initially by 50 percent, and over a longer period by an estimated 90 percent. The consequence was disastrous for the *sacadas* who depended on the industry for their livelihood. Adding to the woes of the sugar industry was the world market crash in 1974 when sugar prices sank from more than 60 cents per pound to 40 cents in 1980 to an abysmal three cents in 1985. The crash drove 85 percent of the Negros population below the poverty line. Sugar in the Philippines has become a feast or famine industry dependent on vagaries of the international market.

SUKHO, CHOI. *See* RAMON MAGSAYSAY AWARD.

SULAIMAN, MONA (1942–). Filipino athlete record holder of the 100-meter dash. Sulaiman was born in Cotabato of Muslim parents. Her athletic prowess was developed in public athletic events in her home province. When her speed became known, she was invited to compete in interscholastic athletic contests where she broke existing records. During a national track and field meet in Manila, she established record-breaking victories in her two favorite events: 11.9 seconds in the 100-meter and 24.6 seconds in the 200-meter dashes. She also competed in the shot put event and tossed the shot to a record 39.11 feet. In the Malaya Open Meet in Kuala Lumpur she won four medals in the 100- and 200-meter races, the shot put and the 4 × 100-meter relay, which she anchored. Later she duplicated her records in the Asian Games held in Djakarta, Indonesia, for which the press dubbed her the "Fastest Woman in Asia." *See also* SPORTS.

SULAIMAN, SAMAON. *See* LIVING TREASURES.

SULTAN BADARUDIN. *See* HADJI BUTU.

SULTAN KUKARAT (1581–1671). Sultan Kudarat united the Moro clans in Cotabato, Lanao, and Basilan and ruled for 50 years. During his reign he led many raids and battles against Spain from 1634 up to 1637. In 1637, he was defeated but was able to escape despite a bullet wound. He was again able to lead his warriors in battles from 1655 to 1668. His leadership inspired the Maranaos to oppose the building of a Spanish fort near Lake Lanao, thus saving Mindanao for Islam.

SULTAN KUDARAT PROVINCE. Located in central Mindanao, Sultan Kudarat province, named after a great Muslim sultan, was sectioned off from the former Cotabato province in 1973. The province occupies 4,288 square kilometers of largely undeveloped land. Its capital, Isulan, is located on the eastern part of this territory. Sultan Kudarat is the cultural center of the Maguindanao who are Muslims and comprise about 40 percent of the province's population, living mostly in coastal towns along the coast. An important minority tribe, the **Tiruray**, live in settlements in the interior regions. *See also* MARAWI.

SULU. A province located in the Sulu Archipelago southwest of Mindanao and comprised of 169 islands and islets, the main islands being Jolo (the largest), Pangutaran, Samales, and Tapul. The province has a combined land area of 1,600 square kilometers and a total population of over 200,000. The capital and main trading center is the city of Jolo, which is situated on the island bearing the same name. The people are mostly Muslims of the **Tausog** and **Samal** ethnic groups. Sultans used to rule these islands as an autonomous sultanate. They strongly resisted Spanish colonial rule. The sultanate was terminated by treaty in April 1940 when the commonwealth government took over possession of the islands. Most of the inhabitants in the islands are engaged in the fishing and seaweed industry. Jolo and Luuk are important fishing ports. Some of the important towns are Indanan, Kalingalan-Caluang, Maimbung, and Siasi.

SUMAKWEL. This is the epic tale of **Panay**, which tells the romantic story of the Bornean datus who came to settle in the island. The author of this tale is the late Pedro Monteclaro who included the story in his manuscript, *Maragtas*, published in the Aklanon language. Besides Sumakwel, the other principal player in the epic is Aeta chief Marikudo, who sold the island for a golden hat (*salakot*). *See also* LABAW DONGGON.

SUMAN. A native food delicacy and centerpiece of Philippine Christmas cooking. The original recipe of *suman* has not changed despite Hispanic and American influences. Also called "*kakanin*," it originated from harvest feasting of the early Filipinos and it has remained as a ritual offering for the important rites. A variety of rice called *Malagkit* is cleaned and polished, wet-milled in a stone grinder to a sticky consistency, mixed with coconut meat, sugar, and salt in delicate proportions, and artfully wrapped in fresh banana or buri leaves. Then it is baked, steamed, or boiled. The suman recipe is not written but handed down from *lola* (grandma) to *apo* (grandchildren). *See also* BALUT; CUISINE.

SUMMER INSTITUTE OF LINGUISTICS (SIL). A nonprofit organization engaged in literacy education of primitive tribes and a 1973 recipient of the **Ramon Magsaysay Award** for international understanding. Its missionary-linguists have worked among the many nonliterate tribes in the Philippines and have developed the alphabet of their language to enable the people to read and write in their own tongue. Employing the science of descriptive linguistics, primers are prepared with glossaries in the tribal tongue. Apt pupils are trained as teachers and help conduct literacy classes for adults and youth. SIL has created dictionaries, folk stories, songbooks, simple readers on arithmetic, hygiene, and Christian scriptures. As in other countries— SIL is in five Asian and 20 countries on five continents—its personnel numbering 150 cooperate with the departments of education, health, and defense, as did their predecessors who came to work in the Philippines two decades ago. Filipino linguists and the Institute of National Language are the principal beneficiaries of their research. At their remote posts they regularly administer first aid and assist in controlling epidemic outbreaks. Field workers are sustained and tribal folks given emergency care by pilots, five aircraft, and 30 stations of their Jungle Aviation and Radio Service. Underwritten by no government or religious denomination, the Institute is supported voluntarily by individuals, church groups, communities, and foundations. *See also* WYCLIFFE BIBLE TRANSLATORS.

SUMUROY (1649–1650). Sumuroy led a rebellion in 1649 against the Spanish in his native province Samar in protest against the forced labor of natives in building the **galleons**, which were used in the galleon trade. Not only were the natives forced to build the ships without any compensation, but they were also put to work in the forests to hew trees. This excessive abuse caused untold miseries to the people, who initially protested to the friars who were responsible for recruiting the shipbuilders. When grave injustices continued, Sumuroy, a skillful sea pilot, gathered a force in his hometown of Palapag, Samar. He battled the Spaniards and for a year successfully put a stop to the shipbuilding in Samar. The rebellion spread to Cavite, another shipbuilding province. A large force of Spanish regulars and mercenaries eventually vanquished Sumuroy. Although the **Royal Audencia** later abolished forced labor of the natives, uprisings continued throughout the Spanish administration. More than a hundred rebellions broke out against the Spaniards' cruel and inhumane treatment of the natives. The Royal Audencia was a government body established by royal decrees in 1583 to restrict the powers of the governor-general and to protect Filipinos from abuses. *See also* DAGOHOY, FRANCISCO; REVOLTS; TAMBLOT.

SUNNI MUSLIMS. *See* TAUSOG.

SUPREME COURT. Under the 1987 constitution of the Philippines, the membership of the court was established at 15 justices. The justices sit en banc or in two divisions. The Constitution also vested in the Supreme Court administrative supervision over all lower courts. A prospective justice is nominated by the Integrated Bar of the Philippines and sent to the president who in turn forwards the nominee to the legislature. The Supreme Court is basically a review court. Its job is mainly affirming, modifying, or reviewing decisions and decrees of lower courts, or other branches of the government, including the Office of the President and Congress as to whether they acted without or in excess of their jurisdiction. Members of the court act and vote independently of each other. About 90 percent of the time, decisions of the court, whether en banc or in division, are unanimous. *See also* DAVIDE, HILARIO JR.; LEGAL EDUCATION.

SURIGAO DEL NORTE. Located on the northeastern tip of Mindanao and including about 100 islands off the Pacific coast, Surigao del Norte is the largest province of which the main islands are Dinagat, Siargao, and Bucas Grande. The province has a combined area of 2,739 square kilometers and a total population of 465,400 people, mostly Visayans who emigrated to the region before World War II attracted by extensive tracks of agricultural land and the discovery of gold. Nickel mining is the major industry. The provincial capital is Surigao City, which was already a thriving settlement before the Spanish arrived in 1521. There are two main indigenous ethnic groups living in the province: the Mamanwa, a Negrito tribe, and the Manobo, a mountain-dwelling people who practice swidden farming and gather forest products. The Surigao Strait was the scene of a major disaster in 1944 for the Japanese navy when U.S. planes destroyed a retreating fleet of aircraft carriers, destroyers, and tankers. Chief towns are Alegria, Burgos, General Luna, Placer, Sison, and Tubod. *See also* BATTLE FOR LEYTE GULF.

SURIGAO DEL SUR. The southern half of the former Surigao province, divided in 1968 into Surigao del Sur and Surigao del Norte. Surigao del Sur is situated on the eastern side of Mindanao facing the Pacific Ocean. It covers 4,552 square kilometers of heavily forested land with limited potential for agriculture. The capital is Tandag. The majority of the province's 469,608 inhabitants are Cebuanos. The indigenous ethnic minorities are the Mamanwas, Manobos, and Tagabaloyes. Surigao del Sur is a major producer of hardwoods and forest byproducts. The city of Bislig is an important timber port and site of a wood processing industry, which produces cut lumber, newsprint, kraft board, veneer, and plywood. The chief towns are Baroto, Lianga, Carmen, and Tago.

SUSTAINABLE DEVELOPMENT. Defined as a method the country must follow to meet the needs of its exploding **population** and implement programs that promote the integration of a sound economy, responsible governance, social cohesion/harmony, and ecological integrity. This involves the protection of the environment and the efficient utilization of natural resources. Sustainable development ignored by previous administrations has been championed for the past decade by many **nongovernmental organizations** in their campaign to control problems of a developing country such as **population growth**, habitat destruction, food shortage, and urban pollution. During the **Fidel Ramos** administration, the Philippine Council for Sustainable Development was created to develop parameters and strategies that resulted in legislations that addressed issues of waste disposal, clean air, **deforestation**, and wildlife conservation. President Gloria Macapagal Arroyo, an economist, promoted legislations for sustainable development programs. The International Monetary Fund (IMF) and World Bank have turned down further loans to the Philippine government unless it sets its house in order by adapting specific programs to protect the environment (pollution prevention) with conservation of natural resources (clean water and reforestation). There are now ongoing projects in 910 barangays in Ilocos Sur, Nueva Vizcaya, Mindoro Oriental and Occidental, and Palawan. The National Environmental Action Plan has also addressed key issues such as degraded ecosystems, protected areas and biodiversity, urban and fresh water ecosystems, coastal, and mineral resources. *See also* PROJECT GOOD ROOTS.

SYLLABARY. Prior to the coming of the Spaniards, the peoples of the Philippine islands wrote in their languages using a syllabary (writing system) in which each symbol represents a syllable. The Ilocanos, Tagalogs, Pangasinenses, Visayans, and Kapampangans shared a similar syllabary, composed of 16 characters (including three vowels, a, e/i, and o/u. In the Tagalog script, syllable final (coda) consonants were not reflected in the orthography, so the three syllable word *pagdating* would be written "pa-da-ti". The ancient Tagalogs used a stylus or sharp stick to incise the symbols on pieces of bark or bamboo. The archaeological evidence of the existence of the syllabary also called *baybayin* is an inscribed pot found in Calatagan, Batangas. Most scholars are reluctant to attribute an origin for the scripts, but they have been compared to the Indic writings in the Edicts of Asoka (500 B.C.), the Batak scripts in Sumatra, and the Buginese scripts in Celebes—all remarkably different from the Philippine scripts. Two Philippine scripts that are also remarkably different from the scripts employed by the Tagalogs and Ilocanos (Luzon) were those of the **Mangyans** (of Mindoro) and the **Tagbanuas** (Palawan). Because of the relative isolation of these ethnic groups, their scripts have flourished. The Mangyans script is still used to this day. *See also* FRANCISCO, JUAN; LANGUAGE; POSTMA, ANTON.

SYMBOLS, NATIONAL. Flower: **Sampaguita**. Adopted as a national flower in 1934. Bird: **Philippine Eagle** (also known as the monkey eating eagle). Tree: **Narra**. The stately tree grows all over the islands and are abundant in Bicol, Mindanao, and the Cagayan Valley. This hardwood is used for furniture making and commonly used also as posts for houses.

– T –

TAAL VOLCANO. Said to be the world's smallest volcano, Taal Volcano is found in Cavite province. Its 406-meter high crater is described as "a crater within an island within a lake" because it stands as an island at Taal Lake. The lake was formed after the volcano, which used to be much larger, collapsed. The ridges around Tagaytay City, which overlooks the lake, are believed to be part of the crater of the old volcano. These ridges now serve as the border of the 18-mile diameter Taal Lake and stretch 32 kilometers from Mount Batulao to

Mount Sungay. Taal Volcano has erupted over 20 times since 1572. *See also* VOLCANOES.

TABON CAVES. Limestone caves found in Lipuun Point, **Palawan**, which yielded the skeletal and fossil remains of a woman, carbon-dated at 22,000 B.C., indicating the presence of Homo sapiens in the Philippines during the **Paleolithic Age** (circa 50,000 to 5,000 B.C.). Other artifacts found included flake pebbled blades, which had a carbon dating of 30,000 B.C. Of the 200 caves discovered by an American, Robert Fox, and his team of archaeologists from the **National Museum** in 1962, only 17 were fully explored and were found to have been used for habitation and/or burial sites by ancient people. The excavations yielded stratigraphic sequences of Upper Paleolithic flake implements covering a period of about 50,000 years of the late Pleistocene and early Post-Pleistocene period. The deepest occupational level excavated has a radiocarbon-14 determination of 30.500+/− 1,100 years (UCLA 958) from charcoal found with flake tools at 121 cm in depth. Subfossil and fossil human and animal bones in association with an industry of flake tools made of chert, basalt chopper-chopping tools, and hammers were found. Preliminary study of the fossil human bones revealed an estimated date of 22,000 to 24,000 years, representative of modern man Homo sapiens. Because of its importance to Philippine history and heritage, the site was declared a Museum Reservation Site by the Philippine government. Some of the artifacts, like Chinese jars, are dated as far back as the late fifth century. The Tabon skullcap and flake tools are stored in the National Museum of the Philippines in Manila. *See also* BUTUAN ARCHAEOLOGGY; PANHUTONGAN ARCHAEOLOGICAL DISCOVERY.

TAFT, WILLIAM HOWARD (1857–1930). When the **Schurman Commission's** work was finished, President William McKinley appointed a second commission, known as the Taft Commission, after its chairman, Ohio Judge William Howard Taft. Its instruction was to establish a civilian government for the Filipinos in accordance with the customs and traditions of the people. The commission was granted legislative and executive powers. Taft and his staff conducted hearings and traveled all over the country to assess the readiness of the Filipinos for self-government. During the period between September 1901 and August 1902, the commission issued 499 laws, which formed the basis of new judicial and civil service systems and a municipal code that provided for the election of local officers. Under Taft's leadership, the Philippine Constabulary was also organized and gradually took over the responsibility for maintaining law and order in the archipelago from United States army units. Another significant action of the commission was the establishment of free elementary education and the design of economic policies to promote the islands' development. When the military governor, Arthur MacArthur, relinquished his legislative powers on September 1, 1901, Taft was appointed the first civilian governor-general by President McKinley. He carried out his policy of the "Philippines for the Filipinos" by appointing Filipino commissioners to his cabinet. New laws were enacted to improve the tax and currency systems. In January 1903, President Theodore Roosevelt appointed Taft the secretary of war, which enabled him to continue taking charge of Philippine affairs. In 1908, Taft was elected president of the U.S. (1909–1913), and later became the chief justice of the U.S. Supreme Court (1921–1930).

TAGALOG. The Tagalogs are the largest ethnolinguistic group indigenous to central and southern Luzon. The language, Tagalog, is spoken by 46 percent of the population and in the United States, where there are 900,000 speakers. Tagalog is a member of the Western group of Malayo–Polynesian languages. The Tagalog people, found by the Spaniards when they conquered Manila in 1571, lived in thriving settlements along the Pasig River from which their name is derived: *taga, ilog* (river dwellers). Chau Ju Kua, a 12th century Chinese historian, described one prosperous community of a thousand families settled along both banks of the Pasig River at a point where Chinese trading junks entered. Tagalog society was ruled by datus and had a social order. They possessed a written form of language and oral folk epics, some of which survive today. Manila was a Tagalog stronghold governed by **Rajah Sulayman**, who was killed defending his city against the Spanish conquistadors. Due to more than 300 years of Spanish colonial rule over the Philippines, the language has incorporated a significant number of Spanish words and expressions. The language also includes words and phrases that are rooted in English and Chinese. However, Tagalog has retained its original form and has remained unchanged as new words have been incorporated. *See also* BUNDOK; FLORANTE AT LAURA; LANGUAGE; SANTOS, LOPE K; SYLLABARY.

TAGBANUA. A tribe that inhabits the central part of the island province of Palawan. Most anthropologists consider this people indigenous to **Palawan**, where they have lived since before Spanish times. The mountainous and hilly regions of the island are the main habitations of the Tagbanuas. A peaceful people, they are mostly farmers who grow rice, maize, and several root crops on small plots of land, although they also engage in commerce, selling their surplus rice as well as a variety of forest products, such as wax, honey, and gum known as "Manila copal," in the town markets. The Tagbanuas have their own syllabic writing. Although they have integrated into Filipino society, they still retain many of their traditional cultural practices and beliefs. Their cosmology includes the worship of spirits and deities and a cult of the dead. Tagbanua communities observe **adat**, a legal and civic code based on traditional customs, which governs complex interpersonal matters such as marriage, divorce, theft, and relations with in-laws. Religion and adat are often closely interrelated. *See also* SYLLABARY.

TAGBILARAN. *See* BOHOL.

TAGLISH. A mixture of Tagalog and English words and expressions. The newspaper *Taliba*, now defunct, popularized Taglish after the end of World War II, and it is used extensively by tabloids. Politicians use Taglish in their speeches and communications to reach the populace. It is widely used in **mass media** and advertising. English words that are difficult to translate or those requiring long translations are liberally used in combination with Tagalog words in written and oral communication

TAGUBA, ANTONIO (1950–). The second highest ranking Filipino–American army officer in the U.S. armed forces. Major General Antonio M. Taguba came into the limelight in May 2004 when he appeared before the United States Senate to report on the alleged human rights abuses of Iraqi prisoners at the Abu Ghraib prison camp by American MP guards. Appointed by the Joint Chief of Staff to investigate the matter, Taguba reported of "blatant, wanton, and criminal acts on the Iraqi prisoners" that caused outrage among the American people. President George W. Bush, who apologized to the Arab world, said that the mistreatment does not reflect the values of the U.S. armed forces and the American nation. Although Taguba's report found that there were only some 12 soldiers and civilian contractors involved, the vivid pictures and video shots of maltreatment shocked the public. General Taguba's impartial and factual report was well-commended by the Senate Investigating Committee that led to the court martial of the perpetrators and dismissal of some officers for failure of command responsibility.

Major General Taguba is the deputy commanding general (support), Third Army, U.S. Army Forces Central Command and Coalition Forces. Before Taguba was commissioned as an army officer, he received an M.A. degree in public administration from Webster University. He began his army career with troop leading assignments in the 1st Battalion, Eight United States Army, in Korea. He is a graduate of the army officer basic and advanced courses, the United States Army Command, and General Staff College, and the U.S. Army War College. The three-star general is a decorated officer having been awarded the Distinguished Service Medal, Legion of Merit (with three oak leaves), and Meritorious Service Medal (with six oak leaves). *See also* FILIPINO–AMERICAN GENERALS.

TAGUM. *See* DAVAO.

TAIWAN. Relations with this northern neighbor are cordial and have been so under several administrations. This friendship is based on their strengths—the Philippines' labor-surplus economy and Taiwan's prosperous industrial economy. There are some 150,000 Filipino construction workers in Taiwan, whereas Taiwan invested $83 million in the year 2002 in the construction of a 100-megawatt cogeneration power plant and plastic products. Philippines' one-China policy does not interfere with their smooth relations on trade and business. *See also* CHINA; SOUTH KOREA; VIETNAM.

TAMARAW (*ANOA MINDORENSIS*). This is the largest endangered land animal in the Philippines—only some 400 head are found in its natural habitat in **Mindoro**. The tamaraw is a close cousin of the carabao, slightly smaller in all aspects, with horns shaped like a "V" curving inward. Ferocious when confronted, the tamaraw was once a diurnal animal but is now primarily nocturnal and feeds mainly on grasses but cogon grass is the most preferred. Except for man, the animal has no known predator. Over hunting and collection of trophies have taken their toll. Although the tamaraw exists only in the island of **Mindoro**, ancient remains—carbon dated at 3,000 years old—were unearthed in a prehistoric settlement in Cagayan indicating that the animal probably roamed Luzon. *See also* CARABAO; PALEOLITHIC CULTURE.

TAMAYO, FELIPE AND JUAN. *See* PULAHAN.

TAMBLOT (1582–1622). Tamblot, a local shaman and **babaylan** in Bohol, became a rebel after refusing to convert to Christianity. In 1621, he and several thousand followers took to the hills and carried on a guerrilla war against the Spanish friars. The rebels continued to destroy church buildings and their contents until an expedition of Spanish soldiers and mercenaries put an end to their depredations. Tamblot's revolt was particularly significant in that it inspired other island chiefs to take up arms against their Spanish overlords. *See also* DAGOHOY, FRANCISCO; DIEGO SILANG; SUMUROY.

TAN, SAMUEL K. *See* JAWI.

TAÑADA, LORENZO (1898–1986). A former senator, Lorenzo Tañada focused his long public service on his devotion to **nationalism** in the mould of Claro Recto. His brand of nationalism was a struggle for liberation from American imperialism represented by egregious enemies—Central Intelligence Agency (CIA), International Monetary Fund (IMF), multinationals, and U.S military bases. He continued his battle against " forces responsible for our lack of independence." until he died. He established and chaired the Movement for the Advancement of Nationalism (MAN) in 1965, which led peaceful demonstrations in Manila against U.S. military bases, excessive privileges of U.S. monopoly firms, and the appropriation of vast tracts of lands by U.S. plantation interests. The cause led by MAN, which was joined by other nationalists organizations, resulted eventually to legislation that dismantled the military bases and curbed the privileges of multinational firms obtained under the controversial **Parity Rights**. *See also* DIOKNO, JOSE; SALONGA, JOVITO.

TANDANG SORA. *See* AQUINO, MELCHORA.

TAPIS. The Filipino wraparound skirt also called *patagyong*, which is worn by women in the Ilocos and Tagalog speaking regions. It is a handy everyday one-piece dress made of cotton material and usually dyed in various colors. The typical Filipina is often portrayed in brochures dressed in colorful *tapis* and *camisa* beside a picturesque **bahay kubo** (nipa hut). *Tapis* is also called *malong* or *sarong* worn by Muslim women in Mindanao. *See also* ABEL, JUSI, RAMIE.

TARLAC. A major agricultural province located in central Luzon and a key producer of sugar and rice, with sugar processing centers at Bamban, Paniqui, and San Miguel. The province occupies 3,053 square kilometers and has a population of 826,502 inhabitants. Its capital, Tarlac, was a Spanish military outpost established to protect settlers from hostile mountain people. Capas, Tarlac, was the destination point of the infamous **Death March** in 1942 during which thousands of captured American and Filipino soldiers perished. This is the homeland of **Carlos P. Romulo, Benigno Aquino Jr., Corazon Aquino**. The chief towns are Tarlac, Concepcion, Camiling, Gerona, and Victoria. *See also* COJUANGCO; HACIENDA LUISITA.

TARUC, LUIS (1913–2005). Commander of the military branch of the Communist party known as Hukbalahap. During the Japanese occupation, he led his rag-tag army of poorly armed peasants in daring raids against the Japanese. After liberation, he laid down his arms, ran for Congress from his district in Pampanga, and won. However, Congress banned him from assuming office because of his previous subversive activities, which forced him to go underground with his Huk army, renamed the *Hukbong Mapagpalayang Bayan*. President

Manuel Roxas, the newly elected president in 1945, tried to crush the Huks but died of a heart attack at Clark Air Base while delivering a speech. Taruc continued his resistance against the government while demanding agrarian reforms, which were ignored by President **Elpidio Quirino**, who waged relentless military campaigns against the Huks. From his headquarters on Mt. Arayat in Pampanga, Taruc, who was called *supremo*, commanded an army of 10,000 guerrillas in raids and ambushes of government troops. The fighters, mostly tenant farmers, joined Taruc not to overthrow the government but simply to obtain justice, a fair share of the harvest, the security of a subsistence living, freedom from landlord and military harassment, and the right to select their own representatives. Because the Huks had effective control of many of the towns in Pampanga and Nueva Ecija, the provinces become known as "Huklandia."

The Huk rebellion came to an end in 1953 when **Ramon Magsaysay** became secretary of defense. He carried out on the government's mailed fist policy. At the same time, he offered amnesty to Huks and their families and the government offered them land in Mindanao. The project known as **EDCOR** was successful in attracting Huks and as a result Taruc and many of his men laid down their arms and reached a peaceful settlement in Mindanao. Taruc has become the leader of the National Farmer's Organization, an affiliate of the **Trade Union Congress** of the Philippines.

TASADAY HOAX. In 1971, Manuel Elizalde Jr., Ferdinand Marcos' cultural minister, claimed to have found a tribe of cave-dwelling primitive people living in the South Cotabato rain forest. They used crude stone tools and subsisted by hunting and gathering. The media latched on to the fantastic story and that year it was also aired in a *National Geographic* TV special. Access to the Tasaday was limited when **martial law** was declared in 1974, but with the overthrow of Marcos 12 years later, visitors found the Tasaday wearing modern clothing, using modern implements, no longer living in caves—and claiming that Elizalde had paid them to act more "primitive." Anthropologists generally agree that the Tasaday was a separate but not totally isolated group that had been exploited for political gain. As for the fate of Elizalde, he fled to Costa Rica where he died in 1997 following the downfall of Marcos.

TAUSOG. A major Muslim ethno-linguistic group, which inhabits the islands of the **Sulu** archipelago consisting of the provinces of Tawi-tawi and Sulu in the southern Philippines. The Tausogs are also called Joloanos in reference to the city of Jolo, which constitutes the cultural and political center of Tausog society. The name Tausog means "people of the current," which describes their traditional lifestyle as ocean-going nomads. Through the centuries, however, they have settled in the fertile islands to become agriculturists and left the small Coralline islands for the more maritime **Samals**. The Tausogs are a culturally unified group with their own distinctive language, customs, and written script, which show strong Malay–Arabic influences. They were early converts to Islam when Arab merchants opened trading posts in the Sulu Archipelago in the 10th century. During the Spanish period, the Tausogs waged continuous warfare against the colonial regime.

The Tausog economy is based primarily on agriculture, fishing, and trade. Their principal cash crops are coconuts, coffee, abaca, and fruit. As in the past, datus and sultans who inherit their positions and rule by Koranic and customary law govern Tausog society. The Tausogs are Sunni Muslims, and the *imam* is an important community leader. Religion traditionally plays a major role in the life of the Tausogs. Thus, the observance of Muslim holidays is mandated: *Ramadan* (fasting), Hari Raya *uasa* (feasting), *Hari Raya Hadji* (feast of sacrifice), and *Maulideen Nab i* (birthday of the Prophet). The Tausogs are known for their showpiece dances, colorful festivals, and entertaining music. *See also* BAJAU; HUSSIN, PAROUK.

TAWI-TAWI. A province of 307 islands and islets in the Sulu Sea Tawi-Tawi, Sanga-Sanga, and Simumul that have a total land area of 1,087 square kilometers and a population of 200,000 people, mostly Muslims. Four ethnic groups are represented: Samal, **Bajau**, Jama-Mapun, and **Tausog** each with its own distinctive lifestyle and language. Fishing is the main industry, although there are also many pearl divers and master boat builders. Tawi-Tawi is the Philippines' southernmost province and is quite close to **Sabah** and the Turtle Islands. Bonggao is the provincial capital of Tawi-Tawi. Other important towns are Balimbing, Cagayan de Tawi-Tawi, Simunul, and Sitangkay.

TAYUG UPRISING. Rural uprising in **Pangasinan**. Early in 1931 there was already widespread discontent among the tenant farmers and against the *kasama* system. From the Visayan Islands to Luzon farmers began to raise protests and demands for land reforms. Since these reforms were not forthcoming, a hundred tenant farmers from Tayug, armed with *bolos* (machetes) and antiquated firearms, took matters into their hands and seized the municipal building and burned the hated land records. They marched into town to the accompaniment of a music band, which helped rally the people to their cause. Government troops quelled the uprising at a cost of six dead farmers and five soldiers. Evidently, this uprising furthered the cause for land reform as more revolts followed in Panay and Negros islands. *See also* CACIQUISM; SAKDALISTA.

TAYLOR, CARSON. *See* NEWSPAPERS.

TAX SYSTEM AND COLLECTION. In 1986, the Corazon Aquino administration formulated a tax reform program that contained some 30 new measures. Most export taxes were eliminated, income taxes were simplified and made more progressive, the investment incentives system was revised, luxury taxes were imposed, and a variety of sales taxes was replaced by a 10 percent **value added tax** (VAT). Problems with the tax system appear to have more to do with collection than with the rates. Estimates of individual tax compliance in the late 1980s ranged between 13 and 27 percent. Assessments of the magnitude of tax evasion by corporate income taxpayers in 1984 and 1985 varied from as low as 1.7 billion pesos ($.07 billion) to as high as 13 billion peso ($0.5 billion). The latter figure was based on the fact that only 38 percent of registered firms in the country actually filed a tax return in 1985. Tax evasion was compounded by mismanagement and corruption. A 1987 government study determined that 25 percent of the national budget was lost to **graft and corruption**. Individual income taxes accounted for only 8.9 percent of tax collections in 1989, and corporate income taxes were only 18.5 percent. Taxes on goods and services and duties on international transactions made up 70 percent of tax revenue.

TECHNOCRATS. Managerial technicians—"new men of knowledge"—with graduate degrees (mainly in economics) from elite Philippine or United States universities who were recruited during the administrations of President **Diosdado Macapagal** and President Ferdinand Marcos to help modernize the Philippine economy. These technocrats were young members of upper middle-class families. As the influence of these highly trained technicians in the private and the public sectors increased in the 1960s, the government began employing them in the economic development program. These technocrats approached problems from a rational-productivity standpoint in contrast to the legal-national perspective that guided the traditional bureaucracy. They described themselves as apolitical for they considered politics a wasteful and irrational use of resources. Many of these technocrats were given cabinet-level positions, and their solutions to issues found their way into public policy, most importantly in the policies of the central banking system. Their noncoercive indicative planning approach has become a model for the government's economic planning. The technocrats' partiality to state power as the engine to promote development attracted criticism from legislators who were bypassed in the planning process. During the Ferdinand Marcos regime, the technocrats established an operations center in the presidential office that monitored the implementation of state projects. This illustrates the gains made by technocracy in centralizing control of the economy. *See also* AGILE.

TECSON, TRINIDAD (1848–1928). A heroine of the revolution. Even though women members of the Katipunan were exempted she signed in 1895 with her own blood (*Sanduguan*) and fought with men in the famous battle of **Biak Na Bato**. Historians reported that she fought in 12 bloody battles in her home province Bulacan. She was wounded and when she recovered she continued to fight side by side with men. Among her exploits was the capture of munitions from Spanish civil guards at Caloocan. Eventually, Tecson organized other women to nurse the wounded and sick soldiers. Her pioneering work in nursing was commended by the American Red Cross after the end of the **Philippine–American Revolution**. *See also* SALAS, QUENTIN.

TEEHANKEE, CLAUDIO (1920–1989). Fifteenth chief justice of the **Supreme Court** appointed by Corazon Aquino, whom he inducted into office as president of the republic. Teehankee was often called the "activist justice" for going against the majority opinion on the court, especially during the time of Ferdinand Marcos. When he retired, he was appointed permanent Philippine ambassador to the United Nations.

TELECOMMUNICATIONS INDUSTRY. The telecommunications industry used to be monopolized by the Philippine Long Distance Telephone Company, a privately owned company that owned as much as 95 percent of the telephone service in the Philippines until 1993. To break the monopoly, President **Fidel Ramos** issued executive orders mandating compulsory interconnection of all telecommunications carriers. The executive orders were reinforced with the passage of the Public Telecommunications Policy Act of 1995, which reiterated the importance of telecommunications and the policy obligations of the government to develop the industry. It also set out the responsibilities of the National Telecommunications Commission (NTC) and the Department of Transportation and Communication. The government action has resulted in a booming telecommunications industry. In three years, the nationwide telephone density index (TDI), or number of lines per 100 persons, grew 230 percent, from 1.4 percent to 4.7 percent. Telephone installations in the national capital region (Metro Manila) grew 200 percent, from 6.9 TDI to 20.8 The government's nationwide TDI target is 5.48 million telephone lines by 2004, representing a national TDI of 10.3. *See also* INFRASTRUCTURE.

THOMASITES. Early American teachers. Predecessors of the **Peace Corps**, the Thomasites were the 1,000 pioneer teachers who arrived in the Philippines in 1901 and 1902 on the army troop ship USS *Thomas* to teach English, science, and the rudiments of the democratic process. They were assigned throughout the islands, and laid the foundation for the modern educational system of the country. Many of them perished due to tropical diseases. Their legacy was the development of leaders, who became prominent in securing the independence of the Philippines. *See also* PENSIONADO.

TIBOLI. The Tiboli tribe inhabits the mountains of **South Cotabato**, and the Lake Sebu region that it calls home. An estimated 200,000 Tiboli inhabit the Tiruray highlands, a 2,000 square kilometers triangle bounded by Surallah, Kiamba, and Polomolok. Most of them live around Lake Sebu, a 365-hectare lake, 900 feet above sea level, which abounds in fish and lake vegetables. The Tiboli tribe is one of the most colorful tribes in the Philippines: they have a wealth of crafts, elaborate ethnic costumes, and lively dances and music. They are also admired for their handsome brassware, which finds its way into figure statuary, heavy belts, chains and noisy anklets. Their famous hand woven "*tinalak*" is made of dyed **abaca** embroidery, including their multicolored abaca basket and beadwork. The Tiboli is one of the few indigenous tribes in Mindanao that still practices polygamy. *See also* GIDA OFONG.

TILAPIA. The so-called poor man's fish, *tilapia* is available all year in Philippine fish markets and sold at a price within reach of most people. It has replaced the common table fare "*galunggong*" (mackerel) that has become scarce due to overfishing. The new *tilapia* is a strain that grows faster and tolerates high salinity, particularly in brackish waters. Before the introduction of saline *tilapia*, fish farmers cultured only the fresh water species. The saline species (*molobicus*) is a hybrid of GIFT (genetically improved farm tilapia), strain of nilotica, locally known as "*pla-pla*," a fresh water and fast-growing fish, and the native "tilapia" or *mossambica*, which is resistant to high salinity. *See also* AQUACULTURE.

TINGGIAN. This ethnolinguistic group inhabits the **Abra** Valley on the western side of the Cordillera Central. The word *tinggian* or *tinguian* means "people living near the Tineg River." They are close relations to the Ilocanos, which is their language too. During the Spanish colonial period, the Itnegs escaped Hispanization and conversion to Christianity by retreating to the mountainous regions of the rugged **Abra** province. There they thrived as hillside swidden farmers and kept to their traditional religion, which consists of many lower gods and one supreme deity, *Kadaklan* The political unit is the village and the head man is the elder *(lakay)*. Tinggian society features child betrothal, the paying of bride prices, female shamans, and bilateral descent. Due to the recent influx of Christian missionaries, many Tinggians have converted to Christianity and adopted Western customs. *See also* ISNEGS.

TINIKLING. It is the national folk dance of the Philippines, and a favorite especially on the island of **Leyte** where it originated. The dance steps imitate the movement of the *tikling* bird (a heron) as it walks between grass stems, runs over tree branches, or dodges bamboo thickets. Thus, dancers emulate the *tikling* bird's legendary grace and speed by skillfully maneuvering between bamboo poles clapped rhythmically to the accompaniment of *tinikling* music. The *tinikling* and **singkil** gained international fame when these dances were performed by the famous **Bayanihan dance troupe** before Western audiences.

TINIO, MANUEL. Appointed brigadier general at the age of 21 by Emilio Aguinaldo during the Philippine–Spanish Revolution in 1896, Tinio was sent to the Ilocos region to lead the fight against the Spanish forces. With the help of his brother Casimiro, who was also appointed a major, they liberated **La Union** and other Ilocos provinces. He was later appointed military governor of Northern Luzon. When the Americans came in 1899, Aguinaldo ordered him to continue the fight for independence by guerrilla warfare. However, he was forced to surrender on May 1, 1901, when he realized the futility of resistance in the face of a superiorly armed enemy.

TIRAD PASS. A lonely mountain pass located at the foot of Three Sisters peak 25 kilometers from the town of Candon, **Ilocos Sur**. This pass was the scene of a famous battle fought on December 2, 1899, by Filipino forces under the command of 24-year old General **Gregorio del Pilar** against overwhelming American forces in pursuit of General **Emilio Aguinaldo**. Together with 60 poorly armed men, General Del Pilar held off an American battalion armed with superior fire power. The young general and his men perished in combat. Del Pilar was cited for his gallantry by his American conquerors and Tirad Pass has been declared a national shrine.

TIRURAY. The Tirurays are a distinct ethnologuistic group with clear Malayan features. They are mostly found in the **Maguindanao** and **Sultan Kudarat** provinces. The Tirurays have a solid social structure as reflected by their socioeconomic activities, which include farming, hunting, fishing, and basket weaving. While many have adapted to the political mainstream, a large number of their population of 76,000 still believe and practice their indigenous customs and ritual. They maintain a traditional culture of their own, characterized by communal households, polygamy, and a distinct legal system. *See also* LUMADS; TIBOLI.

TIZON, ALEX (1958–). A Filipino journalist who won a Pulitzer Prize in 1997 for investigative reporting. As a reporter for 17 years for the *Seattle Times*, Tizon together with fellow Filipino newspaperman Byron Acohido, who also received the prize, wrote articles that advanced the cause of the marginal sectors of American society. They covered youth gangs, immigrant groups, and Native American tribes. They also wrote extensively about race and ethnicity, crime and law enforcement. Among their significant articles were those that exposed widespread fraud in the federal Indian Housing Program. For his numerous articles in the *Seattle Times*, *Pacific, Times Sunday* magazine, *Entertainment Weekly*, *Newsweek*, and CBS News, Tizon received numerous awards: the Phoenix Award, Penny Missouri Lifestyle Awards, and Clarion Award. Tizon hails from **Pampanga.**

TOLENTINO, GUILLERMO (1890–1976). Known as the "father of Philippine sculpture," Tolentino was born in Malolos, **Bulacan**. He graduated with a fine arts degree from the University of the Philippines. It was through his works that Filipino sculpture came to be known in the middle of the 19th century. His signature masterpiece was the Bonifacio monument (**Cry of Balintawak**) in Caloocan City, which is a group of sculptures composed of numerous figures massed around a central obelisk. The Bonifacio monument, completed in 1933, marked the apex of Tolentino's career. Another landmark sculpture was the *Oblation*, which stands at the gate of his alma mater, carved in 1935. The figure is of a naked young man with his hands raised up, a symbolic gesture of sacrificial offering of service to the country and humanity.

TONDO. In the 1800s, Tondo, a suburb of **Manila**, was a poor man's town. People from all over the country who came looking for work in Manila made Tondo their first home. In 1877, some 10,000 Spaniards and their helpers lived in the walled city of **Intramuros,**

and 30,000 people in Tondo. Today, Tondo is just as a crowded—at 45,000 people per square kilometer making it one of the most densely populated places in the world. Serving the medical and health needs of its impoverished residents are Mary Johnston Hospital, a private hospital established by the United Methodist Church in 1906, and the Tondo Medical Center, a government hospital. Historically, Tondo is the site of the first uprising against the Spaniards led by **Magat Salamat** in 1588, and 300 years later **Andres Bonifacio** planned the **Katipunan** in Tondo and successfully carried out the revolution that led to the eventual downfall of the Spanish regime.

TORRE, EDICIO DE LA. A former Roman Catholic priest, who went underground in 1972 and joined the communist revolutionary movement when **martial law** was declared by President Ferdinand Marcos. It was for such involvement that he earned two jail terms that spanned almost a decade. When **Joseph Ejercito Estrada** became president, he appointed De La Torre to serve as director of the Technical Education and Schools Development Authority (TESDA). He directed the successful implementation of the agency's program by improving the training and certification of vocational and technical education with the help of funds provided by the Asian Development Bank. Prior to this post, he was executive director of the Institute for Popular Democracy (IPD), a **nongovernmental organization** (NGO) that he cofounded in 1987.

In 2001, he became the subject of much criticism from Manila's civil society as he refused to give up government service and ignored calls from former NGO colleagues to stop lending credibility to Estrada's administration. De La Torre, a convert to **liberation theology**, wanted to push for pro-poor reforms and did not care whether it was inside government institutions or not. He strongly supported Estrada's anti-poverty programs at the beginning of his administration. But it did not take long for observers to notice that it was impossible for such idealists to achieve major reforms through Estrada's mismanaged government. Estrada failed not only to deliver pro-poor reforms but also managed to turn off legitimate business investors with a leadership style that openly gave undue business advantages to a selected circle of personal friends and political allies. De La Torre was disappointed and finally ceased supporting his idol and returned to his post as director of IPD. *See also* CHRISTIANS FOR NATIONAL LIBERATION.

TORRE, GASPAR DE LA. *See* DAGOHOY, FRANCISCO.

TOURISM. The tourist industry is affected periodically by political unrest but remains an important sector of the economy. The Philippines is a major foreign tourist destination center. More than a million tourists visit the country every year for pleasure or business. From January to December there are cultural and religious **festivals** as well as sports attractions for tourists all over the country. Of the total number of tourists, Americans are in the majority, with Japanese and Germans following in that order. Other visitors come from Hong Kong, Taiwan, and the ASEAN countries. By region, Metropolitan Manila had the biggest number of tourists (1.3 million). Central Visayas ranks second with 350,000 visitors followed by northern Mindanao with 297,000. Of the total number, 87 percent were foreigners and 13 percent were Filipinos. These visitors traveled mainly for business (32 percent), vacation or holiday (32 percent), and to visit relatives or friends (23 percent). December is generally the peak month of tourist influx.

The country has sufficient accommodations for its tourist industry, which is monitored by the Department of Tourism. Interisland transportation is provided by Philippine airlines and ships, which ply the routes between Manila and major local ports. During the term of President Gloria Macapagal Arroyo, she highlighted the tourism industry by making visits to selected tourist destinations. The Department of Tourism's plan for the year 2010 is a tourism industry that establishes the country as a "premier Asian destination," while setting a target of five million visitors for the year, and creating 8.3 million jobs. The department sees the industry as staying on "a **sustainable development** path" that protects the land, culture, and people. *See also* AKLAN; BORACAY; CALAUIT ISLAND; FORT SANTIAGO; GUINTING-GUINTING NATIONAL PARK; HUNDRED ISLANDS NATIONAL PARK; MARAWI; MAYON VOLCANO; PAGSANJAN FALLS, PALAWAN; RICE TERRACES; SAGADA; TAAL VOLCANO; TUBBATAHA REEF; VIGAN.

TRADE UNION CONGRESS OF THE PHILIPPINES (TUCP) *(Katipunang Mangagawang Pilipino).* A labor union founded in 1977 by the Ferdinand Marcos government with a strong anti-Communist and pro-U.S. platform. While other unions faced tremendous repression, this right-wing labor organization enjoyed prodigious support from the Marcos administration. The organization played a key role in upholding Marcos' repressive labor legislation, such as outlawing strikes in vital industries. After the downfall of Marcos, the TUCP switched its progovernment support to Corazon Aquino and Fidel Ramos. Some of its funding came from the American Free Labor Institute, a U.S. organization controlled by the U.S. AFL-CIO. In the 2001 national elections, the TUCP failed to elect a candidate due to the split among the labor parties. In order to retain its mass base of 1.3 million members, the TUCP has concentrated its efforts on agrarian reform and social justice.

TRADE UNIONS. The trade union movement in the Philippines started out as a strong force after the end of World War II. In 1993, the Industrial Peace Act (Republic Act 875) or the magna carta of labor was passed. The working people managed to dismantle compulsory arbitration, institutionalize mediation, and conciliation and succeeded in getting state recognition for collective bargaining, the right to organize, and the right to wage strikes. The labor relations system is based on enterprise unionism. Trade union activities suffered a serious setback when **martial law** was declared in 1972. Nevertheless, there were several strikes; the most dramatic was launched by the workers of Distillera La Tondeña Company. When martial law was lifted in 1981, trade unions asserted their power. A general strike was launched in 1987 to demand an oil price rollback. Then trade unions challenged President Fidel Ramos's economic program, "Philippines 2000," and its bias for free trade (neoliberal globalization).

Trade unionism in the Philippines is highly personalistic—some leaders end up as lifetime leaders. Hence, union federations have been divided, not because of real organizational issues, but because of power struggles among its leaders. Trade unions establish themselves as independent entities at the enterprise level by winning certification elections. These enterprise unions then affiliate with a federation, which can gather the resources to provide legal backup for court hearings on collective bargaining agreements. In the trade union context, there is a regionalistic or clannish attitude, which has often contributed to further division of the trade union movement. Additionally, **political parties** with rigid ideologies tend to overpower trade unions making their party programs more important than the trade unions' needs.

Despite these weaknesses, the movement has contributed greatly in shaping the country's economy, politics, and **culture** by actively participating in discourses of national significance. Trade unions joined **People Power II** in ousting President Joseph Ejercito Estrada. During the past decade, three major organizations have emerged in the workers movement—the Filipino Workers Solidarity, Fraternity of Union Presidents, and National Confederation of Labor. As of 2001, there were 14,606 active trade unions. Among the registered unions, 13,900 were private sector unions, 698 were public sector unions, and 175 were federation or labor unions. *See also* BUKLU-RAN NG MANGAGAWANG PILIPINO (BMP), KILUSANG MAYO UNO (KMU); LABOR.

TRANSACTIONAL POLITICS. This connotes a one-time political transaction between a politician and the voter, whereby the voter is given cash for his vote, otherwise called vote buying. In addition, voters are influenced by free entertainment and campaign giveaways. These practices have been denounced as the source of fraud in national and local elections. *See also* DAGDAG-BAWAS; SOCIAL VALUES; TRAPO.

TRANSPORTATION. Transportation in the Philippines is mainly by ship, railroad, and road. Air travel is confined to major cities. The Philippines has extensive interisland transportation. Ships call regularly at 314 private and 622 public ports, including major ports at Manila, Cebu, Iloilo, Cagayan de Oro, Zamboanga, and Davao. Railroad transportation is found in Luzon and Panay provinces. The government-owned railroads run between Manila and San Fernando, La Union, a distance of 266 kilometers (165 miles) and between Manila and Legaspi City in the south, a distance of 474 kilometers (295 miles). The country has 157,000 kilometers (97,516 miles) of various types of roads and 26,000 kilometers (16,149 miles) are designated national (arterial) roads. About 50 percent of national roads have all-weather surfaces. There are 301 airports of which 237 are served by Philippine Airlines, a government owned agency. There are three major international airports: Ninoy Aquino International

Airport; Manila; Lapu-lapu International Airport, Mactan Island; and Diosdado Macapagal International Airport in Pampanga.

TRAPO. A media word coined for traditional politicians to describe career politicians who belong to **political dynasties** and are obsessed with power by all means. When candidates for political office are branded as *trapo* by the media this often connotes the image of a crooked aspirant and thus make him or her a suspect who cannot be trusted for public office. *See also* DAGDAG-BAWAS; POLITICS.

TREATY OF AMITY, COMMERCE, AND NAVIGATION, PHILIPPINES–JAPAN. Before the expiration of the Reparations Agreement, the Philippines and **Japan** began negotiations on a treaty of amity and commerce. An agreement was reached after 13 years of protracted negotiations; both countries signed the treaty in 1973. Since that time, Japan has been a close trading partner of the Philippines and a primary source of developmental assistance and capital investments. The Philippines and Japan are working closely toward a free-trade agreement as bilateral trade accords gain more popularity in view of the collapse of global negotiations at the World Trade Organization in Cancun, Mexico. The Japan–Philippine Economic Partnership (JPEP) under which the two countries granted duty-free access to each other's products showed mutual benefits in terms of trade volume. Seventy-nine percent of Philippine exports in 2002 to Japan enjoyed a zero tariff while only 51 percent of Japanese exports to the Philippines were granted the same.

TREATY OF PARIS (1898). This treaty, signed on December 10, 1898, in Paris between Spain and the United States effectively ended the Spanish–American War. The U.S. ultimately paid Spain $20 million for possession of the Philippines. Thus, the Philippines came under the control of the United States by right of conquest and purchase. This treaty was signed without the presence of a Filipino agent— **Felipe Agoncillo**—who was sent to Paris by General Emilio Aguinaldo to present the Philippines' case for liberty and independence. Agoncillo's arrival in Paris was too late, and the treaty was already a *fait accompli. See also* MANIFEST DESTINY.

TRECE MARTIRES. When **Cavite** rose up arms in August 1896 under the leadership of Emilio Aguinaldo, the people of Trece Martires united in their support of the uprising against Spain. The Spanish governor general sent a battalion of riflemen who quickly put down the rebellion. Mass arrests and summary executions were carried out. The most notable were the "thirteen martyrs of Cavite" *(trece martires)*, all of them Chinese—31 to 64 years of age—10 of them were masons. In dying for a noble cause the town of Trece Martires was named after them. *See also* GOMBURZA.

TRIBUTES (TRIBUTOS). During the Spanish colonial regime, the Filipinos were vassals of the Spanish crown. They paid *tributos* (tributes), a kind of head tax, to Spain. The rate was originally set as eight reales but was raised to ten in 1602 then to 12 reales in 1851. One tribute was equivalent to one family consisting of the father, wife, and minor children. Every unmarried man over 20 years and every unmarried woman over 25 years paid half of tribute. The natives did not like the way collectors collected tribute. The *encomienderos* made great profits and became rich through the collection of tributes. In addition to the tribute, the natives were forced to provide labor called *polo*. They had to build and repair roads and bridges, cut timber, and work in foundries and shipyards. They were also responsible for building the stone churches. The Filipinos were greatly humiliated because they were never paid for hard work, and they were even deprived of their rice rations by the officials. Another burden imposed on the natives was the *bandala*—the compulsory sale by native farmers of their farm products to the government. Not only were the goods or products undervalued but also in many cases they were not even paid for. *See also* CABEZA DE BARANGAY; CRY OF BALINTAWAK; MANIAGO, FRANCISCO; SUMUROY.

TRIPOLI AGREEMENT (1976). A peace accord entered into in Tripoli by the Philippine government and **Moro National Liberation Front (MNLF)** on December 23, 1976, in which the initial demand for an independent Bangsa Moro Republic composed of Mindanao, Sulu, and Palawan was reduced to regional autonomy comprising 13 provinces and nine cities. Because of differences over the interpretation and implementation of the accord, it failed to resolve the conflict in Mindanao. The Tripoli agreement became the common denominator for all Moro factional demands until the Corazon Aquino administration adopted the stand to use the 1987 Constitution as a basis for negotiations and settlement. *See also* JEDDAH ACCORD.

TSINOY. A word for Tsinong-Pinoy or Chinese Filipino. Though **Chinese** in ancestry, he is *Pinoy* (colloquial word for Filipino) in heart and mind. His features and language may be Tsino (Filipino word for Chinese). In the 1960s to 1970s, some sociologists and anthropologists proposed terms such as Pinsino, Filisino, and various combinations to refer to locally born Chinese who grew up and were educated in the Philippines, whose hearts and minds are Filipino, but who traced their cultural origins to the Chinese. On the other hand, the Filipinos used the term Insik to refer to the Chinese. Although Insik has lost its pejorative connotation over the years, many older-generation Chinese still feel uncomfortable with the term. The terms proposed in the 1960s and 1970s never took off because they sounded too contrived and anglicized. Then in the 1980s, the term Chinese Filipino became popularized. It meant that the person is a Filipino first and foremost and the word Chinese is a modifier to designate his cultural heritage. However, the term Filipino–Chinese had already been well adopted. The term was popularized in the 1980s when many Chinese opted to acquire Filipino citizenship by naturalization after the rash of postindependence **Filipinization** measures. Etymologically, the term was first used to mean two separate entities—Filipinos and Chinese. Many associations adopted the prefix Filipino–Chinese to mean that their membership is composed of Filipino and Chinese citizens. Pinoy is unmistakably Filipino and Tsinoy seems to evoke undoubtedly the image of a Pinoy who is a Tsino in being. Thus, Tsinoy, the term, was born and has been well accepted. *See also* CHUA, QUEENA LEE; GOKONGWEI, JOHN; PARIAN.

TUBA. Filipino beer produced from the sap of coconut trees. This native brew, also known as *lambanog*, is extracted from the unopened coconut bud by lopping the tip off with a sharp knife and allowing the sap to flow into a bamboo container. Four liters of liquid are collected each day from a young coconut tree and drunk on the same day. If it is allowed to ferment for two or three weeks, tuba becomes vinegar. Tuba can also be made from the sap of the **nipa** palm. In the Visayan Islands a variety of *tuba* called *lambanog* is distilled by boiling *tuba*. The result is a smoother derivative, which is used in cocktail mixes. *See also* BASI; COCONUT.

TUBBATAHA REEFS. Located in Central Sulu Sea, these reefs are considered the world's richest biogeographic area. Tubbataha, a **Samal** word meaning "long reef exposed at a low tide," was declared the country's first national marine park in 1988. The marine park covers 33,200 hectares and contains what is believed to be the world's largest grouping of marine life per unit area. Scientists claimed that more than 300 coral species and at least 40 families and 379 species of fish were recorded in the area. Among the species identified in the area were manta rays, sea turtles, sharks, tuna, dolphins, and jackfish. In 1993, the United Nations Educational, Scientific and Cultural Organization (UNESCO) listed Tubbataha Reefs as a world heritage site. *See also* CALAUIT ISLAND; MALAMPAYA SOUND.

TUGUEGARAO. *See* CAGAYAN.

TUWA-ANG. An epic tale of the **Manobo** people who live in the mountains of Davao provinces. The complete song of *Tuwa-ang* in English is about the magnificent adventures of a "maiden of the Buhong Sky" and gives insight into the customs and tradition of the people. *See also* MANUEL, E. ARSENIO; *SANDAYO*.

TYDINGS-MCDUFFIE ACT. The act adopted by the United States Congress in March 1934 was secured by Manuel Quezon. It replaced the Hare-Hawes-Cutting Law. Quezon was able to obtain more favorable provisions. Besides obtaining a **commonwealth** government, Quezon included provisions regarding a constitution, foreign policy, immigration, currency system, and foreign trade, all of which were important issues to Quezon's political party. The act cleared the road to Philippine independence and thus marked a new stage in Philippine–American partnership. *See also* BELL TRADE ACT.

TYPHOONS. The word typhoon comes from the Cantonese phrase *tai fung*, which means "great wind." Annually the Philippines is visited by these destructive winds, which create much havoc and misery for the country and the people. Typhoons develop as weather distur-bances called tropical cyclones in the western Pacific or China Sea. These cyclones intensify in velocity as they travel at speeds of 19–24 kilometers (12–15 miles) per hour in an easterly direction toward the islands of Luzon and Visayas. There are four types of tropical cy-clones: depression with maximum wind speed of 60 kilometers (37 miles) per hour, tropical storms with wind speed ranging from 61–86 kilometers (37–54 miles) per hour, severe tropical storms with wind speed ranging from 87–116 kilometers (54–72 miles) per hour, and a typhoon with wind speed of 117 kilometers (73 miles) per hour. The Philippines is struck by about 20 typhoons per year. *See also* EARTHQUAKES; VOLCANOES.

– U –

UDTOG MATALAM. *See* JABIDAH.

ULOG. See BONTOC.

UNITED NATIONAL ALLIANCE (UNA). Successor of the defunct **United Nationalist Democratic Organization**. It was established by Salvador Laurel and **Juan Ponce Enrile** after a falling-out with the **Laban** and Corazon Aquino in 1988. This new alignment of disen-chanted politicians became a thorn in the side of the Aquino admin-istration, which was in the process of recovering from a series of **coups d'état**. The UNA's agenda included switching from a presi-dential to a parliamentary form of government, legalizing the com-munist party, and extending the U.S. bases treaty. When these ideas failed to attract a substantial following, Laurel abandoned the party and returned to the **Nacionalista party**, the grand old party of the Philippines.

UNITED NATIONALIST DEMOCRATIC ORGANIZATION (UNIDO). Opposition party against Ferdinand Marcos. This party was organized by several of Marcos' opponents: **Lorenzo Tañada**, Francisco Rodrigo, Gerardo Roxas, Eva Kalaw Estrada, and Salvador Laurel. It was an umbrella organization for 12 parties, which came together in united opposition to the New Society Movement (KBL). Marcos felt so secure in 1973 that he tolerated a certain level of dissent. Salvador Laurel took over the leadership of UNIDO to contest the 1982 elections, but the party did poorly in the rural areas. Marcos and his KBL party were still able to wrest a majority of the elected seats. Laurel wanted to run for president in the 1986 elections under the UNIDO banner but because of a weak following he was persuaded by **Jaime Cardinal Sin** to unite with the **Laban** party to endorse and support the more popular political candidate, Corazon Aquino. The unified party had the initials: PDP-LABAN-UNIDO. After the election of Aquino, UNIDO left the coalition. *See also* PILIPINO DEMOCRATIC PARTY.

UNITED STATES. The September 11, 2001, events have significantly altered—for the better—the 50-year-old historic partnership of the Philippines and the United States because of the effect of the worldwide war on terrorism and the mighty military presence of the United States in the region. Earlier the U.S. was forced to close its Philippine bases in 1992, after the Philippine Senate rejected the bases treaty that was the subject of widespread opposition and anti-American activism and left a lingering bitterness. The U.S. government turned over assets worth more than $1.3 billion to the Philippines; however, the Corazon Aquino administration retained its security relationship by keeping the U.S.–Philippine Mutual Defense Treaty that was negotiated before World War II. The war on terrorism triggered the resurgence of the **New Peoples' Army** and Muslim extremist groups that the Philippine armed forces were unable to contain and consequently forced President Gloria Macapagal Arroyo to request U.S. military assistance. The **Balikatan** (Joint Training Exercises) proved to be effective in crushing the **Abu Sayyaf** in Basilan. Her pronouncements marked a shift toward expanded security relations that incensed her critics and led to the resignation of her secretary of foreign affairs **Teofisto Guingona**, an avowed nationalist. The bilateral defense consultative mechanism created by Presidents George W. Bush and Arroyo provided a ten-fold increase in military assistance to the Philippine army. Under the 1998

Visiting Forces Agreement, the U.S. was given access to ports and bases throughout the Philippines, in exchange for financial help to buy U.S. arms. This issue generated anti-American demonstrations in Manila and major cities.

On the other side of the bilateral relationship are the vibrant economic and commercial ties that ironically have the broad support of the Filipino people. Currently the United States is the Philippines' largest trading partner and top export market. One third of all Philippine exports go to, and some 20 percent of all Philippine imports—valued at over $8 billion—come from, the United States. The United States is also the Philippines' largest foreign investor, with an estimated 25 percent share of the Philippines' foreign direct investment stock worth over $3.3 billion. The relatively closed Philippine economy has been opened significantly by foreign exchange deregulation, banking liberalization, and tariff and market barrier reduction. However, a major obstacle has been and will continue to be a constitutional restriction on foreign ownership of public utilities, which limits ownership to 40 percent. Although the current wave of anti-Americanism—considered assertions of national identity—has not lessened, a great majority of Filipinos still support the American military and business presence in the Philippines. *See also* FOREIGN RELATIONS; U.S. PHILIPPINES DEFENSE TREATY.

UNIVERSITY OF SANTO TOMAS (UST). Founded in 1611 by Dominican friars, the UST is called the pontifical and royal Catholic university of the Philippines, and is one of the oldest existing universities in Asia. Named after the famous Dominican theologian, Saint Thomas Aquinas, the institution started as a training school to prepare young men for priesthood. It was elevated to the rank of a university in 1645 by Pope Innocent X and then placed under royal patronage in 1680. The title "royal university" was granted by King Charles III in 1785 for the exceptional loyalty shown by the administration and students who volunteered to defend Manila against the **British invasion**. Years later, the UST was made a "pontifical university" by Pope Leo XII in 1902 and bestowed with the title "the Catholic University of the Philippines" by Pope Pius XII in 1974. The university moved from **Intramuros** to its present site on España Avenue, Manila, in 1927. Despite being a historic academic institution, the walled campus, which occupies 10 city blocks, became a civilian POW camp during World War II. There were some 5,000 internees, mostly Americans and British citizens, who were liberated by the forces of General **Douglas MacArthur** in 1945.

USAFFE. This is the acronym of the United States Army Force in the Far East that was formed by the War Department of the U.S. government in January 1941 as a deterrent to the impending crises in the Pacific due to Japan's expansionist plans of conquering the Asian region, particularly the Philippines. The USAFFE was created by assembling all the Philippine army, scouts, and the American military units—air force, navy, and artillery—under the unified command of General **Douglas MacArthur**, who was called to active duty by President Franklin D. Roosevelt to plan a defense of the Philippines. The defense code named Orange called for combating the Japanese on the Bataan peninsula and waiting for reinforcements promised by General George Marshall, since the USAFFE, which had a force of 50,000 men, was not adequate to defend all the possible landing sites of the Japanese. The USAFFE were still under training and organization when Japanese invasion troops of 130,000 men landed on December 22, 1941, in Lingayen Gulf, Pangasinan, and Dingalan Bay, Quezon, and caught MacArthur by surprise. Orange plan was immediately followed and the Philippine–American troops slowly withdrew to Bataan. The Japanese forces commanded by **General Masaharu Homma** advanced so rapidly that they were on the Bataan perimeter in March. The USAFFE, under the command of General **Jonathan Wainwright** fought a delaying action but they were too poorly armed—no heavy artillery and armor—to stop the fast advance of Japanese tanks. A dwindling food supply further added to the problems of the front line troops. On the other hand, the Japanese were prepared with their artillery and well-supplied troops. In April 1941, General Wainwright saw the futility of further resistance, since the promised reinforcement never came, and so on April 7 he had to capitulate to General Homma, who demanded an unconditional surrender of all USAFFE forces in the Philippines. The USAFFE forces in the Visayas and Mindanao, however, were under separate commanders and Wainwright's authority to surrender was limited to his Bataan command. Meanwhile, General MacArthur had already escaped to

Australia by submarine. And for this failure to capture MacArthur, General Homma was later dismissed from his command and sent to a desk job in Japan. As for the American and Philippine captives, the Japanese forced them on a long 120-kilometer **death march** to prison camps in Capas, Tarlac. *See also* PHILIPPINE SCOUTS.

USAMA BIN LADIN. *See* ABU SAYYAF.

U.S.–PHILIPPINE DEFENSE TREATY. A treaty signed between the United States and the Philippines in 1951. The treaty affirms the strong historical, cultural and personal links between the Philippine and American people and acknowledged the brave contribution of the Filipinos during World War II to freedom and democracy. The alliance has been vital in maintaining peace and stability in the Asia Pacific for the past half a century. *See also* VISITING FORCES AGREEMENT.

URBAN GUERRILLA. The imposition of martial law in 1972 generated an atmosphere of intense opposition by the population toward the Ferdinand Marcos administration. As martial law took its toll of arrests and brutality on the people, it spawned a new opposition of reformist elements in society who called themselves "urban guerrillas," made up of educated, articulate young men and women who patiently studied the latest tactics in urban warfare. Besides contending with the subversive wings of the **communist party**, which continued its deadly hit and run tactics in rural and urban areas, the Marcos government had to face a more subtle enemy, which blazed a swath of destruction in the cities. One small group of urban guerrillas, calling itself the "Light-a-Fire Movement," surfaced in Manila. Using crude incendiary devices it burned several government buildings and hotels, including a luxurious floating casino controlled by the First Lady's brother. Ferdinand Marcos feared the tactics of the urban guerrillas because his defenses were limited against a well-organized destabilization plan. What President Marcos feared actually did happen when urban guerrillas supported by opposition elements from the United States exploded a bomb at a Manila meeting of travel agents. In the audience were President Marcos, the speaker of the House of Representatives, and the United States ambassador, who escaped uninjured. This incident drew a denunciation from the U.S. Urban guerrilla warfare ceased when martial law was lifted in 1981. *See also* LAGMAN, FILEMON.

URTULA, LUCRECIA REYES (1925–1999). Choreographer and dance educator. Lucrecia Reyes Urtula spent almost four decades in the exploration and study of Philippine folk and ethnic dances. She applied her findings to project a new example of an ethnic dance culture that goes beyond simple preservation and into creative growth. Over a period of 30 years, she choreographed suites of mountain dances, Spanish-influenced dances, Muslim pageants and **festivals**, regional variations and dances of the country for the **Bayanihan Philippine Dance Company** of which she was the dance director. These dances have all earned critical acclaim and rave reviews from audiences in their world tours. Among the widely acclaimed dances she has staged are the *singkil*, a Bayanihan signature number; *vinta*, a dance honoring Filipino sailing prowess; *tagabili*, a tale of tribal conflict; *pagdiwata*, a four-day harvest festival; and *salidsid*, a mountain wedding dance. *See also* AQUINO, FRANCISCO.

– V –

VALDERRAMA, PEDRO. *See* LIMASAWA.

VALENZUELA, PIO (1869–1956). A physician by profession, Pio Valenzuela was a close friend and trusted adviser of **Andres Bonifacio** and served as the first propagandist of the Katipunan during the Philippine–Spanish Revolution. It was Valenzuela who suggested to Bonifacio the need of an organ to publicize the **Katipunan**. The name *Kalayaan* was adopted and Valenzuela took charge of the publication and at his suggestion **Marcelo Del Pilar's** name was printed as editor with Yokohama, Japan, as the place of publication. This tactic was to mislead the Spanish authorities. A thousand copies of the first and only issue of *Kalayaan* dated January 18, 1896, came out in mid-March. Its eight pages published news items written by Valenzuela under his nom-de-plume *Madlang Away* entitled *Catuiran*—describing the cruelties of Spanish priests and civil guards. Valenzuela considered the publication of *Kalayaan* as the most important accomplishment of the Secret Chamber of the Katipunan.

Valenzuela also suggested to Bonifacio that the Katipuneros solicit contributions to buy arms and munitions from Japan in order to carry out the revolution. Bonifacio approved the suggestion but asked that it first be submitted for the approval of Dr. Jose Rizal, who was in exile in Dapitan. Since Valenzuela was the most highly educated member of the society, he was chosen as the emissary to consult with Rizal. He undertook the dangerous journey under an assumed name. Rizal advised Valenzuela that the revolution should not be started until sufficient arms had been secured and the support of wealthy Filipinos been achieved. Valenzuela reported to Bonifacio, who assigned him to procure at least 2,000 bolos. Unfortunately, the Spanish authorities discovered the Katipunan before Bonifacio could organize his men. He was caught with other plotters, but because of his valuable training as a physician he was granted amnesty by Governor General Ramon Blanco. He was, however, deported to Spain and imprisoned in Madrid. After the end of the ill-fated revolution he returned to the Philippines in April 1899 and resumed his medical practice, but only for philanthropic purposes. The town of Valenzuela, Bulacan, was named in his honor. *See also* JACINTO, EMILIO.

VALUE ADDED TAX (VAT). Tax reform package. The new tax law passed by the Philippine Congress in 1994 was designed to simplify the complicated 73 layers of sales taxes that had previously been in effect and also to limit sources of graft and corruption. Initially there was considerable opposition to the VAT from affluent businessmen who stood to be most affected by its implementation. A massive public relations campaign launched by the Bureau of Internal Revenue commissioner and staff led to widespread dissemination of information and an acceptance of the new tax package. One of the beneficial effects of the VAT was the elimination of all agricultural export taxes and the exemption of all agricultural products. *See also* TAX SYSTEM AND COLLECTION.

VAN NOORDT, OLIVER. *See* DUTCH; SAN DIEGO WARSHIP.

VELARDE, MARIANO (1947–). The charismatic spiritual leader of El Shaddai, a secular Catholic movement, and better known as Brother Mike, Mariano Velarde built up a phenomenal following for his El Shaddai movement, which he started in 1978 in Manila. By profession, he was a successful real estate developer and following a miraculous recovery from a heart ailment that he attributed to divine providence bought a radio station and started a weekly Bible-quoting radio program. He adopted the name of El Shaddai, a Hebrew word for Almighty God, which attracted followers mostly among the urban poor in Manila and the provinces. In due time his weekly radio show turned into weekly 24-hour prayer vigil and faith-healing rallies that gathered on the grounds of the **Philippine International Convention Center** in Manila. Claiming a following of a million people, Velarde transformed El Shaddai into an economic and political powerhouse thanks to the contributions of his followers and sales of religious trinkets. During national elections politicians sought the group's endorsement. The most notable politicians supported by El Shaddai included **Fidel Ramos**, **Joseph Ejercito Estrada**, and **Gloria Macapagal Arroyo**—all of whom won the presidency. *See also* MANALO, FELIX.

VELEZ, APOLINARIO (1865–1939). During the Philippine–American Revolution, Velez was the commander-in-chief of the west and southwest sector of the Philippine–Revolutionary Army. He organized Filipino volunteers to form the Maguindanao battalion, and led his troop to victory in the battle of Makahambus.

VENECIA JR., JOSE DE (1946–). He was the presidential candidate of the **Lakas ng EDSA National Union of Christian and Muslim Democrats** (Lakas-CMD) party in 1998 but lost to the popular Joseph Estrada. A former journalist, he started in politics by being appointed as diplomat and served as an ambassador to Vietnam. In his post as an economic counselor, he conceived of and implemented his historic dollar remittance program of **Overseas Filipino Workers** worldwide. Then he was elected congressman from his home province, **Pangasinan**, and one of his major accomplishments was to unify seven political parties to form the "rainbow coalition," which was instrumental in promoting beneficial legislations for the people. He was the principal author of the build-operate-transfer law, which brought $3.3 billion in foreign investments to the country. He also authored the Bases Conversion Law, which transformed Subic Naval Base, Clark Air Base, Camp John Hay, and Poro Point into special economic zones. As the Speaker of the House, De Venecia was President Fidel Ramos' chief architect of 101 laws on the economy, women's rights, marginalized people, and poverty alleviation. Venecia was instrumental in the election of Gloria Macapagal Arroyo in the 2004 national elections, and remains as Speaker of the House of Representatives. *See also* DRILON, FRANKLIN.

VER, FABIAN. *See* NATIONALIST REVOLUTIONARY ALLIANCE.

VIETNAM. Diplomatic relations started after the end of the Vietnam war when thousands of refugees (Vietnamese and Cambodians) fled to the Philippines and found temporary asylum in camps set up by the United Nations in Palawan and Bataan. Although the government welcomed them, their presence became a problem with local people who objected to their occupation of valuable land. Some of them returned to Vietnam but some 1,600 remained under the auspices of the United Nations. An official visit in Hanoi by President Gloria Macapagal Arroyo in November 2002 initiated a diplomatic relations that resulted in a bilateral agreement that provided an early resolution to the issue. President Arroyo, however, cleared the issue by assuring that the remaining Vietnamese refugees were still welcome in the Philippines since most of them had expressed a desire to settle in the country. The accord also sealed long-term and strategic cooperation to expand the economic partnership and raised the standards of security cooperation as fellow members of the **Association of Southeast Asian Nations (ASEAN)**. The two countries mapped the direction of their diplomatic, economic, and security ties in the next 25 years and beyond despite territorial disputes—**Spratly Islands**—among various parties in the South China Sea. *See also* VIETNAMESE REFUGEE CENTER.

VIETNAMESE REFUGEE CENTER. Located near Puerto Princesa, Palawan, this center was set up by the Philippine government with the help of the United Nations to accommodate fleeing Vietnamese refugees. At the height of their exodus in the 1970s, there were some 2,000 refugees who were received at the center. Supported by the United Nations, the refugees were provided with food, clothing, and shelter. When the Vietnam crisis was over, many of the refugees were repatriated and others were admitted to the United States and other third countries. However, a number chose to stay in the sprawling center where they have established their communities. The Philippine government granted permanent refugee status to 200 remaining refugees. *See also* VIETNAM.

VIGAN. This historic capitol of Ilocos Sur has the best-preserved example of a planned Spanish colonial town in Asia. The architecture of houses and churches reflects the coming together of the cultural elements of Europe and the Philippines. During the Spanish colonial period, Vigan was the site of the government of the Ilocos region. Vigan lies at the mouth of the Abra River, which is an important trading post along the Ilocos coast. *See also* SILANG, DIEGO.

VIGILANTES. Home defense groups. Paramilitary forces headed by local warlords who operate with government permission and serve as protectors of towns and villages. During the height of the Communist insurgency, the military could not cope with the attacks of the **New Peoples' Army** so they organized vigilante groups made up of local people and gave them arms and equipment to defend themselves. The first and most famous vigilante group to be organized was the 1987 *Alsa Masa* (Masses Arise) in Davao City. Soon there were about 200 vigilante groups with frightening noms de guerre such as *tad-tad* (chop-chop), *el tigre* (tiger), or *pulahan* (red). The vigilante groups were hailed as an answer to the deterioration of law and order in the rural areas. The use of paramilitary forces in counterinsurgency had its roots in the "civilian guards" of the anti-Huk campaign during the 1950s and 1960s. Ferdinand Marcos used the Barrio Self-Defense Units, which were assailed not only for human rights abuses but also for acting as private armies.

Under President Corazon Aquino, a civilian counterinsurgency group was created, the Citizens Armed Force Geographical Unit, composed of volunteer and regular soldiers deployed in barrios for community defense. Aquino described these home-defense groups as an exercise of "People Power." The proliferation of these home-defense units spawned a series of **human rights** violations. Local and international human rights watchdogs expressed alarm as they documented grave cases of abuses, including summary executions. **Amnesty International** publicized incidents of torture, murder, and executions. Some vigilante groups responded by shooting leaders of Amnesty International and even killing President Aquino's secretary of local government. Consequently, the government established strict guidelines defining the role of these paramilitary groups. A distinction was made between ad hoc vigilante groups and civilian volunteer organizations. By 1989, there were 2,000 civilian volunteer organizations under an umbrella organization called the National Alliance for Democracy. Many of these radical vigilante groups have since been disbanded. *See also* SPARROW SQUADS.

VILLA, JOSE GARCIA (1908–1997). Considered one of the finest Filipino poets, Jose Garcia Villa, who wrote under the pen name Doveglion, caught the attention of poetic aficionados and brought literary honor to his home country. Villa was born in Manila but left for the United States in 1929 after being expelled from the University of the Philippines for writing a series of erotic poems. He enrolled at the University of New Mexico where he edited and published a literary magazine. He spent the rest of his life in New York City, where he produced much of his beautiful poetry. The American critic e.e. cummings even wrote a poem, *Doveglion, Adventures in Value*, for Villa. Another American poet, Dame Edith Sitwell, had praised Villa's works as being "amongst the most beautiful written in our time." Among Villa's acclaimed works are *Many Voices* (1939), *Poems* (1941), *Have Come Am Here* (941), and *Doveglion Book of Philippine Poetry* (1962). He received the National Artist Award for Literature in 1973. *See also* BULOSAN, CARLOS, JAVELLANA, STEVEN; JOAQUIN, NICK.

VILLA, RENATO DE. *See* COUP DE ETAT.

VILLALOBOS, RUY LOPEZ DE. Villalobos led the fourth Spanish expedition, and it was he who named the islands Philippines after Philip II, heir to the Spanish throne (1556–1598).

VILLAMOR, JESUS (1914–1971). Ace pilot and war hero. Villamor was one of the fighter pilots who shot down a Japanese plane during the battle of Bataan. He was born in Bangued, **Abra**, where he finished high school, and went to De La Salle University,

Manila. In 1938, the government sent him to the U.S. to learn aviation. He graduated from the U.S. Air Corps Flying School at Randolph and Kelly Field. Upon his return to the Philippines, he was appointed director of the Philippine Air Corps Flying School, which trained the first Filipino air force pilots. When **World War II** broke out, Villamor was promoted to colonel and headed his own squadron in the Philippine Army Air Corps. He gained fame during the Japanese air raids by being the first pilot to get his plane in the air and engage Zero fighters over Manila. For being the first Filipino airman, he was awarded the Medal of Valor, the Distinguished Flying Cross, and the Legion of Merit. After the fall of **Bataan** and **Corregidor**, General Douglas MacArthur took Villamor to Australia where he launched his many trips by submarine to the Philippines to gather intelligence information and prepare guerrilla forces for the coming liberation of the Philippines. Villamor Air Force Base is named after him. *See also* LIBERATION OF THE PHILIPPINES.

VINTA. A popular sailboat used by the people of the **Sulu** archipelago for fishing and local travel. Usually manned by two persons, the characteristic feature of the quintessential vinta is the triangular sail, which is decorated with colorful geometric designs. The sleek construction (wood) and outriggers make it one of the fastest sailboats in the region.

VINZONS, WENCESLAO Q. (1910–1942). Vinzons was known as the freedom fighter of the Bicol region and youngest congressman (31 years old) in the Philippine Legislature at the outbreak of World War II in 1941. After placing third in the bar examinations of 1933, Vinzons became the youngest delegate to the Constitutional Convention the following year, representing **Camarines Norte** province. When the legislature was dissolved, he returned to his province and determined to lead his people to resist Japanese occupation. A reserve officer (first lieutenant) in the Philippine Army, he organized a guerrilla group, which he led in successful forays and pitched battles against the enemy, liberating Daet and other towns from Japanese control. The Japanese tried all manner of ruses to capture him and his men but failed until an informer finally discovered his headquarters.

Vinzons, his family, and several government officials were captured. The Japanese major who led the assault personally executed Vinzons (at age 32), his wife, and their two children. The town of Indan, where he was born, was renamed Vinzons in his honor in recognition of his valiant fight for freedom. The Japanese major was captured by the guerrillas during the liberation and subsequently executed.

VIOLA, MAXIMO (1857–1933). As a medical student in Barcelona, Spain, Viola met **Jose Rizal** and became a close friend. He helped Rizal and other propagandists work for justice and changes in the Spanish colonial government in the Philippines. When he learned Rizal needed money to publish his first novel *Noli Mi Tangere*, Viola readily paid for the printing of 2,000 copies. To thank him, Rizal gave him the first copy with the dedication: "To my friend, Maximo Viola, the first to read and appreciate my work." March 29, 1887. *See also* JAENA, GRACIANO LOPEZ.

VIRAC. *See* CATANDUANES.

VIRATA, CESAR (1925–). Cesar Virata was a high profile figure during the Ferdinand Marcos administration, having served the dictator in various capacities, one of which was as prime minister (1981–1986) under the Marcos engineered constitution. His main responsibility was to finance the budget and debt management by rescheduling and structuring debt, and he developed policies on banking reforms. He also served as secretary minister of finance and member of the monetary board of the Central Bank of the Philippines. His service was characterized by integrity, and was not marked by any of the charges of graft and corruption that followed many of Marcos' **cronies.** Virata then went into business and established his own management company and also served in several banking and investment institutions.

VISAYA (BISAYA). Visaya is the generic name for the language group or the islands that form the Visayan group. There are three linguistic subgroups under the Visayan term: Cebuano of Cebu, Ilonggo of Panay, and **Waray-waray** of Samar-Leyte.

VISAYAN ISLANDS. The islands situated between Luzon and Mindanao, the largest of which Panay, Negros, Cebu, Bohol, Leyte, and Samar comprise six of the Philippines' 11 major islands. The Visayan people fall into three distinct ethnolinguistic groups: Cebuanos, Ilonggos, and Warays. The western Visayas include Panay's four provinces (Antique, Aklan, Capiz, and Iloilo) and Negros Occidental, homeland of the **Hiligaynons**, who speak Ilonggo. The central Visayas include Cebu, Bohol, Siquijor, and Negros Oriental. Cebu is the regional commercial center and the country's most densely populated province. Cebuano is the major language spoken in central Visayas. The major islands of the eastern Visayas are Samar and Leyte, which are divided into three and two provinces, respectively. Tacloban is the area's commercial and cultural center. This region is the homeland of the Warays, who speak the distinctive **Waray-waray** language, although the inhabitants of western and southern Leyte speak Cebuano since most of them come from Cebu. *See also* LANGUAGE.

VISAYAN WRINKLED HORNBILL (*ACEROS WALDINI*). This hornbill is one of the four species of hornbills discovered by a German ornithologist in 1896. Locally called *kalaw*, it used to be found in most islands. However, due to indiscriminate hunting for its distinctive hornbill and wholesale destruction of its primary habitat the Visayan Wrinkled Hornbill is now an endangered species. The surviving birds are estimated at 120–160 and are found only in the Western Visayas Islands of **Panay** and Negros. This beautiful bird measures about 20 inches from the tip of its bill to its tail feathers. The head, neck, throat, and upper breast of the female is dark rufous. The back and wing feathers are black with bluish green gloss. The tail, dark buff with basal and terminal banks, is also black. Breast and belly feathers are black. *See also* FLORA AND FAUNA; PHILIPPINE EAGLE.

VISITING FORCES AGREEMENT (UFA). An agreement between the United States and Philippine governments signed in 2001 that reaffirms the obligations of the U.S. under the 1951 Philippine **Mutual Defense Treaty**. This agreement expands on the provisions of the mutual defense treaty, such as criminal jurisdiction, movement

of vessels and aircraft, and importation and exportation of equipment, materials, and supplies. The key provision is the entry, stay,
and exit of U.S. soldiers in the country. The VFA resumed the annual war games (**balikatan**) that enhanced the ability of the Philippine armed forces to fight communist guerrillas and the terrorist
Abu Sayyaf. Questions were raised by antiadministration elements
about the role of U.S. troops in the country, but the Philippine
Supreme Court upheld their presence and effectively supported the
government position.

VOLCANOES. As part of the so-called "ring of fire" of the Pacific basin,
the Philippines has 22 volcanoes, most of which are located on the eastern or Pacific Rim of the archipelago. Mount Pinatubo caught the
world's attention with its devastating eruption in 1991, followed by a
minor one in 1993. The other volcanoes, their height in meters, and locations are as follows: Babuyan Claro**, 1,160, Babuyan Island, Cagayan; Camiguin de Babuyanes**, 623, Camiguin, Cagayan; Cagua*,
1,158, Gonzaga, Cagayan; Smith**, 670, Babuyan Island; Didicas**,
228, Babuyan Island; Sto. Tomas*, 2,260, Benguet; Makiling*, 1,144,
Laguna and Batangas; Banahaw*, 2,177, Laguna and Batangas; **Taal****,
400, Batangas; **Mayon****, 2,462, Albay; Malinao**, 1,458, Albay; Bulusan**, 1,559, Sorsogon; Biliran*, 1,187, Leyte; Burauen*, 845,
Leyte; Kanlaon**, 2,465, Negros Occidental; Camiguin (Vulcan)*,
580, Camiguin; Hibok-hibok**, 1,330, Camiguin; Musuan**, 302,
Bukidnon; Ragang**, 2,815, North Cotabato; Macaturing**, 1,675,
Lanao del Sur; Mt. Apo*, 2,953, Davao del Sur and North Cotabato;
Bud Dajo*, 399, Sulu. (*Volcano dormant, emitting only a steam and
sulfurous vapors; **volcano active, has erupted in the past and may
erupt again.) See name of provinces for specific locations in the Philippines. *See also* EARTHQUAKES.

– W –

WAINWRIGHT, JONATHAN (1883–1953). Wainwright was the
American general who took command of the beleaguered Philippine–
American forces in **Bataan** and **Corregidor** in 1942 after the departure
of General **Douglas MacArthur** to Australia. Seeing the futility of con-

tinued resistance against a superior foe, General Wainwright surrendered the entire United States Armed Forces in the Far East on May 6, 1942, to General **Masaharu Homma** of the Imperial Japanese Forces. The Japanese imprisoned him in Manchuria until the end of the war. He witnessed the official surrender of Japan on September 2, 1945, in Tokyo Bay on board the battleship USS *Missouri*.

WALING-WALING (*euanthe sanderiana*). Dubbed the "queen of Philippine orchids," the *waling-waling* was discovered by a German botanist Gustav Reicheinback in Mindanao in 1882. Due to habitat destruction, the *waling-waling* has disappeared in the rain forests of Davao. But thanks to Charita Puentispina, a neophyte orchidist, they made a comeback when she successfully pioneered mass production of the *waling-waling* through embryo culture in 1965. In its natural environment the *waling-waling* grows on tree trunks in the rain forests of Davao, Sultan Kudarat, and Cotabato. The orchid grows to a height of 60 to 120 centimeters, and it starts to blossom when it is about 30 centimeters long and has a few sets of flat, channeled, and graceful recurved leaves. The flower, the largest of Philippine orchids, is seven to 12 centimeters wide. The flower is pale purple blotched with dark reddish-purple. The *waling-waling* is widely used in corsages and wedding bouquets. *See also* QUISUMBING, EDUARDO; SAMPAGUITA; Y'LANG Y'LANG.

WALLACE, BEN. *See* PROJECT GOOD ROOTS.

WARAY-WARAY (SAMAREÑO). Language spoken mostly in eastern Leyte and Samar in the eastern Visayas.

WEAVING. In spite of the advent of factory-produced clothing, weaving is still a profitable cottage industry in the Philippines. Weaving originated in precolonial times and is one of the country's living traditions in the Cordillera and northern regions in Luzon, Visayas, and Mindanao. Many tribal groups practice weaving for their native attire. Some of the vintage products are the hand-loomed blankets, tapis, malongs, and men's shirts. The Ilocanos take pride in their sturdy **abel** weave, which is quite popular with overseas Filipinos. *See also* JUSI; PIÑA; RAMIE.

WEIGHTS AND MEASURES. The metric system is used and enforced in the Philippines. Distances are measured in kilometers, meters, centimeters, and millimeters. Liquid is measured either in liters or pints. Areas are measured in square meters and kilometers and in hectares (2.471 acres); weights are indicated in kilograms or kilos (2.2 pounds) and in metric tons; dry measures is indicated in *chupas*, *gantas*, and *cavans*. Eight chupas equal one ganta; 25 gantas equal one cavan; one cavan equals 2.13 bushels or 44 kilos (97 pounds).

WILLOUGHBY, CHARLES. *See* GUERRILLA.

WILWAYCO, EDWIN (1952–). Wilwayco is one of the well-known abstract painters in the Philippines. He took his fine arts degree from the University of the Philippines and started his career as an art director for an advertising firm. Wilwayco was influenced by the likes of Jackson Pollock and Wilhelm de Kooning, which he melded with his native sensibility. Critics noted the bright colors and exuberant rhythms of his canvases. He disrupted the symmetry and traditional conceptions of the Philippine flag and transformed it into a fragmented and colorful pop icon. Wilwayco's important Jeepney Fantasia, featured in the **Ayala Museum** in 1983, was distinguished by the exploded chromatic images of the **jeepney** intermingling with the bird-of-paradise plants and birds while the chaos in the streets were suggested by expressionist brushstrokes. This series based on the jeepney continued and further developed the pop preoccupation of Wilwayco in an oriental baroque direction. His 1992 one-man show, his fifth exhibit at the Ayala Museum**,** centered on floral motifs, which evoked the influence of the Asian painting tradition while the impact of the imagery preserved the American and European influences. *See also* ART GALLERIES; ZOBEL, FERNANDO.

WOMEN. Among Southeast Asian women, the Filipinas counterparts have probably gained more rights and played more significant roles in the struggle against oppression, foreign control, and gender equality. Even before they won **suffrage** in 1937, precolonial women leaders were already involved in village **(barangay)** leadership and development. And their role became more prominent during the revolutions against Spain and America. When Filipino women finally gained universal suffrage, no less than 24 women were elected to various positions. Only World War II broke the momentum of women's run for electoral office. In the ensuing years some 26 congresswomen and four senators were elected. They authored important legislations on women's rights, education, environment, and social amelioration. Some of their notable bills included the right of women to enter into contract without having to seek their husband's permission, opening the **Philippine Military Academy** for women, and reserving for women's projects 5 percent of government departments' budget.

In the 1987 Constitution the five women delegates successfully included Article II, Section 14 that guarantees equality between men and women—"The State recognizes the role of women in nation-building, and shall ensure the fundamental equality before the law of women and men." They also successfully added a provision for the representation of marginalized sectors, including women, through the sectoral representation and the **party-list system**. The Women Empowerment Act of 1993 reserved for qualified women at least one third of appointive positions in national and local government, and included an enabling bill for elections to local boards. **Nongovernmental Organizations (NGO)** like **Gabriela** and **sectoral parties** like **Ang Bagong Pilipina**, **Abanse Pinay** have advanced the cause of Filipino women in the areas of equal opportunity in the work place and educational institutions. Their vigilant demands for electoral reforms and further democratization of the political system have remarkably changed the socioeconomic landscape of the Philippines in the last half century. *See also* BRAID, FLORANGEL ROSARIO; PALABRICA-GO, RAMONA; RASUL, SANTANINA; REGALADO, GEORGIA.

WOMEN IN POWER. *See* SECTORAL PARTIES.

WOOD, LEONARD (1860–1927). American governor-general in the Philippines (1921–1926). Wood distinguished himself as a Rough Rider with Theodore Roosevelt in Cuba, where he led troops during the Spanish–American Revolution. For his feats as a military officer, he was appointed governor of Santiago City and eventually all of Cuba. He then became governor-general in the Philippines, succeeding **Francis Burton Harrison**. Unlike Harrison, Wood was not convinced that the Filipinos were ready for self-government, a conviction that led him on a collision course with Filipino political leaders, notably **Manuel L. Quezon** and **Sergio Osmeña**. Being a military man, Wood surrounded himself with army officers, known as the "khaki cabinet," which did not ingratiate him with Filipino officials. He further alienated himself from the Filipino people by dispensing with the advice and cooperation of the leaders of the Philippine Assembly. However, his term was marked by notable improvements in land reform and law and order in the country, although his administration was marred by his unequivocal support of the military **massacre** of Moros in Sulu.

WORCESTER, DEAN (1866–1924). Although reviled in Philippine history as the ugly American for his role in the famous **Aves de Rapina** case and his strong opposition to early Philippine independence, Dean Worcester was among the most influential American bureaucrats during the American regime. For the first two decades of his service, he accomplished the following: established the **Culion** Leper colony, started the Bureau of Science, the Philippine General Hospital, and the fight against the recurring epidemics of cholera and bubonic plague. He worked for the protection of the culture and habitat of the tribal minorities. Like **Francis Burton Harrison**, Worcester strove to bring probity and strict accountancy to the Philippines government.

WRIGHT, LUKE (1846–1922). American governor-general in the Philippines (1903–1906). Wright was named by President Theodore Roosevelt as a member of the Philippine Commission headed by **William Howard Taft**. Wright succeeded Taft when the latter was appointed secretary of war. During his administration, He antagonized wealthy Filipino businessmen, who protested his decision to tax cigars and alcohol in an effort to make the Philippines financially stable. Obstruction by Filipino politicians made his work as an administrator both difficult and disagreeable. Strong, competent, and unbending, he defied opposition from both Filipinos and Americans.

WYCLIFFE BIBLE TRANSLATORS. This is an international organization founded by William Cameron Townsend in 1942, and it engaged in the translation of the scriptures into the languages of primitive peoples. Their involvement in the Philippines is their work with the **Manobo** tribe in Mindanao. After working with the Manobos for several years, Wycliffe workers with the help of the **Summer Institute of Linguistics** were able to produce the New Testament in January 1989, making the Manobos the first Philippine tribe to have a scripture in their language. Wycliffe continues its work with other tribes in Mindanao.

– X –

XAVIER UNIVERSITY. *See* MISAMIS ORIENTAL.

– Y –

YAKAN. A Muslim ethnolinguistic group living mostly on **Basilan** Island off the northern coast of Zamboanga. They are a peace-loving people who practice agriculture and cattle breeding. They are also known as superb textile weavers whose dresses are distinctive in color and style. Both men and women wear a close-fitting jacket with long, narrow sleeves, striped trousers that become skintight below the knee, and a small betel nut box at the waist. The women's jackets are usually black with gold buttons. Although the Yakans are Muslims, their practice of the faith is intermixed with animist practices.

YAMASHITA, TOMOYUKI (1888–1946). Yamashita was named the "Tiger of Malaya" for his successful invasion and capture of the Malaysian Peninsula from the British during World War II. General Yamashita was sent to the Philippines to relieve the disgraced General **Masaharu Homma** and defend Manila against the massive armed forces of General **Douglas MacArthur**. Finding that his troops were unable to repulse the powerful American and Filipino military force, he retreated to the Mountain Provinces where they made their last stand. However, on their retreat Japanese soldiers inflicted terrible atrocities on the Filipino people and wanton destruction of property. Yamashita was captured on September 2, 1945, and charged with war crimes. He was found guilty by a war crimes tribunal and hanged in Los Baños, Laguna.

Y'AMI. The northernmost point of the Batanes Islands of the Philippine archipelago. The islet, which measures less than one square kilometer, is closer to Taiwan, which is 224 kilometers away, than to Luzon Island. *See also* FUGA ISLAND.

YAP, CONRADO. *See* PEFTOK.

YEN, JAMES. *See* PHILIPPINE RURAL RECONSTRUCTION MOVEMENT.

YLANG-YLANG (ALSO ILANG-ILANG). Pronounced EE LANG EE LANG. A flower of the Ylang-Ylang tree found mostly in highly forested areas. Its yellowish petals exude a distinctive scent and are distilled to make perfume. *See also* SAMPAGUITA; WALING-WALING.

YORAC, HAYDEE (1953–). A Yale-trained lawyer, Yorac was appointed in March 2001 as chair of the **Presidential Commission on Good Government**—the government agency mandated to recover the ill-gotten assets of the Marcos family. Known for her tough nononsense persona, she and her staff pursued the case and were successful in recovering some of the stolen monies and real estate properties. During the Ferdinand Marcos dictatorship she led many rallies against human rights abuses, and as a member of the Human Rights Commission she spearheaded the investigation of alleged abuses of the military in Cagayan valley. As a **COMELEC** commissioner she successfully refereed several election disputes of Muslim candidates in Mindanao. She then served the administrations of Corazon Aquino, Fidel Ramos, and Joseph Estrada as mediator and investigator of electoral conflicts, graft, and corruption of government officials, and human rights violations. Her probity has earned her the respect of the public and set model standards of government service. In recognition of her exceptional integrity in government service and unwavering pursuit of the rule of law in the Philippines, Yorac was a 2004 Ramon Magsaysay Awardee.

YUZON, AMADO. (1906–1979). This many talented man distinguished himself in literature, education, law, and legislation. He was born in Guagua, **Pampanga**, to well-to-do parents. Early on he mastered his own language Kapampangan and English and wrote poetry in both languages with great distinction. His literary production earned him the honor of poet laureate of his province and he later gained international fame as the first Filipino to be crowned "Poet Laureate" of the world at the World Congress of Poets. He obtained a law degree in 1939 and practiced his profession by defending the poor and marginalized people. Yuzon also taught law and English at several universities in Manila. He was elected congressman of his home district. During his tenure he authored bills, which were passed into laws that benefited mostly the poor and the peasants.

– Z –

ZAMBALES. A province located on the west central coast of Luzon with Bataan as its neighbor. Its capital is Iba and the province includes **Subic Bay**, site of a former U.S. naval base. Zambals, Ilocanos, Negritos, and Tagalogs populate the province. Its most famous son was **Ramon Magsaysay** (1907–1957), third president of the Republic of the Philippines. Products, which are exported, include timber and the mineral chromite.

ZAMBOANGA DEL NORTE. This province on the northwest coast of Mindanao has a total land area of 6,075 square kilometers and a population of about 650,000, mostly Cebuano-speaking people. There are two cities: Dipolog, the capital, and Dapitan. The province's main industry is the production of **copra**, which is processed in Roxas. Corn is the staple food of the people. Other cash crops include a variety of fruits such as bananas and mangoes. Yellow-fin tuna are caught in commercial quantities and exported to Japan. Other important towns are Sindangan, Labason, Siocon, and Sibuco.

ZAMBOANGA DEL SUR. The Zamboanga Peninsula covers 8,058 square kilometers and has a population of about 1.7 million people. The provincial capital of Pagadian City is located on Illana Bay and is the trading center for the eastern Zamboanga agricultural region. The province produces copra, rice, abaca, and timber. One distinctive

language spoken in Zamboanga City is **Chavacano**, a kind Spanish Creole. Important towns are Zamboanga City, Alicia, Dimataling, Kabasalan, Margosatubig, Lapuyan, Tukuran, and Malangas.

ZAMBOANGA SIBUGAY. This is one of the newest provinces in Mindanao created out of Zamboanga Del Sur in 2001. The name Sibugay refers to the vast tract of land in the valley, which is the new province's rice granary. The province comprise 16 municipalities, with Ipil as the capital town. The province has an area of 322,830 hectares and a population of 200,000 made up of Christians, **Lumads**, and Muslims. Major crops produced include rice, coconuts, rubber, fruit trees, tobacco, and coffee. The province has an impressive range of excellent **tourist** attractions—waterfalls, caves, stalactites, hot springs, white sand beaches, and fish and sea snake sanctuaries. The area is the ancestral domain of the Subanons and Kalibugans who live in four towns—Titay, Tungawan, Imelda, and RT Lim.

ZAMORA, NICOLAS (1875–1914). Founder of the *Iglesia Evangelica Metodista en las Islas Filipinas* (Evangelical Methodist Church in the Philippine Islands). An early convert to Protestantism, Zamora left his law studies at the **University of Santo Tomas** to work as an evangelist for the Methodists. An American Methodist bishop ordained him in the ministry, and he became the first licensed Methodist minister in the Philippines. Gifted with a stentorian voice and brilliant preaching, Zamora brought many converts to the Methodist faith in evangelistic meetings. He was appointed pastor of Knox Memorial Methodist Church, Manila, becoming the first Filipino Protestant pastor of one of the largest Protestant congregations in the country. In time he felt the need for an indigenous church, and established the *Iglesia Evangelica Metodista en las Islas Filipinas* on February 28, 1909. He became its first bishop. Known today as the IEMELIF church, it has congregations all over the islands and some in California. *See also* MANALO, FELIX.

ZAPOTE. This little town in Cavite is known as the place where hostilities started between **Emilio Aguinaldo's** armed forces and the American Expeditionary Army of General John Pershing. A major battle was fought in Zapote on February 4, 1899, in which the poorly armed Filipino forces suffered heavy casualties and were forced to carry on year-long guerrilla warfare. The capture of Aguinaldo on March 23, 1901, in Palanan, Isabela, effectively ended the **Philippine–American Revolution**.

ZARZUELA (SARSUWELA). This is a form of operatic theater, which combines dramatic performance with music and dance. Introduced into the Philippines by Dario Cespedes, a Spanish poet and playwright who arrived in Manila in 1878, the zarzuela became an instant success. In its initial stages the zarzuela was exactly the same as its Spanish counterpart (one-act pieces), but when Filipino playwrights adopted the form they introduced a format of acts using contemporary Philippine situations highlighted by songs. Early Filipino playwrights wrote their plays in Spanish with Spanish characters, themes, and music. However, as new writers appeared local languages were adopted and the zarzuela became an avenue to express grievances against the Spanish colonial rule and, in particular, against the cruelty of the Spanish friars. Some of these early vernacular playwrights were Mariano Proceso Pabalan, who wrote in Kapampangan; **Severino Reyes**, who wrote in **Tagalog**; Buenaventura Rodriguez, who wrote in Cebuano; Benedicto Sabater, who wrote in Bicol; and Mena Pecson Crisologo, who wrote in **Ilocano**. The most prolific writers were Tagalogs, followed by the Cebuanos. Zarzuelas were staged in theaters or on open-air stages during provincial **fiestas**; those that were anti-Spanish in tone were called the seditious or revolutionary zarzuelas. When the Americans came zarzuela playwrights, such as Juan Matapang Cruz, maintained an anti-imperialist theme to protest American annexation. Realizing the volatile effect of the zarzuela plays, the American authorities suppressed them and even jailed the writers and performers. Later productions tackled social and political problems of the day, often exposing the mistakes and shortcomings of government officials or other well-known personages in the community. With the advent of cinema zarzuelas declined in popularity. *See also* FIESTA; MORO-MORO.

ZIALCITA, LORENZO (1873–1932). Zialcita was an aide-de-camp of **Emilio Aguinaldo** because of his knowledge of the English language. He was commissioned a lieutenant and subsequently promoted to captain at the start of the Philippine–American Revolution. In May 1899, he was one of the delegates who conferred with the Americans on the suspension of hostilities. The conference was unsuccessful and hostilities resumed until Aguinaldo was captured on March 23, 1901. Zialcita was later hired as an interpreter for the Americans.

ZOBEL, FERNANDO DE AYALA (1924–1984). Fernando Zobel was born and educated in the Philippines and Spain. He studied philosophy and letters at Harvard University. A *magna cum laude* graduate, he enjoyed the company of artists and thus was encouraged to try his hand in printing. He explored various printing styles while mingling and exhibiting with artists in the Philippines and United States. In 1960, Zobel retired from the family business and became a full-time artist, devoting his time to abstract art. He founded the *Museo de Arte Abstracto Espanol* in Cuenca, Spain, where he settled and blossomed into a distinguished abstractionist. Many of his works are exhibited at the **Ayala Museum** in **Makati**.

Appendix

Table 1. Population of the Philippines
Census Years 1769 to 2000

Year	Population	Average Annual Rate of Increase (%)
1799	1,502,574	–
1800	1,561,251	3.91
1812	1,933,331	1.80
1819	2,106,230	1.23
1829	2,593,287	2.10
1840	3,096,031	1.62
1850	3,857,424	2.22
1858	4,209,381	1.34
1870	4,712,006	0.78
1877	5,567,685	2.41
1887	5,984,727	0.72
1896	6,261,339	0.50
1903	7,635,426	2.87
1918	10,314,310	2.03
1939	16,000,303	2.11
1948	19,234,182	2.07
1960	27,087,685	2.89
1970	36,684,486	3.08
1975	42,070,660	2.78
1980	48,098,460	2.71
1990	60,703,206	2.35
1995	68,616,536	2.32
2000	76,498,735	2.36

Note: Population from 1799 to 1896 excludes non-Christians
Source: 2002 Philippines Statistical Yearbook

**Table 2. Population by Region
Census Years 1990, 1990, and 2000**

Area	2000 (May 1)	1995 (Sept. 1)	1990 (May 1)
Philippines	76,498,735	68,616,536	60,703,206
National Capital Region	9,332,560	9,454,040	7,948,392
Cordillera Administrative Region	1,365,220	1,254,838	1,146,191
Ilocos Region	4,200,478	3,803,890	3,550,642
Cagayan Valley	2,813,159	2,536,035	2,340,545
Central Luzon	8,083,945	6,932,570	6,199,017
Southern Tagalog	11,796,655	9,943,096	8,263,099
Bicol Region	4,674,855	4,345,307	3,910,001
Western Visayas	6,208,733	5,776,938	5,393,333
Central Visayas	5,701,064	5,014,588	4,584,124
Eastern Visayas	3,610,355	3,366,917	3,054.490
Western Mindanao	3,091,208	2,794,659	2,459,690
Northern Mindanao	2,747,585	2,483,272	2,197,554
Southern Mindanao	5,189,335	4,604.158	4,006,731
Central Mindanao	2,598,210	2,359,808	2,032,958
ARMM*	2,412,159	2,020.903	1,863,930
Caraga Region	2,095,367	1,942,687	1,764,297

*Autonomous Region of Muslim Mindanao

Table 3. Simple Literacy of the Population 10 Years and Over 1989 and 1994 by Percentage

Area/Region	1989			1994		
	Both Sexes	Male	Female	Both Sexes	Male	Female
Philippines	89.8	89.8	89.8	93.9	93.7	94.0
Urban	95.4	"	"	96.5	96.6	96.5
Rural	86.2	"	"	91.2	91.1	91.3
Metro Manila	98.1	"	"	98.8	98.9	98.8
Cordillera Administrative	86.4	"	"	88.8	89.9	87.5
Ilocos Region	90.6	"	"	95.5	96.1	94.8
Cagayan Valley	88.4	"	"	93.3	93.7	92.8
Central Luzon	93.7	"	"	96.3	96.5	96.1
Southern Tagalog	93.2	"	"	96.4	96.8	96.0
Bicol Region	87.3	"	"	96.9	94.8	95.0
Western Visayas	97.7	"	"	91.9	90.8	93.0
Central Visayas	88.0	"	"	93.1	93.4	92.8
Eastern Visayas	81.7	"	"	90.9	89.2	92.7
Western Visayas	80.4	"	"	89.7	89.1	90.1
Northern Mindanao	90.5	"	"	94.6	93.8	95.5
Southern Mindanao	60.5	"	"	92.0	91.6	92.4
Central Mindanao	78.3	"	"	90.8	90.3	91.4
Autonomous Region of Muslim Mindanao	—	"	"	73.5	75.6	71.4

Source: 2002 Philippines Statstical Yearbook

Table 4.   Education

1. Number of public and private schools		
Pre-school	SY 2001-02	12,541
Elementary	SY 2000-02	40,761
Secondary	SY 2000-02	7,683
Tertiary	SY 2001-02	1,603
2. Enrolment in public and private schools		
Pre-school	SY 2001-02	647,533
Elementary	SY 2000-02	12,826,218
Secondary	SY 2000-02	5,813,879
Tertiary	SY 2001-02	2,430,392
3. Number of graduates		
Higher education	SY 99-2000	350,804
Technical & vocational	SY 99-2000	94,803

Source: 2002 Philippines Statistical Yearbook

Table 5. Agriculture

Crop Year	2000	In Thousand Metric Tons
1. Production of agricultural crops		68,112
Cereals		16,900
Palay		12,389
Corn		4,511
Major crops		48,347
Coconut		12,944
Sugarcane		24,491
Banana		4,929
Pineapple		1,559
Coffee		126
Other major crops		4,245
Other crops		2,864
2. Value of production of agricultural crops (in million pesos)		283,141
Cereals		234,700
Palay		105,062
Corn		29,637
Major crops		120,894
Coconut		25,989
Sugarcane		19,837
Banana		20,408
Pineapple		10,455
Coffee		5,552
Other major crops		38,651
Other crops		27,546
3. Fish Production (1,000 metric tons)		2,993
Commercial fishing		946
Municipal fishing		945
Aquaculture		1,100
4. Value of fishing production (million pesos)	2001	107,193
Commercial fishing		36,088
Municipal fishing		34,221
Aquaculture		36,883
5. Livestock and poultry production (thousand metric tons)	2001	
Livestock (liveweight)		2,056
Poultry (liveweight)		1,152
6. Value of livestock and poultry (million pesos) 2001	2001	
Livestock (liveweight)		106,402
Poultry (liveweight)		68,543
Egg		17,379

Table 6.   Natural Resources

Year	2000	Value (in Thousand Pesos)
Land classification (in hectares)	30,000,000	
Alienable and disposable		14,145,027
Forest land		15,854,973
Classified		14,765,804
Unclassified		1,089,169
Area reforested (in hectares)		42,167
Forest Disturbance (in hectares)		11,171
Production of forest products (1,000 cu. m.)		
Logs		730
Lumber		288
Plywood		243
Veneer		89

Source: 2002 Philippines Statistical Yearbook

Table 7. Foreign Trade

		(Million U.S. Dollars)
1. External trade	2001	
Exports		32,150
Imports		29,550
Balance of trade		2,559
2. Total exports	2001	32,150
Coconut products		532
Copra		3
Coconut oil		418
Dessicated coconut		63
Copra meal or cake		36
Others		13
Sugar and sugar products		32
Centrifugal and refine sugar		23
Molasses		9
Forest products		23
Lumber		16
Plywood		3
Veneer sheets/corestock		1
Others		2
Mineral products		537
Copper concentrates		10
Copper metal		256
Gold		95
Iron ore agglomerates		61
Chromium ore		2
Others		112
Fruits and vegetables		552
Canned pineapple		91
Pineapple concentrates		30
Pineapple juice		14
Banana		297
Mangoes		28
Others		93
Abaca fibers		9
Tobacco unmanufactured		15
Petroleum products		242

Table 8.   Industry Sector

1. Index of value of production of key manufacturing enterprises by industry	2001	193
Food		135
Beverages		192
Tobacco		156
Wearing apparel		86
Wood and wood products		101
Furniture and fixtures		97
Paper and paper products		170
Chemical and chemical products		278
Rubber products		58
Petroleum products		271
Non-metallic mineral products		109
Basic metals		90
Transport equipment		115
Electrical machinery		265
Miscellaneous		110
2. Number of newly registered corporations & partnerships	2001	
Corporations		11,727
Partnerships		2,465
3. Capital increases & withdrawals of corporations & partnerships (million of pesos)		
Increases		26,640
Withdrawals		4,506
Net effect		22,135
4. Amount of investments approved under Executive Order 226 (million pesos)	2001	64,935
Local		46,093,425
Foreign		18,841,904

Source: 2002 Philippines Statistical Yearbook

Table 9. Labor and Employment

1. Total labor force (1,000 persons)	2000	33,354
Employed		30,085
Unemployed		3,269
2. Unemployment rate (percent)	2001	
Philippines		9.8
National Capital Region		16.5
Cordillera Administrative Region		6.1
Region 1		9.1
Region 2		4.8
Region 3		10.3
Region 4		10.5
Region 5		7.6
Region 6		9.0
Region 7		9.9
Region 8		8.0
Region 9		7.0
Region 10		7.2
Region 11		9.5
Region 12		6.9
Region 13		8.0
Autonomous Region in Muslim Mindanao		4.0
3. Processed overseas Filipino workers	2001	760,985
Land-based		638,217
Sea-based		222,769
4. Deployed overseas Filipino workers	2001	866,590
Land-based		661,639
Sea-based		204,951
5. Number of strikes/notices filed	2001	620
6. Actual strikes	2001	43

Table 10. Commonwealth and Republic Presidents

1.	Emilio Aguinaldo	1899–1901
2.	Manuel L. Quezon	1935–1944
3.	Sergio Osmeña	1944–1946
4.	Jose P. Laurel	1943–1945
5.	Manuel Roxas	1946–1948
6.	Elpidio Quirino	1948–1953
7.	Ramon Magsaysay	1953–1957
8.	Carlos P. Garcia	1957–1961
9.	Diosdado Macapagal	1961–1965
10.	Ferdinand Marcos	1964–1986
11.	Corazon C. Aquino	1986–1992
12.	Fidel V. Ramos	1992–1998
13.	Joseph Estrada	1998–2000
	Gloria Macapagal Arroyo	2000–2004
14.	Gloria Macapagal Arroyo	2004–2009

Bibliography

PART 1. GENERAL SOURCES OF INFORMATION

A. Bibliographies

Abad, Ricardo G. and Elizabeth U. Eviota. *Philippine Poverty: An Annotated Bibliography, 1970–1983*. Manila: Philippine Institute for Development Studies, 1985.

Ables, Higinio A., ed. *Guide to State Universities and Colleges in the Philippines*. Laguna: University of the Philippines, 1987.

Alcantara, Ruben R. with Nancy S. Alconcel, John Berger. *The Filipinos in Hawaii: An Annotated Bibliography*. Honolulu, Hawaii: Social Sciences and Linguistics Institute, University of Hawaii, 1977.

Angangco, Ofelia, Laura Samson, Teresita M. Albino, assisted by Sheila S. Coronel. *Status of Women in the Philippines: A Bibliography with Selected Annotations*. Quezon City: Alemar Phoenix, 1980.

Ayala Museum. *Filipiniana Collection*. Makati, Metro Manila: The Museum, 1983.

Baradi, Edita. *Southeast Asia Research Tools: The Philippines*. Honolulu: Southeast Asia Studies, University of Hawaii, 1979.

Bell, Walter F. *The Philippines in World War II, 1941–1945. A Chronology and Selected Annotated Bibliography of Books and Articles in English.* Westport, Conn.: Greeewood Press, 1999.

Bernardo, Gabriel. *A Bibliography of Philippine Bibliographies, 1593–1961*. Quezon City: Ateneo De Manila University Press, 1968.

Bernardo, Gabriel and Natividad P. Versoza. *Philippine Retrospective National Bibliography, 1523–1699*. Quezon City: Ateneo de Manila University Press, 1974.

Bibliography of Cebuano Folklore. Cebu City: Cebuano Studies Center, University of San Carlos, 1979.

Bibliography of Library Resouces on Women. Quezon City: Philippine Nartional Women's Information Network, 1986.

Cruikshank, Bruce. *Filipiniana in Madrid: Field Notes on Five Major Manuscript Collections*. Honolulu, Hawaii: University of Hawaii, 1984.

Filipino Women: A Union Catalog. Manila: National Centennial Commission, 1997.

Foronda, Marcelino A. *An Iloko Bibliography: A List of Iloko Materials in the Foronda Collection*. Manila: De La Salle University Library, 1972.

Funtecha, Henry F. *A Bibliographic Guide to the History and Culture of Iloilo*. Iloilo City: The Author, 1999.

Gieser, C. Richard, ed. *Bibliography of the Summer Institute of Linguistics, Philippines 1953–1988*. Manila: Linguistic Society of the Philippines, 1996.

Gupit, Fortunato. *A Guide to Philippine Legal Materials: A Text on Philippine Legal Bibliography. Philippine Legal Hisory, Philippine Legal System, Legal Philosophy, Methods of Legal Research*. Manila: Rex Book Store, 1991.

Headland, Thomas N. and P. Bion Griffin, compilers. *A Bibliography of Agta of Eastern Luzon*. Manila: Summer Institute of Linguistics, 2002.

Hendrickson, Gail R. and Leonard E. Newell. *A Bibliography of Philippine Language Dictionaries and Vocabularies*. Manila: Linguistic Society of the Philippines, 1991.

Johnson, Rex E., compiler. *A Bibliography of Philippine Linguistics*. Manila: Linguistic Society of the Philippines, 1996.

Jose, Regalado Trota. *Impreso: Philippine Imprints, 1593–1811*. Makati, Metro Manila: Fundacion Santiago, 1993.

Lopez Memorial Museum. *Catalogue of Filipiniana Materials*. Pasay City: 1962.

Medina, Isagani R. *Filipiniana Materials in the National Library*. Quezon City: The National Library and the University of the Philippines Press, 1972.

Meixsel, Richard B. *Philippine–American History 1902–1942*: An *Annotated Bibliography*. Jefferson, N.C.; McFrland & Co., 2003.

Nemenzo, Catalina A. *Graduate Theses in Philippine Universities and Colleges*, 1908–1969. An Annotated Bibliography. Quezon City: Philippine Center for Advance Studies, 1974. 4 vols.

Orbase, Lily O. *Bibliography of Philippine Bibliographies, 1962–1985*. Manila: Bibliography Division, National Library, 1987.

Palao, Trinidad. *Bibliography of Philippine Imprints, 1800–1850*. Quezon City: University of the Philippines, 1974. (Master of Library Science thesis).

Pardo de Tavera and Trinidad H. *Biblioteca Filipina*. Washington D.C.: Government Printing Office, 1903.

Perez, Aurora and Perla Patacsil, compilers. *Philippine Migration Studies: An Annotated Bibliography*. Manila: Migration Research Network and Philippine Social Science Council, 1998.

Philippine National Library. *Bibliography of Philippine Bibliographies, 1962–1985*. Compiled by Lily Q. Orbase and Yolanda E. Jacinto. Manila: National Library, Bibliography Division. 1987. (TNL Research Guide Series no. 22).

Postma, Antoon. *Annotated Mangyan Bibliography (1570–1988)*. Panaytayan, Mansalay, Mindoro: Mangyan Assistance and Research Center, 1988.

Quirino, Carlos. *Who's Who in Philippine History*. Ed. Conrado M. Lancion Jr. Manila: Tahanan Books, 1995.

Retana y Gamboa and Wenceslao Emilio. *Aparato Bibliografico de la Historia General de Filipinas; Deducido de la Coleccion que Posee en Barcelona la Compania General de Tabacos de Dichas Islas*, 1906. 3 vols. Impresional offset, Pedro B. Ayada y Compania. Manila: 1964.

Retana y Gamboa and Wenceslao Emilio. *La Imprenta en Filipinas; Investigaciones Historicas, Bibliograficas y. Typografias. Dedichas Islas*. Madrid: Impr. Dela Sucesora de M. Minuesa de Madrid: Libreria General de Victoriano Suarez, 1911.

Robertson, James Alexander. *Bibliography of the Philippine Islands*. New York: Kraus Reprint Co. 1970. Reprint of the 1908 ed, published by Arthur H. Clark Co. Cleveland, Ohio. This is also vol. 53 of *The Philippine Islands, 1493–1898* by Emma Helen Blair and James Alexander Robertson.

Rodriguez, Isacio. O.S.A. *Updated Checklist of Filipiniana at Valladolid*. Manila: National Historical Institute and the Government Printing Office, 1976.

Rony, A. Kohar, compiler. *Philippine Holdings in the Library of Congress, 1960–1941. An Annotated Bibliography*. Washington D.C.; Library of Congress: 1991.

Saito, Shiro and Alice W. Mak. *Philippine Newspapers: An International Union List*. Honolulu: University of Hawaii, 1984.

See, Chinben and Teresita Ang See. *Chinese in the Philippines. A Bibliography*. Manila: China Studies Program, De La Salle University, 1990.

See, Chinben and Teresita Ang See. *Chinese in the Philippines: A Bibliography*. Manila: De La Salle University, 1990.

Stymeist, David H. with Lilia Salazar, Graham Spafford. *A Selected Annotated Bibliography on the Filipino Immigrant Community in Canada and the United States*. Winnipeg, Manitoba, Canada: Department of Anthropology, University of Manitoba, 1989.

Theses and Dissertations on the Philippines at the University of Hawaii at Manoa. Honolulu: Center for Philippine Studies, University of Hawaii, 1998.

Tiamson, Alfredo T. *The Muslim Filipinos: An Annotated Bibliography*. Manila: Office of the Special Assistant on Cultural Communities, Department of Public Information, 1977.

Tubangui, Helen E., editor. *A Catalog of Filipiniana at Valladolid*. Quezon City: Ateneo de Manila University Press, 1996.

Virata, Enrique T. *Agrarian Reform: A Bibliography*. Quezon City: Community Development Research Council, University of the Philippines, 1965.

Yamada, Yukihiro and Cynthia Neri Zayas, editor. *A Bibliography of the Basic Languages and Cultures*. Diliman, Philippines: CSSP Publications, UP Diliman Office for Research and Development, Initiative for the Study of Ethnolinguistic Groups in the Philippines, 1997.

B. Dictionaries

Almario, Virgilio S., ed. *UP Diksyunaryong Filipino*. Pasig City: Sentro ng Wikang Filipino and Anvil Publishing, 2001.

Andres, Tomas Quintin. *D. Dictionary of Filipino Culture and Values*. Quezon City: Giraffe Books, 1994.

Benton, Richard. *Pangasinan Dictionary*. Honolulu, Hawaii: University of Hawaii Press, 1971.

Cabonce, Rodolfo. *An English Cebuano Visayan Dictionary.* Manila: National Book Store, 1983.

Camins, Bernardino S. *Chabacano de Zamboanga Handbook and Chabacano–English–Spanish Dictionary.* Zamboanga City: First United Broadcasting Corp. 1989.

Collins, Millard A., Virginia R. Collins, and Sulfilix Hashim, compilers. *Mapun–English Dictionary.* Manila: SIL VIII, 2001.

Constantino, Ernesto. *Ilokano Dictionary.* Honolulu: University of Hawaii, 1971.

Diksyunaryong ng Wikang Filipino. San Miguel, Manila: Komisyon ng Wikang Filipino, 1998.

Gelad, George P. *Ilokano–English Dictionary.* Manila: CICM Missionaries, Inc. 1993.

Hassan, Irene U. and Seymour A. Ashley. *Tausog–English Dictionary: Kabtangan Iban Manna* 2nd ed. Jolo, Sulu: Notre Dame of Jolo College; Manila: Summer Institute of Linguistics, 1994.

Hidalgo, Cesar A. and Elena Asa Villa Alcantara. *Ivatan–Filipino–English Dictionary: The Culural Dictionary of Batanes.* Manila: Academics Foundation, 1998.

JVP *English–Filipino Thesaurus Dictionary.* Manila: Mhelle L. Publications, 1988.

Laconsay, Greg C. *Iloko–English–Tagalog Dictionary.* Quezon City: Phoenix Publishing House, 1993.

Manuel, E. Arsenio. *Dictionary of Philippine Biography.* Quezon City: Filipiniana Publications, 1955–.

McKaughan, Howard P. and Batua Al-Macarya. *Maranao Dictionary.* Manila: De La Salle University Press, 1996.

Motus, Cecile. *Hiligaynon Dictionary.* Honolulu, Hawaii: University of Hawaii Press, 1971.

Newell, Leonard E. and Frances Bontog Poligon. *Batad Ifugao Dictionary, with Ethnographic Notes.* Linguistic Society of the Philippines. Special Monograph XVII, 744 p. 1993.

Panganiban, Jose Villa. *Diksonaryo-Tesauro Pilipino–Ingles.* Lungsod Quezon: Manlapaz Publishing Co. 1988.

Peralejo, Cezar C. and Pacifico A. Agabin. *English–Filipino Legal Dictionary.* Quezon City: Sentro Ng Wikang Filipino, University of the Philippines, 1995.

Postma, Antoon, editor. *Vocabulario Tagalo: Tagalog–Spanish Dictionary.* Quezon City: Sources of Philippines Studies, 2000.

Rubino, Carl Ralph Galvez. *Ilocano Dictionary and Grammar.* Honolulu: University of Hawaii, 2000.

Santos, Vito. *Pilipino–English Dictionary.* Manila: National Book Store, 1983.

Sullivan, Robert E. *Maguindanaon Dictionary: Maguindanaon–English, English Maguindanaon.* Cotabato City: Notre Dame University, Institute of Cotabato Cultures, 1986.

Svelmoe, Gordon and Thelma Svelmoe, compilers. *Mansaka Dictionary.* SIL Language Data, Asian Pacific Series 16. Dallas: SIL XIV, 1990.

Wolfenden, Elmer P., compiler. *A Masbatenyo–English Dictionary.* Summer Institute of Linguistics, 2001.

Yap, Elsa Paula and Maria Victoria Bunye. *Cebuano–Visayan Dictionary*. Honolulu, Hawaii: University of Hawaii Press, 1971.
Zorc, R. David Paul. *Tagalog Slang Dictionary*. Manila: De La Salle University Press, 1993.

C. Directories

A Guide to Philippine Economic and Business Information Sources. Manila: Makati Business Club, 1990.
Directory of Entrepreneurship Training Institutions for Women in the Philippines. Taguig, Metro Manila: International Cooperation Agency, 1999.
Directory of Non-Government Organizations in the Philippines. Manila: National Economic and Development Authority, 1989.
Directory of Philippines NGOs. 3rd ed., updated. Manila: Philippine Partnership for the Development of Human Resources in Rural Areas (PHILDHRRA), 1988.
Directory of Women's Organizations in the Philippines. Manila: Bureau of Women and Minors, Ministry of Labor and Employment, 1985.
Philippine Directory of Foundations. Prepared by the Association of Foundations; edited by Narzalina Z. Lim. Manila: SCC Development and Research Foundation, 1974.
Philippine Government Directory. Produced by the Office of the Press Secretary, Bureau of Communications Services. Manila: Office of the Press Secretary, 1998.
Philippine Media Profile. Manila: Philippine Information Agency, Media Services Division, 1998.
Women's Resource Directory. 1st ed. Manila: National Commission on the Role of Filipino Women, 1989.

D. Encyclopedias

CCP Encyclopedia of Philippine Art. Manila: Cultural Center of the Philippines, 1994.
Custodio, Teresa M. and Jose Y. Dalisay Jr. *Kasaysayan: The Story of the Filipino People*. Manila: Asia Publishing Co., 1998.
Demetrio, Francisco R., editor. *Encyclopedia of Philippine Folk Beliefs and Customs*. Cagayan de Oro City: Xavier University, 1991.
Galang, Zoilo. *Encyclopedia of the Philippines*. Manila: E. Floro, 1950–1958.
Philippine Encyclopedia of the Social Sciences. Quezon City: Philippine Social Science Council, 1993.
Roces, Alfredo, editor. *Filipino Heritage: The Making of a Nation*. Manila: Lahing Pilipino Publications, 1977.

E. Map Collections, Almanac, and Atlas

Abigan, Eduardo R. *The Philippine Atlas: Features: Colonial maps, and profiles of the 16 regions and 78 provinces of the archipelago*. Manila: Philippine Guides, 1998.

Filway's Philippine Almanac. Makati, Metro Manila: Filway Marketing, 1998.
McFarland, Curtis D. *A Linguistics Atlas of the Philippines*. Tokyo: Institute for the Study of Languages and Cultures of Asia and Africa. Tokyo University of Foreign Studies, 1980.
Metro Manila: Street Atlas. Mandaluyong City: Asiatype Inc., 1997.
Philippines 1:500,000; Special Map, Greater Manila: City of Manila. Scale 1:1,500,000. Singapore: Apa Press: Munich, Austria: Nelles Verlag, 1989.
The Philippine Atlas. Manila: Philippine Guides, 1998.
Philippine Regional Natural Resources Atlas. 2 vol. By Natural Resources Management Center. Manila: JUMC Pr. 1990.

F. Guidebooks and Handbooks

Barreveld, Dirk J. Manila: *Guide to Asia's Most Exciting Capital. Cebu City:* Arcilla Integrated Marketing Inc. 1999.
Guerrero, Amadis Marìa. *Traveler's Choice: From North to South*. Manila, Philippines: Anvil Publishers, 1993.
A Guide to Philippine Economic & Business Information Sources. Manila, Philippines: Joint Forum for Philippine Progress, 1990.
Harper, Peter. *Philippines Handbook*. 2nd ed. Chico, Calif.: Moon Publications, 1994.
The Ins and Outs of Metro Manila. Manila, Philippines: Philippine Guides and Merriam & Webster, 1985.
Investor's Guide to the Philippines. Ermita, Manila, Philippines: Mahal Kong.
Metro Manila: Street Atlas. Mandaluyong City: Asiatype, Inc., 1997.
Peters, James. *The Philippines, a Travel Survival Kit*. 5th ed. South Yarra, Victoria, Australia: Lonely Planet, 1994.
Philippine Business Profiles: 1990–1991. Makati, Metro Manila.
Philippine Company Profiles. Ermita, Manila, Philippines: Mahal Kong Pilipinas, 1993.
Philippine Encyclopedia of the Social Sciences. Quezon City, Philippines: Philippine Social Science Council, 1993.
Philippine Overseas Employment Guidebook: *Compiled Testimony for all Industry Practitioners*. Quezon City, Philippines: AIDEC International Marketing and Management Systems, 1989.
Philippines (Insight Guide Series). 8th rev. ed. Boston, Mass.: Houghton Mifflin, 1994.
Shopping & Travelling the Exotic Philippines. San Luis Obispo, Calif.: Impact Publications, 1995.
Timberman, David G. and Ma. Anne M. Corpuz, eds. *A Guide to Philippine Economic and Business Information Sources*. Manila, Philippines: The Makati Business Club for the Joint Forum for Philippine Progress, 1990.
Verlag, Nelles. *Philippines*. Cincinnati, OH: Seven Hills Book, 1993.

G. Indexes

Fookien Times Yearbook Master Index, 1936–1980. Manila: Fookien Times Yearbook Publishing.

Index to Philippine Periodicals. Quezon City: University of the Philippines Library, 1955–.

Index to Philippine Periodical Literature, 1946–1967. Quezon City: University of the Philippines Library, 1972.

Index to Filipino Poetry in English, 1905–1950. Compiled by Edna Zapanta-Manlapuz, Gemino H. Abad. Manila: National Book Store, 1988.

Index to Philippine Book Reviews, 1972–1982. Compiled by Verna C. Lee. Sydney: Bibliographic Information on Southeast Asia, University of Sydney, 1966.

Index to Philippine Periodicals. Quezon City: University of the Philippines Library, 2002.

Index to Philippine Plays, 1923–1983. Compiled by Maria Nena R. Mata. Manila: National Book Store, 1984.

Index to Plays, 1946–1967. Diliman: University of the Philippines Library, 1970.

Literary Index, 1932–1945. Quezon City: University of the Philippines Library, 1971

Manila Times Index, 1946–1969. Quezon City: University of the Philippines Library.

Philippine Business and Industry Index. Manila: Library Integrated Services Cooperative, 1980.

Philippine Daily Express Index 1972–1984. Quezon City: Ateneo De Manila University Libraries.

Philippine Essay and General Literatue Index. Compiled by Maria Nena R. Mata. Manila: National Book Store, 1984.

Philippine Treaties Index 1946–1982. Manila: Philippine Foreign Service Institute, 1983.

Philippine Short Story Index. Compiled by Maria Nena R. Mata. Manila: Rizal Library, Ateneo de Manila University, 1976.

Tagalog Periodical Literature. Compiled by Teodoro A. Agoncillo. Manila: Institute of National Language, 1953.

H. Statistical Sources

Compendium of Philippine Social Statistics. Manila: National Statistical Coordination Board, Economic and Social Statistics Office.

Factbook Philippines. Quezon City: FactsPhil, 1993.

Fookien Times Philippine Yearbook. Manila: Fookien Times Publishing Co., 2002.

Inventory of Statistics Avaliable in Government. Manila: National Statistical Coordination Board, 1993.

NSO Monthly Bulletin of Statistics. Manila: National Statistics Office. *Provincial Profile.* Manila: National Statistical Office, 1990.

Philippine Agribusiness Factbook and Directory. Manila: CRC.

Philippine Statistical Yearbook. Manla: National Economic and Development Authority, 2002.

Philippine National Statistical Coordination Board. *Inventory of Statistics Available in Government*. Manila: National Statistical Coordination Board. 1983.

PART 2. HISTORY

A. Historiography

Abinales, Patricio N. *State Authority and Local Power in Southern Philippines*. Ithaca, N.Y.: Cornell University, 1997.

Aguirre, Alexander P. and Ismael Z. Villareal. *Readings on Counterinsurgency*. Quezon City, Philippines: Pan Service Master Consultants, 1987.

Amnesty International. *Philippines: Unlawful Killings by Military and Paramilitary Forces*. London: Amnesty International Publications, 1988.

Anderson, James N. *Critical Issues in the Philippine Research: A Selected and Annotated Literature Review on the Women's Movement, Conflict in Luzon's Cordillera, Muslim Autonomy, and the Recent Political Resistance*. Berkeley: Center for South and Southeast Asia Studies, University of California, 1996.

Campomanes, Oscar V. "The New Empire's Forgetful and Forgotten Citizens: Unpresentability and Unassimilability in Filipino–American Post Colonialists" *Critical Mass*. Vol. 2. No. 2 (Spring 1995). 145–200.

Casiño, Eric S. *Mindanao Statecraft and Ecology. Moros, Lumads, and Settlers Across the Lowland Highland Continuum*. Cotabato City: Notre Dame University, 2000.

Costa, Horacio de la. SJ. *The Jesuits in the Philippines 1581–1768*. Cambridge, Mass.: Harvard University, 1967.

Cushner, Nicholas P. *Landed Estates in the Colonial Philippines*. New Haven: Yale University, Southeast Asia Monographs, 1976.

Davis, Leonard. *Revolutionary Struggle in the Philippines*. New York: St. Martin's Press, 1989.

Doeppers, Daniel and Xeros, Peter, eds. *Population and History: The Demographic Origins of Modern Philippines*. Madison, Wisc. Center for Southeast Asian Studies: 1998.

De Castro, Arturo M. "Mistrial: A Case Study of the Assasination of Senator Benigno Aquino, Jr.": *Current Events Digest*, 1986. 120+.

George, Thayil J. *Revolt in Mindanao: The Rise of Islam in Philippine Politics*. Kuala Lumpur, Malaysia: New York, Oxford University Press, 1980.

Gowing, Peter. *Muslim Filipinos–Heritage and Horizon*. Quezon City: New Day, 1979.

Gloria, Heidi K. *The Bagobo: Their Ethnohistory and Acculturation*. Quezon City: New Day, 1987.

Hart, Donn V., ed. *Philippine Studies: History, Sociology, Mass Media and Bibliography*. Occasional Papers, No. 6. 1978.

———. *An Annotated Bibliography of Philippine Bibliographies*. Occasional Papers, No. 4.

Holt, Elizabeth Mary. *Colonizing Filipinas: Ninteenth Century Representations of the Philippines in Western Historiography*. Manila: Ateneo De Manila University Press, 2002.

Hutchcraft, Paul. "Colonial Masters, National Politics, Provincial Lords: Central Authority in the American Philippines, 1900–1913." *Journal of Asian Studies* 59. No. 2, 2000.

Ileto, Reynaldo C. *Filipinos and Their Revolution: Event, Discourse, and Historiography*. Manila: Ateneo De Manila University Press, 1999.

Jones, Gregg R. *Red Revolution: Inside the Philippine Guerrilla Movement*. Boulder, Colo.: Westview Press, 1989.

Kessler, Richard J. *Revolution and Repression in the Philippines*. New Haven: Yale University Press, 1989.

Lande, Carl H., et al. *Southern Tagalog Uprising 1946–1963*. Political Behavior in a Philippine Region. Special Reports, no. 7, 1973.

Larkin, John A., ed. *Perspective in Philippine Historiography; A Symposium*. New Haven: Southeast Asia Monograph, 1979.

Linn, Brian M. *The Philippine War 1899–1906*. Lawrence: University of Kansas Press, 2000.

Malcolm, George A. *First Malaysian Republic. The Story of the Philippines*. Boston: Christopher Publishing House, 1951.

May, Glenn. "The State of Philippine American Studies." *Essays on Philippine History and Historiography*. Quezon City: New Day, 1987.

May, Ronald James. *Vigilantes in the Philippines*. Manoa: University of Hawaii (Philippine Studies Occasional Papers: 12, 1992).

McCoy, Alfred and Ed. De Jesus. *Philippine Social History: Global Trade and Local Transformations*. Quezon City: Ateneo de Manila University Press, 1982.

Miller, Stuart Creighton. "Benevolent Assimilation." *The American Conquest of the Philippines*. New Haven: Yale University Press, 1982.

Molina, Carmen. "Filipino Migrants in Spain." *Philippine Studies*. 40 (First Quarter), 1992. 99–110.

Owen, Norman G., ed. *Compadre Colonialism: Studies on the Philippines Under American Rule*. Ann Arbor, Michigan: 1971.

Paredes, Ruby., ed. *Philippine Colonial Democracy*. New Haven: Yale University, Southeast Asia Studies, 1988.

Pido, Antonio. *The Pilipinos in America: Micro/Macro Dimensions of Integration*. New York: Center for Migration Studies, 1986.

Rafael, Vicente. *White Love and Other Events in Philippine History*. Duham, N.C.; Duke University Press, 2000.

Reyes, Portia. "The Treasonous History of Filipino Historiography. The Life and Times of Pedro Paterno, 1858–1911." *Southeast Asian Studies Program*. National University of Singapore, 2003.

San Juan, Epifanio Jr. "Configuring the Filipino Diaspora in the United States." *Diaspora* 3:2 (Fall), 1994, 117–134.

Scott, William Henry. *Cracks in the Parchment and Other Essays in Philippine History*. Quezon City: New Day, 1982.

———. *Filipinos in China Before 1500*. Manila: De La Salle University Press, 1989.

Simkins, Paul and Wernstedt, Frederick L. *Philippine Migration: The Settlement of Digos-Padada Valley, Davao Province*. New Haven: Yale University Press, 1971.

Thompson, Mark R. *The Anti-Marcos Struggle: Personalistic Rule and Democratic Transition in the Philippines.* New Haven: Yale University Press, 1995.

Tordesillas, Ellen and Greg Hutchinson. *Hot Money, Warm Bodies. The Downfall of Philippine President Joseph Estrada*. Manila: Anvil Press, 2001.

Vellut, J. L. *The Asian Policy of the Philippines 1954–61*. ANU, Canberra: 1965.

Welch, Richard. *Response to Imperialism: The United States and the Philippine–American War 1899–1902.* Chapel Hill, S.C.; University of North Carolina Press, 1979.

Zwick, Jim. "The Anti-Imperialist League and the Origins of Filipino–American Opposition Solidarity." *American Journal* 24 (No. 2), 64–65, 1998.

B. General History

Abueva, Jose V., ed. *The Making of the Filipino Nation and Republic: From Barangays, Tribes, Sultanates, and Colony*. Manila: University of the Philippines Press, 1998.

Aguinaldo, Emilio. *Reseña veridica de la revolucion Filipina: True Version of the Philippine Revolution.* Manila: National Historical Institute, 1899, 2002.

Alejandrino, Jose. *The Price of Freedom*. Manila: Solar Publishing Corp., 1986.

Allen, Francis J. *The Concrete Battleship: Fort Drum, El Fraile Is land*, Manila Bay. Missoula, Mont.: Pictorial Histories Publishing, 1989.

Arcilla, Jose SJ. *An Introduction to Philippine History*. Manila: Ateneo De Manila University Press, 2000.

———. *Rizal and the Emergence of the Philippine Nation*. Manila: Ateneo De Manila University Press, 2001.

Arcilla, José S. *The Fine Print of Philippine History*. Makati, Metro Manila, Philippines: St. Paul Publications, 1992.

Bankoff, Greg and Kathleen Weekley. *Post Colonial National Identity in the Philippines: Celebrating the Centennial of Independence*. Aldershot, UK; Burlington, Vt.; Ashgate, 2002.

Bauzon, Leslie E., ed. *In Search of Historical Truth*. Quezon City: Heritage Publishing House, 1992.

Best, Jonathan. *A Philippine Album: American Era Photographs, 1900–1930*. Makati City: Bookmark, 1998.

Blair, Emma Helen and James Alexander Robertson, eds. *The Philippine Islands, 1493–1803: Explorations by Early Navigators, Descriptions of the Islands and Their Peoples, Their History and Records of the Catholic Missions, as Related in Contemporaneous Books and Manuscripts, Showing the Political, Economic, Commercial and Religious Conditions of Those Islands from Their Earliest Relations with European Nations to the Beginning of the Nineteenth Century*. Manila: s.n., 1962.

Borromeo, Soledad Masangkay. *The Cry of Balintawak: A Contrived Controversay: A Textual Analysis with Appended Documents*. Quezon City: Ateneo De Manila University Press, 1998.

Brainard, Cecilia Manguerra and Edmundo F. Litton. *Journey of 100 Years: Reflections on the Centennial of Philippine Independence*. Santa Monica, Calif.: Philippine–American Women Artists and Writers, 1999.

Brodie, Scott. *Philippines*. London: Watts, 2002.

Brown, John Clifford. *Gentlemen Soldier*. College Station: Texas A&M University Press, 2004.

Burton, Sandra. *Impossible Dream: The Marcoses, the Aquinos, and the Unfinished Revolution*. New York: Warner Books, 1989.

Calero, Ana Mari S. *Three Continents*. Manila: De La Salle University Press, 2001.

Co, Jason. *The Spirit of 1896: A Mirror of the Philippine Past, a Window on its Future*. Quezon City. University of the Philippine Press, 2000.

Constantino, Renato. *A History of the Philippines: From the Spanish Colonization to the Second World War*. New York: Monthly Review Press, 1975.

Costa, Horacio de la SJ. *Readings in Philippine History*. Manila: Bookmark, 1965.

Coronel, Sheila S. *Coups, Cults & Cannibals: Chronicles of a Troubled Decade, 1982–1992*. Manila: Anvil Publishing, 1993.

Corpuz, Onofre D. *The Roots of the Filipino Nation*. 2 vols. Quezon City: Aklahi Foundation, 1989.

Crisostomo, Isabelo T. *Cory—Profile of a President*. Brookline Village, Mass.: Branden Publishing Co. 1987.

Cruz, Neni Sta. Romana and Lorna Kalaw-Tirol. *Tales from EDSA*. Pasig City: Anvil Publishers, 2000.

Custodio, Teresa Ma. and Jose Y. Dalisay. *Kasaysayan: The Story of the Filipino People*. Manila: Asia Publishing Co., Pleasantville, N.Y.: Reader's Digest, 1998.

De La Cruz, Enrique B. and Pearlie Rose Baluyut. *Confrontations, Crossings and Convergence: Photographs of the Philippines and the United States. 1898–1998*. Los Angeles: UCLA Asian American Study Center, 1998.

Diokno, Ma. Serena. *Up From the Ashes*. Pleasantville, N.Y.: Reader's Digest, 1998.

Desuasido, Rodolfo N. *Katipunan: hakbang tungo sa revolusyon*. Quezon City: Adarna Book Services, 1997.

Dolan, Robert E., ed. *The Philippines: A Country Study.* 4th ed. Washington, D.C.: Library of Congress, 1993.

Encarnacion, Emmanuel. *Ang Pamana ni Andres Bonifacio.* Quezon City: Adarna Books Services, 1997.

Escalante, Rene R. *The American Friar Lands Policy: Its Framers, Contexts, and Beneficiaries, 1898–1916.* Manila: De La Salle University Press, 2002.

Fajardo, Reynald S. *Dimasalang. Calasiao, Pangasinan*: CMM Printing, 1999.

Feleo, Anita Kasaysay: *The Story of the Filipino People.* Manila: University of Santo Tomas Press, 1998.

Fenner, Bruce Leonard. *Cebu under the Spanish Flag, 1521–1896: An Economic-Social History.* Cebu City: University of San Carlos, 1985.

Filipino Heritage: The Making of a Nation. 4 vols. Manila: Lahing Filipino Publishing, 1977.

Fisher, Shirley. *When Britain Ruled the Philippines, 1762–1764: The Story of the 18th Century British Invasion of the Philippines.*

During the Seven Years War. Bloomington, Ind.: 1st Books, 2003.

Forest, James H. *Four Days in February: The Story of the Nonviolent Overthrow of the Marcos Regime.* Basingstoke, U.K.: M. Pickering, 1988.

Francisco, Juan R. *The Philippines and India. Essays in Ancient Cultural History.* Manila: National Book Store, 1971.

———. "Notes on the Contact History of Mindanao and Sulu." *Mindanao Journal,* Vol. III, January–June 1977.

———. "Man and God in Pre-Hispanic Manila." *Metro Manila Magazine,* April 1–15 1977, pp. 1–7.

Gagelonia, Pedro A. *Concise Philippine History.* Manila: Far Eastern University Consumers Cooperative, 1970.

Gaspar, Karl. *How Long?: Prison Reflections from the Philippines.* Maryknoll, N.Y.: Orbis Books, 1986.

Guingona, Teofisto. *Laban: Voice of Resistance.* Manila: T. Guingona, 1987.

Go, Bon Juan and Joaquin Sy. *The Philippines in Ancient Chinese Maps.* Manila: Kaisa Para sa Kaunlaran, 2000.

Gonzales, Barbara C. *We're History: A Memoir on History and Culture.* Pasig City: Anvil Publications, 1998.

Hicks, Nigel. *This is the Philippines.* London: New Holland, 1999.

Izon, Esmeraldo Z. *Cartoon History of the Philippines.* Manila: Philippine Free Press, 1993.

Joaquin, Nick. *Culture and History: Occasional Notes on the Process of Philippine Becoming.* Metro Manila: Solar Publishing, 1988.

———. *A Question of Heroes: Essays in Criticism on Ten Key Figures of Philippine History.* Makati: Ayala Museum, Filipinas Foundation, 1977.

Jocano, F. Landa. *Filipino Prehistory. Rediscovering Precolonial Heritage.* Manila: Punlad Research House, 1998.

Kalaw-Tirol, Lorna. *Public Faces, Private Lives.* Quezon City: Anvil Publishing, 2000.

Kasaysayan. *The Story of the Filipino People.* Hong Kong: Asia Publishers, 1998.

Kasaysayan mula sa bayan: History from the People. Manila: National Historical Institute and Philippine National Historical Society, 1998.

King, David. *Philippines: Know and Appreciate Our Homeland.* New York: World Link Books, 2002.

Landicho, Domingo G. *Diskurso sa Pilipinismo: Pagsilang ng Inang Bayan.* Quezon City: University of the Philippines Press, 2001.

Lico, Gerard. *Edifice Complex: Power, Myth, and Marcos State Architecture.* Quezon City: Ateneo De Manila University Press, 2003.

Linn, Brian McAllister. *The Philippine War 1899–1902.* Lawrence: University Press of Kansas, 2002.

Lopez, Salvador P. *The Judgement of History: Elpidio Quirino.* Manila: President Elpidio Quirino Foundation, 1990.

Magno, Alexander R. *A Nation Reborn.* Pleasantville, N.Y.: Reader's Digest, 1998.

Manalo, Ino. *Home of Independence: Emilio Aguinaldo.* House, Kawit, Cavite, Manila: National Historical Insitute, 1998.

Mata, Nestor. *Cory of a Thousand Days.* Manila: Solidaridad Publishing House, 1989.

Mauricio, Luis R. *Renato Constantino and the Marcos Watch.* Quezon City: Karrel Inc, 1986.

May, Glenn Anthony. *A Past Recovered.* Quezon City: New Day Publishers, 1987.

May, R. J. and Francisco Nemenzo, eds. *The Philippines after Marcos.* New York: St. Martin's Press, 1985.

McCoy, Alfred W., ed. *An Anarchy of Families: State and Family in the Philippines.* Madison, Wisc.: University of Wisconsin, Center for Southeast Asian Studies, 1993.

Melchor, Merci and Auri Asuncion Yambao. *Bandila: The Story of thePhilippine Flag.* Manila: Tahanan Books for Young Readers, 1998.

Mojares, Resil B. *Waiting For Mariang Makiling: Essays in Philippine Cultural History.* Manila: Ateneo De Manila University Press, 2002.

Morallos, Chando P. *Treasures of the National Library: A Brief History of the Premier Library of the Philippines.* Manila: National Library, 1998.

Ocampo, Ambeth R. *The Centennial Countdown.* Pasig City: Anvil Publishers, 1998.

Ochosa, Orlino A. and Viva Isabelo Abaya: *A Belated Salute to the Ilocano Hero Snubbed by History.* Quezon City: Giraffe Books, 1999.

Oleksy, Walter. *The Philippines Enchantment of the World.* New York: Children's Press, 2000.

One Hundred Events That shaped the Philippines. Mandaluyong City: National Centennial Commission, 1999.

One Hundred Years (100). Quezon City: Philippine Historical Association in cooperation with New Day Publishers, 1999.

Overholt, William B. "The Rise and Fall of Ferdinand Marcos." *Asian Survey*, 26, No. 11 (November 1986), 1137–1163.

Peralta, Jesus T. and Lucila A. Salazar. *Pre-Spanish Manila: A Reconstruction of the Pre-History of Manila.* National Historical Institute, Manila: 1994, 2nd printing 1993.

Phelan, John Leddy. *The Hispanization of the Philippines: Spanish Aims and Filipino Responses. 1565–1700.* Madison: University of Wisconsin Press, 1967.

Quibuyen, Floro C. *A Nation Aborted: Rizal, American Hegemony, and Philippine Nationalism.* Quezon City: Ateneo De Manila University Press, 1999.

Quisumbing, Jose R. *The American Occupation of Cebu Warwick Barracks, 1899–1917.* Cebu City: J. R. Quisumbing, 1983.

Rafael, Vicente L. "Nationalism, Imagery, and the Filipino Intelligentsia in the Nineteenth Century." *Critical Inquiry* 16 (Spring 1990): 591–611.

Recto, Claro M. *Vintage Recto: Memorable Speeches and Writings.* Quezon City: Foundation for Nationalist Studies, 1986.

Rocha, Eduardo A. *From Britain to the Philippines.* Makati City: ACE Multimedia (HK), 1998.

Rodao, Florentino and Felice Noelle Rodriquez, eds. *The Philippine Revolution of 1896: Ordinary Lives in Extraordinary Times.* Quezon City: Ateneo de Manla University Press, 2001.

Salazar, Z. A. et al. *Himagsikang Filipino: Digma ng mga Anak ng Bayan.* Manila: The Authors, 1996.

San Diego, Salvador E. *Lakas ng sambayanan (people power): alay kay Ninoy Aquino at sa massang Pilipino.* Quezon City: SANDUGO Enterprises, 1987.

Santiago, Miriam Defensor. *Cutting Edge: The Politics of Reform in the Philippines.* Manila: Woman Today Publications, 1994.

Schemenauer, Elma. *The Philippines.* Chanhassen, Minn.: Child's World, 2000.

Schraff, Anne E. *Philippines.* Minneapolis, Minn.: Carolhoda Books, 2000.

Schumacher, John N. *Father Jose Burgos: A Documentary History with Spanish Documents and Their Translation.* Quezon City: Ateneo De Manila Press, 1999.

Schurz, William Lytle. *The Manila Galleon.* New York: Dutton, 1959.

Scott, William Henry. *Barangay, Sixteenth Century Philippine Culture and Society.* Manila: Ateneo De Manila University Press, 1994.

Siegel, Beatrice. *Cory: Corazon Aquino and the Philippines.* New York: Dutton, 1988.

Silliman, Sidney D. "The Philippines in 1983: Authoritarianism Beleaguered." *Asian Survey* 24 No. 2 (February 1984), 148–158.

Steinberg, David Joel. *The Philippines: A Singular and a Plural Place.* 2nd ed. Boulder, Colo.: Westview Press, 1990.

Sullivan, Margaret. *The Philippines Pacific Crossroads.* New York: Dillon Press, 1993.

Tan, Samuel K. *A History of the Philippines.* Quezon City: Manila Studies Association, 1997.

———. *The Critical Decade, 1921–1930.* Quezon City: University of the Philippines and the National Commission on Culture and Arts, 1993.

Totanes, Henry S. *A Timeline of Philippine History.* Pleasantville, N.Y.: Reader's Digest. 1998.

Tope, Lily Rose R. *Philippines*. New York: Marshall Cavendish, 1999.

Torres, Jose Victor Z. *Pananaw: Viewing Points on Philippine History and Culture*. Manila: UST Publication House, 2002.

Villanueva, Rene. *Dagohoy: Ang Mandirigmang Hindi Sumuko*. Quezon City: Adarna House, 2002.

Wild, Mary C. *Philippines*. San Diego, Calif.: Lucent Books, 2004.

Wood, Alan Thomas. *Asian Democracy in World History*. New York, 2004.

Worcester, D. C. *The Philippine Islands*. Vols. I & II. New York: MacMillan, 1914.

Wright, Martin, ed. *Revolution in the Philippines?* Chicago: St. James Press, 1988.

Wu Ching-hong. *A Study Reference to the Philippines in Chinese Sources from Earliest to the Ming Dynasty*. Quezon City: University of the Philippines Press, 1959.

Yoder, Carolyn P. *Filipino Americans*. Chicago: Heinemanm Library, 2003.

Zaide, Gregorio F., ed. *Documentary Sources of Philippine History*. Metro Manila, Philippines: National Book Store, 1990.

——. *Jose Rizal: Life, Works and Writings of a Genius, Writer, Scientist, and National Hero*. Manila: National Book Store, 1984.

Zaide, Sonia M. *The Philippines: A Unique Nation*. Quezon City: All Nations Publishers, 1999.

C. Regional History

Abat, Fortunato U. *The Day We Nearly Lost Mindanao*. The CEMCOM Story: How CEMCOM Checked the Secessionist Attempt to Establish a de Facto Bangsa Moro Republic in Cotabato. 2nd ed. San Juan, Metro Manila: F. U. Abat, 1994.

Alcina, Francisco Ignacio. et al. *History of the Visayan People: Evangelization and Culture at the Contact Period*. Manila: UST Publishing House, 2002.

Aldecoa-Rodriguez, Caridad. *Negros Oriental and the Philippine Revolution*. Dumaguete City, Philippines: Provincial Government of Negros Oriental, 1983.

——. *History of Dumaguete City*. Dumaguete City: Author, 2001.

Almeda, Fernando A., Jr. *Story of a Province: Surigao across the Years*. Diliman, Quezon City: Heritage Publishing House, 1993.

Alunan, Merlie M. and Bobby Flores Villasis, eds. *Kabilin: Legacies of a Hundred Years of Negros Oriental*. Dumaguete City, Philippines: Negros Oriental Centennial Foundation, 1993.

Arenas, Mar D. *Valenzuela: Ang Bayani at ang Bayan*. Metro Manila: Museo Valenzuela Foundation, 1997.

Bonocan, Rhina Alvero and Dwight Diestro David. *A. Nineteenth Century Conditions and the Revolution in the Province of Laguna*. Quezon City: University of the Philippines, Center for Integrative and Development Studies. 2002.

Buchhholdt, Thelma. *Filipinos in Alaska: 1788–1958*. Anchorage, Alaska: Aboriginal Press, 1996.

Calairo, Emmanuel Franco. *Noveleta: Bayan Ng Magdiwang*. Dasmariñas, Cavite: Cavite Historical Society, 2000.

———. *Cavite: El Viejo, Kasaysayan, Lipunan, Kultura*. Dasmariñas, Cavite: Cavite Historical Society, 1998.

Calairo, Rosalina M. et al. *Ang Kasaysayan ng Novaliches: prehistori hanggang sa panahon ng Hapon*. Lunsod Quezon: R. M. Franco-Calairo, 1997.

Carigara: Six Hundred Years of History in a Town in Leyte. Carigara, Leyte, Philippines: Carigara 400, 1995.

Cebu: More Than an Island. Makati City: Ayala Foundation, 1997.

Cojuangco, Margarita R. *Tarlac: Prehistory to World War II*. Tarlac: Provincial Government of Tarlac, 1997.

Contreras, Edward B. *Capiz, Prospect and Retrospect*. Panay, Capiz: E. B. Contreras, 1993.

Corcino, Ernesto I. *Davao History*. Davao City: Philippine Centennial Movement, 1998.

Cortes, Rosario Mendoza. *Pangasinan 1801–1900: The Beginnings of Modernization*. Detroit, Mich.: The Cellar Book Shop, 1991.

———. *Pangasinan 1901–1986: A Political, Socioeconomic and Cultural History*. Detroit, Mich.: The Cellar Book Shop, 1991.

Cuesta, Angel Martinez., trans. *History of Negros*. Manila: Historical Conservation Society, 1980.

Cullamar, Evelyn Tan. *Babaylanism in Negros, 1896–1907*. Quezon City: New Day Publishers, 1986.

Dulawan, Lourdes S. *Ifugao: Culture and History*. Manila: National Commission for Culture and the Arts, 2001.

De Paz, Ernesto L. *Nagcarlan in Perspective*. Manila: De La Salle University Press, 1999.

Doeppers, Daniel F. "Metropolitan Manila in the Great Depression: Crisis for Whom?" *Journal of Asian Studies* 50 (August 1991): 511–535.

Echevarria, Ramon. *Rediscovery in Southern Cebu*. Cebu City: Historical Conservation Society, 1974.

Fenner, Bruce Leonard. *Cebu under the Spanish Flag, 1521–1896: An Economic–Social History*. Cebu City: University of San Carlos, 1985.

Foronda, Marcelino A. *Kasaysayan: Studies on Local and Oral History*. Manila: De La Salle University Press, 1991.

Fry, Howard T. *A History of the Mountain Province*. Quezon City: New Day Publishers, 1983.

Funtecha, Henry Florida and Melanie J. Padilla. *Historical Landmarks and Monuments of Iloilo*. Iloilo City: Visayan Studies Program, U. P. in the Visayas, 1987.

Gabriel, Manuel G. and James Kroeger. *Sons of San Jose: The Josefina Spirit: A Profile*. Quezon City: San Jose Seminary Alumni Association, 2002.

Gonzaga, Violeta B. Lopez. *Land of Hope, Land of Want: A Socio-Economic History of Negros, 1571–1985*. Quezon City: Philippine National Historical Society, 1994.

Griffin, P. Bion and Agnes Estioko Griffin. *The Agta of Northeastern Luzon: Recent Studies*. Cebu City: University of San Carlos, 1985.

Hechanova, Louie G. *The Baclaran Story.* Quezon City: Claretian Publications, 1998.

Joaquin, Nick. *My Manila: A History for the Young.* Manila: Republic of the Philippines. Manila: 1990.

Kellock, Elizabeth. "A Certain Liveliness in Sulu 1876." *Asian Affairs* 22 (February 1991): 46–53.

Luengo, Jose Maria S. *Pedro Calungsod: The Visayo Protomartyr in Tumhon, Guam, April 2, 1672.* Tubigon, Bohol: Mater Dei Publications, 1998.

———. *A History of the Philippines: Focus on PELBURGONZA, Pelaez, Burgos, Gomez, Zamora: The Galvanizers of Filipino Nationalism, Freedom, and Independence, 1582–1872.* Tubigon, Bohol: Slus Insitute Publications, 2000.

Magno, Francisco A. "Politics, Elites and Transformation in Malabon." *Philippine Studies* 41, 2 (1993): 204–216.

Mallari, Francisco A. *Vignettes of Bicol History.* Quezon City: New Day Publishers, 1999.

Martinez, Manuel F.A. *History of Quezon Province.* Parañaque City: MFM Enterprises, 1999.

Mata, Elvira and Chit Lijauco. *Batanes, Philippines.* Batanes: 1997.

May, Glenn Anthony. *Battle for Batangas: A Philippine Province at War.* New Haven, Conn.: Yale University Press, 1991.

Meimban, Adriel Obar. *La Union: The Making of a Province. 1850–1921.* Quezon City: Rex Printing Co. 1997.

Mindanao: A Portrait. Manila: Bookmark, 1999.

Mojares, Resil B. *Casa Gorordo in Cebu: Urban Residence in a Philippine Province 1860–1920.* Cebu City: Ramon Aboitiz Foundation, 1983.

———. *History of Cebu: Bibliographic Guide.* Cebu City: Cebuano Studies Center, University of San Carlos, 1980.

Montebon, Marivir R. *Retracing Our Roots: A Journey into Cebu's Colonial Past.* Cebu City: ES Villver Publication, 2000.

Navarro, Atoy. *Tayabas: Pagmumulat sa Kasaysayan, Himagsikan, at Sentenaryo.* Lunsod Quezon: Limbagang Pangkasaysayan, 1998.

On The Trail to Freedom: People, Places, and Events of the PhilippineRevolution: A Historical Adventure on the Centennial Freedom Trail. Laguna, Manila, Cavite, Batangas, and Bulacan, Manila: Convention & Visitors Corporation, 1998.

Ordoñez, Elmer A. *Toward the First Asian Republic: Papers from the Jakarta International Conference on the Centenary of the Philippine Revolution and the First Asian Republic.* Jakarta: Indonesia, 1997.

Owen, Norman G. *The Bikol Blend: Bikolanos and Their History.* Quezon City: New Day Publishers, 1999.

Pastells, Pablo. *Mission to Mindanao, 1850–1900.* Cebu City: University of San Carlos, 1994.

Provincial Profiles, Philippines. Quezon City: Department of Agriculture, 1988.

Realubit, Maria Lilia F. *Bikols of the Philippines.* City of Naga. A. M. S. Press, 1983.

Reed, Robert R. *City of Pines: The Origins of Baguio as a Colonial Hill Station and Regional Capital.* Berkeley: Center for South and Southeast Asian Studies, University of California, 1976.

Regalado, Felix B. and Quintin B. Franco. *History of Panay*. Iloilo City: Central Philippine University, 1973.

Romero, Ma. Fe Hernaez. *Negros Occidental between Two Foreign Powers (1880–1909)*. Bacolod: Negros Occidental Historical Commission, 1974.

Rood, Steven. "Issues on Creating an Autonomous Region for the Cordillera, Northern Philippines." *Ethnic and Racial Studies* 14 (October 1991): 516–544.

Saleeby, Najeed M. *The History of Sulu*. Manila: Filipiniana Book Guild, 1963.

Schreurs, Peter. *Angry Days in Mindanao*. Cebu City: University of San Carlos, 1987.

Scott, William Henry. *Barangay: Sixteenth-Century Philippine Culture and Society*. Manila: Ateneo de Manila University Press, 1994.

Serag, Sebastian Sta. Cruz. *The Remnants of the Great Ilonggo Nation*. Manila: Rex Book Store, 1997.

Tagarao, Silvestre L. *All This Was Bataan*. Quezon City: New Day Publishers, 1991.

Tantuico, Francisco S., Jr. *Leyte: The Historic Islands*. Tacloban: Leyte Publishing, 1964.

Villacorta, Wilfrido V., Isagani R. Cruz, and Ma. Lourdes Brillantes, eds. *History, People and Culture: The Proceedings of the Manila Studies Conference*. Manila: De La Salle University Press, 1989.

Villarica, F. D. *Oriental Mindoro from the Dawn of Civilization to the year 2000 A.D.* Calapan City: Island Printing Press, 1998

Wolters, Willem G. *Politics, Patronage, and Class Conflict in Central Luzon*. The Hague, The Netherlands: Institute of Social Studies, 1983.

Zaide, Sonia M., ed. *Butuan, the First Kingdom: A Monograph for the City Government of Butuan*. Butuan: City of Butuan, 1990.

D. Spanish Period

Achutegui, Pedro S. de and Miguel A. Bernard. *Aguinaldo and the Revolution of 1896: A Documentary History*. Quezon City: Ateneo de Manila University Press, 1972.

Agoncillo, Teodoro A. Malolos: *The Crisis of the Republic*. Quezon City: University of the Philippines, 1960.

Aguilera Rojas, Javier. *Manila, 1571–1898: Occidente en Oriente*. Madrid: Ministerio de Fomento, Secretaria General Tecnica, Centro Publicaciones, 1998.

Alva Rodriguez, Immaculada. *Vida Municipal en Manila, Siglos XVI–XVII*. Cordoba: Universidad de Cordoba, 1997.

Alvarez y Tejero and Luis Prudencio. *Memoirs of the Philippine Islands*. Valencia, Spain: Caberizo Printing, 1998.

Alvina, Corazon S. *The World of 1896*. Makati City: Quezon City: Bookmark, 1998.

Cabrero, Leoncio. *Histori General de Filipinas*. Madrid: Ediciones de Cultura Hispanica, 2000.

Cariño, Jose Maria A. Jose *Honorato Lozano*: *Filipinas 1847*. Makati City: Ars Mundi, 2002.

Castellanos Escudier, Alicia. *Filipinas. De la Insurreccion a la intervencion de Estados Unidos 1896–1899*. Madrid: Silex, 1998.

Chirino, Pedro. *Historia de la Provincia de Filipinas de la Companya de Jesus 1581–1606*. Barcelona: Portic, 2000.

Churchill, Bernardita Reyes. *Revolution in the Provinces*. Quezon City: National Commission for Culture and the Arts, 1999.

Churchill, Bernardito Reyes and Francis Geologo. *Centernnial Papers on the Katipunan and the Revolution*. Quezon City: National Commission on Culture and the Arts 1999.

Constantino, Renato. *A History of the Philippines: From the Spanish Colonization to the Second World War*. New York: Monthly Review Press, 1975.

Corpuz, Onofre D. *Saga and Triumph: The Filipino Revolution Against Spain*. Quezon City: University of the Philippines Press, 2002.

Costa, Horacio de la, ed. *The Trial of Rizal*. Manila: Ateneo de Manila University Press, 1961.

Cruikshank, Bruce. *Filipiniana in Madrid: Field Notes on Five Major Manuscript Collections*. Honolulu, HI: Philippine Studies Program, Center for Asian and Pacific Studies, University of Hawaii, 1984.

———. *Samar: 1768–1898*. Manila: Historical Conservation Society, 1985.

Cunningham, Charles Henry. *The Audiencia in the Spanish Colonies: As Illustrated by the Audiencia of Manila* (1583–1800). Berkeley: University of California Press, 1919.

Cushner, Nicholas P. *Documents Illustrating the British Conquest of Manila, 1762–1763*. London: Royal Historical Society, 1971.

———. *Isles of the West: Early Spanish Voyages to the Philippines, 1521–1564*. Quezon City: Ateneo de Manila University Press, 1966.

Dery, Luis Camara. *Remember the Ladies and Other Essays in the 1896 Philippine Revolution*. Las Piñas, Metro Manila: M&L Licudine Enterprises, 2000.

Diaz-Trechuelo Spinola, et al. *La Expedicion de Juan Cuellar a Filipinas*. Barcelona: Real Jardin Botanico, Consejo Superior de Investigaciones Cientificas, 1997.

Dizon, Lino.L. *Tarlac and the Revolutionary Landscape: Essays on the Philippine Revolution from a localized perspective*. Tarlac: Center for Tarlaqueños Studies, 1997.

Elizalde, Ma Dolores et al. Obras Clasicas para de la historia de Manila. Madrid: Fundacion Historica Tavera, 1998.

Escoto, Salvador P. *Historical Aspects of the Late 18th Century Philippines: A Collection of Articles*. Northern Illinois University. 2000.

Fernandez de la Reguera, Ricardo. *Heroes de Filipinas: Los Heroes del Desastre*. Barcelona: Planeta, 1998.

Fradera. Josep Maria. *Filipinas La Colonia mas Peculiar. La Hacienda Publica La Definicion de la politica colonial, 1762–1868*. Madrid: Consejo Superior de Investigaciones Cientificas, 1999.

Francisco, Michael C. *Cavite en siglo 19: Translation of Selected 19th Century Documents*. Cavite: Cavite Historical Society, 2002.

Franco, Juan. Muerte *al Castila: La Guerra de Filipinas contada por sus protagonistas*. 1898. Madrid: Parteluz, 1998.

Funtecha, Henry Florida and Melanie Padilla Jalandoni. *The Struggle against the Spaniards and the Americans in the Western Visayas.* Iloilo City: University of the Philippines in the Visayas Centennial Committee, 1998.

Gaspar de San Agustin, et al. *Conquistas de las Islas Filipinas. 1565–1724.* Manila: San Agustin Museum, 1998.

Gonzalez Hurtado, Deogracias. *La Perdida de Filipinas narrada por un soldado extremeño, 1896–1899: Memorias del sargento Deogracias Hurtado.* Merida, Badajoz, España: Editora Regional de Extremadura, 1998.

Gonzalez, Rodriguez y Agustin Ramon. *La Guerra 98: Las Compañas de Cuba, Puerto Rico y Filipinas.* Madrid: Agualarga, 1998.

Guerra, Francisco. *La Educacion Medica en Hispanomerica y Filipinas durante el domino español.Madrid:* Universidad de Alcala, 1998.

Guillermo, Ramon and Soña Almirante Guillermo. *Philippine History and Government.* Manila: Ibon Foundation, 1999.

Hamada, Margarita Ventenilla. *Swatting the Spanish Flies: A Critical Commentary on Some Sweet Lies/Bitter Truths in Philippine History.* Quezon City: Giraffe Books, 2001.

Ileto, Reynaldo Clemeña. *Pasyon and Revolution: Popular Movements in the Philippines, 1840–1910.* Quezon City: Ateneo de Manila University Press, 1979.

——. "Rizal and the Underside of Philippine History." In *Moral Order and the Question of Change: Essays on Southeast Asian Thought.* Ed. by David K. Wyatt and Alexander Woodside. New Haven, Conn.: Yale University Southeast Asian Studies, (1982): 274–377.

——. "The 'Unfinished Revolution' in Philippine Political Discourse." *Southeast Asian Studies* (Kyoto University) 31, 1 (1993): 62–82.

Javellana, Rene B. and Jose Ma. Tan. *Fortress of Empire: Spanish Colonial Fortifications of the Philippines.* Makati City: Bookmark, 1997.

Jerez, Luis Moreno. *The Spanish Prisoners Held by the Tagalogs*: A Historical Narrative of Their Captivity and the Measures Taken for Their Freedom. Manila: National Historical Insitute, 1998.

King, Jenny. *Great and Famous Filipinos.* S.I.: Woodlink Books, 2001.

Leguineche, Manuel. *Yo te dire: La verdadera historia de los ultimos de Filipinas (1898–1998).* Madrid: El Pais-Aguilar, 1998.

Luengo, Jose Maria S. *History of the Philippines: Focus Miguel Ayatumo: The Filipino Profoconfesor, 15963–1609.* Tubigon, Bohol: Leungo Foundation, 2001.

Mallat de Bassilan, Jean Baptiste. *The Philippines: History, Geography, Customs, Agriculture, Industry, and Commerce of the Spanish Colonies in Oceania.* Manila: National Historical Institute, 1983.

Manchado Lopez, Marta M. *La Politica Religiosa del alaves Simon de Anda y Salazar en Filipinas.* Bilbao: Fundacion BB, 1997.

Morga, Antonio de. *Sucesos de las Islas Filipinas.* Madrid: Ediciones Polifemo, 1997.

Noone, Martin J. *The Islands Saw It: The Discovery and Conquest of the Philippines, 1521–1581.* Dublin, Ohio: Helicon Press, 1980.

Nuchera, Patricio. *La Encomienda en America y Filipinas: su impacto sobre la realidad socio-economica del mundo indigena: bibligrafia*. España: Felix Muradas Garcia, 1999.

Ordoñez, Elmer A. *The Philippine Revolution and Beyond: Papers from the International Conference on the Centennial of the 1896 Philippine Revolution*. Manila: Philippine Centennial Commission, 1996.

Perez-Llorca. Jaime. *1898: la estralegia el desastre*. Madrid: Silex, 1998.

Peterson, Don. *Mail and Markings of Private Business Firms of the Spanish*. Eden, N.Y.: International Philippine Philatelic Society, 1998.

Peterson, Don and Geoffrey Lewis. *Postal History of the Spanish Philippines. 1565–1898*. Washington, D.C.: Don Peterson, 2000.

Philippine Insurrection, April 21, 1898–July 4, 1902. St. Paul, Minn.: Paduan Press, 1998.

Ramos-Perez, Demetrio y Emilio Diego. *Cuba, Puerto Rico y Filipinas en las perspectiva del 98*. Madrid: Complutense, 1997.

Reed, Robert Ronald. *Hispanic Urbanism in the Philippines: A Study of the Impact of Church and State*. Manila: University of Manila, 1967.

Reyes Alcantara, Virgilio. *La Revolucion Filipina, 1896–1898: El Nacimiento de una idea*. Santiago de Chile: 2000.

Roces, Alfredo, ed. *Filipino Heritage* v 9. Manila: Lahing Pilipino Publishing, 1990.

Russell, Henry B. *The Story of Two Wars: An Illustrated History of Our War with Spain and Our War with the Filipinos, Their Causes, Incidents, and Results: A Record of Civil, Military, and Naval Operations from Official Sources Including the Life and Career of Admiral Dewey*. Hartford, Conn.: The Hartford Publishing, 1899.

Sales, Colin Oswald. *El movimiento portuario de Acapulco: al progtagonismo de Nueva España en la relacion con Filipinas, 1584–1648*. Mexico: D.F. Plaza y Valdes Editores, 2000.

Salgado, Pedro V. *Cagayan Valley at the Arrival of the Spaniards*. Manila: Socio-Pastoral Institute, 1990.

Schumacher, John N. *The Propaganda Movement: 1880–1895*. Manila, Philippines: Solidaridad Publishing House, 1973.

Scott, William Henry. *Looking for the Prehispanic Filipino: And Other Essays in Philippine History*. Quezon City: New Day Publishers, 1992.

Sierra de la Calle, Blas. *Filipinas 1870–1898: imagenes de la ilustracion Española y Americana*. Valladolid: Museo Oriental Padres Augtinos Filipinos, 1998.

Shaw, Angel Velasco and Luis H. Francia, eds. *Vestiges of War: The Philippine–American War and the Aftermath of an Imperial Dream, 1899–1999*. New York: New York University Press, 2002.

——. *Prehispanic Source Materials for the Study of Philippine History*. Rev. ed. Quezon City: New Day Publishers, 1984.

Soetemo, Greg. *Revolusi Damai: belajar dari Filipina*. Yogyakarta: Penerbit Kanisius, 1998.

Tiu, Macario D. *Davao: 1890–1910: Conquest and Resistance in the Garden of the Gods*. Quezon City: UP Center for Integrative and Development Studies, 2003.

Tope, Lily Rose R. *(Un)framing Southeast Asia: Nationalism and the Postcolonial Text in English*. Quezon City: University of the Philippines, Office of Research and Coordination, 1998.

Villanueva, Alex L. *Bonifacio's Unfinished Revolution*. Quezon City: New Day Publishers, 1989.

Villaroel, Fidel. *The Dominicans and the Philippine Revolution, 1896–1903*. Manila: University of Santo Tomas Press, 1999.

E. American Period

Abb, Madelfia A. *Bringing About Military Learning Organizatio: The U.S. Army in the Philippine War, 1899–1902*. Fort Leavenworth, Kans.: School of Advanced Military Studies, U.S. Army Command and General Staff College, 2000.

Alejandrino, Jose, trans. *The Price of Freedom: Episodes and Anecdotes of Our Struggles for Freedom*. Manila: M. Colcol, 1949.

Araneta, Salvador. A*merica's Double-Cross of the Philippines: A Democratic Ally in 1899 and 1946*. Quezon City: Sahara Heritage Foundation, 1999.

Ataviado, Elias M. *The Philippine Revolution in the Bicol Region*. Quezon City: New Day Publishers, 1999.

Bauzon, Leslie E., ed. *In Search of Historical Truth*. Quezon City: Heritage Publishing House, 1992.

Beck, John Jacob. *MacArthur and Wainwright: Sacrifice of the Philippines*. Albuquerque, N. Mex.: University of New Mexico Press, 1974.

Blount, James H. *The American Occupation of the Philippines, 1898–1912*. With origin of a myth (an introductory essay by Renato Constantino). Manila: Solar Publishing Co., 1991.

Borinaga, Rolando O. *The Balangiga Conflict Revisited*. Quezon City: New Day Publishers, 2003.

Camagay, Maria Luisa T. *French Consular Dispatches on the Philippine Revolution*. Quezon City: University of the Philippines Press, 1997.

Carter, Thomas M. *Land of the Morning: A Pictorial History of the American Regime*. Manila, Philippines: Historical Conservation Society, 1990.

Cartografia Historica Iberoamericana: Cuba, Puerto Rico, Filipinas 1890–1899. Madrid: Ministerio de Defensa, Secretaria General Tecnica, 1999.

Churchill, Bernadita Reyes. *The Philippine Independence Missions to the United States, 1919–1934*. Manila: National Historical Institute, 1983.

Conroy, Robert. *The Battle of Bataan: America's Greatest Defeat*. New York: Macmillan, 1969.

———. *The Battle of Manila Bay: The Spanish–American War in the Philippines*. New York: Macmillan, 1968.

Davis, Lucile. *The Philippines*. Mankato, Minn.: Bridgestone Books, 1999.

Delmendo, Sharon. *The Star Spangled Banner: One Hundred Years of America in the Philippines*. New Brunswick, N.J.: Rutgers University Press, 2004.

Denton, Frank H. and Victoria Villena-Denton. *Filipino Views of America: Warm Memories, Cold Realities.* Washington, D.C.: Asia Fellows, 1986.

Dery, Luis Camara. *The Kris in Philippine History: A Study of the Impact of Moro Anti-colonial Resistance, 1521–1896*. Quezon City: L.C. Dery, 1997.

Diokno, Ma. Serena I. *Voices and Scenes of the Past: The Philippine–American War Retold.* Quezon City: Jose W. Diokno Foundation, 1999.

Diokno, Ma. Serena and Ramon N. Villegas. *Life in the Colony*. Pleasantville, N.Y.: Reader's Digest, 1998.

Evangelista, Oscar L. "The Philippine Revolution (1896–1901) within the Context of Asian History: A Comparative Study of Anti-colonial Movements in Asia, 1857–1918." *Centennial Issue Asian Studies* Vol. 34 1998: 1–15.

Eyre, James K., Jr. *The Roosevelt–MacArthur Conflict*. Chambersburg, Penn.: The Author, 1950.

Feuer, A. B. *America at War. In the Philippines. 1898–1913*. Westport, Conn.: Praeger, 2002

Gates, John Morgan. *Schoolbooks and Krags: The United States Army in the Philippines, 1898–1902.* Westport, Conn.: Greenwood, 1973.

Gibson, Charles Dana. *Overseas: U.S. Army Maritime Operations 1898 through the Fall of Philippines.* Camden, Maine, 2002.

Gleeck, Lewis E., Jr. *The American Governors-General and High Commissioners in the Philippines: Proconsuls, Nation-Builders, and Politicians*. Quezon City: New Day Publishers, 1986.

——. *Laguna in American Times: Coconuts and Revolucionarios*. Manila: Historical Conservation Society, 1981.

——. *Nueva Ecija in American Times: Homesteaders, Haciendros and Politicos*. Manila: Historical Conservation Society, 1981.

Go, Julian. "El Cuerpo, Razon at Kapangyarihan: The Body, Reason and Power of: Filipino Elite Cosmologies of State Under American Colonial Rule, 1890s–1920s" *Centennial Issue Asian Studies*. Vol. 34 1998: 146–170.

Go, Julian and Anne L. Foster. *The American Colonial State in the Philippines: Global Perspectives.* Durham: Duke University Press, 2003.

Gonzales, Joaquin L. *Philippines.* Milwaukee, Wisc.: Gareth Stevens Publication, 2001.

Hoganson, Kristin L. *Fighting for American Manhood: How Gender Politics Provoked the Spanish–American Wars.* New Haven: Yale University Press, 1998.

Ileto, Reynaldo Clemeña. *Knowing America's Colony: A Hundred Years from the Philippine War.* Honolulu: University of Hawaii at Manoa, 1999.

Jenista, Frank Lawrence. *The White APOS: American Governors on the Cordillera*. Quezon City: New Day Publishers, 1987.

Kalaw, Maximo Manguiat. *The Filipino Rebel: A Romance of American Occupation in the Philippines*. Manila: Filipiniana Book Guild, 1964.

Kolb, Richard K. "Blaze in the Boondocks: Fighting on America's Imperial Front in the Philippines, 1899–1913." Kansas City: Mo.: *VFW Magazine*, 2002.

Langelier, John P. *Uncle Sam's Little Wars: The Spanish–American Wars, Philippine Insurrection and Boxer Rebellion, 1898–1902*. Philadelphia: Chelsea House Publishers, 2002.

Lewis, Peter. *Foot Soldier in an Occupation Force: Letters of Peter Lewis, 1898–1902*. Manila: De La Salle University Press, 1999.

Lieurance, Suzanne. *The Philippines*. Berkeley Heights, N.J.: My Reports Links.com Books, 2004.

Linn, Brian McAllister. *The U.S. Army and Counterinsurgency in the Philippine War, 1899–1982*. Chapel Hill, N.C.: University of North Carolina Press, 1989.

McCallus, Joseph P. *Gentleman Soldier: John Clifton Brown and the Philippine–American War*. College Station: Texas A&M University Press, 2003.

McFerson, Hazel M. *Mixed Blessing: The Impact of the American Colonial Experience on Politics and Society in the Philippines*. Westport, Conn.: Greenwood Press, 2002.

Medina, Isagani R. and Mirana Medina. *Espionage in the Philippines, 1896–1902, and Other Essays*. Manila: UST Publishing House, 2002.

Miller, Stuart Creighton. *Benevolent Assimilation: The American Conquest of the Philippines, 1899–1903*. New Haven, Conn.: Yale University Press, 1982.

Mojares, Resil B. *The War against the Americans: Resistance and the Collaboration in Cebu, 1899–1906*. Quezon City: Ateneo De Manila University Press, 1999.

Ninkovich, Frank A. *The United States and Imperialism*. Malden, Mass.: Blackwell Publishers, 2001.

Oswald, Mark G. The "Howling Wilderness" *Courts Martial of 1902*. Carlisle, Penn.: U.S. Army War College, 2001.

Rodao Garcia, Florentino and Felice N. Rodriquez. *The Philippine Revolution of 1896*. Manila: Ateneo De Manila University Press, 2001.

Salamanca, Bonifacio S. *The Filipino Reaction to American Rule, 1901–1913*. Expanded ed. Quezon City: New Day Publishers, 1984.

Salman, Michael. *The Embarrassment of Slavery: Controversies over Bondage and Nationalism in the American Colonial Philippines*. Berkeley: University of California Press, 2001.

Sánchez-Archilla Bernal, José. *Recent Philippine History, 1898–1960*. Manila: Office of Research and Publications, Ateneo de Manila University, 1993.

Scott, William Henry. *Ilocano Responses to American Aggression 1900–1901*. Quezon City: New Day Publishers, 1986.

Shaw, Angel Velasco and Luis Francia. *Vestiges of War: The Philippine–American War and the Aftermath of an Imperial Dream 1899–1999*. N.Y.: New York University Press, 2002.

Sheridan, Richard B. *The Filipino Martyrs: A Story of the Crime of February 4, 1899.* Detroit, Mich.: John Lane: The Bodley Head, 1900.

Soberano, Rawlein G. *The Politics of Independence: The American Colonial Experiment in the Philippines.* New Orleans, La.: Alive Associates, 1983.

Soriano, Evelyn Caldera. *Bicolano Revolutionaires: Arejola, Tomas and Ludovico.* Manila: National Commission for Culture and the Arts, 1999.

Stafford, Janice. *The Attitudes of the Philippine Newspapers, the Manila Times and the Philippines Herald, to the Independence Question, 1921–1927.* Queensland, Australia: James Cook University of North Queensland, 1980.

Stanley, Peter, ed. *Reappraising an Empire: New Perspectives on Philippine–American History.* Cambridge, Mass.: Committee on American–East Asian Relations of the Department of History in Collaboration with the Council on East Asian Studies, Harvard University, 1984.

Thompson, Henry O. *Inside the Fighting First: Papers of Nebraska Private in the Philippine War.* Blair, Nebr.: Dana College, 2001.

Viana, Augusto V. *A Study of Japanese Enterprises in the Philippines before and after the Second World War: Focus on the Manila Area 1935–1951.* Manila: Sumitomo Foundation, 2001.

Victoriano, Enrique L. *Historic Manila: Commemorative Lectures. 1993–1996.* Manila: The Commission, 1999.

Villanueva, Rene O. *Melchora Aquino: Ang Himagsikan.* Quezon City: Adarna House, 2001.

Welch, Richard E. *Response to Imperialism: The United States and the Philippine–American War, 1899–1902.* Chapel Hill, N.C.: University of North Carolina Press, 1979.

F. World War II and Japanese Occupation

Agoncillo, Teodoro A. *The Fateful Years: Japan's Adventure in the Philippines, 1941–1945.* Quezon City: University of the Philippines Press, 2001.

Astor, Gerald. *Crisis in the Pacific: The Battles for the Philippine Islands by the Men Who Fought Them.* N.Y.: Dell Publication, 2002.

Barnes-Payne, Georgia L. *Caught in the Crossfire.* Polk, Mo.: Payne Prairie Publications, 1997.

Bartsch, William H. *MacArthur's Pearl Harbor.* College Station: Texas A&M University Press, 2003.

Bisa, Simplicio P. *Lagablab: Mga Alaala ng Digma (Blast: Remembrance of the War)* Maynila: De La Salle University Press, 1998.

Boisclaire, Yvonne. *In the Shadow of the Rising Sun: The Story of Robert Davis, POW and D Battery 515 CAC, Orphan Unit of Bataan.* Bella Vista, Calif.: Clearwood Publishers, 1997.

Breur, William R. *Retaking the Philippines: America's Return to Corregidor and Bataan, October 1944–March 1945.* St. Martin's, 1986.

Buenafe, Manuel E. *Wartime Philippines.* Manila: Education Foundation, 1950.

Bulkley, Robert J. *At Close Quarters: PT Boats in the United States Navy.* Annapolis, Md.: Naval Institute Press, 2003.

Bumgarner, John R. *Parade of the Dead: A U.S. Army physician's memoir of imprisonment by the Japanese, 1942–1945.* Jefferson, N.C.: McFarland, 1995.

Cleope, Earl Jude Paul L. *Bandit Zone: A History of the Free Areas of Negros Island During the Japanese Occupation, 1942–1945.* Manila: UST Publishing House, 2002.

Cogan, Frances B. *Captured: The Japanese Internment of American Civilians in the Philippines 1941–1945.* Athens, Ga.: University of Georgia Press, 1999.

Connaughton, Richard, John Pimlott, and Duncan Anderson. *The Battle for Manila: The Most Devastating Untold Story of World War II.* London: Bloomsbury Publishing, 1997.

Connaughton, R. M. *MacArthur and Defeat in the Philippines.* Woodstock, N.Y.: Overlook Press, 2001.

De La Costa, Horacio. *Light Cavalry Manila.* National Office of Mass Media, 1997.

Doll, John G. *The Battling Bastards of Bataan: A Chronology of the First Days of World War II in the Philippines.* Springfield, Mass.: Merriam, 1992.

De Vera, Ruel S. *The Zero Hour: The Personal War of Basilio J. Valdez.* Makati City: Bookmark, 2001.

Doscher, Henry J. *Little Wolf at Leyte: Story of the Heroic USS Samuel B. Roberts (DE-413) in the Battle of Leyte Gulf during WW II.* New York: St. Martin's Press, 1996.

Dowlen, Dorothy Dore. *Enduring What Cannot be Endured. Memoir of a Woman Medical Aide in the Philippines in World War II.* Jefferson, N.C.: McFarland, 2001.

Empie, Evelyn Berg, Stephen M. Mette, and Xavier Aboitiz. *A Child in the Midst of Battle: One Family's Struggle for Survival in War-torn Manila.* Rolling Hills Estates, Calif.: Satori Press, 2001.

Escoda, Jose Ma. *Warsaw of Asia: The Rape of Manila.* Quezon City: Giraffe Books, 2001.

Espaldon, Ernesto M. *With the Bravest: The Untold Story of the Sulu Freedom Fighters of World War II.* Quezon City: Ateneo De Manila University Press, 1997.

Ephraim, Frank. *Escape to Manila: From Nazi Tyranny to Japanese Terror.* Urbana: University of Illinois Press, 2003.

Eyot, Canning and Jim Zwick. *The Story of the Lopez Family: A Page from the History of the War in the Philippines.* Manila: Platypus Publication, 2001.

Firth, Robert H. *A Matter of Time: Why Philippines Fell, the Japanese Invasion 1941–1942.* Walnut, Calif.: R. H. Firth, 1981.

Flanagan, E. M. *Angels at Dawn: The Los Baños Raid.* Novato, Calif.: Presidio, 1999.

Foronda, Marcelino A., Jr. *Cultural Life in the Philippines during the Japanese Occupation 1942–1945.* Manila: Philippine National Historical Society, 1975.

Gajudo, Nena, et al. *The Women of Mapanique: Untold Crimes of War.* Quezon City: Asian Center for Women's Human Rights, 2000.

Garcia, Joaquin L. *It Took Four Years for the Rising Sun to Set 1941–1945: Recollection of an Unforgettable Ordeal.* Manila: De La Salle University Press, 2001.

Garcia, Mauro, ed. *Documents on the Japanese Occupation of the Philippines.* Manila: Philippine Historical Association, 1965.

Gautier, James Donovan and Robert Whitmore. *I Came Back from Bataan.* Greenville, S.C.: Emerald House Group, 1997.

Hartendrop, A. V. H. *The Japanese Occupation of the Philippines.* 2 vols. Manila: Bookmark, 1967.

Henson, Maria Rosa. *Comfort Woman: A Filipina's Story of Prostitution and Slavery under the Japanese Military.* Lanham: Rowman & Littlefield Publishers, 1999.

Holland, Robert B. *Rescue of Santo Tomas: Manila WW II: The Flying Column: 100 Miles to Freedom.* Paducah, Ky.: Turner, 2003.

Ingles, Gustavo C. *Memoirs of Pain: Kempei-tai Torture in the Airport Studio, Fort Santiago and the Old Bilibid Prison, to Redemption in Muntinlupa.* San Juan, Metro Manila: Mauban Heritage Foundation, 1992.

Ikehata, Setsuho and Ricardo Jose. *The Philippines under Japan: Occupation Policy and Reaction.* Quezon City: Ateneo De Manila University Press, 1999.

Ishida, Jintaro; Makiko Okuyama: *Reynald-Ventura; The Remains of War: Apology and Forgiveness.* Guilford, Conn.: 2002.

Jacinto, Pacita Pestaño. *Living with the Enemy: A Diary of the Japanase Occupation.* Pasig City: Anvil Publications, 1999.

Jose, Ricardo Trota. *The Japanese Occupation.* Pleasantville, N.Y.: Reader's Digest, 1998.

Jose, Ricardo Trota and Lydia Yu-Jose. *The Japanese Occupation of the Philippines: A Pictorial History.* Manila: Ayala Foundation, 1997.

Kapunan, Sal. *Surviving World War II as a Child Swamp Hermit.* Bloomington, Ind.: lst Books Library, 2002.

King, Otis H. *Alamo of the Pacific: The Story of the Famed "China Marines" on Bataan and Corregidor and What They Did to the Enemy as POWs.* Fort Worth, Tex.: Branch Smith, 1999.

Lapham, Robert and Bernard Norling. *Lapham's Raiders: Guerrillas in the Philippines, 1942–1945.* University Press of Kentucky, 1996.

Laurel, Jose P. *Talaarawan ng Digmaan.* Maynila: Lyceum ng Pilipinas, 1997.

Lear, Elma. *The Japanese Occupation of Leyte, 1941–1945.* Ithaca, N.Y.: Cornell University, 1961.

Malay, Armando J. *Occupied Philippines: The Role of Jorge B. Vargas during the Japanese Occupation.* Manila: Filipiniana Book Guild, 1967.

Mallonee, Richard C. *Battle for Bataan: An Eyewitness Account*. Novato, Calif.: Presidio, 1997.

Manikan, Gamaliel L. *Guerilla Warfare on Panay Island in the Philippines: Historical Account of the Organization and Operations of the Wartime Sixth Military District, Philippine Army, Otherwise Known as the "Free Panay Guerilla Forces," during World War II in the Philippines, in 1942–1945*. Quezon City: Bustamante Press, 1977.

Mann, David B. *Avenging Bataan: The Battle of Zigzag Pass*. Raleigh, N.C.: 2001.

Martinez, Carlos Manuel. *Filipino Collaboration and Resistance Movement against the Japanese During World War II*. Dissertation, 2001. Ann Arbor: University Microfilms.

Maynard, Mary McKay. *My Faraway Home: An American Family's WW II Tale of Adventure and Survival in the Jungles of the Philippines*. Guilford, Conn.: Lyons Press, 2001.

Miller, J. Michael. *From Shanghai to Corregidor: Marines in the Defense of the Philippines*. Washington D.C.; History and Museum Division, Marine Corps Historical Center, 1997.

Monahan, Evelyn and Rosemary Neidel-Greenlee. *U.S. Nurses Imprisoned by the Japanese*. Lexington, Ky.: University Press of Kentucky, 2000.

Morris, Eric. *Corregidor: The American Alamo of World War II*. New York: Cooper Square Press, 2000.

Morrison, Samuel Eliot. *The Liberation of the Philippines, Luzon, Mindanao, the Visayas: 1944–1945*. Edison, N.J.: 201.

———. *Leyte: June 1944– January 1945*. Edison, N.J.: 2001.

Nieva, Antonio A. *The Fight for Freedom: Remembering Bataan and Corregidor.* Quezon City: New Day Publishers, 1997.

Norling, Bernard, *The Intrepid Guerrillas of North Luzon*. Lexington: University of Kentucky Press, 1999.

Norman, Elizabeth M. *We Band of Angels: The Untold Story of American Nurses Trapped on Bataan by the Japanese*. New York: Random House, 1999.

Nuval, Beulah D. et al. *Vision & Conviction: An Anthology on World War in North Luzon*. Quezon City: BBCL Publication, 1998.

Prevost, Ann Marie. "Race and War Crimes: The 1945 War Crimes Trial of General Tomoyuki Yamashita." *Human Rights Quarterly* 14 (August 1992): 303–338.

Rios, Eliseo D. *Rays of a Setting Sun: Recollections of World War II*. Manila: De La Salle University Press, 1999.

Roces, Alfredo R. *Looking for Liling: A Family History of World War II Martyr Rafael Roces*. Pasig City: Anvil Publishers, 2000.

Sacro, Aurora Lopez. *Bumitalag: Miracles of War: From the Diary of Aurora Lopez Sacro*. Manila: Interformat, 2001.

Salazar, Generoso P., et al. *World War II in the Philippines: Manila, Bicolandia and the Tagalog Province*. Manila: Heritage Publishing House, 1995.

Santos, Angelito L., et al. *Under Japanese Rule: Memories and Reflections*. Quezon City: Foundation for Nationalist Studies, 1992.

Sasser, Charles W. *Raider: The True Story of the Legendary Soldier Who Performed More POW Raids Than Any Other American in History*. New York: St. Martin's Paperbacks, 2002.

Schwab, Jane Sarmiento. *Filipino American Literature in the Shadow of Empire*. Dissertation, Ann Arbor: University Microfilms, 2003.

Schom, Alan. *The Eagle and the Rising Sun: The Japanese–American War 1941–1943. Pearl Harbor Through Guadalcanal*. New York: W.W. Norton, 2004.

Sheldon, Sayre P. *Her War Story: Twentieth-century Women Write About War*. Carbondale: Southern Illinois University Press, 1999.

Setsuho, Ikebata and Ricardo Trota Jose. *The Philippines under Japan: Occupation policy and reaction*. Quezon City: Ateneo De Manila University Press, 1999.

Sides, Hampton. *Ghost Soldiers: The Forgotten Epic Story of World War II's Most Dramatic Mission*. New York: Doubleday, 2001.

Smith, Steven Trent. *The Rescue: A True Story of Courage and Survival in World War II*. New York: J. Wiley, 2001.

Stahl, Bob. *Fugitives: Evading and Escaping the Japanese*. Lexington: University of Kentucky Press, 2001.

Steinberg, David Joel. *Philippine Collaboration in World War II*. Ann Arbor: University of Michigan, 1967.

Steinberg, Rafael. *Return to the Philippines*. Alexandria, Va.: Time-Life Books, 1998.

Syjuco, Felisa A. *The Kempei Tai in the Philippines, 1942–1945*. Quezon City: New Day Publishers, 1988.

Tillman, Barrett. *The Marianas Turkey Shoot, June 19–20, 1944: Carrier Battle in the Philippine Sea*. St. Paul, Minn.: Phalanx Publishing, 1994.

Vanderbergh, William J. *A Willingness to Sacrifice: The 194th Tank Battalion in Action on Bataan: An Example of Army Values*. Dissertation, 2002 Ann Arbor: University Microfilms.

Viloria, Benjamin Nisce. *They Carried On: Silliman University Men and Women in the Negros Resistance Movement, 1941–1945*. Manila: Veterans Federation of the Philippines, 1998.

Wainwright Papers. Quezon City: New Day Publishers, 1980–1982.

War Crimes on Asian Women: Military Sexual Slavery by Japan during World War II: The Case of the Filipino Comfort Women. Manila: Women Human Rights Council, 1998.

Whitfield, Evelyn. *Three Years Picnic: American Woman's Life inside Japanese Prison Camps in the Philippines during WW II*. Corvallis, Ore.: Premiere Editions International, 1999.

Wodnik, Bob. *Captured Honor: POW Survival in the Philippines and Japan*. Pullman: Washington State University Press, 2003.

World War II in the Philippines (Part 1). Washington D.C.: Library of Congress, 1998.

Young, Robert. *They Too Fought the Japanese: The American Army's War in the Southwest Pacific.* Dissertation.2000. Ann Arbor: University Microfilms.

Yu-Jose, Lydia N. *Japan Views the Philippines, 1900–1944.* Manila: Ateneo de Manila University Press, 1992.

G. After Independence

Abueva, Jose V. *Filipino Nationalism: Various Meanings,Constant and Changing Goals, Continuing Relevance. Nasyonalismong Pilipno: Sari-saring Kahulugan, Patuloy at Nagbabagong mga layon, at dumadaloy ng kaugnayan.* Quezon City: University of the Philippines Press, 1999.

Aquino, Belinda. *Politics of Plunder: The Philippines under Marcos.* Diliman, Quezon City: University of the Philippine Press, 1992.

Bankoff, Greg and Kathleen Weekley. *History, State and National Identity in the Philippines.* London: C. Hurst, 2000.

Baron, Cynthia Sta. Maria and Melba Morales Suazo. *Nine Letters: The Story of the 1986 Filipino Revolution.* Quezon City: G. P. Baron, 1986.

Bonner, Raymond. *Waltzing with a Dictator: The Marcoses and the Making of American Policy.* New York: Vantage Books, 1988.

Bresnan, John, ed. *Crisis in the Philippines: The Marcos Era and Beyond.* Princeton, N.J.: Princeton University Press, 1986.

Brillantes, Alex B., Jr. "The Philippines in 1992: Ready for Take Off?" (Part of a Symposium: A Survey of Asia in 1992), *Asian Survey* 33 (February 1993): 224–230.

Buendia, Rizal R. *Ethnicity and Sub-Nationalist Independence Movements in the Philippines and Indonesia: Implications for Regional Security.* Manila: De La Salle University Press, 2002.

Burton, Sandra. *Impossible Dream: Marcos, Aquino, the Unfinished Revolution.* New York: Warner Books, 1988.

Carroll, John J. *Looking beyond EDSA.* 2 vol. Metro Manila, Philippines: Human Development Research and Documentation, 1986–1987.

Carson, Jayne A. *Nation Building: The American Way.* Carlisle, Penn.: U.S. Army War College, 2003

Celoza, Albert F. *Ferdinand Marcos and the Philippines: The Political Economy of Authoritarianism.* London: Praeger, 1997.

Chaplin, George. *The Philippines under President Cory Aquino: Problems & Potential: A Series of Articles.* Honolulu, Hawaii: Honolulu Advertiser, 1986.

Chapman, William. *Inside the Philippine Revolution.* New York: Norton, 1987.

Constantino, Renato. *Demystifying Aquino.* Quezon City: Karrel, 1989.

Constantino, Renato, et al. *Ang Bagong Lumipas.* Quezon City: University of the Philippines Pres, 1997.

Crouch, Harold A. *The Continuing Crisis in the Philippines*. Kuala Lumpur, Malaysia: Institute of Strategic and International Studies, 1985.

Davis, Leonard. *Revolutionary Struggle in the Philippines*. New York: St. Martin's Press, 1989.

Davis, Stephen R., L. L. Dieterich, and T. Mitchell, eds. *The Philippines in Southeast Asia*. Washington, D.C.: U.S. G.P.O., 1989.

The EDSA Revolution Four Years Later. Pansol, Calamba, Laguna, Sunday, February 18, 1990. Manila: Senate of the Philippines, 1990.

Fenton, James. *The Snap Revolution*. Cambridge, England: Granta, 1986.

Feria, Dolores Stephens. *The Barbed Wire*. Manila: JTL Printing, 1998.

From Revolution to a Second Colonization: The Philippines under Spain and the United States. Manila: National Historical Institute, 1990.

Gleeck, Lewis E., Jr. *The Third Philippine Republic, 1946–1972*. Quezon City: New Day Publishers, 1993.

Goodno, James B. *The Philippines: Land of Broken Promises*. Atlantic Highlands, N.J.: Zed Books, 1991.

Guerrero, N. and John Schumacher. *Reform and Revolution*. Manila: Asia Publishing Co. 1998.

Johnson, Bryan. *The Four Days of Courage: The Untold Story of the People Who Brought Marcos Down*. New York: Free Press, 1987.

Kerkvliet, Benedict J. *Everyday Politics in the Philippines*. Berkeley: University of California Press, 1990.

Lawson, Don. *The New Philippines*. 2nd ed. New York: F. Watts, 1986.

Lyons, John and Karl Wilson. *Marcos and Beyond: The Philippines Revolution*. Kenthurst, England: Kangaroo Press, 1987.

Macdonald, Douglas J. *Adventures in Chaos: American Intervention for Reform in the Third World*. Cambridge, Mass.: Harvard University Press, 1992.

Maramba, Asuncion David, ed. *On the Scene: The Philippine Press Coverage of the 1986 Revolution*. Metro Manila: Solar Publishing, 1987.

Martinez, Manuel Festin. *The Grand Collision: Aquino vs. Marcos*. Quezon City: Martinez, 1987.

May, R. J. and Francisco Nemenzo, eds. *The Philippines after Marcos*. New York: St. Martin's Press, 1985.

McPherson, Hazel M. *Mixed Blessings: The Impact of the American Colonial Experience in Politics and Society in the Philippines*. Westport, Conn.: 2002.

Mercado, Monina Allarey, ed. *People Power: The Philippine Revolution of 1986: An Eyewitness History*. New York: Tenth Avenue Editions, 1986.

Muego, Benjamin N. *Spectator Society: The Philippines under Martial Rule*. Athens, Ohio: Center for International Studies, Ohio University, 1988.

Muñoz, Alfredo N. *The Philippine Dilemma*. Los Angeles, Calif.: Mooncrest, 1986.

Nagara, Bunn. "The Revolt in the Philippines." *Asian Defence Journal* (February 1990): 4–15.

Nakpil, Carmen Guerrero. *Centennial Reader: Selected Essays*. Manila: C. G. Nakpil, 1998.

Ocampo, Ambeth R. *Looking Back*. Manila: Anvil Publishing, 1990.

Ordoñez, Sedfrey A. *Trial of the Assassins*. Manila: Sedfrey A. Ordoñez, 1993.

The Philippines under Aquino: Five Papers. Kent, New Zealand: University of Kent at Canterbury, 1989.

Pomeroy, William J. *The Philippines: Colonialism, Collaboration, and Resistance*. New York: International Publishers, 1992.

Rempel, William C. *Delusions of a Dictator: The Mind of Marcos as Revealed in His Secret Diaries*. Boston, Mass.: Little Brown, 1993.

Reid, Robert H. and Eileen Guerrero. *Corazon Aquino & the Brushfire Revolution*. Baton Rouge, La.: Louisiana State University Press, 1995.

Rivera, Filomena V. *Jose Rizal's Immortal Legacy*. Mandaluyong City: National Book Store, 1997.

Robles, Eliodoro G. *The Philippines in the Nineteenth Century*. Quezon City: Malaya Books, 1969.

Roces, Alfredo P. *Felix Resurreccion Hidalgo and the Generation of 1872*. Pasay City: Eugenio Lopez Museum Foundation, 1998.

Rodriguez, Ernesto O. *Working with Heroes and Exiles*. New York: Vantage Press, 1989.

Rodriguez, Filemon C. *The Marcos Regime: Rape of the Nation*. New York: Vantage Press, 1985.

Romulo, Beth Day. *Inside the Palace: The Rise and Fall of Ferdinand & Imelda Marcos*. New York: Putnam, 1987.

Rosca, Ninotchka. *Endgame: The Fall of Marcos*. New York: F. Watts, 1987.

Salanga, Alfredo Navarro. *A Personal Chronicle, 1971–1987*. Manila: De La Salle University Press, 1990.

Schumacher, John N. *The Making of a Nation: Essays on Nineteenth-Century Filipino*. Manila: Ateneo de Manila University Press, 1991.

Seagrave, Sterling. *The Marcos Dynasty*. New York: Harper & Row, 1988.

Soriano, Marcelo B. *The Unused Guns of the 4-Day EDSA Revolt: The Story of the Unused Guns of the Civilians at the Scene of the Four-Day Revolt That Ousted a 20-Year Dictator*. Quezon City: M. B. Soriano, 1986.

Sta. Maria, Felice. *Visions of the Possible: Legacies of Philippine Freedom*. Makati City: Studio 5 Publication, 1998.

Tarrazona, Hector M. *After EDSA: A Military Reformist's Personal Account of the EDSA Revolution and Some Views on the Problems of the Filipino Society*. Pasay City: H.M. Tarrazona, 1989.

Timberman, David G. "The Philippines in 1989: A Good Year Turns Sour." *Asian Survey* 30, 2 (February 1990): 167–177.

Trafton, William Oliver. *We Thought We Could Whip Them in Two Weeks*. Quezon City: New Day Publishers, 1990.

Veneracion, Jaime B. *Agos Ng Dugong Kayumanggi: Isang kasaysayan ng sambayanang Pilipino*. Quezon City: Abiva Publishing House, 1997.

Von Brevern, Marilies. *The Turning Point: Twenty-Six Accounts of the February Events in the Philippines*. Greenhills, San Juan, Metro Manila: Von Brevern, 1986.

Zaide, Gregorio F. *The Philippine Revolution*. Rev. ed. Manila: Modern Book, 1968.

H. Politics and Political Science

Abaya, Hernando J. *Looking Back in Anger*. Quezon City: New Day Publishers, 1992.

Abinales, Patricio N. *State Authority and Local Power in Southern Philippines, 1900–1972*. Dissertation, 1997. Ann Arbor: University Microfilms.

Abinales, Patricio, ed. *The Revolution Falters: The Left in Philippine Politics after 1986*. Ithaca, N.Y.: Cornell University: Southeast Asia Program Publications, 1996.

———. *Making Mindanao: Cotabato and Davao in the Formation of the Philippine Nation-State*. Quezon City: Ateneo De Manila University Press, 2000.

Active Non-Violence in Action: The Philippine Experience. Manila: World Council for Curriculum and Instruction, Philippine Chapter, 1987.

Adaza, Homobono. *A Time for Decision*. Manila: H. Adaza, 1986.

Adorable, Violeta H. *Political Opportunity and Political Welfare in an Upland Community*. Baguio City: Cordillera Studies Center, University of the Philippines College Baguio, 1990.

Agpalo, Remigio E. *Adventures in Political Science*. Diliman, Quezon City: University of the Philippines Press: College of Social Sciences and Philosophy, 1992.

Aquino, Corazon Cojuangco. *Tearing Down the Dictatorship, Rebuilding Democracy*. Manila: Biblio-Filipino, 1986.

———. *In the Name of Democracy and Prayer: Selected Speeches of Corazon Aquino*. Manila: Anvil Publishing, 1995.

Aquino, Belinda A. "The Philippines in 1987: Beating Back the Challenge of August." In *Southeast Asian Affairs*. Singapore: Institute of Southeast Asian Studies, 1988: 191–215.

———. *An Anarchy of Families: State and Family in the Philippines*. Madison: University of Wisconsin, Center for Southeast Asian Studies,1993.

Aruiza, Arturo C. *Ferdinand E. Marcos: Malacañang to Makiki*. Quezon City: ACA Enterprises, 1991.

Avila, John Laurence. "A Gathering Crisis in the Philippines." *Southeast Asian Affairs*. Singapore: Institute of Southeast Asian Studies, 1990: 257–273.

Barreveld, Dirk J. *Philippine President Estrada Impeached: How the President of the World's 13th Most Populous Country Stumbles over His Mistresses, Chinese Conspiracy and the Garbage of His Capital*. San Jose, Calif.: Writer's Club Press, 2001.

Brilliantes, Alex B. *Dictatorship and Martial Law: Philippine Authoritarianism in 1972*. Quezon City: Philippine Great Books Publishers, 1987.

Buendia, Rizal G. "Philippines." In *Rethinking Political Development in Southeast Asia*. Ed. Norma Mahmood. Kuala Lumpur, Malaysia: University of Malaysia Press, 1994: 81–113.

Cariño, Ledivina V. *Bureacracy for a Democracy: The Struggle of the Philippine Political Leadership and the Civil Service in the Post-Marcos Period*. Manila: University of the Philippines Press, 1988.

Celoza, Albert F. *Ferdinand Marcos and the Philippines: The Political Economy of Authoritarianism*. Westport, Conn.: Praeger, 1997.

Cendran, David. "The Cult of Celebrity." *Media* (January–March 2001), Philippine Center for Investigative Journalism.

Collins,Joseph. *The Philippines: Fire on the Rim*. San Francisco: Institute for Food and Development Policy. 1989.

Coronel, Sheila S. "Triumph of Illusion." *Public Eye* (July–September 1998), Philippine Center for Investigative Journalism.

———. "The Politics of Spoils." *Public Eye* (April 26–27, 2004), Philippine Center for Investigative Journalism.

Coronel, Sheila S. et al. *Boss 5: Case Studies of Local Politics in the Philippines*. Manila: Philippine Center for Investigative Journalism, 1995.

Crisostomo, Isabelo T. *President Joseph Ejercito Estrada, from Stardom to History: The Saga of a Child of Destiny*. Quezon City: J. Kritz Publishers,1999.

Cruz, Uro de la. "The Myth of Ang Palay." *Public Eye* (October–December 2002) Philippine Center for Investigative Journalism.

Damiani, Brian P. *Advocates of Empire: William McKinley, the Senate, and the American Expansion, 1898–1899*. New York: Garland Publications, 1987.

Davis, Leonard. *The Philippines: People, Poverty, and Politics*. New York: St. Martin's Press, 1987.

De Guzman, Raul P. and Mila A. Reforma. eds. *Government and Politics of the Philippines*. Singapore: Oxford University Press, 1988.

Dejillas, Leopoldo J. ed. *Role of Political Parties, Government and Society*. Makati City: Institute for Development Research and Studies, Konrad Adenuer Foundation, 1995.

De La Torre, Edicio. *Touching Ground, Taking Root*. Quezon City: Socio-Pastoral Institute, 1988.

De Los Santos, Jaime S. and Adonis Rizon-Bajao. *Command and Leadership*. Quezon City: Jaime De Los Santos: Adonis Rizon-Bajao, 2002.

Democracy and Development in East Asia: Taiwan, South Korea and the Philippines. Washington D.C.: AEI Press, 1991.

Dictatorship and Revolution: Roots of People Power. Manila: Conspectus, 1988.

Diokno, Ma. Serena, I. *The 1986–1987 Peace Talks: A Reportage of Contention*. Quezon City: University of the Philippines Center for Integrative and Development Studies and the U.P. Press, 1994.

Dohner, Robert and Stephan Haggard. *The Political Feasibility of Adjustment in the Philippines*. Paris: Development Centre of the Organization for Economic Co-operation and Development, 1994.

Door, Steven R. and Deborah J. Mitchell, eds. *The Philippines in a Changing Southeast Asia: Conference Papers*. Washington, D.C.: Defense Academic Research Support Program, 1989.

Druckman, Daniel. *Political Stability in the Philippines: Framework and Analysis.* Denver, Colo.: University of Denver, 1987.

Elwood, Douglas J., ed. *Alternatives to Violence: Interdisciplinary Perspectives on Filipino People Power.* Quezon City: New Day Publishers, 1989.

Espinosa-Robles, Raissa. *To Fight without End: The Story of a Misunderstood President.* Makati: Ayala Foundation, 1990.

Espiritu, Augustus Fauni. *Expatriate Affirmations: The Performance of Nationalism and Patronages in Filipino Intellectual Life.* Dissertation, 2000. Ann Arbor: University Microfilms.

Ferrer, Miriam Coronel. *The Southern Philippines Council for Peace and Development: A Response to the Controversy.* Quezon City: UP Center for Integrative and Development Studies Peace, Conflict Resolution and Human Rights Program and the Mindanao Studies Program, 1997.

Flamiano, Dolores and Donald Goertzen, eds. *Critical Decade: Prospects for Democracy in the Philippines in the 1990s.* Berkeley: Philippine Resources Center, 1990.

Franco, Jenny. *Philippine Electoral Politics and the Peasant-Based Civic Movement in the 1980s.* Quezon City: Philpine Peasant Institute, 1994.

Garcia, Edmundo. *Dawn over Darkness: Paths to Peace in the Philippines.* Quezon City: Claretian Publications, 1988.

Gerona, Danilo M. "Text and Politics: Transactions of Power in the Early Provincial Philippines." *Asian Studies* 34, 1998: 15–77.

Guillermo, Alice. *The Covert Presence and Other Essays on Politics and Culture.* Manila: Kalikasan Press, 1989.

Gutierrez, Eric U., Ildefonso C. Torrente, and Noli G. Narca. *All in the Family: A Study of Elites and Power Relations in the Philippines.* Quezon City: Institute for Popular Democracy, 1992.

Hamel, William Christopher. *Race and Responsible Government: Woodrow Wilson and the Philippines.* Dissertation, 2002 Ann Arbor: University Microfilms.

Hernandez, Carolina G. "The Philippines in 1987: Challenges of Redemocratization." *Asian Survey* 28, 2 (February 1988): 229–241.

———. The Philippines in 1988: Reaching Out to Peace and Economic Recovery." *Asian Survey* 29, 2 (February 1989): 154–164.

Jacob, Malou Leviste. *Anatomy of Corruption.* Manila: St. Scholastica, 1992.

Junker, Laura Lee. *Raiding, Trading, and Feasting: The Political Economy of Philippine Chiefdom.* Honolulu: University of Hawaii Press, 1989.

Kalaw, Maximo M. *The Development of Philippine Politics.* Manila: Solar Publications, 1986.

Kerkvliet, Benedict J. *Everyday Politics in the Philippines: Class and Status Relations in a Central Luzon Village.* Berkeley: University of California Press, 1990.

Kerkvliet, Benedict J. and Resil B. Mojares, eds. *From Marcos to Aquino: Local Perspectives on Political Translation in the Philippines.* Quezon City: Ateneo de Manila University Press, 1991.

Kie-Duck, Park. *Fading Reformism in New Democracies: Comparative Study of Regime Consolidation in Korea and the Philippines.* Manila: ACA Publications, 1993.

Lande, Carl R. *Leaders, Factions, and Parties: The Structure of Philippine Politics.* Southeast Asian Studies Monograph Series, No. 6, New Haven: Yale University, 1964.

Lumbrera, Bienvenido. *Revaluation 1997.* Manila: University of Santo Tomas Press, 1997.

Magno, Alexander R. *Power without Form: Essays on the Filipino State and Politics.* Manila: Kalikasan Press, 1990.

Manlapaz, Romeo L. *The Mathematics of Deception: A Study of the 1986 Presidential Election Tallies.* Quezon City: Third World Studies Center, University of the Philippines, 1986.

Martinez, Manuel F. *A Political History of Our Time: Presidential Policies from Aquino to Ramos to Estrada: A Study in Leadership.* Manila: MFM Enterprises, 1999.

Mata, Elvira. "Meteor Mutiny." *Public Eye* 14, 3 (July–September), Philippine Center for Investigative Journalism.

McDougal, Charles. *The Buddha, the Gold, & the Myth.* San Francisco: San Francisco Publishers, 1997.

Mcpherson, *Hazel Mixed Blessing: The Impact of the American Colonial Experience in Politics and Society in the Philippines.* Westport, Conn.: Greenwood Press, 2002.

Mercado, Monina Allarey, ed. *People Power: An Eyewitness History of the Philippine Revolution of 1986.* New York: Tenth Avenue Editions, 1986.

Miranda, Felipe B., ed. *Democratization: Philippine Perspectives.* Quezon City: University of the Philippines Press, 1997.

Muego, Benjamin N. *Spectator Society: The Philippines under Martial Law.* Athens: Ohio University Center for International Studies, 1988.

O'Brien, Thomas M. *Crises and Instability: The Philippines Enters the Nineties.* Davao City: Philippine International Forum. 1990.

Ordoñez, Marcelo A. *People Power: A Demonstration of the Emerging Filipino Ideology:* Quezon City: Sampaguita Printing Press, 1986.

People Power Uli: Scrapbook about EDSA 2: With Jokes, Text Messages, Photos, Digital Images and More. Quezon City: Philippine Center for Investigative Journalism, 2001.

Pertierra, Raul. *Religion, Politics, and Nationality in a Philippine Community. Quezon City:* Ateneo De Manila University Press, 1988.

Philippine Colonial Democracy. New Haven, Conn.: Yale University, Yale Center for International and Area Studies, 1988.

Philippine Legislature, 100 years. Quezon City: Philippine Historical Association, New Day Publishers, 2000.

Rama, Napoleon G. *A Time in the Life of the Filipino.* Makati, Metro Manila, Philippines: Ayala Foundation, 1990.

Ramos, Fidel V. *A Call to Duty: Citizenship and Civic Responsibility in a Third World Country.* Manila: Friends of Steady Eddie, 1993.

——. *Toward Philippines 2002: A Resurgence of Optimism and Growth*. Manila: Bureau of Communications Services, 1994.

Rivera, Temario C. *Political Opposition in the Philippines: Contestation and Cooperation*. Madison: University of Wisconsin, 1987.

Rimban, Luz. "The X-Men." Philippine Center for Investigative Journalism Special Issue (January–June 2004).

Roach, Frank R. *Benevolent Meddling: The United States Involvement in the 1986 Overthrow of Ferdinand Marcos*. Dissertation, 2000. Ann Arbor: University Microfilms.

Robinson, Thomas W., ed. *Democracy and Development in East Asia: Taiwan, South Korea, and the Philippines*. Washington, D.C.: The AEI Press, 1991.

Rocamora, Joel. *Breaking Through: The Struggle within the Communist Party of the Philippines*. Manila: Anvil Publishers, 1994.

Roces, Alfredo R. and Irene Roces. *Medals and Shoes: Political Cartoons of the Times of Ferdinand and Imelda Marcos, 1965–1992*. Manila: Anvil Publishing, 1992.

Rodriguez, Ernesto O. *Commodore Alcaraz: First Victim of President Marcos*. New York: Vintage Press, 1986.

Simbulan, Roland.G. *Ang Tagumpay Laban Sa Sandatang Nukleyar at U.S. Bases*. Manila: Nuclear Free Philippines Coalition, 1993.

Thompson, Mark R. *The Anti-Marcos Struggle: Personalistic Rule and Democratic Transition in the Philippines*. New Haven, Conn.: Yale University Press, 1995.

Rodolfo, Kelvin S. *Pinatubo and the Politics of Lahar*. Quezon City: University of the Philippines Press, 1995.

Romero Salvosa, Benjamin. *Politics of Unfinished Revolutions*. Baguio City: BCF Press, 1990.

Rood, Steven. "The 'Mini-Marshall Plan' for the Philippines." *Southeast Asian Affairs,* 1990. Singapore: Institute of Southeast Asian Studies, 1990: 274–291.

San Juan, Epifanio. *Filipino Insurgency: Writing against Patriarchy in the Philippines: Selected Essays*. Quezon City: Giraffe Books, 1998.

——. *Crises in the Philippines: The Making of a Revolution*. South Hadley, Mass.: Bergin & Garvey, 1986.

Santos, Antonio Lumicao. *Power Politics in the Philippines: The Fall of Marcos*. Quezon City: Center for Social Research, 1987.

Saulo, Alfredo B. *Communism in the Philippines: An Introduction*. Quezon City: Ateneo De Manila University, 1990.

Shalom, Stephen Rosskam. *The United States and the Philippines: A Study of Neocolonialism*. Philadelphia Institute for the Study of Human Issues, 1981.

Sussman, Gerald. "Politics and the Press: The Philippines Since Marcos." *Bulletin of Concerned Asian Scholars* 20, 4 (1988): 34–43.

Tancangco, Luzviminda G. *The Anatomy of Electoral Fraud: Concrete Bases for Electoral Reforms*. Manila: MJAGM, 1992.

Tapales, Proserpina. et al. *Modern Management in Philippine Local Government*. Quezon City: University of the Philippines Press. 1996.

Tatad, Francisco S. *Guarding the Public Trust: The Making of Public Policy.* Quezon City: Raya Books, 2000.

Tate, C. Neal. "The Judicialization of Politics in the Philippines and Southeast Asia (Part of a Symposium on the Judicialization of Politics)." *International Political Science Review* 15 (April 1994): 187–197.

The Philippines and the World in 1997. Metro Manila: Manila Times, 1997.

Timberman, David G. *A Changeless Land: Continuity and Change in Philippine Politics.* Armonk, N.Y.: M. E. Sharpe, 1991.

Tolentino, Roland B. *National/Transnational: Subject Formation, Media and Cultural Politics in and on the Philppines.* Quezon City: Ateneo de Manila University Press, 2001.

Vann, Jason. *The Philippines and Its Public Enemy No. 1.* Redondo Beach, Calif.: Ten Star Books, 1991.

Vigan, Georges. *Quo vadis Philippines.* Thiers, France: Cercle Cultural Promaethaee, 1990.

Vitug, Marites Danguilan. *The Politics of Logging, Power from the Forest.* Philippine Center for Investigative Journalism. 1993.

Vizmanos, Danilo. *Martial Law Diary. Part One.* Quezon City: Popular Book Store, 2003.

Worsening Poverty and Intensified Exploitation: The Situation of Women under the Philippines Ramos Administration. Quezon City: Center for Women's Resources, 1998.

Wurfel, David A. *Filipino Politics: Development and Decay.* Ithaca, N.Y.: Cornell University Press, 1988.

Youngblood, Robert L. *Marcos against the Church: Economic Development and Political Repression in the Philippines.* Ithaca, N.Y.: Cornell University Press, 1990.

Yuson, Alfred A. *FVR, Erap, Jawao and Other Peeves.* Pasig City: Anvil Publishers, 1997.

I. Government and Administration

Abletez, Jose P. *Foundations of Freedom: A History of Philippine Congresses.* Manila: Merriam & Webster, 1989.

Abueva, Jose V. and Emerlinda R. Roman, eds. *The Aquino Presidency and Administration (1986–1992): Contemporary Assessments and "The Judgement of History?"* Diliman, Quezon City: University of the Philippines Press, 1993.

———. *Corazon C. Aquino: Early Assessments of Her Presidential Leadership and Administration and Her Place in History.* Quezon City: University of the Philippines, 1993.

Agpalo, Remigio E. and Petronilo Daroy. *The Philippine Senate.* Manila: Dick Baldovino Enterprises, 1997.

Apostol, Eugenia D. *Reports of the Fact-Finding Board on the Assassination of Senator Benigno S. Aquino, Jr.* Metro Manila: Mr. & Ms. Publishing, 1984.

Aquino, Belinda A., ed. *Presidential Leadership and Cory Aquino.* Diliman, Quezon City: University of the Philippines, Center for Integrative and Development Studies, 1990.

Aquino, Benigno S. *A Garrison State in the Make and Other Speeches.* Makati, Metro Manila: Benigno S. Aquino, Jr. Foundation, 1985.

Aquino, Corazon Cojuangco. *Speeches of President Corazon C. Aquino.* 8 vol. Manila: National Printing Office, 1989.

Arroyo, Gloria Macapagal. "Policy Statements by the President on the Republic of the Philippines." Manila: *Journal of Diplomacy and Development*, 2001.

The Aquino Administration: Record and Legacy (1986–1992). Diliman, Quezon City: University of the Philippines, 1992.

Bautista, Victoria A., et al., eds. *Introduction to Public Administration in the Philippines: A Reader.* Quezon City: University of the Philippines Press, 1993.

Brillantes, Alex B. and Bienvendia M. Amarles-Ilago. *1898–1992: The Philippine Presidency: Background, Political Influences on, and Administrative Growth of the Philippine Presidency.* Quezon City: College of Public Administration, University of the Philippines, 1994.

Caraque, Guillermo N. *Development in Philippine Government Budgeting under the Aquino Administration.* Manila: Department of Budget & Management, Public Information Service, 1991.

Carlos, Clarita A. *History of Electoral Reforms: Pre-Spanish to 1998.* Makati City: Konrad Adenaur Foundation, 1998.

Castro, Arturo M. de. "Mistrial: A Case Study of the Assassination of Senator Benigno S. Aquino, Jr." Manila: *Current Events Digest,* 1986.

Decentralization: Examining and Maximizing Decentralization Efforts of the Philippine Government. Manila, Philippines: National Economic and Development Authority Training and Development Issues Project, 1989.

Correa, Monina Clavides. *Lupang Hinirang: Kasaysayan at Pamahalaan.* Pasig City: Anvil Publishers, 2000.

The Failed December Coup: View from the UP Community. Diliman, Quezon City: Office of the Vice President for Public Affairs, in Conjunction with Center for Integrative and Development Studies, 1990.

Guerrero, Guillermo I. *Legislation on Local Government in the Eighth Philippine Congress.* Quezon City: Congressional Research and Training Service, 1993.

Guillermo, Gelacio. *The Literature of National Democracy.* Manila: Kalikasan Press, 1990.

Hawes, Gary. "Aquino and Her Administration: A View from the Countryside." *Pacific Affairs* 62 (Spring 1989): 9–28.

———. *The Philippine State and the Marcos Regime: The Politics of Export.* Ithaca, N.Y.: Cornell University Press, 1987.

Hill, Gerald N. and Kathleen Thompson Hill. *Aquino Assassination: The True Story and Analysis of the Assassination of Philippine Senator Benigno S. Aquino, Jr.* Sonoma, Calif.: Hilltop, 1983.

Honculada, Jurgette A. et al. *Transforming the Mainstream: Building a Gender-Responsive Bureacracy in the Philippines, 1975–1998.* Bangkok: UNIFEM. 2000.

Journal and Record of the House of Representatives. 2nd Regular Session (1988–1989). Manila, Philippines: Publication and Editorial Division, 1989.

Kessler, Richard J. *The Philippines under Corazon Aquino: An Assessment of the First Two Years and the Challenges Ahead.* New York: Asia Society, 1988.

Kimura, Masataka. "Philippine Political Parties and the Party System in Transition: Leaders, Factions and Blocs." *Pilipinas* 18, (1992): 43–66.

Lane, Max. "The Philippines 1990: Political Stalemate and Persisting Instability." In *Southeast Asian Affairs.* Singapore: Institute of Southeast Asian Studies, 1991: 223–239.

Laurel, Jose P. *Days of Our Years: The Laurel Legacy.* Manila: s.n., 1989.

Leyco-Reyes, Soccoro. *Legislative Agenda on Womens's Issues for the New Philippine Congress.* Quezon City: Congressional Research and Training Service, 1992.

Local Government in the Philippines: Four Best Practices in Service Delivery. Quezon City: Ateneo De Manila Center for Social Policy and Public Affairs, 1998.

Magno, Alexander R. *Power without Form: Essays on the Filipino State and Politics.* Manila: Kalikasan Press, 1991.

Mamot, Patricio R. *The Aquino Administration's Baptism of Fire.* Metro Manila: National Book Store, 1987.

McDougald, Charles C. *The Marcos File: Was he a Philippine Hero or Corrupt Tyrant?* San Francisco, Calif.: San Francisco Publishers, 1987.

Miranda, Felipe B. "Democratization in the Philippines: Recent Developments, Trends and Prospects." *Asian Journal of Political Science* 1, 1 (June 1993): 85–112.

Montiel, Cristina. *Monitoring Congress: A Cluster Analysis of Legislative Voting Patterns during the Aquino Administration.* Quezon City: Center for Social Policy and Public Affairs, Ateneo De Manila University Press, 1990.

Montinola, Gabriella R. "The Foundations of Political Corruption: Insights from the Philippine Case." *Asian Journal of Political Science* 2, 1 (June 1994): 86–113.

Pamalong, Elly Velez. *Meritocracy of the Masses: A Government for the Masses, by the Masses, and of the Masses.* San Francisco: U.S. Nationals, 1992.

Paredes, Ruby R., et al., eds. *Philippine Colonial Democracy.* New Haven, Conn.: Yale University Southeast Asia Studies, Yale Center for International and Area Studies, 1988.

Pensar, Jed. *Manila Colonialism: The Dark Side of the Flag.* Philippines: L. P. Dacudao, 1988.

Rajaretnam, M., ed. *The Aquino Alternative.* Singapore: Institute of Southeast Asian Studies, 1986.

The Role of the Military in a Third World Economy: The Philippine Experience. January 20, 1990, Pansol, Calamba, Laguna. Manila: Senate of the Philippines, 1990.

Rood, Steve. "Perspectives on the Electoral Behavior of Baguio City (Philippines) Voters in a Transition Era." *Journal of Southeast Asian Studies* 22 (March 1991): 86–108.

Salgado, Pedro V. *Cory Aquino, Militarization, and Other Essays*. Philippines: P. V. Salgado, 1986.

Salonga, Jovito R. *The Senate That Said No: A Four-Year Record of the First Post-EDSA Senate*. Quezon City: University of Philippines Press, 1995.

Sibal, Jose Agaton R. *Local Government: With Constitutional Provisions and Explanatory Notes on Local Government, Local Government Provisions in Administrative Code of 1987*. Quezon City: Central Lawbook Publishing, 1988.

Speeches of the Senators: A Collection of Speeches by the Senators of the Philippines. Manila: Senate of the Congress of the Philippines, 1990.

Suter, Keith D. "The New Government in the Philippines." *Contemporary Review* 248 (May 1986): 225–230.

Thompson, W. Scott. *The Philippines in Crisis: Development and Security in the Aquino Era, 1986–92*. New York: St. Martin's Press, 1992.

Turner, Mark, ed. *Regime Change in the Philippines: The Legitimization of the Aquino Government.* Canberra, Australia: Department of Political and Social Change, Research School of Pacific Studies, Australian National University, 1987.

Van der Kroef, Justus M. *Aquino's Philippines: The Deepening Security Crisis.* London, England: Centre for Security and Conflict Studies, 1988.

Veneracion, Jaime B. *Merit or Patronage: A History of the Philippine Civil Service.* Cubao, Quezon City: Great Books, 1988.

Villegas, Bernado M. "The Philippines in 1985: Rolling with the Political Punches." *Asian Survey* 26, 2 (February 1986): 127–140.

J. Constitution and Law

A Compilation of Laws on Natural Resources and Indigenous Peoples' Rights: A Field Handbook. Quezon City: Legal Rights and Natural Resources Center, 1997.

Abueva, Jose Veloso and Ermelinda R. Roman. *The Post-EDSA Constitutional Commissions, 1986–1992: Self-Assessments and External Views.* Quezon City: University of the Philppines Press, 1999.

Arguillas, Carolyn O. *Turning Rage into Courage: Mindanao under Martial Law.* Davao City: Minda News Publications, 2002.

1992 & Beyond: Forces and Issues in Philippine Elections. Manila: *Philippine Center for Investigative Social Policy and Public Affairs, 1992.*

Arabani, Bensaudi I. *Commentaries on the Code of Muslim Personal Laws of the Philippines with Jurisprudence and Special Procedure*. Manila: Rex Book Store, 1990.

Arroyo, Basilisa C. and Perla S. Frianeza. *Topical Index, 1986 Presidential Is-suances (February 25 to December 31, 1986): Executive Orders, Proclamations, Memorandum Orders, Memorandum Circulars, Administrative Orders.* Quezon City: Law Center, University of the Philippines, 1987.

Bas, Mauricio O. *Philippine Martial Law.* New York: Vantage Press, 1984.

Bernas, Joaquin G. *A Living Constitution: The Cory Aquino Presidency.* Pasig City: Anvil Publishers, 2000.

Carbonell-Catilo, Maria Aurora A., Josie H. de Leon, and Eleanor E. Nicolas. *Manipulated Elections.* Philippines: s.n., 1986.

Carmen, Rolando V. del. "Constitutionality and Judicial Politics." 85–112. In *Marcos and Martial Law in the Philippines.* Ed. David A. Rosenberg. Ithaca: Cornell University Press, 1979.

Casenas, Michael H. *Philippine Laws.* Makati, Metro Manila: J. M. Robles, 1989.

Chan, Manuel T. *The Audencia and the Legal System in the Philippines, 1583–1900.* Manila: M.T. Chan, 1998.

Constantino, Renato. *Dissent and Counter-Consciousness.* Quezon City, Malaya Books, 1970.

Church and State and Other Public Issues and Concerns: Proposals to the 1986 Constitutional Commission. Quezon City: Consultation on the Constitution, National Council of Churches in the Philippines, 1986.

Comparative Study of the 1987, 1973 and 1935 Philippine Constitutions. Diliman, Quezon City: Law Publishing House, Legal Resources Center, 1988.

Coronel, Irma C. *Forecasting Report: 1986 Presidential Election.* Manila: Research Center, De La Salle University, 1986.

Cruz, Isagani A. *Constitutional Law.* 1985 ed. Quezon City, Philippines: Central Lawbook Publishing, 1985.

———. *Philippine Political Law.* 1984 ed. Quezon City: Central Lawbook Publishing, 1984.

Elma, Magdangal B. *The Aquino Presidency and the Constitution.* Manila: Rex Book Store, 1993.

Espiritu, Augusto Caesar. *How Democracy Was Lost: A Political Diary of the Constitutional Convention of 1971–1972.* Quezon City: New Day Publishers, 1993.

Feliciano, Myrna S. "The Legal System of the Philippines." In *Modern Legal Systems Cyclopedia.* Ed. Kenneth Robert Redden. Buffalo, N.Y.: Hein, 1985.

Flamiano, Dolores and Donald Goertzen, eds. *Critical Decade: Prospects for Democracy in the Philippines in the 1990s.* Berkeley, Calif.: Philippine Resource Center, 1990.

Garcia, Ed. *Imperfect Document: Unfinished Quest.* Quezon City: Claretian Publications, 1989.

Gillman, Howard. "On Constructing a Science of Comparative Judicial Politics: Tate & Haynie's 'Authoritarianism and the Functions of Court'." *Law & Society Review* 28, 2 (1994): 355–376.

Herrera, Oscar M. *Treatise on Historical Development and Highlights of Amendments of Rules on Criminal Procedure of the Revised Rules on Criminal Procedure*. Manila: Rex Book Store, 2001.

The History of Philippine Judiciary. Manila: Philippine Judiciary Foundation, 1998.

Laws and Jurisprudence on Built Heritage. National Commission on Culture and the Arts. Public Information Office, and the Supreme Court of the Philippines. Manila: The Commission, 2001.

Leyco-Reyes, Socorro. *Local Legislative Advocacy*. Quezon City: Center for Legislative Advocacy, 1997.

Majul, Cesar A. *The Political and Constitutional Ideas of the Philippine Revolution*. Quezon City: University of the Philippine Press, 1967.

Martin, Ruperto G. *Philippine Constitutional Law*. Rev. ed. Manila: Premium Book Store, 1985.

The Miriam Defensor Santiago Dictionary. Quezon City: Movement for Responsible Public Service, Youth Organization for Unity, Truth, and Honesty, 1991.

Monta, Flor Amor B. *Philippine Government and Constitution*. Makati City: Grandwater Publications and Research Corp., 1999.

The NAMFREL Report on the February 7, 1986 Philippine Presidential Elections. Manila: National Citizens Movement for Free Elections, 1986.

Navarro, Napoleon Y. "The Philippines 1991: Anticipating the Elections." *Southeast Asian Affairs*. Singapore: Institute of Southeast Asian Studies, 1992: 257–280.

The New Constitution of the Philippines. Annotated. Metro Manila: National Book Store, 1990.

Nolledo, Jose N. *The Constitution of the Republic of the Philippines: With Annotations*. Manila: Rex Book Store, 1987.

Pasimio, Renato R. *The Philippine Constitution (Its Evolution and Development) and Political Science*. Manila: National Book Store, 1991.

Reyes, Zenaida S., ed. *Philippine Laws for the Muslims*. Diliman, Quezon City: Z. S. Reyes, 1989.

Rodriguez, Rufus B. *Investment Laws of the Philippines*. Manila: Rex Book Store, 1997.

Schirmer, Daniel B. "Military Access: The Pentagon Versus the Philippine Constitution." *Monthly Review* 46 (June 1994): 22–37.

Senate Blue Ribbon Report on the Activities of the Presidential Commission on Good Government in Connection with the Implementation of Section 26, Article XVIII of the Constitution. Manila: Senate Publication and Editorial Division, 1989.

Tate, C. Neal and Stacia L Haynie. "Authoritarianism and the Functions of Courts: A Time Series Analysis of the Philippine Supreme Court, 1961–1987." *Law & Society Review* 27, 4 (1993): 707–740.

The Supreme Court Centenary Reader, 1901–2001. Manila Judiciary Foundation: Makiling Books, 2001.

Tupaz, Antonio R. and Edsel C. Tupas. *Fundamentals on Impeachment*. Quezon City: Central Lawbook Publication, 2001.

Valero, Gerardo M. C. *Spratly Archipelago: Is the Question of Sovereignty Still Relevant?:* A Roundtable Discussion. Diliman, Quezon City: Institute of International Legal Studies, University of the Philippines Law Center, 1993.

Villacorta, Wilfrido V. "The Dynamics and Processes of Writing the 1987 Constitution." *Philippine Journal of Public Administration* 32, 3–4 (July/October 1988): 299–309.

Wiber, Melanie. *Politics, Property and Law in the Philippine Uplands*. Waterloo, Canada: Wilfrid Laurier University Press, 1993.

Wurfel, David. "Martial Law in the Philippines: The Methods of Regime Survival." *Pacfic Affairs* 50, 1 (Spring 1977) 5–30.

K. Bases

Agreements on United States Military Facilities in Philippine Military Bases, 1947–1985. Rev. ed. Manila, Philippines: Foreign Services Institute, 1985.

Bacho, Peter. "U.S.–Philippine Relations in Transition: The Issue of the Bases." *Asian Survey* 28, 6 (June 1988): 650–660.

The Bases of Their Decisions: Manila. Legislative Publications Staff, Secretariat, Senate of the Philippines, 1991.

Berry, William E. *American Military Bases in the Philippines, Base Negotiations, and Philippine–American Relations*. Boulder, Colo.: Westview Press, 1988.

———. *U.S. Bases in the Philippines: The Evolution of the Special Relationship*. Boulder, Colo.: Westview Press, 1989.

Bengzon, Alfredo R. A. with Raul Rodrigo. *A Matter of Honor: The Story of the 1990–1991 Bases Talk*. Manila: Anvil, 1997.

Calit, Harry S. *The Philippines: Current Issues and Historical Background*. New York: Nova Science Publishers, 2003.

Colbert, Evelyn S. *The United States and the Philippine Bases*. Washington, D.C.: Foreign Policy Institute, School of Advanced International Studies, Johns Hopkins University, 1987.

Constantino, Letizia R. *The 1988 Bases Review Agreement*. Quezon City: Education Forum, 1988.

Corning, Gregory P. "The Philippine Bases and U.S. Pacific Strategy." *Pacific Affairs* 63 (Spring 1990): 6–23.

Fallows, James. "The Bases Dilemma." *The Atlantic Monthly* (February 1988): 18–27.

Garcia, Ed. *The Sovereign Quest: Freedom from Foreign Military Bases*. Quezon City: Claretian Publications, 1988.

Gonzales, Salvador Roxas. *The Philippines: Democracy in Asia*. Fallsington, Penn.: Burgos & Burgos Ltd. 1987.

Greene, Fred, ed. *The Philippine Bases: Negotiating for the Future American and Philippine Perspectives.* New York: Council on Foreign Relations, 1988.

Gregor, A. James and Virgilio Aganon. *The Philippine Bases: U.S. Security at Risk.* Washington, D.C.: Ethics and Public Policy Center, 1987.

Henry, Donald Putnam. *The Philippine Bases: Background for Negotiations: Executive Summary.* Santa Monica, Calif.: Rand, 1989.

Jimenez, Pilar R. and Maria Elena Chiong-Javier. *Social Benefits and Costs: People's Perceptions of the U.S. Military Bases in the Philippines.* Manila: Research Center, De La Salle University, 1988.

Kirk, Donald. *Looted: The Philippines after the Bases.* New York: St. Martin's Press, 1998.

On Wastes and National Dignity: Views and Voices on the US Military Bases. Manila, Philippines: International Affairs Desk, National Council of Churches in the Philippines, 1988.

Paez, Patricia Ann. *The Bases Factor: Realpolitic of RP–US Relations.* Manila: Center for Strategic and International Studies of the Philippines, 1985.

Santiago, Miriam Defensor. "Comments on Immigration and Deportation." In *Fookien Times Philippine Yearbook.* Ed. Betty Go Belmonte. Manila: Fookien Times, 1989, 128.

Schirmer, Daniel B. *U.S. Bases and Intervention in the Philippines.* Manila: Socio-Pastoral Institute, 1986.

Schirmer, Boone, Megan van Frank, and Michael Bedford. *U.S. Bases in the Philippines: In Whose Interest?* Cambridge, Mass.: Third World Reports, 1989.

Simbulan, Roland G. *The Bases of Our Insecurity: A Study of the US Military Bases in the Philippines.* 2nd ed. Metro Manila: Balai Fellowship, 1985.

Tatad, Francisco S. *The Philippines in 1986: Prospects for National Reconciliation and Regional Stability.* Singapore: Heinemann Asia, 1986.

The Philippines: U.S. Policy during the Marcos Years, 1965–1986. Washington D.C., 2000.

Thompson, Williard Scott. *The Philippines in Crises: Development and Security in the Aquino Era, 1986–1992.* New York: St. Martin's Press, 1992.

The U.S. Military Bases in the Philippines: Issues and Scenarios: Proceedings of the Symposium Held on August 14, 1985. Quezon City: International Studies Institute of the Philippines, 1986.

Webb, Katharine Watkins. *Are Overseas Bases Worth the Bucks?: An Approach to Assessing Operational Value and an Application to the Philippines.* Santa Monica, Calif.: Rand, 1993.

L. Armed Forces

Baclagon, Uldarico S. *Military History of the Philippines.* Manila: Saint Mary's Publishing, 1975.

Berry, William E., Jr. "The Changing Role of the Philippine Military during Martial Law and the Implications for the Future." In *The Armed Forces in Contemporary Asian Societies*. Ed. Edward A. Olsen and Stephen Jurika, Jr. Boulder, Colo.: Westview Press, 1986: 215–240.

Brillantes, Alex B. *Dictatorship & Martial Law: Philippine Authoritarianism in 1972*. Quezon City: Great Books, 1987.

Carlos, Corina and Rodolfo Obaniana. *Philippine Army: The First 100 Years*. Manila: Philippine Army, 1997.

Ghormley, Ralph M. *The Military Order of the Carabao: Centennial History*. Washington D.C.: Military Order of the Carabao, 2000.

Hernandez, Carolina G. "Arms Procurement and Production Policies." In *Arms and Defense in Southeast Asia*. Ed. Chandran Jeshrun. Singapore: Institute of Southeast Asian Studies, 1989: 125–151.

Jarque, Rene N. *Defending the Philippines at the Dawn of the 21st Century: Challenges for the Armed Forces*. Camp Aguinaldo, Quezon City: Armed Forces of the Philippines, 1997.

Jose, Ricardo Trota. *The Philippine Army, 1935–1942*. Manila: Ateneo de Manila University Press, 1992.

McCoy, Alfred W. *Closer Than Brothers: Manhood at the Philippine Military Academy*. New Haven, Conn.: Yale University Press, 1999.

Mettraux, Guenael. *U.S. Courts-Martial and the Armed Conflict in the Philippines, 1899–1902*. Oxford: Oxford University Press, 2003.

Miranda, Felipe B. *Development and the Military in the Philippines: Military Perceptions in a Time of Continuing Crisis*. Diliman, Quezon City, Philippines: Social Weather Stations, 1988.

Montiel, Cristina. *Filipinos' Attitude toward the military*. Quezon City: Claretian Publications, 1988.

Nemenzo, Eldon Luis G. *The Philippine Air Force Story*. Pasay City: The Office, 1992.

Pobre, Cesar P. *History of the Armed Forces of the Filipino People*. Quezon City: New Day Publishers, 2000.

Rood, Steven. "Absorptive Capacity of the Philippines: Institutions and Security." In *Leadership and Security in Southeast Asia: Institutional Aspects*. Ed. Stephen Chee. Singapore: Institute of Southeast Asian Studies, 1991: 87–113.

Said, Shuhud. "The New Armed Forces of the Philippines and Part 1: Oplan Mamamayan and the Unfinished Revolution." *Asian Defence Journal* (January 1987): 4–32.

Santos, Ramon G. *Confidence-Building Measures in Philippine Security*. Carlisle, Penn.: U.S. Army War College, 1998.

Selochan, Viberto. *Could the Military Govern the Philippines?* Quezon City: New Day Publishers, 1989.

———. *The Armed Forces of the Philippines: The Perceptions of Governing and the Prospects for the Future*. Clayton, Australia: Monash University, 1989.

Van der Kroef, Justus M. "The 'Rambo Mystique': Philippine Para-Military and Society." *Internationales Asienforum* 21, 1–2 (1990): 5–37.

Villacorta, Wilfrido V. "The Management of National Security in the Philippines: The Role of Leadership Styles." In *Leadership Perceptions and National Security: The Southeast Asian Experience*. Ed. Mohammed Ayoob and Chaianan Samudavanija. Singapore: Institute of Southeast Asian Studies, 1989: 57–82.

Yabes, Criselda. *The Boys from the Barracks: The Philippine Military after EDSA*. Manila: Anvil Publishing, 1991.

M. Insurgency

Abueva, Jose V., et al. *Ending the Armed ConfliConn.: Peace Negotiations in the Philippines*. Quezon City: UP Center for Integrative and Development Studies: University of the Philippines, 1992.

Aventajado, Roberto N. and Teodoro Y. Montelibano. *140 Days of Terror. In the Clutches of the Abu Sayyaf*. Pasig City: Anvil Publishing, 2004.

Azama, Rodney S. *The Huks and the New People's Army: Comparison of Two Postwar Insurgencies*. CSC 1985. Marine Corps Development and Education Command. Quantico, Va.: 1985.

Bacho, Peter. "Rural Revolt in the Philippines: Threats to Stability?" *Journal of International Affairs* 40 (Winter/Spring 1987): 257–278.

Benson, Nichols. *A Clumsy War: An Inquiry on the Operational Ambiguities of America's Counterinsurgency Campaign in the Philippines and Its Opaque History*. Dissertation. Ann Arbor: University Microfilms, 2003.

Boudreu, Vincent. *Grass Roots and Cadre in the Protest Movement*. Manila: Ateneo De Manila University Press, 2001.

Churchill, Bernardita Reyes and Gil D. Golangco. *Resistance and Revolution*. Manila: National Commission for Culture and the Arts, 2002.

Corpuz, Arturo G. "De-Maoization and Nationalist Trends in the CPP." *Journal of Contemporary Asia* 18 (1988): 412–429.

Davis, Leonard. *Revolutionary Struggle in the Philippines*. New York: St. Martin's Press, 1989.

Fay, Chip. *Counter-Insurgency and Tribal Peoples in the Philippines*. Washington, D.C.: Survival International USA, 1987.

Ferrer, Miriam Coronel and Antoinette Raquiza, eds. *Motions for Peace: A Summary of Events Related to Negotiating the Communist Insurgency in the Philippines, 1986–1992*. Metro Manila: Coalition for Peace: Education for Life Foundation, 1993.

Gaspar, Karl. Elpidio A. et al. *Mapagpakamalinawon: A Reader for the Mindanawon Peace Advocate*. Davao City: Alternate Forum for Research in Mindanao, 2002.

Greenberg, Lawrence M. *The Hukbalahap Insurrection: A Case Study of a Successful Anti-Insurgency Operation in the Philippines, 1946–1955*.

Washington, D.C.: Analysis Branch, U.S. Army Center of Military History, 1987.

Hamilton, Donald W. *The Art of Insurgency: American Military Policy and the Failure of Strategy in Southeast Asia.* Westport, Conn.: Praeger, 1998.

Hawes, Gary. "Theories of Peasant Revolution: A Critique and Contribution from the Philippines." *World Politics* 42 (January 1990): 261–298.

Hilsdon, Anne Marie. *Madonnas and Martyrs: Militarism and Violence in the Philippines.* Quezon City: Ateneo De Manila University Press, 1995.

Jones, Gregg R. *Red Revolution: Inside the Philippine Guerrilla Movement.* Boulder, Colo.: Westview Press, 1989.

Kessler, Richard J. *Rebellion and Repression in the Philippines.* New Haven, Conn.: Yale University Press, 1989.

Kintanar, Galileo C. et al. *Lost in Time: From Birth to Obsolescene: The Communist Party of the Philippines.* Quezon City: Truth and Justice Foundation, 2000.

Kowalewski, David. "Counterinsurgent Paramilitarism: A Philippine Case Study." *Journal of Peace Research* 29 (February 1992): 71–84.

——. "Cultism, Insurgency, and Vigilantism in the Philippines." *Sociological Analysis* 52 (Fall 1991): 241–253.

Lee, Albert C. "Notes from the Underground Economy." *Philippine Panorama* (September 15, 1985).

Magno, Jose P., Jr. and A. James Gregor. "Insurgency and Counterinsurgency in the Philippines." *Asian Survey* 26 (May 1986): 501–517.

Malajacan, Marcelino Q., Jr. *Anti-Communist Vigilantes in the Philippines.* Fort Leavenworth, Kans.: United States Army Command and General Staff College, 1988.

Marks, Thomas A. *Maoist Insurgency since Vietnam.* Portland, Ore.: Frank Cass, 1996.

McCallus, Joseph P. "The Propaganda of the National Democratic Front: A Study of Rhetorical Method in Liberation, 1989–1991." *Pilipinas* 20 (Spring 1993): 23–42.

Molloy, Ivan. "Revolution in the Philippines: The Question of an Alliance between Islam and Communism." *Asian Survey* 25 (August 1985): 822–833.

——. "The Decline of the Moro National Liberation Front in the Southern Philippines." *Journal of Contemporary Asia* 18, 1 (1988): 59–76.

Morris, Stephen J. "The Soviet Union and the Philippine Communist Movement." *Communist and Post-Communist Studies* 27 (March 1994): 77–93.

Ochoa, Cecilia S. Siglo-saka: *A Century of Peasant Struggle and Contributions to Philippine Nationhood.* Quezon City: Philippine Peasant Institute, 1998.

Pimentel, Benjamin. *Rebolusyon!: A Generation of Struggle in the Philippines.* New York: Monthly Review Press, 1991.

Philippine Centennial Commission. Saga and Triumph: The Filipino Revolution Against Spain. Manila: Philippine Centennial Commission, 1999.

Philippine Radical Papers in the University of the Philippines. Diliman Main Library: A Subject Guide. Quezon City: University of the Philippines Press, 1998.

Porter, Gareth. *The Politics of Counterinsurgency in the Philippines*. Honolulu, Hawaii: Center for Asian and Pacific Studies, University of Hawaii, 1987.

Rangel-Suarez, Alfredo. *Guerra Insurgente: Conflictos en Malasia, Peru. Filipinas, El Salvador y Colombia*. Bogota: Book Libraries Worldwide 25, 2001.

Salgado, Pedro V. *Militarization and other Essays*. Quezon City: R. P. Garcia Publishing Co., 1986.

Sison, Jose Maria. *The Implosion of the Communist Party of the Philippines: An Interview with Jose Maria Sison, by David Glanz*. Clayton, Victoria, Australia: Centre of Southeast Asian Studies, Monash University, 1995.

Sison, Jose Maria and Ranier Werning. *The Philippine Revolution: The Leader's View*. New York: Crane Russak, 1989.

Stephen, Robert B. *Counterinsurgency in the Philippines: Problems and Prospects*. Langley Air Force Base, Va.: United States Army and Air Force Center for Low Intensity Conflict, 1989.

Stilwell, Richard G. "Averting Disaster in the Philippines: What Government and Army Must Do to Defeat the Communists." *Policy Review* 43 (Winter 1988): 20–24.

Taruc, Luis. *He Who Rides the Tiger*. New York: Praeger, 1967.

Taylor, John Rodgers Meigs. *The Philippine Insurrection against the United States*: A compilation of documents with notes and introduction by John R. Taylor. 5 vol. Pasay City: Lopez Museum, 1971.

Van der Kroef, Justus M. "Aquino and the Communists: A Philippine Strategic Stalemate?" *World Affairs* 151 (Winter 1988/89) 117–129.

———. "The Philippine Vigilantes: Devotion and Despair." *Contemporary Southeast Asia* (Singapore) 10, 2 (September 1988), 162–180.

Valeriano, Napoleon and Charles T. R. Bohannan. *Counter-guerrilla Operations: The Philippine Experience*. New York: Praeger, 1962.

Vitug, Marites Dañgulan and Glenda Gloria. *Under the Crescent Moon: Rebellion in Mindanao*. Quezon City: Ateneo Center for Social Policy & Public Affairs: Institute for Popular Democracy, 2000.

Yuk-Wai, Yung L., ed. *The Huaqiao Warriors: Chinese Resistance Movement in the Philippines, 1942–45*. Philadelphia: Coronet Books, 1995.

N. Human Rights

A Let-Down in Peace, No Let-Up in War: A Human Rights Report on the First Year of the Ramos Government, July 1, 1992–June 30, 1993. Manila: Philippine Alliance of Human Rights Advocates, 1993.

Amnesty International. *The Philippines: A Summary of Amnesty International's Concerns*. AI Series. London: March 1990.

———. *Philippines: Unlawful Killings by Military and Paramilitary Forces*. AI Series. New York: 1988.

Anderson, Benedict. "Cacique Democracy in the Philippines: Origins and Dreams." *New Left Review* 169 (May–June 1988), 3–31.

Angeles, Leonora C. *The Quest for Justice: Obstacles to the Redress of Human Rights Violations in the Philippines*. Manila: UP-CIDS and the U.P. Press, 1994.

Annotated Human Rights Bibliography. New York: Open Society Institute 1996.

Bad Blood: Militia Abuses in Mindanao, the Philippines. New York: Human Rights Watch, 1992.

Bakker, Jan Willem. *The Philippine Justice System: The Independence and Impartiality of the Judiciary and Human Rights from 1986 till 1997*. Geneva: PIOOM Center for the Independence of Judgess and Lawyers, 1997.

The Challenge of Rural Democratization: Perspective from Latin America and the Philippines. Portland, Ore.: F. Case, 1990.

Claude, Richard Pierre. "Human Rights Education: The Case of the Philippines." *Human Rights Quarterly* 13 (November 1991): 453–524.

Diokno, Jose W. *A Nation for Our Children: Human Rights, Nationalism, Sovereignty: Selected Writings*. 3rd ed. Quezon City: Jose W. Diokno Foundation, 1987.

Enriquez, Antonio Reyes. *The Unseen War and Other Tales from Mindanao*. Quezon City: Giraffe Books, 1996.

Espiritu, Augusto Caesar. *Law and Human Rights in the Development of ASEAN: With Special Reference to the Philippines*. Singapore: Friedrich-Naumann-Stiftung, 1986.

Garcia, Ed. *A Distant Peace: Human Rights and People's Participation in Conflict Resolution*. Diliman, Quezon City: University of the Philippines Press, 1991.

———. *The Filipino Quest, a Just and Lasting Peace*. Quezon City: Claretian Publications, 1988.

Jacob, Malou Leviste. *Anatomy of Corruption*. Manila: St. Scholastica, 1992.

Leyco-Reyes, Socorro. *Local Legislative Advocacy*. Quezon City: Center for Legislative Development, 1997.

O'Brien, Niali. *Seeds of Injustice: Reflections on the Murder Frame-Up of the Negros Nine in the Philippines: From the Prison Diary of Nieali O'Brien*. Dublin: O'Brien Press, 1985.

Pearson, Nancy et al. *Recipes for Healing: Gender Sensitive Care for Survivors of Torture*. Quezon City: University of the Philippines Press, 1998.

The Philippine Peasants Human Rights Situation: An Overview. Quezon City: Forum for Fund Concerns, Human Rights Desk, 1989.

Philippines, Human Rights Violations & the Labour Movement. New York: Amnesty International, 1991.

Philippines: Testimonies on Human Rights Violations. Geneva, Switzerland: Commission of the Churches on International Affairs, World Council of Churches, 1986.

Philippines: Unlawful Killings by Military and Paramilitary Forces. New York: Amnesty International, 1988.

The Philippines: Violations of the Laws of War by Both Sides. New York: Asia Watch, 1990.

Pumipiglas: Political Detention and Military Atrocities in the Philippines, 1981–1982. Quezon City: Task Force Detainees of the Philippines, 1986.

Ruiz, Lester Edwin J. "Right-Wing Vigilantism and the Betrayal of Democracy": Notes on a Fact-Finding Mission to the Philippines. Quezon City: *Human Rights Desk.* National Council of Churches in the Philippines, 1987.

Salman, Michael. *The Embarrassment of Slavery: Controversies over Bondages and Nationalism in the American Colonial Philippines.* Berkeley: University of California Press, 2003.

Sarmiento, Rene V., et al. *Torment and Struggle after Marcos: A Report on Human Rights Trends in the Philippines under Aquino, March 1986–June 1992.* Quezon City: Task Force Detainees of the Philippines, 1993.

Shaffer, Steve M. *One Grain of Sand: A Peace Corps Philippine Experience.* Orlando, Fla.: Gasat, 1988.

Silliman, Sidney G. and Lela Garner Noble, eds. *NGOs, Civil Society, and the Philippine State.* Honolulu: University of Hawaii Press, 1998.

Taro, Fe Ann. *Human Rights: The Philippine Perspective.* Metro Manila: National Book Store, 1991.

Toh Swee-Hin and Virginia Floresca-Caragas. *Peace Education: A Framework for the Philippines.* Quezon City: Phoenix Publishing House, 1987.

Torment and Struggle after Marcos: A Report on Human Rights Trends in the Philippines under Aquino, March 1989–June 1992. Quezon City: Task Force Detainee of the Philippines, 1993.

Trott, Reinhold. *The Pain Will Go on until Justice is Done: What Can We Do to Enforce Human Rights to the Philippines?* Quezon City: National Council of Churches in the Philippines, 1987.

Varley, Pamela and Carolyn Mathiasen. *The Sweatshop Quandary: Corporate Responsibility on the Global Frontier.* Washington, D.C.: Investor Responsibility Research Center, 1998.

Vigilantes in the Philippines: *A Threat to Democratic Rule.* New York: Lawyers Committee for Human Rights, 1988.

PART 3. FOREIGN RELATIONS

A. General

Antolik, Michael. *ASEAN and the Diplomacy of Accommodation.* Armonk, New York: Sharpe, 1990.

Annuar Nik Mahmud. *Tunturan Filipina ke Atas Borneo Utara.* Bangi: Penerbit Universiti Kebangsaan Malaysia, 2001.

Australia and the Philippines: The Situation in the Philippines and Its Implication. Australia Parliament Joint on Foreign Affairs and Defence. Canberra: Australian Government Publication Service, 1986.

Burton, Sandra. "Aquino's Philippines: The Center Holds." *Foreign Affairs* 65, 3 (1987): 524–537.

Coronel, Sheila S. "Dateline Philippines: The Lost Revolution." *Foreign Policy* 84 (Fall 1991): 166–185.

Francisco, Juan R. *Indian Influence in the Philippines.* Quezon City: University of the Philippines Press, 1964.

History of the Department of Foreign Affairs, 1898–1991. Manila, Philippines: Foreign Service Institute, Department of Foreign Affairs, 1991.

Ingles, Jose D. *Filipino Advocate and Spokesman: Selected Articles and Statements on Foreign Policy and World Politics.* Manila: Philippine Branch of the International Law Association, 1992.

Jacobson, Matthew Frye. *Barbarian Virtues: The United States Encounters Foreign Peoples at Home and Abroad 1876–1917.* New York: Hill and Wang, 2001.

Krenn, Michael L. *Race and Foreign Policy in the Ages of Territorial and Market Expansion 1840–1900.* New York: Garland Publication, 1998.

Ledesma, Antonio L. and Karl Osner, eds. *Ways and Steps towards Solidarity: Experiences and Impetus from a German–Philippine Exposure and Dialogue Program.* Quezon City: Claretian Publications, 1988.

Leyva, Lozano. *Conspiracion en Filipinas.* Barcelona: Ediciones Salamandra, 2001.

Malay, Armando S. Jr. "How CPR Could Have Averted the Vietnam War." *Centennial Issue Asian Studies* 34 (1998): 100–120.

Manning, Robert A. "The Philippines in Crisis." *Foreign Affairs* 63 (Winter 1984/1985): 392–410.

Marcos Diplomacy: Guide to Philippine Bilateral Relations. Manila, Philippines: Foreign Service Institute, 1983.

Minami, Ryoshin and Kwan Kim S. *Growth, Distribution and Political Change: Asia and the Wider World.* New York: Macmillan Press, 1999.

Nardin, Denis. *France and the Philippines from the Beginning to the End of the Spanish Regime,* trans. from the French by Maria Theresa J. Cruz. Ermita, Manila: National Historical Institute, 1989.

Nisperos, Nestor Martinez. *Philippine Foreign Policy on the North Borneo Question.* Dissertation. University of Pittsburgh, 1969.

Noble, Lela Garner. *Philippine Policy Toward Sabah: A Claim to Independence.* Association for Asian Studies Monograph, No. 33. Tucson: University of Arizona Press, 1977.

Ople, Blas. *Global but Parochial: Selected Writings and Speeches on Foreign Policy.* Quezon City: Institute for Public Policy, 1994.

Palongpalong, Artemio. *Forgotten Neighbors: The Philippines Relations with South Asia.* Manila: Center for Research and Communication, 1992.

Philippine Diplomacy: Chronology and Documents, 1972–1981. Manila: Foreign Service Institute, 1981.

Philippine Perspectives on the Emerging World Order. Manila, Philippines: People's Diplomacy Training Program for Philippine NGOs, 1992.

Polo, Lily Ann. *A Cold War Alliance: Philippine–South Korean Relations, 1948–1971*. Diliman, Quezon City: Asian Center, University of the Philippines, 1984.

Rosenberger, Leif. "Philippine Communism and the Soviet Union." *Survey* 29 (Spring 1985): 113–145.

Samad, Paridah and Darusalam Abu Bakar. "Malaysia–Philippines Relations: The Issue of Sabah." *Asian Survey* 32 (June 1992): 554–567.

Simbulan, Roland G. *The Continuing Struggle for an Independent Philippine Foreign Policy*. Philippines: Nuclear Free Philippines Coalition (NFPC), 1991.

Suhrke, Astri. "Political Rituals in Developing Nations: The Case of the Philippines." *Journal of Southeast Asian Studies* 2, 2 (September 1971), 126–141.

Tarling, Nicholas. *Sulu and Sabah: A Study of British Policy Toward the Philippines and North Borneo from the late 18th Century*. Kuala Lumpur: Oxford University Press, 1978.

Van der Kroef, Justus Maria. *Since Aquino, the Philippine Tangle and the United States*. Baltimore: School of Law, University of Maryland, 1986.

Wadi, Jukipli M. and Aileen S. Baviera. *Pilippine External Relations: A Centennial Vista*. Pasay City: Foreign Service Institute. 1998.

Weatherbee, Donald E. "The Philippines and ASEAN: Options for Aquino." *Asian Survey* 27 (December 1997): 1223–1239.

B. Relations with China

Churchill, Bernardita Reyes, ed. *Philippine–China Relations, 1975–1988: An Assessment*. Manila: De La Salle University Press, 1990.

Coquia, Jorge. "Maritime Boundary Problems in the South China Sea." *University of British Columbia Review* 24, 1 (1994): 117–125.

Cordner, Lee G. "The Spratly Islands Dispute and the Law of the Sea." *Ocean Developments and International Journal* 25, 1 (1994): 61–74.

Cruz de Castro, Renato. "The Controversy in the Spratlys: Exploring the Limits to ASEAN's Engagement Policy." *Issues and Studies* 34, 9 (September 1998): 95–123.

Ferrer, Neil Frank R., ed. "The Philippines and the South Sea Islands." *Overview and Documents*. Manila: Foreign Service Institute, 1993.

Furtado, Xavier. "International Law and Dispute over the Spratly Islands: Whiter UNCLOS?" *Contemporary Southeast Asia* 21, 3 (December 1999): 386–404

Godley, M. R. "Reflections on China's Changing Overseas Chinese Policy." *Solidarity* 123 (July–September 1989): 108–112.

Jie, Chen. "China's Spratly Policy: With Special Reference to the Philippines and Malaysia." *Asian Survey* 34 (1999): 893–903.

Johnson, Christopher C. " The Spratly Dispute: Rethinking the Interplay of Law, Diplomacy, and Geo-Politic in the South China Sea." *The International Journal of Marine and Coastal Law* 13, 2 (May 1998): 193–236.

——. "The Spratly Island Dispute in the South China Sea." *Integrated Coastal Zone Management.* Spring 2000: 85–90.

Liao, Shubert S. C., ed. *Chinese Participation in Philippine Culture and Economy.* Manila: Bookman, 1964.

Magno, Francisco. "Environmental Security in the South China Sea." *Orbis* 28, 1 (Summer 1996): 97–112.

Mangahas, Maria F. "Traditional Marine Tenure and Management in ASEAN." *World Bulletin* 10, 5–6 (September–December 1994): 29–40.

Marston, Geoffrey. "Abandonment of Territorial Claims: The Cases of Bouvet and Spratly Islands." *British Yearbook of International Law* (1986): 337–356.

Muyot, Alberto T. "The Extinction of Criminal Liability in Non-International Conflicts." *World Bulletin* 10, 5–6 (September–December 1994): 41–47.

Narine, Shaun. "ASEAN and the Management of Regional Security." *Pacific Affairs* 11, 2 (Summer 1998): 195–214.

Narine, Shaun. "ASEAN and the ARF. The Limits of the 'ASEAN Way.'" *Asian Survey* 37, 10 (October 1997): 961–979.

Nathan, Andrew J. and Robert S. Ross. *The Great Wall and the Empty Fortress: China's Search for Security.* New York: WW Norton, 1997.

Shi-Ching, Hsiao. *Chinese–Philippine Diplomatic Relations: 1946–1975.* Quezon City: Bookman Printing House, 1975.

South to South: 10 Years of Philippine–China NGO Cooperation for Development: An Anniversary Publication of the Philippine–China Resource Center. Quezon City: Phil–China Resource Center, 2000.

Wong, Kwok-Chu. *The Chinese in Philippine Economy, 1898–1941.* Quezon City: Ateneo De Manila University Press, 1999.

C. Relations with Japan

Asis, Leocadio De. *The Thread of Fate: A Personal Story in Philippine–Japanese Relations.* Makati, Metro Manila: Philippine Foundation of Japan Alumni, 1986.

Dingman, Roger. "The Diplomacy of Dependency: The Philippines and Peacemaking with Japan, 1945–52." *Journal of Southeast Asian Studies* 17 (September 1986): 307–321.

Friend, Theodore. *The Blue Eyed Enemy: Japan against the West in Java and Luzon.* Princeton: Princeton University Press, 1988.

Ikehata, Setsuko and Lydia Yu-Jose, eds. *Philippines–Japan Relations.* Honolulu: University of Hawaii Press, 2003.

Jensen, Richard and Jon Davidann. *Transpacific Relations: America, Europe and Asia in the Twentieth Century.* Westport, Conn.: Praeger, 2003.

Macdonald, Charles C. *Asian Loot: Unearthing the Secrets of Marcos. Yamashita and the Gold.* San Francisco: San Francisco Publishers, 1993.

Potter, David. *Japan's Foreign Aid to Thailand & the Philippines.* New York: St. Martin's Press, 1996.

Rebuilding Bridges: 50 Years of Philippine–Japan Relations, 1948–1998. Manila: Yuchengco Center for East Asia, De La Salle University Press, 1999.

Terami, Motoe. "The Cultural Front in the Philippines, 1942–1945: Japanese Propaganda and Filipino Resistance in Mass Media." Thesis (M.A.) University of the Philippines, 1984.

Yu-Jose, Lydia N. *Japan Views the Philippines, 1900–1944.* Revised Edition. Manila: Ateneo De Manila University Press, 1999.

———. Filipinos in Japan and Okinawa, 1880s–1972. Tokyo: Research Institute for the Languages and Cultures of Asia and Africa, Tokyo University of Foreign Studies, 2002.

D. Relations with the United States

Andrade, Pio, Jr. *The Fooling of America: The Untold Story of Carlos P. Romulo.* Philippines: P. Andrade, 1990.

Bacho, Peter. "U.S.–Philippine Relations in Transition: The Issue of the Bases." *Asian Survey* 28 (June 1988): 650–660.

———. "U.S. Policy Options toward the Philippines." *Asian Survey* 27 (April 1987): 427–441.

Bello, Walden F. *U.S. Sponsored Low-Intensity Conflict in the Philippines.* San Francisco: Institute for Food and Development Policy, 1987.

Blitz, Amy. *The Contested State: American Policy and the Regime Change in the Philippines.* Lanham: Rowman & Littlefield, 2002.

Brands, H. W. *Bound to Empire: The United States and the Philippines.* New York: Oxford University Press, 1992.

Bonner, Raymond. *Waltzing with a Dictator: The Marcoses and the Making of American Policy.* Times Book, 1987.

Carlson, Keith T. *The Twisted Road to Freedom: America's Granting of Independence to the Philippines.* Honolulu: University of Hawaii Press, 1995.

Cullather, Nick. "America's Boy? Ramon Magsaysay and the Illusion of Influence." *Pacific Historical Review* 62 (August 1993): 305–338.

———. *Illusions of Influence: The Political Economy of United States–Philippines Relations, 1942–1960.* Stanford, Calif.: Stanford University Press, 1994.

Cullather, Nick, ed. *Managing Nationalism: United States National Security Council Documents on the Philippines, 1953–1960.* Quezon City: New Day Publishers, 1992.

Doty, Roxanne Lynn. "Foreign Policy as Social Construction: A Post-Positivist Analysis of U.S. Counterinsurgency Policy in the Philippines." *International Studies Quarterly* 37 (September 1993): 297–320.

Flamiano, Dolores and Donald Goertzen, eds. "Critical Decade: Prospects for Democracy in the Philippines in the 1990's: Papers and Discussions from the Critical Decade Conference," March 16–18, 1990, University of California at Berkeley. Berkeley, Calif.: Philippine Resource Center, 1990.

Golay, Frank H. *Face of Empire: United States–Philippine Relations*. Madison: University of Wisconsin, 1998.

Hallenberg, Virginia S. Capulong. *Philippine Foreign Policy toward the U.S. 1972–1980: Reorientation?* Stockholm, Sweden: Department of Political Science, University of Stockholm, 1987.

Ladd-Taylor, Molly. *Retrieving the American Past: A Customized U.S. History Reader*. Boston: Pearson Custom Publication, 2001.

Landé, Carl H., ed. *Rebuilding a Nation: Philippine Challenges and American Policy*. Washington, D.C.: Washington Institute Press, 1987.

Lim, Benito. *Philippine–U.S. Relations: An Overview of Philippine Foreign Policy*. Quezon City: Journals and Publications Division, President's Center for Special Studies, 1984.

Lim, Robyn. *Australian Relations with the Philippines during the Marcos Years: A Study in the Implications of the Nixon Doctrine*. Nathan, Queensland, Australia: Griffith University, School of Modern Asian Studies, Centre for the Study of Australian–Asian Relations, 1987.

Pareñas, Caesar. *Restructuring for Stability: Economic, Political, and Security Dimensions of Japanese–Philippine–U.S. Relations in the 1990s*. Metro Manila: Southeast Asian Science Foundation, 1992.

"The Philippines Facing the Future: An Assessment of the Prospects for the Philippines and for Philippine–America Relations: A Report of the Findings of a Study Mission to the Philippines Sponsored by the Asia Society of New York and the Center for Research and Communication, Manila, Philippines." New York: Asia Society, 1986.

Schirmer, Daniel B. "Korea and the Philippines: A Century of U.S. Intervention." *Monthly Review* 43 (May 1991): 19–32.

PART 4. JOURNALS AND NEWSPAPERS

A. Scholarly Journals

Asian Studies. Quezon City: University of the Philippines, semi-annually.
Budhi. Quezon City: Ateneo De Manila, quarterly.
Far Eastern Law Review. Manila: Far Eastern University, semiannually.
Journal of Research in Science Teaching. Manila: De La Salle University, quarterly.
Kasarinlan. Quezon City: Third World Studies, University of the Philippines, quarterly.
Kinaadman. Cagayan de Oro: Xavier University, quarterly.

Kritika Kultura. Manila: Cultural Center of the Philippines, quarterly.
Philippine Agriculturist. Los Baños: University of the Philippines, semiannually.
Philippine Economics Journal. Manila: Philippine Economics Society, quarterly.
Philippine Historical Review. Manila: Philippine Historical Institute, semiannually.
Philippine Journal of Biotechnology. Los Baños: Philippine Council for Advanced Science and Technology, semiannually.
Philippine Journal of Business Administration. Quezon City: University of the Philippines, quarterly.
Philippine Journal of Nutrition. Manila: Philippine Association of Nutrition Inc., semiannually.
Philippine Journal of Psychology. Manila: Psychologial Association of the Philippines, semiannually.
Philippine Journal of Science. Manila: De La Salle University, quarterly.
Philippine Journal of Veterinary and Animal Sciences. Los Banos: Philippine Society of Animal Science, semiannually.
Philippine Law Journal. Quezon City: semiannually.
Philippine Political Science Journal. Quezon City: Philippine Political Science Association, quarterly.
Philippine Quarterly of Culture and Society. Cebu City: University of San Carlos, quarterly.
Philippine Sociological Review. Manila: Philippine Sociological Society, quarterly.
Philippine Yearbook of International Law. Manila: Philippine Society of International Law, quarterly.
Pilipinas: A Journal of Philipine Studies. Sydney, Australia: University of Sydney, semiannually.
Santo Tomas Journal of Medicine. Manila: University of Santo Tomas, quarterly.
Silliman Journal. Dumaguete: Silliman University, quarterly.

B. Newspapers

English Language

Daily Tribune, Manila.
Malaya, Manila.
Manila Bulletin, Manila.
Manila Chronicle, Manila.
Manila Standard, Manila.
Manila Times, Mandaluyong City.
Philippine Daily Inquirer, Makati City.
Philippine Journal, Manila.
Philppine Star, Manila.
Sun Star, Manila.
Today, Makati City.

Tabloids

Abante, Manila.
Balita, Makati City.
Bandera, Makati City.
Bomba, Manila.
Bulgar, Quezon City.
Diaryo Uno, Quezon City.
Kabayan, Manila.
People's Balita, Quezon City.
People's Journal, Manila.
People's Taliba, Manila.
Pilipino Star Ngayon, Manila.
Remate, Manila.
Remate Tonight, Manila.
RP Daily Expose, Manila.
Saksi Ngayon, Manila.
Tenpo, Manila.
Text Tonight, Manila.

Provincial Newspapers
English Language

Batangan, Batangas City.
Bohol Times, Tagbilaran City.
Capiz Times, Roxas City.
Cebu Daily News, Cebu City.
Daily Dipologan, Dipolog City.
Freeman, Cebu City.
Independent Post, Cebu City.
Mindanao Gold Star, Davao City.
Mindanao Star, Dipolog City.
Mindanao Times, Davao City.
Palawan Sun, Puerto Princesa City.
San Carlos City Interactive, San Carlos City.
South Herald, Zamboanga City.
Sun Star, Bacolod City.
Sun Star, Baguio City.
Sun Star, Cagayan de Oro City.
Sun Star, Cebu City.
Sun Star, Davao City.
Sun Star, Dumaguete City.
Sun Star, General Santos City.

Sun Star, Kalibo City.
Sun Star, Iloilo City.
Sun Star, Pampanga.
Sun Star, Pangasinan.
Sun Star, Zamboanga City.
Visayan Daily Star, Dumaguete City.

Chinese Newspapers

Chinese Commercial News, Manila.
Siong Po, Manila.
World News Publication, Manila.

PART 5. SCIENCES

A. Flora and Fauna

Alava, M. N. R. and A.S.S.P. Yaptinchay. "Marine Mammals." *Philippine Red Data Book*. Makati City: Bookmark, 1997.

Albert, Dean C. and John R. Moring. "The U.S. Fish Commission Steamer Albatross: A History." *Marine Fisheries Review*, Seattle, Wash.: NMFS, Scientific Publications Office, 1999.

Alcala, A. C. *A Guide to Philippine Flora and Fauna: Amphibians and Reptiles*. Vol. 10, Natural Resources Management Center and University of the Philippines. Quezon City and Manila. XIV (1986) 195.

Alcala, A. C. and Pedro Alviola. "Notes on the Birds and Mammals of Boracay, Caluya, Carabao, Semirara and Sibay Islands, Philippines." *Silliman Journal* 17, 3 (1970), 444–454.

Alcala, A. C. "Aspects of Ecology of the Insectivorous Bat (Scotophilus Temminckii) in Southern Negros, Philippines." *Philippine Biota* 5 (1970), 5–11.

Alcala, A. C., G. Joerman, and J. Brzoska. "Mating Calls of Certain Philippine Anurans." *Silliman Journal* 33 (1986), 31–44.

Alcala, A. C. and W. C. Brown "Early Life History of Two Philippine Frogs with Notes on Deposition of Eggs." *Herpetologica* 12 (1956), 241–246.

Alcala, A. C. and W. Sanguila "The Birds of Small Islands off the Eastern Coast of Panay." *Silliman Journal* 16 (1969), 375–383.

Alcala, A. C. "Some Facts and Fancies about Philippine Snakes." *Silliman Journal* 16 (1969), 257–262.

Balete, D. S. et al. "Diversity and Conservation of Philippine Land Vertebrates: An Annotated Bibliography." *Silliman Journal* 36:129–149.

Bondad, N. D. A Mango-Based Cropping System. *Philippine Geographical Journal* 34 (1990), 121–125.

Brown, W. C. and A. C. Alcala 1983. "Modes of Reproduction of Philippine Anurans." In *Advances in Herpetology and Evolutionary Biology*. Essays in honor of E. E. Williams, A. G. J. Rhodin, and K. Miyata, eds. *Museum of Comparative Zoology*. Harvard University, Cambridge, Mass. (1983), 416–428.

Brown, R. M., Diesmos, A. C. and Alcala, A. C. "The State of Philippine Herpetology and the Challenges for the Next Decade." *Silliman Journal* 42 (2001), 18–87.

Brown, W. C. and A. C. Alcala "The Zoogeography of the Herpetofauna of the Philippine Islands, a Fringing Archipelago." *Proceedings of the California Academy of Sciences* 38 (1970):105–130.

———. "Population Ecology of the Frog Rana Eerythraea in Southern Negros, Philippines." *Copeia* 4 (1970), 611–622.

———. "Comparison of the Herpetofaunal Species Richness of Negros and Cebu Islands, Philippines." *Silliman Journal* 33 (1986), 74–86.

Brzoska, J., G. Joerman, and A. C. Alcala "Structure and Variability of the Calls of Polypedates Luecomystax (Amphibia: Rhacophoridae) from Negros, Philippines." *Silliman Journal* 33 (1986), 87–103.

Carumbana, E. and A. C. Alcala 1974. "An Ecological Study of Certain Game Birds in Southern Negros Island." *Silliman Journal* 21 (1974), 139–173.

Christenson, T. D. and T. Lund. *A Comparison of Avian Communities in Different Rain Forest Types in the Northern Sierra Madre Mountains, Philippines*. M. Sc. Thesis. Zoological Museum, University of Copenhagen, Denmark.

Crook, P. G. and A. C. Alcala " Endoparasites of Philippine Land Vertebrates: A Preliminary Survey of Southern Negros." *Silliman Journal* 15, 323–342.

Custodio, C. C. et al. *Bubalus Mindorensis. Mammalian Species* 520 (1996), 1–5.

Danielson, F. et al. "Conservation of Biological Diversity in the Sierra Madre Mountains of Isabela and Southern Cagayan Province, Philippines." *Bird Life International*. Manila and Copenhagen, 1994.

Dickinson E. C., R. S. Kenndy, and K. C. Parkes. "The Birds of the Philippines: An Annotated Checklist." *British Ornithologists' Union*. Tring, 1991.

Estrada, C. G. "New Development in Mango Research." *Tropical Fruits Newsletter* 25 (1997) 6–20.

Ferner, J. W. et al. "A New Genus and Species of Moist Closed Canopy Forest Skinks from the Philippines." *Journal of Herpetology* 31 (1997), 187–192.

Fooden, J. "Systematic Review of Philippine Macaque (Primates, Cercopithecidae: Macaca Fascicularis Subspp." *Fieldiana: Zoology* 64, 1–4.

Gonzales, R. B., P. L. Alviola, and A. C. Alcala. "Notes on the Food Habits of Certain Philippine Birds." *The Philippine Biota* 3 (1968), 20–25.

Gonzales, R. B. and A. C. Alcala. "The Foraging Deployment of Velvet-Fronted Nuthatches and Elegant Titmice." *Silliman Journal* 16 (1969), 402–408.

———. "Rare and Threatened Philippine Vertebrates." *The Philippine Biota* 4 (1969), 6–13.

Gonzales, P. C. "Birds of Catanduanes." *Zoological Papers, National Museum*. Manila 2 (1986), 1–125.

Goodman, S. M. and P. C. Gonzales. "The Birds of Isarog National Park, Southern Luzon, Philippines." *Fieldiana Zoology* 60 (1990), 1–39.

Guerrero, Luzviminda and A. C. Alcala. "Food Habits of Pteropid Bats." *The Philippine Biota* 7 (1970), 139–142.

Guzman, E. de, R. M. Umali, and E. D. Sotalbo. "Philippine Dipterocarps. In Guide to Philippine." *Flora and Fauna* 3 (1989) 1–74.

Heaney, Lawrence R. "Mammalian Diversity on Mount Isarog: A Threatened Center of Endemism on Southern Luzon Island, Philippines." Chicago: *Field Museum of Natural History*, 1999.

——. "A Synopsis of the Mammalian Fauna of the Philippine Islands." *Fieldiana Zoology*, n.s. No. 88, 1998.

Ingle, N. R. "The Natural History of Bats on Mt. Makiling, Luon Island, Philippines." *Asia Life Sciences* 2 (1993), 215–222.

Magsalay, P. M. "Rediscovery of Four Endemic Birds (Philippines)." *Asia Life Sciences* 2, 141–148.

McGuire, J. A. and Alcala. A. C. "A Taxonomic Revision of the Flying Lizards (Iguania: Agamidae: Draco) of the Philippine Islands, with a Descripion of a New Species." *Herpetological Monographs* 14 (2000), 81–138.

Oliver, W. L. R. and L. R. Heaney. "Biodiversity and Conservation." *Philippines International Zoo News* 43, 329–337.

Rabor, Dioscoro. *Philippine Birds and Mammals*. Quezon City: University of the Philippines Press, 1977.

Rickart, Eric. "A Review of the Genera Crunomys and Archboldomys (Rodentia: Muridae: Murinae) with Descriptions of Two New Species from the Philippines." Chicago: *Field Museum of Natural History*, 1998.

Rickart, Eric A. "Diversity Patterns of Mammals along Elevational and Diversity Gradients in the Philippines.: Implications for Conservation." *Asia Life Sciences* 2, 251–260.

Ross, C. A., A. C. Alcala, and R.V. Sison. "Distribution of Zaocys Luzonensis (Serpentes: Colubridae) in the Visayan Islands, Philippines." *Silliman Journal* 34 (1987) 29–31.

Santos, J. V. "Philippine Bamboos." *Guide to Philippine Flora and Fauna* 4, 1–43.

Tan, B. C., E. S. Fernando, and J. P. Rojo. "An Updated List of Endangered Philippine Plants." *Yushiana* 3, 2, 1–5.

Wildlife Conservation Society of the Philippines. *Philippine Red Data Book,* Makati City: Bookmark, 1997.

B. Ecology

Abanes, Jamelah Emma D. "Public-Private Partnershiop as an Approach in Social Delivery in Environmental Conservaton and Protection: Ecological Waste Management in Puerto Princesa City, Palawan." *Philippines Regional Development Dialogue* 21, 2 (2000), 23–34.

Alcala, Angel C. and Edgardo Gomez. *Marine Reserves in the Philippines: Historical Development, Effects, and Influence on Marine Conservation Policy.* Makati City: Bookmark, 2001.

Alcala, A.C. "Blast Fishing and Other Destructive Fishing Methods." *Silliman Journal* 41 (2000), 26–47.

Alcala, A. C. and G. R. Russ. "Status of Philippine Coral Reef Fisheries." *Asian Fisheries Science* 15 (2000), 177–192.

Allen, M.S. "The Rain Forest of Northeast Luzon and Agta Foragers." In *The Agta of Northeastern Luzon Recent Studies*. Ed. P. B. Griffin and A. A. Estioko-Griffin. Cebu City: University of San Carlos Press, 1985.

Arquiza, Yasmin D. "Toll on the Atoll." *Far Eastern Economic Review* 147, 11 (March 1990), 32–34.

Arquiza, Yasmin and Alan White. *Tales from Tubbataha: Natural History, Resource Use, and Conservation of the Tubbataha Reefs, Palawan, Philippines*. Cebu City: Sulu Fund for Marine Conservation Foundation, 1999.

Ballesteros, Andre Gerard. *All that Glitters: Understanding the Myth of "Sustainable Mining" in the Philippines*. Quezon City: Legal Rights and Natural Resources Center, 1997.

Bennagen, Ma. Eugenia. *Estimates of Environmental Damages from Mining Pollution: The Marinduqque Island Mining Accident*. Singapore: Economy and Environment Program for Southeast Asia, 1998.

Cassey, Michael, ed. *The Philippine Coral Reefs in Watercolor*. Quezon City: Jacoby Publishing House, 1997.

Contreras, Antonio R. *Locating the Political in the Ecological Globalization: State-Civil Society Articulation and Environmental Governance in the Philippines*. Manila: De La Salle University Press, 2002.

Crua, Ismael. et al. *Minding Mining: Lessons from the Philippines*. Quezon City: Philippine International Forum, 1999.

Domingo, Estrella V., ed. *Environmental and Natural Accounting: The Cordillera Experience*. Makati City: ENRA, 2001.

Environmental Degradation due to Selected Economic Activities. Makati City: National Statistical Coordination Board. 2000.

Evans, Geoff and James Goodman. *Moving Mountains: Communities Confront Mining and Globalisation*. London: Zed Books, 2002.

Evans, T. D. et al. "Philippine Rain Forest Project Final Report." *Bird Life International*. Cambridge: 1991.

Fairbanks, R. G. "A 17,000 Glacio-Eustatic Sea Level Record: Influence of Glacial Melting on the Younger Dryas Event and Deep-Sea Circulation." *Nature* 342, 637–642.

Gamalinda, E. and Sheila Coronel, eds. "Saving the Earth: The Philippine Experience, Third Edition." Philippine Center for Investigative Journalism. Makati City, 1993

Gomez, Alino. et al. "A Review of the Status of Philippine Reef." *Marine Pollution Bulletin* 29 1–3 (1998), 65–66.

Guerrero, Rafael D. "100 years of Philippine Fisheries and Marine Science." Los Baños, Laguna: Philippine Council for Aquatic and Marine Research and Development.

Headland, Thomas N. *Why Foragers Do Not Become Farmers: A Historical Study of a Changing Ecosystem and Its Effects on a Negrito Hunter-Gatherer Group in the Philippines.* Dissertation. University of Hawaii, 1986.

———. *Tropical Deforestation and Culture Change among the Agta of the Sierra Madre, Eastern Luzon: A Photographic Depiction.* Summer Institute of Linguistics, 2002.

Integrating Environmental Considerations into Economic Policy Making Processes: Background Readings. New York: United Nations, 1999.

Joyce, C. *Earthly Goods: Medicine Hunting in the Rain Forest.* Boston: Little, Brown, 1994.

Kummer, D. M. *Deforestation in the Postwar Philippines.* Chicago: University of Chicago Press, 1992.

Kummer, D. M. and B. L. Turner. "The Human Causes of Deforestation in Southeast Asia." *Bioscience* 44 (1994), 323–328.

Ledesma, G. I. et al. "Danjugan Island Marine Reseerve, Western Visayas Reefs." In *Atlas of Philippine Coral Reefs.* Philippine Coral Reef Information (Phil Reefs). Ed. P. M. Aliño. Quezon City: Goodwill Reading, 2002.

Lewis, Martin W. *Wagering the Land: Ritual, Capital, and Enviroment Degradation in the Cordillera of Northern Luzon.* Berkeley: University of California Press, 1992.

Magsalay, P. M. "Rediscovery of Four Cebu Endemic Birds (Philippines)." *Asia Life Sciences* 2 (1993), 141–148.

Manalo, E. B. "The Distribution of Rain Forest in the Philippines." *Philippine Geographical Journal* 4 (1996) 104–166.

Maypa, A. P., G. R. Russ, A. C. Alcala, and H. P. Calumpong. "Long Term Trends in Yield and Catch Rates of the Coral Reef Fishery on Apo Island, Central Philippines." *Marine Freshwater Research* 53 (2002), 207–213.

Mendiola, Franco. *Meeting the Challenges: Mining, the Community and the Environment.* Pasig City: Chamber of Mines of the Philippines, 1998.

Mining Revisited: *Can an Understanding of Perspectives Help?* Quezon City: Environmental Science for Social Change, 1999.

Mitchell, C. D. *Survey of Non-Timber Forest Product Use in the North Negros Forest Reserve, Negros Occidental, Philippines.* MSc. Theses, University of Edinburgh, 2002.

Myers, N. "Environmental Degradation and Some Economic Consequences in the Philippines." *Environmental Conservation* 15 (1988), 205–214.

Newhall, L. P. and R. S. Punongbayan. *Fire and Mud: Eruptions and Lahar of Mount Pinatubo, Philippines.* Philippine Institute of Volcanology and Seismology. University of Washington Press, 1996.

Otto, James and Maria Luisa Batarseh. *Global Mining Taxation Comparative Study.* Golden, Colo.: Colorado School of Mines, 2000.

Orteza, Edna J. *Forests Forever: A Resource Book on the Environment.* Metro Manila: Spectrum Publishing, 1992.

Pajaro, P. et al. "Using Education to Stop Destructive Fishing Practices: A Partial Success in Several Community-Based Management of Coral Reefs of Coastal Fisheries in Asia and the Pacific." *Concepts, Methods, and Experiences* 56, 3 (1997), 333–343.

Pasicolan, Paulo N. et al. *Devolution: Creation of Spaces for Grassroots Empowerment in NRM.* Laguna: Seameo Searca, 2001.

Philippine Mining Act of 1995 and Related Laws. Manila: Central Book Supply, 1998.

Porter, G. and D. J. Ganapin Jr. *Resources, Population, and the Philippines' Future: A Case Study.* World Resources Institute: Washington, 1988.

Pulling the Plug on Water Mining: A Groundwater Conservation Strategy from the Philippines. Singapore: Economy and Environment Program for Southeast Asia, 2003.

Punongbayan, Raymundo S. "Impacts of Volcanic Eruption and Earthquakes and Disaster Management in Mitigation Measures in Metropolitan Areas for the 21st Century." UNCRD Proceedings Series, No. 1, Nagoya, Japan,1994.

Repetto, R. *The Forests for the Trees? Government Policies and the Misuse of Forest Resources.* Washington, D.C.: World Resouces Institute, 1998.

Slade, E. *The Effect of Logging on Butterfly Diversity and Distribution in a Sub-Montane Tropical Rain Forest in the Philippines.* MSc. Theses, University of Aberdeen, 2001.

Tan, B. C. and Z. Iwatsuki. "A New Annotated Philippine Moss Checklist." *Harvard Papers on Botany* 3 (1991) 1–64.

Tejada, Frank C. *The Treasures of Lamon Bay.* Manila: UST Publishing House, 2001.

Tujan, Antonio A. *Globalizing Philippine Mining.* Manila: IBON Foundation, Databank, and Research Center, 2002.

Werner, Timothy B. and Gerald Allen. "A Rapid Marine Biodiversity Assessment of the Coral Reefs of the Calamianes Islands, Palawan Province, Philippines." Washington, D.C.: Conservation International Department of Conservation Biology, 2000.

Velasquez, German T., ed. "The Challenge of Mindoro: Report of the Quick Response of Mindoro Island Earthquake in the Philippines on November 15, 1994." *UNCRD Research Report Series* 11, Philippine Institute of Volcanology and Seismology (PHILVOCS), 1995.

Vitug, M. D. *Power from the Forest: The Politics of Logging.* Philippine Center for Investigative Journalism. Manila: 1993.

White, Alan T. *Philippine Coral Reefs: A Natural History Guide.* Makati City: Bookmark, 2001.

Whitmore, T. C. *Tropical Rain Forest in the Far East.* Oxford: Clarendon Press, 1984.

Wildmann, Peter. *A Guide to the Ecosystems of Palawan, Philippines Baybay, Leyte: VISCA-GTZ Program on Applied Ecology.* Visayas State College of Agriculture, 1998.

World Bank. *Philippine Environment and National Resource Management Study*. The World Bank, Washington: 1989.

C. Geology

Alejandro, Reynaldo C., and Alfred Yuson. *Pasig: River of Life*. Manila: Unilever Philippines, 2000.

Aquino, R. S. "Geology and Gold Mineralization of Manila Mining Corporation's Placer Project Area, Surigao del Norte." *Philippine Geologist* 37, 2 (1989), 6–19.

Angeles, C. A. Jr. et al. "Geology and Alteration Mineralization Characteristics of the Nalesbitan Gold Deposit, Camarines Norte, Philippines." In *Gold '97 in the Philippine Setting*. Manila: 1987, Proc. Vol. 1, Philippine Institute of Mining and Metallurgy, Geology, 1987, 1115–1515.

Barcelon, Jose S. "Minerals and Mining Industry." In *Shadows on the Land: An Economic Geography of the Philippines*. Ed. Robert E. Huke. Manila: Bookmark, 1963, 97–119.

Cruz, Ismael. *Minding Mining: Lessons from the Philippines*. Quezon City: Philippine International Forum, 1999.

Domingo, E. G. and J. Sato. "Gold-Silver Deposits of the Philippines and Japan: A Comparative Study of Their Geology, Ore, Mineralogy and Fluid Inclusions." In Regional Conference on the Geology of Southeast Asia. Manila. *Geologic Society Philippines* (1982) 547–567.

Hall, R. "Reconstructing Cenozoic SE Asia." In *Tectonic Evolution of Southeast Asia*. Ed. R. Hall and D. Blendell. Geological Society Special Publications, 106, 1–566.

Hargrove, Thomas V. *The Mysteries of Taal: A Philippine Volcano and Lake, Her Sea Life and Lost Towns*. Quezon City: Bookmark, 1991.

Harper, P. and E. S. Peplow. *Philippines Handbook*. Moon Publications. Chico, Calif.: 1991.

Indigenous Peoples Extractive Industries and the World Bank. Oxford, England (April 18, 2003).

Ramos, Emmanuel R. "Application of Remote Sensing of Volcanic and Earthquate Disaster Mitigation in the Philippines." Quezon City: Philippine Institute of Volcanology and Seismology (PHILVOCS), 1998, 33–97.

Rantucci, Giovanni. *Geological Disasters in the Philippines: The July 1990 Earthquake & the June 1991 Eruption of Mount Pinatubo*. Upland, Penn.: Diane, 1995.

Rovillos, Raymundo D. et al. "When the 'Isles of Gold' Turn into 'Isles of Dissent': A Case Study on the Philippines Mining Act of 1995."

D. Anthropology and Archaeology

Alonso, Ana Maria. "The Politics of Space, Time and Substance." *Annual Review of Anthropolgy* 23 (1994), 379–405.

Allison, Karen J. "A View from the Island Culture: Tawi-Tawi." *International Museum of Cultures Publication* 15, 1984.

Azurin, Arnold Molina. *Just Vexations: Essays on Political Culture*. Manila: Kalikasan Press, 1990.

Bailen, Jerome B. *A Tasaday Folio*. Quezon City: Department of Anthropology, University of Philippines, 1986.

Beyer, Henry Otley. *Ethnography of the Negrito-Aeta Peoples*: A Collection of *Original Sources*. Manila: Asia Microfilm, 1918.

Beyer, Henry Otley. *Dean of Philippine Anthropology: A Commemorative Issue*. Cebu City: University of San Carlos, 1968.

Brown, Roxanna M. Guangdon. *Ceramics from Butuan and Other Philippine Sites*. Singapore: Oxford University Press, 1989.

Brown, Peter J. and Marcia Claire Inhorn. *The Anthropology of Infectious Diseases: International Health Perspective*. Amsterdam: Overseas Publishers Association, 1997.

Chinese and Southeast Asian Greenware Found in the Philippines: The Oriental Ceramic Society of the Philippines Third Members' Exhibition Held at the Ayala Museum, February 26, 1991, in Cooperation with the National Museum and Ayala Foundation. Metro Manila: Oriental Ceramic Society of Philippines, 1991.

Dakudao, Michaelangelo E. "The Development of Cemeteries in Manila before 1941." *Philippine Quarterly of Culture & Society* 20, 2/3 (June/September 1992), 133–150.

Dizon, Eusebio. "A Decade of Archaeological Research in the Philippines, 1982–1992," *Philippine Quarterly of Culture and Society* 22 (1995), 197–222.

Dumont, Jean Paul. *Visayan Vignettes: Ethnographic Traces of a Philippine Island*. Chicago: University of Chicago Press, 1992.

Evangelista, Alfredo. "Philippine Archaelogy up to 1950." *Philippine Journal of Science*.

Francisco, Juan R. *Philippine Paleography*: Special Monograph Issue No. 3. Quezon City: Philippine Linguistic Society, 1973.

Galende, Pedro G. *Angels in Stone: Architecture of Augustinian Churches in the Philippines*. Metro Manila, Philippines: G. A. Formoso Publishing, 1987.

———. *San Augustin: Noble Stone Shrine*. Metro Manila, Philippines: G. A. Formoso Publishing, 1989.

Goda, Toh. *Cordillera: Diversity in Culture Change: Social Anthropology of Hill People in Northern Luzon*. Quezon City: New Day Publishers, 2001.

Goddio, Franck, et al. *Sunken Treasure: 15th Century Chinese Ceramics from Lena Cargo*. London: Periplus, 2000.

Gunn, Mary N. *The Development of Social Networks: Subsistence Production and Exchange between Sixth and Sixteenth Centuries A.D. in the Tanjay Region, Negros Oriental, Philippines*. Ann Arbor: University Microfilms, 2000.

Hutterer, Karl L. "Philippine Archaeology: Status and Prospects." *Journal of Southeast Asian Studies* 18 (September 1987): 235–249.

Jocano, L. Landa. *Anthropology of the Filipino People*. Manila: Punlad Research House, 2001.

———. *Philippine Prehistory. An Anthropological Overview of the Beginnings of Filipino Society and Culture*. Quezon City: Philippine Center for Advanced Studies, 1975.

Kramer, Paul A. *The Pragmatic Empire: U.S. Anthropology and Colonial Politics in the Occupied Philippines, 1898–1916*. Dissertation, Northern Illinois University.

Longacre, William A. *Kalinga Ethnoarchaeology: Expanding Archaeological Method & Theory.* Washington, D.C.: Smithsonian Institution Press, 1994.

Mercado, Leonardo M. "Soul and Spirit in Filipino Thought." *Philippine Studies* 39, 3 (1991): 287–302.

The Miagao Church: Historical Landmark. Manila, Philippines: National Historical Institute, 1991.

Mijares, Armand Salvador. *The Minori Cave Expedient Lithic Technology*. Quezon City: University of the Philippines Press, 2002.

Muldar, Niels. *Inside Philippine Society: Interpretations of Everyday Life*. Quezon City: New Day Publishers, 1997.

Omana, Luis T. "Geological Study on the Megalithic Structures in Agsalanan, Dingle, Iloilo." *National Museum Papers* 3, 2 (1992), 80–88.

Polenda, Francisco C. "A Voice from the Hills: Essays on the Culture and Worldview of Western Bukidnon Manobo People." *Linguistic Society of the Philippines: Special Monograph Issue* 29, 18, 375.

Postma, Antoon. "The Laguna Copper-Plate Inscription: Text and Commentary." *Philippine Studies* 40, 2 (1992), 183–203.

Prill-Brett, June. *An Ethnoarcheological Report on Adult Jar Burial Practice in the Central Cordillera, Northern Philippines.* Baguio City: Cordillera Studies Center, 2000.

Rodell, Paul A. *Culture and Customs in the Philippines*. Westport, Conn.: Greenwood Press, 2002.

Rosaldo, Renato. "Ideology, Place, and People without Culture." *Cultural Anthropology* 3, 1 (1988), 77–87.

Santiago, Luciano P. R. "The Painters of Flora de Filipinas (1877–1883)." *Philippine Quarterly of Culture & Society* 21, 2 (June 1993), 87–112.

Sluka, Jeffrey A. *Death Squad: The Anthropology of State Terror*. Philapdelphia: University of Pennsylvania Press, 2000.

Snow, Bryan E. and Richard Shutler, Jr. *The Archaeology of Fuga Moro Island: New Approaches for the Isolation and Explanation of Diagnostic Ceramic Assemblages in Northern Luzon, Philippines*. Cebu City: San Carlos University Publications, 1985.

Somera, Rene D. *Bordered Aging: Ethnography of Daily Life in a Filipino Home for the Aged.* Manila: De La Salle University Press, 1997.

Stark, Miriam T. "Ceramic Production and Community Specialization: A Kalinga Ethnoarchaeological Study." *World Archaeology* 23 (June 1991), 64–78.

Ushijima, Iwao and Cynthia Neri Zayas, eds. "Fisheries of the Visayas; Visayas Maritime." *Anthropological Studies* I: 1991–1993. Diliman, Quezon City: University of the Philippines Press, 1994.

E. Geography and Demography

Alota, Carlito A. "The Nuclear Science of Technology: Perspective and Prospects." In *Challenges of Nuclear Technology for the 21st Century. Proceedings of the 2nd Philippine Nuclear Congress, December 10–12, 1996*. Ed. Elvira S. Sombito et al.

Doeppers, Daniel F. *Population and History: The Demographic Origins of the Modern Philippines.* Madison: University of Wisconsin, Center for Southeast Asian Studies, 1998.

Jalandoni, Luis. *Science and Technology for the People: Papers Presented at the Forum on Science and Ttechnology in the Philippines.* Manila: Aklat ng Bayan Publications, 1998.

Pertierra, Raul. *Texting Selves: Cellphones and Philippine Modernity.* Manila: De La Salle University Press, 2002.

Philippine Plants: Their Medicinal, Culinary, and Cosmetic Values. Manila: Rex Books, 1959.

Philippine Science Encyclopedia. Manila: National Research Council of the Philippines. 1999.

Philippine Inventions. Manila: Department of Science and Technology, 2000.

Rodrigo, Maria Mercedes T. *Information Technology Usage in Metro Manila and Private Schools.* Ann Arbor: University Microfilms, 2002.

Tagura, Pablito M. *A Critical Analysis Of Technology Transfer, Ideology, and Development in the Context of Communication Technology in the Philippines.* Dissertation 1997. Ann Arbor: University Microfilms

Wernstedt, Frederick L. and J. E. *Spences. The Philippine Island World: Physical, Cultural, and Regional Geography.* Berkeley: University of California Press, 1967.

F. Public Health and Medicine

Arriola, Fe Maria and Lan S. Mercado. *Isis and Other Guides to Health Helpful Hint on the Road to Well-Being.* Stamford, Conn.: 1998.

Atkins, C. and L. Wallack, eds. *Mass Communication and Public Health Complexities.* Newbury Park: Sage, 1994.

Bolong ang Herbal (Herbal Medicine). Manila: Agutaynen Translation Advisory Committee; Summer Institute of Linguistics, 1998.

Dauz-Williams, Phoebe A. and Arthur Williams. *Individual, Family, and Community: Promoting and Restoring Health and Well-Being.* Quezon City: JMC Press, 2001.

Coronel, Sheila S. *From Loren to Marimar*. Quezon City: Philippine Center for Investigative Journalism, 1999.

Dayrit, Conrado S. et al. *History of Philippine Medicine, 1899–1999: With Landmarks in World Medical History*. Pasig City: Anvil Publishers, 2002.

De Bevoise, Ken. *Agents of Apocalypse: Epidemic Disease in the Colonial Philippines*. Quezon City: New Day Publishers, 2002.

De Padua, Ludivina S. *Handbook on Philippine Medicinal Plants*. 4 vol. Los Baños Documentation and Information Section, Office of the Director of Research, University of the Philippines at Los Baños, 1977.

Flavier, Juan M. *Let's DOH (Department of Health) It: How We Did It*. Manila: Department of Health, 1998.

———. *Doctor to the Barrios*. Quezon City: New Day Publishers, 1978.

Gray, Jason, Rechor Umpan, and Melchor Bayawan. *Mgo itulon moka-atag to moppiyon kodiolaawa (Stories of Good Health)*. Kidapawan City: Obo Manobo Active Language Resource and Community Development, 2001.

Guerra, Francisco. *Bibliografia medica Americana y Filipina: periodo formativo. Medical Bibliography of the Americas and the Philippines*. Madrid: Ollero y Ramos, 1999.

Haverland, Nicole and Diana Measham. *Responding to Cairo: Case Studies of Changing Practice in Reproductive Health and Family Planning*. New York: Population Council, 2002.

The Healing Cut: Filipino Surgeons Write about the Human Drama, Humor, and Controversy Surrounding Actual Cases. Pasig City: Anvil Publications, 1999.

Hornik, Robert C. *Public Health and Communication: Evidence of Behavior Change*. Mahwah, N.J.: Eribaum Associates, 2002.

Jimenez, Pilar R. *Immunization in the Philippines: The Social and Cultural Dimension*. Amsterdam: Het Spinhuis, 1999.

Lee-Chua, Queena. *Ten Outstanding Filipino Scientists*. Manila: Anvil Publishers, 2002.

Magallanes, Josefina. "Human Nutrition: The Impact of Family and Income on Dietary Intake." *Philippine Sociological Review* 32: 1–4 (January–December 1984), 69–80.

Manuel, Mauro F. *A Century of Veterinary Medicine in the Philippines, 1898–1998*. Quezon City: University of the Philippines Press, 2002.

McDivitt, J. A. et al. "Explaining the Impact of a Communication Campaign to Change Vaccination Knowledge and Coverage in the Philippines." *Health Communication* 9 (2) 95–118. 1997.

Medicine and Public Health in the Philippines (Part 2). Washington D.C. Library of Congress Office; Photoduplication Service, 1998.

Mejia, Raymundo Corazon. *Unsafe Abortion in the Philippines: A Threat to Health*. Quezon City: University of the Philippines Population Institute, 2001.

Mojica, Mariluz P. ed. *Contemporary Issues in STD-HIV/AIDS and Prevention: Focus on Philippine Experience*. Quezon City: University Center for Women Studies, University of the Philippines, 2002.

Nadarajah, M. *Pathways to Critical Media Education and Beyond: Deliberations on Media Reforms and the Manila Initiative. Kuala Lumpur*: Cahayasuara Communications Centre for Asian Communication Network, 2003.

Nolledo, Jose N. *Traditional and Alternative Medicine Act (TAMA) of 1997*. Republic Act no. 8423, with implementing regulations. Manila: Rex Book Store, 2000.

Ortigas, Carmela D. and L. A. Carandang, eds. *Essence of Wellness: Essays in Philippine Clinical and Counseling Psychology*. Quezon City: Ateneo De Manila University Press, 1993.

Palaganas, Erlinda Castro. *Mainstreaming Indigenous Health Knowledge and Practices*. Quezon City: UP Center for Integrative and Development Studies, 2001.

Reyes, Diwan, ed. *Women's Issues and Medical Practice*. Quezon City: University of the Philippines Press, 2002.

Rimon, J. G. et al. "Promoting Sexual Responsibility in the Philippines through Music: An Enter-Educate Approach." Baltimore, MD: Johns Hopkins School of Public Health, Occasional Paper Series No. 3.

Silverman, Milton. *Bad Medicine: The Prescription Drug Industry in the Third World*. Stanford University Press, 1992.

Tan, Michael. *Good Medicine: Pharmaceuticals and the Construction of Power and Knowledge in the Philippines*. Amsterdam: Het Spinhuis, 1999.

Tiglao, Teodora. *A Century of Public Health in the Philippines*. Manila: University of the Philippines, 1998.

Twelve Steps to Understanding Aids: For Media Practitioners. Manila: AIDS Society of the Philippines, 2001.

Vincent, Amanda C. and Marie-Annick Moreau. Proceedings of the First International Workshop on the Management and Culture of Marine Species Used in Traditional Medicines: July 4–9, 1998, Cebu City, Philippines.

Vitug, M. D. *Power from the Forest: The Politics of Logging*. Philippine Center for Investigative Journalism, Manila: 1993.

PART 6. ECONOMY

A. Agriculture

Agenda for Action for the Philippine Rural Sector. Los Banos, Philippines: University of the Philippines at Los Banos Agricultural Policy Research Program and Philippine Institute for Developmental Studies, 1989.

Agrarian Reform Country Models: Proceedings of the Conference Seminar-Workshop on Agrarian Reform Models Held February 2–4, 1988, at the University of the Philippines at Los Banos (UPLB), College, Laguna, Philippines. Quezon City, Philippines: Center for Social Policy and Public Affairs, Ateneo de Manila University, 1988.

Agrarian Reform Implementation in Negros Occidental: Innovations, Lessons, and Experiences. Manila, Philippines: Institute for Social Research and Development, University of St. La Salle, 1993.

Balbin, Remedios C. and Dominador A. Clemente, Jr. *Agribusiness, Philippines Experience: Legal and Policy Notes.* Metro Manila, Philippines: National Book Store, 1986.

Balisacan, Arsenio M. "Agricultural Growth, Landlessness, Off-Farm Employment, and Rural Poverty in the Philippines." *Economic Development and Cultural Change* 41 (April 1993): 533–562.

———. "Survey of Philippine Research on the Economics of Agriculture, Part 1." *The Philippine Review of Economic and Business* 26, 1 (June 1989): 14–46.

Baretto, Felisa R. *An Analytical Study of the Rice Wage Formula.* Manila: Department of Trade, Bureau of Census and Statistics, 1974.

Bondad, N. D. "A Mango-based Cropping System." *Philippine Geographical Journal.* 34 (3) 1990: 121–125.

Bouis, Howarth E. and Lawrence J. Haddad. *Agricultural Commercialization, Nutrition, and the Rural Poor: A Study of Philippine Farm Households.* Boulder, Colo.: Lynne Rienner Publishers, 1990.

Castillo, Gelia T. *Beyond Manila: Philippine Rural Problems in Perspective.* Ottawa: International Development Research Center, 1979.

Castillo, Leopoldo S. "Annotated Bibliography on Philippine Biodiversity Livestock and Poultry." *Agrobiodiversity* 1949–1997. Dairy Cattle, 2001.

Conelly, W. Thomas. "Agricultural Intensification in a Philippine Frontier Community: Impact on Labor Efficiency and Farm Diversity." *Human Ecology* 20 (June 1992): 203–223.

Corpuz, O. D. "Land and Agriculture in the Philippines: An Economic History Perspective." *The Philippine Review of Economics and Business* 29, 2 (December 1992): 137–160.

Cruz, M.S. et al. "Management Options for the Golden Apple Snail on the Native Soil, Vivipora Castata (Quay and Gainard)." *Philippine Entomologist* 14 (2), 2001: 149–157.

David, Cristina C., Eliseo R. Ponce, and Ponciano S. Intal, Jr. *Organizing for Results: The Philippine Agricultural Sector.* Makati, Metro Manila, Philippines: Philippine Institute for Development Studies, 1992.

Developing the Countryside: A Strategy. Metro Manila: Department of Agriculture, 1989.

Development Indicators in Philippine Agriculture. 2nd ed. Manila: Department of Agriculture, Bureau of Agricultural Statistics, 1988.

Eder, James F. "Family Farming and Household Enterprise in a Philippine Community, 1971–1988: Persistence or Proletarianization?" *The Journal of Asian Studies* 52, 3 (August 1993): 647–671.

———. *Who Shall Succeed? Agricultural Development and Social Inequality on a Philippine Frontier.* Cambridge University Press, Cambridge: 1982.

———. *Agricultural Intensification and Labor Productivity in a Philippine Vegetale Garden Community*. Cambridge University Press, Cambridge: 1991.

Fegan, Brian. "Land Reform and Technical Change in Central Luzon: The Rice Industry under Martial Law." *Philippine Sociological Review* 31, 1–2 (January–June 1986): 67–86.

Ferguson, Carol A. "Water Allocation, Inefficiency and Inequity in a Government Irrigation System (Philippines)." *Journal of Development Economics* 38 (January 1992): 165–182.

Gilding, Simeon. *Agrarian Reform and Counter-Reform under the Aquino Administration: A Case Study in Post-Marcos Politics*. Canberra, Australia: Department of Political and Social Change, Division of Politics and International Relations, Research School of Pacific Studies, Australian National University, 1993.

Gloria, Heidi K. and Fe R. Magpayo. *Kaingin, Ethnoecological Practices of 7 Upland Communities in Mindanao*. Davao City: Ateneo De Davao University, 1997.

Gonzaga, Violeta B. Lopez. *Capital Expansion, Frontier Development, and the Rise of Monocrop Economy in Negros (1850–1898)*. Bacolod City, Philippines: La Salle Social Research Center, 1987.

Gonzaga, Violeta Lopez, et al. *Agrarian Reform Implementation in Negros Occidental: Innovations, Lessons, and Experiences*. Bacolod City, Philippines: Institute for Social Research and Development, University of St. La Salle, 1993.

Habito, Cielito Flores and Rosario G. Manasan. *Agricultural Taxation in the Philippines:* A Report for the Policy Analysis Division, FAO Economic and Social Policy Department. Rome: FAO, 1992.

Hanks, L. M. *Rice and Man: Agricultural Ecology in Southeast Asia*. Aldine, Chicago: 1972.

Hayami, Yujiro, Ma. Agnes R. Quisumbing, and Lourdes S. Adriano. *Toward an Alternate Land Reform Paradigm: A Philippine Perspective*. Quezon City: Ateneo de Manila University Press, 1990.

Jefremovas, Villia. *Riding the Green Tide: Strategies among the Sagada Vegetable Gardeners of Northern Luzon*. Baguio City, Philippines: Cordillera Studies Center, University of the Philippines College Baguio, 1993.

Jopillo, Sylvia Ma. G. *Partnership in Irrigation: Farmers and Government in Agency-Managed Systems*. Quezon City, Philippines: Institute of Philippine Culture, Ateneo de Manila University, 1988.

Joven, Jose Romero. *Agrarian Reform Laws in the Philippine Setting: With Supreme Court Decisions on Agrarian Cases, Executive and Administrative Orders, and Other Related Laws*. Rev. ed. Manila, Philippines: Rex Book Store, 1993.

Korten, Frances F. and Robert Y. Sily, Jr., eds. *Transforming a Bureaucracy: The Experience of the Philippine National Irrigation Administration*. Manila, Philippines: Ateneo de Manila University Press, 1989.

Larkin, John A. *Sugar and the Origins of Modern Society*. Quezon City: New Day Publishers, 2001.

Ledesma, Antonio J. and Ma. Lourdes T. Montinola, eds. *The Implementation of Agrarian Reform in Negros: Issues, Problems, and Experiences.* Bacolod City, Philippines: Social Research Center, University of St. La Salle, 1988.

Leviste, Jose P. *Food for Thought: Management of Philippine Agriculture: An Alternative for the Third World.* Los Baños, Laguna, Philippines: Southeast Asian Regional Center for Graduate Study and Research in Agriculture, 1985.

Lewis, Henry T. *Ilocano Irrigation: The Corporate Resolution.* Honolulu: University of Hawaii Press, 1991.

Lewis, Martin W. "Agricultural Regions in the Philippine Cordillera." *The Geographical Review* 82 (January 1992): 29–42.

——. Wagering the Land: Ritual, Capital, and Environmental Degradation in the Cordillera of Northern Luzon, 1900–1986. Berkeley: University of California Press, 1992.

Librero, Aida R. and Agnes C. Rola, eds. *Agricultural Policy in the Philippines: An Analysis of Issues in the Eighties.* Los Banos, Laguna, Philippines: University of the Philippines at Los Banos, 1991.

Livestock Sector Study of the Philippine Agricultural Department Division 1. Manila: Asian Development Bank, 1994.

Martinez, E. G. et al. "Testing the Link Between Public Intervention and Food Price Variability: Evidence from Rice Markets in the Philippines." *American Journal of Agricultural Economics.* 80 (5) 1998: 1180.

Martinez, E. G. and W. A. Shively. "Irrigation, Employment, and the Environment in Southern Palawan." *Journal of Agricultural Economics.* 26 (1) 1998: 112–135.

Mendoza, Meyra S. and Mark W. Rosegrant. Pricing Behavior in Philippine Corn Markets: Implications for Market Efficiency. Washington, DC: International Food Policy Research Institute, 1995.

Miranda, Fraternidad A., et al. *Philippine Agrarian Reform Program: Towards Evaluation and Expansion, an Annotated Bibliography.* Laguna, Philippines: Institute of Agrarian Studies, College of Economics and Management, University of the Philippines at Los Banos, 1987.

Modina, Rolando B. and A. R. Ridao. *IRRI Rice: The Miracle That Never Was.* Quezon City, Philippines: ACES Foundation, 1987.

Nagarajan, Geetha, Cristina David, and Richard L Meyer. "Informal Finance through Land Pawning Contracts: Evidence from the Philippines." *The Journal of Development Studies* 29 (October 1992): 93–107.

Nazarea-Sandoval, Virgina D. *Local Knowledge and Agricultural Decision Making in the Philippines: Class, Gender, and Resistance.* Ithaca, N.Y.: Cornell University Press, 1995.

Nazarea, V. et al. "Defining Culturally Relevant Indicators of Sustainability: What are we waiting for?" *Human Organization* 58 (2) 1999: 219–220.

Ofreneo, Rene E. *Deregulation and the Agrarian Crisis.* Metro Manila, Philippines: Institute of Industrial Relations, University of the Philippines, 1987.

———. *Problems and Prospects of Agrarian Reform Implementation at the Village Level in the Philippines*. Diliman, Quezon City, Philippines: U.P. School of Labor and Industrial Relations, 1991.

Otsuka, Keijiro, Hiroyuki Chuma, and Yujiro Hayami. "Permanent Labour and Land Tenancy Contracts in Agrarian Economies: An Integrated Analysis." *Economica* 60 (February 1993): 57–77.

Otsuka, Keijiro, Violeta Cordova, and Cristina C. David. "Green Revolution, Land Reform, and Household Income Distribution in the Philippines." *Economic Development and Cultural Change* 40 (July 1992): 719–741.

Agricultural Development Project (HADP). Baguio City, Philippines: Cordillera Resource Center, University of the Philippines College Baguio, 1989.

Ranis, Gustav and Frances Stewart. "Rural Nonagricultural Activities in Development: Theory and Application." *Journal of Development Economics* 40 (February 1993): 75–101.

Reyes, Romana P. delos. and Sylvia Ma. G. Jopillo. *An Evaluation of the Philippine Participatory*. Pandan, Raymundo T., Jr., ed. *The Agrarian Reform Process in Negros Occidental: A Program Review and Analysis*. Bacolod City: University of St. La Salle, 1991.

Philippine Agribusiness Factbook and Directory, 1989–90. Manila: Center for Research and Communication, 1989.

Pimentel, David and Marcia Pimentel. *Food, Energy and Society*. New York: John Wiley, 1979.

Pingali, R. & A. C. Rola. *Pesticides, Rice Productivity and Farmers' Health and Economic Assessment*. International Rice Research Institute, Los Baños: 1993

Pitzel, James. *A Captive Land: The Politics of Agrarian Reform in the Philippines*. Manila: Ateneo de Manila University Press, 1992.

Poudel, D.D. et al. "Farmer Participatory Research to Minimize Soil Erosion on Steep Land Vegetable Systems in the Philippines." *Agriculture, Ecosystems and Environment* 79, 2000: 113–127.

Prill-Bret, June. Common Property Regimes among the Bontok of the Northern Philippine Highlands and State Policies. Baguio City: Cordillera Studies Center, University of the Philippines College Baguio, 1993.

———. *Coping Strategies in the Bontok Highland Agroecosystem: The Role of Ritual*. *Baguio City, Philippines*: Cordillera Studies Center, University of the Philippines College Baguio, 1987.

Prill-Brett, June, et al. *A Comparative Study of Agricultural Commercialization in Selected Highland Communities of the Cordillera-Ilocos Region*. Baguio City: Cordillera Studies Center, University of the Philippines College Baguio, 1994.

Primer on the Highland Communal Irrigation Program. Quezon City, Philippines: Institute of Philippine Culture, Ateneo de Manila University, 1986.

Pursuing Agrarian Reform in Negros Occidental. Quezon City: Institute of Philippine Culture, Ateneo de Manila University, 1991.

Rice in Asia: Lives of Seven Farmers. Singapore: Times Academic Press for the Asian Media Information and Communication Centre, 2000.

Riedinger, Jeffrey M. *Agrarian Reform in the Philippines: Democratic Transitions & Redistributive Reform.* Stanford, Calif.: Stanford University Press, 1995.

Rola, A. *Water and Food Security. Policy Form: Center for Policy and Development Studies.* University of the Philippines, 1997.

Rood, Steven. *Indigenous Practices and State Policy in the Sustainable Management of Agricultural Lands and Forests in the Cordillera: A Summary Report.* Baguio City, Philippines: Cordillera Studies Center, University of the Philippines College Baguio, 1995.

Salamon, Sonya. "Ethnic Communities and the Structure of Agriculture." *Rural Sociology* 50 (1985) 323–340.

Samson, Josefina A. "Agrarian Reform and Market Formation in the Philippines." *Journal of Contemporary Asia* 21, 3 (1991): 344–370.

Shivelt, Gerald E. "Poverty, Consumption Risk, and Soil Conservation." *Journal of Development Economics* 65 (2) 2001: 265–290.

Subbarao, Kalanidhi, Akhter U. Ahmed and Tesfaye Teklu. *Selected Social Safety Net Programs in the Philippines: Targetting, Cost-Effectiveness, & Option for Reform.* Washington, D.C: The World Bank, 1995.

Svendsen, Mark. "The Impact of Financial Autonomy on Irrigation System Performance in the Philippines (National Irrigation Administration)." *World Development* 21 (June 1993): 989–1005.

Tadem, Eduardo C. *Grains and Radicalism: The Political Economy of the Rice Industry in the Philippines, 1965–1985.* Quezon City: Third World Studies Center, University of the Philippines, 1986.

Tomlinson, Timothy R. and Olayiwolo Akerere. *Medicinal Plants: Their Role in Health and Biodiversity.* Philadelphia: University of Pennsylvania Press, 1998.

Top, Gerhard van den. *The Social Dynamics of Deforestation in the Philippines.* Honolulu: University of Hawaii Press, 2003.

Torres, Ricardo E., Jr. *Talking Points for Development in the Cordillera.* Baguio City: Cordillera Studies Center, University of the Philippines College Baguio, 1988.

Wheatley, Helen. *Agriculture, Resource Exploitation, and Environmental Change.* Aldershot, Hampshire, Great Britain; Brookfield, Vt.: Variorum, 1997.

Wiber, M. G. "Levels of Property Rights, Levels of Law: A Case Study from the Northern Philippines." *Man* 26 (September 1991): 469–492.

Wurfel, David A. "Land Reform: Content, Accomplishments, and Prospects under Marcos and Aquino." *Pilipinas* 12 (Spring 1989): 35–54.

Veneracion, Jaime B. *Philippine Agriculture during the Spanish Regime.* Quezon City: University of the Philippines Press, 2001.

B. Aquaculture

Agbayani, R. F. and F. F. Abella. "Status of the Sanitation and Marketing of Mollusc in the Philippines." Regional Seafaring Development and Demonstration

Project (Oct. 15–28, 1989), Bangkok, Thailand: Network of Aquaculture Centres in Asia and the Pacific, 98–110.

Agbayani, R. F., U. Hatch, and A. Belleza. "Economic Analysis of Prawn (Penaeus Monodon) Culture in the Philippines. Hatchery Operations." *Asian Fisheries Science* 8:191–200 1995.

Agbayani, R. F. "Economics of Milkfish Culture in the Philippines." In *Proceedings of the Regional Workshop on Milkfish Development in the South Pacific*. Ed. Tanaka U. Tarawa, Kirbali: 1988.

———. "Community Fishery Resource Management in Malalisan Island, Philippines." In *Towards Sustainable Aquaculture in Southeast Asia and Japan*. Ed. T. U. Bagarinao and E. E. Flores. Iloilo City: Southeast Asian Fisheries Development Centre, Aquaculture Department 1990, pp. 209–219.

Agbayani, R. F. and R. M. Lim. "Fishery Cooperatives in the Philippines." Report of an APO Seminar, (March 8–16, 1994) Tokyo, Japan: Asian Productivity Organization, pp. 183–193.

Agbayani, R. F. et al. "Economic Feasibility Analysis of the Monoculture of Mudcrab (Scylla serrata)." *Aquaculture* 91: 223–231.

Agbayani, et al. "Economic Assessment of Shrimp (*Penaeus monodon*) Hatchery Industry in Panay Island." *Report Series*. Vol. 22. 1994.

———. "An Economic Analysis of Modular Pond System of Milkfish Production in the Philippines." *Aquaculture* 83: 249–259. 1989.

———. "Economic Analysis of an Integrated Milkfish Broodstock and Hatchery Operation as a Public Enterprise." *Aquaculture* 99: 235–248, 1991.

Aguero, M. and A. Cruz. "The Economic Impact of Alternative Management and Marketing Decisions under Varying Conditions: A Case Study of Fish Culture in the Philippines." In *Towards an Integrated Management of Tropical Coastal Resources*. Ed. L. M. Chou. Singapore: National University of Singapore, 1991.

Alih, K. J. "Economics of Seaweed (Eucheuma) Farming in Tawi-Tawi in the Philippines." The Second Asian Fishery Forum. Manila: *Asian Fishery Society*. Tawi-Tawi College of Technology and Oceanography, Mindanao State University, 1990.

Aragon, C. T. et al. "Tilapia Marketing in Laguna Province, Philippines." Philippine Tilapia Economics. Philippine Council for Agriculture and Resources and Development. University of the Philippines at Los Baños, 1985.

———. "Economics of Tilapia Cage Culture in Laguna Province." Philippine Tilapia Economics. Philippine Council for Agriculture and Resource and Development, University of the Philippines at Los Baños, 1985.

Aypa, S. M. "Aquaculture Development in the Philippines: Status, Constraints, and Prospects." Proceedings of the 7th Biennial Conference of the International Institute for Fisheries Economics and Trade. Taiwan: National University, 1992, 14–70.

Baliao, D. D. et al. "The Economics of Retailing Milkfish Growth Fingerling Production in Brackish Ponds." *Aquaculture* 62: 195–205,1992.

Baluyut, E. A. "Recent Development in Inland Fisheries and Aquaculture in the Philppines." FAO Fisheries Report No. 370. Rome, Italy: 1987.

Bimbao, G. B. and M. M. Dey. "Philippine Tilapia Hatchery and Grow-Out System: A Macro-level Analysis." International Centre for Living, Aquatic Resource Management, Makati City: 1997.

Fermin, F. "The Introduction of Integrated Backyard Fishponds in Lowland, Cavite, Philippines." *Philippine Tilapia Economics*, Los Baños: Philippine Council for Agriculture and Resource and Development, 1995.

Ferrer, E. M. "Territorial Use Rights in Fisheries and Management of Artificial Reefs in the Philippines. Towards an Integrated Management of Tropical Coastal Resources." Manila: International Centre for Living, *Aquatic Resource Management* 22, 299–302.

Jara, R.S. "Aquaculture and Mangrove in the Philippines." Proceedings of the Workshop on Productivity of the Mangrove Ecosystem, Penang, Malaysia: University of Sains Malaysia. (1984). 97–107.

Juliano. R. O. "Observation of the Brackish Water Farming Industry in the Philippines." *Fish Today* 5 (2) University of the Philippines. 228–236.

Sunderlin, W. D. and M. L. Gorospoe. "'Fishers' Organization and Modes of Co-Management: The Case of San Miguel Bay, Philippines." *Human Organization* 56 (3) 1997: 333–343.

C. Finance and Banking

Batalia, Eric C. *The Politics of Financial Liberalization: Foreign Banking in Japan and the Philippines.* Manila: De La Salle University Press, 2002.

Blanco, Rhenee. *Rural Deposit Mobilization in the Philippines, 1977–1986.* Makati, Metro Manila: Philippine Institute for Development Studies, 1988.

Boyce, James K. "The Revolving Door? External Debt and Capital Flight: A Philippine Case Study." *World Development* 20 (March 1992): 335–349.

Broad, Robin. Unequal Alliance: *The World Bank, the International Monetary Fund, and the Philippines.* Berkeley, Calif.: University of California Press, 1988.

Cabanilla, Alex Ramon Q. "Innovative Financing: The Case of Metropolitan Manila Development Authority." In Financing Metropolitan Development: Private-Public Sector Roles. Edited by Josefa S. Edralin. UNCRD Research Report Series No. 35, 1999, 101–111.

De Dios, Emmanuel S. and Joel Rocamora. *Of Bonds & Bondage: A Reader on Philippine Debt.* Quezon City: Transnational Institute Philippine Center for Policy Studies Freedom from Debt Coalition, 1992.

Department of Finance and Banking Celebrating a Proud History, Building a Solid Future. Makati City: Nova Productions International and Department of Finance Centennial Committee, 1997.

Dohner, Robert S. *Philippine External Debt: Burdens, Possibilities, and Prospects.* New York: The Asia Society, 1989.

Floro, Sagrario L. and Pan A. Yotopoulos. *Informal Credit Markets and the New Institutional Economics: The Case of Philippine Agriculture.* Boulder, Colo.: Westview Press, 1991.

Hutchcroft, Paul D. *Booty Capitalism: The Politics of Banking in the Philippines.* Ithaca; London: Cornell University Press, 1998.

Khanser, Marites A. *Dance of Chaos: The Application of Chaos Theory in the Philippine Foreign Exchange Market.* Cagayan de Oro City: Khanser Publishing House, 1999.

Lee-Chua, Queena N. *Successful Family Business: Dynamic of Five Filipino Busines Families.* Quezon City: Ateneo De Manila University Press, 1997.

Licuanan, Victoria A. *Unlocking Doors: Filipino Women in Business.* Makati City: Asian Institute of Management, 1998.

Manansan, Rosario G. *Financing Public Sector Development Expenditure in Selected Countries: Philippines.* Manila: Asian Development Bank, 1988.

Montes, Manuel F. *Financing Development: The Political Economy of Fiscal Policy in the Philippines.* Manila: Philippine Institute for Development Studies, 1991.

———. "The Philippines Goes for Growth." *Euromoney* (May 1993): 1–36.

Nagano, Yoshiko. *Philippine "Colonial Banking" During the American Period.* Quezon City: University of the Philippine, School of Economics, 1999.

Patrick, Hugh and Honorata A. Moreno. "Philippine Private Domestic Commercial Banking, 1946–1980 in Light of Japanese Historical Experience." *Philippine Economic Journal* 27, 2–3 (1984) 87–104.

San Jose, Armida S. "Monetary Instrument and the Control of Liquidity in the Philippines: Focus on Open Market Operations." *Journal of Philippine Development* 17, 1 (1990): 133–146.

Talib, Azizah. "Philippine Monetary Policy in the Eighties: An Update." In *Monetary Policy in the SEACEN Countries: An Update.* Kuala Lumpur, Malaysia: The South East Asian Central Banks (SEACEN), 1993: 371–414.

Tan, Edita A. *Bank Concentration and the Structure of Interest.* Metro Manila: School of Economics, University of the Philippines, 1989.

The Philippine Banking Sector. Manila: IBON Books, 2003.

Yotopoulos, Pan A. and Sagrario L. Flora. "Income Distribution, Transaction Costs and Market Fragmentation in Informal Credit Markets." *Cambridge Journal of Economics* 16 (September 1992): 303–326.

D. Industry and Trade

Aguilar, Filomeno V. *Clash of Spirits: The History of Power and Sugar Planter Hegemony on a Visayan Island.* Honolulu: University of Hawaii Press, 1998.

Bautista, Germelino M. "The Forestry Crisis in the Philippines: Nature, Causes, and Issues." *The Developing Economies.* Kyoto, Japan, 28, No. 1 (March 1990), 67–94.

Billig, Michael S. Barons. *Brokers, and Buyers: The Institutions and Cultures of Philippine Sugar.* Honolulu: University of Hawaii Press, 2003.

Boquiren, R. R. *The History and Political Economy of the Vegetable Industry.* CSC Working Paper 14. Baguio City: Cordillera Studies Center. University of the Philippines College, 1997.

Capistrano-Baker, Florina H. *Basketry of Luzon Cordillera, Philippines.* Los Angeles: Fowler Museum of Cultural History, 1998.

Clarete, Ramon C. "The Economic Effects of Trade Liberalization on Philippine Agriculture." *The Philippine Review of Economics and Business* 26, 2 (December 1989): 208–235.

Dayrit, Manuel M. and Guilbert P. Aquitania. "The Pharmaceutical Industry: Public Policy and Proposed Legislation." *Solidarity* 118 (May–June 1988), 432–433.

De Dios, Emmanuel S., et al. *Poverty, Growth, and the Fiscal Crisis.* Makati, Metro Manila: Philippine Institute for Development Studies and International Development Research Center, 1993.

De Jesus, Ed. C. *The Tobacco Monopoly in the Philippines: Bureaucratic Enterprise and Social Change, 1766–1880.* Quezon City: Ateneo de Manila University, 1980.

Dejillas, Leopoldo J. *Trade Union Behavior in the Philippines, 1946–1990.* Manila: Ateneo de Manila University Press, 1994.

Effective Mechanisms for the Enhancement of Technology and Skills in the Philippines. Singapore: ASEAN Secretariat and Japan Institute of International Affairs in Collaboration with ASEAN Economic Research Unit, Institute of Southwest Asian Studies, 1987.

Espejo, Roman. *The Age of Reform and Industrialization 1896–1920.* San Diego: Greenhaven Press, 2003.

Galang, Roberto and Chani Marie Solleza. *Deregulation Under Fire: An Assessment of Downstream Oil Industry.* Makati City: Asian Institute of Management. 2001.

Godinez, Zinnia R. "Privatization and Deregulation in the Philippines." ASEAN *Economic Bulletin* 5, 3 (March 1989): 259–289.

Hamilton, Roy W. *From the Rainbow's Varied Hue: Textiles of the Southern Philippines.* Los Angeles: UCLA Fowler Museum of Cultural History, 1998.

Industry Trends. Manila, Philippines: Republic of the Philippines, National Statistics Office, 1987.

Intal, Ponciano S. *A Decomposition Analysis of Philippine Export and Import Performance, 1974–1982.* Manila: Philippine Institute for Development Studies, 1985.

Intal, Ponciano S., Jr. and John H. Power. *Trade, Exchange Rate, and Agricultural Pricing Policies in the Philippines.* Washington, D.C.: World Bank, 1990.

Kunio, Yoshihara. *Philippine Industrialization, Foreign and Domestic Capital.* Quezon City: Ateneo de Manila University Press, 1985.

Kuo, Cheng-Tian. *Global Competitiveness & Industrial Growth in Taiwan & the Philippines.* Pittsburgh, Penn.: University of Pittsburgh Press, 1995.

Legarda, Benito J. *After the Galleons: Foreign Trade, Economic Change and Entreprenuership in the Nineteenth Century Philippines*. Quezon City: Ateneo De Manila Press, 1999.

Lim, Elena S. *Business in the Real World: My Own Way: Profile of a Filipino Entrepreneur*. Manila: s.n., J. 1996.

Lim, Jospeh Y. *The Distributive Implications of Export-Led Industrialization in a Developing Economy*. Quezon City: University of the Philippines, School of Economics, 1985.

Leuken, Scott M. *The Persistence of Sharecropping in the Philippine Sugar Industry under Agrarian Reform*. Dissertation 2001. Northern Illinois University.

Lyman, R. Ashley. "Philippine Electric Demand and Equivalence Scales." *Southern Economic Journal* 60 (January 1994): 596–611.

Matejowsky, Ty Stephens. *Commerce and Society in the Urban Philippines: A Comparative Study*. Dissertation 2001. Ann Arbor: University Microfilms.

Mercado-Aldaba, Rafaelita. "EC 1992: Its Impact on Trade and Investment in the Philippines." *Journal of Philippine Development* 18, 1 (1991): 51–72.

Owen, Norman G. *Prosperity without Progress: Manila Hemp and Material Life in the Colonial Philippines*. Berkeley, Calif.: University of California Press, 1984.

Paderanga, Antonio R. and Cayetano W. Paderanga Jr. "The Oil Industry in the Philippines." *Philippine Economic Journal* 27, 1–3, 1988, 89–107.

Pernia, Ernesto M. *Factors Influencing the Choice of Location: Local and Foreign Firms in the Philippines*. Manila, Philippines: Asian Development Bank, 1987.

Pertierra, Raul. *The Work of Culture*. Manila: De La Salle University Press, 2002.

Quiason, Serafin D. *English 'Country Trade' with the Philippines, 1644–1765*. Quezon City: University of the Philippines Press, 1966.

Reyes, Christine. *Towards an Invigorated Housing Industry: An Action Agenda*. Makati City: Asian Institute of Management, 2001.

Rutten, Rosanne. *Artisans and Entrepreneurs in the Rural Philippines: Making a Living and Gaining Wealth in Two Commercialized Crafts*. Amsterdam: VU University Press: Centre for Asian Studies Amsterdam, 1990.

———. "Provincial Entrepreneurs in Philippine Crafts." *Philippine Studies* 40, 4 (1992): 480–500.

Saldana, Cesar G. "Rent Seeking Public Policies and Corporate Conduct in the Philippine Flour Milling Company." *Journal of Philippine Development* 17, 1 (1990): 89–132.

Sanchez, Aurora. "The Textile Industry in the Philippines and Thailand: A Comparison." *Journal of Philippine Development* 17, 1 (1990): 67–87.

Sta. Maria, Felice. *Dynamic Partnership: A Fusion of Vision and Power. The Petron Story*. Manila: Petron Corp. 1999.

Tan, Michael L. *Dying for Drugs: Pill Power and Politics in the Philippines*. Quezon City, Philippines: Health Action Information Network, 1988.

The Philippine Government and Trade Industries. Manila: IBON Foundation, 2001.

Tolentino, Rolando B. *National/Transnational: Subject Formation and Media in and on the Philippines.* Manila: Ateneo De Manila University Press, 2001.

Trade and Industry in the Philippines. Part 1. Washington D.C.: Library of Congress Office: Photoduplication Service, 1998.

Trade Liberalization and the Environment: Lessons Learned from Bangladesh, Chile, India, Philippines, Romania and Uganda: A Synsthesis Report. New York: United Nations, 1999.

Valencia, Ernesto M. *Trade & Philippine History & Other Exercises.* Quezon City: Giraffe Books, 2002.

E. Labor and Trade Unions

Andres, Tomas D. *Dealing with Filipino Workers.* Quezon City: Giraffe Books, 1997.

Buhay at Dugo ng anakpawis-Alay Sa Bayan. Manila: Commission on Trade Union and Human Rights, 1997.

Cagoco-Guiam, Rufa. *Philippine Child Soldiers in Central and Western Mindanao: A Rapid Assessment.* Geneva.: International Labor Organization, 2002.

Castillo, Evangeline et al. *Case Investigation on the participation of Women in the Reforestation in the Philippines.* Quezon City: Development Bureau, 1999.

Elmhirst, Rebecca and Ratna Saptari. *Labour in Southeast Asia: Local Processes in a Globalised World.* London: Routledge Curzon, 2004.

Espejo, Roman. *The Age of Reform and Industrialization 1896–1920.* San Diego: Greenhaven Press, 2003.

Fujita-Rony, Dorothy B. *American Workers, Colonial Power: Philippine Seattle and the Transpacific.* West Berkeley: University of California Press, 2003.

Go, Stella P. "Of Barangays, Institutional Mechanisms, and International Labor Migration." The Philippine Experience in Cross National Labor Migration in Asia and Regional Development Planning: Implications for Local Level Management. Edited by Toshio Yotari. UNCRD. Research Report Series No. 10. Nagoya, Japan. 1995, 41–61.

Gunn, Susan E. and Ostos Zenaida. "Dilemmas in Tackling Child Labour: The Case of Scavenger Children in the Philippines." *International Labour Review* 131, 6 (1992): 629–646.

Into Workers' Clothes. Quezon City: Socio-Pastoral Institute, 1999.

Jardiniano, P. F. and N.S. Tayag, eds. *Dictionary of Philippine Labor Terms.* Manila: Rex Book Store, 1997.

Jennings, Norman S. *Child Labour in Small-Scale Mining: Examples from Niger, Peru, and Philippines.* Geneva, Ill., 1999.

Kerkvliet, Benedict J. *Land Struggles and Land Regimes in the Philippines and Vietnam during the 20th Century.* Amsterdam: CASA-Centre for Asian Studies, 1997.

Kimura, Masataka. "Philippine Peasant and Labor Organizations in Electoral Politics: Players of Traditional Politics." *Pilipinas* No. 14 (Spring 1990), 61–63.

Lindo-McGovern, Ligaya. *Filipino Peasant Women: Exploitation and Resistance.* Philadelphia: University of Pennsylvania Press, 1997.

Lim, Jospeh Y. *The East Asian Crises and Employment: The Gender Dimension.* Quezon City: Philippine Center for Policy Studies, 2000.

Macaraya, Bach M. *Workers' Participation in the Philippine People Power Revolution: An Examination of the Roles Played by Trade Unions in the Philippine "People Power" Revolution.* Manila: Fiedrich Ebert Stiftung, 1988.

Paderanga, Cayetano W., Jr. *Employment in Philippine Development.* Metro Manila: School of Economics, University of the Philippines, 1989.

Ponciano, Ronnie and Cherie M. Espino. "The Philippine Rural Reconstruction Movement Community-based Intervention to Combat Child Labor in Small-Scale Gold Mining Communities in Camarines Norte, Philippines." *Regional Development Dialogue* 20. No. 2 (2000) 119–130.

Ramos, Elias T. *Dualistic Unionism and Industrial Relations.* Quezon City: New Day, 1990.

Shively, Gerald E. "Agricultural Change, Rural Labor Markets, and Forest Clearing: An Illustrative Case from the Philippines." *Land Economics* 77 (2) 2001: 268–284.

The Socialist Vision and Other Documents. Quezon City: Bukluran sa ikauunlad ng Sosyalistang Isip at Gawa, 1987.

The Congress for a People's Agrarian Reform. Manila: Ateneo De Manila University Press, 2001.

Villegas, Egberto M. *The Political Economy of Philippine Labor Laws.* Quezon City: Foundation for Nationalist Studies, 1988.

West, Lois A. *Militant Labor in the Philippines.* Philadelphia: Temple University Press, 1997.

F. Development

Alcala, A. C. *Conserving Philippine Marine Environment and Resources.* Quezon City: Rex Printing, 2001. 117 Illustrated.

Alcala, A. C. *Science, Conservation, and Development in the Philippine Setting.* Silliman University Press. Dumaguete City, 2000.

Balisacan, Arsenio M. *Poverty, Urbanization and Development Policy: A Philippine Perspective.* Quezon City: University of the Philippines Press, 1994.

Boguslauski, Michael von. "Regional Development under Participation: Some Experiences from the Philippines." In *New Regions: Concepts, Issues, and Practices.* Vol. 3. Edited by David Edgington, et al., 147–163. Westport, Conn.: Greenwood Press, 2001.

Briones, Leonor M."The Role of Government Owned or Controlled Corporations in Development." *Philippine Economic Journal* 25, 1–2 (1986) 51–89.

Broad, Robin. "The Poor and the Environment: Friends or Foes?" *World Development* 22 (June 1994): 811–822.

Bulan, Mila. "A Study of Official Development Assistance to the Philippines FY 1952–1972)." *Philippine Economic Journal* 8, 3 (1974), 206–268.

Castro-Palaganas, Erlinda et al. *Mainstreaming Indigenous Health Knowledge and Practices.* Quezon City: University of the Philippines, Center for Integrative and Development Studies, 2001.

Clark, Gracia. *Gender at Work in Economic Life.* Walnut Creek, Calif.: Altamira Press, 2003.

The Congress for a People's Agrarian Reform. Manila: Ateneo De Manila University Press, 2001.

Cordillera People's Industrial Enterprises: Paper Presented at the "GO-NGO Forum." Held at the University of the Philippines College Baguio, Baguio City, 8 July 1992. Baguio City: Cordillera Studies Center, University of the Philippines College Baguio, 1993.

Corpuz, Arturo G. *The Colonial Iron Horse: Railroads and Regional Development in the Philippines, 1875–1935.* Quezon City: University of the Philippines Press, 1999.

Cosalan, Peter M. *Development Concerns, Needs and Priorities in the Cordillera.* Baguio City: Cordillera Studies Center, University of the Philippines College Baguio, 1993.

Costello, Michael A. "Economic Development and Income Inquality in Northern Mindanao." *Philippine Sociolgical Review* 51, 1–2 (January June 1983), 53–66.

Crouch, Harold A. *Economic Change, Social Structure, and the Political System in Southeast Asia: Philippine Development Compared with the Other ASEAN Countries.* Singapore: Institute of Southeast Asian Studies, 1985.

Dubsky, Roman. *Technocracy and Development in the Philippines.* Diliman, Quezon City: University of the Philippines Press, 1993.

Eder, James F. ed. *Patterns of Power & Politics in the Philippines: Implications for Development.* Tempe, Ariz.: Arizona State University Program for Southeast Asian Studies, 1994.

Elkins, Richard E. "Culture Change in a Philippine Folk Society." *Philippine Sociological Review* 14:160–66. SIL 1966.

Evangelista, Oscar L. *Building the National Community: Problems and Prospects and Other Historical Essays.* Quezon City: New Day Publishers, 2002.

European Official Development Assistance to the Philippines. Manila: Transnational Institute and Council for People's Development, 1992.

Felizmeña, Amelia Delda and Belen Dayauon P. "Women Power in Social Welfare and Development." Quezon City: Department of Social Welfare and Development, 1999.

Flowers, Nancy M. Review of "Population Dynamics of a Philippine Rain Forest People: The San Ildefonso Agta" by John D. Early and Thomas N. Headland. *Human Ecology* 27 (1) 189–92 1999.

Fostering Gender Fairness in Coastal Resource Management: A Community-based Project in the Philippines. Washington D.C.; Centre for Development and Population Activities, 1999.

Galorport, Ryan C. and Diolia D. Galorport, compilers. *Community Health Education and Promotion Manual*. XV. Manila: Translators Association of the Philippines XV (1997).

Gonzales, Lulu. *Official Development Assistance in the Philippines: Land Resource Ownership and Access Rights among the Igorots of the Itogon Mining Area.* Baguio City: Mining Communities Development Center, 1996.

Hayumi,Yujiro and Masao Kikuchi. "A Rice Village Saga: Three Decades of Green Revolution in the Philippines." Basingstake, England: McMillan XVII, 2000.

Hayumi, Yujiro et al. *Toward an Alternate Land Reform Paradigm: A Philippine Perspective.* Quezon City: Ateneo De Manila University Press, 1990.

Hilhorst, Dorothea. *The Real World of NGOs: Discourses, Diversity, and Development*. London: Zed Books, 2003.

International Institute of Rural Reconstruction. "Towards Better Enterprises: Business Development, Marketing and Microfinance Practices." Manila: Citigroup Foundation, 2001.

Ishii, Alichir, et al. *National Development Policies and the Business Sector in the Philippines*. Tokyo, Japan: Institute of Developing Economies, 1988.

Kintanar, Noel Eli. "Looking at Private Sector Participation into Infrastructure Development in the Philippines." *Transport and Communications Bulletin for Asia and the Pacific*. no. 12 (2003) 37–55.

Kwiatkowski, Lynn. *Struggling with Development: The Politics of Hunger and Gender in the Philippines.* Quezon City: Ateneo De Manila University Press, 1999.

Lacson, Daniel L. *The Philippines Yesterday, Today, and Tomorrow: Political and Socio-Economic Developments.* Singapore: Times Academic Press for the Institute of Policy Studies, 1991.

Lamgerte, Mario B., et al. *Decentralization and Prospects for Regional Growth*. Makati, Metro Manila, Philippines: Philippines Institute of Development Studies, 1993.

Lane, Max R. *The Urban Mass Movement in the Philippines, 1983–87*. Canberra, Australia: Department of Political and Social Change Research School of Pacific Studies, Australian National University, 1990.

Lindsey, Charles W. "Commodities, Technology and Trade: Transnational Corporations and Philippine Economic Development." *The Philippine Review of Economics and Business* 26, 1 (June 1989): 67–108.

Llanto, Gilberto M. *The State of Philippine Housing Programs: A Critical Look at How Philippine Housing Subsidies Work*. Makati City: PIDS, Philippine Institute for Development Studies, 2001.

Magdaluyo, Raymund E. et al. *An Inquiry into the Competitivenes of Emerging Philippine Cities.* Makati City: Philippine Institute for Development Studies, 2001.

Major Development Programs and Projects, 1986–1992. 95 v. Manila: Office of the President, 1992.

Mani, Devyani and Teruhiko Yoshimura. "Achieving Human Security for the Urban Poor in Naga City." *Regional Development Dialogue* 22, 2 (Autumn 2001) 11–21.

Mercado, Eliseo R. *Southern Philippines Question: The Challenge of Peace and Development*. Cotabato City: Notre Dame Press, 1999.

Mohr, Tamara and Paul Osborn. *Encyclopedia of Sustainability: A World of Experience*. Amsterdam: Both ENDS, 2002.

National Physical Framework Plan, 1993–2022. Manila: National Land Use Committee, National Economic and Development Authority, 1992.

Olson, David R. and Nancy Torrance. *The Making of Literate Societies*. Malden, Mass.: Blackwell, 2001.

Philippine Development Report, 1988. Metro Manila: National Economic and Development Authority, 1989.

Philippine Rural Development: Problems, Issues, and Directions. Los Baños: University of the Philippines, Los Baños, 1991.

Reyes, Ed Aurelio and Araceli Cadahing-Ocampo. *Philippine Development Assistance Programme*. Manila: National Economic Development Authority, 2000.

Rocamora, Joel, Hanneke van Eldik Thieme, and Ernesto M. Hilario, eds. *European Official Development Assistance to the Philippines*. Manila, Philippines: Transnational Institute and Council for People's Development, 1992.

Sambahaginan: An Experience in Community Development Work. Quezon City: Institute for Studies in Asian Church and Culture, 1992.

Serrano, Isagani R. *Pay Now, Not Later: Essays on Environment and Development*. Quezon City: Philippine Rural Reconstruction Movement, 1994.

Southeast Asia: The Role of Foreign Direct Investment Policies in Development. Paris: Organization for Economic Co-operation and Development, 1999.

Strassmann, W. Paul, Alistair Blunt, and Raul Tomas. "Land Prices and Housing in Manila." *Urban Studies* 31 (March 1994) 267–285.

Sycip, Ly. *The Measurement of Filipino Well-Being: Technical Report*. Quezon City: University of the Philippines, Center for Integrative and Development Studies, 2000.

Tendero, Avelino P., Dolores A. Reyes, and Maria Socorro F. Manas. *Philippine Development Issues: An Inquiry*. Metro Manila: National Book Store, 1984.

Towards Better Enterprises: Business Development, Marketing and Microfinance Pratices. Manila: Citigroup Foundation, International Institute of Rural Reconstruction, 2001.

Updates of the Philippine Development Plan, 1990–1992. Manila: National Economic and Development Authority, 1990.

Umali, Celia L. "Balanced Agro-Industrial Development to Strengthen Regional Economies." *Regional Development Studies*. (1994–95) 107–129. University of the Philippines Institute for Science and Mathematics.

Zamora, Mario D. *Perspectives and Cultural Change and Development: Focus on the Philippines.* New Delhi: Reliance Publishing House, 1993.

PART 7. SOCIETY

A. Population

Carballo, Roque L. "The Population Debate: Growth or Control?" *Solidarity* 126 (April–June 1990), 147–159.

1990 Census of Population and Housing: Population by City, Municipality, and Barangay. 102 v. Manila, Philippines: National Statistics Office, 1992.

Concepcion, Mercedes B. "The Philippine Population Problem: Myth or Reality." *Philippine Studies* 42, 2 (1994): 139–154.

Constantino-David, Karina and Valte. "Poverty, Population Growth and the Impact of Urbanization in the Philippines (Part of a Symposium on: Population: Issues and Policies)." *International Social Science Journal* 46 (September 1994): 413–421.

Doeppers, Daniel F. and Peter Xenos. *Population and History: The Demographic Origins of the Modern Philippines.* Quezon City: Ateneo De Manila University Press, 1998.

Eagle, Julian. A *Smouldering Land: Lessons from the Philippines.* London: Catholic Insitute for International Relations, 1987.

Early, John D. and Thomas N. Headland. *Population Dynamics of a Philippine Rain Forest People: The San Ildefonso Agta.* Gainesville: University Press of Florida, 1998.

Hackenberg, Robert A. and Henry F. Magalit. *Demographic Responses to Development: Sources of Declining Fertility Rates in the Philippines.* Boulder, Colo.: Westview Press, 1985.

Hirtz, Frank. "Rural Population in the Philippines and the Role of State Intervention in Rural Social Policy." *Pilipinas* 12 (Spring 1989): 155–171.

Johnson, Mark. *Beauty and Power: Transgendering and Cultural Transformation in the Southern Philippines.* Oxford, England; New York: Berg, 1997.

Kaneshiro, Edith Mitsuko. *Our Home Will the Five Continents: Okinawan Migration to Hawaii, California and the Philippines, 1899–1941.* Dissertation, 1999. Ann Arbor: University Microfilms.

Lopez, Maria Elena and Ana Maria R. Nemenzo. *The Formulation of Philippine Population Policy.* Manila: Institute of Philippine Culture, Ateneo de Manila University, 1986.

Mason, Andrew. *Population Change and Economic Development in East Asia.* Stanford: Stanford University Press, 2001.

Mijares, Tito A. *The Population of the Philippines: Its Growth and Development.* Manila: Bureau of Census and Statistics, 2001.

Perez, Aurora Esquivel and Perla C. *Patacsil. Philippine Migration Studies: An Annotated Bibliography.* Manila: Philippine Migration Research Network, 1998.

Pertierra, Raul, Minda Cabilao, and Marna Escobar, eds. *Remittances and Returnees: The Cultural Economy of Migration in Ilocos.* Quezon City: New Day Publishers, 1992.

Population Projections by Province, City, Municipality, 1980–2000. Manila: National Census and Statistics Office.

Porter, Gareth and Delfin J. Ganapin, Jr. *Resources, Population, and the Philippines' Future. A Case Study.* Washington, D.C.: World Resources Institute, 1988.

Pugne, Melina S. *The Communication Planning Process in the Philippine Commission on Population.* Honolulu, HI: East–West Center, East-West Communication Institute, 1983.

The Thirteenth Asian Parliamentarians' Meeting on Population and Development. Kobe, Japan, March 17–18, 1997. Tokyo: Asian Population and Development Association.

Trager, Lillian. *The City Connection: Migration and Family Interdependence in the Philippines.* Ann Arbor, Mich.: University of Michigan Press, 1988.

Villegas, Bernardo M. *The Philippine Vision of Sustainable Development.* Manila: Southeast Asian Science Foundation, 1993.

B. Chinese

Alejandrino, Clark. *A History of the 1902 Chinese Exclusion Act: American Colonial Transmission and Deterioration of Filipino–Chinese Relations.* Manila: Kaisa Para sa Kaunlaran, 2003.

Amyot, Jacques. *The Chinese Community of Manila: A Study of Adaptation of Chinese Familism to the Philippine Environment.* Chicago, Ill.: Philippine Studies Program, Department of Anthropology, University of Chicago, 1960.

Armstrong, M. Jocelyn and R. Warwick Armstrong. *Chinese Populations in Contemporary Southeast Asian Societies: Identities, Interdependence, and International Influence.* Richmond: Curzon, 2001.

Angliongto, Jose L. *Integration of Philippine Chinese Ethnic Elements into the National Socio-Political Community.* Fort Bonifacio, Philippines: Rizal National Defense College of the Philippines, 1975.

Baviera, Aileen S. P. *Contemporary Political Attitudes and Behavior of the Chinese in Metro Manila.* Quezon City: Philippine–China Development Resource Center, 1994.

Carino, Theresa. *Chinese in the Philippines.* Manila, Philippines: DLSU University Press with Assistance of Research Dissemination Office of De La Salle University Research Center, 1985.

———. "The Chinese in the Philippines: A Survey of the Literature." *Journal of the South Seas Society* 43 (1988): 43–54.

Chen Ching Ho. *The Chinese in the Philippine Life, 1850–1898.* New Haven, Conn.: Yale University Press, 1965.

Cheng, Charles L. and Katherine V. Bersamin. *The Ethnic Chinese and the Cordillera Philippines: The Untold Story of Pioneers.* Baguio City: Unique Printing Press, 1997.

Cheong, Caroline Mar Wai Jong, et al. *The Chinese-Cantonese Family in Manila: A Study in Culture and Education.* Manila, Philippines: Centro Escolar University Research and Development Center, 1983.

Chirot, Daniel and Anthony Reid. *Essential Outsiders: Chinese and Jews in the Modern Transformation of Southeast Asia and Central Europe.* Seattle: University of Washington Press, 1997.

Djao, Wei. Being Chinese: *Voices from the Diaspora.* Tucson: University of Arizona Press, 2003.

Felix, Alfonso, Jr., ed. *The Chinese in the Philippines.* 2 v. Manila: Solidaridad Publishing House, 1966.

Gomez, Edmund Terence and Xinhuang Xiao. *Chinese Business in Southeast Asia: Contesting Cultural Explanations, Researching and Entrepreneurship.* Richmond, Surrey: Curzon, 2001.

Huff, W. G. *Currency Boards and Chinese Banking Development in Pre-World War II Southeast Asia: Malaysia and the Philippines.* Glasgow: University of Glasgow, 2003.

Jensen, Irene Khin Khin Myint. *The Chinese in the Philippines during the American Regime: 1898–1946.* San Francisco, Calif.: R and E Associates, 1975.

Li Yuk-Wai. "The Chinese Resistance Movement in the Philippines during the Japanese Occupation." *Journal of Southeast Asian Studies* 23 (September 1992): 308–321.

Omohudro, John T. *Chinese Merchant Families in Iloilo: Commerce and Kin in a Central Philippine City.* Athens, Ohio: Ohio University Press, 1981.

Ong, Aihwa and Donald Nonini. *Ungrounded Empires: The Cultural Politics of Modern Chinese Transnationalism.* New York: Routledge, 1997.

Sa-Onoy, Modesto P. *The Chinese in Negros.* Bacolod City, Philippines: St. John's Institute and Negros Occidental Historical Commission, 1980.

See, Chinben and Teresita Ang See. *Chinese in the Philippines: A Bibliography.* Manila: China Studies Program, De La Salle University, 1990.

See, Teresita Ang. *Chinese in the Philippines: Problems and Perspectives.* Manila, Philippines: Kaisa Para Sa Kaunlaran, 1990.

Tan, Antonio S. *The Chinese in the Philippines, 1898–1935: A Study of Their National Awakening.* Quezon City: R. P. Garcia, 1972.

———. *The Chinese in the Philippines during the Japanese Occupation.* Quezon City: University of the Philippines Press Asian Center, 1981.

———. *The Chinese Mestizos and the Formation of the Filipino Nationality.* Diliman, Quezon City: Asian Center, University of the Philippines, 1984.

Tan-Gatue, Belen. "The Social Background of Thirty Chinese–Filipino Marriages." *Philippine Sociological Review* III, 3. (July 1955), 3–13.

Weightman, George H. "Changing Patterns of Internal and External Migration among Philippine Chinese." *Crossroads* 2, 3 (1986): 83– 114.

Wickberg, Edgar. *The Chinese in Philippine Life, 1850–1898*. New Haven, Conn.: Yale University Press, 1965.

———. "The Chinese Mestizo in Philippine History." *Journal of Southeast Asian History* 5, 1 (March '64): 62–100.

C. Muslims

Aide Memoire on the Mindanao Peace Talks: Position of the Philippine Government Panel. Manila: Peace and Development Panel for Mindanao and the Cordilleras, 1987.

Antonio, Isabelita Solamo. *Gender, Muslim Laws and Reproductive Rights*. Davao City: PILIPINA Legal Resources Center, 2001.

Antonio, Isabelia Solamo and Norma Maruhom. *Muslim Personal Laws and Justice for Muslim Women*. Davao City: PILIPINA Legal Resources Center, 2000.

Arce, Wilfredo F. *Before the Secessionist Storm: Muslim-Christian Politics in Jolo, Sulu, Philippines, 1961–62*. Singapore: Maruzen Asia, 1983.

Bacho, Peter. "The Muslim Secessionist Movement." *Journal of International Affairs* 41 (Summer/Fall 1987): 153–164.

Baclagon, Uldarico S. *Christian–Moslem Guerrillas of Mindanao*. Manila: U. S. Baclagon, 1988.

Basman, Taha M. *Autonomy for Muslim Mindanao: The RCC Untold Story*. Manila, Philippines: B-Lal Publishers, 1989.

Bauzon, Kenneth E. *Liberalism and the Quest for Islamic Identity in the Philippines*. Durham, N.C.: Acron Press, 1991.

Boac, Ernesto D. *The East Timor and Mindanao Independence Movements: A Comparative Study*. Carlisle Barracks, Penn.: U.S. Army War College, 2001.

Che Man, W. K. *Muslim Separatism: The Moros of Southern Philippines and the Malays of Southern Thailand*. Singapore: Oxford University Press, 1990.

Dale, Stephen Frederic. "Religious Suicide in Islamic Asia: Anticolonial Terrorism in India, Indonesia, and the Philippines." *The Journal of Conflict Resolution.* 32 (March 1988): 37–59.

Dery, Luis Camara. *The Kris in Philippine History: A Study of the Impact of Moro Anti-Colonial Resistance, 1571–1896*. Manila: Luis Camara Dery, 1997.

Diaz, Patricio P. *What Ails Muslim Autonomy?* General Santos City: P.P. Diaz, 1998.

Episodes in the Moro Wars: Eyewitness Accounts of the Siege of Palumpong and of the Battle of Iligan as Reported by the Jesuit Parish Priests of These Places. Manila: Historical Conservation Society, 1991.

George, T. J. S. *Revolt in Mindanao: The Rise of Islam in Philippine Politics*. Singapore: Oxford University Press, 1980.

Gomez, Rafael R. *Peaceful Conflict Transformation: Civil Society Respnses to the Conflict in Mindanao*. Essen: Asienhaus Essen, 2001.

Gowing, Peter G., ed. *Understanding Islam and Muslims in the Philippines*. Quezon City: New Day Publishers, 1988.

Gowing, Peter Gordon and Robert D. McAmis, eds. *The Muslim Filipino: Their History, Society and Contemporary Problems*. Manila: Solidaridad Publishing House, 1974.

Gutierrez, Eric U. *Rebels, Warlords and Ulama: A Reader on Muslim Separatism and the War in Southern Philippines*. Quezon City: Institute of Popular Democracy, 2000.

———. *The Re–Imagination of the Bangsamoro: 30 Years Hence*. Quezon City: Institute for Popular Democracy, 1999.

Jocano, F. Landa, ed. *Filipino Muslims: Their Social Institutions and Cultural Achievements*. Quezon City: Asian Center, University of the Philippines, 1983.

Jubair, Salah. *Bangsamoro, a Nation under Endless Tyranny*. Lahore, Pakistan: Islamic Research Academy, 1984.

Kamlian, Jamail A. *Bangsamoro Society and Culture: A Book of Readings on Peace and Development in Southern Philippines*. Iligan City: Iligan Center for Peace Education And Resarch, 1999.

Lacar, Luis Q. "Culture Contact and National Identification among Philippine Muslims." *Philippine Studies* 42, 4 (1994): 431–451.

———. *Muslim Christian Marriages in the Philippines*. Quezon City: New Day Publishers, 1980.

———. "Neglected Dimensions in the Development of Muslim Mindanao and the Continuing Struggle of the Moro People for Self-Determination." *Journal of Institute of Muslim Minority Affairs* 9, 4 (July 1988): 296–310.

Lacar, Luis Q. and Carmelita S. Lacar. "Maranao Muslim Migration and Its Impact on Migrant Children." *Philippine Studies* 37, 1 (1989): 3–14.

———. "Muslim Christian Marriages in the Philippines." Quezon City: New Day, 1980.

LaRousse, William. *Walking Together Seeking Peace: The Local Church of Mindanao-Sulu Journeying in Dialogue with the Muslim Community, 1965–2000*. Quezon City: University of the Philippines Press, 2001.

Macapado, Abaton. *The Moro Armed Struggle in the Philippines: The Nonviolent Autonomy Alternative*. Marawi City: Mindanao State Universsity, 1994.

Majul, Cesar Adib. *The Contemporary Muslim Movement in the Philippines*. Berkley: Mizan Press, 1985.

———. *Muslims in the Philippines*. Manila: Ateneo De Manila University Press, 1998.

McKenna, Thomas M. "Martial Law, Moro Nationalism, and Traditional Leadership in Cotabato." *Pilipinas* 18 (1992): 1–18.

———. *Muslim Rulers and Rebels: Everyday Politics and Armed Separatism in the Southern Philippines*. Berkeley: University of California Press, 1998.

———. "Persistence of an Overthrown Paradigm: Modernization in a Philippine Muslim Shantytown." *Journal of Anthropological Research* 44 (Fall 1988): 287–309.

Mastura, Michael O. *Muslims Filipino Experience: A Collection of Essays.* Manila, Philippines: Ministry of Muslim Affairs, 1984.

Sadain, Mehol K. "The Muslim Filipinos and the Development of Philippine Nationalism." *Diliman Review* 39, 3 (1991): 40–45.

Sakili, Abraham P. "Deceptive Nationalism and the 1998 Philippine Centennial Commemoration: A Philippine Muslim's View," *Centennial Issue Asian Studies* 34 1998: 112–120.

Selected Documents and Studies for the Conference on the "Tripoli Agreement, Problems and Prospects," September 12–13, 1985. Diliman, Quezon City, Philippines: International Studies Institute of the Philippines, Law Complex, University of the Philippines, 1985.

Silva, Rad D. *Two Hills of the Same Land: Truth Behind the Mindanao Problem.* Davao City: Mindanao-Sulu Center of Critical Studies and Research Group, 1999.

Tan, Samuel K. *Decolonization and Filipino Muslim Identity.* Cubao, Quezon City: Journals and Publications Division, President's Center for Special Studies, 1985.

———. "Internationalization of the Bangsamoro Struggle." Diliman, Quezon City: Center for Integrative and Development Studies, University of the Philippines Press, 1993.

Tanggol, Sakamo D. *Muslim Autonomy in the Philippines: Rhetoric and Reality.* Marawi City: Mindanao State University, 1993.

Tuban, Rita. "A Genealogy of the Sulu Sultunate." *Philippine Studies* 42, 1 (1994): 20–38.

Ugarte, Eduardo. "Muslims and Madness in the Southern Philippines." *Pilipinas,* 19 (1992): 1–23.

Yegar, Moshe. *Between Integration and Secession: The Muslim Communities of the Southern Philippines, Southern Thailand, and Western Burma/Myanmar.* Lanham, Md.: Lexington Books, 2002.

D. Ethnic Groups

A Look at the World of Indigenous Women: A Research in Selected Areas of Ifugao, Maguindanao, and Bacolod City. Quezon City: Center for Women's Resources, 1999.

Agta of Northeastern Luzon: Recent Studies. Cebu City: San Carlos Publications, University of San Carlos, 1985.

Alan, Mercedes. *Mindanao Ethnic Communities: Patterns of Growth and Change.* Quezon City: University of the Philippines, Center for Integrative and Development Studies, 2001.

Angeles, Brenda Jay C. and Charmian K. Gloria. "Ancestral Domain: The Tenurial Rights of Indigenous Communities." *Tambara: Ateneo de Davao University Journal* 10 (December 1993): 1–60.

Anima, Nid. *The Headhunting Tribes of the Philippines*. Quezon City: Cultural Foundation for Asia, 1985.

Azurin, Arnold Molina. *Beddeng: Exploring the Ilocano-Igorot Confluence*. Philippines: Museo ng Kalinangang Pilipino, Sentrong Pangkultura ng Pilipinas, 1991.

Ballard, Arlene. "How the Ibaloi Language Reflects the Basic Values: Behavioral Profile." Dallas: SIL 1979.

Buenconsejo, Jose S. *Songs and Gifts at the Frontier: Person and Exchange in the Agusan Manobo Possession Ritual, Philippines*. New York: Rutledge, 2002.

Casal, Gabriel. *Kayamanan: Ma'i-Panoramas of Philippine Primeval*. Metro Manila: Ayala Museum, 1986.

Dandan, Virginia B., ed. *Readings on the Tasaday*. Manila: Tasaday Community Care Foundation, 1989.

de Raedt, Jules. *Similarities and Differences in Life Styles in the Central Cordilleras from Different Perspectives*. Baguio: Studies Center, 1984.

Conklin, Jean M. *An Ifugao Notebook*: Bloomington: 1st Books, 2003.

Disoma, Esmail R. *The Maranao: A Study of Their Practices and Beliefs*. Marawi City: Department of Sociology, College of Social Sciences and Humanities, Mindanao State University, 1990.

Duhaylongsod, Levita and David Hyndman. "Creeping Resource Exploitation in the Tiboli Homeland: Political Ecology of the Tasaday Hoax." In *The Tasaday Controversy: Assessing the Evidence*, 59–75. Ed. Thomas N. Headland. *American Anthropological Association*, Scholarly Series 28. Washington, D.C. 1992.

Dubois, Carl D. "Death and Burial Customs of the Sarangani Manobo." *Kinaadman* 12:33–35.1990.

Dumont, Jean Paul. *Visayan Vignettes: Ethnographic Traces of a Philippine Island*. Chicago, Ill.: University of Chicago Press, 1992.

Eder, James F. *On the Road to Extinction: Depopulation, Deculturation, and Adaptive Well-Being among the Batak of the Philippines*. Berkeley: University of California Press, 1987.

Elkins, Richard C. "Conversion or Acculturation? A Study of Culture and Its Effect on Evangelism in Mindanao Indigenous Societies." *Missiology* 22:167–76. 1994.

Filipino Tradition and Acculturation: Reports on Changing Societies. Tokyo: Philippine Studies Program, Institute of Social Sciences, Waseda University, 1983.

Gastardo-Conaco, Cecilia and Pilar Ramos-Jimenez. *Ethnicity and Fertility in the Philippines*. Singapore: Institute of Southeast Asian Studies, 1986.

Gaza, Teofredo A. and Yukihiro Yamada. *Atlas of Itbayat Place-Names, Batanes, Philippines*. Himeji, Japan: Himeji Dokkyo University, 1999.

Gibson, Thomas. *Sacrifice and Sharing in the Philippine Highlands: Religion and Society among the Buid of Mindoro*. Dover, N.H.: Athlone Press, 1986.

Headland, Thomas N. A Review of "On the Road to Tribal Extinction: Depopulation, Deculturation and Adaptive Well-Being among the Batak of the Philippines." *Journal of Asian History* 22: (1988) 93–95.

Hemley, Robin. *Invented Eden: The Elusive, Disputed History of the Tasasay.* New York: Farrar, Straus and Giroux, 2003.

Hornedo, Florentino H. *Laji: Anu Maddaw Ka Mu Lipus: An Ivatan Folk Lyric Tradition.* Manila: University of Santo Tomas Press, 1997.

Igorot: A People Who Daily Touch the Earth and Sky. 3 v. Baguio City; Cordillera Schools Group, 1986–1987.

Indigenous Peoples' Rights, Mining. Quezon City: Legal Rights and Natural Resources Center, 1997.

Jocano, F. Landa, et al. *The Hiligaynon: An Ethnography of Family and Community Life in Western Bisayas Region.* Diliman, Quezon City: Asian Center, University of the Philippines, 1983.

———. *Filipino Indigenous Ethnic Communities: Patterns, Variations, and Typologies.* Punlad Research House, 1998.

Johnson, Nan E. and Linda M. Burton. "Religion and Reproduction in Philippine Society: A New Test of the Minority-Group Status Hypothesis." *Sociological Analysis* 48, 3 (Fall 1987): 217–233.

Kikuchi, Yasushi. *Philippine Kinship and Society.* Quezon City: New Day Publishers, 1989.

———. *Uncrystallized Philippine Society: A Social Anthropological Analysis.* Quezon City: New Day Publishers, 1991.

Lopez-Gonzaga, Violeta B. *Peasants in the Hills: A Study of the Dynamics of Social Changes among the Buhid Swidden Cultivators in the Philippines.* Quezon City: University of the Philippines Press, 1983.

———. *The Negrense: A Social History of an Elite Class.* Manila Institute for Social Research and Development, 1991.

Lumangdong, Tony. "The Meaning of Education for Tribal Filipinos." *Solidarity* 122 (April–June 1989), 61–62.

Maceda, Marcelino N. "The Culture of the Mamanua (Northeast Mindanao) as Compared with That of Other Negritos of Southeast Asia." *Journal of Polynesian Society.* 75 (1966) 243–44.

Mammanteo, Lydia Buteng. *The Courageous BIBAK of Montreal: Its Beginning and Growth 1991–1999.* Dorval, Quebec: Dalida Publishing House, 2000.

Masferré, E. *People of the Philippine Cordillera: Photographs, 1934–1956.* Makati, Metro Manila: Devcon, 1988.

Mendoza, Julus and Athena Lydia Casambre. *Thoughts on Indigenous Knowledge.* Baguio City: Cordillera Studies Center, UP College, 2002.

Ness, Sally Ann A. *The Sinulog Dancing of Cebu City, Philippines.* Dissertation, University of Washington, 1987. Ann Arbor: University Microfilms.

Nimmo, H. Arlo. *Magosaha: An Ethnography of the Tawi-Tawi Dilaut.* Manila: Ateneo De Manila University Press, 2001.

Oracion, Enrique Galen. "Ethnicity, Intermarriage, and Change in the Biosocial Structure of the Contemporary Negrito Population in Southern Negros." *Silliman Journal* 31, 3–4 (1983) 102–110.

Pablo, Renato Y. and Richard C. Gardner. "Ethnic Stereotypes of Filipino Children and Their Parents." *Philippine Studies* 35 (1987): 332–347.

Postma, Antoon. "Formal Education among the Mangyans." *Solidarity* 122 (April–June 1989). 54–60.

Prill-Brett, June. *Baguio, a Multi-Ethnic City and the Development of the Ibaloy as an Ethnic Minority*. Baguio City, Philippines: Cordillera Studies Center, University of the Philippines College Baguio, 1990.

———. *Preliminary Perspectives on Local Territorial Boundaries and Resource Control*. Baguio City, Philippines: Cordillera Studies Center, University of the Philippines College Baguio, 1988.

Resurreccion, Babette P. *Transforming Nature, Redefining Selves: Gender and Ethnic Relations, Resource Use and Environmental Change in the Philippines Uplands*. Maastricht. Netherlands: Shaker Publication, 1999.

Reyes, Lynda Angelica N. *The Textiles of Southern Philippines: The Textile Traditions of the Bagobo, Mandaya and Bilaan of the Philippines*. Quezon City: University of the Philippines Press, 1992.

Rodil, B. R. *The Minoritization of the Indigenous Communities of Mindanao and the Sulu Archipelago*. Mindanao: Alternate Forum for Research in Mindanao, 1994.

Rye, Ajit Singh. "The Indian Community in the Philippines." In *Indian Communities in Southeast Asia*. Singapore: Institute of Southeast Asia, 1993: 708–775.

Salazar, Z. A., ed. The Ethnic Dimension: Papers on Philippine Culture, History and Psychology. Cologne, Germany: Counselling Center for Filipinos, Caritas Association for the City of Cologne, 1983.

Salibad, Rogelio B. *The Cordillera in Transition*. Baguio City: Tribu Publications, 1989.

Schlegel, Stuart A. *Children of Tulus: Essays on the Tiruray People*. Quezon City, Philippines: Giraffe Books, 1994.

Scott, William Henry. *Of Igorots and Independence: Two Essays*. Baguio City: ERA, 1993.

Shimizu, Hiromu. *Pinatubo Aytas: Continuity and Change*. Quezon City, Metro Manila: Ateneo de Manila University Press, 1989.

Teo, Saladin S. *The Life-Style of the Badjaos: A Study of Education and Culture*. Manila: Centro Escolar University Research and Development Center, 1989.

Valderrama, Ursula Cinco. *The Colourful Mandaya: Ethnic Tribe of Davao Oriental*. Davao City: U. C. Valderrama, 1987.

Warren, James Francis. *Iranun and Balangingi: Globalization, Maritime Raiding and the Birth of Ethnicity*. Quezon City: New Day Publishers, 2002.

Yengoyan, Aram A. "Shaping and Reshaping the Tasaday; A Question of Cultural Identity. A Review Article." *Journal of Asian Studies* 50, 3 (Aug. 1991): 565–573.

Zahalka, Anne. *Woven Threads: Picturing Tribal Women in Mindanao*. Fitroy, Vic.: Community Aid Abroad, 1997.

Zaragoza, Ramon Ma. *The Philippines: Images of the Past*. Makati, Metro Manila: Ramaza, 1993.

E. Education

Abueva, Jose Veloso. "Internationalizing Higher Education Values and Ethics." *Philippine Studies Newsletter* 17, 2 (June 1989): 22–29.

Angeles-Bautista, Fenny delos, ed. *Multigrade Teacher's Handbook*. Manila: Department of Education, Culture and Sports, 1994.

Arguelles, Clariza Alcantara. *Education a Worthwhile Investment: Evidence from Cebu, Philippines*. Dissertation, 2001. Ann Arbor: University Microflms.

Bago, Adelaida L. *Curriculum Development: The Philippine Experience*. Manila: De La Salle University Press, 2001.

Barsaga, Eligio B. and Debbie P. Lacuesta. *An Evaluation of the Multigrade Program in Philippine Education*. Monograph. Manila: Regional Center for Educational Innovation and Technology, 1999.

Benton, Richard. "The Philippine Bilingual Education Program: Education for the Masses or Preparation for New Elite?" *Philippine Journal of Linguistics* 11, 2 (December 1984): 1–14.

Bicomong, Gregorio E. *The Arrival of Don Bosco in the Philippines: Requests Made to the Salesians 1891–1951*. Makati City: Don Bosco Press, 2001.

Canieso-Doronila, Maria Luisa. *The Limits of Educational Change: National Identity Formation in a Philippine Public Elementary School*. Quezon City: University of the Philippine Press, 1989.

Cariño, Isidro D. *A Business Executive Joins the Cabinet: His Joy and Pains*. Mandaluyong, Metro Manila: Cacho Hermanos, 1992.

Cooney, R. P. and E. Paqueo-Arreza. "Higher Education Regulation in the Philippines: Issues of Control, Quality Assurance, and Accreditation." In *East Asian Higher Education: Traditions and Transformations*. Ed. Albert H. Yee. New York: Published for the IAU Press, Pergamon, 1995: 165–178.

Cortes, Josefina R. *Education and Development: The Philippine Experience and Future Possibilities*. Quezon City: Publisher's Printing, 1987.

———. *Explorations in the Theory and Practice of Philippine Education, 1965–1993*. Quezon City: University of the Philippines Press, 1993.

Cruz, Isagani R. and Mandy Navasero. *Building a Nation: Private Education in the Philippines*. Makati City: Fund For Assistance to Private Education, 1997.

Diagnostic Studies on Educational Management, Country Studies: Philippines. Bangkok: Unesco Regional Office for Education in Asia and the Pacific, 1984.

Duka, Cecilio D. *Historical, Philosophical and Legal Foundations of Education*. Quezon City: Phoenix Publishing House.

Education in the Philippines. Manila, Philippines: Republic of the Philippines, Ministry of Education, Culture and Sports, 1986.

Estioko, Leonardo R. *Essays on Philippine Education*. Manila: Divine Word Publications, 1989.

Gaerlan Barbara. Philippines: *The History of English as the Medium of Instruction and the Challenge Mounted by the Filipino*. Dissertation. Ann Arbor: University Microfilms,1998.

Garcia, Robert Francis. *Of Maps and Leap Frog: Popular Education and Other Descriptions*. Quezon City: Popular Education for People's Empowerment, 1999.

Gonzales, James Arthur. *Colonial Education and Filipino Sudent Immigration in the Early Twentieth Century*. Dissertation. Ann Arbor: University Microfilms.

Gregorio, Herman C. and Cornelia M. Gregorio. Principles of Elementary-Secondary Education. rev. ed. Quezon City: R. P. Garcia Publishing, 1989.

Kurian, George Thomas, ed. The Philippines." In *World Education Encyclopedia*. New York: Facts on File, 1988: 992–1005.

Morris, Greta N. *The American Contribution to Philippine Education. 1898–1998.* Manila: U.S. Information Service, 1998.

NFE Accreditation and Equivalency Learning Material. Pasig City: Nonformal Education Project. Department of Education, Culture nd Sports, 2001.

Oleksy, Walter G. *The Philippines*. New York: Children's Press, 2000.

Peralta, Jesus T. "Ethnicity Maintenance and National Education." *Solidarity* 122 (April–June 1989), 48–53.

Postma, Antoon. "Formal Education among the Mangyans." *Solidarity* 122 (April–June 1989): 54–60.

Racelis, Maria and Judy Celine. *Bearers of Benevolence: The Thomasites and Public Education.* Pasig City: Anvil Publishers, 2001.

Reyes, Flordiliza C. *Unveiling Teacher Expertise: A Showcase of Sixty-Nine Outstanding Teachers in the Philippines*. Manila: De La Salle University Press, 2002.

Santiago, Luciano P. R. "The Beginnings of Higher Education in the Philippines (1601–1772)." *Philippine Quarterly of Culture & Society* 19, 2 (June 1991) 135–145.

Sullivan, Margaret W. *Pacific Crossroads*. Parsippany, N.J.: Dillon Press, 1998.

Sutaria, Minda C., Juanita S. Guerrero, and Paulina M. Castano, eds. *Philippine Education: Visions and Perspectives*. Metro Manila: National Book Store, 1989.

Synott. John P. *Teacher Unions, Social Movements, and the Politics of Education in Asia: Philippines, South Korea, and Taiwan*. Aldershot, Hampshire, Great Britain; Burlington, Vt.; Ashgate, 2002.

To Islands Faraway: The Story of the Thomasites and Their Journey to the Philippines. Manila: Public Affairs Section, U.S. Embassy, 2001.

Wee, Jessie. *Philippines.* Philadelphia: Chelsea House Publishers, 1999.

F. Religion

Abad, Ricardo G. "Religion in the Philippines." *Philippine Studies* 49 (2000), 337–367.

Achutegui, Pedro S. de. "The Miracle of the Philippine Revolution: Interdisciplinary Reflections" Symposium Organized by the Loyola School of Theology. Manila: Loyola School of Theology, Ateneo de Manila University, 1986.

Achutegui, Pedro S. de and Miguel A. Bernad. *Religious Revolution in the Philippines: The Life and Church of Gregorio Aglipay, 1860–1960.* 2nd rev. and enl. ed., 4 v. Manila: Ateneo de Manila, 1961–1972.

Alvarez, David. "Purely a Business Matter: The Taft Mission to the Vatican." *Diplomatic History* 16 (Summer 1992) 357–369.

Apilado, Mariano Casuga. *Revolutionary Spirituality: A Study of the Protestant Role in the American Colonial Rule of the Philippines.* Quezon City: New Day Publishers, 1999.

Banzuelo, Edilberto V. *The Beginnings of Evangelical Christianity in the Philippines.* Valenzuela, Bulacan: FEBIAS College of the Bible, 1998.

Bauzon, Kenneth E. "Knowledge and Ideology in Philippine Society." *Philippine Quarterly of Culture & Society* 19, 3 (September 1991): 207–234.

Beckford, James A. and Araceli Suzara. "A New Religious and Healing Movement in the Philippines." *Religion* 24 (April 1994) 117–141.

Belita, Jaime A., ed. *And God Said: Hala!* Manila: De La Salle University Press, 1991.

Bickert, Robert Andrew. *Perception and Response to Receptivity: The History and Growth of the Wesleyan Church in the Philippines, 1932–1994.* Manila: Dissertation. Ann Arbor: University Microfilms.

Brenan, Joseph William. *Christianaity in the Philippines in the Twentieth Century: Why is the Only Christian Nation in Asia in Need of Evangelism.* Dissertation, 2000. Ann Arbor: University Mircofilms.

Brewer, Carolyn. *Shamanism, Catholicism and Gender Relations in Colonial Philippines 1521–1685.* Aldershot, Hants, England; Burlington, Vt.: Ashgate, 2004.

———. *Holy Confrontation: Religion, Gender, and Sexuality in the Philippines.* Manila: St. Scholastica's College Institute of Women's Studies, 2001.

Bulatao, Jaime. "Roman Theology Meets Animistic Culure." *Kinaadman* 6, 1 Cagayan de Oro: 1994, 102–110.

Bunda, Nestor Distor. *A Mission History of the Philippine Baptist Churches 1898–1998: From a Philippine Perspective.* Aachen: Verl. An der Lottbek, 1999.

Cajes, Prisco S. *Anitism and Perichoresis: Towards a Filipino Christian Eco-Theology of Nature.* Quezon City: Dissertation, 2002. Ann Arbor: University Microfilms.

Cariño, Feliciano V. *The Sacrifice of the Innocent: Themes on Christian Participation in the Philippine Struggle.* Hong Kong: World Student Christian Federation, Asia/Pacific Region, 1984.

Casper, Gretchen. "The Changing Politicization of the Philippine Roman Catholic Church, 1972–1988." *Pilipinas* 13 (Fall 1989), 43–56.

Clymer, Kenton J. *Protestant Missionaries in the Philippines, 1898–1916: An Inquiry into the American Colonial Mentality.* Urbana, Ill.: University of Illinois Press, 1986.

Commission on Evangelism and Ecumenical Relations: Exploring the New Religious Movements in the Philippines. Philippines: National Council of Churches in the Philippines, 1989.

Coronel, Hernando M. *Boatmen for Christ: The Early Filipino Priests: A Chronicle of the History of the Diocesan Priesthood and the Role of the Seminary in Forming the First Filipino Clergy.* Manila: Reyes Publication, 1998.

Costa, Horacio de la and John N. Schumacher. *The Filipino Clergy: Historical Studies and Future Perspectives.* Manila Loyola Papers Board of Editors, 1982.

Cruikshank, Bruce. *Spanish Franciscans in the Colonial Philippines,1578–1898: Catalog and Analysis for a History of Filipinos in Franciscan Parishes.* Hastings, Neb.: Cornhusker Press, 2003.

Cummins, J. *Christianity and Missions 1450–1800.* Aldershot, Great Britain; Brookfield, Vt: Ashgate Variorum, 1997.

Cunningham, Floyd T. "The Early History of the Church of the Nazarene in the Pilippines." *Philippine Studies* 41, 1 (1993): 51–76.

Dagdag, Edgardo E. "The Politicization of the Philippine Catholic Church." *Centennial Issue Asian Studies* 34 1998: 50–77.

Dañguilan, Marilen J. *Women in Brackets: A Chronicle of Vatican Power and Control.* Pasig City: Center for Investigative Journalism, 1997.

De la Torre, Edicio. *Touching Ground, Taking Root: Theological and Political Reflections on the Philippine Struggle.* Quezon City: Socio-Pastoral Institute, 1986.

De La Torre, Visitacion R. *Faith Enshrined: Churches of Pangasinan.* Makati City: Tower Book House, 1997.

Diaz-Trechuelo Spinola, Maria Lourdes, y Diego Baselenque. *Evangelizacion y misiones en Iberoamerica y Filipinas Textos Historicos.* Madrid: Fundacion Historica Tavera, 1999.

Elesterio, Fernando G. *Three Essays on Philippine Religious Culture.* Manila: De La Salle University Press, 1989.

Fajardo, Reynold S. *The Brethren.* Manila: E. L. Locsin and the Grand Lodge of Free and Accepted Masons of the Philippines, 1999.

The Favor of the Gods: Essays in Filipino Religious Thought and Behavior. Manila: University of Santo Tomas Press, 2001.

Felix, Maria Leny E. *Footprints of a Pilgrim People: The Socio-Pastoral Apostolates of the Missionary Benedictinre Sisters of the Philippines.* Manila: St. Scholastica's Priory, 2001.

Giordano, Pasquale T. *Awakening to Mission: The Philippine Catholic Church, 1965–1981.* Quezon City: New Day Publishers, 1988.

Gleeck, Lewis E. *Sainthood Postponed.* Manila: Ateneo De Manila University Press, 1992.

Gomez, Martin de Jesus H. *Worship and Weave: Towards Filipino Liturgical Vestments.* Makati City: Ayala Foundation and Monastery of the Transfiguration, 2001.

Guillermo, Artemio R. ed. *Churches Aflame.* Nashville: Abingdon Press, 1991.

———. "Protestantism in the Philippines." *Journal College of Liberal Arts*, University of the East, Manila: II, 1, 1965.

Hardy, Richard P., ed. *The Philippine Bishops Speak, 1968–1983*. Quezon City: Maryhill School of Theology, 1984.

Hernandez, Policarpio F. and Marionette Ocampo Martinez. *The Augustinians in the Philippines and Their Contribution to the Printing Press, Philology, Poetry, Religious Literature, History, and Sciences*. Makati City: Colegio San Agustin, 1998.

Hornedo, Florentino H. *On the Trail of Dominican Engineers, Artists & Saints in the Cagayan Valley & Batanes*. Manila: University of Santo Tomas Press, 2002.

Image and Reality in the Ecumenical Movement. Quezon City: National Council of Churches in the Philippines, 1987.

Javellana, Rene B., ed. *Morality, Religion, and the Filipino*. Quezon City: Ateneo De Manila University Press, 1994.

Jocano, F. Landa. *Folk Christianity: A Preliminary Study of Conversion and Patterning of Christian Experience in the Philippines*. Quezon City: Trinity Research Institute, Trinity College of Quezon City, 1981.

Jones, Anne Wayne. *Christian Missions in the American Empire: Episcopalians in Northern Luzon, The Philippines, 1902–1946*. Dissertation 2001. Ann Arbor: University Microfilms.

Jose, Regalado Trota. *Images of Faith: Religious Ivory Carvings from the Philippines*. Pasadena, Calif.: Pacific Asia Museum, 1990.

Karotemprel, S. *Heralds of the Gospel in Asia*. Ban Phatthaya, Thailand: Shillong, 1997.

Kroeger, James H. *The Philippine Church and Evangelization, 1965–1984*. Rome: Pontifical Gregorian University, 1985.

Kroger, Daniel. *Disarming Peter: Retrieving a Christian Ethic of Nonviolence in the Philippine Context*. Manila: De La Salle University Press, 2002.

Kwantes, Anne C. *Chapters in Church History*. Colorado Springs, Colo.: International Academic Publishers, 2002.

Larousse, William. *Walking Together Seeking Peace: The Local Church of Mindanao-Sulu Journeying in Dialogue with the Muslim Community*. Quezon City: Claretian Publications, 2001.

La, Sunghwan. *A Case for the Independence of the Philippine United Methodist Church from Expatriate Control for Healthy Growth*. Dissertation, 2002. Ann Arbor: University Microfilms.

Lee-Chua, Queena N. *Cogito Ergo Sum and Other Musings on Science*. Manila: Ateneo De Manila University Press, 2002.

Lorenzo Garcia, Santiago. *La Expulsion de los Jesuitas de Filipinas*. Alicante: Universidad de Alicante, 1999.

Ma, Julie C. *When the Spirits Meet the Spirits: Pentecostal Ministry among the Kankan-ey Tribe in the Philippines*. New York: P. Lang, 2000.

McCoy, Alfred William. *Priests on Trial*. Ringwood, Victoria, Australia: Penguin Books, 1984.

Missionary Files of the Methodist Episcopal Church Missionary Correspondence, 1846–1912: Philippines, Africa, Europe, India, Malaya, Mexico, South America and West Indies. Wilmington, Del.; Scholarly Resources, 1999.

Miranda-Feliciano, Evelyn. *Filipino Values and Our Christian Faith.* Manila: OMF Literature, 1990.

Montoya, Michael Ariel. *"As the Bamboo Breaks" toward Retrieving a Filipino Theological Anthropology Using the Story of Malakas and Maganda.* Dissertation 2002. Ann Arbor: University Microfilms.

Muir, Fredric John. *Aglipay Universalist: The Unitarian Universalist Church of the Philippines.* Annapolis, Md.: F. J. Muir, 2001.

Nimmo, H. Arlo. "Religious Beliefs of the Tawi-Tawi Bajau." *Philippine Studies* 38, 1 (1990) 3–27.

——. "Religious Rituals of the Tawi-Tawi Bajau." *Philippine Studies* 38, 2 (1990): 166–198.

O'Brien, Niall. *Island of Tears, Island of Negros: Living the Gospel in a Revolutionary Situation.* Maryknoll, N.Y. Orbis Books, 1993.

Orteza, Edna J., ed. *What Do We Mean When We Say Sacred. A Resource Handbook on Culture and Identity.* Geneva, Switzerland: World Council of Churches, 1998.

Pertierra, Raul. *Religion, Politics, and Rationality in a Philippine Community.* Honolulu, HI: University of Hawaii Press, 1988.

Porras, José Luis. *The Synod of Manila of 1582.* Manila: Historical Conservation Society, 1990.

Quibuyen, Floro C. "And Women Will Prevail over Men: Symbolic Sexual Inversion and Counter-Hegemonic Discourse in Mt. Banahaw": *The Case of the Ciudad Mistica de Dios.* Manoa, HI: Center for Philippine Studies, School of Hawaiian, Asian and Pacific Studies, University of Hawaii at Manoa, 1991.

Rafael, Vicente L. "Confession, Conversion, and Reciprocity in Early Tagalog Colonial Society." *Comparative Studies in Society and History* 29 (April 1987): 320–339.

——. *Contracting Colonialism: Translation and Christian Conversion in Tagalog Society under Early Spanish Rule.* Durham, N.C.: Duke University Press, 1993.

——. *Laying the Foundations: Kapampangan Pioneers in the Philippine Church, 1592–2001.* Angeles City: Juan D. Nepomuceno Center for Kapampangan Studies, Holy Angel University, 2002.

Robledo, Liwliwa Tubayan and Phebe Gamata Crismo. *Celebrating a Century of God's Faithfulness: Harris Memorial College and the Deaconess.* Dolores, Taytay, Rizal: Harris Memorial College, 2003.

Rosana, Amalia Tessa. *Towards a De-clone-ialized Theological Education for the Philippines: In Search of a Methodology.* Dissertation, 2002. Ann Arbor: University Microfilms.

San Buenaventura, Steffi. "Filipino Folk Spirituality and Immigration: Mutual Aid to Religion." *Amerasia Journal* 22, 1 (1996).

Santiago, Luciano P. R. *The Hidden Light: The First Filipino Priests.* Quezon City: New Day Publishers, 1987.

Schreurs, Peter. *Carago Antigua, 1521–1910: The Hispanization and Christianization of Agusan, Surigao and East Davao.* Cebu City, Philippines: University of San Carlos, 1989.

Schumacher, John N. "Foreign Missionaries and the Politico-Cultural Orientations of the Roman Catholic Church, 1910–70." *Philippine Studies* 38, 2 (1990): 151–165.

Sin, Jaime L., ed. *A Cry A Song: Selected Writings of Jaime Cardinal L. Sin.* Quezon City: Vibal, 1989.

Sitoy, T. Valentino, Jr. *A History of Christianity in the Philippines: The Initial Encounter.* Quezon City: New Day Publishers, 1985.

Suarez, Oscar S. *Protestantism and Authoritarian Politics; the Politics of Repression and the Future of Ecumenical Witness in the Philippines.* Quezon City: New Day Publishers. 1999.

Suico, Joseph R. *Institutional and Individualistic Dimensions of Transformational Development: The Case of Pentecostal Churches in the Philippines.* Dissertation. 2003. Ann Arbor: University Microfilms.

The Philippine Revolution and the Involvement of the Church. Manila: Social Research Center, University of Santo Tomas, 1986.

The Centernnial Book of the Churches of Christ in the Philippines, Special Commemorative Publication on the Centennial Anniversary of the Churches of Christ in the Philippines, Manila: Centennial Book, 2002.

Trinidad, Ruben F. *A Monument to Religious Nationalism: History and Polity of the IEMELIF Church.* Quezon City: Evangelical Methodist Church in the Philippines, 1999.

Uy, Antolin V. *The State of the Church in the Philippines, 1850–1875: The Correspondence between the Bishops in the Philippines and the Nuncio in Madrid.* Tagaytay City: Divine Word Seminary, 1984.

Vaño, Manolo O. *Christianity, Folk Religion, and Revolution: An Oppressed Nation's Struggle for Liberation.* Quezon City: Giraffe Books, 2002.

Vergara, Alex R., ed. *Waves 1888–1988. The United Methodist Church of Hawaii: A Centennial Jubilee.* Kauai, Hi.: Taylor Publishing, 1988.

Wiegele, Katharine L. *Investing in Miracles: El Shaddai and the Transformation of Popular Catholicism in the Philippines.* Honolulu: University of Hawaii Press, 2004.

Women Journeying in Faith II. Manila: National United Women's Society of Christian Service Publications, 2000.

Youngblood, Robert L. "The Corazon Aquino 'Miracle' and the Philippine Churches." *Asian Survey* 27 (December 1987): 1240–1255.

G. Sociology and Social Conditions

Abihay, Iluminada. *Responsiveness of Rural People to the Folk Media, Folk Drama and the Balitao as Channels for Development Information.* Theses. University of the Philippines at Los Baños, 1978.

ADB (Asian Development Bank) *Poverty and Well-being in the Philippines with Focus on Mindanao Manila: 2001.*

A Look at the World of Indigenous Women: A Research in Selected Areas of Ifugao, Maguindanao, and Bacolod City. Quezon City: Center for Women's Resources, 1999.

Adem, Elisea S. *Urban Poverty: The Case of the Railway Squatters.* Manila: Social Research Center, University of Santo Tomas, 1992.

Aguilar, Filomeno V. Jr., ed. *At Home in the World: Filipinos in Global Migration.* Quezon City: Philippine Migration Research Network and Philippine Social Science Council, 2002.

Alejo, Albert E. SJ. *Generating Energies in Mount Apo: Cultural Politics in a Contested Environment.* Manila: Ateneo De Manila University Press, 2001.

Aluit, Alphonso J. *The Conscience of a Nation: A History of the Red Cross in the Philippines, 1896–1997.* Manila: Galleon Publications, 1997.

Andres, Tomas Quintin D. *Understanding the Filipino.* Quezon City: New Day Publishers, 1987.

Arens, Richards. *Folk Practices and Beliefs of Leyte and Samar.* Tacloban City: Divine Word University, 1982.

Barrios, Maria Josephine and Odine de Guzman. *Body Politics: Essays on Cultural Representations of Women's Bodies.* Quezon City: UP-Center for Women's Studies, 2002.

Brewer, Carolyn. *Holy Confrontation: Religion, Gender, and Sexuality in the Philippines, 1521–1685.* Manila: St. Scholastica's College Institute of Women's Studies, 2001.

Cabigon, Josefina V. *Social Science in Health.* Quezon City: CSSP Publications, University of the Philippines, 1999.

Choy, Catherine Ceniza. *Empire of Care: Nursing and Migration in Filipino–American History.* Durham: Duke University Press, 2003.

Cordova, Dorothy F. and Yosun Park. *The Filipino Community in the United States.* Seattle: Cross Cultural Health Care Program, 2000.

Bishop, Ryan and John Philips. *Postcolonial Urbananism: Southeast Asian Cities and Global Processes.* New York: Routledge, 2003.

Borromeo-Buehler, Soledad. "The Inquilinos of Cavite: A Social Class in Nineteenth-Century Philippines." *Journal of Southeast Asian Studies* 16 (March 1985): 69–98.

Broad, Robin. *Plundering Paradise: The Struggle for the Environment in the Philippines.* Berkeley: University of California Press, 1993.

Campos, J. Edgardo, ed. *Corruption: The Boom and Bust of Asia.* Manila: Ateneo De Manila University Press, 2001.

Canlas, Mamerto. *Land, Poverty, and Politics in the Philippines.* Quezon City: Claretian Publications, 1988.

Castro, Leonardo D. *Social Science in the Philippines.* Quezon City: CSSP Publications, University of the Philippines Press, 1998.

Clark, Gracia. *Gender at Work in Economic Life*. Walnut Creek, Calif.: Altamira Press, 2003.

Clausen, Heather Lynn. *Un(convent)ional Sisterhood: Feminist Catholic Nuns in the Philippines*. Dissertation, 1998. Ann Arbor: University Microfilms.

Collins, Joseph. *The Philippines: Fire on the Rim*. San Francisco: Institute for Food and Development Policy, 1989.

David, Fely and Fely Chin. *Economic and Psychosocial Influences of Family Planning on the Lives of Women in Western Visayas*. Research Triangle Park, N.C.: Women's Studies Project, Family Health International, 1998.

Davis, Leonard. *The Philippines: People, Poverty, and Politics*. Houndmills, Basingstoke, Hampshire: Macmillan, 1987.

De Dios, Emmanuel S., et al. *Poverty, Growth, and the Fiscal Crisis*. Makati, Metro Manila, Philippines: Philippine Institute for Development Studies and International Development Research Center, 1993.

Depth of Field: Photographs of Poverty, Repression, and Struggle in the Philippines. Manila: Photobank Philippines: NCCP/Human Rights Desk, 1987.

Dery, Luis C. "Prostitution in Colonial Manila." *Philippine Studies* 39, 4 (1991): 475–489.

De Vera, Arleen Garcia. *Constituting Community: A Study of Nationalism, Colonialism, Gender and Identity Among the Filipinos in Calfornia, 1919–1946*. Dissertation, 2002. Ann Arbor: University Microfilms.

Dunn, Caroline. *The Politics of Prostitution in Thailand and the Philippines: Policies and Practice*. Clayton, Victoria, Australia: Centre of Southeast Asian Studies, Monash University, 1994.

Dy, Manuel B. *Values in Philippine Culture & Education*. Washington, D.C.: Council for Research in Values & Philosophy, 1994.

Elkins, Richard E., compiler. *A Sampling of Philippine Kinship Patterns*. Manila: Summer Institute of Linguistics VIII, 239 p., 1984.

Ellevera,-Lambverte, Exaltacion. "Marco-level Indication of Upland Poverty." *Philippine Sociological Review* 31, 1–2 (January–June 1983), 19–52.

Espiritu, Yen Le. "Colonial Oppression, Labor Importation, and Group Formation: Filipinos in the U.S." *Ethnic and Racial Studies*. 19:1, 1996.

Filipino Tradition and Acculturation: Reports on Changing Societies. Tokyo: Philippine Studies Program, the Institute of Social Sciences, Waseda University, 1985.

Findley, Sally E. *Rural Development and Migration: A Study of Family Choices in the Philippines*. Boulder, Colo.: Westview Press, 1987.

Fitzgerald, John M. *Family in Crises: The United States, the Philippines, and the Second World War*. Bloomington, Ind.: 1st Books, 2002.

Fox, Robert B. *Religion and Society among the Tagbanuwa of Palawan Island, Philippines*. Manila: National Museum, 1982.

Francisco, Josefa S. and Shalimar Vitan. *Gender Equity and Economic Reforms: Engineering Policy Critique and Advocacy of Philippine NGOs*. Quezon City: Oxfam Great Britain, 1999.

Garcia, Manuel B., Francisco M. Zulueta, and Cynthia T. Caritativo. *Sociology: Focus on Filipino Society and Culture*. Manila: National Book Store, 1984.
Go, Stella P. *The Filipino Family in the Eighties*. Manila: De La Salle University, 1993.
González, N. V. M. *The Father and the Maid: Essays on Filipino Life and Letters*. Diliman, Quezon City: University of the Philippines Press, 1990.
Griffiths, Stephen L. *Emigrants, Entrepreneurs, and Evil Spirits: Life in a Philippine Village*. Honolulu: University of Hawaii Press, 1988.
Guerrero, Sylvia H. and Patricia Licuanan. *Towards Feminist Consciousness: Filipino Mothers and Daughters Tell Their Story*. Manila: UP-University Center for Women Studies, 1997.
Gutierrez, Eric U. *All in the Family: A Study of Elites and Power Relations in the Philippines*. Quezon City: Institute for Popular Democracy, 1992.
Hasik-Kasarinlan: *The Center for Community Services, a Decade of Commitment, 1978–1988*. Quezon City: Center for Community Services, 1989.
Hilario, Vicente M. and Eliseo Quirino, eds. *Thinking for Ourselves: A Collection of Representative Filipino Essays*. 2nd ed. Metro Manila: Cacho Hermanos, 1985.
Hunt, L. Chester, et al., eds. *Sociology in the Philippine Setting*. Quezon City: Phoenix Publishing House, 1987.
Industan, Edmund Melig. "The Family among the Ata Manobo of Davao del Norte." *Philippine Quarterly of Culture & Society* 20, 1 (March 1992): 3–13.
Inosanto, Dan. *Filipino Martial Arts: Serrado Escrima*. Los Angeles, Calif.: Know Now Publishing, 1994.
Jimenez-David, Rina. *Nightmare Journeys: Filipina Sojourns through the World of Trafficking*. Quezon City: Northern Illinois University, 2002.
Joaquin, Nick. *Culture and History: Occasional Notes on the Process of Philippine Becoming*. Manila: Solar Publishing, 1989.
Jocano, F. Landa. *Social Organization in Three Philippine Villages: Explorations in Rural Anthology*. Manila: Centro Escolar University, Research and Development Center, 1988.
———. *Filipino Value System: A Cultural Definition*. Manila: Punlad Research House, 2000.
———. *Filipino Social Organization; Traditional Kinship and Family Organization*. Manila: Punlad Research House, 1998.
Kikuchi, Yasushi, ed. *Philippine Kinship and Society*. Quezon City: New Day Publishers, 1989.
Kiley, Henry W., ed. *Filipino Tribal Religious Experience: II, Sickness, Death and After-Death: Proceedings of the Second Annual Colloquium between Social Scientists and Theologians*. Quezon City: Giraffe Books, 1994.
Labor, Teresa and Jerry Jacobs. "Preserving Multiple Ancestry: Intermarriages and Mixed Births in Hawaii." *Journal of Comparative Family Studies*. 29:3, 1998.
Labrador, Roderick N. *Constructing "Home" and "Homeland": Identity-Making among Filipinos in Hawaii*. Honolulu: University of Hawaii Press, 2003.

Lane, Max R. *The Urban Mass Movement in the Philippines. 1983–1987.* Canberra: Australian National University, 1990.

Loanzon, Jeanette Isabelle. *Hanap-Buhay 2001: Securing the Economic Contributiona of Poor Women through an Innovative, Community-Based, Self-Help, Non-Governmental Development Cum Cooperative.* Manila: UST Publication House, 2001.

Lynch, Frank S.J. *Philippine Peace Corps Survey.* Honolulu: University of Hawaii Press, 1966.

Mangahas, Mahar, *The Philippine Social Climate: From the SWS Surveys.* Manila: Institute for Social Research and Development, 1991.

McAndrew, John P. "Urbanization and Social Differentiation in a Philippine Village." *Philippine Sociological Review* 37, 1–2 (January–June 1989): 26–37.

McCoy, Alfred W. and E. C. de Jesus, eds. *Philippine Social History: Global Trade and Local Transformations.* Honolulu: University of Hawaii Press, 1982.

Medina, Belen T. G. *The Filipino Family: A Text with Selected Readings.* Diliman, Quezon City: University of the Philippines Press, 1991.

———. "The New Wave: Latest Findings on Filipino Immigration in the United States," *Philippine Sociological Review* 32, 1–4 (January–December 1984), 135–143.

Megatrends: The Future of Filipino Children. Manila: Katha Publication, 1998.

Miralao, Virginia A. et al. *The Philippine Social Sciences in the Life of the Nation.* Quezon City: Philippine Social Science Council, 1999.

Mojares, Resil B. *Theater in Society, Society in Theater: Social History of a Cebuano Village 1840–1940.* Quezon City: Ateneo de Manila University Press, 1985.

Nacu, Juanita Santos. *Storytelling: Project Heart to Heart: A Means to Bridge Generational Gap in Post-1995 Filipino Immigration Families.* U.S.: 1998.

Nebres, Bienvenido F.SJ, et al. *Managing Conflict, Building Consensus: The Xavier University House Project.* Cagayan de Oro: Xavier University Press, 2002.

"NGO Futures: Beyond Aid" (Special Topic). *Third World Quarterly: Journal of Emerging Areas* 21, 4 (August 2000).

NGO Study of Selected Villages in the Philippines. Makati, Metro Manila.

Orendain II, Antonio E. *Zamboanga Hermosa: Memories of the Old Town.* Metro Manila: Filipinas Foundation, 1984.

Ortigas, Carmela D. *Poverty Revisited: A Social Psychological Approach to Community Empowerment.* Manila: Ateneo De Manila University, 2001.

Paguntalan, Aileen May. *Nimble Fingers, Clenched Fists: Dynamics of Structure, Agency, Women's Spaces in a Manufacturing Company.* Quezon City: UP-Center for Women's Studies, 2002.

Parreñas, Rhacel Salazar. *Servants of Globalization: Women, Migration, and Domestic Work.* Stanford, Calif.: Stanford University Press, 2001.

Perlas, Gloria Kathleen. *Fostering Community and Identity: Filipino Radio Programs in Hawaii.* M.A. thesis. University of Hawaii at Manoa, 1998.

Pertierra, Raul and Eduardo F. Ugarte, eds. *Cultures & Texts: Representations of Philippine Society.* Honolulu: University of Hawaii Press, 1995.

Philippine Economic and Social Conditions, 1989–90: Findings from Four Surveys. Quezon City: Social Weather Stations, 1990.

Philippine Social Sciences in the Life of the Nation. Quezon City: Philippine Social Science Council, 1999.

Philippine Society: Reflections on Contemporary Issues. Quezon City: Institute of Religion and Culture, 1990.

Rafael, Vicente L. *Figures of Criminality in the Philippines, Indonesia, and Colonial Vietnam.* Ithaca, N.Y.: Southeast Asia Program Publications, Cornell University, 1999.

Reyes, Soledad B., ed. *Reading Popular Culture.* Quezon City: Office of Research and Publications, Anteneo de Manila University, 1991.

Roces, Alfredo & Grace. *Culture Shock! Philippines.* Portland, Ore.; Graphic Arts Center Publishing, 1994.

Rodriguez, Jocelyn Alma A. and Richard L. Meyer. *The Analysis of Saving Behavior: The Case of Rural Households in the Philippines.* Makati, Metro Manila: Philippine Institute for Development Studies, 1988.

Rosaldo, Renato. *Cultural Citizenship in Island Southeast Asia: A Nation Belongs to the Hinterlands.* Berkeley: University of California Press, 2003.

Russel, Susan D. and Clark E. Cunningham, eds. *Changing Lives, Changing Rites: Ritual and Social Dynamics in Philippine and Indonesian Uplands.* Ann Arbor, Mich.: Center for South and Southeast Asian Studies, University of Michigan, 1989.

Salman, Michael. *The Embarrasment of Slavery: Controversies over Bondage and Nationalism in the American Colonial Philippines.* Manila: Ateneo De Manila University Press, 2001.

San Juan, Epifanio. *Only in Struggle: Reflections on Philipine Culture, Politics and Society in a Time of Civil War.* Quezon City: Giraffe Books, 2002.

Schlimgen, Veta. *Filipino American "Nationals" and Transnationals: Forging Community and Citizenship during the Interwar Period.* Dissertation, 2002. Ann Arbor: University Microfilms.

Schult, Volker. *Mindoro, a Social History of a Philippine Island in the 20th Century: A Case Study of a Delayed Developmental Process.* Manila: Divine Word Publications, 1991.

Stoop, Chris De. *They are So Sweet, Sir: The Cruel World of Traffickers in Filipinas and Other Women*; tr. from the French version by Francois & Louise Hubert-Baterna. Manila: Limitless Asia, 1994.

Sibayan, Bonifacio. "Philippine National Cultural Communities." In *Language in Global Perspective: Papers in honor of the 50th Anniversary of the Summer Institute of Linguistics, 1935–1985.* Ed. Benjamin Elson. 613–26. Dallas: SIL 1986.

Silliman, Sidney and Lela Garner Noble. *Organizing for Democracy: NGOs, Civil Society and the Philippine State.* Honolulu: University of Hawaii Press, 1998.

Talisayan, Serafin D. "Distinct Elements of Filipino Values: Cross National Comparisons." Series on Filipino Spiritual Culture No. 3. Quezon City, 1998.

Thapan, Anita Raina. *Sindhi Diaspora in Manila, Hong Kong, and Jakarta.* Manila: Ateneo De Manila University Press, 2002.

Turner, Mark M. *National Level Elites in the Philippines, 1945–84: A Framework for Analysis.* Hull, England: University of Hull, Centre for South-East Asian Studies, 1984.

Warren, James Francis. *Iranum and Balangigi: Globalization, Maritime, Raiding and the Birth of Ethnicity.* Singapore: Singapore University Press, 2002.

Yengoyan, Aram A. and Perla Q. Makil, eds. *Philippine Society and the Individual: Selected Essays of Frank Lynch, 1949–1976.* Ann Arbor: University of Michigan Press, 1984.

H. Women

Abao, Carmele V.; Karen N. Tañada.; Jurgette Honculada A. *Networking towards Women's Empowerment: A Profile of the Women's Action Network Development.* Manila: Diwata Foundation, 1997.

Abaya, Ma. Concepcion O. *Feminine Voices: Towards a New Millenium.* Manila: NCCA, 2001.

Aguilar, Delia D. "Engendering the Philippine Revolution: An Interview with Vicvic (Interview with Victoria Justiniani)." *Monthly Review* 45 (September 1993): 25–37.

Ancheta, Herminia M. and Michaela Beltran-Gonzalaz. *Filipino Women in Nation Building: A Compilation of Brief Biographies: Dedicated to the Decade of Women Proclaimed by the United Nations, 1975–1985.* Quezon City: Phoenix Publishing House, 1984.

Anderson, James N., Robert R. Reed and Gaspar L. Sardalla. *Critical Issues in Philippine Research: A Selected & Annotated Literature Review on the Women's Movement, Conflict in Luzon's Cordillera, Muslim Autonomy & Recent Political Resistance.* Berkeley: University of California, Berkeley: Centers for South & Southeast Asia Studies, 1996.

Angangco, Ofelia Regala, Laura L. Samson and Teresita M. Albino. *Status of Women in the Philippines: A Bibliography with Selected Annotation.* Quezon City: Alemar-Phoenix, 1980.

Añonevo, Estrella and Augustus Añonuevo. *Coming Home: Women, Migration, and Reintegration.* Manila: Balikbayan Foundation, 2002.

Barrameda, Teresita V. and Lea Espallardo. *Breaking Silence: A Nationwide Informance Tour for the Prevention of Violence Against Women in the Family.* Quezon City: Philippine Educational Theater Association, 2000.

Bobis, Merlinda C. *Flights Is Song (Ang Lipad ang Awit Sa Apat na Hangin).* Manila: St. Scholastica, 1990.

Brigham, Susan. *Women Migrant Workers in the Global Economy: The Role of Critical Feminist Pedagogy for Filipino Domestic Workers*. Dissertation, 2002. University Microfilms.

Buensalido, Joy and Abe Florendo. *100 Women of the Philippines: Celebrating Filipina Womandhood in the New Millennium*. Makati City: Buensalido & Associates, 1999.

Buttny, Richard. "Legitimation Techniques for Intermarriage: Accounts of Motives for Intermarriage from U.S. Servicemen and Philippine Women." *Communication Quarterly* 35 (Spring 1987): 125–143.

Cabaraban, Magdalena C. and Maria Teresa Sharon Linog. *Experiences in Charity Health Care: Legal and Ethical Implications*. Manila: Reproductive, Health, Rights and Ethics Center for Studies and Training, University of the Philippines, 2001.

Cabaraban, Magdalena C. and Chona Echavez. *Situation Analysis of Women in Low-Income Communities in the Visayas and Mindanao*. Cagayan de Oro City: Xavier University, 1999.

Carbo, Nick and Eileen Tabios. *Babaylan: An Anthology of Filipina American Writers*. San Francisco: Aunt Lute Books, 2000.

Castillo, Evangeline T. et al. *Case Investigation of the Participation of Women in Reforestation in the Philippines*. Laguna: Rexel O. Publication, 1999.

Caycayan, Agnes Miclat. *The Shaman's Woman's Dream: How Can We Worship God without the Forest?* Davao City: Hinabi Women's Circle. 2002.

Choy, Catharine Ceniza. *The Export of Women Power: A Transitional History of Filipino Nurses Migrating in the United States*. Dissertation, 1998. Ann Arbor: University Microfilms.

Corcuera, Sigrid M. *Anger in Filipino Women. A Phenomentological Study*. Dissertation. 2001. Ann Arbor: University Microfilms.

Cruz, Coring V. *The Emerging Woman: A Book by a Woman for Women & about Women*. Metro Manila: SVC Center for Self-Management, 1985.

Diaz, Josefina C. *Kababaihan: Kababaihan para sa Kalayaan: Filipino Women in the Struggle for Freedom*. Manila: Socio-Pastoral Insitute, 1997.

Doan, Rebecca Miles and Barry M. Popkin. "Women's Work and Infant Care in the Philippines." *Social Science & Medicine* 36, 3 (February 1993): 297–304.

Doran, Christine. "Spanish and Mestizo Women of Manila." *Philippine Studies* 41, 2 (1993): 269–286.

Edwards, Louise P. and Mina Roces. *Women's Suffrage in Asia: Gender, Nationalism, and Democracy*. New York: Routledge, 2004.

Ehrenreich, Barbara and Arlie Hochschild. *Global Woman: Nannies, Maids, and Sex Workers in the New Economy*. New York: Metropolitan/Owl Books, 2004.

Ehrenreich, Barbara and Arlie Hochschild. *Global Woman*. New York: Russell Publication, 2001.

Eviota, Elizabeth Uy. *The Political Economy of Gender; Women and the Sexual Division of Labour in the Philippines*. London, England: Zed Books, 1992.

Exploratory Survey on the Skill Training Needs of Rural Women in a Selected Area. Manila: Bureau of Women and Minors, Ministry of Labor and Employment, 1985.

Feliciano, Myrna S. and Flordeliza Trinidad. *Laws on Women.* Manila: C. Vargas Publication and National Commission on the Role of Women, 2001.

Fernandez, Doreen and Jonathan Chua. *Feasts and Feats: Festschrift for Doreen Fernandez.* Manila: Ateneo De Manila University Press, 2002.

From the Eyes of the Cordillera Women: Cordillera Women's Education and Resource Center. Baguio City: Cordillera Women's Education and Resource Center, 1991.

Hidalgo, Cristina Pantoja *Pinay.* Manila: Ateneo De Manila University Press, 2002.

Hidalgo, Rosa Linda P. *The Integration of Women in Philippine Development.* Quezon City: University of the Philippines School of Economics, 1985.

Hutchison, Jane. "Women in the Philippines Garments Exports Industry." *Journal of Contemporary Asia* 22, 4 (1992): 471–489.

Illo, Jeanne Frances I. *Impact of Irrigation Development on Women and Their Households: The Case of the Aslong Project.* Quezon City, Philippines: Institute of Philippine Culture, Ateneo de Manila University, 1987.

Illo, Jeanne Frances I., et al. *Fishers, Traders, Farmers, Wives: The Life Stories of Ten Women in a Fishing Village.* Manila, Philippines: Institute of Philippine Culture, Ateneo de Manila University, 1990.

Jimenez-David, Rina. *Community-based Approaches to Violence against Women: The Pilipina Experience.* Quezon City: PILIPINA, 1999.

———. *Overview of the Philippine Women's Movement.* Quezon City: PILIPINA, 1999.

———. *Chronicle of the Women's Party.* Quezon City: PILIPINA, 1999.

Labayen, Fe Corazon Tengco. *In Every Women: Asian Women's Journey to Feminist Awakening.* Manila: Institute of Women' Status. St. Scholastica College, 1998.

Lacar, Luis Q. "The Emerging Role of Muslim Women." *Philippine Studies* 39, 1 (1991): 3–22.

Lacsamana, Anne E. *Colonialism, Globalization, and the Filipina Mail-Order Bride.* Dissertation, 2000. Ann Arbor: University Microfilms.

Leyco-Reyes, Soccoro. *Strengthening the Linkage between Selected Women's Groups and Women in Government.* Quezon City: Congressional Research and Training Service, 1991.

Lindo-McGovern, Ligaya. *Filipino Peasant Women: Exploitation and Resistance.* Philadelphia: University of Pensylvania Press, 1997.

Lucero, Rosario Cruz. *Herstory.* Manila: St. Scholastica, 1990.

Miralao, Virginia A. *Male and Female Status and Changing Roles of Women.* Quezon City: Institute of Philippine Culture, Ateneo de Manila University Press, 1985.

Pagaduan, Maureen. "National Liberation and Women's Liberation: The Split View." *Diliman Review* 40, 4 (1992): 26–35.

Philippine Development Plan for Women, 1989–1992. Manila: Republic of the Philippines, 1989.

Philippine Development Report on Women. Manila, Philippines: Office of the President, National Commission on the Role of Filipino Women, 1989.

Popkin, Barry M., David K. Guilkey and John S. Akin. "Nutrition, Lactation, and Birth Spacing in Filipino Women." *Demography* 30 (August 1993): 333–352.

Quintos,-Deles, Teresita. *Filipino Women's Advocacy and Action for Peace.* Quezon City: PILIPINA, 1999.

Richter, Linda K. "The Constitutional Rights of Women in the Post-Marcos Philippines." *Pilipinas* 11, 1 (Fall 1990): 33–46.

Salleh, Ariel. *Ecofeminism as Politics: Nature, Marx and the Postmodern.* Manila: St. Scholastica, 1999.

Santiago, Lilia Quindoza. *Sa Ngalan ng Ina: Sandaang Taon ng Tulang Feminista sa Pilipinas, 1889–1979.* Quezon City: University of the Philippines Press, 1997.

Santos, Aida Fulleros. *The Debt Crisis: A Treadmill of Poverty for Filipino Women.* Manila: KALAYAAN, 1989.

Situation of Children and Women in the Philippines 1990. Government of the Republic of the Philippines, United Nations Children's Fund. Manila: Government of the Philippines, 1990.

Soriano, Rafaelita Hilario, ed. *Women in the Philippine Revolution.* Manila: Heritage Publishing House, 1995.

Spring, Anita. *Women Farmers and Commercial Ventures: Increasing Food Security in Developing Countries.* Boulder, Colo.: L. Rienner Publishers, 2002.

Sulong Filipina! A Compilation of Filipina Women Centennial Awardees. Manila: National Centernnial Commission, 1999.

Tan, Emily Ledesma. *Feminist Consciousness: Motifs from Philippine Postcolonial Literature Written in English by Filipina Women.* Dissertation, 2001. Ann Arbor: University Microfilms.

Tengco, Labayen. *In Every Woman: Asian Women's Journey to Feminist Awakening.* Manila: St. Scholastica, 1990.

Torres, Amaryllis Tiglao, et al. *Mga Ina ng Bayan: Life Stories of Filipino and Japanese Women Community Leaders.* Quezon City: Milflores Publication. 2002.

Williams, Lindy and Lita J. Domingo. "The Social Status of Elderly Women and Men within the Filipino Family." *Journal of Marriage and the Family* 55 (May 1993): 415–426.

Women's International Solidarity Affair in the Philippines (WISAP) February 25–March 8, 1986. GABRIELA Third National Congress, March 13–14, 1986. San Juan, Philippines: GABRIELA, 1986.

Villanueva, Marianne and Virginia Cerenio. *Going Home to a Landscape: Writings by Filipinas.* Corvallis, Ore.: CALYX Books, 2003.

I. Mass Media and Journalism

Barrameda, Nes. *Media in Court: The Criminal Justice System: Guidebook for Reporters.* Manila: Center for Media Freedom & Responsibility, 1997.

Block, De Los Reyes, Mamerta. *The Price of Freedom: The Story of a Courageous Manila Journalist*. Manassas, Va.: Trinity Rivers Publication, 2003.

The Book of Philippine Newspaper Cartoons. Manila: Samahang Kartunista ng Pilipinas and the Philippine Press Institute, 1990.

Braid-Rosario, Florangel and Ramon Tuazon R. *Media as a Battlefield: Coverage of War in Iraq*. Manila: Philippine Communication Centrum, 2003.

Braid-Rosario, Florangel, ed. *Comunication and Society*: The Philippine Context, Manila: Cacho Publishing House, 1991.

Buhain, Dominador D. *A History of Publishing in the Philippines*. Quezon City: D.D. Buhain, 1998.

Calero, J. J. *Movers and Shakers in the History of Philippine Advertising*. Manila: GMA Foundation and J. Walter Thompson Co., 2000.

Campbell, Dennis. *International Communication Law*. London: Ashford Press, 1999. *Changing Lenses: Women's Perspectives on Media*. Quezon City: Isis International Manila, 2001.

Coronel, Sheila S. *From Loren to Marimar: The Philippine Media in the 1990s*. Quezon City: Philippine Center for Investigative Journalism, 1999.

De La Cruz, Pennie Azarcon. *GMA Gold: Fifty Years of Broadcast History*. Manila: GMA Network, 2001.

———. *Images of Women in Philippine Media*. Manila: Asian Social Institute, 1988.

Deocampo, Nick. *Cine: Spanish Influences on Early Cinema in the Philippines*. Manila: National Commission for Culture and the Arts, 2003.

Engendering Communication Policy in Asia: Papers Presented at the Media and Gender Policy Conference in Antipolo, Philippines: The Asian Network of Women in Communication, 1997.

Foundation for Media Alternatives, Philippines. Manila: Foundation for Media Alternatives, 2001.

Garth, Jowett and James M. Linton. *Movies as Mass Communication*. 2nd edition. New York: Sage, 1992.

Guillermo, Artemio R. *A Readership Survey of Taliba: A Philippine Newspaper.* Dissertation, 1972. Syracuse University. Ann Arbor: University Microfilms.

———. "Decline and Fall of the Freest Press in Asia." *Quill* 63, 4 (April 1975).

———. "Worcester Libel Case and Philippine Journalism." *Bulletin American Historical Collecion* III, 3 (July 1975).

———. "The Tagalog Press of the Philippines." *Silliman Journal* XXI, 4 (4th Quarter, 1974).

Kudeta: the Challenge to Philippine Democracy. Manila: Philippine Center for Investigative Journalism, 1990.

Lucas, Francis B. *A Radio Broadcasting Model for Rural Women and Farm Households: A Philippine Case Study on Distance Education*. Bangkok; FAO, 1999.

Harnett, Richard M. and Billy Ferguson. *Unipress, United Press International Covering the 20th Century.* Golden, Colo.: Fulcrum Publishers, 2003.

Katz, Elihu and Tomas Szesko, eds. *Mass Media and Social Change*. New York: Sage, 1981.

Maslog, Crispin C. *A Manual for Peace Reporting in Mindanao*. Manila: Philippine Press Institute, 1990.

Matutina, Cecile. *Pinoy Television: The Story of ABS-CBN: The Medium of Our Lives*. Quezon City: ABS-CBN Broadcasting, 1999.

Minges, Michael. *Pinoy Internet Philippines case study*. Geneva, Switzerland: International Communication Union, 2002.

Navarro, Atoy. *Wika, Panitikan, Sining, at Himagsikan*. Lunsod Quezon: LIKAS, 1998.

Rao, Madanmohan. *News Media and New Media*. Singapore: Eastern Universities Press, 2003.

Reyes, Cid. *Adboard: 25 Years of Self-Regulation*. Makati City: Advertising Board of the Philippines, 2000.

Rodriguez, Isacio Rodriquez y Jesus Fernandez Alvarez. *La Revolucion Hispano–Filipina en la prensa: Diario de Manila y Heraldo de Madrid*. Madrid: Agencia Española de Cooperacion Internacional, 1998.

Santos, Teodoro M. and Ma. Catalina Tolentino. *The State of Book Writing and Publishing in the University of the Philippines*. Quezon City: Office of Research Coordination University of the Philippines, 1997.

Smith, Desmond. *Democracy and the Philipine Media, 1983–1993*. Lewiston, N.Y.: Edwin Mellen Press, 2000.

Tagura, Pablito M. *A Critical Analysis of Technology Transfer Ideology, and Development in the Context of Communication Technology in the Philippines*. Dissertation, 1997. Ann Arbor: University Microfilms.

Tan, Bienvenido A. *The Public Has the Right to Know*. Manila: Bookmark, 1985.

Teodoro, Luis V. and Rosalinda *Kabatay. Mass Media Laws and Regulations in the Philippine*. Singapore: Asian Media Information and Communication Centre, 1998.

Teodoro, Luis and Melinda Q. de Jesus, eds. *The Filipino Press and Media, Democracy, and Development*. Pasig City: Anvil Publications, 2001.

Terrorism and Media. Manila: Philippine Communication Centrum, 2002.

Tolentino, Roland B. *National/Transnational: Subject Formation, Media and Cultural Politics in and on the Philippines*. Quezon City: Ateneo De Manila University Press, 2001.

Transition, 1986–1990: The Chronicle as an Agent of Change. Manila: Chronicle Publishing, 1990.

Yambot, Isagani and Letty Magsanoc-Jimenez. *Page One: Philippine Daily Inquirer Front Pages. 1985–1995*. Makati City: Philippine Daily Inquirer, 1998.

PART 8. CULTURE

A. Architecture

Araneta-Cruz, Gemma. *Stones of Faith: Roman Catholic Churches in the Philippines*. Manila: PAMATEC, 1998.

Brody, David Eric. *Fantasy Realized: The Philippines, Orientalism, and Imperialism in Turn-of-the-Century Visual Culture.* Dissertation, 1997. Ann Arbor: University Microfilms.

Dacanay, Julian E., Jr. *Ethnic Houses and Philippines Artistic Expression.* Kapitolyo, Pasig, Metro Manila: One-Man Show Studio, 1988.

De Viana, Lorelei D. C. *Three Centuries of Binondo Architecture, 1594–1898. A Socio-Historical Perspective.* España, Manila: University of Santo Tomas Press, 2001.

Ebro-Dakudao, Michaelangelo. "Pre-War Japanese Housebuilders in the Philippines: Views and Images." *Philippine Quarterly of Culture & Society* 21, 2 (June 1993): 113–145.

Funtecha, Henry Florida and Melanie J. Padilla. *Historical Landmarks and Monuments of Iloilo.* Iloilo City, Philippines: Visayan Studies Program, U. P. in the Visayas, 1987.

Ipac-Alarcon, Norma. *Philippine Architecture during the Pre-Spanish and Spanish Periods.* Manila: Santo Tomas University Press, 1991.

Jose, Regalado Trota. *Simbahan: Church Art in Colonial Philippines, 1565–1898.* Metro Manila, Philippines: Ayala Foundation, 1992.

———. *Visita Iglesia Bohol: A Guide to Historic Churches.* Manila: National Commission for Culure and the Arts, 2001.

Klassen, Winand. *Architecture in the Philippines: Filipino Building in a Cross-Cultural Context.* Cebu City, Philippines: USC, 1986.

Santos, Ruperto C. *Manila Cathedral: Basilica of the Immaculae Conception.* Manila: The Archdiocesan Archives of Manila, 1987.

B. Arts

Aldecoa, Ena Maria R. and Corazon R. Dioquino. *Compendium of the Humanities: Musical Arts.* Metro Manila: National Research Council of the Philippines, 1998.

Capino, Jose Bernard T. *Cinema and the Spectacle of Colonialism: American Documentary Film and (Post) Colonial Philippines, 1898–1998.* Dissertation, 2002. Ann Arbor: University Microfilms.

Casal, Gabriel, et al. *The People and Art of the Philippines.* Los Angeles: Museum of Cultural History, University of California, Los Angeles, 1981.

Centennial Honor for the Arts. Manila: Cultural Center of the Philippines, 1999.

CPP Encyclopedia of Philippine Art. 10 v. Manila, Philippines: Cultural Center of the Philippines, 1999.

David, Joel. *Wages of Cinema: Film in Philippine Perspective.* Quezon City: University of the Philippines Press, 1998.

Enriquez, Milagros S. *Bulakeña: Anyo at Kasaysayan ng Baro't Saya.* Malolos, Bulacan: Center for Bulacan Studies, 1999.

Flores, Patrick D. *Painting History: Revisions in Philippine Colonial Art.* Quezon City: University of the Philippines, 1998.

Francisco, Juan R. *Selected Essays on Mindanao Art and Culture.* Marawi City: Mindanao State University. *Mindanao Journal* 14, 1988.

Galende, Pedro G. and Jose Regalado. *San Agustin Art & History*. Manila: San Agustin Museum, 2000.

Guillermo, Alice C. *Sining Biswal: An Essay on Philippine Visual Arts*. Manila: Sentrong Pangkultura ng Pilipinas, 1989.

———. *Image to Meaning*. Manila: Ateneo De Manila University Press, 2001.

Guillermo, Alice C. et al. *Sculpture in the Philippines: From Anito to Assemblage, and Other Essays*. Manila: Metropolitan Museum of Manila, 1991.

Jose, Regalado Trota. *Images of Faith Religious Ivory Carvings from the Philippines*. Pacific Asia Museum, 1994.

Kasilag, Lucretia R. "The Performing Arts Scene: 1987–1988. In *Fookien Times Philippine Yearbook*, 1987–1988. Ed. Betty Go Belmonte.

Leitz, Rudolf J. The Philippines in the 19th Century: A Collection of Prints. Mandaluyong City: RLI Gallery Systems, 1998.

Matilac, Rosalie S. *San Miguel de Mayumo: Growth, Decline and Renewal of a Museum Town: An Environmental Perspective*. Quezon City: Environmental Center of the Philippines Foundation, 1997.

Pilar, Santiago Albano and Imelda Cajipe-Endaya. *Limbag Kamay: 400 Years of Philippine Printmaking*. Philippines: Cultural Center of the Philippines, 1993.

Ramas. Wilhelmina Q. *Studies in Pre-war Sugbuanon Theatre*. Quezon City: University of the Philippines, 2001.

———. *Sugbuanon Theatre from Sotto to Rodriguez and Kabahar: An Introduction to Pre-War Sugbuanon Drama*. Quezon City: University of the Philippine Press, 1982.

Reyes, Cid. *Conversations on Philippine Art*. Manila: Cid Reyes and the Cultural Center of the Philippines, 1989.

Reyes, Soledad S. *Pagbasa ng Panitikan at Kulturang Popular: Piling Sanaysay, 1976–1996*. Quezon City: Ateneo De Manila University Press, 1997.

Sampung Taon Cine: Philippine CinSema. 1990–1999. Manila: National Commission for Culture and the Arts, 2002.

Tolentino, Roland B. *Geopolitics of the Visible: Essays on Philippine Film Culture*. Quezon City: Ateneo De Manila University Press, 2000.

Ty-Navarro, Virginia and Paul C. Zafaralla. *Carlos V. Francisco, the Man and Genius of Philippine Art*. Makati, Metro Manila: Ayala Museum, 1985.

Wiley, Mark V. *Arnis: History and Methods of the Filipino Martial Arts*. Rutland, Vt.: Charles F. Tuttle, 2001.

Zafra, Galileo S. *Balagtasan: Kasaysayan at Antolohiya*. Quezon City: Ateneo De Manila University Press, 1999.

C. Customs and Festivals

Demetrio, Francisco R. "The Bukidnon Myths of Sickness, Death and Afterlife." *Philippine Studies* 42, 4 (1994): 415–430.

Fernandez, Doreen. *Palayok: Philippine Food through Time, on Site and on the Pot.* Makati City: Bookmark, 2000.

Funtecha, Henry F. and Zoilo S. Andrada. *Popular Festivals in Western Visayas.* Iloilo City, Philippines: Center for West Visayan Studies, College of Arts and Sciences, University of the Philippines in the Visayas, 1992.

Gatan, Marino. *Ibanag Indigenous Religious Beliefs: A Study in Culture and Education.* Manila: Centro Escolar University Research and Development Center, 1981.

Gorospe, Vitaliano R. "Mount Banahaw: The Power Mountain from Ritualism to Spirituality." *Philippine Studies* 40, 2 (1992): 204–218.

Javellana, Rene, Fernando N. Zialcita, and Elizabeth Reyes. *Filipino Style.* Singapore: Periplus Editions, 1997.

King, Richard and Timothy Craig. *Global Goes Local: Popular Culture in Asia.* Vancouver: UBC Press, 2002.

Lawless, Robert. "A Comparative Analysis of Two Studies on 'Utang Na Loob'." *Philippine Sociological Review* 29, 3 (July 1966), 14–16.

Lieben, Richard W. *Cebuano Sorcery: Malign Magic in the Philippines.* Quezon City: New Day Publishers, 1994.

Marinas, Amante P. *Pananandata: History and Techniques of the Daga, Yantok, Balisong, and Other Traditional Weapons of the Philippines.* Boulder, Colo.: Paladin Press, 2002.

Mercado, Leandro N., ed. *Old Culture, Renewed Religions: The Search for Cultural Identity in a Changing World.* Manila: Logos Publications, 2001.

Miranda-Feliciano, Evelyn. *Of Songs, Words and Gestures: Rethinking Filipino Liturgy.* Quezon City: Institute for Studies in Asia Church and Culture, 2000.

Mojares, Resil B. *Waiting for Mariang Makiling: Essays in Philippine Cultural History.* Quezon City: Ateneo De Manila Press, 2002.

O'Boyle, Lily Gamboa, et al. *Philippine Hospitality: A Gracious Tradition of the East.* New York: Acacia, 1988.

Peterson, Jean Treloggen. "Generalized Extended Family Exchange: A Case from the Philippines." *Journal of Marriage and the Family* 55 (August 1993): 570–584.

Philippine Folk Science. Quezon City: University of the Philippines, Institute for Science and Mathematics Education Development, 1998.

Prill-Brett, June. *The Bontok Chuno Feast in the Context of Modernization.* Baguio City, Philippines: Cordillera Studies Center, University of the Philippines College Baguio, 1989.

Quirino, Carlos. *The Manners and Customs, and Beliefs of the Philippine Inhabitants of Long Ago; Being Chapters of a Late 16th Century Manila.* Manuscript Transcribed and Translated and Annotated by Carlos Quirino and Mauro Garcia. Manila: Bureau of Printing, 1961.

Quisumbing, Agnes R. "Intergenerational Transfers in Philippine Rice Villages: Gender Differences in Traditional Inheritance Customs." *Journal of Development Economics* 43 (April 1994): 167–195.

Ramos, Maximo D. *Creatures of Philippine Lower Mythology*. Quezon City: University of the Philippines Press, 1971.

Russell, Susan D. "The Grand Cañao: Ethnic and Ritual Dilemmas in an Upland Philippine Tourist Festival." *Asian Folklore Studies* 48, 2 (1989): 647–663.

Smart, John E. "The Flight from Agiwan: A Case Study in the Socio-Cultural Dynamics of an Isneg Marriage Negotiation." *Philippine Quarterly of Culture & Society* 21, 4 (December 1993): 330–343.

Sontohot, Felicitas S. "Rites and Rituals of the Sangils." *Philippine Studies* 42, 2 (1994): 177–193.

Torre, Visitacion R. de la. *The Barong Tagalog: The Philippines' National Wear.* Manila: V. R. de la Torre, 1986.

Wiley, Mark. *Arnis: History and Development of the Filipino Martial Arts*. Boston: Tuttle Publishers, 2001.

D. Music and Dance

Aldecoa, Ena Maria R. and Corazon R. Dioquino. *Compendium of the Humanities: Musical Arts*. Metro Manila: National Research Council of the Philippines, 1998

Baes, Jonas. "Ya-ye-yo-na-i-yu-nan: Swaying in the Vocal Music of the Iraya People of Mindoro, Philippines." *Ethnomusicology* 31 (Spring/Summer 1987): 229–239.

Baes, Jonas and Amapola Baes. "East and West Syntheses or Cultural Hegemony? Questions on the use of Indigenous Elements in Philippine Popular Music." *Perfect Beat* 4 (1) 1988. 4–55.

Baños, Raymundo C. *Filipino Music and Theater*. Quezon City: Manlapaz Publishing, 1969.

Buenaventura, Cristina Lacónico. *The Theatre in Manila, 1846–1946*. Manila: De La Salle University Press, 1994.

Castro, Christi-Ånne Salazar. *Music, Politics, and the Nation at the Cultural Center of the Philippines.* Dissertation, 2001. Ann Arbor: University Microfilms.

Dioquino, Corazon C. "Musicology in the Philippines." *Acta Musicologica* v. 54 (1982): 1–15.

Feliciano, Francisco. *Four Asian Composers: The Influence of Tradition in Their Works*. Quezon City: New Day Publishers, 1983.

Fernandez, Doreen. "Philippine Popular Culture: Dimensions and Directions." *Philippine Sudies* 29, 1981.

Gamboa-Alcantara, Ruby. *Ritual Sayaw sa Lumang Makati: Isang Panata para kina San Pedro, San Pablo, at Virgen de la Rosa* 55. Manila; Rex XII, 1994.

Goquingco, Leonor Orosa. *The Dances of the Emerald Isles: A Great Philippine Heritage*. Quezon City, Metro Manila: Ben-Lor Publishers, 1980.

Hess, Sally. *Body, Movement, and Culture: Kinesthetic and Visual Symbolism in a Philippine Community*. Philadelphia: University of Pennsylvania Press, 1992.

Hila, Antonio C. *Musika: An Essay on Philippine Music.* Manila: Sentrong Pangkultura ng Pilipinas, 1989.

Kalinangang Pilipino: Cultural Resources and Communications Services: Cultural Center of the Philippines: The National Coordinating Center for the Arts, 1989.

Lockard, Craig A. *Dance of Life: Popular Music and Politics in Southeast Asia.* Honolulu: University of Hawaii Press, 1998.

Maceda, Jose. *Gongs and Bamboo: A Panorama of Philippine Musical Instruments.* Quezon City: Ateneo De Manila University Press, 1999.

Mangahas, Fe. "The State of Philippine Music: Politics and Culture: The Philippine Experience." Manila: Educational Theater Association, 1984.

McAndrew, John P. *People of Power: A Philippine World-View of Spirit Encounters.* Manila: Ateneo De Manila University Press, 2001.

Mirano, Elena Rivera. *Ang mga tradisyonal na musikang pantinig sa lumang Bauan, Batangas.* Manila: National Commission on Culture and the Arts, 1997.

Mirano, Elena Rivera and Neal M. Oshima. *Subli: Isang Sayaw Sa Apat Na Tinig— One Dance in Four Voices.* Manila: Museo ng.

Ness, Sally Ann. "Originality in the Postcolony: Choreographing the Neoethnic Body of Philippine Ballet." *Cultural Anthropology* 12, 1 (1997): 64–108.

Otto, Steven Walter. *The Maranao Kakolingtang: An Approach to the Repertoire.* Iligan City, Philippines: Coordination Center for Research & Development, Mindanao State University, 1985.

Reichl, Karl. *The Oral Epic: Performance and Music.* Berlin: VWB, Verlag fur Wissenschaft und Bildung, 2000.

Santos, Ramon P. "Philippine Traditional Music: Sources and Resources Revivalism and Modernism in the Musics of Post-Colonial Asia." *Bulawan* 2. *Philippine Arts and Culture*, Manila: National Commission for Culture and the Arts. 34–61, 1991.

Reyes, R. "Philippine Sound and the Musical Gold Rush." *Far Eastern Economic Review* 17 (11), 1988.

Sunico, Raul M., et al. *Mga Awit Himagsikan: Songs of the Philippine Revolution of 1896–1898.* Quezon City: Tawid Publications, 1997.

Union Catalog on Philippine Culture: Music. Manila: Cultural Center of the Philippines Library, 1989.

Villa, Lila. "Romance and Corrido: A Comparison of Some Folktales Motifs in English and the Philippine metrical romances." *Social Science and Humanities Review* 17 (1952), 8 20.

E. Language and Linguistics

Antworth, Evan L. ed. *Folktale Texts. Studies in Philippine Linguistics* 2 (2). Manila: Linguistic Society of the Philippines and SIL. VII, 210 p.

Benton, Richard. "The Philippine Bilingual Education Progra: Education for the Masses or Preparation of a New Elite?" *Philippine Journal of Linguistics* 11, 2 (December 1984), 1–14.

Bernabe, Emma J. Fonacier. *Language Policy Formation, Programming, Implementation, and Evaluation in Philippine Education (1565–1974).* Manila: Linguistic Society of the Philippines, 1987.

Busenitz, Marilyn J. "Core Bibliograpphy of the Philippines" *Notes on Linguistics* 7:3–20, 1978.

Burton, Scott Lynn. "A Case Study of Lexical Borrowing between Languages: The East Mindanao and Manobo Languages. M.A. Thesis. University of Texas at Arlington XII, Summer Institute of Linguistics, 1996.

De Leon, Bayani. *Baybayin. The Ancient Script of the Philippines. A concise manual.* Bycynthium Treasures, Paramus, N.J.: 1992.

Enrique, Virgilio C. "Filipino Values: Towards a New Interpretation (Using Local) Language as a Resource." *Philippine Studies Newsletter* 16, 3 (October 1988), 29–34.

Espiritu, Precy. *Intermediate Ilokano: An Integrated Language and Culture Reading Text.* Honolulu: University of Hawaii Press, 2004.

Francisco, Juan R. "Bhinneka Tunggal Eka: The Development of a National Language in the Philippines." *Centennial Issue Asian Studies* 34 (1998): 112–120.

Gonzales, Andrew. "An Overview of Language and Development." *Journal of Multilingual and Multicultural Development* 14, 5–23.

Gonzalez, Andrew. *Language Surveys in the Philippines, 1966–1984.* Manila: DLSU Press, 1986.

———, ed. *The Role of English and Its Maintenance in the Philippines: The Transcript, Consensus, and Papers on the Solidarity Seminar on Languages and Development.* Manila: Solidaridad Publishing House, 1989.

Hall, William C. "Ethnic Minority Languages within the Wider Philippine Social Context." *International Journal of Sociology of Language* 88: 59–68, 1991.

Hidalgo, Cristina Pantoja and Priscelina Patajo-Legasto, eds. *Philippine Post-Colonial Studies: Studies on Languages and Literature.* Quezon City: University of the Philippines Press, 1993.

Manuel, E. Arsenio. *Chinese Words in the Tagalog Language.* Manila: Filipiniana, 1948.

Metillo, Loreben Daday and Wynn D. Laidig. *Understanding Cebuano Grammar II. Book 2. Advanced Grammar.* Davao City: Philippine Baptist Mission SBC, V, 118 p., 1996.

Maramba, R. E. "Filipino or Tagalog with a New Label?" *Sunday Philippine Inquirer Magazine,* August 7, 1994.

McFarland, Curtis D. "Subgrouping and Number of the Philippine Languages or How Many Philippine Languages Are There?" *Philipine Journal of Linguistics.* 25 (1994) 75–84.

Milambiling, Joyce. "Language Diversity, Educational Policy, and Language Rights in the Philippines." The Linguistic Association of Korea (2002) 6, 62–84.

Newell, Leonard E., comp. *Batad Ifuago Dictionary with Ethnographic Notes.* Manila, Philippines: Linguistic Society of the Philippines, 1993.

Pallesen, A. Kemp. Culture Contact and Language Convergence. Manila: Linguistic Society of the Philippines, 1985.

Parnes, Samuel Will. *A History of Filipino Rondalla Music and Musicians in Southern Califorua.* Dissertation, 2000.

Peñaflorida, Andrea H. *Points of Departure: Essays on Language Pedagogy.* Manila: De La Salle University Press, 2002.

Pittman, Richard S. *Notes on the Dialect Geography of Philippines.* Grand Forks: Summer Institute of Linguistics of the University of North Dakota, X, 116 p., 1953.

Ramos, Teresita V. *Conversational Tagalog: A Functional-Situational Approach.* Manila: Merriam & Webster, Filipino Word Book. Honolulu: Bess Press, 1993.

Rosales, Antonio-Ma. *A Study of a 16th Century Tagalog Manuscript on the Ten Commandments: Its Significance and Implications: Juan de Oliver's "Declaracion de Los Mandamientos de la Ley de Dios."* Quezon City: University of the Philippines Press, 1984.

Schachter, P. *Tagalog.* In *The World's Major Languages.* Ed. B. Comrie. 936–935. New York: Oxford University Press.

Schirmer, P. and S. R. Shalom, eds. *The Philippine Reader.* Boston: South End Press, 1987.

Schwalm, Claudia. *Tagalog–English Picture Dictionary.* Alameda, Calif.: Cultural Connections, 1994.

Scott, M. "Confusion of Tongues: "English vs. Filipino in the Language Debate." *Far Eastern Economic Review* 145 (July 6, 1989) 44–46.

Sibayan, Bonifacio and Andrew Gonzales. English Language Teaching in the Philippines." A Succession of Movements. In *Teaching and Learning English Worldwide.* Ed. J. Britton, R. Shafer and K. Watson. Clevedon: Multilingual Matters, 269–298.

———. "Language Policy, Language Engineering and Literacy in the Philippines." In *Advances in Language Planning.* Ed. J. Fishmen. The Hague: Mouton ede Gruter.

Trosdal, Mimi B. *Formal-Functional Cebuano–English Dictionary*: With an English–Cebuano Lexicon and Special Articles, the Cebuanos, the Semantic-Cultural Content of a Lexical Entry, a Brief History of the Cebuano–Bisayan Language. Cebu City: M. B. Trosdal, 1990.

———. "Reflections, Assertions, and Speculation on the Growth of Pilipino." *Southeast Asian Journal of Social Science.* 13: 1 (1985), 40–51.

F. Literature

Abad, Gemino H., ed. *The Likhaan Anthology of Philippine Literature from 1900 to the Present. Quezon City*: University of the Philippines Press, 1999.

Abad, Gemino H. et al. *Memories, Visions, and Scholarship and Other Essays.* Quezon City: University of the Philippines, Center for Integrative and Development Studies, 2001.

Abad, Gemino and Edna Manlapaz. *Man of Earth.* Quezon City: Ateneo De Manila Unversity Press, 1989.

Abesamis, Marilen and Lorna Kalaw-Tirol. *Women on Fire.* Pasig City: Anvil Publications, 1997.

Abueg, Efren R. *Sila-noon: Oral na kasaysayan ng 9 na manunulat sa Tagalog.* Malate, Manila: De La Salle University Press, 2001.

Aguilar-Cariño, Maria Luisa. *Cordillera Tales.* Quezon City: New Day Publishers, 1990.

Alburo, Erlinda K. "Continuing and Emerging Directions in Contemporary Philippine Folklore Studies." *Philippine Quarterly of Culture & Society* 20, 2/3 (June/September 1992): 210–225.

Alburo, Erlinda K. and Resil B. Mojares. "List of Published Literary Translation to/from Cebuano." *Philippine Quarterly of Culture & Society* 18, 2 (June 1990): 82–96.

Aldecoa, Ena Maria R. and Corazon R. Dioquino. *Compendium of the Humanities: Musical Arts.* Metro Manila: National Research Council of the Philippines, 1998.

Alegre, Edilberto N. and Doreen G. Fernandez. *The Writer and His Milieu: An Oral History of First Generation Writers in English.* Manila: De La Salle University Press, 1984.

Almario, Virgilio S., et al., eds. *Bumasa at Lumaya: A Sourcebook on Children's Literature in the Philippines.* Manila: Anvil Publishing, 1994.

Armengol, Pedro Ortiz. *Noli Me Tangere (Jose Rizal 1861–1896).* Valencia, Barcelona: Circulo de Lectores: Galaxia Gutenberg, 1998.

Arquiza, Yasmin and Alan White. *Tales from the Tubbataha.* Puerto Princesa: Bandillo ng Palawan Foundation, 1994.

Aviado, Virgilio, Ben Cabrera, and Alfred A. Yuson, eds. *Eros Pinoy: An Anthology of Contemporary Erotica in Philipine Art and Poetry.* Manila: Anvil Publishing, 2001.

Axelsson, Magull. *Rosario Is Dead.* Pasig City: Anvil Publishing, 1997.

Balde, Abdon M. *Mga pangarap at pangitain.* España, Manila: Inilimbag at ipinamamahagi ng UST Publishing House, 2001.

Barrios, Joi. *Bailaya.* Quezon City: University of the Philippines Press, 1997.

Basa, Juliet V. "Cebuano Children's Rhymes: Wonder and Irreverence." *Philippine Quarterly of Culture & Society* 20, 4 (December 1992): 277–299.

Bautista, Cirilo F. *Breaking Signs: Lectures on Literature and Semiotics.* Manila: De La Salle University Press, 1990.

Bejarano, Valorie Slaughter, ed. *The Beginning and Other Asian Folktales.* Santa Monica, Calif.: PAWWA, 1995.

Bobis, Merlinda. *Cantata of the Warrior Woman Daragang Magayon.* Manila: St. Scholastica, 1993.

———. *Summer Was a Fast Train.* North Melbourne Victoria: Spinifix Press, 1998.

Borinaga, Irah. *Shifting Sands: A Novel.* Quezon City: Giraffe Books, 1997.

Brainard, Cecilia Manguerra. *Contemporary Fiction by Filipinos in America*. Pasig City: Anvil Publishing,1997.
———. *When the Rainbow Goddess Wept*. New York: Dutton, 1994.
Bresnahan, Roger J. *Angles of Vision: Conversations on Philippine Literature*. Quezon City: New Day Publishers, 1992.
Brown River, *White Ocean: An Anthology of Twentieth-Century Philippine Literature in English*. New Brunswick, N.J.: Rutgers University Press, 1993.
Bulusan, Carlos. *America Is in the Heart*. Seattle: University of Washington Press, 1943.
Burns, Gerald T. "The Repatriate Theme in Contemporary Philippine Fiction." *Philippine Studies* 40, 3 (1992): 320–332.
Cariño, Maria Luisa Aguilar. *Blood Sacrifice*. Quezon City: University of the Philippines Press, 1997.
Casper, Leonard. *Firewalkers: Literary Concelebrations 1964–1984*. Quezon City: New Day Publishers, 1987.
———. *The Circular Firing Squad*. Quezon City: Giraffe Books, 1999.
Castillo, T. and B. Medina Jr. *Philippine Literature from Ancient Times to the Present*. Quezon City: Del Castillo & Sons, 1968.
Chua, Jonathan, comp. and ed. *The Critical Villa: Essays in Literacy Criticism*. Manila: Ateneo De Manila University Press, 2002.
Chung, Lilia Hernandez. *Facts in Fiction: A Study of Peninsular Prose Fiction of the Philippines, 1859–1897*. Manila: De La Salle University Press, 2001.
Corcuera, Sigrid M. *Anger in Filipino Women: A Phenomentological Study*. Dissertation, 2001. Ann Arbor: University Microfilms.
Crogan, R. *The Development of Philippine Literature in English*. Manila: Ateneo De Manila, 1975.
Cruz, Alberto Segismundo. *Piling Nobela: Lakandula, Halimuyak, ang Bango*. Quezon City: Ateneo De Manila University Press, 1997.
Dalisay, Butch. *Best of Barfly*. Pasig City: Anvil Publishers, 1997.
Demetrio, Francisco R. "On Human Values in Philippine Epics." *Asian Folklore Studies* 45, 2 (1986): 205–225.
DiDominicus, Lynn. *The Far Side of the Sea: From the Philippines to Ukraine*. Kansas City: Nazarene Publication House, 2003.
Edwards, William. *The Miracle of EDSA: A Novel*. Daly City, Calif.: Milrose Publication, 2000.
Enriquez, Antonio Reyes. *The Night I Cry and Other Stories*. Quezon City: New Day Publishers, 1989.
Eugenio, Damiana L. "Philippine Folktales: An Introduction." *Asian Folklore Studies* 44, 2 (1985): 155–177.
Evasco, Marjorie M. *Ochre Tones*. Pasig City: GEBA Printing, 1999.
Fajardo, Herminia R. and Erlinda Panlilio. *Holding Up Half the Sky: Success Stories in the Economic Empowerment of Women*. Quezon City: Milflores Publication, 2001.
Feria, Dolores Stephens. *The Long Stag Party*. Manila: St. Scholastica, 1991.

Flavier, Juan. *Back to the Barrios*. Quezon City: New Day Publishers, 1978.

Forsberg, Vivian. *T'boli Medicine and the Supernatural*. M.A. Theses. Fuller Theological Seminary, V. 173, p. 1988.

Francisco, Juan R. *From Ayodhaya to Pulu Agamaniog. Rama's Journey to the Philippines*. Quezon City: Philippine Asian Center, 1994.

——. *Maharadia Lawana*. Quezon City. Quezon City: Philippine Folklore Society, 1969.

——. "Ancient Tales from the Land by the Lake." *Salam*. Vol. II and III 1976.

Galdon, J. *Filipino Fiction*. Quezon City: Ateneo De Manila University Press, 1972.

Garcia, J. Neil. *Kaluluwa: New and Selected Poems*. Manila: University of Santo Tomas Press, 2001.

——. *Myths and Metaphors*. Manila: University of Santo Tomas Publishing House, 2002.

Gloria, Heidi K. "The Myths of the Bagobo, Tagakaulo and Mandaya: An Ethnological Analysis." *Tambara: Ateneo de Davao University Journal* 10 (December 1993): 76–91.

Gonzales, N.V.M. *The Bamboo Dancers*. Manila: Republic Book Supply, 1977.

——. *A Grammar of Dreams and Other Stories*. Quezon City: University of the Philippines Press, 1997.

Goschnick, Hella E. "The Poetic Conventions of Tina Sambal." *Linguistic Society of the Philippines,* Special Monograph Issue 27. Manila: Linguistic Society of the Philippines VIII, p. 452, 1989.

Gotera, Vince. *Dragonfly*. San Antonio, Tx.: Pecan Grove Press, 1995.

Grow, L. M. *Distillation & Essence: World-view in Modern Philippine Literature*. Quezon City, Giraffe Books, 2002.

Guerrero, Leon Ma. *We Filipinos*. Manila: Daily Star Publishing, 1986.

Guevara, Joe. *Point of Order*. Manila: Magna Ventures International, 1987.

Guillermo, Artemio R., ed. *Epic Tales of the Philippines*. Lanham, Md.: University Press of America, 2003.

Guillermo, Artemio R., and Nimfa M. Rodeheaver. *Tales From the 7,000 Isles*. Santa Rosa, Calif.: Vision Books International, 1997.

Hagedorn, Jessica Tarahata. *Dream Jungle*. New York: Viking, 2003.

Hall, Luisa J. Mallari. *From Domicile to Domain: The Formation of Malay and Tagalog Masterpiece Novels in Post-independence Malaysia and the Philippines*. Bangi: Penerbit Universiti Kebangsaan Malaysia. 2002.

Hart, Donn V. *Riddles in Filipino Folklore: An Anthropological Analysis*. Syracuse, N.Y.: Syracuse University Press, 1964.

Hau, Cristine S. *Necessary Fictions: Philippine Literature and the Nation 1946–1980*. Manila: Ateneo De Manila University Press, 2001.

Hayes, Kevin J. *Folklore and Book Culture*: Knoxville: University of Tennessee Press, 1997.

Holmes, Margarita Go Singco. *Bed Bold Brazen*. Pasig City: Anvil Publishers, 1997.

Holthe,Tess Uriza. *When Elephants Dance: A Novel*. New York: Henry Holt, 2002.

Hornedo, Florentino H. *Pagmamahal and Pagmumura: Essays.* Quezon City: Office of Research and Publication, Ateneo De Manila University Press, 1978.

Hosillos, Lucila V. *Originality as Vengeance in Philippine Literature.* Quezon City: New Day Publishers, 1984.

Jacob, Ave Perz. *Sibol sa mga Guho.* Manila: De La Salle University Press, 1997.

Jayme, Freda. *Catch Me a Butterfly and Other Stories.* Makati City: Bookmark, 1998.

Joaquin, Nick. *La Orosa: The Dance-Drama That Is Leonor Goquingco.* Manila: Anvil Publishing and National Commission for Culture and the Arts, 1994.

———. *The Way We Were: Writers & Their Milieu: An Oral History of Second Generation Writers in English*, ed. E.N. Alegre & D. Fernandez. Manila: De La Salle University Press, 1987, pp. 1–9.

———. *The Woman Who Had Two Navels.* Manila: Soledaridad, 1972.

———. *Tropical Gothic.* St. Lucia, Queensland: University of Queensland Press, 1972.

———. *Collected Verse.* Quezon City: Ateneo de Manila University Press, 1987.

Kahayon, Alicia H. *Philippine Literature: Choice Selections from a Historical Perspective.* Manila, Philippines: National Book Store, 1989.

Kintanar, Thelma B. *Women's Bodies, Women's Lives: Anthology of Philippine Fiction and Poetry on Women's Health Issues.* Quezon City: UP-Center for Women's Studies, 2001.

Lacson-Locsin, Ma. Soledad and Raul L. Locsin, *Noli Me Tangere.* Honolulu: University of Hawaii Press, 1997.

Lim, Paulino Jr. *Sparrows Don't Sing in the Philippines.* Quezon City: New Day Publishers, 1994.

———. *Requiem for a Rebel.Priest.* Quezon City: New Day Publishers, 1996.

Llavan, Peregrina A. Ranto. *Ginotay-gotay (A Collection of Poems in Agutayenen: Filipino and English).* Manila: Agutayenen Translation Advisory Committee and Institute of Philippine Languages and Department of Education, Culture and Sports. VI, p. 143, 2000.

Locsin-Nava, Ma. Cecilia. *History & Society in the Novels of Ramon Muzones.* Quezon City: Ateneo De Manila University Press, 2001.

Lumbrera, Bienvenido, ed. *Filipino Writing: Philippine Literature from the Regions.* Pasig City: Anvil Publishing, 2001.

Lumbrera, Bienvenido and Cynthia Lumbrera. *Philippine Literature: A History and Anthology.* Manila:. National Bookstore, 1982.

Mabanglo, Elynia S. *Invitation of the Imperialist: Poems. Text in Tagalog and English.* Manila: Ateneo De Manila University Press, 1999.

Manlapaz, Edna Z. "Our Mothers, Our Selves: A Literary Genealogy of Filipino Women Poets Writing in English, 1905–1950." *Philippine Studies* 39, 3 (1991): 321–336.

Manuel, E. Arsenio and Gilda Cordero-Fernando. *Filipino Myths & Folktales: Treasury of Stories.* Manila: Anvil Publishing, 1995.

———. *History and Form: Selected Essays*. Quezon City: Ateneo De Manila University Press, 1996.

Maramba, A. *A Philippine Contemporary Literature*. Manila: Bookmark, 1962.

Matibag, Eugenio. "El Verbo del Filibusterismo"; "Narrative Ruses in the Novels of Jose Rizal." *Revista Hispanica Moderna* (December 1995), pp. 250–264.

Matute, Epifanio G. *Mga Kislap ng Panulat*. Quezon City: University of the Philippine Press, 2001.

———. *Kuwentong Kutsero*. Quezon City: University of the Philippine Press, 1997.

Matute, Genoveva Edroza. *Sa ilalim ng araw na pula*. Manila: Bookmark, 2001.

McKaughan, Howard P., compiler. *Stories from the Darangen*. Manila: De La Salle University Press X, 194, 1988.

Medina, Buenaventura S. *Salingdugo*. Quezon City: University of the Philippines Press, 1997.

Meñez, Herminia. *Explorations in Philippine Folklore*. Manila: Ateneo De Manila University Press, 1996.

Mojares, Resil B. "From Cebuano/to Cebuano: The Politics of Literary Translation." *Philippine Quarterly of Culture & Society* 18, 2 (June 1990): 75–81.

———. *Origins and Rise of the Filipino Novel: A Generic Study of the Novel until 1940*. Quezon City: University of the Philippines Press, 1983.

Nakpil, Carmen Guerrero. *Whatever: A New Collection of Later Essays*. Manila: Ateneo De Manila University Press, 2002.

Nery, Peter Solis. *Moon River, Butterflies, and Me*. Quezon City: New Day Publishers, 1997.

Netzorg, Morton J. *Backward, Turn Backward*. Manila: National Book Store, 1985.

Nicanor, Precioso M. *The Philippines, My Beloved Country*. Manila: Philippines Premier Publications, 1986.

Nimmo, Harry. *The Songs of Salanda: And Other Stories of Sulu*. Seattle: University of Washington, 1994.

Ocampo, Ambeth R. *Makamisa: The Search for Rizal's Third Novel*. Manila: Anvil Publishers, 1992.

Ocampo, Manuel. *Heridas de la Lengua (Wounds of the Tongue)*: Selected Works; essays by Chon A. Noriega and Kevin Power; dialogue with Manuel Ocampo and Daniel J. Martinez; ed. By Pilar Perez. Santa Monica, Calif.: Smart Art Press, 1997.

Omaois, Marina B.and Cynthia Villamor. *Homecoming: Brief Histories and Special Place*. Manila: University of the Philippines, 1998.

Ong, Charlson. *Woman of Am-Kaw and Other Stories*. Pasig City: Anvil Publishing, 1995.

Ordoñez, Elmer A. *The Other View: Notes on Philippine Writing and Culture*. Manila, Philippines: Kalikasan Press, 1989.

Ordoñez, Elmer A., ed. *Many Voices: Towards a National Literature*. Manila: Published for the Philippine Writers Academy by the National Commission for Culture and the Arts, Committee on Literary Arts, 1995.

————. *Emergent Literature: Essays on Philippine Writing.* Quezon City: University of the Philippines Press. 2001.

————. *With Hearts Aflame: A Historical Novel.* Manila: Anvil Publishers, 2002.

Ordaz, Jorge. *Perdido Eden.* Barcelona: Ediciones del Bronce, 1998.

Ortiz-Armengol, Pedro. *Letras en Filipinas. Madrid: Direccion General Relaciones Culturales y Cientificas.* Ministerio de Asuntos Exteriores de España, 1999.

Pantoja-Hidalgo, Cristina. *A Gentle Subversion: Essays on Philippine Fiction in English.* Quezon City: University of the Philippines Press, 1998.

Patajo-Legasto, Priscelina. Filipiniana Reader: A Companion Anthology of Filipiniana Online. Quezon City: University of the Philippines, 1998.

Pithaya (Ambition). Quezon City: National Commission on Culture and the Arts, 1997.

Polenda, Francisco Col-om. "Ulegingen: A Prose Retelling of a Mindanao Epic," tr. and ed. by Richard E. Elkins. *Kanaadman Journal* 14, 2 (1994): 101–168.

Polotan, Kerima. *Author's Choice: Selected Writings of Kerima Polotan.* Quezon City: University of the Philippines Press, 1998.

Realubit, Maria Lilia F. "A Survey of Contemporary Bikol Writing: A Bibliographical Note." *Philippine Studies* 38, 4 (1990): 500–528.

————, ed. *Haliya: Anthology of Bikol: Poets and Poems.* Quezon City: National Committee on Literary Arts, 1999.

Regalado, Iñigo ed. *Damdamin mga pilig nila.* Quezon City: Ateneo de Manila University Press, 2001.

————. *El Filibusterismo.* Hong Kong: Sing Cheong Printing, 1965.

Reyes, Gracianus. R. *Scattered Brain Showers.* Quezon City: Giraffe Books, 1999.

Reyes, Lina Sagaral. *Storya and Other Poems.* Manila: St. Scholastica, 1992.

Reyes, Raymundo. *Castles in the Cordilleras.* Quezon City: Giraffe Books, 1997.

Reyes, Soledad S. *Tellers of Tales, Singers of Songs. Selected Critical Essays.* Manila: De La Salle University Press, 2001.

Rizal, Jose. *Noli Me Tangere.* Hong Kong: Sing Cheong Printing, 1961.

Roces, Mina. "Filipino Identity in Fiction, 1945–1972." *Modern Asian Studies* 28 (May 1994): 279–315.

Romero, Sophia C. *Always Hiding: A Novel.* New York: William Morrow, 1998.

San Juan, Epifanio. *Toward a People's Literature: Essays in the Dialectics of Praxis and Contradiction in the Philippine Writing.* Quezon City, Philippines: University of the Philippines Press, 1984.

————. *The Radical Tradition of Philippine Literature.* Quezon City: University of the Philippines Press, 1985.

Santos, Aida F. *Spaces: Earthbound, Skybound.* Manila: St. Scholastica, 1998.

Santos, Bienvenido N. *You Lovely People.* Manila: Benipayo Press, 1955.

Santos, Ildefonso. Sa tabi ng dagat at iba pang tula. Quezon City: Ateneo De Manila Press, 2001.

Sionil, F. Jose. *Dusk: A Novel.* New York: Modern Library, 1984.

————. *The Samsons. Two Novels in the Rosales Saga.* New York: Modern Library, 2000.

Sulit, Loreto Paras. *Harvest and Other Stories*. Manila: De La Salle University Press, 2001.

Smyth, David. *The Canon in Southeast Asian Literatures: Literatures of the Philippines, Burma, China, Cambodia, Indonesia, Laos, Malaysia, Thailand and Vietnam*. Dekalb, Ill.: Northern Illinois University, 2000.

Tabios, Eileen R. *Beyond Life Sentences: Contemporary Philippine Poetry*. Pasig City: Anvil Publishing, 1998.

Tabujara, Milagros Gonzalez. *Visayan Folklore*. Quezon City: Folklore Studies Program, College of Social Sciences and Philosophy, University of the Philippines, 1985.

Tan, Susie L. *Asian Hearts: A Review of Filipino and Chinese Folktales*. Manila: De La Salle University Press, 1998.

Tan, Edwardson. *Visitation: Essays and Poems*. Quezon City: Giraffe Books, 1999.

Teoxon, Lucio F. *The Quest for Truth: A Study of Six Contemporary Novels in English*. Quezon City: New Day Publishers, 1990.

Torrevillas, Rowena Tiempo. *Flying Over Kansas: Personal Views*. Quezon City: Giraffe Books, 1998.

Tiempo, Edith L. *Marginal Annotations and Other Poems*. Quezon City: Giraffe Books, 2001.

———. *A Blade of Fern: A Novel about the Philippines*. Quezon City: Giraffe Books, 1998.

Tiempo, Edilberto K. *To Be Free*. Quezon City: New Day Publishers, 1972.

Tonogbanua, Francisco G. *Philippine Literature in English*. Rev. ed. Manila: Dena Enterprises, 1984.

Versus: Philippine Protest Poetry, 1983–1986. Quezon City: Ateneo De Manila University Press, 1986.

Vida, Vendela. *And Now You Go: A Novel*. New York: Knopf, 2003.

Villa, Jose Garcia and Jonathan Chua. *The Critical Villa: Essays in Literary Criticism*. Quezon City: Ateneo De Manila University Press, 2002.

Wilson, Laurence Lee. *Ilongot Life and Legends*. Manila: Bookmark, 1967.

Wrigglesworth, Hazel J. and Pengenda Mengsenggilid. *Good Character and Bad Character: The Manobo Storytelling Audience as Society's Jurors*. Manila: Linguistic Society of the Philippines, 1993

———, compiler. *Anthology of Ilianen Folktale. Humanities Series II*. Cebu City: University of San Carlos Press XII, p. 299, 1981.

Yuson, Alfred A. *The Word on Paradise: Essays 1991–2000 on Writers and Writing*. Pasig City: Anvil Publishing, 2001.

PART 9. WEBSITES

www.gov.ph   Official government portal of the Republic the Philippines. Online information on the Philippine government.

www:filipinolinks.com   Complete links to the Philippines.

www.sunstar.com.ph   Internet home of community newspapers. Website pools news and other information from twelve Sun Star newspapers.

www.filipinolanguages.com   Learn the Filipino language.

http://.www.angelfire.com/biz5pinoystocks   Philippine stocks online.

jaguar@languagelinks.org   Translation from English to major Philippine languages.

http://www.philsol.n/OF.htm   Overseas Filipinos.

www.frrick.net/catholic/index.html   Catholic links.

http://www.worldwife.edu/ci/philippines/index.html   Universities, language institutions, professionals, and adult education.

http://www.geocitiescom/icasocot/home.html   Survey of Philippine literature.

http//www.asiatraveltips.com/Philippines.html   Travel tips.

http://www.philexport.phl   Philippine exports online.

http//www.chanrobles.com/index/.htm   Chan Robles virtual law library

http://pinoylit.webmanila.com   Provides information on Filipino writers.

About the Authors

Artemio R. Guillermo began his educational journey as a scholar at Silliman University, Dumaguete City, Philippines, (B.A. English-Anthropology) and as a Fulbright-Crusade scholar at Syracuse University, Syracuse, New York (M.A. Journalism and Ph.D. Communication). He did graduate work at Medill School of Journalism, Northwestern University, Evanston, Illinois, and postdoctoral graduate research on Philippine history at Michigan State University. He was a lecturer under the Asian Visiting Professors Program at Indiana University and Cortland College. He taught communication courses at three state universities at Bowling Green State University, Arkansas State University, and University of Northern Iowa. Since retiring, he has continued his writing and produced four books. This revision of the historical dictionary marks his fifth major work.

May Kyi Win (1948–2002) was former associate professor and curator of the Donn V. Hart Southeast Asia Collection at Northern Illinois University Libraries and was a principal author of the first edition. Her excellent bibliography provided the model on which this revised and expanded version was developed. During her tenure at the University Libraries, she contributed to the Burmese collection, considered the world's largest and best collection outside of Burma (Myanmar), and the Mainland Southeast Asia collection through her expertise in languages and her knowledge of the literature of the region. In addition to being an author of this dictionary, she was also the author of the *Historical Dictionary of Thailand* and was working on a revised edition at the time of her death.